Advances in Entrepreneurship
Volume II

Wherever possible, the articles in these volumes have been reproduced as originally published using facsimile reproduction, inclusive of footnotes and pagination to facilitate ease of reference.

For a list of all Edward Elgar published titles visit our site on the World Wide Web at http://www.e-elgar.co.uk

Advances in Entrepreneurship Volume II

Edited by

Paul Westhead

Professor of Entrepreneurship
University of Stirling, Scotland, UK

and

Mike Wright

Professor of Financial Studies and Director of the Centre for Management Buy-Out Research
University of Nottingham Business School, UK

An Elgar Reference Collection
Cheltenham, UK • Northampton, MA, USA

Published by
Edward Elgar Publishing Limited
Glensanda House
Montpellier Parade
Cheltenham
Glos GL50 1UA
UK

Edward Elgar Publishing, Inc.
136 West Street, Suite 202
Northampton
Massachusetts 01060
USA

A catalogue record for this book is available from the British Library.

Library of Congress Cataloguing in Publication Data

Advances in entrepreneurship / edited by Paul Westhead and Mike Wright.
p. cm. — (An Elgar reference collection) (Elgar mini series)
Includes bibliographical references and index.
1. Entrepreneurship. 2. New business enterprises—Management. I. Westhead, Paul, 1962– II. Wright, Mike, 1952– III. Series. IV. Series: Elgar mini series

HB615 .A375 2000
658.4'21—dc21 00–024526

ISBN 1 84064 031 6 (3 volume set)

Printed and bound in Great Britain by MPG Books Ltd, Bodmin, Cornwall

Contents

Acknowledgements

The editors and publishers wish to thank the authors and the following publishers who have kindly given permission for the use of copyright material.

Academy of Management and the Copyright Clearance Center, Inc. for article: William B. Gartner (1985), 'A Conceptual Framework for Describing the Phenomenon of New Venture Creation', *Academy of Management Review*, **10** (4), October, 696–706.

Blackwell Publishers Ltd for article: M.E. Beesley and R.T. Hamilton (1984), 'Small Firms' Seedbed Role and the Concept of Turbulence', *Journal of Industrial Economics*, **XXXIII** (2), December, 217–31.

Carfax Publishing Ltd, Taylor and Francis Group for article: David Keeble and Sheila Walker (1994), 'New Firms, Small Firms and Dead Firms: Spatial Patterns and Determinants in the United Kingdom', *Regional Studies*, **28** (4), July, 411–27.

Elsevier Science Ltd for articles: Arnold C. Cooper (1985), 'The Role of Incubator Organizations in the Founding of Growth-Oriented Firms', *Journal of Business Venturing*, **1** (1), Winter, 75–86; Robert Ronstadt (1986), 'Exit, Stage Left: Why Entrepreneurs End Their Entrepreneurial Careers Before Retirement', *Journal of Business Venturing*, **1** (3), Fall, 323–38; Paul D. Reynolds (1987), 'New Firms: Societal Contribution Versus Survival Potential', *Journal of Business Venturing*, **2** (3), Summer, 231–46; Mel Scott and Richard Bruce (1987), 'Five Stages of Growth in Small Business', *Long Range Planning*, **20**, Number 3, June, 45–52; James J. Chrisman, Alan L. Carsrud, Julio DeCastro and Lanny Herron (1990), 'A Comparison of Assistance Needs of Male and Female Pre-Venture Entrepreneurs', *Journal of Business Venturing*, **5** (4), July, 235–48; Carolyn Y. Woo, Arnold C. Cooper and William C. Dunkelberg (1991), 'The Development and Interpretation of Entrepreneurial Typologies', *Journal of Business Venturing*, **6** (2), March, 93–111; Per Davidsson (1991), 'Continued Entrepreneurship: Ability, Need, and Opportunity as Determinants of Small Firm Growth', *Journal of Business Venturing*, **6** (6), November, 405–29; Andrew H. Van de Ven (1993), 'The Development of an Infrastructure for Entrepreneurship', *Journal of Business Venturing*, **8** (3), May, 211–30; Arnold C. Cooper (1993), 'Challenges in Predicting New Firm Performance', *Journal of Business Venturing*, **8** (3), May, 241–53; Sue Birley and Paul Westhead (1994), 'A Taxonomy of Business Start-Up Reasons and their Impact on Firm Growth and Size', *Journal of Business Venturing*, **9** (1), January, 7–31; Michael Harvey and Rodney Evans (1995), 'Strategic Windows in the Entrepreneurial Process', *Journal of Business Venturing*, **10** (5), September, 331–47; Nancy M. Carter, William B. Gartner and Paul D. Reynolds (1996), 'Exploring Start-Up Event Sequences', *Journal of Business Venturing*, **11** (3), May, 151–66; Paul Westhead and Mike Wright (1998), 'Novice, Portfolio, and Serial Founders: Are They Different?', *Journal of Business Venturing*, **13** (3), May, 173–204.

Entrepreneurship Theory and Practice, Baylor University for articles: Howard E. Aldrich (1990), 'Using an Ecological Perspective to Study Organizational Founding Rates', *Entrepreneurship Theory and Practice*, **14** (3), Spring, 7–24; Pamela Hammers Specht (1993), 'Munificence and Carrying Capacity of the Environment and Organization Formation', *Entrepreneurship Theory and Practice*, **17** (2), Winter, 77–86; Devi R. Gnyawali and Daniel S. Fogel (1994), 'Environments for Entrepreneurship Development: Key Dimensions and Research Implications', *Entrepreneurship Theory and Practice*, **18** (4), Summer, 43–62; W. Gibb Dyer, Jr. (1994), 'Toward a Theory of Entrepreneurial Careers', *Entrepreneurship Theory and Practice*, **19** (2), Winter, 7–21; Jerome A. Katz (1994), 'Modelling Entrepreneurial Career Progressions: Concepts and Considerations', *Entrepreneurship Theory and Practice*, **19** (2), Winter, 23–39; Gaylen N. Chandler (1996), 'Business Similarity as a Moderator of the Relationship Between Pre-Ownership Experience and Venture Performance', *Entrepreneurship Theory and Practice*, **20** (3), Spring, 51–65.

Helbing and Lichtenhahn Verlag AG Basel for article: C. Mirjam Van Praag and Hans Van Ophem (1995), 'Determinants of Willingness and Opportunity to Start as an Entrepreneur', *Kyklos*, **48** (4), 513–40.

Kluwer Academic Publishers for articles: David M. Flynn (1993), 'A Critical Exploration of Sponsorship, Infrastructure, and New Organizations', *Small Business Economics*, **5** (2), June, 129–56; Steven J. Davis, John Haltiwanger and Scott Schuh (1996), 'Small Business and Job Creation: Dissecting the Myth and Reassessing the Facts', *Small Business Economics*, **8** (4), August, 297–315; Paul D. Reynolds (1997), 'Who Starts New Firms? – Preliminary Explorations of Firms-in-Gestation', *Small Business Economics*, **9** (5), October, 449–62.

University of Chicago Press for article: Michael T. Hannan and John Freeman (1977), 'The Population Ecology of Organizations', *American Journal of Sociology*, **82** (5), March, 929–64.

John Wiley and Sons Ltd for articles: Jeffrey G. Covin and Dennis P. Slevin (1989), 'Strategic Management of Small Firms in Hostile and Benign Environments', *Strategic Management Journal*, **10** (1), January–February, 75–87; Sue Birley and Paul Westhead (1990), 'Growth and Performance Contrasts Between "Types" of Small Firms', *Strategic Management Journal*, **11** (7), November–December, 535–57.

Woodcock Publications Ltd for article: Paul Westhead and David Storey (1996), 'Management Training and Small Firm Performance: Why is the Link So Weak?', *International Small Business Journal*, **14** (4), July–September, 13–24.

Every effort has been made to trace all the copyright holders but if any have been inadvertently overlooked the publishers will be pleased to make the necessary arrangement at the first opportunity.

In addition the publishers wish to thank the Library of the London School of Economics and Political Science, the Library of the London Business School, the Marshall Library of Economics, Cambridge University and the Library of Indiana University at Bloomington, USA for their assistance in obtaining these articles.

Part I
Entrepreneurial Careers

[1]

Toward a Theory of Entrepreneurial Careers

W. Gibb Dyer, Jr.

Parallel streams of theory and research regarding entrepreneurship and careers has led to a dearth of comprehensive theories regarding the careers of entrepreneurs. This article describes four core dimensions of theory that are essential in developing a comprehensive theory of entrepreneurial careers: (1) a theory of career choice; (2) a theory of career socialization; (3) a theory of career orientation; and (4) a theory of career progression from entry to exit. A general model is presented that articulates various aspects of theory building along each of these four dimensions. Implications for both theory and practice regarding entrepreneurial careers is also discussed.

For the past several decades there has been considerable research and theorizing on the topics of entrepreneurship and careers. Career theorists have generally studied careers in organizational contexts to better understand the conflicts and challenges people encounter as they fill new roles while ascending the corporate hierarchy (Van Maanen & Schein, 1979; Arthur, Hall, & Lawrence, 1989a). Since entrepreneurs start at the top and grow a hierarchy beneath them, entrepreneurship researchers have studied those factors that would motivate someone to start an entrepreneurial career rather than focusing on career progression and advancement. Historically, entrepreneurship research has attempted to articulate the individual factors that influence people to embark on entrepreneurial careers (e.g. Miller, 1963; Sexton & Bowman, 1984); however, more recent research has identified the social and economic factors that give rise to entrepreneurship (Secrest, 1975; Aldrich, Rosen, & Woodward, 1986; Kirchoff, 1991).

Despite the long tradition of research in the two fields of careers and entrepreneurship, most of this work has been done in parallel. Little has been done using theory from both fields to build a comprehensive theory of entrepreneurial careers. Because entrepreneurship researchers have put so much emphasis on understanding the factors that influence someone to start a new business, little work has been done to understand how these individuals progress through various roles throughout their careers. The study of entrepreneurs seems to end once a business has been started and achieved some measure of success (or failure). Career researchers, on the other hand, seem to be more comfortable studying careers that have clear career paths, roles, and socialization practices. Occupations such as lawyers, doctors, and police officers along with managerial careers have received the most attention. A recent anthology of research on careers virtually ignored the entrepreneur (Arthur, Hall, & Lawrence, 1989a).

The purpose of this article is to bring these two streams of research together to develop a theory of entrepreneurial careers. Before doing so, however, it is important to clearly define what we mean by the terms "entrepreneur" and "career." While there is considerable debate on the definition of entrepreneurship (Kilby, 1971; Gartner, 1988), the core attribute of an entrepreneur is the ability to found new enterprises. Thus, the theory of entrepreneurial careers presented here will describe the careers of those who found organizations.

While some career theorists see careers only in terms of the work one performs (Arthur, Hall, & Lawrence, 1989b), an entrepreneurial career is greatly influenced by what is occurring in the person's personal life and family as well. For example, many entrepreneurs hire family members to work in their businesses, which creates overlapping and at times conflicting roles. Thus, a theory of entrepreneurial careers should employ a broad definition of career to encompass these more complex roles and dynamics. Goffman (1961, p. 127) defines a career as being "any social strand of a person's course through life" which provides the broader context that we need for studying entrepreneurial careers. Using a definition that illuminates the interaction of the entrepreneur's work, family, and personal life will provide a more robust theory of career than merely focusing on work roles (Schein, 1978).

BUILDING A THEORY OF ENTREPRENEURIAL CAREERS

A comprehensive theory of entrepreneurial careers should contain the following four "sub-theories":

(1) *A theory of career choice*. A theory of careers typically starts by explaining why someone would choose a particular occupation. In the context of an entrepreneurial career, a theory is needed to articulate the individual, social, and economic factors that influence individuals to found organizations.

(2) *A theory of career socialization*. A theory of entrepreneurial careers should describe the kinds of socialization experiences that would prepare someone to fill entrepreneurial roles.

(3) *A theory of career orientation*. As one starts a particular career and accepts various roles, there are generally several different ways to play those roles. For example, some who take the role of college professor choose to see themselves primarily as teachers and act accordingly, while others see themselves primarily as researchers and organize their activities around this research role. Thus, the theory must explain the different career orientations an entrepreneur might adopt.

(4) *A theory of career progression*. As Solomon (1968, p. 5) notes, "A career always consists of a sequence of roles." Thus, a theory of entrepreneurial careers should provide an understanding of how entrepreneurs' roles—business, family, and personal—change over the course of the careers (Schein, 1978). Moreover, the theory should articulate the kinds of role dilemmas and conflicts that are likely to be encountered over time.

Given this introduction, we will now proceed to developing a broad framework which is founded on these four basic ideas.

ENTREPRENEURIAL CAREERS: A MODEL

In Figure 1, a model describing the dynamics of entrepreneurial careers is presented. This model identifies four major areas: (1) the antecedents that influence career choice; (2) career socialization; (3) career orientation; and (4) career progression, which outlines the primary dilemmas that affect entrepreneurial roles from entry to exit from the career. The purpose of this model is to provide the skeleton from which to examine entrepreneurial careers. Such a framework is not designed to provide all the answers, but is formulated to raise questions and issues that need to be addressed in order to add flesh to the skeletal frame.

Figure 1
A Model of Entrepreneurial Careers

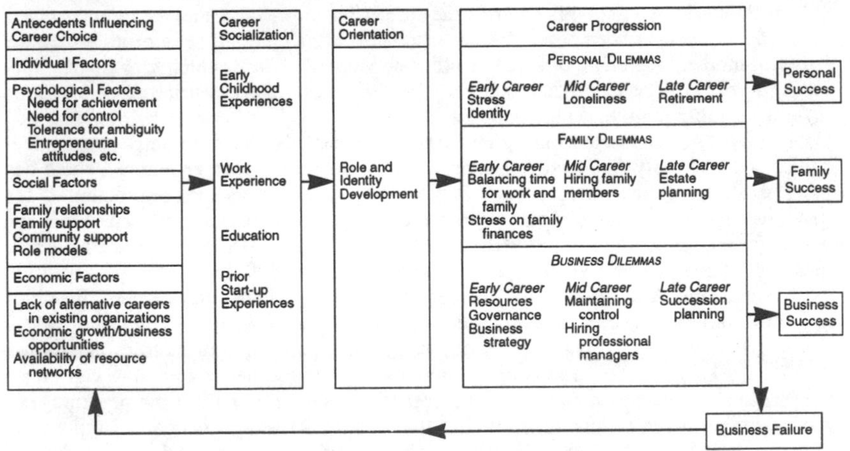

Antecedents Influencing Career Choice

There are three factors that appear to influence the decision to become an entrepreneur. These factors have either an individual, social, or economic basis.

Individual factors. Historically, studies of entrepreneurship have emphasized those psychological factors that stimulate one to seek an entrepreneurial career. For example, studies have shown that those individuals that have high needs for control, achievement, the ability to take risks, and a tolerance for ambiguity will be more likely to engage in entrepreneurial activity (Brockhaus, 1982; Brockhaus & Horwitz, 1986; Scherer, Brodzinski, & Wiebe, 1991; Bird, 1989). Schein (1990) also notes that certain individuals have an entrepreneurial "career anchor"—the driving force behind one's career choices—which motivates them to start an entrepreneurial career.

Recent writings have noted the disappointing results of those studies that have attempted to link individual traits to entrepreneurial behavior (e.g. Gartner, 1988). Some writers have noted that attitude measures may be more predictive of entrepreneurial behavior than mere psychological traits while others have suggested that social cognition and cognitive processes are significant factors in career choice (Robinson, Stimpson, Huefner, & Hunt, 1991; Shaver & Scott, 1991). Moreover, recent research on gender differences suggests that there are significant differences in the orientations and motivations of male and female entrepreneurs (Brush, 1992). While it is clear that research that has attempted to link individual characteristics to entrepreneurial behavior has not lived up to its early promise, individual factors do play a role in the selection of an entrepreneurial career and should not be overlooked in developing a theory of entrepreneurial careers.

Social factors. There also appear to be a variety of social factors that influence one's decision to become an entrepreneur (Reynolds, 1991). Early studies by Collins and Moore (1964) noted that many entrepreneurs came from social environments that could be described as "deprived"—their childhoods filled with poverty and parental neglect. Kets de Vries (1977) extended this argument when he noted that entrepreneurs grow up in a world where the dominant themes concern desertion, death, and neglect. Such an upbringing causes an individual to be highly impulsive, reject authority figures, and have persistent feelings of rejection and isolation. Individuals who grow up under such social conditions are motivated to take control over what they consider to be a hostile and uninviting world. To gain this control, they create businesses that they can mold to their own will. It has also been noted that entrepreneurs often come from families where the father or mother was self-employed (Collins & Moore, 1970; Roberts & Wainer, 1968; Shapero, 1972). The children of entrepreneurs are more likely to see such a career as more acceptable than working for someone else.

Family support for the entrepreneurial career can also have an impact on career choice. Often family financial resources are used in starting a new venture, which can put great strains on the entrepreneur's family, and the long hours and commitment to the new business may cause discontent on the part of the spouse and children. Thus one reason for not launching an entrepreneurial career is the lack of support for the career by members of the prospective entrepreneur's family (Dyer, 1992).

Thomas and Alderfer's (1989) discussion of race, culture, and careers illustrates how race and culture can have a significant impact on the kinds of roles adopted by entrepreneurs and the strategies and tactics they use to perform in those roles. Stevenson (1987) also indicates that a lack of community support for the new venture can create barriers to a successful entrepreneurial career. Studies have noted that the percentage of Asian entrepreneurs is four times higher than that of African American entrepreneurs (Kotkin, 1986). Much of this difference can be attributed to the social networks and support that the respective communities give to local entrepreneurs (Aldrich & Waldinger, 1990). Asian Americans support with their dollars those businesses started by members of their communities, while African Americans tend to support businesses started by other racial and ethnic groups. There also tend to be highly visible, successful entrepreneurial role models in the Asian community, while successful African American entrepreneurs often leave their communities of origin and migrate to the suburbs. Such role models encourage members of the community to seek the status that can be gained from owning one's own business.

Economic factors. A third set of factors that will encourage or inhibit entrepreneurial activity is economic in origin. The early work of Stinchcombe (1965) outlined the environmental and economic conditions that give rise to the creation of new organizations while more recent writings by Wilken (1979), Aldrich (1990), and Kirchoff (1991) have elaborated the economic factors that stimulate entrepreneurial activity.

Such writings note that entrepreneurial careers are launched when there is a lack of opportunities for employment in existing organizations. For example, certain ethnic groups—particularly immigrant groups such as Asian Americans and Jews—were often discriminated against as they sought employment. Thus, they were compelled to seek their livelihoods outside established organizations and began to create their own businesses. To the extent that there are not viable careers within existing organizations, people will be more likely to start their own enterprises.

Economic growth that creates business opportunities can also spawn entrepreneurial careers. We find that the extent to which a nation's economy is expanding and there is more demand for goods and services is reflected in the likelihood that someone will seize the opportunity to start an entrepreneurial career.

Another factor, that of resource networks, can also encourage someone to start a new business (Aldrich & Zimmer, 1986; Birley, 1985). Without the basic resource requirements of labor, capital, and raw materials, few organizations can survive for long, and few individuals would be willing to risk starting a new enterprise without at least some access to these resources. The more an individual has access to resource networks, the more likely that individual will be to engage in entrepreneurial activity (Aldrich, Rosen, & Woodward, 1986).

Socialization Into an Entrepreneurial Career

A theory of entrepreneurial socialization has not been developed fully, unlike various models of organizational socialization (Van Maanen & Schein, 1979). However, there do appear to be certain socialization experiences that would prepare someone to choose an entrepreneurial career.

As cited previously, the work of Collins and Moore and Kets de Vries suggests that certain early childhood experiences can encourage entrepreneurial behavior. In studying the career histories of a panel of entrepreneurs, Dalton and Holdaway (1989) found that many had received significant responsibilities at a young age and had even started some entrepreneurial ventures in their youth. These entrepreneurs reported that these experiences influenced their choice of an entrepreneurial career.

Other research has indicated that various work experiences and training can influence career choice (Cooper, 1970; Lamont, 1972; Brockhaus & Nord, 1979; Roberts, 1969; Chambers, Hart, & Denison, 1988). Specialized courses in entrepreneurship or training in how to start a business may give some people the confidence they need to start their own companies. Furthermore, a study of the CEOs of the *INC. 500* companies noted that these individuals generally had developed some type of expertise and had solid business experience before they embarked on their entrepreneurial careers (Case, 1989). For some, their negative work experiences in large companies convinced them that an entrepreneurial career would be more satisfying (Dyer, 1992). Studies by Starr (1990) have shown that those who have previously started a business are more likely to start a new business. Thus, prior experience in a start-up appears to lead to further entrepreneurial activity. Moreover, the experience of working for an entrepreneur may also influence one to choose an entrepreneurial lifestyle.

Although there does not appear to be a single sequence or pattern of experiences that would lead one to become an entrepreneur, previous research does seem to indicate that early family and childhood experiences, education and training, and certain work experiences encourage entrepreneurial behavior. Further research on entrepreneurial socialization would likely lead to models that would be more predictive of entrepreneurial behavior than those models that have been based solely on individual factors.

Career Orientation

While the preceding discussion described the individual factors and socialization experiences that would influence one to become an entrepreneur, we will now turn our attention to understanding how individuals orient themselves to the role of an entrepreneur. One of the difficulties in studying entrepreneurs lies in the fact that those who engage in entrepreneurial activity often do not define themselves as entrepreneurs (Duffy & Stevenson, 1984; Carland, Hoy, Boulton, & Carland, 1984). They see themselves as real estate developers, retailers, engineers, and so forth, who just happened to start a business. They see themselves this way largely because of the previous career experiences that they have had in a given occupation. Thus, they may be more oriented to an occupational career than to an entrepreneurial career (Van Maanen & Barley, 1984). In contrast, when researchers study police officers, firefighters, doctors, or lawyers, they can be reasonably certain that those who they study use the same cover terms to describe their occupation and that the attributes of the various career roles are reasonably stable and can be generalized. With the variation in entrepreneurial careers, however, we can envision entrepreneurs approaching their roles in a host of different ways.

Given the likelihood of different orientations toward the role of an entrepreneur, we can postulate that one's orientation to an entrepreneurial role occurs in two stages.

The first stage concerns the acceptance by an individual of what might be called the "general entrepreneurial role." This role—that of creating an organization, and owning it—is one that must be accepted by all those who could be defined as entrepreneurs (Stevenson, 1987). Whether or not an individual defines himself or herself as an entrepreneur, if they create and own an organization, they have accepted an entrepreneurial role. This role may be either full time or part time. For example, many entrepreneurs start their careers by "moonlighting"—creating their own businesses while keeping their regular employment. Thus, they may adopt several occupational identities over the course of their careers.

The second stage in the development of an entrepreneurial role is what might be called the creation of a "specific entrepreneurial role." Previous research by Vesper (1980), Derr (1984) and others has noted that there is no single orientation toward an entrepreneurial career. Some start their careers because they enjoy developing a new technology, others do so because they enjoy building an organization and owning their own company. Still others enjoy making deals and starting new ventures, but dislike managing them. Van Maanen (1983) has described how the "culture of orientation" that people bring with them to a new role influences how they develop that role for themselves. He notes, for example, that those learning the sport of windsurfing learn how to windsurf differently depending on whether they had previously learned to snow ski, surf, or sail. How they learned those other sports influenced how they learned to become a proficient windsurfer. Thus, we will likely need to understand the impact of previous socialization experiences on entrepreneurs in order to better understand how they will accept and adopt various entrepreneurial roles.

Goffee and Scase's (1985) study of women entrepreneurs illustrates how one's orientation to the career can have a profound impact. They discovered that the women they studied differed dramatically depending on how they saw their roles in relation to their families and to their work. Some of the women had decided to put family as first priority and the business second priority while others reversed the order of importance. Those that put family first tended to run businesses out of their homes and organized their work around family needs and activities. Those women who put the business as their first priority worked away from the home and were "married to the business." Family needs were subservient to business concerns. Such differences in orientation lead to very different careers.

It is also important to understand entrepreneurs' orientations toward their careers, since the roles they will potentially adopt and dilemmas that they will encounter as they progress in the career will differ somewhat depending on their orientation. For example, those entrepreneurs who are only interested in making deals will typically avoid many of the problems related to growing a business, since an organization is not necessary for them to continue their entrepreneurial endeavors. In contrast, technical entrepreneurs need the resources of an organization in order to bring their products to the marketplace.

Career Progression

While research on managerial careers has led to the development of several models that outline the stages of a managerial career (Dalton, Thompson, & Price, 1977; Dalton & Thompson, 1986), little work has been done to understand the dynamics of an entrepreneurial career from entry to exit. A theory of entrepreneurial careers should describe the kinds of roles adopted by an entrepreneur over time. Hughes (1937) suggests that career theory should have a "moving perspective" outlining the changes in the interaction between the person and society over time. As societal institutions change, so too do the roles of those who interact with those institutions.

Common roles entrepreneurs play include a business owner, a wife/husband, a father/mother, a community leader, a manager, and so forth. Depending on how far entrepreneurs have progressed in their careers, they may have had to adopt several different roles as a result of changes in their families, in their businesses, and in their personal lives. As cited previously, work by Schein (1978) describes careers as encompassing the personal, family, and work dilemmas that one encounters over a lifetime. These dilemmas reflect the changing nature of a person's role. My own work applies these ideas to the study of entrepreneurial careers (Dyer, 1992). As I tracked the careers of over 100 entrepreneurs, I discovered that the changing nature of their roles involved the personal, family, and business dilemmas that they encountered at different stages of their careers. These dilemmas are noted in Figure 1. While this list of dilemmas is clearly not exhaustive—there are undoubtedly many others—it does suggest that those who study entrepreneurial careers should understand how the dilemmas facing an entrepreneur do change over the course of a career as a function of their changing roles. The following discussion summarizes how these dilemmas can affect an entrepreneurial career.

Early Career Roles and Dilemmas

As one begins an entrepreneurial career, there are several new roles and career dilemmas that are encountered. Personal dilemmas revolve around managing the stress and tension that accompanies an entrepreneurial career. Moreover, the entrepreneur often must cope with the insecurity and ambiguity that accompanies the acquisition of new roles as a business owner and manager.

The entrepreneur's family also feels the effects of an entrepreneurial career. Family finances are often used to fund the new venture, which can place strains on the family. Entrepreneurs often start new ventures in their twenties and thirties—about the time that they start to have children. Thus they can feel pulled between the demands of work and the demands of family as they try to fulfill their roles in both worlds. Some entrepreneurs in late career lament the fact that they did not manage this dilemma well (Dyer, 1992). They report that they sacrificed their families for their businesses.

Business dilemmas in early career typically concern gaining resources—labor, capital, raw materials—to start the new enterprise (Egge & Simer, 1988; Terpstra & Olson, 1993). Kazanjian's (1988) research noted that sales, marketing, and finance problems were most salient in early career. McCarthy, Krueger, and Schoenecker (1990) suggested that entrepreneurs use their time quite differently depending on the stage of their firm's development. Early stage entrepreneurs are more focused on customer issues than are later stage entrepreneurs.

Questions regarding the governance of the business also tend to arise early in the career. If the business is a partnership, how will partnership relations be managed? Will there be a board of directors? If so, who will be on the board and how will decisions be made? One study noted that entrepreneurs who have partners are four times more likely to be successful than those who start alone (Blotnick, 1987). However, many of the entrepreneurs that I studied told "horror stories" about partner relationships (Dyer, 1992). Thus, how the entrepreneur manages the role of owner and interacts with other owners is a key feature of an entrepreneurial career.

Midcareer Roles and Dilemmas

The roles of an entrepreneur appear to change in mid-career. As the entrepreneur's business grows, strategic planning, solving employee problems, and various administrative tasks become part of the entrepreneur's role (Kazanjian, 1988; McCarthy, Krueger, & Schoenecker, 1990). As entrepreneurs begin to accept more administrative duties they tend to face additional tension and stress as their roles change. The stress and weight of responsibility is often manifested in a sense of loneliness. Boyd and Gumpert (1984) noted that 54% of the entrepreneurs they studied experienced a recurrent sense of profound loneliness.

In a growing organization, the entrepreneur may need to use new forms of control through systems, information, or culture in order to manage operations. Entrepreneurs who lead growing enterprises frequently report that they are frustrated by the fact that they don't feel in control of their expanding businesses (Dyer, 1992). To manage growth, entrepreneurs often must change from a "doing role" to a "delegating role" since they must rely on others to get work accomplished.

Some entrepreneurs decide to hire professional managers to handle many of the functions of a growing business. This can also pose a unique set of problems since the orientation and values of professional managers are often different from those of the entrepreneur. Several studies have noted that the ability (or inability) of entrepreneurs to integrate the skills of professional management into their businesses can spell the difference between success or failure (Dyer, 1989).

The decision whether or not to hire family members also emerges as the business begins to grow. This can create another unique set of problems (Dyer, 1986; Ward, 1987). Family and business dynamics are often disrupted since these two systems generally function under a different set of assumptions. Families exist to nurture and support family members; love is unconditional. A business exists to be efficient and profitable; rewards are contingent upon performance. Hence, how well the entrepreneur manages the conflicts between family and business roles may determine whether or not the entrepreneur has a satisfying career.

Late Career Dilemmas

Retirement and disengagement from a career are often very stress-producing experiences since such changes involve adopting a new set of roles personally, professionally, and in the family (Schein, 1978). For the entrepreneur, retirement has often been equated with "preparing for one's own death" or "committing suicide" (Beckhard & Dyer, 1983; Lansberg, 1983). One study of entrepreneurs who had graduated from Harvard University noted that 48.9% had no plans to ever retire, and another 25% had not even thought about retirement or were not planning to retire until well after age 65 (Duffy & Stevenson, 1984). My own work suggests that entrepreneurs experience retirement much like the terminally ill patients described by Elizabeth Kübler-Ross (Dyer, 1992; Kübler-Ross, 1969). Kübler-Ross found her patients going through the stages of denial, anger, bargaining, depression, and acceptance as they attempted to come to terms with their life-threatening illnesses—although some patients never got beyond the denial stage. Entrepreneurs appear to go through similar psychological stages, although some may be unwilling to recognize their own mortality and prepare their businesses and their families for a future without them.

Early research by Trow (1961) noted that those businesses where the leader had not developed or shared the succession plan did worse financially after succession than those businesses where the leader had carefully planned for succession. Other case study data indicate that a lack of succession planning can lead to disaster (Ward, 1987). Lansberg

(1983) points out how family members, coworkers, and other owners of a business can conspire to prevent the entrepreneur from engaging in succession planning. Likewise, certain personality characteristics—such as a need for power and control—can affect the entrepreneur's ability to start a succession planning process (Peay & Dyer, 1989).

There is clear evidence that a lack of estate planning can undermine family relationships as well. The entrepreneur's family can be thrown into turmoil without a clear understanding of how assets are to be divided and who is to maintain control of those assets (Ward, 1987). Thus, entrepreneurs can lead relatively successful lives and careers, only to wreck havoc on their businesses and their families if they don't successfully plan for retirement and succession.

Business Failure

The model in Figure 1 has an arrow leading from the business dilemmas to what has been labeled "business failure." The careers of entrepreneurs are fraught with business failure. Many entrepreneurs start several unsuccessful businesses before launching a successful enterprise. Ronstadt (1982) indicated that this is a common pattern in the entrepreneurs that he has studied.

When the entrepreneur's business fails, the individual, social, and economic factors that affect career choice again come into play. For example, an entrepreneur's needs for autonomy, the encouragement of the community to start a new enterprise, the availability of other forms of employment, and economic conditions in general could all combine to determine whether the entrepreneur will attempt to start a new business, or work for others until conditions are right to launch a new venture. Certain new socialization experiences may also encourage the entrepreneur to try again. Of course, in some cases, an entrepreneur will forever leave the entrepreneurial career path in favor of a more traditional career.

It is also important to note that business failure (or success) is only one aspect of an entrepreneurial career. Personal and family satisfaction also plays a significant role. In a study conducted by Peay (1987), seventy-one entrepreneurs were surveyed. Of that sample, over 90% were either quite satisfied or very satisfied with their lives in general, over 90% were quite satisfied or very satisfied with their marriages, and over 90% were either quite satisfied or very satisfied with their family life. Thus it appears that many entrepreneurs are handling these dilemmas quite well. However, one study by Boyd and Gumpert (1983) reported a number of problems experienced by entrepreneurs. The majority of the entrepreneurs they studied reported numerous physical ailments from which they suffered regularly. A smaller percentage reported increased use of alcohol and tobacco since starting an entrepreneurial career. Twelve percent reported that they were undergoing regular psychiatric counseling. Furthermore, numerous studies have reported how entrepreneurs significantly damaged family relationships, which undermined their sense of career success and accomplishment. Thus a theory of entrepreneurial careers should provide an understanding of the potential outcomes of the particular career choices and career paths.

Variations on the Stages of Career Progression

While the stages of career progression just presented suggest a temporal ordering, it should be noted that with certain entrepreneurs these stages may overlap or occur simultaneously. For example, a person who starts a business later in life and has grown children may have to deal with issues related to hiring family members as he or she starts the business. Also, succession planning and estate planning may need to be done fairly soon. Furthermore, we may find that what may appear to be a dilemma for one entrepreneur may not be a dilemma for another because of differing skills, background, or psychological make-up. Thus, while discovering the common dilemmas facing entrepreneurs may prove to be a fruitful way to study their careers, one must recognize the potential for great variation in the kinds of dilemmas and problems that different entrepreneurs encounter.

FUTURE DIRECTIONS FOR RESEARCH ON ENTREPRENEURIAL CAREERS

The purpose of this article has been to present an overall framework for understanding the nature of entrepreneurial careers. As one can tell by this brief review, much additional work needs to be done. The following list of questions outlines those issues that need to be addressed in future research:

(1) What is the relative influence of the various antecedents on career choice? Which factors—individual, social, or economic—have the greatest impact? How do these factors interact with one another to motivate someone to start an entrepreneurial career? By what processes can these antecedents be changed or influenced? Rather than focusing on just one of the antecedents of career choice as has generally been the case in the past, future theories will need to be more robust, taking into account all the factors in career choice and understanding the relationships between them.

(2) Are there common socialization experiences for all entrepreneurs? Do these experiences follow any particular sequence? Do certain types of socialization experiences determine whether or not an entrepreneur will be successful? To answer these questions a theory of career socialization, much like Van Maanen and Schein (1979) developed for organizational careers, needs to be created for entrepreneurs.

(3) What are the different orientations that entrepreneurs have towards their careers? Do entrepreneurs with different orientations (e.g., technical entrepreneur versus a deal maker) differ with regard to the roles they adopt and the dilemmas they face throughout their careers? By better understanding how entrepreneurs develop a career orientation, we might be able to better predict the course of their careers and possibly help entrepreneurs adapt more quickly to various entrepreneurial roles. Research into the orientations of entrepreneurs might lead us to conclude that there is no single theory of entrepreneurial careers, but, in fact, multiple theories are needed to delineate the career dynamics of different types of entrepreneurs.

(4) What are the significant roles assumed by entrepreneurs during the course of their careers? Can we develop a better understanding of the personal, family, and business dilemmas encountered by entrepreneurs? How do they interpret these roles and dilemmas? How do they cope with role conflicts and career dilemmas? What coping strategies seem to work? Are there certain personal, family, or business characteristics that make it more difficult to succeed in an entrepreneurial career?

Of course there are a myriad of factors that can influence how we might answer each of these questions, and research has already been conducted that lays a good foundation to answer such questions. It is clear, however, that for us to better understand the dynamics of an entrepreneurial career, much more research and theorizing needs to be done.

There are several methodological issues that need to be addressed in studying entrepreneurial careers. Goffman (1961) suggests that careers can be studied primarily from two vantage points: the "internal" or subjective dimensions of a career and the "external" or objective aspects of a career.

If one were to study entrepreneurial careers from a subjectivist or interpretive perspective, the focal point of such research would be to understand how entrepreneurs interpret their experiences as they pursue their careers. In terms of the model presented earlier, this would imply that one would attempt to understand the impact of the antecedents of career choice by studying how entrepreneurs interpreted those factors that influenced them to become entrepreneurs. Entrepreneurial roles and the various career dilemmas could be studied from an interpretive perspective by gathering oral histories, participant observation, semiotic analysis, or other such ethnographic methods. Such an approach to research would give us a deeper understanding of what it is like to be an entrepreneur from the "native's point of view."

From an objectivist perspective, one might attempt to discover the relative impact of the antecedents of career choice by gathering data concerning each of these factors and then comparing them across states, regions, industries, countries, and so forth. The goal would be to see which of these factors has the greatest influence on start-up activity. This would require the creation of large data sets on each of these factors, which are not now readily accessible.

Questionnaires could be developed and administered to entrepreneurs to measure such factors as the degree of role conflict they experience, the kinds of dilemmas they face, or how they orient themselves to the career. Data might also be gathered from members of entrepreneurial families and those who work with entrepreneurs to discover their perceptions about the entrepreneur's role. Perhaps they see the entrepreneur's role quite differently than the entrepreneur. This approach would allow the researcher to compare and contrast the responses from a large number of entrepreneurs and those who live and work with them, and possibly lead to more general theories of entrepreneurial careers.

The trade-offs inherent in using either an objectivist or subjectivist stance are apparent. Objectivist approaches allow us to broadly sample the population of entrepreneurs, develop clear, measurable constructs, and develop general models and theories. However, often such an approach can miss the rich, contextual data that provide deeper insights. In contrast, by using a subjectivist perspective, one can get closer to the phenomenon under investigation, but the problems associated with analyzing and presenting such "messy" data can undermine such research efforts.

Because of the drawbacks and advantages inherent in both methodological stances, and the dearth of previous research on entrepreneurial careers, it would appear that research should be carried out using both approaches, and that theories and methods from various disciplines and fields such as psychology, family systems theory, anthropology, economics, sociology, and so forth need to be applied to the study of entrepreneurial careers. Regardless of the method, there is a need for more longitudinal studies. For example, Edgar Schein's (1978) research approach of tracking a panel of graduates from the Sloan School of Management at MIT over time and gathering data from them at regular intervals appears to be one of the more fruitful ways to understand how careers develop and change over time. Without longitudinal data, we will be unable to gain insights into complex career dynamics, and will, as a result, end up with fairly shallow and incomplete theories.

CONCLUSION

The purpose of this paper has been to present a general model to understand the dynamics of entrepreneurial careers and to suggest some research questions and methodological concerns that will likely shape much of the research in this area. From a theoretical standpoint, we need to discover the complex interplay between individual, social, and economic factors that influences entrepreneurial behavior. We also need to come to a deeper understanding of how entrepreneurs manage their roles and develop their career identities, and how they attempt to cope with the complex personal, family, and business dilemmas that they encounter during the course of their lives. From a practical standpoint, such research may help in initiating policies that can stimulate entrepreneurial activity, particularly in areas that are economically depressed or disadvantaged, and help entrepreneurs be more successful—not just in business, but in their personal and family lives as well.

REFERENCES

Aldrich, H. E. (1990). Using an ecological perspective to study organizational founding rates. *Entrepreneurship Theory and Practice, 14*(3), 7-24.

Aldrich, H. E., Rosen, B., & Woodward, W. (1986). The impact of social networks on business founding and profit: A longitudinal study. In R. Ronstadt, J. A. Hornaday, R. Peterson, and K. H. Vesper (Eds.), *Frontiers of entrepreneurship research*, pp. 154-168. Wellesley, MA: Babson College.

Aldrich, H. E., & Waldinger, R. (1990). Ethnicity and entrepreneurship. *Annual Review of Sociology, 16*, 111-135.

Aldrich, H. E., & Zimmer, C. (1986). Entrepreneurship through social networks. In D. Sexton & R. Smilor (Eds.), *The art and science of entrepreneurship*, pp. 3-23. Cambridge, MA: Ballinger.

Arthur, M. B., Hall, D. T., & Lawrence, B. S. (Eds.). (1989a). *Handbook of career theory*. Cambridge: Cambridge University Press.

Arthur, M. B., Hall, D. T., & Lawrence, B. S. (1989b). Generating new directions in career theory: The case for a transdisciplinary approach. In M. B. Arthur, D. T. Hall, & B. S. Lawrence (Eds.). *Handbook of career theory*, pp. 7-25. Cambridge: Cambridge University Press.

Beckhard, R., & Dyer, W. G., Jr. (1983). SMR Forum: Managing change in the family firm—Issues and strategies. *Sloan Management Review, 24*(3), 59-65.

Bird, B. J. (1989). *Entrepreneurial behavior*. Glenview, IL: Scott, Foresman.

Birley, S. (1985). The role of networks in the entrepreneurial process. In J. A. Hornaday, E. B. Shils, J. A. Timmons, & K. H. Vesper (Eds.), *Frontiers of entrepreneurship research*, pp. 325-337. Wellesley, MA: Babson College.

Blotnick, S. (1987). Two for the money. *Forbes*, February 23, p. 166.

Boyd, D. P., & Gumpert, D. E. (1983). The effects of stress on early age entrepreneurs. In J. A. Hornaday, J. A. Timmons, & K. H. Vesper (Eds.), *Frontiers of entrepreneurship research*, pp. 180-191. Wellesley, MA: Babson College.

Boyd, D. P., & Gumpert, D. E. (1984). The loneliness of the start-up entrepreneur. In J. A. Hornaday, F. Tarpley, Jr., J. A. Timmons, & K. H. Vesper (Eds.), *Frontiers of entrepreneurship research*, pp. 478-487. Wellesley, MA: Babson College.

Brockhaus, R. (1982). The psychology of the entrepreneur. In C. Kent, D. Sexton, & K. Vesper (Eds.), *Encyclopedia of entrepreneurship*, pp. 39-57. Englewood Cliffs, NJ: Prentice Hall.

Brockhaus, R., & Horwitz, P. (1986). The psychology of the entrepreneur. In D. L. Sexton & R. W. Smilor (Eds.), *The art and science of entrepreneurship*, pp. 25-48. Cambridge, MA: Ballinger.

Brockhaus, R., & Nord, W. R. (1979). An exploration of factors affecting the entrepreneurial decision: Personal characteristics vs. environmental conditions. *Proceedings of the National Academy of Management*, 364-368.

Brush, C. (1992). Research on women business owners: Past trends, a new perspective and future directions. *Entrepreneurship Theory and Practice*, *16*(4), 5-30.

Carland, J., Hoy, F., Boulton, W., & Carland, J. (1984). Differentiating entrepreneurs from small business owners: A conceptualization. *Academy of Management Review*, *9*(2), 354-359.

Case, J. (1989). The origins of entrepreneurship. *INC.*, June, 51, 52.

Chambers, B. R., Hart, S. L., & Denison, D. R. (1988). Founding team experience and new firm performance. In B. A. Kirchoff, W. A. Long, W. E. McMullan, K. H. Vesper, & W. E. Wetzel, Jr. (Eds.), *Frontiers of entrepreneurship research*, pp. 106-118. Wellesley, MA: Babson College.

Collins, O. F., & Moore, D. G. (1964). *The enterprising man*. East Lansing: Michigan State University.

Collins, O. F., & Moore, D. G. (1970). *The organization makers*. New York: Appleton-Century-Crofts.

Cooper, A. C. (1970). The Palo Alto experience. *Industrial Research*, *12*(5), 58-61.

Dalton, G. W., & Holdaway, F. (1989). Preliminary findings—Entrepreneur study. Working paper, Brigham Young University, Department of Organizational Behavior.

Dalton, G. W., & Thompson, P. H. (1986). *Novations: Strategies for career management*. Glenview, IL: Scott, Foresman.

Dalton, G. W., Thompson, P. H., & Price, R. (1977). The four stages of professional careers. *Organizational Dynamics*, Summer, 19-42.

Derr, C. B. (1984). Entrepreneurs: A careers perspective. Paper presented at the meeting of the Academy of Management, Boston, Massachusetts.

Duffy, P. B., & Stevenson, H. H. (1984). Entrepreneurship and self employment: Understanding the distinctions. In J. A. Hornaday, F. Tarpley, Jr., J. A. Timmons, & K. H. Vesper (Eds.), *Frontiers of entrepreneurship research*, pp. 461-477. Wellesley, MA: Babson College.

Dyer, W. G., Jr. (1986). *Cultural change in the family firms: Anticipating and managing business and family transactions*. San Francisco: Jossey-Bass.

Dyer, W. G., Jr. (1989). Integrating professional management into a family owned business. *Family Business Review*, *2*, 221-235.

Dyer, W. G., Jr. (1992). *The entrepreneurial experience*. San Francisco: Jossey-Bass.

Egge, K. A., & Simer, F. J. (1988). An analysis of the advice given by recent entrepreneurs to prospective entrepreneurs. In B. A. Kirchoff, W. A. Long, W. E. McMullan, K. H. Vesper, & W. E. Wetzel, Jr. (Eds.), *Frontiers of entrepreneurship research*, pp. 119-133. Wellesley, MA: Babson College.

Gartner, W. B. (1988). Who is an entrepreneur? is the wrong question. *American Journal of Small Business*, *13*, Spring, 11-32.

Goffee, R., & Scase, R. (1985). *Women in charge*. London: George Allen and Unwin.

Goffman, E. (1961). The moral career of the mental patient. In E. Goffman, *Asylums*, p. 127. New York: Anchor Books.

Hughes, E. C. (1937). Institutional office and the person. *American Journal of Sociology*, *43*, 404-413.

Kazanjian, R. K. (1988). Relation of dominant problems to stages of growth in technology-based new ventures. *Academy of Management Journal*, *31*(2), 257-279.

Kets de Vries, M. F. R. (1977). The entrepreneurial personality: A person at the crossroads. *Journal of Management Studies, 14*, 34-57.

Kilby, P. (1971). Hunting the heffalump. In P. Kilby (Ed.), *Entrepreneurship and economic development*. New York: Free Press.

Kirchoff, B. A. (1991). Entrepreneur's contribution to economics. *Entrepreneurship Theory and Practice, 16*(2), 93-112.

Kotkin, J. (1986). The reluctant entrepreneurs. *INC.*, September, 81-86.

Kubler-Ross, E. (1969). *On death and dying*. New York: Macmillan.

Lamont, L. M. (1972). The role of marketing in technical entrepreneurship. In A. C. Cooper & J. L. Komives (Eds.), *Technical entrepreneurship: A symposium*, pp. 150-164. Milwaukee, WI: Center for Venture Management.

Lansberg, I. (1983). The succession conspiracy. *Family Business Review, 1*(2), 119-143.

McCarthy, A. M., Krueger, D. A., & Schoenecker, T. S. (1990). Changes in the time allocation patterns of entrepreneurs. *Entrepreneurship Theory and Practice, 15*(2), 7-18.

Miller, M. (1963). *The way of enterprise*. London: Deutsch.

Peay, R. T. (1987). *The power needs of entrepreneurs and their effects upon the transfer of leadership power in entrepreneurial firms*. Unpublished doctoral dissertation, Brigham Young University.

Peay, R. T., and Dyer, W. G., Jr. (1989). Power orientations of entrepreneurs and succession planning. *Journal of Small Business Management, 27*(1), 47-52.

Reynolds, P. D. (1991). Sociology and entrepreneurship. *Entrepreneurship Theory and Practice, 16*(2), 47-70.

Roberts, E. B. (1969). Entrepreneurship and technology. In W. Gruber & D. Marquis (Eds.), *Factors in the transfer of technology*, pp. 219-237. Cambridge, MA: MIT Press.

Roberts, E. B., & Wainer, H. A. (1968). New enterprise on Rte. 128. *Science Journal, 4*(12), 78-83.

Robinson, P. B., Stimpson, D. V., Huefner, J. C., & Hunt, H. K. (1991). An attitude approach to the prediction of entrepreneurship. *Entrepreneurship Theory and Practice, 15*(4), 13-32.

Ronstadt, R. (1982). Does entrepreneurial career path really matter? In K. H. Vesper (Eds.), *Frontiers of entrepreneurship research*, pp. 540-567. Wellesley, MA: Babson College.

Schein, E. H. (1978). *Career dynamics: Matching individual and organizational needs*. Reading, MA: Addison-Wesley.

Schein, E. H. (1990). *Career anchors: Discovering your real values*. San Diego, CA: University Associates.

Scherer, R., Brodzinski, J., & Wiebe, F. (1991). Examining the relationship between personality and entrepreneurial career preference. *Entrepreneurship and Regional Development, 3*(2), 195-206.

Secrest, L. (1975). Texas entrepreneurship. In J. W. Schrier & J. Susbauer (Eds.), *Entrepreneurship and enterprise development: A worldwide perspective*, pp. 51-65. Milwaukee, WI: Center for Venture Management.

Sexton, D. L., & Bowman, N. B. (1984). The effects of preexisting psychological characteristics on new venture initiations. Paper presented at the meeting of the Academy of Management, Boston, Massachusetts.

Shapero, A. (1972). The process of technical company formation in a local area. In A. C. Cooper & J. L.

Komives (Eds.), *Technical entrepreneurship: A symposium*, pp. 63-95. Milwaukee, WI: Center for Venture Management.

Shaver, K. G., & Scott, L. R. (1991). Person, process, choice: The psychology of new venture creation. *Entrepreneurship Theory and Practice*, *16*(2), 23-46.

Solomon, D. (1968). Sociological perspectives on occupations. In H. S. Becker, B. Geer, D. Riesman, & R. S. Weiss (Eds.), *Institutions and the person*, pp. 3-13. Chicago: Aldine.

Starr, J. (1990). Resource parsimony and resourcefulness in new venture creation: Lessons from habitual entrepreneurs. Unpublished dissertation proposal, The Wharton School, University of Pennsylvania.

Stevenson, H. H. (1987). General management and entrepreneurship. Working Paper, Harvard University, Department of Organizational Behavior.

Stinchcombe, A. L. (1965). Social structure and organizations. In J. March (Ed.), *Handbook of organizations*. Chicago: Rand McNally.

Terpstra, D. E., & Olson, P. D. (1993). Entrepreneurial start-up and growth: A classification of problems. *Entrepreneurship Theory and Practice*, *17*(3), 5-20.

Thomas, D. A., & Alderfer, C. P. (1989). The influence of race on career dynamics: Theory and research on minority career experiences. In M. B. Arthur, D. T. Hall, & B. S. Lawrence (Eds.), *Handbook of career theory*, pp. 133-158. Cambridge: Cambridge University Press.

Trow, D. B. (1961). Executive succession in small companies. *Administrative Science Quarterly*, September, 228-239.

Van Maanen, J. (1983). Doing new things in old ways: The chains of socialization. Office of Naval Research Report TR-ONR-17.

Van Maanen, J., & Barley, S. R. (1984). Occupational communities: Culture and control in organizations. In B. Staw & L. Cummings (Eds.), *Research in organizational behavior*, vol. 6, pp. 287-365. Greenwich, CT: JAI.

Van Maanen, J., & Schein, E. H. (1979). Toward a theory of organizational socialization. In B. Staw (Ed.), *Research in organizational behavior*, vol. 1, pp. 209-264. Greenwich, CT: JAI.

Vesper, K. (1980). *New venture strategies*. Englewood Cliffs, NJ: Prentice Hall.

Ward, J. L. (1987). *Keeping the family business healthy: How to plan for continuing growth, profitability, and family leadership*. San Francisco: Jossey-Bass.

Wilken, P. H. (1979). *Entrepreneurship: A comparative and historical study*. Norwood, NJ: Ablex.

W. Gibb Dyer, Jr. is Professor and Chair of the Department of Organizational Behavior at Brigham Young University.

This paper was originally presented at the ICSB meetings in Las Vegas, Nevada, on June 22, 1993. I would like to thank Thomas Monroy and several anonymous reviewers for their help with earlier drafts of this article.

[2]

Modelling Entrepreneurial Career Progressions: Concepts and Considerations

Jerome A. Katz

Studying entrepreneurship longitudinally is in effect a study of entrepreneurial *careers*, but there is little vocational theory specific to self-employment, much less entrepreneurship. Using Edgar Schein's Career Anchor Theory as a starting point, the existing anchors of autonomy and entrepreneurship are adapted to facilitate secondary analysis using existing longitudinal datasets. A model of career progression or trajectory, which would permit analysis of the self-employed as well as others, is developed using six variables. The first three come from Schein's "career cone" model of vocational movement—hierarchy, function, and centrality. Three new variables are derived from a diverse literature on entrepreneurship—employment duration, job multiplicity, and self-employment emergence. One approach to the operationalization of these six variables is shown using the Panel Study of Income Dynamics, and implications for future research and theorizing on entrepreneurial career progression are given.

Studying entrepreneurs longitudinally is becoming more prevalent as a research *desiderata* (Bygrave, 1989) and as a practical possibility (Carroll & Mosakowski, 1987; Katz, 1992). But what remains largely unasked is what set of theories should be used to study entrepreneurs over time. Whether commonsense approaches, sometimes with sophisticated statistical underpinnings, are used to study firm and job creation (Birch, 1987; Reynolds, 1988), or economic modelling is used (Evans & Leighton, 1989), these are not approaches grounded in the actual study of the internal processes and decisions of the entrepreneurs themselves. What are needed to complement the growing capacity for primary and secondary analysis of entrepreneurs longitudinally are theories to complement the datasets and statistical methods.

There are several variants in the social sciences used to study people over time. The specific field concerned with the longitudinal study of people in work situations is called vocational or career theory (Ornstein & Isabella, 1993; Osipow, 1973; Schein, 1978). To date, however, little work has been reported in career theory related to entrepreneurs. Covering 1989-1992, Ornstein and Isabella (1993) found only two such papers, one of which was the precursor of this manuscript. What is needed is the adaptation of career theory to better consider the people and processes of entrepreneurship.

Fortunately one major career theory does provide an explicit consideration of types much like both the "entrepreneurs" and "small business owners" of longstanding debate (Carland, Hoy, Boulton, & Carland, 1984; Gartner, 1988)—the career anchor theory of Edgar Schein (1978). Schein's model provides both a means to conceptualize different types of self-employeds in a manner consistent with existing entrepreneurship research, and a widely recognized and accepted set of variables for describing the nature of an individual's career and the individual's movement through it, called the career cone.

Using Schein's model as a base, this paper will pursue two goals. One goal is to adapt Schein's vocational model to analyze in finer detail a greater range of entrepreneurial career progressions and subsidiary analytic issues. To do this definitions of the three major career cone variables of hierarchy, function, and centrality will be expanded to fit with career-relevant findings from entrepreneurship research, and three additional variables—employment duration, job multiplicity, and self-employment emergence—will be introduced to better account for the nature of entrepreneurship in the workforce. The other goal will be to demonstrate how these variables can be operationalized to facilitate ***theory-based*** secondary analyses of entrepreneurial careers using the growing collection of longitudinal datasets of the workforce. The effort starts with introducing and adapting Schein's theory.

ADAPTING SCHEIN'S CAREER THEORY

The Schein model is uniquely suited for research in entrepreneurial careers because it is one of the few models that explicitly considers self-employed individuals. In fact, Schein's two types of career anchors for the self-employed, entrepreneurial endeavors and autonomy, closely follow the conventional entrepreneur/small business owner dichotomy common in entrepreneurship research.

Schein's general model for career cycles forms the basis for developing a theory-driven model for analyzing longitudinal datasets. Schein (1978) characterizes the individual's career progression using what is called a Career Cycle Cone (Figure 1) reflecting movement along one or more of three dimensions: **Hierarchy**, which reflects the total control or power available to the person in the job; **Functional/Technical Area**, which reflects the type of activity performed in the job; and **Centrality/Inclusion**, which reflects movement toward or away from the "core" of the organization or profession.

The first two variables have a long-established history in vocational and economic theory. For example, in one of the most detailed recent economic models of career mobility using the Panel Study of Income Dynamics (Sicherman & Galor, 1990), change was measured using differences across time in occupational code (a technical measure[1]) and a derived measure of "level" of the occupation based on the education necessary for employment in that occupation.

In addition to the three variables making up the Career Cone, Schein found that all the self-employed fell into one of two Career Anchors. A career anchor is "the pattern of self-perceived talents, motives, and values [which] serves to guide, constrain, stabilize and integrate the person's career" (Schein, 1978, p. 127). Uniquely among personality-based characteristics, career anchors cannot be successfully identified in students, since stable anchors emerge only with work experience. The two anchors favored

1. One problem of such approaches is that they categorize all self-employeds in one group, with equal status. In many cases this underestimates the average status and the variance in status of the self-employed because it fails to consider the higher status of self-employed professionals such as doctors or lawyers in private practice. In some occupations, such as dentistry, the self-employed dominate, while in most professions in the U.S. the self-employed occur near the national average of 12%.

Figure 1.
Schein's (1978) Career Cycle Cone

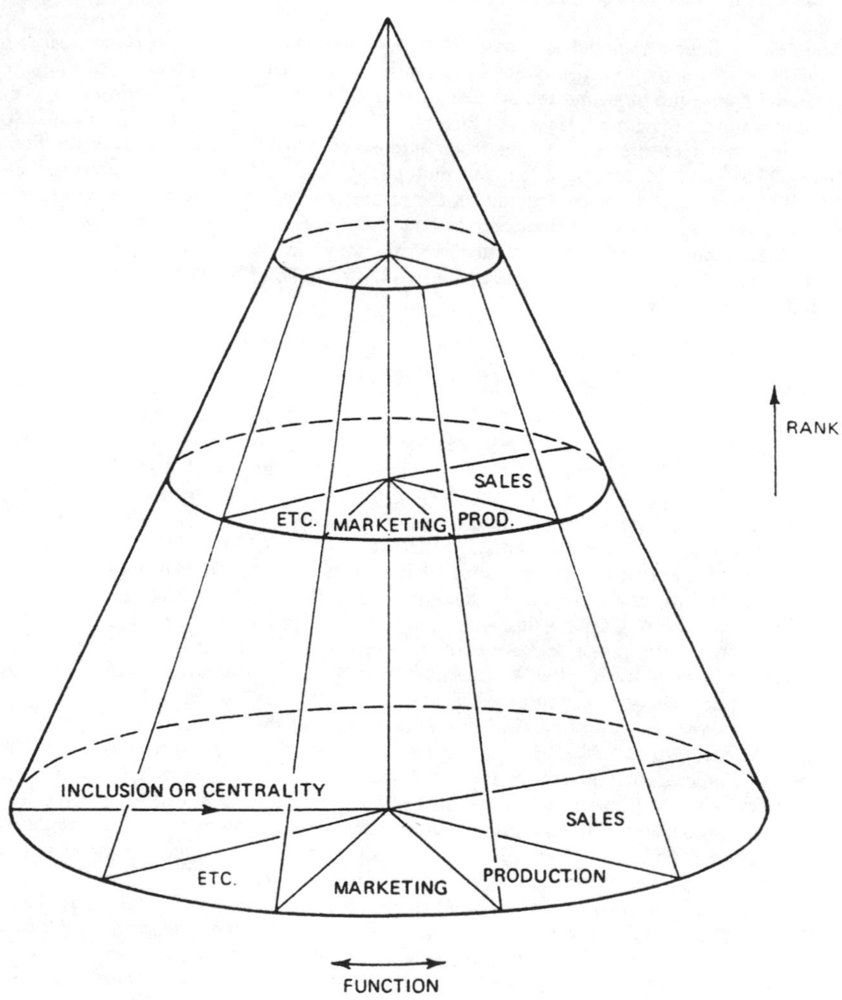

by the self-employed are: **Autonomy/Independence**, which is a desire for freedom from rules and the control of others; and **Entrepreneurship** (originally called Creativity), which focuses on the creation of "something new, involving the motivation to overcome obstacles, the willingness to run risks, and the desire for personal prominence in whatever is accomplished" (Schein, 1985a, p. 30).

These two anchors closely follow respectively the "Craftsman" and "Opportunistic" entrepreneurial orientations originally developed by Smith (1967) and refined in the works of Smith and Miner (1983). The distinction also closely follows the small business owner vs. entrepreneur distinction articulated by Hoy and others (Carland, Hoy, Boulton, & Carland, 1984).

This section considers the dimensions of hierarchy, function, and centrality and the career anchors from the perspective of fine tuning their adaptation to the self-employed, and operationalizes the measures to make possible analysis using established longitudinal surveys of individuals.

Hierarchy

Self-employment by definition places the individual at the top of the firm's hierarchy. In one-person firms (Katz, 1984; Star, 1979), which account for over half of all business firms, growth occurs by adding levels below the top of the hierarchy.

This situation rooted in the extreme case offers an approach for adapting hierarchy to the study of the self-employed. In studying the self-employed, hierarchy is best measured by growth in organizational size. This approach measures the number of people over whom the self-employed exercises leadership or power. The owner of a one-person firm would be seen as having power over no one. Hence the owner of a one-person firm has less hierarchy than the owner of a 100-employee firm.

The advantage of accepting such a size measure means that differences between large- and small-business CEOs become matters of degree along a clearly operationalizable dimension, instead of requiring different sets of theory for the two classes of CEOs. Additionally, such an approach fits well with wealth-centered (Stevenson, Roberts, & Grousbeck, 1989; Timmons, Muzyka, Stevenson, & Bygrave, 1987) and political economy (Birch, 1987) definitions of entrepreneurship. The measure is also included in most surveys of the self-employed and is relatively unambiguous in its meaning, measurement, and interpretation.

There are, however, three problems related to the use of such a size measure. First, organizations, especially small ones, can grow substantially in ways that do not add employees. For example, small businesses often grow through the use of independent contractors or through the use of automation such as answering machines or computers. Second, particularly in new firms, number of employees may be an inferior size measure compared to sales. As new firms establish themselves in the market, a fixed number of employees often produce substantially greater sales with additional experience and customer awareness. Finding such firms in samples would require having information on the age of the firm in addition to its size. Third, in most organizational theory research, hierarchy is measured directly or inferred using some rule of thumb about the span of control. This approach is likely to be impractical for application in smaller enterprises for three reasons. First, the self-employed remains at the first level of hierarchy regardless of the number of levels below. Second, few of the longitudinal surveys of individuals contain information about number of hierarchical levels in firms, although most of these surveys do ask the self-employed for the number of employees in their firm. Third, while some established norms exist for converting number of employees into number of levels, those norms are based on large, often publicly held and professionally managed firms. When this approach to organizational design is contrasted to the models common in small business, it is commonly found that smaller, owner-managed firms tend to have exceptionally flat (Mintzberg, 1979) or simple (Jaques, 1976) structures, with few levels of hierarchy.

Therefore, unless new, separate norms can be established for smaller, owner-managed firms, the least ambiguous way to measure hierarchy of the self-employed is to use the number of employees.

Function

Function is perhaps the weakest of the three dimensions because the rules of thumb underlying research differ by country. For example, in some countries occupational classification schemes differentiate between the activities of salaried and self-employed managers in the same type of vocation (e.g., Carroll & Mosakowski, 1987), while the American system, based on census classifications, does not. A self-employed plumber in America becomes a "proprietor," even though the vast bulk of the individual's work is no different from that of a wage-or-salaried plumber without managerial duties. Does employment status make a difference in the functions performed by the individual?

Looking at American vocational theory, one might guess the answer to be "no." Little conceptual work has been done to document or analyze differences between wage-or-salaried and self-employed individuals in what are ostensibly the same occupation. And in practice, the continuing reliance on 2-digit Census Occupational Codes in most American surveys means that there is little opportunity to compare functional differences between wage-or-salaried and self-employed individuals. The major known problem stemming from the use of the 2-digit classification relates to those individuals who are classified as proprietors rather than as self-employeds practicing a particular occupation, as in the case of the plumbers mentioned above. Worse yet, while coding of this variable appears consistent within organizations (e.g., ISR, NORC), it may differ between organizations.

Despite the oversight in theory and census coding, the little research to date suggests that employment status does alter function. Eden (1975), using data from the Quality of Employment Surveys, has shown that salaried and self-employed work do have some systematic differences. In Eden's parlance, wage-or-salaried work can be referred to as "maintenance-free employment." This means that while a self-employed individual must worry about maintaining the firm, meeting payrolls, paying licenses and firm fees, the employee does not. The burden of maintaining the workplace as an ongoing institution falls on the self-employed, not the wage-or-salaried.

Centrality

Centrality, like hierarchy, loses some meaning when the owner is the central figure in the firm. From an inter-firm or longitudinal perspective, however, the solution follows the logic applied to hierarchy. Over time the defining characteristic of centrality of the self-employed is their relation to their *expertise*. If centrality is proximity to the critical expertise of the firm or the career, the adaptation becomes clearer. Entrepreneurs' careers can be measured in terms of deviations from their central expertise.

The adaptation is clearest when studying entrepreneurs in the nonbusiness professions. A dentist who opens a dental practice has directly applied expertise. In taking on and supervising subordinate dentists, the entrepreneur-dentist is doing some dentistry, but is also doing supervision, requiring some generalization of the lessons learned in dental school. A dentist who creates a multimember dental plan (the dental equivalent of an HMO) has generalized on the core expertise even more, to the extent that some may see the dentist now more as a manager than as a practicing dentist.

Dentists may also branch out from their profession. For example, for almost two decades Holiday Inns' largest franchisee was a Memphis dentist. Another Memphis dentist, Winfield Dunn, served as governor of the state. In both cases the business owner and the politician reported that their analytic abilities and people-oriented skills were directly based on what they learned as dentists.

Centrality information is variably available in longitudinal surveys. For example, in the work detail supplements of the Panel Study of Income Dynamics (PSID) and the

National Longitudinal Studies (NLS), there are detailed entries about the type of work done, permitting the possibility of evaluating centrality. In life history datasets such as the German one described by Carroll and Mosakowski (1987), such details are available for coding. However, most longitudinal studies, such as those listed by Katz (1992) as particularly relevant for entrepreneurship researchers, would not permit centrality analyses. Overall, the effectiveness of this measure will depend on the biographical and qualitative nature of the data being used.

Career Anchors

Career anchors have been assessed through two methods. Originally, career anchors were assessed only through the use of an extensive interview or self-study protocol (Schein, 1978). Later, a somewhat simplified dyadic interview protocol was developed (Schein, 1985a) and included a 41-item questionnaire, the Career Orientations Inventory (COI). The COI, however, is a poor method for assessing career anchors when using secondary data analyses; psychometric information on the COI is scarce; its relation to other personality or vocational instruments is not known; and it has not been used in major national surveys. For these reasons, the interview protocol and its scoring system will be discussed here.

Analysis of the interview protocols has always proceeded in a holistic, qualitative fashion. The goal has been to identify major themes in the history, and to seek to establish whether these themes form any consistent patterns across the person's working life. These patterns, where they exist, are weighed, and the dominant one is labelled the individual's career anchor.

This approach has the potential for adaptation to existing datasets through pattern matching. In pattern matching, profiles of typical behaviors for Autonomy- and Entrepreneurship-oriented individuals are developed, and individuals' career histories are compared to the two profiles. With a few exceptions, the major longitudinal studies do not code answers verbatim or ask the types of questions that would permit a direct application of career anchor thematic analysis approaches. However, given sufficient points of comparison, classification into one of two categories should be possible. Such taxonomic methods have been applied in organizational studies by McKelvey (1982). An example of such patterns based on Schein's work (1978, 1985a, 1985b) is given below in Table 1.

Table 1

Prototype for Career Anchor Pattern Asssessment

	Autonomy	Entrepreneurship
Status Changes in Wage-or-salaried Employment Moves	Little	Changes to Higher Status Frequent
Firm Sales Show Substantial Growth	Typically No (esp. after start-up)	Typically Yes
Income	Low-to-Moderate (for industry)	High (for industry)
Firm Sole Proprietorship	Typically Yes	Typically No
Number of Employees	Low-to-Moderate (for industry)	High (for industry)
Habitual Entrepreneur Pattern	Owns Firms Serially	Owns Multiple Firms Simultaneously
Multiple Business Sites	Typically No	Typically Yes

To explain the reasoning behind the entries, the prototypical autonomy-oriented individual would tend to emphasize freedom rather than financial or status achievement. Therefore, such a person, when employed by others, is less likely to change jobs to increase his or her level of autonomy. As Smith (1967) pointed out, to control a business, its size must be kept manageable. This means one site, where the owner is always present, only enough employees to be directed personally, and growth limited to what is needed to provide a consistent living, and this is likely to "top out" at moderate levels. If the individual has multiple episodes of self-employment, they are handled one-at-a-time, in order to maximize control over the firm and the demands placed on the owner by work. Rather than share control with partners or directors, the autonomy-oriented person seeks control through a sole proprietorship.

Those with an entrepreneurship anchor are likely to change salaried work for greater pay or status, and are more likely to pursue opportunity. Their firms are more often designed for growth, for example being incorporated to facilitate raising capital. Their firms are likely to show growth in sales, number of sites and employees, and where successful are likely to show high levels of each. When entrepreneurs have multiple episodes of self-employment, they are more likely than others to have more than one firm going at the same time.

The problem in this approach is determining the degree of correspondence necessary to classify the career anchor as autonomy or entrepreneurship, and not one of the other six anchors, or even the unclassifiable 4.6% who appear to have no clear anchor (Schein, 1985b, p. 7). One demanding but workable approach is to develop classification schemes for all anchors to assure the discriminant quality of the two anchors of interest.

A final concern around Schein's anchors and mainstream entrepreneurship research centers on the incidence of autonomy and entrepreneurship anchors. Based on 14 studies with a total of 348 individuals, Schein (1985b) reported an incidence of entrepreneurship anchors of 7.7% across the groups, while autonomy anchors appeared in 11.1% of participants. The incidence of entrepreneurship in this sample is roughly twice the incidence rate projected for the population in large-scale studies such as Reynolds (1988) or Cooper and Dunkelberg (1981).

Sample differences most probably account for much of this difference. Schein's samples are generally MIT graduates, managers, or professionals. Virtually all have college degrees, and many have even more education. These individuals are drawn from the wage-and-salaried as well as the self-employed. Cooper and Dunkelberg (1981) surveyed only self-employeds, including many self-employeds with minimal education, who were further preselected as NFIB members, while Reynolds surveyed owners or managers of small businesses identified through Dun and Bradstreet reports. Among these studies, there emerges a demonstrated need to compare methods for determining the incidence of entrepreneurship from different approaches to improve the accuracy of self-employment projections. The differences identified between the career anchor and other approaches suggest the form such a comparison might take.

ADDITIONS TO THE SCHEIN MODEL

While the three cone variables and career anchors explain much about career dynamics, there remain untouched but important elements of careers, particularly those of the self-employed. Three key variables of entrepreneurial careers, derived from the literature below, serve as a starting point. They are duration, multiplicity, and emergence.

The literature underlying these three additional variables is eclectic, drawing from virtually all areas of the social sciences, as well as from a number of research efforts in entrepreneurship itself. The data sources used to identify the additional variables needed to analyze the nature of organizational careers for the self-employed fall into two main categories: research works and anecdotal works. Research works included empirical mainstream entrepreneurship models (Dyer, 1992; Katz, 1992; Katz & Gartner, 1988; Roberts, 1991; Ronstadt, 1984b, 1985, 1988; Savage, 1979; Schein, 1978; Scherer, Bordzinski, & Weibe, 1991; Smith, 1967); models from labor economics (Evans & Leighton, 1989); and models from organizational theory on organizational formation and self-employment (Carroll & Mosakowski, 1987; Perkins, Nieva, & Lawler, 1978; Sarason, 1972; Van deVen, Hudson, & Schroeder, 1984). Anecdotal works included biographic compilations (Fucini & Fucini, 1985; Gervitz, 1984; Silver, 1985); mainstream historical biographies (Livesay, 1979); business cases (Ronstadt, 1984a; Stevenson, Roberts, & Grousbeck, 1989); and journalistic essays from *Inc.* and *Entrepreneur* magazines.

Research works tend to be grounded in theoretical or empirical efforts by academics, while anecdotal works can be developed by academics, as cases usually are, or by journalists or even the entrepreneurs themselves.

Duration

Duration is the time that the person is self-employed. For example, Ross Perot or An Wang can be seen as long-duration self-employeds, while Donald Burr, who started People Express, was self-employed for a much shorter period. Since short-lived efforts may well represent failure, or lessons that could be learned only by direct experience, these short-duration episodes are likely to have a substantial impact on career decision making, and need to be covered wherever possible.

However, for secondary analysts duration poses a special problem related to the between-interview interval. An enduring issue in the analysis of firm formation or organizational emergence is the ability to monitor *all* efforts to create firms, to accurately gauge which organizational forms or mutations have been tried, and which succeed and which fail (Katz & Gartner, 1988). In developing entrepreneurial sampling frames, a key problem is gathering information on firms that were attempted, or were created but died, within a between-interview interval. For example, Aldrich (1990) shows that telephone books and D&B lists may miss firms that are very short-lived.

One of the few empirically based efforts to identify the rate of short-lived business is seen in a footnote to Evans and Leighton (1989, p. 525). Using the *Current Population Survey* data on the unincorporated self-employed white males, they estimated a 41.4% exit rate within 12 to 21 months. Conversely, Carroll and Mosakowski (1987) reported that the self-employed were generally among the most stable workers in the sample, staying in their firm longer than typical wage-or-salaried individuals stay in their jobs. The difference between these types of findings most probably represents the "liability of newness" argument of Singh, Tucker, and House (1986).

Another duration-related area which has received little focus but where theory may be usefully applied is in the seasonality of self-employment. For example, many short-duration yard-maintenance people work primarily in spring and summer. In contrast, tax preparers may work primarily in winter and early spring. What distinguishes these types of work is that they are of limited duration and the likely durations can be specified in advance. To date, little effort has been made to develop seasonal adjustments for self-employed work, although such adjustments for wage-or-salaried estimates are common.

Multiplicity

Multiplicity is the number of jobs concurrently held by the self-employed individual. About one in five self-employeds also works at a wage-or-salaried job. A variant of this pattern is called by Jennifer Starr (1992) the "habitual entrepreneur," the person who is self-employed in more than one business at a time.

Multiplicity can occur with a mixture of wage-or-salaried and self-employment, as well as with a mix of simultaneously held self-employed positions. Autonomy- and entrepreneurship-anchored individuals both appear likely to "try out" self-employment while at work in a wage-or-salaried job. Likewise, there does not appear to be any theory-drive argument suggesting differences in the incidence of non-moonlighting self-employment.

Where the greatest likelihood for a difference to exist between entrepreneurship and autonomy-anchored individuals is in the pattern for owning a number of firms through a career span. Studies such as Katz (1990) suggest that most self-employeds operate only one business at a time, although there is a contingent of people who return to self-employment repeatedly. However, Starr's habitual entrepreneurs, who arguably represent the extreme case of entrepreneurship-anchored individuals, often have more than one personally owned business operating at a time.

From the career anchor perspective, it is unlikely that an autonomy-oriented individual would be interested in owning a number of firms simultaneously. Control of diverse firms, particularly if they are in different locations, would be difficult. Additionally, with more firms to operate, each probably requiring some minimum additional increment of the owners' time, autonomy-oriented individuals would find less of their time under their control. This type of person might own several firms across a lifetime, but they would be owned one-at-a-time, to maximize control over the firm and one's own life. When the autonomy-anchored person is involved in two organizations simultaneously, it commonly represents the person using self-employment as an income supplement, through "moonlighting," or the individual's testing out self-employment by dabbling in it part-time.

For the entrepreneurship-oriented person, multiplicity may simply reflect the strong drive to create firms. Since here the creation is important, the time costs of multiplicity would not be a consideration, although concerns about the survival of the different firms would remain an issue. For these people, the potential for simultaneous multiple firm ownership is viable. This analysis is supplemented by available information that virtually all of Starr's habitual entrepreneurs demonstrate strong identification with the entrepreneurship anchor (Starr, 1992).

Emergence

Emergence in careers means actual entry into self-employment. It represents a more general case of the concept of organizational emergence offered by Katz and Gartner (1988), and like that earlier version is characterized by the presence of four characteristics: intention to enter self-employment, boundary between the role of self-employed person and other life roles, resource dedication to the self-employment activity, and goods or service or financial exchange across the self-employment boundary. The organizing process (Weick, 1979) for a new firm requires the four characteristics to come together. With one or more element missing, the individual is in the process of organizing a firm.

The emergence variable is important because its four characteristics help conceptually differentiate incomplete and failed efforts at achieving self-employment from efforts that go through to completion. While several studies have noted the "gestational" period prior to self-employment entry (Perkins, Nieva, & Lawler, 1978; Van deVen, Hudson, & Schroeder, 1984), little work has been done looking at the pre-entry period. Two exceptions, which look at the start-up process in very limited fashion, are studies of venture-capital-backed efforts, and business planning.

Katz and Gartner (1988) have suggested that a useful means of analyzing emergence comes from the sequence in which the four properties come into the process. Using the autonomy and entrepreneurship career anchors, an autonomy-oriented individual is more likely to be driven by the desire to have freedom from control by others. This type of intention often is at the forefront in histories of small business owners. A variant of this is the assertion of or desire for territoriality, "a place of my own," which reflects a boundary consideration. For the autonomy-oriented, issues of market opportunity (exchange) or asset accumulation (resources) are less likely to be their first considerations in starting a firm.

For those with an entrepreneurship anchor, the opportunity-recognition process (Gilad & Levine, 1986) or wealth-creation process (Stevenson, Roberts, & Grousbeck, 1989) is foremost in their consideration. Often these people report themselves "pulled" into ownership by the external pressures of market (exchange) or wealth (resources). Even those entrepreneurs who become self-employed as a reaction to rejection of the firm's service or product by the individual's former employer, such as Apple founders Jobs and Wozniak, often describe the need to see their idea go forth into the market as their driving force.

Application

Taken together, duration, multiplicity, and emergence offer substantial additional information to the career cone variables of hierarchy, function, and centrality, and the career anchors of autonomy and entrepreneurship. Table 2 summarizes the comparison of autonomy-anchored to entrepreneurship-anchored individuals using the career cone variables and the additional variables introduced in this analysis.

Collectively, these variables make possible the analysis of career dynamics of the self-employed at a more sophisticated level. Fundamental analyses of self-employment entry have been reported by researchers interested in occupational mobility (Markey & Parks, 1989; Sicherman & Galor, 1990), and in more focused analyses by Carroll and Mosakowski (1987) and Katz (1990). However, occupational mobility analysts tend to consider only emergence and functional changes, while self-employment entry analyses have looked only at duration of episodes, and in the case of the Katz analysis considered partially emergent cases.

One useful integration of these variables is in the extension of Schein's career cycle concept into the specific processes of career trajectory (DiPrete, 1987; Juhasz, 1989). Among the wage-or-salaried, the concept of career progressions is well understood, and relatively easy to describe. In most of these models, the progression is made easy because of a succession of positions of greater hierarchy and/or centrality. For the self-employed, the reliance on centrality and hierarchy minimizes the interpretability of the progression or trajectory, since self-employeds are by definition at the top and most central position in the firm from its inception. Because of the reduction in variance, the inclusion of other variables, such as function, duration, multiplicity, and emergence, is needed to produce an analysis of the self-employeds' trajectories that matches the detail of conventional analyses of the wage-or-salaried.

Table 2

Summary of Career Anchor Differences on Key Variables

	Autonomy	Entrepreneurship
"Career Cone" Variables		
Hierarchy	At Top of Smaller Firm, Simple Structure Likely	At Top of Larger Firm, Simple Structure Likely More Complex Structure Possible
Function	Managerial/Proprietor Less Likely	Managerial/Proprietor More Likely
Centrality	Less Variation from Core Occupation	Greater Variation from Core Occupation
Additional Variables		
Multiplicity	Less Likely. Person Usually Owns Firms Serially	More Likely. Person Usually Owns Multiple Firms Simultaneously
Duration	Longer Duration Within Self-Owned Firm	Shorter Duration in Self-Owned Firm (or until multiplicity occurs)
Emergence	Intention and Boundary Likely Before Resources or Exchange	Resources or Exchange Likely Before Boundary or Intention

In addition, the lesson of the two career anchors predominating among the self-employed suggests substantially different types of career trajectories. As is best seen in Smith's (1967) work, autonomy-oriented individuals are inclined to grow a business to a psychologically comfortable level (best defined as "just as much as I can personally control, and not one bit more") and then stop growth. Entrepreneurship-oriented individuals, or opportunistic entrepreneurs in Smith's sample, will continue to grow the firm, using delegation, advertising, and other techniques. In Smith's analysis of manufacturers, the average sales for the two types differed by a factor of ten, with opportunistic types, Schein's entrepreneur-anchored people, reporting the larger sales.

From the Starr (1992) work on habitual entrepreneurs, it is evident that those entrepreneurs sampled were inclined toward an entrepreneurship anchor. Their use of multiple, simultaneous firm ownership reflects one special type of trajectory. To differentiate this approach from the autonomy-anchored individual who "wears many hats" such as mechanic, real estate agent, and farmer, the size of the firm (a hierarchical measure) would be needed in analysis.

There are other likely trajectories.

Intermittent. Individuals alternate between wage-or-salaried and self-employed work, because (1) they may be marginally capable of work as often described in sociological and psychological literature (Shapero & Sokol, 1982) or (2) their work is strongly seasonal (e.g., tax preparers, lawn services, fruit stands) and they intersperse the two forms of employment.

Helical. Work-related changes are affected by family or personal factors, altering their timing or size and making the individual's career trajectory appear erratic (Juhasz, 1989; Schein, 1978, p. 24).

Downward. The business fails or is downscaled (Ronstadt, 1985).

Ambiguous. The individual is unsure of his or her self-employment.

Obscured. The individual is either unsure of self-employment or is pursuing it as part of the "underground economy" and is resistant to public admission of self-employment.

Jump-started. The individual enters self-employment in an existing and substantial business through purchase or inheritance.

These approaches contrast with the traditional models of entrepreneurial entry (Cooper & Dunkelberg, 1981) by focusing on the total career process. The analysis of trajectory and the authentication of these potential trajectories defined by cross-sectional or small sample models depend on the ability to usefully create the Schein variables and their extensions described above. The potential for doing that is explored in the next section.

IMPLICATIONS

The goal in the above efforts was to develop a theoretically grounded model for analyzing the careers of self-employeds which has potential for analysis using existing longitudinal datasets. The theory chosen is that of Edgar Schein, specifically his model for career mobility using the variables of hierarchy, function, and centrality, and his concept of career anchors. To this were added three variables found useful in dynamic analyses of entrepreneurship: duration, multiplicity, and emergence. In developing these variables for analysis of the self-employed, several distinctions were made between autonomy-anchored and entrepreneurship-anchored individuals, and these serve as hypotheses for test in the future. Similarly, several cautions regarding the measurement or conceptualization of the variables were identified, and where possible, suggestions for how problems can be evaluated or resolved were given.

There remains a practical question—can the variables be operationalized successfully using existing longitudinal datasets? In this section, the variables introduced above will be operationalized using variables from the Panel Study of Income Dynamics (PSID).

The PSID (Morgan, 1972) is a longitudinal survey conducted yearly by the Survey Research Center of the University of Michigan since 1968. Its subjects are a panel of 3426 households that were representative of the American population in 1968 (with low-income households oversampled). Spinoffs of the original households are kept in the panel, and the data can be weighted to provide population estimates.[2] The surveys, which are conducted by phone, have a core set of questions that remains consistent year-to-year, and another set of questions that varies each year. Fortunately, the information needed to operationalize the majority of the variables comes from the core question set of the study. In addition to the standard questions, a special PSID work history supplement was gathered in 1987, and serves as a separate dataset.

Building on the adapted and new variables introduced in this paper and summarized in Table 2, Table 3 demonstrates both the potential and the shortcomings of secondary analysis done from an *a priori* theoretical framework. The best measured variables in

2. Among the datasets mentioned in Katz (1992) as applicable to the study of the self-employed, the PSID is one of the two most useful. The other survey, the National Longitudinal Survey (NLS) from Ohio State University (Parnes, 1976) generally has many of the same core variables as the PSID, but has substantially different non-core information. Additionally, the NLS is organized by cohorts of older men, mature women, and young men and women. In general, the findings for variables based on the PSID approximate what could be done using the NLS.

Table 3

Summary of Variable Operationalizations for Key Variables

	Description of Operationalization in the PSID dataset
"Career Cone" Variables	
Hierarchy	None
Function	Occupation (Census 2-digit Code), Industry (Census 3-digit code)[1]
Centrality	Prior occupations can be compared to present occupation
Additional Variables	
Multiplicity	Each income source is separately listed
Duration	Interview date—When current job started[2] = Time in current job
	Current job start data—prior job end date = Time between current job and last job
	Prior job start date—Prior job end date = Time in prior job
Emergence	
Intention	Job plans for the next year, Part-time self-employment
Boundary	Self-employment (full or part-time), Whether business is incorporated
Exchange	Income from self-employment, Non-cash transfers (in and out of business)
Resources	General assets available, Income

[1] The PSID also asks respondents "What are your most important activities or duties?" but does not code the responses.

[2] This measure is of course subject to right censoring for survival type analyses.

Table 3 are intention and duration, for which direct measures are available, and are consistent with the theory or established methods of prior research. However, key variables such as hierarchy cannot be gleaned from the information available in the PSID. Other variables, such as resources or exchange, can only be studied in the most superficial way, or in the case of boundary, only for established businesses.

Variables such as function or centrality represent approximations of the desired variables. In the case of function, occupation is a longstanding, surrogate measure. Centrality requires developing a novel measure. Since the codes are based on the 1970 Census of Occupation, the codes reflect two characteristics simultaneously. Most importantly, the numerical classification generally reflects a Census and Department of Labor classification of job families, where similar jobs are grouped together.[3] A second classification is a job status hierarchy, with the highest status workers (professionals and technical workers) at the top and the lowest status workers (private household workers) at the bottom. Either way, centrality can be measured as differences in the ordinal scale

3. The result remains an ordinal scale with all its attendant problems. For example, differences between job families are more substantial than differences within a job family. Thus a 10-point difference within a job family would have less import than a 2-point difference that puts the person into another job family. However, the ordinal scale can be weighted to produce an approximation of an interval scale, for example, by separating job families by arbitrary differences of 100 points, while leaving point differences within families unchanged.

values for current and prior jobs, in terms of job family difference scores, or status differences. The smaller the difference, the more central the current job.

Although not covered in Table 3, the PSID offers considerable opportunity for indirectly classifying the career anchors of autonomy and entrepreneurship from attitudinal information. The study includes raw item results for items included in an Atkinson model achievement motivation questionnaire, as well as an additional set of attitude questions about economic decision making.

Other operational measures introduced in Table 3 that can be directly measured from existing PSID variables are status changes in employment moves, income, and habitual entrepreneurship. Where an individual's income growth can be accepted as a surrogate for a firm level measure, firm sales growth can be estimated, and incorporated firms can be distinguished from sole-proprietorship and partnerships. Given national statistics indicating the small percentage of partnerships in the population of firms, this measure can be adapted to reflect an estimated number of sole proprietorships. Of the potential variables listed in Table 3, only number of employees and multiple business sites could not be measured or derived from the PSID.

These problems of lack of variable coverage are the common problems of secondary analysis in general. What makes such compromise palatable is the faster access to longitudinal data. Depending on the type of information sought, having information of a few key variables for a 20-plus-year period may provide useful information.

In this specific instance, is the fit of Schein's career dynamics model to secondary analysis likely to be a useful one? The value of theory in general, and Schein's theory of career dynamics in particular, is that it provides coherence to the structuring of research. The potential threat to the secondary analyst is the slide into "dustbowl empiricism," the search for statistical significance rather than conceptual meaningfulness. To date, most career analyses of the self-employed have relied solely on studies of entry. Once in self-employment, few of the existing theories have explanatory power. Ronstadt's (1988) observation of the corridor principle[4] is an exception to this, however it describes only one component of the career development process.

As was shown above with PSID data, some meaningful analyses of models inspired by Schein's work can be generated with existing data, and without using elaborate proxies based on chains of suppositions. Other datasets, such as those described by Katz (1992), offer opportunities, especially in cross-sectional analyses, for more detailed testing of the Schein model.

The extension of Schein's three career cone variables to include multiplicity, duration, emergence, and the integrated concept of trajectory is grounded in the idea of operationalizing the actions assumed in the Schein model, for example entry in the case of emergence, and duration in the positions held. The concept of trajectory within a career, and the impact of life and family elements on career issues, are already considered by Schein, although the specific implications for the self-employed are not elaborated in his existing work.

It is in this elaboration process that findings from mainstream entrepreneurship research, and the related works of labor economists, sociologists, and organizational ecologists become the basis for specific content descriptions of the potential forms the career processes might take. In the example of potential trajectory forms, virtually all the

4. Ronstadt's discovery of the corridor principle demonstrates the typical gulf between entrepreneurship researchers studying entrepreneurial careers and those who make career research their focus. In one of the definitive review texts on theories of career development, Osipow (1973) detailed the opening of opportunity contingent on prior decisions, what Ronstadt calls the corridor principle, as a structural derivative of his own systems approach to career development.

career cone variables, the extended variables, the career anchors, and the findings of other researchers come into play to identify empirically and theoretically derived trajectories. In this case, the Schein model serves as the unifying element. With the extensions elaborated here, it possesses the requisite variables to accommodate the piecemeal contributions of the different disciplines and still provide an overarching, integrated, and consistent model that permits the creation of new knowledge from the works of others. From the standpoint of a secondary analysis approach, that is all that one can ask.

REFERENCES

Aldrich, H. E. (1990). Using an ecological perspective to study organizational founding rates. *Entrepreneurship Theory and Practice, 14*(3), 7-24.

Birch, D. L. (1987). *Job creation in America: How our smallest companies put the most people to work.* New York: Free Press.

Bygrave, W. D. (1989). The entrepreneurship paradigm (II): Chaos and catastrophes among quantum jumps? *Entrepreneurship Theory and Practice, 14*(2), 7-30.

Carland, J. W., Hoy, F., Boulton, W. R., & Carland, J. C. (1984). Differentiating entrepreneurs from small business owners: A conceptualization. *Academy of Management Review, 9*(2), 354-359.

Carroll, G. R., & Mosakowski, E. (1987). The career dynamics of self-employment. *Administrative Science Quarterly, 32*, 570-589.

Cooper, A., & Dunkelberg, W. C. (1981). A new look at business entry. In K. H. Vesper (Ed.), *Frontiers of entrepreneurship research*. Wellesley, MA: Babson College.

DiPrete, T. A. (1987). Horizontal and vertical mobility in organizations. *Administrative Science Quarterly, 32*, 422-444.

Dyer, W. G. (1992). *The entrepreneurial experience*. San Francisco: Jossey-Bass.

Eden, D. (1975). Organizational membership *vs*. self-employment: Another blow to the American dream. *Organizational Behavior and Human Performance, 13*, 79-94.

Evans, D. S., & Leighton, L. S. (1989). Some empirical aspects of entrepreneurship. *American Economic Review, 79*(3), 519-535.

Fucini, J. J., & Fucini, S. (1985). *Entrepreneurs: The men and women behind famous brand names and how they made it*. Boston: G. K. Hall.

Gartner, W. B. (1988). "Who is an entrepreneur?" is the wrong question. *American Journal of Small Business, 12*(1), 11-32.

Gervitz, D. (1984). *The new entrepreneurs: Innovation in American business*. New York: Penguin.

Gilad, B., & Levine, P. A. (1986). Behavioral model of entrepreneurial supply. *Journal of Small Business Management, 24*(4), 45-53.

Jaques, E. (1976). *A general theory of bureaucracy*. New York: Halsted.

Juhasz, A. M. (1989). A role-based approach to adult development: The triple helix model. *International Journal of Aging and Human Development, 29*(4), 301-315.

Katz, J. A. (1984). One person organizations: A resource for researchers and practitioners. *American Journal of Small Business, 18*(3), 24-30.

Katz, J. A. (1990). Longitudinal analysis of self-employment follow-through. *Entrepreneurship and Regional Development, 2*(1), 15-25.

Katz, J. A. (1992). Secondary analysis in entrepreneurship: An introduction to data bases and data management. *Journal of Small Business Management, 30*(20), 74-86.

Katz, J., & Gartner, W. B. (1988). Properties of emerging organizations. *Academy of Management Review, 13*(3), 429-441.

Livesay, H. C. (1979). *American made: Men who shaped the American economy*. Boston: Little Brown.

McKelvey, W. (1982). *Organizational systemics: Taxonomy, evolution, classification*. Berkeley: University of California Press.

Markey, J. P., & Parks, W. II (1989). Occupational change: Pursuing a different kind of work. *Monthly Labor Review*, September, 3-12.

Mintzberg, H. (1979). *The structuring of organizations*. Englewood Cliffs, NJ: Prentice Hall.

Morgan, J. N. [Principal Investigator] (1972). *A panel study of income dynamics: Study, design, available data: 1968-1972 interviewing years (Volumes 1 and 2)*. Ann Arbor, MI: Survey Research Center, ISR.

Ornstein, S., & Isabella, L. A. (1993). Making sense of careers: A review 1989-1992. *Journal of Management, 19*(2), 243-267.

Osipow, S. H. (1973). *Theories of career development* (2nd ed.). Englewood Cliffs, NJ: Prentice Hall.

Parnes, H. S. (1976). *Handbook for the national longitudinal surveys*. Columbus: Ohio State University.

Perkins, D. N. T., Nieva, V. F., & Lawler, E. E. (1978). *Causal forces in the creation of a new organization*. Ann Arbor, MI: ISR.

Reynolds, P. D. (1988). Organizational births: Perspectives on the emergence of new firms. In F. Hoy (Ed.), *Academy of Management Best Paper Proceedings 1988*, pp. 69-73. Athens, GA: Academy of Management.

Roberts, E. B. (1991). *Entrepreneurs in high technology*. New York: Oxford University Press.

Ronstadt, R. C. (1984a). *Entrepreneurship: Text, cases and notes*. Dover, MA: Lord.

Ronstadt, R. C. (1984b). Ex-entrepreneurs and the decision to start an entrepreneurial career. In J. A. Hornaday, F. Tarpley, Jr., J. A. Timmons, & K. H. Vesper (Eds.), *Frontiers of entrepreneurship research*, pp. 437-460. Wellesley, MA: Babson College.

Ronstadt, R. C. (1985). Every entrepreneur's nightmare: The decision to become an ex-entrepreneur and work for someone else. In J. A. Hornaday, E. B. Shils, J. A. Timmons, & K. H. Vesper (Eds.), *Frontiers of entrepreneurship research*, pp. 409-434. Wellesley MA: Babson College.

Ronstadt R. C. (1988). The corridor principle. *Journal of Business Venturing, 13*(1), 31-40.

Sarason, S. B., and associates (1972). *The creation of settings and the future societies*. San Francisco: Jossey-Bass.

Savage, D. (1979). *Founders, heirs and managers: French industrial leadership in transition*. Beverly Hills, CA: Sage.

Schein, E. H. (1978). *Career dynamics: Matching individual and organizational needs*. Reading, MA: Addison-Wesley.

Schein, E. H. (1985a). *Career anchors: Discovering your real values*. San Diego, CA: University Associates.

Schein, E. H. (1985b). *Career anchors: Trainer's manual*. San Diego, CA: University Associates.

Scherer, R. F., Bordzinski, J. D., & Weibe, F. A. (1991). Assessing perception of career role-model performance: The self-employed parent. *Perceptual and Motor Skills, 72*(2), 555-560.

Shapero, A., & Sokol, L. (1982). The social dimensions of entrepreneurship. In C. Kent, D. Sexton, & K. Vesper (Eds.), *Encyclopedia of entrepreneurship*. Englewood Cliffs, NJ: Prentice Hall.

Sicherman, N., & Galor, O. (1990). A theory of career mobility. *Journal of Political Economy, 98*(1), 169-192.

Silver, A. D. (1985). *Entrepreneurial megabucks: The 100 greatest entrepreneurs of the last twenty-five years*. New York: Wiley.

Singh, J. V., Tucker, D. J., & House, R. J. (1986). Organizational legitimacy and the liability of newness. *Administrative Science Quarterly, 31*, 171-193.

Smith, N. R. (1967). *The entrepreneur and his firm*. E. Lansing, MI: Bureau of Business and Economic Research, MSU.

Smith, N. R., & Miner, J. B. (1983). Type of entrepreneur, type of firm, and managerial innovation: Implications for organizational life cycle theory. In J. A. Hornaday, J. Timmons, and K. Vesper (Eds.), *Frontiers of entrepreneurship research*, pp. 51-71. Wellesley, MA: Babson College.

Star, A. D. (1979). Estimates of the number of quasi and small businesses, 1948 to 1972. *American Journal of Small Business, 4*(2), 44-52.

Starr, J. A. (1992). Climbing the occupational ladder: Career development of habitual entrepreneurs. Paper presented at the annual meeting of the Academy of Management, Las Vegas, Nevada, August 11.

Stevenson, H. H., Roberts, M. J., & Grousbeck, H. I. (1989). *New business ventures and the entrepreneur* (3rd ed.). Homewood, IL: Irwin.

Timmons, J. A., Muzyka, D. F., Stevenson, H. H., & Bygrave, W. D. (1987). Venture capital and the search for potentially successful ventures: The characteristics of successful ventures. Paper presented at the Babson Entrepreneurship Research Conference.

Van deVen, A. H., Hudson, R., & Schroeder, D. M. (1984). Designing new business startups: Entrepreneurial, organizational, and ecological considerations. *Journal of Management, 10*(1), 87-107.

Weick, K. E. (1979). *The social psychology of organizing* (2nd ed.). Reading, MA: Addison-Wesley.

Jerome A. Katz is Professor of Management and Associate Director of the Jefferson Smurfit Center for Entrepreneurial Studies at Saint Louis University.

Thanks are extended to Gibb Dyer, Jennifer Starr, Ed Schein, Norris Krueger, Bill Olbrecht, and Cheryl Nietfeldt for their help in the development of the ideas used in this paper, although the resulting ideas are solely the responsibility of the author. A version of this work was presented as part of the Symposium: New Directions in Research on Entrepreneurial Careers, at the 1992 Annual Meeting of the Academy of Management, Las Vegas, August 11, 1992. Support for this work came from the Jefferson Smurfit Center for Entrepreneurial Studies, the Department of Management and Decision Sciences, the Beaumont Faculty Development Fund, and the Summer Research Grant Fund of the School of Business and Administration, Saint Louis University.

[3]

STRATEGIC WINDOWS IN THE ENTREPRENEURIAL PROCESS

MICHAEL HARVEY
University of Oklahoma

RODNEY EVANS
University of Oklahoma

INTRODUCTION

Being prepared and knowing when to act are both dimensions of becoming an entrepreneur. Just as learning should be a lifelong process, entrepreneurship should be viewed as a career long opportunity. The essence of entrepreneurship is its dynamic nature. The environment, process, and event of entrepreneurial activities require a holistic analysis rather than a simplistic analysis of the individual elements of entrepreneurship (Bygrave 1989b). The creativity, risk-taking, innovation, and market-niching of many entrepreneurs are the hallmarks of the entrepreneurial process. Many times, discontinuous unique events that present themselves to the prospective entrepreneur seem to be rigid. The temporal dimensions of the entrepreneurial process envelops both the dynamic nature of environment for entrepreneurs as well as the career lifecycle of the prospective entrepreneur. The principal goals of an entrepreneurial venture are growth, profit, and innovative strategies (Carland et al. 1984). Therefore, the entrepreneur is one who manages a business for the principal purpose of profit and growth (Carland et al. 1984). A static model as basis for a discussion of entrepreneurial opportunity is a disservice. There are multiple opportunities, i.e., strategic windows, to becoming an entrepreneur.

The concept of strategic windows was introduced in the strategic management literature to focus attention on the fact that there are only limited periods during which the "fit" between key requirements of a market and the particular competencies of a firm competing in a market is at an optimum (Abell 1978). The ability to predict future market needs and to make an objective assessment of the firm's capabilities to meet the needs of this future market provides the fundamental foundation for success of an organization. It is proposed in this research that the same anticipation of the future market needs as well as preparing oneself to become an entrepreneur are critical to new entrepreneurial ventures.

A great deal has been written about the attributes, characteristics, and qualities of being a successful entrepreneur (Chell and Haworth 1987; McClelland 1987; Evans and Leighton 1989). Recently, there has been a number of efforts to develop an integrated model/paradigm of entrepreneurship (Moore 1986; Wortman 1987; Sexton 1988; Low and MacMillian 1988; Bygrave 1989a, 1989b; Bygrave and Hofer 1991; Covin and Slevin 1991; Bygrave 1993).

Address correspondence to Michael Harvey, College of Business Administration, University of Oklahoma, Norman, OK 73019.

Journal of Business Venturing 10, 331–347

655 Avenue of the Americas, New York, NY 10010

0883-9026/95/$9.50
SSDI 0883-9026(95)00037-9

One outcome of these research efforts is that there has been a division between the entrepreneurial process and the entrepreneurial event. The latter involves the creation of a new organization to pursue an opportunity, whereas, the former involves all functions, activities, and actions associated with perceiving opportunities and the creation of organizations to pursue an opportunity (Bygrave 1993). By emphasizing the temporal dimensions of the entrepreneurial process, the anticipation of future market needs is highlighted, as well as the point that there may be multiple opportunities to enter an entrepreneurial venture (Bygrave 1989a; 1989b; Covin and Slevin 1991; Bygrave and Hofer 1991; Bygrave 1993).

Although there is no agreement on a "grand model" of entrepreneurship, important discoveries were made during the model building: (1) the domain of entrepreneurship should no longer be restricted in a conceptual sense to independent new venture creation (Covin and Slevin 1991); (2) entrepreneurship is a dynamic rather than a static system (Bygrave 1989b); (3) a central ingredient in the concept of entrepreneurship is innovation (Moore 1986); (4) the entrepreneurship process is discontinuous, i.e., not a smooth, continuous, ordinary process (Low and MacMillian 1988); and (5) a "triggering" event typically activates the entrepreneurship process (Quinn 1985; Moore, 1986). Although there were other issues that were discussed, these five concepts are essential elements in this research effort.

This study examines the entrepreneurial process relative to the career lifecycle of a potential entrepreneur. This approach illustrates that there are "unique" times in a career lifecycle when the opportunity to become an entrepreneur is most favorable. The preparation for becoming an entrepreneur can, therefore, also be described as a dynamic process because the entrepreneurial process itself is dynamic. There is not one set of skills or experiences, but rather an array of past experiences/skills needed to be a successful entrepreneur relative to the stage of the career lifecycle of the individual. The study also examines the discontinuous opportunities to becoming an entrepreneur and how to prepare for such events. Finally, the various entrepreneurial entry modes are examined to illustrate that to become an entrepreneur does not necessarily mean one has to start a new venture, as has been accentuated by college curriculum while focusing on entrepreneurship (see, for example, Plaschka and Welsch 1990). These entrepreneurial entry modes are then matched to the career lifecycle of potential entrepreneurs.

STRATEGIC WINDOWS OF OPPORTUNITY IN BUSINESS

The concept of strategic windows of opportunities was introduced into the business literature more than 20 years ago (Abell 1978). The essence of the concept is that there are only limited periods during which the "fit" between the key requirements of a market and the particular competencies of a firm competing in a market are at an optimum (Abell 1978). To benefit during these periods, a company must undertake a dynamic analysis of both the external and internal environment, attempting to forecast nonincremental changes in the marketplace that will present future opportunities for the firm. Being prepared for unexpected opportunities in the marketplace and responding to them to gain competitive advantage is the essence of strategic windows.

There is an implicit temporal dimension in the discussion of strategic windows, in that targets of opportunity will present themselves and organizations prepared to react to the opportunities presented will be able to do so. As competition increases and demand is fulfilled, the strategic windows of opportunity close to firms that did not anticipate the demand in the marketplace. It is critical that organizations anticipate when these "strategic windows" will be open to them and prepare their organizations to react in a timely fashion to these unique market opportunities. Modifying the distinctive competency of the organization to the unique aspects of the new demand creates a relative competitive advantage for the company – however fleeting that advantage may be. It can be argued that the more entrepreneurial firms may even create demand for this product/service by analyzing the latent demand characteristics of niches of market demand. By better understanding the unique desires of these market segments, the entrepreneurial firm can produce products/services that fulfill that particular demand. Therefore, entrepreneurs must anticipate strategic market opportunities and in some instances preempt the competition by "creating" demand for innovative product offerings. Strategic windows for entrepreneurial organizations may be due in part to their risk-taking, proactivity, and innovation as well as a change in the marketplace (Slevin and Covin 1990).

Just as businesses move through cycles that create "strategic" windows, individual managers also evolve through a career development cycle. The primary research on career development is based on research in vocational psychology and sociology. This research (Hall and Nougaim 1968; Dalton, et al 1977; Ference, et al 1977) has found that an individual's wants and needs from a job will vary depending on the person's particular career situation – that is, the jobs they have held, their current position, and the career direction in which they are moving (up, plateaued, down).

Career theorists have described that individuals will, under normal circumstances, experience four career stages: (1) exploration; (2) establishment; (3) maintenance; and (4) disengagement (Hall 1976; Schein 1971; Baird and Kram 1983). Each of these phases presents opportunities for the individual to learn, modify expectations, and change career goals. These stages of career development are also useful indicators when assessing the opportunity/motivation to become an entrepreneur. Career plateauing may be a particularly interesting stage to stimulate an individual to undertake an entrepreneurial venture (Warren, et al 1975; Near 1980; Reid and Evans 1983; Barbwick 1983).

The following research propositions relate to multiple opportunities in a career lifecycle for undertaking an entrepreneurial venture:

> Proposition 1: Individuals pass through a career lifecycle that has distinct stages, each of which may create an opportunity to undertake an entrepreneurial venture.
>
> Proposition 2: Individuals possess different skill inventories during various stages of their career lifecycle that impact their preparedness to become an entrepreneur.

STRATEGIC WINDOWS IN ENTREPRENEURIAL CAREERS

When are there opportunities to become an entrepreneur? Presenting students with only the choice of being an entrepreneur at the time of graduation deflects them from the sensitivity to seek and identify opportunities – strategic windows – to becoming an entrepreneur later in their careers. Becoming an entrepreneur is not an event. The entrepreneurial process may be viewed in much the same way as the employee turnover process: (1) job dissatisfaction; (2) thinking of quitting; (3) intention to search; (4) probability of finding an acceptable alternative; (5) intention to quit/stay; and (6) quit and stay (Mobley, Horner, and Hollingsworth 1978; Schneider and Schmitt 1986). In fact, the two processes may be complementary for some individuals who use the prospect of entrepreneurial activity as one alternative to their present employment situation.

A number of variables have been identified as antecedents to organizational commitment (Mowday et al. 1982; Glisson and Durrick 1988; Mathieu and Zajac 1990). These variables –

the individual, job, organization, and nonjob factors – can be analyzed to determine the level of satisfaction/dissatisfaction with the individual's position. The individual elements center on the tenure with the organization as a prediction of turnover (Becker 1960; Mowday et al. 1982; Mathieu and Zajac 1990). The longer the tenure in the organization, the less likely it is that the individual will leave. Job characteristics are also important correlates of commitment to an organization (Jackson and Schuler 1985; King and King 1990; Mathieu and Zojac 1990). Essentially, Salancik (1977) agrees that the more characteristics of the job enhance a sense of responsibility, the more an individual will exhibit commitment to the organization in which that job is performed (Gregersen 1992).

The organization, particularly an entrepreneurial organization, can play a significant role in the turnover of individuals. The degree to which the organization is perceived as dependable and supportive, will influence individuals to exhibit organizational commitment (Angle and Perry 1983; Eisenberger, Fasolo, and Davis-LaMastro 1990). The other set of variables relative to the organization centers on individuals' ability to identify with the goals and objectives of that organization. Therefore, if the entrepreneurs does not share their "vision" with key employees, their willingness to remain committed to the organization may diminish. Nonjob variables have not been researched extensively (Mowday et al. 1982; Mathieu and Zajac 1990) but researchers have identified personal relationships, organizational culture, and *esprit de corps* as important ingredients in commitment to stay with an organization.

Developing an understanding of commitment and turnover are important issues because an individual may not only leave but may start their own entrepreneurial venture in direct competition with the company they just left. The incentive to start a new venture may be dissatisfaction with their present organization because it no longer satisfies personal needs and nonjob expectations of the individual (Mowday, Porter, and Steers 1982). It should be recognized that disgruntled employees of an entrepreneurial firm may not only leave the company but may start their own new venture with the knowledge attained while working for the entrepreneur.

The prospective entrepreneur: (1) conceptualizes new business venture; (2) evaluates alternative entry modes; (3) assesses financial ramifications of entering business; (4) prospects for capital; (5) finalizes company and/or product concept; (6) forms an intention to enter new venture; and (7) enters/does not enter a new business venture. The process of becoming an entrepreneur is a process of discrete decisions that may take an extended length of time in the move from one to the other. And, just as with the employee turnover model, not everyone moves through all the stages of the process. In fact, individuals may start the process many times without actually quitting and starting a new entrepreneurial venture. So, although there are parallels between the turnover and entrepreneurial processes, there is an important distinction raised in this study. The concept of strategic windows suggests that the windows occur and, except for the chronological relationship, they may be unrelated to one another.

Entrepreneurial opportunities should also be viewed as a series and/or a process involving a number of critical junctures where becoming an entrepreneur is logical, and the educational process should identify these unique opportunities (Plaschka and Welsch 1990). Such a series of entrepreneurial strategic windows (Figure 1), illustrates the number of incremental opportunities available during a career to "logically" plan on going into business for one's self. The process of preparing to become an entrepreneur can also be started at many points throughout one's career. The opportunities to do so present themselves in a predictable pattern.

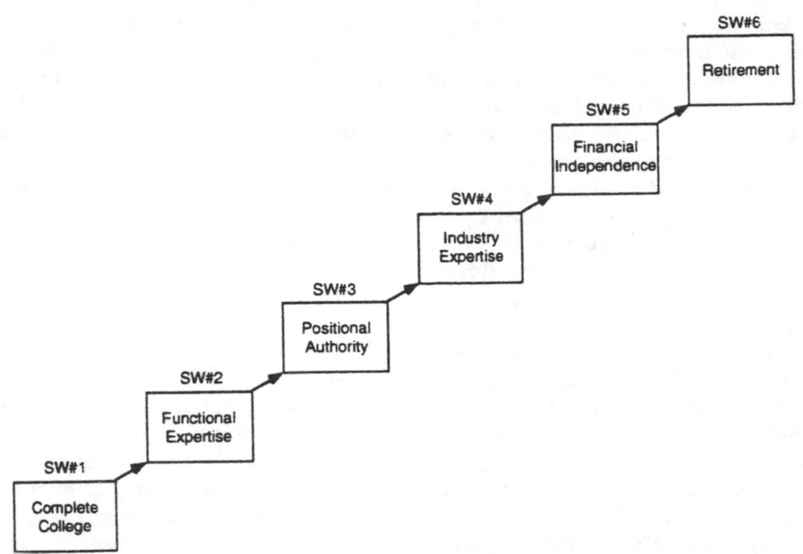

FIGURE 1. Entrepreneurial strategic windows of opportunity.

Many young people display entrepreneurial tendencies even as early as the preteenage years. The usual lemonade stand still appears on a hot summer day. Individual students excel in fund raising projects, in part because they step outside the organized system and devote excess energy to the process; and occasionally, a high school student will develop an entrepreneurial idea so completely that an opportunity to continue it into the future is impossible to ignore. For many reasons, however, the experience of attending college represents the beginning of a series of life events that may be viewed as the start of strategic windows of opportunity for the would-be entrepreneur. The college experience is a prominent event – the process of attending a college is a broadening experience that includes the development of personal skills that would be helpful if an entrepreneurial venture was undertaken. One does not have to graduate or for that matter study business while attending college; the mere experience of independence, being exposed to new ideas and people as well as coming to the realization that the adolescence stage of life is ending, may motivate the student to consider an entrepreneurial venture. After college, there are fewer opportunity costs, high motivation, high level of energy, and drive and, if unsuccessful, the damage to one's career can be contained. Conversely, of course, the would-be entrepreneur's relevant business and managerial experience is low, store of resources is limited, and ability to deal with unexpected events is unknown. It could also be said that if individuals are successful in their entrepreneurial efforts, they will be less likely to be able to handle success.

At the other end of the career lifecycle continuum, retirees have extensive business experiences, have faced a number of critical decisions that may have had a material impact on careers, resources are more extensive than at earlier stages of careers, and they may better understand the inherent risks in an entrepreneurial venture better than younger individuals. Positioning the college attendee and the retiree as polar extremes provides a convenient beginning and end to the career evolution process. In many ways, these extremes are easiest to define and describe, and they lack the shortcoming of being related to chronological age. The college experience presumably makes one the recipient of new but untested skills and therefore eligible for new entry level positions no matter at what age it occurs. Retirement implies some level of economic success; one has the income for food and shelter, and it implies the desire to step out of active economic pursuit. There will always be exceptions to these generalized characteristics. In fact, the most successful entrepreneurs will likely not exhibit an identical set of weaknesses and strengths but the majority of individuals in these two stages have a similar set of personal/behavioral characteristics.

Determining the occurrence of the intermediate phases of the entrepreneurial career process is more difficult. What is the level of functional/industry expertise? How much positional authority is necessary, and for how long? How much money makes one financially independent? Does every individual experience most or all of the phases? Is the sequence consistent across individuals? Are there reasonable time periods one can expect to spend between phases? These questions tend to be grouped into two categories: (1) timing and (2) intensity of experience. With respect to timing, the obvious judges are the individuals themselves. Quasi indicators may help to determine a relevant time-frame event that would alert the prospective entrepreneur that they were at a critical juncture. For example, being given additional responsibility and authority that broadens or enhances their job or being promoted for the first time from an entry level position may be indicators of mastering functional skills. For example, an entry level accountant passes the CPA exam, has been conducting client audits for 4 years, and is assigned larger, more important clients or is promoted to account manager. The organization and the individual's profession have signaled to the individual of having reached a function expertise plateau. A financial analyst observes advertised qualifications for positions at a rival firm to be below his/her own. A sales representative observes a contemporary with similar performance and experience being shifted to a larger, more lucrative territory; although it was a lateral movement, the new position still connotes advancement in the organization. A scientist begins to read and understand the *Wall Street Journal*. All of these are indications of growth and show an independent assessment of the appropriateness of the prospective entrepreneur's background to date. Many companies are replacing vertical hierarchies with horizontal networks – linking together traditional functions through interfunctional teams (Hirschhorn and Gilmore 1992). Therefore, the delineation between being transferred and promoted might make this personal assessment more difficult. But, with the reduced levels in many organizational hierarchies, horizontal "promotion" may also be an appropriate signal that the would-be entrepreneur may be ready to undertake an entrepreneurial venture. A strategic window may be open where those new required skills may give the individual a relative advantage in the marketplace.

The typical salesperson's career helps to illuminate the concept of positional authority. Salespeople who are successful often will move into the management of the sales force – the logic being that these individuals will be able to identify, develop, and motivate behavior similar to their own. After a series of promotions in the sales management arena, i.e., district manger to regional manager to national manager, the individual may be considered for general management in the organization. At each of these junctures, there may be an opportunity for this individual to take the acquired skills and become an entrepreneur. Judgment on when to become an entrepreneur may be one of the critical skills necessary to being a success – knowing when to act. The important issue is that there are times when the window is open if the individual is prepared and motivated to become an entrepreneur. The action of becoming an entrepreneur may occur many times throughout the entire career life-cycle.

Career Life-Cycle 'Strategic Windows'	Family Life-Cycle	Organization Life-Cycle						
		Early Stages			*Middle Stages*		*Late Stages*	
		Planning	Establishment	Survival	Organ. Redefinition	Growth	Plateaued	Maturity
	Single	0 part time assistance (learning business)		0 'unpaid' employee	0 open new markets	0 loyalty to company	0 replace more costly employees	0 assist in shutting down operations
College Experience		= energy/ enthusiasm	= new technical skills	= dedication to stay with company	= strength to take on difficult task	= special projects	= technical impact on reducing cost	= cost control measures
	Married	0 full time employment		0 husband/wife team	0 relocate to open new facilities	0 feedback from the field	0 provide for succession	0 advisory to entrepreneur
Functional Expertise		= Assists in Development/ Implementation System		= mfg. technology/ new 'concept' process	= introduction of new technology	= establish control systems	= means to reduce cost	= increase control
	Married w/ Children	0 advisory/ part-time employment		0advise on improving operations	0 associated with professionalization of management		0 stability/ control	0 board-of-directors
Positional Authority		= management techniques/processes		= organizational/employee motivation	= leadership	= experience dealing with success	= mentorship	= board-of-directors
	Married w/ Older Children	0 introduction of next generation to business		0 training new employee/generation	0 assist in dealing with conflict	0 arbitrator in family conflict	0 mentorship	0 board-of-directors
Industry Expertise		= transplant knowledge to new business 'how to'		= open new mkts	= introduce new technology	= hire experts from social network	= prescribe means to reduce cost	= member of audit committees
	'Empty Nest'	0 relocation to assist in stabilizing company		0 investment/sign for debt	0 open in new locations	0 travel to make location assessments	0 help to ensure continued development of personnel	
Financial Independence		= investment	= access to 'others' capital	= co-signing bank loans	= capital for expansion	= supplement cash-flow requirements	= purchase stock for investment	= estate planning for next generation
	Sole Survivor	0 board-of-directors		0 part-time employment	0 'new' career	0 support to entrepreneurs	0 arbiter to the business	0 advisory conflict
Retirement		= moral support		= member of the board-of-directors	= strategy consultation	= assistance with success coping	= ment or next generation	='wisdom'

FIGURE 2. Lifecycle analysis and contribution to the entrepreneurial venture.

The financially independent career juncture affords the individual the economic freedom to undertake an entrepreneurial venture. Typically, the critical issue at this stage of the career life-cycle is to what degree will the independence of the individual be hampered by the entrepreneurial venture. As with many new ventures, the principals have to make commitments backed by their personal assets to help insure the viability of the entrepreneurial venture. The freedom to explore and enter an entrepreneurial effort may spell the end of personal financial independence.

If the career life-cycle strategic windows and standard family life-cycle are related to the organizational life-cycle of an entrepreneurial organization, the potential contributions of the would-be entrepreneur at various stages can be illustrated (see Figure 2). For example, a single individual with college experience, during the early stages of the entrepreneurial organization lifecycle, could provide energy, enthusiasm, and dedication to stay with the company as well as new technical skills, either as a part-time employee or in some cases an "unpaid" employee. The parallel to this situation would be a sole survivor in retirement, during the later stage of the organization's lifecycle, e.g., plateaued, maturity contributing mentoring, arbitration of conflict, and in general providing the "wisdom" of their experience. Figure 2 demonstrates the various contributions of an individual relative to their strategic windows life-cycle and their family life-cycle to different needs of the entrepreneurial organization.

It should also be noted that, whereas the prospective entrepreneur is at one of their career "critical junctures," it does not mean that they should become an entrepreneur. There may be personal reasons for not becoming an entrepreneur such as: (1) lack of funding, (2) debt obligations, (3) family commitments, and the like. But another major concern of the candidates should be, "Is the market conducive to my entrepreneurial expertise?" Will a new entrepreneur's distinctive competence meet the needs of the potential target market (Figure

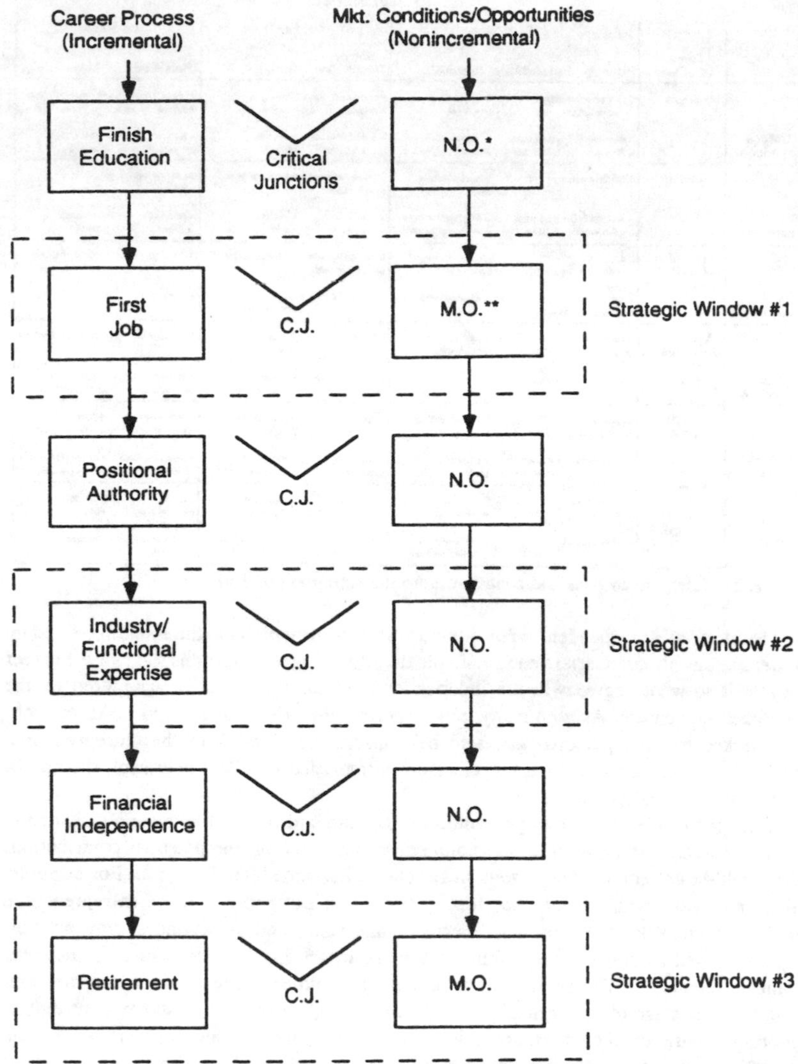

FIGURE 3. Strategic windows: critical entrepreneurial career junctions and market opportunities.

3) to create a competitive advantage? Timing becomes critical, not only for the individual, but also for the environment. The distinctive competency of the individual must correspond to market demand or there will not be a relative advantage for the entrepreneurial venture. Would-be entrepreneurs may need a set of distinctive competencies that differentiate their business venture from others in the marketplace. Too often, entrepreneurs focus extraordinary amounts of time and effort analyzing personal issues without a commensurate effort on the

need to meet customers' expectations concerning a unique product/service utility package. Better understanding of the target market needs is essential but may be insufficient in itself to guarantee success of the entrepreneurial effort.

Still, the concept of strategic windows is very useful for individuals. It helps define the process of seeking entrepreneurial opportunity in the context of the more customary career development process. Consequently, a person who actively anticipates career events is, at the same time, well positioned to consider a response to the upcoming entrepreneurial windows. At bare minimum for individuals managing their professional lives, this provides a kind of dual track of opportunity. One rail is preparation for the next promotion or assignment, and the other rail is the sensitivity to entrepreneurial opportunity. We do not believe these are in conflict. On the contrary, they appear to be remarkably complementary.

The following research propositions relate to "critical junctures" in career life-cycles and their impact on becoming an entrepreneur:

> Proposition 3: Individuals may enter a "critical juncture" of their career life-cycle, yet may be constrained on a personal basis, i.e., lack of funds, debt obligations, etc., and therefore be unable to undertake an entrepreneurial venture.
>
> Proposition 4: Individuals may enter a "critical juncture" of the career life-cycle and not enter an entrepreneurial venture because their unique skills inventories do not fit with demands of the marketplace.
>
> Proposition 5: Individuals may prepare themselves for "critical junctures" in their careers that afford them the opportunity to become entrepreneurs.

ASSESSMENT OF PREPARATION IN BECOMING AN ENTREPRENEUR

Knowing that windows of opportunities will present themselves to an individual at various times during their career life-cycles, the question becomes how to prepare for these occasions. What skills/attributes should be inventoried to allow the individual to make the decision to take on an entrepreneurial activity? The accumulated set of skills and attributes inventoried for each stage of the strategic window process will vary, but the individual should attempt to assess a set of skills and improve the chances of success in an entrepreneurial venture. But in general, how could such a personal skill plan be implemented? Table 1 illustrates an approach that would-be entrepreneurs might use to assess their level of preparedness for a venture into the entrepreneurial world. The assessment matrix depicted in Table 1 is divided into two sources of skills and attributes, business experience and personal skills and attributes, and then subdivided into tangible and intangible skills. The skills and attributes listed in Table 1 are generalized to provide the reader with an understanding of what would be included

TABLE 1 Enterpreneurial Skills and Attributes Matrix

Source	Tangible Skills and Attributes	Intangible Skills and Attributes
Business	• functional expertise (CPA) • international expertise • supervisory/management expertise • project management expertise	• corporate political awareness • ethical business behavior • business "networking"
Personal	• health • IQ • educational background • stage of lifecycle • personal financial position	• perceptiveness • communication skills • decisionmaking style • creativity • personal/social "networking"

in a generic entrepreneurial assessment. There may be additional skills and the attributes of each skill may vary throughout the entrepreneurial career lifecycle, but skills inventory and assessments are essential to the process. A brief discussion of the matrix illustrates the importance of taking an inventory of skills/attributes before entering an entrepreneurial activity.

The tangible skills derived from one's business experience are an accumulation of skills obtained from all prior employers. The tangible dimensions of the company, i.e., organization structure, size, rate of growth, profitability, all impact the experience base of the employee. At the same time, the positions occupied imply an identifiable skill level as well as level of performance over time; the latter, for example, is shown by enlargement or enrichment of one's present position or by promotion from one level to another within the organization. The impact of the organizational structure is related to the degree of formal as well as informal authority employees/managers are given in decision-making. The more decentralized the organization generally, the greater the degrees of latitude in making decisions and the better prepared the individuals could be for operating their own business. The organizational boundaries describe which activities are conducted within a firm's hierarchy and which are conducted outside the hierarchy (Williamson 1975, 1985). Therefore, horizontal movement by the individual within the organization may also be an indicator of acquired skills necessary in an entrepreneurial venture. An additional asset that can be accumulated by the prospective entrepreneur is functional expertise. This "corporate merit badge" increases the inventory of skills and, logically, increases the readiness of the individual to become an entrepreneur.

At the same time that these tangible resume-oriented skills are being stockpiled, intangible skills are also accruing to the individual. These skills, although less obvious, nonetheless influence the experience base of the prospective entrepreneur. The corporate culture and climate may strongly influence the individual's ability to discern the political atmosphere of a situation. Entrepreneurs will use opportunities to improve their skills as managers to improve the probability of success in their new organization: "If I ever had my own company, we would never. . ." is a common comment. Social networking during the corporate years of the future entrepreneur's career can have a significant impact on the new entrepreneur and, in many cases, represent a valuable resource once the new business entity is developed. These influential individuals may become partners, financial investors, board-of-directors' members, or may provide a myriad of other types of resources to the entrepreneur. Not surprisingly, the corporate career path functions as a "training" ground not only for the employing company itself, but in the development of personal skills, contact, and cultural and ethical perspectives of individual employees, which are internalized as if they were their own. These skills, contacts, and cultural and ethical perspectives are then transported with the employee either to the next position or, it is suggested, to the entrepreneurial opportunity. The "training" organizations and their personnel, in this way, are high potential contributors to the new business venture.

Just as the business experience inventory is being established, a set of personal skills are also accumulating. Some of these attributes, such as intelligence, are innate; others are acquired personal traits. These elements, including education and personal financial position, help to prepare the individual to deal with running a business. Intangibles are harder to quantify, but most assuredly have an influence on the careers of the entrepreneurs. The communication skills, perceptiveness, creativity, and personal/social networking are important ingredients for the prospective entrepreneur.

AWARENESS/PREPARATION FOR UNPLANNED STRATEGIC WINDOWS

To this point it has been assumed that the opportunity to become an entrepreneur evolves incrementally from one stage of the carer life-cycle to the next. But the avenue to an entrepreneurial venture may be precipitated by a nonincremental event. These less predictable events are normally beyond the control/influence of the individual but, nonetheless, create a window (maybe strategic) to become involved entrepreneurially. Such events as involuntary termination of employment, death in the family, inheritance or divorce can create career vacuums that can produce entrepreneurial opportunity.

The loss of one's job has obvious consequences: a negative impact on self-image, restructured social networks, and decreased, if not eliminated, income flow–among others. But this event also creates a critical juncture in a career life-cycle. The stress and tension associated with this event frequently pushes individuals to find another job and not reflect on the future and what they want to do. But with "early retirements," extended job furloughs, and other creative dismissals with severance pay, prospective entrepreneurs have the time to undertake a critical assessment of their future goals and owning their own businesses. This puts the otherwise employee-status individual on the same road with the preparing entrepreneur who uses the job loss as the trigger to "go do what I always wanted." So even though the resultant attitude may be very different, from fear, stress and disappointment on the one hand, to anger, resentment and relief on the other, the results are similar: new entrepreneurs are created. Recent history is replete with stories of highly skilled, mid- and upper-level managers being dismissed in record numbers. This strengthens the position that every individual should be an active career manager. And keeping options active and open should be a focal part of the career management process.

Other career modifying events come unexpectedly but nonetheless present the individual with the self-employment career options. One that has been chronicled frequently is that of a divorced individual starting a business to support dependent children. This critical time in a family unit sometimes drives the choice of "radical" means to meet present needs and alters the future in a fundamental way. Multiple jobs and higher risk-taking characterize this position. The thought of going into one's own business at least part-time, is appealing, and the additional money that is generated may be perceived as a substitute for the contributions of a spouse.

Just as with incremental predictable phases, the prospective entrepreneur can make some preparation for the nonincremental opportunities. A starting point of preparation is to have an aptitude/personality assessment completed early in one's career. These standardized tests help highlight careers for which an individual has an aptitude or may have an interest in developing in the future. Importantly, these formats also help identify areas for which individuals are not well suited. By having this inventory complete and updated on a timely basis, the prospective entrepreneur can accomplish two important tasks: (1) address weaknesses discovered in the skills section of the testing and (2) become informed/educated in business sectors that could "someday" be where they would start a business. Some people do no more than keep "clipping files" of articles relevant to interesting business segments for future potential entrepreneurial activity. Others take training courses, attend trade shows, and interview with companies that are already in the business. In both cases, they are building an inventory of skills/knowledge on a business concept that may be of interest in the future.

To prepare for nonincremental entrepreneurial opportunities is a lifelong process. Actions and attitudes stimulate the development of one's portfolio of business knowledge. Constant attention is also given to building the motivation to become an entrepreneur, even though this process might take a negative turn through divorce, death, or other misfortune, and converting that into the drive and desire to become an entrepreneur.

The following research propositions relate to the nonincremental events that occur in a career lifecycle and how they impact becoming an entrepreneur:

Proposition 6: There are nonincremental events that occur throughout a career lifecycle that may precipitate the opportunity to undertake an entrepreneurial venture.

Proposition 7: Nonincremental opportunities to become an entrepreneur can also be prepared for by the individual.

ENTREPRENEURIAL MODES OF ENTRY

The prospective entrepreneur assembles experiences/resources to prepare for a critical career juncture. How to most effectively execute the opportunity into an entrepreneurial business remains an issue. As in strategic windows of business opportunity, entrepreneurs must focus their attention on an entry strategy that most closely fits their capabilities. The company defines its distinctive competency and enters a strategic window with a structure that matches, or is complementary to, its strengths (Abell 1978). So must entrepreneurs select organizational entry strategies that complement their strengths and increase their distinctive competencies as entrepreneurs. The appropriate entry strategy is also tied to the critical juncture that has occurred in the candidate's career life-cycle. One's career position can directly influence the mode of entry, as can the inventory of personal skills/experiences. The entry mode strategy should compliment the strengths of the aspiring entrepreneur to provide the support to reduce the probability of failure. For example, an individual with limited marketing/sales experience might have a higher probability of success purchasing a franchise that has established market identity, sales promotion, and advertising programs for the franchisee. Conversely, a person with extensive marketing/sales experience could benefit more from acquiring an existing manufacturing facility that has had a weak selling effort in the past.

Figure 4 illustrates a decision process in making the selection of an appropriate mode of entry for the would-be entrepreneur. The external factors depicted in the model are the environmental variables that can influence the decision to enter business. These external factors included general economic conditions, availability of capital from traditional sources, competitive environment, governmental regulations, consumer demand, and other elements external to the firm that will impact the business.

The next step in the entry mode selection process focuses attention on prospective entrepreneurs and their personal/psychological attributes, their stage of career and personal life-cycles, a skills assessment inventory, and the goals and level of motivation of becoming an entrepreneur. In an effort to select the most appropriate entry strategy, external market conduciveness and the level of "preparedness" of the entrepreneurial candidate must be integrated. As was discussed in Figure 3, the critical juncture stage of career life-cycle and market opportunity needs to be aligned before the new venture is undertaken.

Once the environment/entrepreneur assessment is completed, only appropriate modes of entry will remain in the analysis. Each of these entry modes are then analyzed individually for strengths and weaknesses relative to the analysis of the first two stages of the decision process. For example a prospective entrepreneur may not select franchising as an option because of the high initial cost, even though that mode of entry would fit the external/internal factor analysis. The remaining set of considerations relate to which entry mode will best facilitate accomplishing economic and non-economic goals established by the would-be entre-

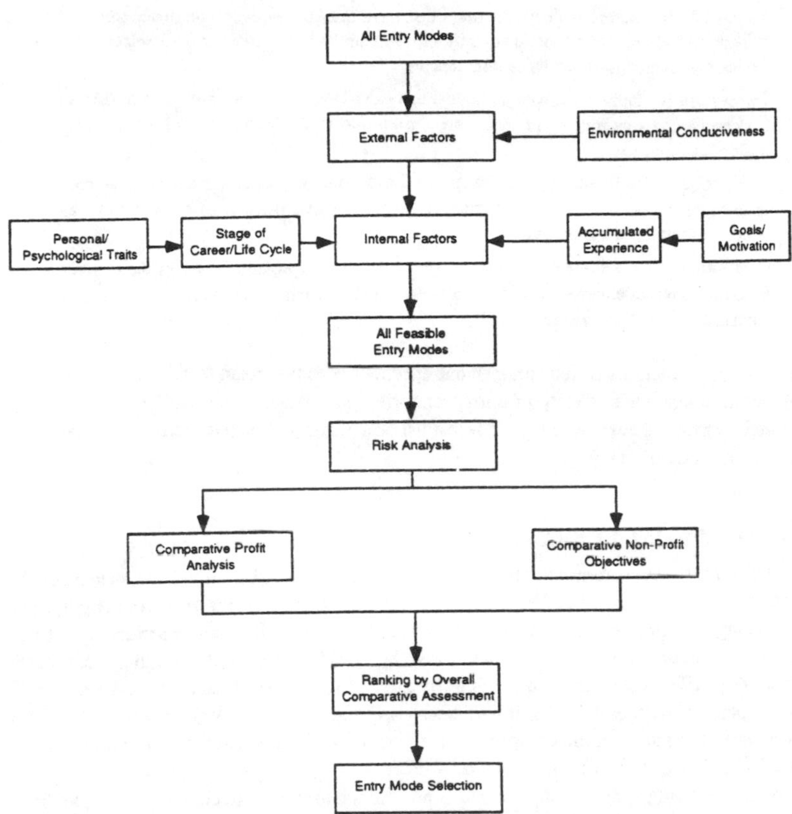

FIGURE 4. Decision process for selecting appropriate entrepreneurial entry mode.

preneur. Economic goals may be reached at a certain level of profit, whereas non-economic expectations may make decisions independent of influence by the type of entry mode, i.e., franchisor expecting compliance by franchisee on key operating procedures/policies. The selection process is a system of elimination of particular modes of entry that attempts to "fit" the entry mode with the expectations of the entrepreneur in a particular environmental setting.

In an effort to tie entry modes to the strategic windows of entrepreneurial opportunity outlined in this study, each entry made must be analyzed illustrating its advantages and disadvantages. Table 2 profiles the pros/cons of entry modes as an illustration of the type of assessment the prospective entrepreneur might make while assessing entry modes. The final step is to compare the strengths and weaknesses of the entrepreneur at each strategic window. In an effort to demonstrate the outcome of the entry mode decision process and entrepreneurial opportunity, the following research propositions are presented:

> Proposition 8: The selection of a mode of entry for the entrepreneur should complement their past experiences, stage of career/life-cycles and the environmental conditions present at that time.

Proposition 9: Prospective entrepreneurs that have limited business experience (finished college education, after functional training) and limited resources should select entry modes that compensate for these deficiencies.

Proposition 10: Individuals with positional authority have an opportunity to undertake an entrepreneurial opportunity in their corporation due to the power associated with the positional authority.

Proposition 11: Individuals with industry and functional expertise have greater latitude in selecting a model of entry and therefore have the largest number of entry vehicles to select from in the decision process.

Proposition 12: Would-be entrepreneurs who want to enter at later stages of their career (financial independence and/or retirement) may select from part-time enterprises to outright purchases of existing operations.

The most important issue is that being an entrepreneur does not mean that a start-up operation is required. There are a variety of entrepreneurial entry modes that can be considered by prospective entrepreneurs. Above all, there must be a match between the individual's capabilities and the mode of entry.

SUMMARY/CONCLUSIONS

Preparation for the opportunity to become an entrepreneur should be actively pursued throughout one's business career. There are skills that will help to prepare for the career opportunity of becoming an entrepreneur. Assessment of the intangible skills and experiences that can be acquired during "corporate life" should also be closely monitored. Building a corporate inventory of skills/experience helps to improve the probabilities of success for the entrepreneur. Hoping or wanting to be "your own boss" is frequently not enough to base a successful entrepreneurial venture in the competitive markets in the United States. There are cases of "blind luck," but that is just what they are—luck.

Simply desiring to be an entrepreneur is not enough to insure success, nor is preparation. Sensitivity to the multiple opportunities that will present themselves is an essential ingredient for success. But, equally essential is a match with the market demand for what the entrepreneurial effort is going to supply—whether it be product or service. The distinctive competency of the individual is not a means for differentiation or a relative advantage in the marketplace unless the market is seeking the skill set of the new entrepreneur. When the individual comes to one of the critical career lifecycle junctions, there may not be an opportunity to enter an entrepreneurial venture. It is important to be prepared and understand that there will be additional windows of opportunity. There is not one time or, for that matter, only one way to start a new venture to becoming an entrepreneur.

Starting a new venture is a popular vehicle to teach students about entrepreneurship, but, in reality, the entrepreneurial venture may be started through a variety of modes of entry to be coordinated with the career life-cycles of potential entrepreneurs. These modes provide different advantages, infrastructures, and all have their own inherent disadvantages.

Just as learning should be a lifelong process, entrepreneurship should be viewed as a careerlong process. Being prepared and knowing when to act are both dimensions of becoming an entrepreneur. The corporate "rightsizing" and reduced opportunities for hierarchical advancement in organizations may stimulate many individuals to want to start their own busi-

TABLE 2 Analysis of Entry Modes: Selected Advantages/Disadvantages

ENTRY MODE/ PROS & CONS	Start-Up	Part-Time	Franchises	Acquisition	Intrapreneurial
Advantages of entry mode	• No historic "artifacts" to deal with	• Less personal risk	• Established identity in market	• Established customer/ supplier base	• Test personal skills essential to entrepreneurial ventures
	• Limit costs of "essentials"	• Continue existing full-time employment	• Procedures/processes established	• Immediate cash flow	• Develop skills that are deficient
	• Selection of all personnel	• High level of personal interest	• Assistance from franchisor	• Personnel in-place	• Low monetary risk
	• Shape company image to differentiate from competitors	• "Test market" for full-time venture	• Advertisement/promotion "umbrella"	• Infrastructure to conduct business	• Means to differentiate from other corporate managers
Disadvantages of entry mode	• Extensive time commitment to organization/ personnel	• Not important enough to make commitment	• Past performance to build on • Lack of flexibility	• Resistance to change inside acquired company	• Risk to owners if venture is unsuccessful
	• Cost of every-thing to operate is needed	• Not considered a "real" company by customers/suppliers	• Continuing "payment" for your success	• Corporate culture that may not be consistent	• Behavior may not be rewarded by corporation
	• No systems in place to assist employees	• Lack of adequate assistance to grow business	• Corporate mistake impacts franchise	• Difficult to alter market perception	• Considered "outsider"/unconventional by peers
	• Unknown entity to customers/suppliers • Financial resources may be dissipated in the planning and start process	• Lack of business infrastructure • Divided loyalty • May not reach threshold of sales needed for success	• Higher factor input cost if purchased from franchisor	• Potential loss of key personnel due to acquisition	• If venture is successful, become disinfranchised with "normal" corportate decision-making and incentives

nesses. Today, wanting to go into business and having the necessary skills, experience and understanding of the marketplace may be two completely different things.

REFERENCES

Abell, D. 1978. Strategic windows. *Journal of Marketing* July:21–26.

Ahiarah, S. 1989. Strategic management and entrepreneurship courses at the undergraduate level: can one inform the other. *Proceedings* Arlington, VA: Small Business Institute Director's Association National conference, pp. 60–66.

Angle, H., and Perry, J. 1983. Organizational commitment: individual and organizational differences. *Work and Occupations* 10:123–146.

Baird, L., and Kram, K. 1983. Career dynamics: managing the superior/subordinate relationship. *Organizational Dynamics* Spring:46–64.

Bardwick, J. 1983. Plateauing and productivity. *Sloan Management Review* Spring:67–73.

Beam, H., and Carey, T. 1989. Could you succeed in small business? *Business Horizons* September-October:65–69.

Becker, H. 1960. Notes on the concept of commitment. *American Journal of Sociology* 66:32–42.

Bygrave, W., and Hofer, C. 1991. Theorizing about entrepreneurship. *Entrepreneurship: Theory and Practice* 15:7–25.

Bygrave, W. 1989a. The entrepreneurship paradigm (I): a philosophical look at its research methodologies. *Entrepreneurship: Theory and Practice* 14:7–26.

Bygrave, W. 1989b. The entrepreneurship paradigm (II): chaos and catastrophe among quantum jumps? *Entrepreneurship: Theory and Practice* 14:7–30.

Bygrave, W. 1993. Theory building in the entrepreneurship paradigm. *Journal of Business Venturing* 8:255–280.

Carland, J.W., Hoy, F., Boulton, W., and Carland, J.C. 1984. Differentiating entrepreneurs from small business owners: a conceptualization. *Academy of Management Review* 9(2):354–359.

Chell, E., and Haworth, J. 1987. Entrepreneurship and entrepreneurial personality – a review. In *London School of Small Business Bibliography 1985–1986*. London School of Economies Library.

Covin, J., and Slevin, D. 1991. A conceptual model of entrepreneurship as a firm behavior. *Entrepreneurship: Theory and Practice* 15.

Dalton, G., Thompson, P., and Price, R. 1977. The four stages of professional careers – a new look at performance by professionals. *Organizational Dynamics* Summer:19–42.

Eisenberger, R., Fasolo, P., and Davis-LaMastro, V. 1990. Perceived organizational support and employee diligence, commitment, and innovation. *Journal of Applied Psychology* 75:51–59.

Evans, D., and Leighton, L. 1989. Some empirical aspects of entrepreneurship. *American Economic Review* 79:(3):519–535.

Ference, T., Stoner, J., and Warren, K. 1977. Managing the career plateau. *Academy of Management Review* (2):602–612.

Glisson, C., and Durrick, M. 1988. Predictors of job satisfaction and organizational commitment in human service organizations. *Administrative Services Quarterly* 31:61–81.

Gregersen, H. 1992. Commitments to a parent company and a local work unit during repatriation. *Personal Psychology* 45:29–54.

Hall, D., and Nougaim, K. 1968. An examination of Maslow's need hierarchy in an organizational setting. *Organizational Behavior and Human Performance* 3:12–35.

Hall, D., *Careers in Organizations 1976*. Pacific Palisades, CA: Goodyear.

Hills, G.E. 1988. Variations in university entrepreneurship education: an empirical study of an evolving field. *Journal of Business Venturing* 3:109–122.

Hirschhorn, L., and Gilmore, T. 1992. The new boundaries of the "boundaryless" company. *Harvard Business Review* May-June:104–115.

Jackson, S., and Schuler, R. 1988. A meta-analysis and conceptual critique of research on role ambiguity and role conflict in work settings. *Organizational Behavior and Human Decision Processes* 36: 16–78.

Katz, J. 1989. Endowed positions: entrepreneurship and relative fields. *Entrepreneurship: Theory and Practice* Spring:53-67.

King, L., and King, D. 1990. Role conflict and role ambiguity: a critical assessment of construct validity. *Psychological Bulletin* 107:48–64.

Low, M., and MacMillian, I. 1988. Entrepreneurship: past research and future challenges. *Journal of Management* 14(2):139–161.

Mathieu, J., and Zajac, D. 1990. A review and meta-analysis of the antecedents, correlates, and consequences of organizational commitment. *Psychological Bulletin* 108:171–194.

McClelland, D. 1987. Characteristics of successful entrepreneurs. *Journal of Creative Behavior* 21(3): 219–233.

Moore, C. 1986. Understanding entrepreneurial behavior. In J. Pearce, and R. Robinson, eds., *Academy of Management Best Papers Proceedings*. Chicago, IL: 46th Annual Meeting of the Academy of Management.

Mosakowski, E. 1991. Organizational boundaries and economic performance: an empirical study of entrepreneurial computer firms. *Strategic Management Journal* 12:115–133.

Mowday, R., Porter, L., and Steers, R. 1982. *Employee-Organizational Linkages: The Psychology of Commitment, Absenteeism, and Turnover*. New York: Academic Press.

Near, J. 1980. The career plateau: career and effects. *Business Horizons* October:53–77.

Plaschka, G., and Welsch, H. 1990. Emerging structures in entrepreneurship education: curricular designs and strategies. *Entrepreneurship: Theory and Practice* Spring:55–79.

Quinn, J. 1985. Managing innovation: controlled chaos. *Harvard Business Review* May-June:73–84.

Reid, R., and Evans, M. 1983. The plateaued manager. *The Cornell H.R.A. Quarterly* August:83–91.

Salancik, G. 1977. Commitment and the control of organizational behavior and belief. In B. Shaw, and G. Salancik, eds., *New Directions in Organizational Behavior*. Chicago, IL: St. Clair Press, pp. 1-54.

Schein, E. 1971. The individual, the organization, and the career: a conceptual scheme. *Journal of Applied Behavioral Sciences* 7:401–426.

Sexton, D. 1988. The field of entrepreneurship: is it growing or just getting bigger? *Journal of Small Business Management* 26(1):5–8.

Vesper, K. 1990. *Summary of Entrepreneurial Education Survey*. Seattle, University of Washington, Department of Management and Organization.

Vesper, K. 1993. *Entrepreneurial Education*. University of California, Los Angeles, CA: Entrepreneurial Studies Center, The Anderson School.

Warren, K., Ference, T., and Stoner, J. 1975. Case of the plateaued performer. *Harvard Business Review* January-February:5–13.

William, O. 1995. *Markets and Hierarchies: Analysis and Antitrust Implications*. New York: Free Press.

Wortman, M. 1987. Entrepreneurship: integrating topology and evaluation of the empirical research in the field. *Journal of Management* 13:259–279.

Williamson, O. 1985. *The Economic Institutions of Capitalism*. New York: Free Press.

[4]

EXIT, STAGE LEFT: WHY ENTREPRENEURS END THEIR ENTREPRENEURIAL CAREERS BEFORE RETIREMENT

ROBERT RONSTADT
Babson College

EXECUTIVE SUMMARY

This article examines the process of entrepreneurship from a different perspective. It considers evidence not only about practicing entrepreneurs but also about ex-entrepreneurs: individuals who have ended their entrepreneurial pursuits to work for someone else.

Why entrepreneurs ended their entrepreneurial careers is understood by examining not only their expressed reasons for leaving, but also by observing how they exited, when they exited, and who exited compared to who remained.

The study's findings are tentative. They are published now because they have important implications for potential entrepreneurs, for practicing entrepreneurs, and for those working with entrepreneurs either directly or indirectly (e.g., policymakers) who must make important decisions before more evidence is available. Overall, the findings indicate that a high-risk profile exists that distinguishes ex-entrepreneurs, particularly those with brief careers, from "more seasoned" entrepreneurs who have experienced longer lives as entrepreneurs.

Perhaps the most important implication is that early-career start-ups may be better than previously thought. Preexisting profiles of the "ideal entrepreneurs" place them in their mid- to late thirties at the time of venture start up. But this start-up age (and older ages) were highly correlated in this study with very short, aborted careers compared to practicing entrepreneurs and ex-entrepreneurs who started earlier.

A second implication is related to the first: those who started earlier were able to do a better job of anticipating their future entrepreneurial pursuits than were those who started later, mainly because they were sensitized to entrepreneurship as a career possibility at a much earlier age. Early planning for an entrepreneurial career is correlated with longer careers not just because they start earlier but because they last longer.

Address reprint requests to Robert Ronstadt, Babson College, Babson Park, Mass. 02157.

This article combines and expands upon work published in two earlier articles that appeared originally in *Frontiers of Entrepreneurship Research* (Ronstadt 1984a; 1985). Generous support was provided for all three articles by Babson College's Board of Research. I also wish to thank Prof. John McKenzie who provided insights regarding the statistical analysis. Any deficiencies, of course, are mine alone.

Journal of Business Venturing **1**, 323–338 (1986) 0883-9026/86/$03.50

A third implication is the need to scale down the scope (and risk) of the first venture. Such venture "downsizing" can lessen financial requirements while also giving new entrepreneurs the flexibility to start another, often better, venture after they get into business and learn about new opportunities, contacts, and skills that they could not foresee or develop before starting their first ventures.

A fourth implication reinforces existing notions about the relative perils of the first few years of an entrepreneurial career. Survival rates increase considerably after the completion of the second year and the probability of a long career rises substantially after the sixth year of entrepreneurial life.

A final implication is that the overall costs, risks, and dangers of entrepreneuring have been overstated. Career exit rates are much lower than venture exit rates. Relatively few ex-entrepreneurs apparently suffered truly catastrophic career exits, at least to the extent that they felt that their careers had been very unrewarding and that they had ruled out ever entrepreneuring again.

INTRODUCTION

Practicing entrepreneurs have been asked what it would take to induce them to leave their entrepreneurial pursuits and to go to work for someone else. The usual response suggests that they would prefer some mild form of hara-kiri. At the very least they demand the opportunity "to write their own ticket": one that would ensure, to no one's surprise, their autonomy and financial freedom on a scale most Middle East potentates would envy. When asked what they would do if their current venture failed, the usual reply is, "I'd start another" (Shapero 1985).

Yet individuals do leave their entrepreneurial careers to work for others rather than starting other ventures and remaining in an "entrepreneurial career mode." Who they are and why they leave entrepreneurship is not clearly understood. Our understanding of entrepreneurship, however, will never be complete until these "fatalities" are studied and explained in sufficient numbers. Unfortunately, very few post mortems have been conducted. When it comes to "discontinued" entrepreneurial careers, the cadavers have a way of disappearing.

To the best of my knowledge, this descriptive study represents the first exploratory analysis of a substantial number of entrepreneurs who not only left one or more ventures, but also left their entrepreneurial careers to work for someone else. It also marks the first time large numbers of ex-entrepreneurs have been identified and examined in terms of their similarities to and differences from practicing entrepreneurs. Let me emphasize, however, that the study does *not* focus on venture failure or even on career failure. Rather than failure, the study examines the incidence of venture birth and death throughout the careers of ex-entrepreneurs that sometimes ended in venture failure but in other instances ended on a more positive note.

Definitions

In this study, ex-entrepreneurs were defined as individuals who had started one or more entrepreneurial ventures but who had returned to work for someone else by 1982.

Practicing entrepreneurs were defined as individuals who "started from scratch" an independent venture or acquired one at a time in which sales and assets were not very large at the time of acquisition. These individuals were still pursuing their entrepreneurial careers in 1981 and had started them over the 1928–1980 period.

The Data Base and Its Relevance to U.S. Entrepreneurs

The data base for this study is comprised of Babson College alumni. The ex-entrepreneurs were identified from a blind mailing to 3500 alumni who appeared (by title and affiliation) to be working for someone else. This initial mailing identified about 200 ex-entrepreneurs. A second mailing was made to this group and contained a five-page questionnaire. This second mailing resulted in 95 usable responses from ex-entrepreneurs.

The practicing entrepreneurs were identified from a listing of approximately 550 alumni who identified themselves as "self-employed." A single mailing to this group produced 208 usable responses.

Two key points will be made regarding the relevance of the Babson data base to other U.S. entrepreneurs. First, unlike many other studies of entrepreneurs, the one contains data drawn from a relatively homogeneous group. For instance, the effects of many differentiating (and possibly confounding) variables are held constant because Babson alumni share:

1. A common educational background in that they studied the same programs at the same institution: all were members of an academic institution that has specialized exclusively in business education since its founding in 1919;
2. A similar profile in terms of geographic and other locational factors; and
3. A similar orientation toward business generally, including a distinct inclination for some kind of business career at a relatively early age.

Second, such homogeneity provides an opportunity to at least assess the ways in which the sample groups mirror perceptions about the majority of U.S. entrepreneurs. This study and earlier ones (Ronstadt 1982; 1983) indicate several possible areas of common ground with the majority of U.S. entrepreneurs. For example, Babson entrepreneurs show distinct preferences for starting independent ventures from scratch. They tend to start these ventures without partners. In addition, their ventures tend to be smaller businesses with modest initial goals, utilizing low to medium technologies as opposed to high-tech ventures, team-dominated start-ups, and/or venture capital funded enterprises that other studies show are a small minority of all the ventures created by entrepreneurs.

Likely areas of differences also appear to exist. For example, Babson entrepreneurs are not driven by displacement forces to the same extent as the majority of U.S. entrepreneurs apparently are. They probably have a far greater share of parents who are or were entrepreneurs. They approach their entrepreneurial pursuits armed with a relatively strong business education. And they are probably starting their first ventures at earlier ages and on different career paths than are the majority of U.S. entrepreneurs.

The Study's Limitations and Future Research

Despite the advantages derived from a fairly homogeneous sample, some important limitations exist regarding the data base and the research methodology. For instance, the data are confined 100% to *male* alumni who are *non-minorities* and who graduated from an "entrepreneurially inclined" business school. The analysis is limited further by a subjective approach regarding the selection of predictor variables. As such, it may not capture the interaction of other unknown variables. Finally, more powerful statistical techniques are needed to assess the combined impact of the selected variables on the study's independent variable: entrepreneurial career duration.

These limitations will be reduced or avoided in the future. Research still under way will expand the data base to include alumni from other schools. Eventually, non-college graduates will be added. In addition, more sophisticated multivariate techniques will be used to assess the interactive effects of numerous variables that seem to influence both venture life and entrepreneurial career duration. Consequently, this study is exploratory and "descriptive" (i.e., it describes this sample only). The reader should be wary of making inferences about individual variables and their impacts on venture or career length, particularly for other non-Babson entrepreneurs.

PRIOR RESEARCH

The literature discusses venture continuance versus discontinuance from two perspectives: 1) by identifying success and/or failure factors associated with individual ventures and/or particular entrepreneurs; and 2) by identifying the incidence of venture birth and death based on larger sample studies. Both approaches provide information about who might be an ex-entrepreneur, as well as how, when, and why they might leave their entrepreneurial careers.

Success and Failure Factors

Most efforts here conclude that "poor or incompetent management" is the primary cause of business failure (Church 1984; Van Voorhis 1980). In turn, poor management means weaknesses in any of several areas: business planning, cash management, sales generation, or inventory management, for example. Other researchers trace these deficiencies in management skills to weak personal qualities and experience; for example, weakness in drive, perserverence, creativity, intelligence, personality, and communication skills, plus inadequate technical, industry, business, and entrepreneurial experience (Ames and Wellsfry 1983; Vesper 1980; Olm and Eddy 1985).

Many of the same researchers report other factors that contribute directly to venture success or failure. For instance, besides "management practices" and "individual makeup," Vesper (1980) cites six other factors in a review of the literature: 1) choice of business; 2) education and experience; 3) collaboration; 4) location; 5) starting capital; and 6) external forces.

This last factor has been the focus of empirical work at different levels. At the macroeconomic level, one study has shown that business failures are a function of reduced growth in GNP, reduced money supply, reduced capital market activity, and increased business formations, all of which increase competition, limit access to capital, and limit opportunities to raise prices to cover debt and other expenses with cheaper dollars (Altman 1983). At the macropolitical level, case studies document how threshold capitalization requirements and operation costs are increased by the introduction of new government regulations for mail order businesses, franchising, and professional service ventures. Similar case studies show how changes in social values can increase or decrease a community's support for an entrepreneurial venture and play a direct role in the subsequent success or failure of the venture (Ronstadt 1984; Pavan 1983).

Overall, the body of work on venture success and failure factors indicates the existence of multiple factors and multiple underlying causes. Although some may be dominant, the sheer number coupled with comments of former entrepreneurs suggests that any particular venture failure is more likely an outcome produced by a combination of factors than by any single cause. For instance, one entrepreneur made the following remark about his bankrupt business:

> We fell victim to a combination of problems, which, if individually experienced, wouldn't have been so fatal but collectively these problems were terminal (Sweeney 1984).

Venture Dissolution: Larger Sample Studies

The President's Report on the State of Small Business in 1984 made the following distinctions between venture dissolution, venture failure, and venture bankruptcy:

> Ninety percent of the approximately 400,000 businesses that dissolve each year do so for voluntary reasons, such as retirement of the owner or a desire to enter a more profitable field. Almost 10 percent of the businesses that annually cease operations do so for involuntary reasons: they may file for bankruptcy or be considered a business failure if the organization ceases to operate and leaves outstanding debt. Ninety nine percent of failed businesses have fewer than 100 employees and over 80 percent are under ten years old (United States 1984).

Although the data base and precise numbers are suspect (Birley 1984), the vast majority of venture exits are probably "voluntary" as defined in the president's report. But such may not be the case for career exits.

In addition, what constitutes venture failure is less clear and is partly responsible for great divergence about venture exit rates, at least as they are expressed in terms of venture age. Shapero and Giglierano (1982) document these differences and conclude that they are overstated. But whatever the actual venture exit rates for different industries or geographic regions, they will remain overstated when considered from an entrepreneurial career perspective. For example, hearing about the "venture failure" of a particular entrepreneur followed by a success later in the same entrepreneur's career is not uncommon.

From an entrepreneurial perspective, meaningful venture exit rates should disclose not only the risks of pursuing a certain venture in a particular industry or geographic area, but should also give some indication of the likelihood of career continuance or discontinuance. Venture exits may be high in a certain industry, but career exits may be quite low. In other industries or geographic areas, the opposite may be true.

A career perspective does something else. It allows us to focus on another measure that is just as important as the rate of venture discontinuance: the rate of venture continuance *after* a career exit. A set of ventures are created, as we shall see, that live beyond the career departure of ex-entrepreneurs.

Limitations of Previous Research

The prior work on venture dissolution does not capture the effects of multiple ventures created by a single entrepreneur. The same problem exists for those who have focused on venture success and failure factors. In short, the factors that may have been responsible for an initial venture failure may not be the same for subsequent venture failures by the same entrepreneur. Nor may these factors be the same for a venture exit that is also a career exit, as opposed to the venture termination that leads to another venture and continuance of an entrepreneurial career.

Beyond these considerations, one must admit the likelihood that most, if not all, the larger-scale studies of success and failure factors cannot possibly uncover the real or fundamental causes of all venture failures. No incentive exists for people to admit the truth when it is particularly painful, and I doubt that, unobtrusive measures notwithstanding, the cleverest of surveys or interviews will not elicit such responses as, "I failed because I was an alcoholic"; "I failed because of infidelity with my partner's spouse"; "I failed or exited because I could no longer live with my unethical behavior"; or "I exited because I thought the IRS was getting too close." More likely, such surveys or interviews will misread the data they are allowed to see and will simply chalk up another failure due to "management incompetence." Should anyone think this likelihood improbable, consider the words of one ex-entrepreneur who revealed what I believe most would not:

> Having lived through the disease of alcoholism and recovered, I find on reflection that having my own business and making my own hours, etc., was perfect for my main mission—drinking. This may be a concept of entrepreneurship which you may not have even thought to explore and justly so. There are many such people in business to facilitate their habit and to satisfy a highly inflated ego. Some die trying, some fail as I did, and a very few make it. It is a sad experience to say the least.

This Research

Because this study is descriptive, it does not attempt to explain the causes of venture or career success, failure, or even discontinuance. Its purpose is simply to describe a particular group of individuals and provide some insights regarding 1) Who specifically is exiting from an entrepreneurial career: younger entrepreneurs (in terms of both chronological and entrepreneurial age) or older ones? 2) Are the exits occurring among those who have started single ventures or among those who have already created additional ventures? 3) When, how, and why are they exiting? and 4) Are their career exits "voluntary"?

A basic hypothesis of the study is that career exits are not voluntary in the usual sense of the word. Ventures may end for positive reasons, but the presumption of this study is that entrepreneurial careers end because negative forces "displace" entrepreneurs into new careers.

A related hypothesis is that ex-entrepreneurs will be displaced into new careers when a combination of negative factors, rather than a single reason, exists.

WHO ARE THE EX-ENTREPRENEURS?

We know that the 95 ex-entrepreneurs in the study ranged in age from 33 to 73 in 1982 (the survey year). As their varying ages might suggest, they had been entrepreneurs for considerably different lengths of time, ranging from less than one year to 32 years. One might speculate without losing much sleep that considerable difference probably existed between the ex-entrepreneur who exited after one or two years versus the ex-entrepreneur who lasted 32 years. It was this presumption that led us:

1. To organize the description of ex-entrepreneurs by entrepreneurial career length; and then
2. To observe the number of ventures they started, continued, and discontinued; as well as,
3. To observe the extent to which venture-goal changes, different factor intensities and technology levels, and other variables were associated with varying career lengths and numbers of ventures created and discontinued.

Entrepreneurial Career Length

Table 1 describes the ex-entrepreneurs in terms of the amount of time they spent as entrepreneurs. It shows the possible existence of four other groups of ex-entrepreneurs in terms of career length: 33% were *fast exits:* those leaving before three years; about 40% were *early exits:* those exiting between three and six years; about 20% were *mid-range exits:* those exiting between seven and 15 years; and approximately 7% were *late exits:* those exiting after over 15 years of entrepreneurial experience.

Although these groupings are potentially interesting, we should not lose sight of the following:

1. The vast majority of career exits were among "younger" ex-entrepreneurs in terms of career length or "entrepreneurial age";
2. Over one-third exited before three years; over two-thirds exited by six years; and
3. If we define "seasoned entrepreneurs" as people having at least seven years of entrepreneurial experience, then such individuals accounted for less than one-third of all career exits in this sample.

Consequently, the longer careers were the exception rather than the rule. In statistical terms, the seven late exits are "outliers" that can misrepresent the bulk of the sample in terms of measures of career duration. Excluding them produces an average (mean) career of five years for most ex-entrepreneurs (92% of the sample) with careers from 0 to 15 years. The median career for this group, however, is still a year less, indicating continued skewness (to the right) for the sample. In fact, the mean and median values of career length do not equalize until the 7-to-15-year group of mid-range exits are also excluded. This exclusion still leaves us with 73% of the sample population with an average career of three years (S.D. = 1.45).

TABLE 1 Entrepreneurial Career Length (ECL)

Exit Group	ECL in Years	Number	Percentage	Cum. Percentage
Before 3 years	1	8	9.1%	9.1%
(Fast Exits)	2	21	23.9	33.0
3 to 6 years	3	12	13.6	46.6
(Early Exits)	4	11	12.5	59.1
	5	9	10.2	69.3
	6	3	3.4	72.7
7 to 15 years	9	2	2.3	75.0
(Mid-Range Exits)	10	5	5.7	80.7
	11	4	4.5	85.2
	12	1	1.1	86.4
	13	2	2.3	88.6
	15	3	3.4	92.0
Over 15 years *(Late Exits)*	20 to 32 yrs	7	8.0	100.0
Total		88	100.0	

TABLE 2 The Number of Ventures Created by Ex-Entrepreneurs

Single	51%	Single	51%	1 Venture	51%
Multiple	49	Sequential	22	2 Ventures	22
		Overlapping	27	3 Ventures	18
				4 Ventures	6
				5 Ventures	5
				6 Ventures	2
				7 Ventures	1

The Number of Ventures

Approximately 51% of the ex-entrepreneurs started only a single venture during their careers. The other 49%, however, started from two to seven ventures. These subsequent ventures were split fairly evenly between sequential versus overlapping startups. The exact distributions are shown in Table 2.

All together, the 95 ex-entrepreneurs started a total of 193 ventures. They discontinued 143 of these ventures (74%) before the end of their entrepreneurial careers. Fifty ventures were continued (26%) after their career exits occurred.

Venture discontinuance rates were similar to those reported by Hoad and Rosko (1964), Churchill (1955), and the United States (1984). The rate of venture discontinuance as a percentage of all ventures discontinued is shown specifically in Table 3.

These rates dropped noticeably, however, when all ventures started by ex-entrepreneurs were considered; that is, those continued after a career exit in addition to those discontinued during it (see Table 4).

At this point, we can say that, on average, each ex-entrepreneur created two ventures (193 / 95) during his or her career. Approximately 1.5 (143 / 95) of these two ventures were discontinued, whereas 0.5 (50 / 95) were continued after the career exit. Of course, there can be considerable variance around these averages, as the actual number of ventures created suggests. For instance, half the ex-entrepreneurs created only one venture. Another 32% created three or more.

Did creating additional ventures help to shorten or extend entrepreneurial careers? No clear answer exists. Instances can be cited for both ex-entrepreneurs and practicing entrepreneurs in which starting additional ventures was detrimental for a career. In other cases, the second or third venture clearly saved or extended the career.

Some evidence is emerging, however, that suggests that multiple ventures may be more beneficial than previously thought under certain conditions. Thus far we know that both practicing entrepreneurs and ex-entrepreneurs had tendencies to start more than one venture in their careers (see Table 5). Approximately 40% of both groups with careers under

TABLE 3 Unadjusted Exit Rates (in Percentages)

	Babson Ex-Entrepreneurs Venture Exit Rate[a]	Other Studies' Venture Exit Rates
Year 3	46%	43% (Hoad)
Year 6	70	74 (Churchill)
Year 10	82	80 (United States)

[a]Defined as a percentages of all ventures ended.

TABLE 4 Adjusted Exit Rates

Year	Net Venture Exit Rate[a]	% Difference from Unadjusted Exit Rate
Year 3	34%	26% Decline
Year 6	53%	24% Decline
Year 10	61%	26% Decline

[a]Defined as a percentage of all ventures created, including those that survived the ex-entrepreneurs. A complete distribution of the data is provided in Ronstadt (1985).

three years started at least a second venture. The share remained nearly equal and rose to 50% for both practicing entrepreneurs and ex-entrepreneurs with careers between three and six years. After seven years, however, practicing entrepreneurs had a higher tendency to start additional ventures compared to ex-entrepreneurs.

At the same time, the largest relative number of venture births came from ex-entrepreneurs who started at a younger age. The data in Table 6 shows that a relatively higher share of multiple ventures were created by individuals who started their first venture before their twenty-sixth birthdays. Those who started over 40, by contrast, were more likely to have exited from their entrepreneurial careers without having created more than a single venture.

The final and connecting piece of evidence is presented in the next section. It indicates that the ex-entrepreneurs who started earlier (under 26) also created a higher share of multiple ventures but lasted longer as entrepreneurs.

WHEN DID THE EX-ENTREPRENEURS EXIT?

The ages of the ex-entrepreneurs in this study ranged from 25 to 66 years when they ended their entrepreneurial careers. The years during which the ex-entrepreneurs exited were from 1952 to 1982. During this time, they had been removed from their entrepreneurial careers for as little as one year to as many as 30 years before the survey year (1982). However,

TABLE 5 Entrepreneurial Career Length and Number of Ventures Created by Practicing Entrepreneurs and Ex-Entrepreneurs

	<3 Years	3–6 Years	7–15 Years	>15 Years
By Practicing Entrepreneurs				
% Single Ventures	62	49	35	35
% Multiple Ventures	38	51	65	65
N = (203)	(21)	(65)	(60)	(57)
% = 100%	10%	32%	30%	28%
By Ex-Entrepreneurs				
% Single Ventures	59	51	44	57
% Multiple Ventures	41	49	56	43
N = (87)	(29)	(35)	(16)	(7)
% = 100%	33%	40%	18%	8%

TABLE 6 Start Up Age and the Number of Ventures Started

Age Started First Venture	Single Venture Created	Multiple Ventures Created
Under 26	19%	30%
26 to 32	34	33
33 to 40	23	24
Over 40	23	13
N = (94)	(48)	(46)

75% had exited within 12 years of 1982. Approximately 10% exited by their thirtieth birthdays. An additional 50% left by their fortieth birthdays, with another 30% exiting by their fiftieth birthdays. The final 10% exited after their fifty-first birthdays.

A related question at this point is: How old were the ex-entrepreneurs when they exited relative to the number of years they had spent as entrepreneurs? The data in Table 7 show an unexpected relationship. For instance, one might expect a high positive correlation (from colinear effects if nothing else; that is, on average, those with longer careers would also be older). But this relationship didn't exist except for the *late exits* (over 15 years). The *early exits* (3 to 6 years) were actually younger than the *fast exits* (below 3 years). Even the *mid-range exits* (7 to 15 years) were less than two years older than the *fast exits* (actually no older in terms of median age, both 38), despite having entrepreneurial careers that lasted from four to 12 years longer than the *fast exits*.

These variations exist between average exit age and career length because a weak but negative linear relationship exists for ex-entrepreneurs between career length and another variable, their start-up ages (correlation coefficient = .24). The data in Table 8 show that *as ex-entrepreneurs started their first ventures at older ages, their entrepreneurial careers became increasingly shorter*.

HOW DID THE EX-ENTREPRENEURS EXIT?

The vast majority of the 95 ex-entrepreneurs exited mainly by "selling out" or liquidating their ventures. Only a few exited via bankruptcy. Of course, the possibility exists that ex-entrepreneurs who experienced bankruptcy may have been less likely to respond to the questionnaire.

TABLE 7 Exit Age by Entrepreneurial Career Duration (In Years)

	All Exits	<3 Yrs. *(Fast Exits)*	3–6 Yrs. *(Early Exits)*	7–15 Yrs. *(Mid-Range Exits)*	>15 Yrs. *(Late Exits)*
Median Age at Exit	38	38	36.0	38.0	55.0
Mean Age at Exit	39.7	38.7	37.6	40.5	56.5
Standard Deviation	8.9	7.8	8.1	7.2	7.4

TABLE 8 Career Start-Up Age Classified by Entrepreneurial Career Length

Age Started	Median ECL	Mean[a] ECL	Standard Deviation	Number of Observations
Under 26	8.2	9.6	7.3	16
26 to 33	4.0	6.6	7.1	37
34 to 40	3.5	5.8	6.4	22
Over 40	3.0	3.4	2.9	17
				92

[a] $F = 2.61$ with $DF = 3,88$. Significant at .10 (Ho rejected that the means are equal except for chance sampling variation).

Sold Out[a]	44	46%
Liquidation	41	43%
Bankruptcy	5	5%
Unclear	5	5%

How does the mode of career exit relate to the amount of time spent as an entrepreneur? The data in Table 9 provide the following observations:

1. Three of the four bankruptcies occurred under seven years. Those three occurred in years 4 and 5, whereas the fourth bankruptcy occurred in the ninth year. The number of bankruptcies is small; however, the clustering does make some sense. The absence of bankruptcies before three years may reflect the need to build up sizable debt of sufficient magnitude to force bankruptcy. The absence of bankruptcy at the other end of the time spectrum suggests that sufficient assets have been accumulated to permit a sell out or liquidation when a final disposition becomes necessary.
2. A higher relative proportion of liquidations occurred during the early career years (that is, before seven years) compared to sell-outs. This observation makes intuitive sense because it is no doubt more difficult to sell a newly created venture than one with an established record regarding sales and profits.
3. Nevertheless, the percentage of sell-outs in early years (45%) may be surprising to some readers.

TABLE 9 Exit Mode Classified by Entrepreneurial Career Length for Ex-Entrepreneurs (Excludes 21 in "Other" Category; in Percentages)

	< 3 Yrs. (Fast Exits)	3–6 Yrs. (Early Exits)	7–15 Yrs. (Mid-Range Exits)	> 15 Yrs. (Late Exits)
Bankruptcy	0%	10%	7%	0%
Liquidation	55	45	29	17
Sell-Out	45	45	64	83
N	(20)	(29)	(14)	(6)

TABLE 10 Exit Reasons of Ex-Entrepreneurs

1: Financial Reasons	2: Personal and Family Reasons	3: Environmental and Venture-Related Reasons	4: Combination of Sets of Reasons
Finance related	Family Problems; Time Needs; Divorce; Personality Conflicts; Lack Experience; Lack Education; Illness	Idea/Concept; Legal Problems; Competition; Market Decline; Other Opportunity; Fire; Real Estate/Site Problems	1 & 2 1 & 3 2 & 3 1, 2, & 3

WHY DID THE EX-ENTREPRENEURS EXIT?

Ex-entrepreneurs were asked to note the reason or reasons that were instrumental in causing them to leave their entrepreneurial careers. These reasons are summarized in Table 10.

The respondents had the opportunity to make multiple responses. Many took advantage of this option. A few limited their responses to a single factor; others limited their responses to a single set or group (e.g., personal/family related). Nevertheless, the single largest group was the *Combination of Reasons* category (43% of the total).

Disaggregating the combinations of reasons provides a breakdown of exit reasons by the seven categories as shown in Table 11.

Nearly three-fourths (74%) claimed that financial reasons and some interplay of financial and other related considerations played a role in their decisions to end their entrepreneurial careers. Other combined sets of reasons were nearly as frequently cited or more frequently cited than personal/family or venture/environmental reasons. For example, financial reasons plus personal/family reasons were nearly twice as frequent as personal/family reasons alone. No one, however, claimed that the last combined set (personal/family or venture/environmental reasons) played a role in their exit decisions.

Exit Reasons by Entrepreneurial Career Length

The distribution of exit reasons categorized by entrepreneurial career duration (the data in Table 12) supports a hypothesis that sees earlier exits hampered more by financial concerns, whereas later exits experienced greater difficulties with personal and family problems. The

TABLE 11 The Distribution of Exit Reasons

Exit Reasons	Number	Percentage	Cumulative Percentage
1. Financial Alone	27	31%	31%
2. Financial, Personal/Family	18	21	52
3. Financial, Venture/Environmental	11	13	65
4. Financial, Personal/Family, Venture/Environmental	8	9	74
5. Venture/Environmental Alone	13	15	89
6. Personal/Family Alone	9	11	100
7. Personal/Family, Venture/Environmental	0	0	100

TABLE 12 Exit Reasons Classified by Entrepreneurial Career Length (Percentage Distribution)

Exit Reasons	< 3 Years	3–6 Years	7–15 Years	>15 Years	Total
Finance Alone	34%	43%	25%	0%	31%
Finance Personal/Family	21	19	20	17	21
Finance Venture/Envir.	16	14	10	0	13
All Three Groups	11	0	10	33	9
Venture/Envir. Alone	13	19	10	33	15
Personal/Family Alone	5	5	25	17	11
Total	100	100	100	100	100
Total *N*	(38)	(21)	(20)	(6)	(85)

rationale for this hypothesis is that later exits were less encumbered by cash-flow constraints, having solved these difficulties earlier in their careers. Rather, changes in their personal and family lives forced them to make new decisions about the reinvestment of their time and capital.

This position is supported by additional data that reveal the perceptions of ex-entrepreneurs about their banking and financial contacts and whether or not they viewed their entrepreneurial careers as financially disappointing.

For instance, Table 13 shows that a substantial share of earlier exits (before seven years) felt that they did have good financial contacts; however, higher shares of these earlier exits also felt that they did *not* have good banking/financial contacts compared to later exits. Specifically, about one-third of the earlier exits indicated that they did not enjoy good contacts in these areas.

The data in Table 14 confirm that a majority (61%) of all exits found their entrepreneurial careers to be financially disappointing. Again, exits before seven years experienced a somewhat higher share of financial disappointment compared to the mid-range, 7-to-15-year group (about 70% versus 53%).

SUMMARY

Most Babson ex-entrepreneurs (about 70%) felt significantly prepared to start their entrepreneurial pursuits. A near-equal share (72%) believed, in retrospect, that they were not ill advised to start entrepreneurial careers. Both perceptions possibly come from the fact that, as a group, they possessed considerable business experience and formal education in business.

TABLE 13 Financial Contacts by Entrepreneurial Career Length (in Percentages)

Yes, Good Financial Contacts	All Exits	< 3 Yrs. Fast Exits	3–6 Yrs. (Early Exits)	7–15 Yrs. (Mid-Range Exits)	> 15 Yrs. (Late Exits)
Strong Agree	27%	10%	30%	41%	43%
Moderate Agree	28	31	27	23	14
Neutral	19	24	12	23	43
Moderate Disagree	16	14	21	12	0
Strong Disagree	10	21	9	0	9
(Number of Observations)	(93)	(29)	(33)	(17)	(7)

TABLE 14 Financial Disappointment Classified by Entrepreneurial Career Length (in Percentages)

Did ex-entrepreneurs view their entrepreneurial careers as financially disappointing?

Yes, Financially Disappointing	All Exits	< 3 Yrs. (Fast Exits)	3–6 Yrs. (Early Exits)	6–15 Yrs. (Mid-Range Exits)	> 15 Yrs. (Late Exits)
Strong Agree	27%	33%	33%	18%	29%
Moderate Agree	34	37	36	35	29
Neutral	0	0	0	0	0
Moderate Disagree	16	17	15	12	14
Strong Disagree	23	12	15	35	29
N	(88)	(24)	(33)	(17)	(7)

Despite this experience plus good financial and banking contacts, ex-entrepreneurs encountered a mix of financial and other constraints that were beyond their abilities or desires to resolve. The result was a difficult decision to leave their ventures and, rather than start other ventures, return to work for someone else.

This particular sample of ex-entrepreneurs left their careers well before "retirement age" to work for someone else. Over 60% exited by age 40 and 90% left by age 50. The data also indicate that most ex-entrepreneurs, which is also to say those with careers under seven years, departed more for involuntary and negative reasons than for voluntary ones. A few noted positive, opportunistic reasons for their career shifts. But most tended to leave due to a variety of pressures that had produced financial disappointment, personal hardships, and family strain. Although they started their entrepreneurial careers for mainly opportunistic reasons (Ronstadt 1984a), they ultimately were driven from these careers by displacement forces that emanated from multiple sources. Despite these negative forces, most still did not view their careers as entrepreneurs as entirely disappointing or frustrating. In fact, a large share (57%) had not ruled out resuming these careers at some point in the future. Another 20% were uncertain, and only 23% noted that another venture in the future was unlikely.

Earlier Career Exits versus Later Career Exits

Seasoned entrepreneurs with seven or more years of entrepreneurial experience were not ending their entrepreneurial careers in large numbers to work for someone else. Among ex-entrepreneurs, most career exits occurred in the earlier years of an entrepreneurial career. Approximately two-thirds exited before seven years and nearly one-third exited before three years.

Earlier exits also tended to end their careers via liquidation to a greater extent than did later exits. Financial factors were clearly more associated with earlier exits, even among those who managed to sell out. Personal and family factors were more important for later exits, though financial considerations often played a role in their exits.

A high percentage of earlier exits also created multiple ventures (nearly half the sample). Even among ex-entrepreneurs with careers shorter than three years, over 40% started at least one other venture. This rate of venture creation, however, was no different than the rate for practicing entrepreneurs with careers of equivalent length. (Although practicing entrepreneurs with careers longer than seven years did have higher rates of new venture creation than ex-entrepreneurs with comparable careers.)

Approximately one-fourth (26%) of all ventures started by ex-entrepreneurs were continued after they exited from their entrepreneurial careers. Although venture exit rates were similar to those presented in several other studies, they dropped considerably when venture continuance was factored into the exit rate. And nearly half (46%) of the ex-entrepreneurs saw at least one venture survive them. *The likelihood is that these adjusted exit rates will fall still further once the venture histories of practicing and retired entrepreneurs are also included.*

The distinctions between different modes of exit pale when one considers the timing of a career departure. For instance, the difference among earlier exits between a liquidation and a sell-out appears to be insignificant in many instances. Whatever significance exists is apparently insufficient to alter financial expectations about the career in any meaningful way.

Finally, longer careers among ex-entrepreneurs were associated with earlier start-up ages, particularly for those who started under 26 years of age. In addition, this age group was characterized by a greater share of multiple ventures that were "low-tech" enterprises. Prior work showed that these younger entrepreneurs were on different pathways than those who started at older ages. The younger startups tended to begin their careers as first careers or explicitly anticipated them by choosing a prior career as preparation for an entrepreneurial one (Ronstadt 1984a).

Overall, the evidence suggests that *under certain conditions,* earlier starts are better than late starts; that anticipated starts are better than unanticipated ones; and that late starts that are unanticipated are particularly precarious. Their danger may reside in a need by older individuals to scale up the goals of their first ventures, to maintain these goals for subsequent ventures rather than to downgrade them, and to employ "medium technologies" in ventures that eventually run into financial difficulties for any number of possible reasons.

REFERENCES

Altman, Edward I. 1983. Why businesses fail. *Journal of Business Strategy.*

Ames, Michael D., and Wellsfry, Norval L. 1983. *Small Business Management.* New York: West Publishing Co.

Birley, Sue. 1984. New firms and job generation in St. Joseph County. *Frontiers of Entrepreneurship Research 1984.* Wellesley, Mass.: Center of Entrepreneurial Studies, Babson College.

Church, Olive D. 1984. *Small Business Management and Entrepreneurship.* Chicago: Science Research Associates.

Churchill, B.C. December 1955. Age and life expectancy of business firms. *Survey of Current Business* 35 (12).

Hoad, William, N., and Rosko, Peter. 1964. *Management Factors Contributing to the Success and Failure of New Small Manufacturers.* Ann Arbor, Mich.: Bureau of Business Research, University of Michigan.

Olm, Kenneth W., and Eddy, George G. 1985. *Entrepreneurship and Venture Management: Text and Cases.* Columbus, Ohio: Merrill Publishing Co.

Pavan, Robert. 1983. Social responsibility: Who should pay? In *Introduction to Business: A Case Approach,* Robert Ronstadt and Laurence J. Stybel, eds. Dover, Mass.: Lord Publishing.

Ronstadt, Robert. 1982. Does career path really matter? *Frontiers of Entrepreneurship Research.* Wellesley, Mass.: Babson College.

Ronstadt, Robert. 1983. The decision *not* to become an entrepreneur. *Frontiers of Entrepreneurship Research.* Wellesley, Mass.: Babson College.

Ronstadt, Robert. 1984a. Ex entrepreneurs and the decision to start an entrepreneurial career. *Frontiers of Entrepreneurship Research.* Wellesley, Mass.: Babson College.

Ronstadt, Robert. 1984b. *Entrepreneurship: Text, Cases, & Notes*. Dover, Mass.: Lord Publishing.

Ronstadt, Robert. 1985. Every entrepreneur's nightmare: The decision to become an ex entrepreneur and work for someone else. *Frontiers of Entrepreneurship Research*. Wellesley, Mass.: Babson College.

Shapero, A. Winter 1985. Why entrepreneurship, *Babson Bulletin,* Wellesley, MA: Babson College.

Shapero, Albert, and Giglierano, Joseph. 1982. Exits and entries: A study in yellow pages journalism. *Frontiers of Entrepreneurship Research*. Wellesley, Mass.: Babson College.

Star, Alvin D., and Narayana, Chem L. October 1983. Do we really know the number of small business starts? *Journal of Small Business Management*.

Sweeney, Harry M. February 1984. Why I went out of business. *Computer Dealer*.

United States. 1984. *The State of Small Business: A Report of the President*. Washington, D.C.: U.S. Government Printing Office.

Vesper, Karl. July-August 1979. New venture ideas: Do not overlook the experience factor. *Harvard Business Review*.

Vesper, Karl. 1980. *New Venture Strategies*. Englewood Cliffs, N.J.: Prentice-Hall.

Van Voorhis, Kenneth R. 1980. *Entrepreneurship and Small Business Management*. Boston: Allyn and Bacon.

[5]

KYKLOS, Vol. 48 – 1995 – Fasc. 4, 513 - 540

Determinants of Willingness and Opportunity to Start as an Entrepreneur

C. Mirjam Van Praag and Hans Van Ophem*

I. INTRODUCTION

Since new firm formation has been recognized for a long time as an important source of economic growth and labor demand, the topic of self-employment or entrepreneurship has gained considerable theoretical as well as political interest. Governments are by and large of the opinion that new firm formation is necessary for a healthy economy and that the 'natural' entrepreneurship supply is insufficient. As a result, governments started to provide encouragement programmes for self-employment and studies to evaluate the programmes' effectiveness became desirable. This calls for insight in the individual decision process. Empirical microeconomic studies have started to supply these insights. The objective of self-employment encouragement programmes is to stimulate potential successful entrepreneurs to switch to this occupational status, or to provide promising and enthusiastic would-be entrepreneurs with an opportunity to become self-employed. In order to recruit programme participants efficiently, these categories of would-be entrepreneurs should be located. Hence, it is of interest to identify individual determinants of both opportunity and willingness to become self-employed.

This paper attempts to empirically separate the effects of opportunity and willingness on becoming an entrepreneur. Observing someone as being self-employed implies that the individual both has been willing and has had the opportunity to switch to this occupational status. If either *willingness* (motivation) or *opportunity* (ability and/or capital) is absent, the individual will not become self-employed. We define the unobserved concepts of opportunity and

*Drs. and Dr., Tinbergen Institute and Departments of Economics of the University of Amsterdam, Roetersstraat 11, 1018 WB Amsterdam, The Netherlands. We should like to thank Mars Cramer, Joop Hartog, Hessel Oosterbeek, Andrew Oswald and Gerard Van Den Berg for their helpful comments.

willingness such that their levels should both surpass a given threshold for somebody to become self-employed: opportunity and willingness are each necessary conditions and together they are sufficient to switch to self-employment. We wish to identify the contribution of these unobservable concepts to the decision of a wage worker to start as an entrepreneur. This is done by estimating the bivariate probit model with partial observability (cf. Poirier, 1980). Do individuals who 'decide' not to become self-employed lack the opportunity or rather the willingness or both? And what are the observable variables that constitute the unobserved underlying concept 'opportunity' and what variables explain the 'willingness' to become self-employed? These are the questions we intend to answer. We do so by means of a dynamic approach. Using the observation of switches to self-employment, we explain the probability of becoming an entrepreneur rather than the probability of being one.

The paper is organized as follows. Section II defines opportunity and willingness to become self-employed and explains why we distinguish between them. We relate our model to a long tradition in economics of entrepreneurship, going back to Say (1803), Marshall (1890), Schumpeter (1911) and Knight (1921).

Section III describes Poirier's (1980) bivariate probit model that is used to distinguish the unobservable phenomena of opportunity and willingness.

Section IV describes the data (the U.S. National Longitudinal Survey of Youth) and the variables we used. The model is estimated from a subsample of white men (between 20 and 31 years old) who were (un)employed in any year from 1985 to 1988 and who were either (un)employed or self-employed in the next year (1986-1989). We focus on white male labor force participants for homogeneity reasons and for comparability with related studies. The survey, selected because it contains appropriate information on a large number of observations, imposes the restriction on age. Its panel character makes it possible to focus on the dynamics of starting as an entrepreneur.

Both in theoretical and empirical studies various definitions have been used in order to define the concept of 'entrepreneur'[1]. We do not aim at finding a theoretical concept ourselves; we merely focus on an appropriate empirical counterpart of entrepreneurship. The empirical observed phenomenon, closely related to entrepreneurship, that we use (and has been used in most empirical research) is self-employment. Following De Wit (1993), we include in the group

1. Extensive discussions on the various existing theoretical notions can be found in Casson (1991), Barreto (1989) and Hébert and Link (1989).

of self-employed both individuals who report being self-employed and those who are sole owners of their incorporated businesses: these persons perform no other function than the self-employed and they often incorporate their businesses for the sake of fiscal advantages only.

Section V discusses the maximum likelihood estimates of the empirical model. The results reveal that for most individuals opportunity is the more constraining factor in the selection process into self-employment. Opportunity in turn is dependent on the availability of capital (assets and real estate). These capital requirements can be compensated for by a low regional unemployment rate and by self-employment experience. The results are in accordance with the historical views of Say and Knight. Section VI concludes and summarizes the main findings.

II. OPPORTUNITY AND WILLINGNESS

Opportunity is defined as the possibility to become self-employed if one wants to. Important variables determining opportunity are starting capital, entrepreneurial ability and the (macro)economic environment. Young men who are willing to become self-employed have an opportunity to do so whenever they possess enough capital, or can borrow it. It is likely that loans are dependent on the perceived (entrepreneurial) ability of the would be-entrepreneur, given economic conditions. This implies that ability and own capital are substitutes[2]: the opportunity to start as an entrepreneur increases with a (weighted) sum of both.

Willingness to start as an entrepreneur is defined as the valuation of work in self-employment versus remaining (un)employed, for otherwise identical situations. Willingness is positive whenever self-employment is seen as the best available (career) option. Consequently, willingness is dependent on both individual preferences for the special features of self-employment as well as on the available outside options and their perceived attractiveness.

Our wish to distinguish entrepreneurial willingness from opportunity within a dynamic framework is based on our own intuition and on our reading of the important (classical) literature. Before the more recent revival of entrepreneurship research, several important economists; Say (1803), Marshall (1890), Schumpeter (1911) and Knight (1921) have laid the basis. And in contrast with

2. Another explanation for substitutability could be that the 'smarter entrepreneurs' need less capital for a venture. In Evans and Jovanovic (1989) capital and entrepreneurial ability are assumed to be positively correlated; a test reveals a significant negative correlation.

recent contributions, the distinction between opportunity and willingness is quite prominent in this literature. Say (1971) stresses the importance of the availability of a scarce combination of certain moral qualities (ability) necessary for being an entrepreneur. Capital may be borrowed, but only by people who have some additional qualities.

> 'It is commonly requisite for the entrepreneur himself to provide the necessary funds. Not that he must be already rich, for he may work upon borrowed capital; but he must at least be solvent, and have the reputation of intelligence, prudence, probity and regularity;... These requisites shut out a great many competitors.' (Say 1971, p 330).

Marshall's view (1930) largely agrees with Say's. They both argue that ability (though defined differently) is a restricting factor for the supply of individual entrepreneurship. Marshall's entrepreneur may borrow capital, though surviving as an entrepreneur is easier for those who supply their own capital. Schumpeter (1934) argues that ability does not play a significant role, while capital can be borrowed easily. For Schumpeter, the prime restriction on the supply of entrepreneurs is a scarce combination of motivating forces (willingness) of pursuing indirect instead of direct consumption. Knight (1921) argues that capital, due to moral hazard (see LeRoy and Singell, 1987), and willingness, unlike ability, are necessary to just start as an entrepreneur.

> 'Willingness plus power to give guarantees, not backed up by ability, will evidently lead to a dissipation of resources, while ability without the other two factors will be merely wasted.' (Knight 1971, p 283).

Our empirical estimates will identify the relative importance of opportunity (ability and capital) and willingness and the estimates will thereby show which of the diverging views is sustained by our findings.

Current empirical entrepreneurship research within the economics tradition[3] is not in a position to separate the effects of opportunity and willingness on entrepreneurship dynamics. The majority of studies is based on cross-sectional data and can therefore not capture these dynamics. They do not permit distinguishing factors determining survival in entrepreneurship from those that determine the start as an entrepreneur.

Empirical (person oriented) analyses that are based on duration data and consequently in a position to capture dynamics, are scarcer and do not decompose the propensity to become self-employed into willingness and opportunity. Evans and Leighton (1989) study the individual determinants of observed

3. An overview is found in Van Praag (1994).

switches from wage employment to entrepreneurship and compare these results to their findings concerning selection and earnings. One of their key findings is that the availability of more assets results in a larger probability of switching from wage employment to the occupational status of entrepreneur. Evans' and Jovanovic's (1989) (dynamic) study aims at determining whether liquidity constraints play a role in the decision process to become an entrepreneur (and to start at the most profitable scale). They find empirical support for binding liquidity constraints as capital assets have a positive effect on the wage worker's probability to start a business. Holtz-Eakin et al. (1994) study the individual determinants of business formation in order to determine whether an individual's wealth affects the probability of becoming an entrepreneur. They employ a unique sample of people who received inheritances. They find that the probability of becoming an entrepreneur rises with the size of the inheritance.

Blanchflower and Oswald (1994) study the determinants of being an entrepreneur as well as being happy as an entrepreneur. Like Holtz-Eakin et al. (1994), they find inheritances to be a major determinant of the occupational status of entrepreneur.

We shall contribute to this empirical research base by means of the following potential innovations: The first is the identification of the contribution of opportunity and willingness aspects in the decision process of a labor force participant to become self-employed. The survey material used by Blanchflower and Oswald (1994) indicates that there are more people who would like to become self-employed than the actual number of self-employed. Their analysis based on satisfaction data also points at serious impediments to entrepreneurship. We supply an additional instrument to verify whether indeed opportunity rather than willingness forms the bottleneck in this process.

The only 'serious impediment' however which Blanchflower and Oswald (1994) isolate is the liquidity constraint. Moreover, Evans and Jovanovic (1989), Evans and Leighton (1989) and Holtz-Eakin et al. (1994) all find evidence that capital constraints bind, each using different approaches. With our model, we are in a position to uncover whether there are other impediments to self-employment opportunity, keeping motivation or preferences for switching to self-employment constant. This leads to answering the question: is it possible to compensate a lack of capital by, for instance, entrepreneurial ability?

A third contribution is to evaluate what observable variables affect the probability to switch through opportunity and what variables do so through willingness. For example, if we observe within a univariate framework that married men are more inclined to become self-employed than bachelors, is this due to their superior willingness, due to more perceived opportunities or are they less willing but do they face far more opportunities?

We do not know, unless we differentiate between opportunity and willingness in an estimable model. Differentiating between these two concepts helps also to find out whether the effects of certain observable individual characteristics on willingness and opportunity are adverse.

III. THE MODEL

The concepts of willingness and opportunity are not (separately) observed. We only observe whether an individual becomes self-employed or not. And we know that, by definition, men who choose to become self-employed have more willingness and more opportunity than their threshold levels (arbitrarily set at zero). We also know that men who choose not to become self-employed have either less than zero willingness or less than zero opportunity or both. We need an empirical model that uses the available information (revealed preferences) as an input but is able to identify the unobserved underlying concepts as well. Poirier (1980) discusses a (joint-decision) model which meets these requirements. It is known as the bivariate probit model with partial observability[4].

Define two individual specific latent variables, I_{1i}^* representing the opportunity to switch to self-employment and I_{2i}^* reflecting willingness to become self-employed, where i distinguishes individuals. These constructs can be related to observed regressor variables Z by a linear relation:

$$I_{1i}^* = Z_{1i}\gamma_1 - \varepsilon_{1i} \quad (1)$$

$$I_{2i}^* = Z_{2i}\gamma_2 - \varepsilon_{2i} \quad (2)$$

where Z_{ji} $(j=1,2)$ is the vector of regressors, γ_j is a vector of unknown parameters and ε_{ji} is an error term with mean 0 and (normalized) variance 1. We assume that the error terms have a bivariate standard normal distribution with correlation ρ and are independent from one observation to another. Define two (still unobserved) dummy variables

4. Although this model is well known in the econometric literature, we have not encountered an empirical application thus far. Maddala (1983), who describes this model extensively, does not mention an empirical application either.

$$I_{ji} = \begin{cases} 1 & \text{if and only if } I^*_{ji} > 0 \\ 0 & \text{otherwise.} \end{cases} \quad (3)$$

Hence, I_{1i} equals one for a young man with (sufficient) opportunity to become self-employed and it equals zero for a man without (sufficient) opportunity. I_{2i} equals one if and only if a young man is (sufficiently) willing to become self-employed and is zero otherwise. We observe whether an individual becomes self-employed or not, i.e., the realization of the dichotomous variable $I_i = I_{1i} * I_{2i}$. Consequently, the probability of switching to self-employment equals:

$$Pr(I_i = 1) = Pr(\min[I^*_{1i}, I^*_{2i}] > 0) =$$
$$Pr(\varepsilon_{1i} < Z_{1i}\,\gamma_1, \varepsilon_{2i} < Z_{2i}\,\gamma_2) = F(Z_{1i}\,\gamma_1, Z_{2i}\,\gamma_2, \rho) \quad (4)$$

where F(.,.,.) is the standard normal cumulative distribution function. Maximum likelihood estimates of γ_1, γ_2 and ρ can be obtained by maximizing the loglikelihoodfunction:

$$\log L = \sum_{i=1}^{N} \left\{ I_i \log[F(Z_{1i}\,\gamma_1, Z_{2i}\,\gamma_2, \rho)] + (1 - I_i) \log [1 - F(Z_{1i}\,\gamma_1, Z_{2i}\,\gamma_2, \rho)] \right\}$$

where N is the number of observations.

Poirier (1980) has shown that γ_1, γ_2 and ρ are identified as long as Z_{1i} and Z_{2i} do not contain exactly the same variables and the explanatory variables exhibit sufficient variation[5].

Maddala (1983, p. 279) discusses an alternative model that deals with multiple decision functions and partial observability; it is nested in Poirier's model (an empirical example of this model can be found in Abowd and Farber (1982)), unlike the univariate probit model. Maddala defines Poirier's model as the joint case and the model estimated by Abowd and Farber as the sequential case. In the sequential case I^*_{2i} is a useful concept only for those observations

5. Moreover, the exogenous variables must take on at least as many distinct data configurations as there are unknown parameters in the model, indicating that if a model contains a number of variables taking on many different values, no identification problems will occur (cf. Poirier, 1980, p 215).

that meet the condition $I_{1i}^* > 0$. For instance, consider the question whether a certain individual is matched to a particular job or not. Suppose the job vacancy is (exclusively) advertised in a newspaper. In order for the match to be realized the individual should first of all apply for the job and secondly be hired by the employer. Individuals who do not apply will certainly not be hired: $I_{1i}^* \leq 0$ and therefore I_{2i}^* can never take on a positive value. 'Nothing ventured, nothing gained'. This sequential case is obtained from the joint case by the parameter restriction $\rho = 0$. However, this parameter restriction is not a necessary but a sufficient condition for obtaining the sequential case, for ρ captures not only the correlation between the error terms but also between the omitted variables in both equations[6]. Section V will show which one of the two bivariate models with partial observability suits the survey data best.

IV. THE DATA: CONSTRUCTION AND CHOICE OF VARIABLES

The empirical model is estimated on a sample drawn from the *National Longitudinal Survey of Youth* (NLSY). The first interview amongst the approximately 12,000 respondents was held in 1979 when they were between 14 and 22 years old. Afterwards these rather extensive interviews have been repeated annually. The last year at our disposal is 1989. For homogeneity reason, we use a subsample of 3790 white males.

The observed dependent variable, which we call 'switch', takes on the value 1 in year t if a white male labor force participant, who was not self-employed in year t, reported to be self-employed[7] in year $t+1$. It takes on the value 0 for labor force participants (excluding self-employed) in year t who have not become self-employed in year $t+1$[8]. The observable variable 'switch' summarizes for each young man whether the required amounts of opportunity and willingness are present in a given year. Switch=1 if and only if both conditions are met: opportunity and willingness surpass their threshold values. The following table shows that switches are rather scarce[9].

6. We thank Gerard Van den Berg who revealed this point to us.
7. Individuals who start incorporated businesses are included.
8. Switch is probably an underestimate of the real fraction of starters, because self-employment spells that started but ended between interviews are not counted.
9. The reason why the table starts in 1985 will be given in due course.

DETERMINANTS OF WILLINGNESS AND OPPORTUNITY

Table 1

Self-Employment and Switches in the NLS

Year	Labor Force	Self-Employed	Switches
n=3790			
1985	3488	171	71
1986	3561	196	77
1987	3597	208	96
1988	3630	231	74
1989	3643	246	
total			318

Therefore, we are forced to pool observations from the last five years. We proceeded as follows: The frequency of observation is once a year. We assume that a switch between year t and year $t+1$ (self-employed in year $t+1$ but not in t) by labor force participant i is best explained by the values of the variables applying to this individual i in year t. We sampled all individuals for whom switch=1 in either 1985, 1986, 1987 or 1988. The year t-values were assigned to the explanatory variables of these switchers, while the observed dependent variable takes on value 1. Of the 24 individuals who switched more than once, we randomly retained one year of observation and deleted the other[10]. This left us with 294, (318-24), observations for whom switch=1. For the remaining observations (individuals for whom switch=0 during all periods under study), four sets of regressor values (1985, 1986, 1987 and 1988) are available. We have randomly assigned one of these four sets to each of these individuals. Individuals

10. The way we have defined a 'switch' renders a maximum of two switches per individual in the four subsequent observations. The number of men who switched two times is very small. It hardly makes sense to treat double switches as a separate state, consequently we chose to randomly select one of the switches. Due to the correlation of the error terms we can not treat a double switcher as two observations.

in the resulting sample, consisting of 3451 labor force participants who are not currently self-employed, are between 20 and 31 years old. We created a 'year dummy' variable that denotes the year of observation to check whether time effects exist. The procedure yields a switch percentage of $100\% \times \frac{294}{3451} = 8.5\%$. The origins of the pooled data are summarized in *Table 2*.

Table 2

Origins of Pooled Data

Year	Not Self-Employed Labor Force Participants Including Switchers	Switches
1985	842	59
1986	872	75
1987	884	92
1988	853	68
total	3451	294

Apart from the time dependent explaining variables we have time independent information like parental background variables, formal education etc. We also constructed some longitudinal variables like experience in self-employment. The variables that we use in the final analysis are defined in *Table A* in the *Appendix.* After deleting observations with missing values for at least one variable, 2244 out of 3451 observations remained. *Table B (Appendix)* shows the descriptive statistics for this subsample.

Besides the differences between the groups of switchers and non-switchers, there is another interesting comparison between the switchers before they have switched and afterwards. They are shown in *Table 3*.

Table 3

Switchers Before and After the Switch

Variable	Before	After
Industry		
Agriculture	5.7%	9.4%
Construction	25.9%	34.0%
Manufacturing	13.8%	6.7%
Transportation/Communication	2.7%	5.1%
Trade	22.6%	12.5%
Business and Repair	8.8%	15.5%
Professional Services	7.7%	5.7%
Others	12.8%	11.1%
Occupation		
Professional/Technical	9.1%	11.1%
Managers	9.4%	14.8%
Craftsmen, Foremen	34.7%	40.7%
Operatives	12.5%	9.4%
Farmers	2.6%	2.5%
Sales	6.7%	4.7%
Service Workers	7.7%	4.7%
Others	17.3%	12.1%
Job Satisfaction (1-4)	3.3	3.6
(Hourly) Rate of Pay	$8.6	$11.6
Rate of Pay's Stand. Dev.	$4.9	$8.6
Mortgage Loan	$4,500	$65,100

Switchers stem from a variety of industrial and occupational origins, though especially from the industries construction and trade (wholesale and retail) and the occupation 'craftsman'. Furthermore, 45% of the switchers remain within their own industry, 45% within their occupation and 28% remain within one industry and one occupation. On average, these (self-selected) individuals gain both in satisfaction and in rate of pay as they switch; but their mortgages increase considerably.

To identify our empirical model, and indeed to identify opportunity and willingness, we have to impose at least one exclusion restriction. We make two assumptions:

A The opportunity equation is dependent on the variable 'self-employment experience measured in years' and the willingness equation on the dummy variable 'ever been self-employed'. This is a sensible assumption to make: the ability to borrow money ('opportunity') is likely to depend upon previous experience as an entrepreneur. The relation between willingness and previous length of self-employment experience is less obvious, although the fact that a person has been self-employed is likely to have an impact on willingness.

B Following Knight (1921) and more recent empirical research, we expect wealthier people to have a higher propensity to become self-employed. We assume capital to affect this propensity exclusively through opportunity and not through willingness[11].

We want to stress that the identification of 'opportunity' and 'willingness' critically depends upon the exclusion restrictions. In principle it is possible to estimate the model only under restriction A. However, in that case identification becomes very thin. Furthermore, the estimated coefficients pertaining to capital variables were not significant in the willingness equation.

With respect to the explanatory variables we make the following comments. Some of these comments relate a variable directly to 'opportunity' or 'willingness'. But keep in mind that we initially use every variable in both the 'opportunity' and the 'willingness' equation. The explanatory variables mentioned in assumptions A and B above are exceptions.

Psychological variables. Social psychologists strongly believe that a measure of internality of someone's locus-of-control beliefs is a determinant of successful entrepreneurship; of entrepreneurship ability. The Rotterscale (1966) is such a measure. The lower an individual's Rotterscale, the less internal are his locus-of-control beliefs and the more he perceives the outcome of an event as

11. We disregard the possibility that wealthier people might have lower absolute risk aversion, making them more willing to become self-employed (as in Kihlstrom and Laffont 1979, and Kanbur 1979).

beyond his personal control. The dichotomous Rotterscale measure derived from the NLS is equal to 1 for more internal individuals.

Moreover, social psychologists (see Hornaday and Aboud 1971) have found a low religious value amongst entrepreneurs. We include a dummy for people who adhere to stricter religions (Lutheran and Methodist) to verify whether these are less willing to become self-employed. The descriptive statistics suggest to include a dummy that differentiates men that have been extremely outgoing children from the more shy ones.

Human capital variables. Human capital variables, such as age, education, or experience in self-employment are supposed to explain both opportunity and willingness to switch to self-employment. This kind of variables is included in the opportunity equation because human capital is supposed to affect the (by the lender perceived) entrepreneurial abilities. Inclusion of human capital variables in the willingness equation is justified by its expected effect on the availability and desirability of outside options. Education, self-employment experience, the respondent's age and the frequency of former job changes are included in the (final) willingness equation.

Situational variables. There are other variables which can be believed to directly influence a potential lender's decision (perhaps because they affect entrepreneurship ability) and also one's willingness to start as an entrepreneur: these are whether a person is currently unemployed, whether he works in the public sector (instead of the private sector), whether he has severe health limitations or not and whether he is married or not. An individual's central city citizenship (SMSA) might have an impact on both opportunity and willingness.

More macro-oriented indicator for the regional (and temporal) unemployment rate, included in the NLS, may directly affect the opportunity for an individual to become self-employed.

Table C of the *Appendix* contains the results of the saturated model in which all explanatory variables listed above, except for the ones relating to the assumptions, were part of both equations. On the basis of this model we chose the specification presented in the next section: we imposed 6 restrictions and the likelihood-ratio statistic is 2.688. The restricted model is not rejected in favor of the saturated model.

V. ESTIMATION RESULTS AND INFERENCES

Table 4 summarizes the final estimation results[12] We comment on the key results reflected in this table.

Financial variables. The estimated assets coefficient does not diverge from the recent empirical findings by Evans and Jovanovic (1989), Evans and Leighton (1989), Holtz-Eakin et al. (1994) and Blanchflower and Oswald (1994): a lack of assets restrains the opportunity to become self-employed. But the effect turns out to be relatively small as soon as we add the dummy for real estate ownership. This variable gives scope to the possibility that the additional security that real estate owners can offer to potential lenders (in case of future bankruptcy) influences individual business formation opportunity. Black, De Meza and Jeffreys (1993) find in their more macro-oriented study that the supply of collateral significantly affects business formation in the U.K. *Table 3* showed that mortgage loans are indeed considerably increased by young men who switch to self-employment. *Table 4* shows that ownership of collateral affects individual (perceived) business opportunities to a large extent.

Psychological variables. The Rotterscale, measuring respondents' internal-locus-of-control beliefs, has no significant effect: neither on opportunity nor on willingness. Evans and Leighton (1989) found no significant effect either of being an 'internal' individual on the transition probability. We thought of the possibility that this insignificance was due to unidentified opposing forces of internality on opportunity and willingness. However, the related variable 'outgoing as a child', which has not been implemented in this type of studies before, has a highly significant and positive effect on willingness to switch. Men who were outgoing as kids are significantly more willing to become self-employed.

The negative coefficient of the religion dummy variable in the willingness equation (taking on value one for the two strict religions) renders some weak empirical support for a low entrepreneurial interest among believers.

Variables related to self-esteem are omitted because they lacked any significance, unlike Say's predictions (1971, p 241-243).

12. The estimates shown are obtained in Gauss. We used Limdep to verify the results. Differences are negligible. The reported t-values are based on White's heteroskedastic consistent estimate of the covariance matrix.

DETERMINANTS OF WILLINGNESS AND OPPORTUNITY

Table 4

Estimation Results: Bivariate Probit

	Opportunity Equation			Willingness Equation		
Variable	Coefficient	(t-Value)	Derivative	Coefficient	(t-Value)	Derivative
Financial Variables						
Assets	0.006	(1.72)	0.001			
Real Estate	0.825	(2.91)	0.125			
Psychological Variables						
Rotter	-0.352	(-1.70)	-0.053	0.467	(1.48)	0.028
Lutheran/Methodist				-0.277	(-1.79)	-0.017
Outgoing Child	-0.335	(-1.40)	-0.051	1.217	(2.11)	0.073
Human Capital Variables						
Age	-1.686	(-2.04)	-0.255	1.741	(2.12)	0.105
Age Squared/10	0.354	(2.12)	0.054	0.374	(-2.34)	-0.022
Education	-0.014	(-0.40)	-0.002	-0.031	(-0.63)	-0.002
Self-Empl. Exp.	0.353	(2.18)	0.053			
Dummy Self Exp.				0.574	(1.17)	0.034
Job Changes				0.054	(3.26)	0.003
Situational Variables						
Unemployed	0.116	(0.27)	0.017	-0.374	(-0.64)	-0.022
Public Sector	-0.503	(-1.79)	0.076	0.632	(1.37)	0.038
Married	0.177	(0.76)	0.027	-0.526	(-1.72)	-0.032
Handicap	0.223	(1.10)	0.034			
Low Unemp. Rate	0.731	(2.12)	0.110			
SMSA	-0.329	(-1.29)	-0.050	0.998	(2.30)	0.060
Constant	19.653	(1.91)	2.970	-19.664	(-1.88)	-1.181
Rho	-0.757	(-3.33)				
Log-Likelihood	-692.18					
Number of Cases	2244					

Human capital variables. The data show that the individuals with age 24 have the worst opportunities to start a business. On the other hand individuals of 23 are the most willing to do so across all ages. The majority of young men in our sample is older than 24. Therefore, opportunity is an increasing function of age and willingness is a decreasing function of age for most individuals in our sample. Our findings with respect to age are consistent with both Evans' and Jovanovic's (1989) presumptions and with Miller's (1984) occupational choice model.

Education does not affect the probability to become self-employed; neither through willingness, nor through opportunity. Self-employment experience is a significant determinant of opportunity[13]. For the average young male in the sample, one additional year of experience in self-employment increases the probability of having the opportunity to enter self-employment again by a significant 5.3%[14]. Say (1971) already pointed at the importance of 'knowledge of business' for successful entrepreneurship. An alternative explanation for this positive effect is unobserved heterogeneity. This alternative explanation is however not sustained by a significant influence of former self-employment experience on willingness. The dummy for self-employment experience included in the willingness equation shows that the fact that one has been self-employed in the past does not affect the motivation to become self-employed again. On the one hand, individuals may have become very enthusiastic, even though they quitted; on the other hand, they may have become disillusioned.

The frequency of former job changes has a positive effect on the willingness to become self-employed. This is both consistent with a positive approach, i.e., entrepreneur types change jobs frequently because they like changes (as in Schumpeter 1934) and with the negative approach that frequent job changers are associated with displaced persons (as in Evans and Jovanovic 1989, Shapero 1975).

Situational variables. Unemployed young white males in the U.S. do not face less opportunities and are not more willing to become self-employed in com-

13. Self-employment experience is gathered before 1985 (but as of 1979). The 24 observations that have switched twice may also have gathered this experience afterwards, depending on whether their first or second switch has randomly been selected.
14. The measurement of this variable is not perfect: we increased self-employment experience by the number of weeks between the current and previous interview divided by 52 whenever one reported to be self-employed.

parison to their (privately) employed counterparts[15]. Public sector workers have somewhat less opportunity to switch to self-employment than wage workers in the private sector. This result is corroborated by the finding that 71% of the founders of the fastest growing U.S. companies got their entrepreneurial idea, which is part of the opportunity, through previous employment (Bhide 1994). This source of ideas is generally not available for public sector workers. Public sector workers are not significantly less willing to make the transition.

We predicted married men to have more opportunity to become self-employed than bachelors for husbands do have wives who either save personnel cost or supply the family with a fixed income. Moreover, we presumed married men to be less willing to engage in a (risky) entrepreneurial venture due to their family responsibility. The empirical evidence only renders (marginally) significant support for the second presumption.

A low (regional and temporal) unemployment rate, defined as a rate lower than 3%, raises the opportunity to start a business significantly: some 11% for the average sampled individual. The effect of living in SMSA is not significant on opportunity and positive on willingness. Whether an individual is physically disabled or not does not seem to influence his opportunities to start a business.

By means of alternative specifications of the opportunity and willingness equations, we found some additional results: the interview year that corresponds to each individual selected in the sample is not significant in explaining opportunity and willingness. Parental background (measured as father's and mother's education level, father's occupation and language usage at home) does not add anything to the explanation either. Brockhaus' finding (1980) that extremely unsatisfied wage workers are pushed into self-employment is not sustained by our data either: low reported job satisfaction did not affect willingness to become self-employed.

Table 4 demonstrates ρ to be negative and significant. Apparently the error terms of the willingness and opportunity equations are correlated. Consequently, our model differs significantly from the nested bivariate probit model with partial observability: the sequential case.

Figure 1 shows what kind of distribution within the willingness and opportunity region the estimates generate.

15. We also included 'unemployment experience' in the relationships and found that this does not affect willingness nor opportunity. Surveys on the (ambiguous) relation between unemployment and self-employment can be found in Meager (1992) and Storey (1991).

Figure 1

Distribution of Obsevations by Imputed Opportunity and Willingness

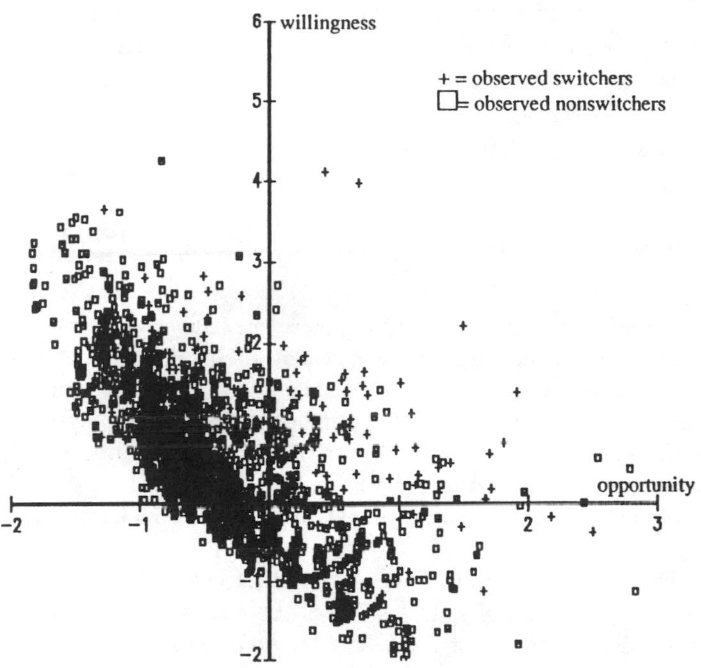

Apparently, there are far more individuals willing to become self-employed than individuals who have an opportunity. The number of entrepreneurial starts would be almost seven times as high if everyone who wishes to start had the opportunity to do so. This finding is consistent with research results by Blanchflower and Oswald (1994): there are more individuals who wish to switch to self-employment than the actual number of switchers. This result is also consistent with the several stories about capital restrictions and higher satisfaction amongst self-employed (Blanchflower and Oswald 1994).

The following *Table* shows which percentage of individuals, self-employed and employed in reality, belongs to each of the quadrants in *Figure 1*.

DETERMINANTS OF WILLINGNESS AND OPPORTUNITY

Table 4a

Estimated Percentages in Each of the Quadrants in *Figure 1*

Quadrant	Total	Self-Employed	Employed
Willingness > 0, Opportunity > 0	7.7%	28.0%	5.0%
Willingness < = 0, Opportunity > 0	12.3%	6.4%	13.1%
Willingness > 0, Opportunity < = 0	69.0%	61.7%	69.9%
Willingness < = 0, Opportunity < = 0	11.0%	3.8%	12.0%

In order to compare our study to others, we have also estimated a univariate probit with identical independent variables. This is not nested in the bivariate model. However, we have also estimated which percentage of actual self-employed people is predicted by this model to be self-employed. The resulting percentage is 10.6%, much lower than the comparable estimate of 28% resulting from the bivariate approach. This is some indicator that the bivariate approach is superior indeed. Univariate probit estimation results are shown in *Table 5*.

The parameter estimates themselves differ from the bivariate approach with respect to a number of variables. The effect of the stricter religions is significant here: adhering to one of the stricter religions goes together with a significant lower probability to switch to self-employment. The coefficient of the bivalent variable that indicates whether one has self-employment experience or not has become significant, besides self-employment experience measured in years. Higher educated young men have a significant lower probability to switch to self-employment. The coefficient for the dummy variable that indicates whether a young man is married or not is significantly negative. This is consistent with both the findings by Evans and Jovanovic (1989) and Evans and Leighton (1989).

Our decomposition of effects is not easily derived from this aggregate approach by inspection: some surprises remain. This was also the case in the application of Abowd and Farber (1982). Meant as an instrument to decompose regressor effects on the propensity to start as an entrepreneur into effects on opportunity and willingness, the bivariate approach is also a valid instrument to find significant effects that are hidden as insignificant effects in the aggregate.

Table 5

Estimation Results: Unvariate Probit

Variable	Coefficient	(t-Value)	Derivative
Financial Variables			
Assets	0.007	(2.22)	0.001
Real Estate	0.739	(5.99)	0.128
Psychological Variables			
Rotter	-0.075	(-0.86)	-0.012
Lutheran/Methodist	-0.202	(-1.95)	-0.035
Outgoing Child	0.302	(2.82)	0.052
Human Capital Variables			
Age	-0.156	(-0.64)	-0.027
Age Squared/10	0.028	(0.58)	0.005
Education	-0.037	(-2.24)	-0.006
Self-Empl. Exp.	0.218	(2.99)	0.037
Dummy Self Exp.	0.520	(3.35)	0.089
Job Changes	0.038	(4.29)	0.006
Situational Variables			
Unemployed	-0.124	(-0.89)	-0.021
Public Sector	-0.107	(-0.70)	-0.018
Married	-0.198	(-2.44)	-0.034
Handicap	0.180	(0.90)	0.030
Low Unemp. Rate	0.755	(2.26)	0.129
SMSA	0.175	(1.62)	0.030
Constant	0.830	(0.27)	0.142
Log-Likelihood	-707.53		
Number of Cases	2244		

Inferences. What can we infer from our estimation results? To investigate this, we compare the simulated probability to become self-employed of a reference individual with this probability of an individual who deviates from the reference one with respect to one variable only. The reference individual is defined as having average values for continuous variables and the modal outcome for categorical variables.

Table 6

Simulated Probabilities to Become Self-Employed

Individual	Pr(switch)	Difference with Ref. Ind.	(t-Value)
Reference	0.075		
Financial Variable			
Real Estate	0.302	0.227	(3.62)
Assets + σ	0.102	0.027	(1.65)
Assets - σ	0.071	-0.004	(-1.83)
Psychological Variable			
Outgoing as a Kid	0.097	0.022	(0.81)
Human Capital Variable			
Self-Empl. Exp. + σ	0.387	0.312	(3.00)
Situational Variable			
Low Unemp. Rate	0.269	0.194	(1.08)

The table shows the differences in probability due to changes in one of the independent variables in each category. This difference is large (and significant) if the reference individual suddenly becomes an owner of real estate: this renders a probability difference of almost 23%. A reference individual who faces a capital increase of one standard deviation, experiences a probability increase of 2.7% only (σ = \$11,250). Both self-employment experience (measured in years) and a low regional unemployment rate (dummy variable) can compensate for a lack of assets and real estate: they both strongly increase the probability to become self-employed, by 31% and 19% respectively.

Policy Implications. What can be learnt from our results by institutions with a mission to increase the U.S. number of young starters in entrepreneurship? As we have obviously revealed opportunity rather than willingness to be the bottleneck, opportunity should be improved by manipulating its instruments.

- The government should take a measure to improve borrowing facilities for starters, as banks and participation companies seem to undersupply this market. The government has a valid incentive to create, for instance, a 'risk fund', since positive external effects of entrepreneurship (economic growth and less unemployment) are obviously present.
- The fact that self-employment experience may serve as a substitute for capital and/or collateral suggests that the United States banks and participation companies believe that entrepreneurship can be learned through experience[16]. Courses that really simulate the entrepreneurial venture should be organized. A qualification from such a course should lead to 'easier borrowing' comparable to the borrowing probabilities of 'experienced starters'. For instance, by having the 'risk fund' come within reach only for 'course graduates'.
- It appears that authorities striving after low unemployment rates serve entrepreneurship opportunities as well. However, authorities want to reduce unemployment by stimulating entrepreneurship and a circle results. Anyhow, starting as an entrepreneur appears to be an upswing activity: entrepreneurship start-ups are stimulated by a low (regional) unemployment rate.

VI. CONCLUSIONS

Individuals whom we observe to start as entrepreneurs have not only perceived enough opportunity to do so, they also have perceived this career option as the most attractive one. In our words, they have the opportunity and willingness to become self-employed. Individuals whom we observe not to switch to self-employment are either not willing or do not face the opportunity or both. This paper separates the unobserved concepts of opportunity and willingness for young

16. Or that they can screen for superior entrepreneurship qualities by means of this indicator if they believe that its positive effect is due to unobserved heterogeneity.

white male Americans. We assume that opportunity and willingness can be explained by a (partly distinct) set of observed explanatory variables. Opportunity includes variables that are observed equivalents for both capital and entrepreneurial ability, given economic conditions. It is argued that the opportunity to start as an entrepreneur is positively present for men having sufficient assets. If not, capital lenders should be convinced that the potential lender has enough entrepreneurial ability. Whereas opportunity and willingness are both necessary conditions (and together sufficient) to become entrepreneur, capital and ability are assumed to be potential substitutes for meeting the necessary opportunity condition.

A bivariate model with partial observability is estimated on a subsample of the National Longitudinal Survey of Youth. The annual data are pooled in a particular way to obtain a sufficient number of observed switches. The resulting sample includes 264 switches. The key empirical results are:

- By far the majority of young men in the U.S. are willing to become self-employed. Given the opportunity to anyone, the realized amount of switchers would multiply by seven. Opportunity evidently forms the bottleneck in the individual decision process.
- Opportunity is largely determined by capital requirements. These in turn are primarily dependent on real estate ownership. The opportunity for entrepreneurship is also affected by the regional unemployment rate and by entrepreneurial ability, mainly through self-employment experience and age. Willingness is positively affected by outgoingness, by the number of job changes and by one's central citizenship (SMSA). Older people (as of 23) are less and less willing to become self-employed. Religious and or married people have a lower probability to be willing to become self-employed, though not very significantly so. Other variables are insignificant.
- Entrepreneurial ability serves to a certain extent as a substitute for capital requirements. The kind of entrepreneurial ability that increases the opportunity to start largely coincides with entrepreneurship experience.
- As capital seems to be a necessary requirement for becoming self-employed (for starters without experience in entrepreneurship) and since willingness is no constraining factor, we conclude that the U.S. evidence supports Knight's ideas. A first start in entrepreneurship requires assets or collateral. This finding, pointing at binding capital constraints, is in accordance with other empirical estimates by Evans and Jovanovic (1989), Evans and Leighton (1989), Blanchflower and Oswald (1994) and Holtz-Eakin et al. (1994). However, the additional finding that experience in entrepreneurship results in a perceived entrepreneurial ability that can serve as a substitute for own capital or real estate is in accordance with the related ideas of Say. Schum-

peter's vision is empirically not supported: motivational factors appear not to be the prime constraints in the individual supply of entrepreneurship.

Future research should demonstrate the individual determinants of lasting and successful entrepreneurship for the subsample of individuals that have shown to be willing and in a position to start as an entrepreneur.

APPENDIX

Table A

Definition of the Variables Selected

Variable	Definition
Switch	dependent variable; =1 if respondent switches from wage employment or unemployment to self-employment
Assets	total amount of assets (in $ 1,000)
Real Estate	dummy:=1 if respondent owns some real estate
Rotter	dummy:=1 if respondent feels: 'direction of life is in control'
Lutheran or Methodist	dummy:=1 if respondent's religion is Lutheran or Methodist
Outgoing Child	dummy:=1 if respondent reports to have been an extremely outgoing child
Age	respondent's age (in years)
Education	number of years of formal education
Labor Exp.	years of total labor experience
Self-Empl. Exp.	years of self-employment experience
Dummy Self Exp.	dummy:=1 if resp. has self-employment experience
Job Changes	reported number of different jobs ever had
Unemployed	dummy:=1 if respondent is unemployed
Public Sector	dummy:=1 if respondent is public sector worker
Married	dummy:=1 if respondent is married
Handicap	dummy:=1 if respondent has health limitations
Low Unemp. Rate	dummy:=1 if regional unemployment rate is less than 3%
SMSA	dummy:=1 if respondent lives in SMSA, central city

DETERMINANTS OF WILLINGNESS AND OPPORTUNITY

Table B

Descriptive Statistics

Variable	Mean Switchers	(s.d.)	Mean	(s.d.) Non Switchers	Mean All	(s.d.)
Observations	264			1980	2244	
Switch					0.118	(0.32)
Assets	6.24	(25.33)	3.20	(7.60)	3.56	(11.28)
Real Estate	0.19	(0.39)	0.051	(0.22)	0.066	(0.25)
Rotter	0.75	(0.44)	0.77	(0.42)	0.76	(0.42)
Lutheran or Methodist	0.14	(0.34)	0.19	(0.39)	0.18	(0.39)
Outgoing Child	0.17	(0.38)	0.10	(0.30)	0.11	(0.31)
Age	25.46	(2.65)	25.32	(2.61)	25.34	(2.62)
Education	12.59	(2.46)	12.79	(2.45)	12.77	(2.45)
Self-Empl. Exp.	0.61	(1.16)	0.12	(0.49)	0.17	(0.63)
Dummy Self Exp.	0.32	(0.47)	0.079	(0.27)	0.11	(0.31)
Job Changes	8.24	(4.87)	6.69	(3.88)	6.87	(4.03)
Unemployed	0.072	(0.26)	0.084	(0.28)	0.082	(0.28)
Public Sector	0.053	(0.22)	0.085	(0.28)	0.081	(0.27)
Married	0.37	(0.48)	0.44	(0.50)	0.43	(0.50)
Handicap	0.038	(0.19)	0.029	(0.17)	0.030	(0.17)
Low Unemp. Rate	0.019	(0.14)	0.006	(0.08)	0.008	(0.09)
SMSA	0.16	(0.37)	0.11	(0.31)	0.12	(0.32)

C. MIRJAM VAN PRAAG AND HANS VAN OPHEM

Table C

Estimation Results of the Saturated Model: Bivariate Probit

	Opportunity Equation			**Willingness Equitation**		
Variable	Coefficient	(t-Value)	Derivative	Coefficient	(t-Value)	Derivative
Financial Variables						
Assets	0.007	(1.68)	0.000			
Real Estate	0.864	(2.85)	0.123			
Psychological Variables						
Rotter	-0.374	(-1.17)	-0.053	0.526	(1.08)	0.029
Lutheran/Methodist	-0.053	-0.66)	-0.007	-0.228	(-0.25)	-0.013
Outgoing Child	0.031	(-0.33)	-0.044	1.328	(1.46)	0.073
Human Capital Variables						
Age	-1.605	(-1.60)	-0.228	1.780	(1.81)	0.098
Age Squared/10	0.340	(1.66)	0.048	-0.382	(-1.92)	0.021
Education	-0.023	(-0.36)	-0.003	-0.024	(-0.30)	-0.001
Labor Exp.	-0.022	(-0.26)	-0.003	-0.010	(-0.08)	-0.000
Self-Empl. Exp.	0.362	(1.82)	0.051			
Dummy Self Exp.				0.635	(0.95)	0.035
Job Changes	0.011	(0.02)	0.002	0.045	(1.44)	0.002
Situational Variables						
Unemployed	0.178	(0.57)	0.025	-0.056	(-0.65)	-0.031
Public Sector	-0.435	(-1.21)	-0.062	0.547	(0.98)	0.030
Married	0.139	(0.45)	0.020	-0.509	(-0.80)	-0.028
Handicap	0.091	(0.12)	0.013	0.200	(0.18)	0.011
Low Unemp.rate	0.316	(0.39)	0.045	0.777	(0.40)	0.043
SMSA	-0.302	(-1.08)	-0.043	1.032	(1.72)	0.057
Constant	18.647	(1.49)	2.648	20.116	(-1.54)	-1.108
Rho	-0.679	(-1.88)				
Log-Likelihood	-690.84					
Number of Cases	2244					

DETERMINANTS OF WILLINGNESS AND OPPORTUNITY

REFERENCES

Abowd J.M. and H.S. Farber (1982). Job queues and the union status of workers, *Industrial and Labour Review*. 35: 354-367.

Barreto, H. (1989). *The entrepreneur in economic theory. Disappearance and explanation*. London: Routledge.

Bhide, A. (1994). How Entrepreneurs Craft Strategies That Work, *Harvard Business Review*. 150-161.

Black, J, D. de Meza and D. Jeffreys (1993). House prices, the supply of collateral and the enterprise economy, working paper, University of Exeter.

Blanchflower, D.G. and A.J. Oswald (1994). What makes an entrepreneur? Evidence on Inheritances and Capital Constraints, *Journal of Labor Economics*. forthcoming.

Brockhaus, R.H., Sr. (1980). The effect of job dissatisfaction on the decision to start a business, *Journal of Small Business Management 18*.

Casson, M. (1991). *The entrepreneur, an economic theory*. Worcester: Billing & Sons Ltd.

De Wit, G. (1993). Models of self-employment in a competitive market, *Journal of Economic Surveys*. 7: 367-397.

Evans, D.S. and L.S. Leighton (1989). Some empirical aspects of entrepreneurship, *American Economic Review*. 79: 519-535.

Evans, D.S. and B. Jovanovic (1989). An estimated model of entrepreneurial choice under liquidity constraints, *Journal of Political Economy*. 97: 808-827.

Hébert, R.F. and A.N. Link (1988). *The entrepreneur, Mainstream Views and Radical Critiques*. New York: Praeger.

Holtz-Eakin, D.D. Joulfaian and H.S. Rosen (1994). Entrepreneurial decisions and liquidity constraints, *Rand Journal of Economics*. 25: 334-347.

Hornaday, J.A. and J. Aboud (1971). Characteristics of successful entrepreneurs, *Personnel Psychology 24*.

Kanbur S.M. (1979). Of risktaking and the personal distribution of income, *Journal of Political Economy*. 87: 760-797.

Kihlstrom, R.E. and J.J. Laffont (1979). A general equilibrium entrepreneurial theory of new firm formation based on risk aversion, *Journal of Political Economy*. 87: 304-316.

Knight F.H. (1921). *Risk, Uncertainty and Profit*. In: G.J. Stigler (ed.) (1971), Chicago: University Press of Chicago.

Leroy, S.F. and L.D. Singell Jr. (1987). Knight on risk and uncertainty, *Journal of Political Economy*. 95: 394-406.

Maddala, G.S. (1983). *Limited-dependent and qualitative variables in econometrics*. Cambridge University.

Marshall, A. (1930). *Principles of Economics*. London: Macmillan and co., limited, (first edition 1890).

Meager, N. (1992). Does unemployment lead to self-employment, *Small Business Economics*. 4: 87-103.

Miller, R.A. (1984). Job matching and occupational choice, *Journal of Political Economy*. 92: 1086-1120.

Poirier, D.J. (1980). Partial observability in bivariate probit models, *Journal of Econometrics*. 12: 209-217.

Rotter, J.B. (1966). Generalized Expectancies for Internal vs. External Control of Reinforcement, in: *Psychological Monographs:* General and Applied, whole 609 80, No 1 (1966).

Say, J-B. (1971). *A treatise on political economy or the production, distribution and consumption of wealth*. New York: Augustus M. Kelley Publishers, (first edition 1803).

Schumpeter, J. (1934). *The theory of economic development*. Cambridge Mass: Harvard University Press.

Shapero, A. (1975). The displaced, uncomfortable entrepreneur, *Psychology Today*. 9: 83-88.

Storey D.J. (1991). The birth of new firms- Does unemployment matter? A review of the evidence, *Small Business Economics*. 3: 167-178.

Van Praag, C.M. (1994). Determinants of self-employment duration: a competing risks model, Discussion Paper, Tinbergen Institute, Amsterdam, The Netherlands, TI 94-115.

SUMMARY

This paper develops an empirical model to separate the unobserved factors of 'opportunity' and 'willingness' in the decision of labor force participants to become self-employed or not. The estimation results suggest that the majority of young Americans is willing to switch to self-employment but that opportunity is a major constraint, especially through finance. Entrepreneurial ability aspects that can compensate for a lack of capital are scarce.

Part II
Types of Entrepreneurs

[6]

Who Starts New Firms? – Preliminary Explorations of Firms-in-Gestation

Paul D. Reynolds

ABSTRACT. Little is known about the factors which lead individuals to start a new firm. This hiatus is due to an absence of data about the gestation processes that precedes a firm birth. Most analyses have used reported self-employment as an indicator of entrepreneurial behavior and resorted to linear additive models to account for "entrepreneurship." The resulting models have not been very successful for predictions and the conception is at odds with the most salient characteristics of entrepreneur's start-up stories. These personal accounts emphasize the unique combination of events that led to a new businesses start-up. A pilot study that identified those developing new firms provides information on firms-in-gestation. Preliminary analysis using Automatic Interaction Detection (AID) explores the unique combinations of events that underlay a decision to start a new firm. Seven-in-ten startups in the U.S. may be initiated by those 25–34 years old with full-time jobs, part-time jobs, or managing another business. There is some limited support for an impact of unemployment or a "liquidity constraint" on initiating start-ups.

Introduction

Every year millions of new firms are started in market economies around the world. There is a strong suspicion that those starting new firms are unique individuals or in distinctive situations. The efforts, however, to understand how or which individuals decide to become involved in a new firm start-up have not been very successful – or satisfying. There is, for example, very little overlap between the "entrepreneurial success stories" and the systematic efforts to explore factors leading to entrepreneurial behavior (e.g. self-employment) in large scale random samples.

Final version accepted on February 19, 1996

Center for Entrepreneurial Studies
Babson College
Wellesley, MA 02157-0310
U.S.A.

A recent comprehensive overview of research on new and small firms (Storey, 1994) provides a summary of four efforts to analyze representative samples to determine the nature of individuals involved in self-employment (a surrogate for entrepreneurship used by Evans and Leighton, 1989; Dolton and Makepeace, 1990; Blanchflower and Oswald, 1990; and Blanchflower and Meyer, 1991). All four studies were based on representative samples in the thousands (from the U.S., U.K. and Australia) and included data related to a range of personal and background characteristics affecting the "probability of entry into self-employment." The resulting multi-variate analyses produced different variation of the linear additive models developed from multiple regression analysis.

A variety of operational definitions and analysis procedures were utilized in the different studies, the reviewer summarized the results by indicating only when a variable included in a linear model was statistically significant, as shown in Table I. The good news is the absence of conflicting results. That is, there are no cases where one study finds a significant positive effect and the other a significant negative effect. Despite the diverse operational definitions and procedures, the patterns are complementary.

There are, however, several other problems with this strategy. One is the extent to which the resulting models help to explain the phenomena under consideration. The concept of "explain" can be considered to have two interpretations. First, in terms of a formal model that can account for or control the variation in the observed phenomena. Frequently referred to as the amount of variance explained by a formal model. This information is rare in these analyses, in part because the concept

Small Business Economics 9: 449–462, 1997.

TABLE I
Analysis of factors affecting self-employment

	Statistically significant		Not statistically significant	Not included
	Positive	Negative		
Married	1		2	1
Divorced	1			3
Educational attainment	2		2	
Children			3	1
Unemployed	2		1	1
Higher employed wages		1	1	2
Experience	1		1	2
Age	1		3	
Ethnic background			4	
Gender	1		3	
Social class	1			3
School type (public/private)	1			3
Urban region	1		2	1
Inheritance/liquidity	2			2
Personality	1			3
Managerial background			2	2
Family business background			1	3

Adapted from Storey, 1994, Table 3.3.

of "variation" as a feature of a distribution is more appropriate when the variable is continuous, such as predisposition toward self-employment (an attitude) or income from self-employment. It is not so useful when the dependent variable is dichotomous, as whether or not a person is involved in entrepreneurship (or reports they are self-employed).

One analysis was completed on data from 150,275 employed white men 25–60 years old in the United States from 1968–1987 (Evans and Leighton, 1989, p. 527). This Current Population Survey data includes information on the individuals employment status in the survey week and the previous year. A linear probability model was developed to estimate the probability of becoming self-employed (considered an indicator of entrepreneurship). Variables that were statistically significant in the equation (at least at the 0.05 level) included personal income, personal income squared, net family assets (liquidity), dropping out of college, finishing college, post graduate education, urban residence, married and, military veteran. Not statistically significant individually, but left in the model as adding to the overall significant, were age, age squared, and whether or not the individual dropped out of high school. The resulting model was statistically significant and explained 0.286% of the variance, this left 99.7% of the variance in reported self-employment unexplained by this linear model. Confronted with this modest level of overall predictive success, it is reasonable to expect the analyst to focus on hypothesis testing – where there is no ambiguity over the relative impact of a independent variable in a model. This leads to the type of summary presented in Table I, which focus on the occurrence of statistically significant effects.

The amount of explained variance is, of course, only one of several criteria one might use to examine the adequacy of a modeling exercise. Another that is often used is a statistical test to determine whether or not the overall model is statistically significant, compared to the patterns that would be generated by random processes. This is usually reported as the F-test. On the other hand, the results of these efforts are often presented as the definitive statements regarding who might becomes involved in starting new businesses, even when over 99% of the variation remains unaccounted for in the analysis. Clearly, this is a misleading posture given the success of these models for predicting entry into self-employment, or "entrepreneurship."

A second problem reflects the criticisms of such models by entrepreneurs. They seldom recognize themselves in this type of conceptual framework. Linear additive models imply that a set of factors encourage a shift toward self-employment and when enough of these "forces" are added together, it will trigger an individual decision to be "self-employed." So when work experience, gender (maleness), family tradition of entrepreneurship, need for achievement, educational attainment, personal wealth, and the like are all found in the same individual the pressure to be entrepreneurial may be great enough to cause them to cross the threshold to pursue self-employment.

The resulting image is not very consistent with the stories told by most that pursue entrepreneurship and start a new venture. These discussions usually emphasize a unique combination of circumstances that lead a person to pursue a firm start-up, often focusing upon the opportunities or attractions of entrepreneurial options. While every entrepreneur likes to think their own situation and reactions are unique, their may be some common features in these "conception stories."

This may be related to the third and perhaps most important problem with these analyses. Reported self-employment from large scale surveys is a very poor indicator of "entrepreneurial behavior." The most elementary concept of entrepreneurial behavior are actions to implement a new business. Creating a business where none existed in the past. It is to be expected that many of these efforts, despite the investment in time and money, will not lead to a firm birth. So be it. The concept of entrepreneurial behavior clearly implies attempts to start new ventures and does not require that every attempt be successful.

The following will report on a preliminary analysis of a pilot study, one that uses a new survey research technique to identify "nascent entrepreneurs" engaged in behavior to start a new firm. Reported self-employment is treated as reporting "small business ownership" and not entrepreneurship. Two analysis strategies are utilized. The first is a additive linear model providing results similar to that outlined in Table I. A second procedure provides a systematic method for identifying the most significant interactions. The results focus – in the following analysis – on the unique situations that lead individuals to pursue, or not pursue, a new firm start-up. The results are more successful – in terms of predictive power – than a linear regression modeling procedure and give a greater sense of the unique set of factors that lead individuals to pursue new firm start-ups. There is more confidence that a situation that would trigger a decision to start a new firm has been identified.

Sources of data

The major stumbling block to a precise description of the entrepreneurial or firm start-up process has been locating nascent entrepreneurs. A procedure has been developed that starts with a random selection of households, followed by a random selection of an adult member of the household (Palit and Reynolds, 1993; Reynolds and White, 1993). In the course of a phone interview, this person is asked about their work activity. The questions allow a person to indicate multiple work activities, full-time work and part-time work, full-time work and business ownership, and so forth.

At an appropriate point in the interview, they are asked: "Are you, alone or with others, now trying to start a business?" If they answer yes, they are then asked (1) if they have "given serious thought to the new business" and (2) if a number of different behaviors associated with starting a new firm (such as sought a bank loan, filed for incorporation, leased equipment, hired employees, and the like) have been "initiated" or "completed." They are also asked the month and year all reported actions are initiated. Those that report two or more firm gestation behaviors are considered "nascent entrepreneurs." They are also asked if the new business is, to their knowledge, included in any of the standard lists of businesses: Dun and Bradstreet files, unemployment insurance files, social security files, or the federal tax return listings. This can be used to determine the percentage of the sample that are engaged in the gestation process and, in turn, the proportion of the population that may be considered nascent entrepreneurs.

The results of this procedure for a representative sample of U.S. adults (18 and older) is presented in Table II. It shows the proportion of respondents who said they were starting a new

TABLE II
Firm gestation events: U.S. Sample, 1993

	Order asked	Percentage (n = 40)
Gestation (start-up) activity		
Serious thought about business	1	99%
Looked for facilities/equipment	4	75
Initiated savings to invest	16	68
Invested own money in the new firm	7	66
Organized start-up team	3	58
Written business plan	2	56
Bought facilities/equipment	5	50
Sought financial support	8	41
License, patent, permits applied for	14	38
Developed first model or prototype	10	35
Received money from sales	12	33
Achieved positive monthly cash flow*	–	22
Devoting full time to new business	13	32
Received financial support	9	29
Other start-up behaviors initiated	17	22
Rented or leased facilities/equipment	6	15
Created a new legal entity	15	14
Hired employees to work for wages	11	11
Incorporation with lists of businesses		
Know that firm on Dun & Bradstreet lists	18	2%
Paid first state unemployment insurance taxes	19	16
Paid first federal social security taxes	20	15
Filed first federal income tax return	21	18

* Cash income exceeds cash expenses.

business and reported initiating each gestation (or start-up) activity. This U.S. sample was developed from the October and November 1993 University of Michigan Survey of Consumers[1] (Curtin, 1982) and 64 actually completed these questions. But after eliminating those reporting (a) less than two behaviors or (b) a positive monthly cash flow prior to 1993, only 40 remained. The items are presented in the order of "popularity" among the respondents, the order of presentation in the interview is indicated in the first column of numbers. About 95% of those reporting they are "now trying to start a new business" indicate two or more start-up behaviors, the average was 6.7 (range from 1–15).

The types of businesses represented by these start-up efforts are compared with existing U.S. businesses in Table III. The start-ups, given the small sample, are typical for the U.S. as 74% are in construction, retail, or services (Reynolds, 1995), compared to 70% for existing U.S. businesses (U.S. Small Business Administration, 1994, Table 2.1). This is a typical finding among new

TABLE III
Economic sector of new firm start-ups

Economic sector	Active firms US* Total	Start-up firms US Sample
Agricultural, forestry, fishing	2%	8%
Mining	1	–
Construction	11	5
Manufacturing	6	5
Transportation, communications, utilities	3	2
Wholesale	7	5
Financial, insurance, real estate	8	–
Retail, including restaurants, bars	22	27
Services	37	42
Other, can't classify	2	5
Total	100%	99%

* Table 2.1, Office of Advocacy, U.S. Small Business Administration, *Handbook of Small Business Data: 1994*, based on 4,991,474 firms (not establishments) with employees in 1988.

businesses, that they reflect the existing structure of business activity very closely.

Univariate analysis

It is possible to estimate the prevalence of adults (number/100 or percents) that are nascent entrepreneurs trying to start new firms. Using various background characteristics helps to explore the personal attributes or contextual factors that encourage individuals to become a nascent entrepreneur and pursue the gestation of a new firm. These are presented in Table IV. It should be noted that low rates of prevalence, almost all are below ten in a hundred or 10%, and samples in the hundreds are associated with very wide standard errors of the mean.

Most important, the overall prevalence of nascent entrepreneurs for the United States is 3.9%, confirming an earlier survey of Wisconsin adults that found a prevalence of 4.3% (Reynolds and White, 1993). This is, for the U.S. in 1993, one-in-25 adults or about 7.2 million adults. As the average start-up involves 2.2 adults, this represents about 3.3 million firms-in-gestation (FIGs). The success of these start-up efforts and the time required to implement a viable new firms are the subject of another analysis (Carter, Gartner and Reynolds, 1995).

Statistically significant differences associated with the prevalence of nascent entrepreneurs are related to gender (higher for men); age (highest for 25–34 year olds); educational attainment (higher for post high school); county tenure (length of residence in the county); region of the United States (higher levels in West and Northeast, lower levels in North Central and South); labor force status (highest for the self-employed); martial status (absent for those widowed); and kids in the household (highest for households with one or two kids). No statistically significant differences are found in this analysis for ethnic status, household income, occupational status, consumer confidence index[2] rating, number of financial reserves (a count of the presence of IRA/Keogh retirement plan, company pension, money market funds, mutual funds, stocks, or certificates of deposit), or the number of adults in the household.

Sources of nascent entrepreneurs, a different question, can be explored by examining the proportion provided by each category associated with each of these variables. This is presented in the right column of Table IV. Some differences are striking. For example, even though the prevalence of men reporting they are trying to start a new firm is twice that of women (5.6% versus 2.7%), because there are more women in the adult population they are responsible for two in five (40%) of efforts to start a new firm. Perhaps more dramatic is the effect of age. While the prevalence of start-ups among those 25–34 years old is over twice the average (9.7%), they are responsible for seven in ten of all reported start-ups (71%). Similarly, those reporting they are self-employed have a high rate of participating in start-ups (12.1%), but are responsible for one-third (36%) of all reported start-ups. In fact, those with full-time, part-time, or self-employment account for about four-fifths (82%) of all start-ups. Starting a new firm is clearly a secondary activity for those already involved in the world of work. Those unemployed account for about one-in-twenty (6%) of the efforts to start a new firm.

Multivariate analysis: logistic regression models

The potential for high levels of inter-correlation among these independent variables leads immediately to a multivariate analysis. Logistic regression models, a specialized version of discriminate analysis, has been developed for dichotomous dependent variables and are appropriate for this situation (Norusis, 1992, pp. 1–34). Using the complete sample the results of stepwise logistic regression procedures using SPSS PC V5.0 are presented in Table V. Note that the results vary depending upon whether a forward procedure, new variables added to increase the fit and predictions of the model, or a backwards procedure, variable eliminated from a full variable model until there is a decrease in the fit and predictions, is utilized.

The results, a set of variables selected as optimal for a linear additive model, are very similar to Table I. The models are statistically significantly different from a random model assuming no systematic relationship. In fact, the ability to accurately predict the outcome appears impressive, as both models make correct predictions for 96% of the cases.

TABLE IV
Prevalence of nascent entrepreneurs: U.S. 1993

		N cases	Prevalence	P (Chi-square)	Proportion
Overall		1,016*	3.9%		100%
Gender	Men	431	5.6%		60%
	Women	585	2.7	0.02	40
Age	18–24 yrs old	106	3.3%		8%
	25–34 yrs old	290	9.7		71
	35–44 yrs old	174	3.0		13
	45–54 yrs old	95	2.1		6
	55 and up	349	0.3	0.00000	2
Ethnic status	White	798	3.6%		73%
	Black	128	6.3		20
	Other	76	4.3	0.39	7
Educational attainment	Less than high school	151	1.4%		5%
	High school degree	383	2.3		21
	Post high school	223	6.4		35
	College degree	168	6.2		28
	Post college experience	85	5.1	0.02	11
Household income	Up to $10K/yr	216	3.3		17%
	$10–35K/yr	490	3.7		46
	$35K–50K/yr	111	3.6		12
	$50K and up/yr	160	5.6	0.72	25
County tenure	0–5 yrs	234	5.2%		31%
	6–15 yrs	180	4.9		22
	16–30 yrs	257	5.6		37
	31 yrs and up	320	1.4	0.02	10
Region of U.S.	Northeast	200	6.0%		31%
	South	356	2.7		23
	North Central	262	2.1		13
	West	197	6.6	0.02	33
Labor force status	Full time job	388	3.3%		34%
	Part-time job	131	3.9		12
	Self-employed	115	12.1		36
	Unemployed	37	7.5		6
	Homemaker	66	0.9		1
	Retired	149	0.4		1
	Student	27	10.1		6
	Disabled	84	2.0	0.0002	4
Occupational status	Prof-Tech	160	3.0%		14%
	Manager-administrator	151	6.5		24
	Clerical-sales	241	3.3		22
	Foreman-craftsman	107	5.5		14
	Operators-unskilled work	160	2.4		8
	Service-household work	150	5.3	0.38	18
Consumer confidence index	High	306	5.1%		40%
	Medium	363	2.5		22
	Low	337	4.6	0.16	38
Financial reserves	None	426	4.5%		46%
	One	227	2.0		11
	Two	187	3.9		20
	Three	93	5.3		13
	Four-Six	82	4.6	0.48	10

TABLE IV *(Continued)*

		N cases	Prevalence	P (Chi-square)	Proportion
Martial status	Never Married	187	5.0%		23%
	Married	500	3.4		45
	Separated, divorced	180	7.4		32
	Widowed	144	0.0	0.0007	–
Kids under 18 in household	None	627	2.8%		45%
	One	168	6.2		25
	Two	145	6.8		24
	Three or more	74	3.2	0.06	6
Adults in household	One	365	3.7%		32%
	Two	502	3.7		49
	Three	116	5.6		15
	Four or more	33	4.1	0.84	4

* Total cases for some categories is less than total sample due to missing data.

TABLE V
Linear model coefficients with Logistic Regression Analysis

	Forward stepwise		Backwards stepwise	
	Beta	Sign	Beta	Sign
Constant	–0.7944	0.16	–1.9761	0.002
Gender			0.7507	0.05
Age	–0.0757	0.0000	–0.0837	0.0000
North central resident	–1.0848	0.03		
West resident			1.0963	0.008
Northeast resident			1.0920	0.010
Self-employed	1.6137	0.0000	1.5463	0.0001
Unemployed			1.2638	0.07
Managerial-administrative occupation			0.8408	0.05
Consumer confidence			–0.3702	0.10
Divorced	1.0175	0.01	1.3445	0.001
Overall chi-square	55.634	0.0000	70.031	0.0000
Percentage correct predictions	96.02%		96.02%	

SPSS PC 5.0.2 Logistic Regression with standard defaults.

This predictive accuracy is somewhat misleading, however, since it is done by predicting that none of the individuals are nascent entrepreneurs – the model predicts that all 1,016 are NOT involved in starting a new firm. Misclassification of 4% that are involved in a new firm start-up results in accurate predictions 96% of the time. Hardly an impressive indication of the value of this modeling procedure for predicting who gets involved in a firm start-up.

An alternative procedure can be used to give this exploratory procedure a more severe test. This is to randomly divide the 96% of those that are not nascent entrepreneurs into groups of 40. These are then combined with the single group of 40 nascent entrepreneurs and the analysis procedure is completed for each smaller group, 24 distinct comparisons in this case. As the probability of successfully predicting if a person in each group is a nascent entrepreneur is 50%, this gives the procedure a more challenging set of predictions. When this is done, using the forward stepwise procedure, the average correct predictions are 75%, a 50% improvement over the 50% expected by chance. The variables chosen for the 24 linear models varies slightly: age has a negative impact in 21 of the 24; self-employment a positive impact in 20; not living in the north central region in 7; fewer kids in the household in 5; working in a domestic or service occupation in 5; presence of financial reserves in 4; shorter residence tenure in the county in 4; lower levels of consumer confidence in 3; living in the western region in 3; higher levels of household income in 3; male respondents in 3; and so forth. Two variables have inconsistent patterns, homemaker and never-married appear with both positive and negative signs, reflecting the diversity to be expected in these small randomly selected comparison groups.

In either case, the results are hard to interpret in terms of the circumstances that trigger the decision to work on a new firm start-up. It is clear that being younger and currently self-employed (running a business of one's own) seems to have a major impact. But many young people and self-employed are not starting businesses. Perhaps more important (as indicated in Table IV), two-thirds of the start-ups efforts are reported by those that are NOT self-employed.

Multivariate analysis: automatic interaction detection analysis

It is quite clear that a number of factors are related to the decision to start a new firm. A more complete understanding will require attention to the possible interaction effects among a large number of independent variables: gender, age, educational attainment, household income, labor force status, residential tenure, occupational status, and the like as presented in Table IV. The number of possible interactions is substantial – in the hundreds – and the modest research literature on this first transition in the start-up process is not a very useful source of hypotheses.

This is exactly the situation that led to the development of the Automatic Interaction Detection (AID) technique. This procedure is designed for the analysis of representative samples to identify the major combinations among multiple independent variables that affect a single dependent variable (Sonquist and Morgan, 1964; Sonquist, 1970). The procedure involves two stages. First, initial analysis (such as found in Table IV) is used to create nominal or ordinal independent variables. A hierarchy of analysis is then completed. With the SPSS CHAID (*CHi*-square *A*utomatic *I*nteraction *D*etection; Magidson, 1992) at each stage the independent variable that provides the most statistically significant relationship to the dependent variable is used to divide the sample – one subgroup for each independent variable category. Each subgroup is then examined to determine which of the remaining independent variables will provide the most significance divisions among the further subgroups. This procedure is continued until no further statistically significant divisions of the sample are possible. Different independent variables may be involved in different paths of the analysis hierarchy. The procedure does not assume a linear impact or any particularly form of interaction. The second stage involves using a one-way analysis of variance utilizing the resultant subgroups to determine the extent to which subgroup differences are statistically significant.

This procedure was carried out with this U.S. sample, and is presented in Exhibit 1. Age is clearly the dominate factor affecting decisions to start a new firm. The impact of age, however, is not monotonic but curvilinear, with the highest proportion, almost 10%, occurring among those 25–34 years old. The rate is one-third this level, about 3%, among those 18–24 or 35–54 years old. Nascent entrepreneurs are virtually non-existent among those 55 and older. The impact of other factors varies with the age of the respondent, indicating the significance of these interactions. Among the youngest adults, 18–24 years old, the presence of other adults in the household is critical. Among the oldest respondents, 55 and up, the availability of financial reserves is critical. Among the mid-life adults, their occupational status has a major effect, with self-employment substantially increasing the probability of attempting to start a new firm. But for those young adults, 25–34 years old with full or part time work, educational attainment is critical, for almost one in eight that have completed high school are also attempting to start a new business. Among those in later middle years, 35–54 years old, and *not* self-employed, those new to a county (the United States has 3,124 counties) are more likely to be starting a new firm, particularly if they are men.

While two of the variables with great emphasis in the univariate analysis (Table IV) or the linear

EXHIB. 1

Interaction of factors and presence of nascent entrepreneurs. Based on U.S. random sample from October–November 1993 Survey of Consumers. Number of cases in each group in parentheses. Letter appearing before the number of cases identifies category in next exhibit. Collapsing sample weights into 9 categories for use in the CHAID analysis procedure slightly increased the overall prevalence from 3.9% to 4.1%. For this exploratory analysis, CHAID was allowed to develop a 6 level analysis, use Chi-square values of 0.20 for both predictors and significance of categories, and subgroup sizes were limited to 50 before splits and 25 after splits.

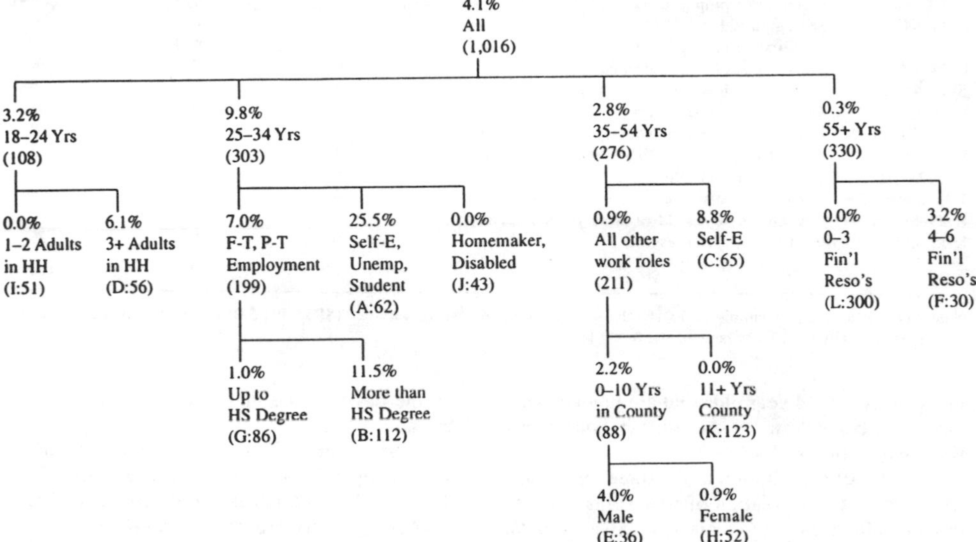

models developed from logistic regression (Table V) have a major impact in this search for interaction – age and self-employment – it is also important that a number of others do not. For example, gender does not appear in this model, partially because those 55 and over, who are not trying to start new businesses, are dominated by women. Two-thirds (67.4%) of those 55 and over are women; one-third (38.1%) of all women in the sample – and the adult population – are 55 and over. In all other age categories the genders are relatively evenly balanced.

The second phase of the analysis, comparing the 12 subgroups developed in the first stage, is presented in Table VI. When the groups are ranked on the basis of the prevalence of nascent entrepreneurs and a one-way analysis of variance is completed, the results are statistically significant beyond the 0.0000 level and about 12% of the variance is accounted for. This is substantially more than the analysis of self-employment with the Current Population Survey data from 150,000 respondents, described above, that left 99.7% of variance *unexplained.*

The ranking presented in Table VI demonstrates the extent to which efforts to start new firms are concentrated in unique groups in the adult population. Seven-in-ten of new firm start-ups (69%) are provided by one-sixth (17%) of the adult population; those 25–34 that are self-employed, unemployed, or students (group A) or with employment and more than a high school degree (group B). If those 35–54 reporting self-employment (group C) are added, five-sixths (83%) of start-ups are provided by less than one-quarter (23%) of the adult population. Equally dramatic is identifying that 50% of the adult population that fail to generate any efforts to start a new firm: those 55 and over with no financial reserves; those 35–54 not self-employed and with over 10 years

TABLE VI
Population groups and prevalence of nascent entrepreneurs

Group	Description	Prop nascent entre's	Percent total nascent entre's	Percent sample
A 25–34 yrs;	Self-employed, unemployed, student	26%	38%	6%
B 25–34 yrs;	Full or part-time employment; more than Hi Sch Degree	12	31	11
	(Cumulative proportions)		(69%)	(17%)
C 35–54 yrs;	Self-employed	9	14	6
	(Cumulative proportions)		(83%)	(23%)
D 18–24 yrs;	3 or more adults in household	6	8	6
E 35–54 yrs;	Not self-employed; 0–10 yrs in county; male	4	3	4
F 55-up yrs;	4 or more financial reserves	3	2	3
G 25–34 yrs;	Full or part-time employment; up to HS degree	1	2	9
H 35–54 yrs;	Not self-employed; 0–10 yrs in county; female	1	1	5
I 18–24 yrs;	1–2 adults in household	0	0	5
J 25–34 yrs;	Homemaker, disabled	0	0	4
K 35–54 yrs;	Not self-employed; 11 or more years in county	0	0	12
L 55-up yrs;	0–3 financial reserves	0	0	29
Total		4%	99%	100%

Note: This is a weighted sample of 1,016. Using a one-way analysis of variance (SPSS PC 5.0) the total explained variance is 11.6%; statistically significant beyond the 0.000 level.

in a county; 25–34 year olds that are homemakers or disabled; and those 18–24 living in households with one or two adults.

The unique contribution of the three top groups (A, B & C) to the creation of new firms justifies more careful attention to their distinctive features. In each group a minority are involved in a new firm startup (nascent entrepreneurs, NascE) and the majority are not (Other). They are compared on the basis of the major independent variables in Table VII.

Most of the differences in Table VII, due to small sample sizes, are not statistically significant. The first three variables merely confirm what the CHAID analysis provided: Groups A and B are restricted to those 25–34 years old, group C to those 35–54 years old; Group B is composed of those reporting full- or part-time employment,

TABLE VII
Selected group comparisons: others and nascent entrepreneurs (NascE)

		A Group		B Group		C Group	
		Other	NascE	Other	NascE	Other	NascE
Overall		46	16	100	13	59	6
Age	25–34 yrs old	100%	100%	100%	100%		
	35–44 yrs old					54%	75%
	45–54 yrs old					46	25
Labor force status	Full time job			87%	81%		
	Part-time job			13	19		
	Self-employed	73%	67%			67%	72%
	Unemployed	18	16				
	Homemaker						
	Retired						
	Student	9	16				
	Disabled					33	28

TABLE VII *(Continued)*

		A Group		B Group		C Group	
		Other	NascE	Other	NascE	Other	NascE
Educational attainment	Less than high school	5%	10%			11%	8%
	High school degree	34	27			42	52
	Post high school	30	38	36%	32%	22	15
	College degree	19	19	42	42	15	25
	Post college experience	11	5	22	26	10	–
Gender	Men	44%	46%	45%	60%	55%	77%
	Women	56	54	55	40	45	23
Ethnic status	White	71%	59%	80%	87%	81%	100%
	Black	15	41	14	13	15	–
	Other	14	–**	7	–	4	–
Consumer confidence index	High	48%	46%	46%	49%	30%	37%
	Medium	37	49	27	7	48	8
	Low	15	6	27	45	22	55*
County tenure	0–5 yrs	24%	30%	48%	46%	8%	15%
	6–15 yrs	17	38	22	6	35	8
	16–30 yrs	40	32	21	41	20	25
	31 yrs and up	19	–*	8	7	37	52
Household income	Up to $10K/yr	16%	34%	8%	–%	20%	31%
	$10–35K/yr	53	44	43	58	43	33
	$35K–50K/yr	17	11	20	14	13	–
	$50K and up/yr	13	11	30	28	24	36
Financial reserves	None	54%	62%	22%	28%	47%	58%
	One	22	11	27	–	20	–
	Two	4	27	32	20	13	17
	Three	12	–	11	32	8	25
	Four-Six	8	–**	8	20**	14	–
Occupational Status	Prof-Tech	23%	16%	37%	20%	21%	–%
	Manager-administrator	20	22	17	35	28	17
	Clerical-sales	15	6	19	33	11	45
	Foreman-craftsman	22	30	6	–	11	8
	Operators-unskilled work	12	–	12	–	14	15
	Service-household work	9	27	8	12	14	15
Martial status	Never married	25%	16%	27%	35%	11%	–%
	Married	54	32	60	46	55	63
	Separated, divorced	17	52	13	20	31	37
	Widowed	4	–**	–	–	2	–
Kids under 18 in household	None	25%	19%	57%	68%	52%	62%
	One	16	48	20	7	27	23
	Two	48	16	15	26	12	15
	Three or more	10	16**	8	–	9	–
Adults in household	One	38%	52%	28%	20%	30%	37%
	Two	56	42	59	68	55	40
	Three	4	–	7	12	10	23
	Four or more	2	6	6	–	6	–

Chi-square statistical significance: * 0.10; ** 0.05; *** 0.01.

Groups A and C those that report self-employment but Group A also includes those unemployed or students; those in Group B reported educational attainment beyond high school.

But these three groups of nascent entrepreneurs appear to be somewhat different. The sixteen in the A group, those 25–34 in the labor force but not working for others, are 40% Black, confident about their economic future, less likely to have lived their whole life in the same county, have lower household income and financial reserves, 70% are not married, 70% have no kids in the household, and half live with no other adults. They would appear to be optimistic, independent, and with a career emphasis on managing and starting new firms – a commitment to the entrepreneurial life.

In contrast, the thirteen in the B group, who are the same age but with full-time or part-time jobs and education beyond high school are more likely to be men, have high or low confidence in their economic future, higher levels of household income and more financial reserves, more likely to have white collar work, be married or living with another adult but without children in the household. They would appear to be pursing a new firm either as a sideline to their existing work or as a hedge against potential problems with their day job – entrepreneurship as a hobby or a hedge.

The six in the C group, composed of those 35–54 that are self-employed, seem more diverse, for they may be pursing a new firm as they find a new opportunity or as a hedge against problems with their existing business activity. All white and mostly men, they are long term residents of their counties with diversity in both their financial situations and confidence in the economy. All have been married but now 40% live without another adult and usually without children. This group probably includes both those who, when they were younger, had a commitment to an entrepreneurial career as well as those for whom new firms were a hobby or hedge (Group A or B individuals at a later stage in their life).

While tentative, this overview seems to provide a more complete understanding of the factors affecting the decision to pursue a new firm start-up.

This analysis helps illuminate the significance of at least two variables given a great deal of attention in the economics literature related to new firm start-ups – unemployment and personal liquidity. The assumption that increases in unemployment leads to greater entrepreneurship (reported self-employment) is generally based on aggregated analyses, has focused on the relationship between the unemployment rate and rates of new firm births (Reynolds, Storey and Westhead, 1994; Storey, 1991; Storey, 1994). While it is true that statistically significant relationships can be found between measures of unemployment and firm birth rates, and that unemployed (as an individual characteristic) is statistically significant in linear additive models associated with transitions into self-employment (see Table I), it is clear that the majority of efforts to start new firms are *NOT* initiated by the unemployed. As discussed above in relation to Table IV, over 80% of those trying to start a new firm are engaged in full- or part-time work or are self-employed.

Adam Smith apparently suggested the only difference between the local shopkeeper and the "great merchant" was the availability of capital (Shorrocks, 1988, p. 256); leading to the liquidity constraint hypotheses – that lack of financial resources will constrain entrepreneurship (Jovanovic, 1982). There seems to be little doubt that this is a statistically significant factor (Evans and Leighton, 1989; Evans and Jovanovic, 1989). One analysis has found that reporting of substantial inheritances on Internal Revenue Service estate returns increases the probability that subsequent personal returns of the beneficiaries will include, for the first time, a business expense schedule, indicating new business activity (Holtz-Eakin *et al.*, 1994). Although these analyses have found statistically significant effects of increased liquidity on reported self-employment, the amount of explained variance has been modest. The conditions under which the availability of funding triggers self-employment has not been identified.

The analysis completed above finds that two indicators of financial well-being, household income and the availability of financial resources, plays a minor role in the decision to initiate a new firm start-up. But the impact of financial reserves appears to have opposite effects on the group A and B entrepreneurs considered in Table VII. Those nascent entrepreneurs in Group A have more modest financial reserves in relationship to their comparison group while those in Group B have more significant financial reserves than their comparison group. Given this result, it is no wonder that the empirical support for the "liquidity effect" has been modest.

The use of the automatic interaction detection procedure has identified unique situations where participation in new firm start-ups in enhanced. The results have improved understanding in two ways. First, the variance accounted for by personal and contextual factors has increased substantially, from less than 1% to over 10%. Second, the combination of factors defining those groups where nascent entrepreneurs are most likely to ge found produces an interpretation that is more closely related to most descriptions of the start-up process.

One caution is in order. The AID procedure, designed to facilitate the "search for structure" has the same drawbacks as other similar techniques, stepwise multiple regression techniques or cluster analysis or factor analysis. The results may be idiosyncratic if the sample is idiosyncratic. To reduce the risk that a distinctive sample may provide a misleading interpretation, the procedure can be applied several times to different samples or to subsets of the same sample. This was not possible in this situation because of the small size of the sample of nascent entrepreneurs, 40 out of a representative sample of over 1,000. Larger samples in future studies will make this possible.

Conclusion

This is, as should be clear, a preliminary analysis of a research program in development. Nonetheless, several conclusions seems justified. First, it is technically feasible to study the pre-organization or start-up or entrepreneurial process in some detail. While there are some costs – each nascent entrepreneur in the random samples the U.S. adult population represents about $250 in direct costs – they are not so high as to preclude further research. These costs, compared to the billions in public funds devoted to encouraging new firms and entrepreneurship in the European Union and the United States, are rather modest.

Second, participation in the entrepreneurial process is a major activity for those in the U.S. labor force. (Participation in other countries is less clear at this time.) If the 1 in 25 estimate is accurate, then over seven million U.S. adults are involved in the entrepreneurial process at any given time – this is greater than the annual number that get married or have children. Just as with marriage and childbearing, however, new firm start-ups are concentrated among young adults. Further, these individuals are not – as some have suggested – driven, amoral economic sociopaths wreaking havoc on society (Baumol, 1990) or "misfits cast off from wage work" (Evans and Leighton, 1989), but mainstream adults seeking new options in their work careers.

Third, preliminary evidence suggests that the processes leading to the initiation of a start-up reflect complex interactions among personal, life course, and contextual factors. They seem to fall into a small set of well defined groups. Satisfying explanations or useful predictions are unlikely to be provided by simple linear, additive models.

Finally, public policies oriented toward enhancing the number of new firms or encouraging entrepreneurial activity may be the most effective if directed toward a small number of well defined groups, primarily those 25–34 years old. Further research, including follow-up contact with the firms-in-gestation, will be required to determine the success of these start-ups (Carter, Gartner and Reynolds, 1995).

Notes

1 These two data sets, one for each month, are available from the archives maintained by the Inter-university Consortium for Political and Social Research [ICPSR] at the University of Michigan Institute for Social Research; P.O. Box 1248; Ann Arbor, MI 48106 USA.

2 This index has been used as an indicator of economic well-being for the U.S. since 1948 and is now reported semi-monthly (Curtin, 1982). The items for the index are: (1) We are interested in how people are getting along financially these days. Would you say that your (and your family living there) are better off or worse off financially than you were a year ago? Why would you say so? (2) Now looking ahead – do you think that a year from now you (and your family living there) would be better off financially, or worse off, or just the same as now? (3) Now turning to business conditions in the country as a whole – do you think that during the next 12 months we'll have good times financially, or bad times, or what? (4) Looking ahead, which would you say is more likely – that in the country as a whole we'll have continuous good times during the next five years or so, or that we will have periods of widespread unemployment or depression, or what? (5) About the big things people buy for their homes – such as furniture, a refrigerator, a stove, television, and things like that. Generally speaking, do you think now is a good or a bad time

for people to buy major household items? Why do you say so? Responses for each item are on a scale from 1 (positive) to 5 (negative). The index was created by standardizing each item with a zero mean and standard deviation of 1 and then taking the average of the responses for each respondent. Any respondent answering three or more of the five items was included. Standardized Chronbach's Alpha, a measure of reliability, was 0.54 for this sample.

References

Baumol, William J., 1990, 'Entrepreneurship: Productive, Unproductive, and Destructive', *Journal of Political Economy* **98**(5, part 1), 893–921.

Blanchflower, D. G. and D. B. Meyer, 1991, 'Longitudinal Analysis of Young Entrepreneurs in Australia and the United States', *Working Paper* No. 3746. Cambridge, MA: National Bureau of Economic Research.

Blanchflower, D. G. and A. J. Oswald, 1990, 'Self Employment in the Enterprise Culture', in R. Jowell, S. Witherspoon and L. Brook (eds.), *British Social Attitudes: The Seventh Report*, Gower/Aldershot: SCPR.

Carter, Nancy M., William B. Gartner and Paul D. Reynolds, 1996, 'Exploring Start-Up Event Sequences', *Journal of Business Venturing* (In Press).

Curtin, Richard, 1982, 'Indicators of Consumer Behavior: The University of Michigan Surveys of Consumers', *Public Opinion Quarterly* **46**, 340–362.

Dolton, P. J. and G. H. Makepeace, 1990, 'Self-Employment Amongst Graduates', *Bulletin of Economic Research* **42**(1), 35–53.

Evans, David S. and B. Jovanovic, 1989, 'An Estimated Model of Entrepreneurial Choice under Liquidity Constraints', *Journal of Political Economy* **94**(4), 808–827.

Evans, David S. and Linda S. Leighton, 1989, 'Some Empirical Aspects of Entrepreneurship', *American Economic Review* **79**(3), 519–535.

Holtz-Eakin, Douglas, David Joulfaian and Harvery S. Rosen, 1994, 'Sticking it Out: Entrepreneurial Survival and Liquidity Constraints', *Journal of Political Economy* **102**(1), 53–76.

Jovanovic, Boyan, 1982, 'Selection and the Evolution of Industry', *Econometrica* **50**(3), 649–670.

Magidson, Jay, 1992, *SPSS/PC+ CHAID: Version 5.0.*, Chicago: SPSS Inc.

Norusis, Marija J., 1992, *SPSS/PC+ Advanced Statistics: Version 5.0.*, Chicago: SPSS Inc.

Palit, Charles and Paul Reynolds, 1993, 'A Network Sampling Procedure for Estimating the Prevalence of Nascent Entrepreneurs', *Proceedings of the International Conference on Establishment Surveys*, pp. 657–661, Alexandria, VA, USA: American Statistical Association.

Reynolds, Paul D., 1995, *The National Study of U.S. Business Start-Ups: Background and Progress Report*, Conference on Dynamics of Employment and Industry Evolution, 19–21 January, Mannheim: University of Mannheim.

Reynolds, Paul, David J. Storey and Paul Westhead, 1994, 'Cross-national Comparisons of the Variation in New Firm Formation Rates', *Regional Studies* **28**(4), 443–456.

Reynolds, Paul and Sammis White, 1993, *Wisconsin's Entrepreneurial Climate Study*, Final Report to Wisconsin Housing and Economic Development Authority, Milwaukee: Marquette University Center for the Study of Entrepreneurship.

Shorrocks, Anthony, 1988, 'Wealth Holdings and Entrepreneurial Activity', in D. Kessler and A. Masson (eds.), *Modeling the Accumulation and Distribution of Wealth*, pp. 241–258, Oxford: Clarendon Press.

Sonquist, John A., 1970, *Multivariate Model Building: The Validation of a Search Strategy*, Ann Arbor: University of Michigan Institute for Social Research.

Sonquist, John A. and James N. Morgan, 1964, *The Detection of Interaction Effects*, Monograph No. 35, Ann Arbor: University of Michigan Institute for Social Research.

Storey, David J., 1991, 'The Birth of New Firms – Does Unemployment Matter?', *Small Business Economics* **3**, 167–178.

Storey, David J., 1994, *Understanding the Small Business Sector*, London: Routledge.

U.S. Small Business Administration, Office of Advocacy, 1994, *Handbook of Small Business Data*, Washington DC: U.S. Government Printing Office.

[7]

EXPLORING START-UP EVENT SEQUENCES

NANCY M. CARTER
Marquette University

WILLIAM B. GARTNER
San Francisco State University

PAUL D. REYNOLDS
Babson College

EXECUTIVE SUMMARY

This research analyzed new venture start-up activities undertaken by 71 nascent entrepreneurs. Nascent entrepreneurs are individuals who were identified as taking steps to found a new business but who had not yet succeeded in making the transition to new business ownership. Longitudinal data for the study comes from a secondary data analysis of two representative samples, one of 683 adult residents in Wisconsin (Reynolds and White 1993) and the other of 1016 adult residents of the United States (Curtin 1982). These surveys were conducted between 1992 and 1993, and the nascent entrepreneurs were reinterviewed six to 18 months after their initial interview.

Three broad questions were addressed: (1) What activities do nascent entrepreneurs initiate in attempting to establish a new business? (2) How many activities do nascent entrepreneurs initiate during the gestation of the start-up? and (3) When are particular activities initiated or completed?

Between the first and second interview, 48% of the nascent entrepreneurs reported they had set up a business in operation. Over 20% had given up and were no longer actively trying to establish a business. Almost a third of the respondents reported they were still trying to establish a firm.

As a way to summarize the results and as a springboard toward some insights into the implications of this research for practice and future research, we developed the following activity profiles of the three types of nascent entrepreneurs studied. These profiles are offered as a combination of both fact and some intuition about the findings.

STARTED A BUSINESS. Nascent entrepreneurs who were able to start a business were more aggressive in making their businesses real. They undertook activities that made their businesses tangible to others: they looked for facilities and equipment, sought and got financial support, formed a legal entity, organized a team, bought facilities and equipment, and devoted full time to the business. Individuals who started businesses seemed to act with a greater level of intensity. They undertook more activities than those individuals who did not start a business. The pattern of activities seem to indicate that individuals who started firms put themselves into the day-to-day process of running an ongoing business as quickly as they could and that these activities resulted in starting firms that generated sales (94%

Address correspondence to Nancy M. Carter, School of Business Administration, Marquette University, 606 North 13th St., Milwaukee, WI 53233.

Journal of Business Venturing 11, 151–166

655 Avenue of the Americas, New York, NY 10010

0883-9026/96/$15.00
SSDI 0883-9026(95)00129-8

of the entrepreneurs) and positive cash flow (50% of the entrepreneurs). What is not known is how successful or profitable these new firms will be over time. For example, 50% of the firms that were started had not reached positive cash flow and these firms may have been started by individuals who were foolhardy and rushed into operation of a business that would not be sustainable.

GAVE UP. The pattern of activities for the group of entrepreneurs who gave up seem to indicate that these entrepreneurs discovered that their initial idea for their businesses would not lead to success. The finding that the activity of developing a model or prototype differentiated individuals who gave up from those who were still trying would suggest that those who gave up had "tested" their ideas out and found that they would not work according to their expectations. Nascent entrepreneurs who gave up seemed to be similar in their activity patterns compared with those who started their firms, that is, individuals who gave up pursued the activities of creating a business in an aggressive manner at the beginning of the process. But as the business unfolded over time, these entrepreneurs decreased their activities and then ceased start-up activities. This group of individuals might be seen as either having the wisdom to test their ideas out before jumping into something that might lead to failure or lacking the flexibility to find more creative ways to solve the problems that they were confronted with.

STILL TRYING. It would seem that those who are still trying are not putting enough effort into the start-up process in order to find out whether they should start the business or give up. Those still trying had undertaken fewer activities than individuals in the other two groups. The still trying entrepreneurs were devoting their short-term efforts toward activities internal to the start-up process (e.g., saving money and preparing a plan) and less effort toward activities that would make the business real to others. The still trying entrepreneurs may be all talk and little action. Or these still trying entrepreneurs might be involved in developing businesses that take longer for these particular opportunities to unfold. (It should be noted that there was no industry effect across the three groups.)

Our advice to individuals considering business start-up is that the results seem to provide evidence that nascent entrepreneurs should aggressively pursue opportunities in the short-term, because they will quickly learn that these opportunities will either reveal themselves as worthy of start-up or as poor choices that should be abandoned. Individuals who do not devote the time and effort to undertaking the activities necessary for starting a business may find themselves perennially still trying, rather than succeeding or failing.

What entrepreneurs do in their day-to-day activities matters. The kinds of activities that nascent entrepreneurs undertake, the number of activities, and the sequence of these activities have a significant influence on the ability of nascent entrepreneurs to successfully create new ventures. This study suggests that the behaviors of nascent entrepreneurs who have successfully started a new venture can be identified and differentiated from the behaviors of nascent entrepreneurs who failed. We believe that future studies will more precisely identify the kinds of behaviors appropriate for certain new venture conditions. If such contingency information can be generated, entrepreneurship research is likely to have significant benefits for entrepreneurship practice, education, and public policy.

INTRODUCTION

This study focused on nascent entrepreneurs and the process of organization creation. Other terms for this period of time are: organizational emergence (Gartner, Bird, and Starr 1992); the preorganization (Katz and Gartner 1988; Hansen 1990), the organization in vitro (Hansen and Wortman 1989), prelaunch (McMullan and Long 1990), gestation (Reynolds and Miller 1992; Whetten 1987), and start-up (Van de Ven, Angle, and Poole 1989; Vesper 1990). Organization creation involves those events before an organization becomes an organization, that is, organization creation involves those factors that lead to and influence the process of starting a business.

Reynolds (1994) estimates that nearly 4% of working age adults in the United States are, at any one time, actively involved in the process of starting a business. He found that nearly 10% of the nascent entrepreneurs in his study reported a new firm in place within 12 to 18 months of initial contact, whereas it took, on average, over two years before nascent entrepreneurs indicated they had given up on efforts to start a business. Coupled with Birch's (1987) findings that, on average, over one million businesses are founded in the United States each year, substantial efforts are undertaken and resources utilized (both successfully and unsuccessfully) to create new organizations.

This study explored the activities undertaken by nascent entrepreneurs during the organization creation process. Three broad questions were addressed: (1) What activities do nascent entrepreneurs initiate in attempting to establish a new business? (2) How many activities do nascent entrepreneurs initiate during the gestation of the start-up? and (3) When are particular activities initiated or completed?

LITERATURE REVIEW

A number of scholars have offered frameworks for exploring the characteristics of the organization creation process. Gartner (1985) outlined a framework of four dimensions that should be accounted for when studying new ventures: the individuals involved in the creation of the new venture, the activities undertaken by those individuals during the new venture creation process, the organizational structure and strategy of the new venture, and the environmental context of the new venture. Van de Ven et al. (1989) suggested that researchers explore the business creation process by looking at " (1) how a business idea (or strategy) emerges over time, (2) when and how different functional competencies are created to develop and market the first proprietary product, (3) when and how these functional competencies are redeployed to develop subsequent new products in a family of products believed to result in a sustainable business, and (4) how these business development efforts both influence and are constrained by organization and industry contexts" (pp. 224–225). Vesper (1990) argued that a new company is composed of five key ingredients: (1) technical know-how, (2) a product or service idea, (3) personal contacts, (4) physical resources, and (5) customer orders, and he offers some insights into various start-up sequences that occur among the five key ingredients. Katz and Gartner (1988) explored the organization theory and entrepreneurship literature to identify a theoretical and empirically based framework for identifying the properties that would indicate an organization in the process of creation. Their literature review found that most theories on organizations assume complex properties that occur only after organizations achieve some particular size (e.g., Mintzberg 1979; March and Simon 1958; Miles 1980), rather than some minimal set of characteristics that might differentiate an emerging organization from other types of social situations. Katz and Gartner (1988) suggested four emergent properties that would be indicators that an organization is in the process of coming into existence: *intention* to create an organization, assembling *resources* to create an organization, developing an organizational *boundary* (e.g., incorporation), and *exchanges* of resources across the boundary (e.g., sales).

Subsequent empirical explorations (Reynolds and Miller 1992; Reynolds and White 1993, Reynolds 1994) of the Katz and Gartner (1988) framework have found that no one pattern or sequence of events is common to all emerging organizations. Whereas the most common first event in the creation of an organization is a personal commitment by individuals involved in the new venture (five out of six new firms), some emerging organizations (two in five) reported the first event as having sales, whereas others began with hiring or financial support (one in four). The most common last events in the creation of an organization were likely to be hiring first employees and first sales income (one-half of new ventures), financial support (two in five), and a major personal commitment to the venture (one in four new ventures). In general, the average time a firm was in the process of emergence was one year, though 20% completed gestation within one month, and 90% completed gestation within three years. In contrast, Van de Ven et al. (1989) in a study of high-technology ventures found that entrepreneurs engaged in a set of activities for nearly four years before business initiation.

We sought to reexamine the literature on entrepreneurial behaviors and develop linkages between certain cogent entrepreneurial behaviors and their efficacy for organization creation. The theoretical and empirical literature on entrepreneurial behaviors is very diverse, and few efforts have been undertaken to identify and validate a set of comprehensive and parsimonious behaviors necessary to create new businesses (Gatewood, Shaver, and Gartner 1995; Gartner and Starr 1993). As discussed in the methodology section, we had available for analysis 14 activity measures taken from two previous studies of nascent entrepreneurs (see Table 1). The theoretical basis for our exploration is grounded in Weick's theory of organizing (Weick 1979). In Weick's view, an organization is an ongoing process of interactions among individuals. We see the process of organization formation as analogous to Weick's process of "enactment"–the generation of specific patterns of interlocked behaviors among individuals. In general, one would expect that some behaviors would be more effective in enacting an organization compared to others. For example, Aldrich and Fiol (1994) suggest that entrepreneurs seek to gain cognitive legitimacy for their organizations by developing trust among those involved in the start-up. In broad terms, a view of organization formation as "enactment" would assume that entrepreneurs who were involved in behaviors that demonstrated to others that the emerging business was "real" would be more likely to create an organization (Gartner, Bird, and Starr 1992, p. 17). For example, a behavior such as buying facilities and equipment might be a more significant indicator to others that a nascent business is real than undertaking a behavior such as planning. Buying facilities may show others that the entrepreneur has made a significant commitment to creating a new business compared to what might be a less public demonstration of commitment like planning. A fully developed logic for linking theoretical ideas about organizing with specific hypotheses and measures awaits development.

Our primary objective was to explore the three questions listed earlier: What activities were undertaken? How many activities were undertaken? When were these activities undertaken? It was our assumption that nascent entrepreneurs who were able to get a business up and running undertook different behaviors (or sequences of behaviors) in starting their businesses than those nascent entrepreneurs who failed to start a business. What specific behaviors or sequences of behaviors would result in the successful creation of a business would be discovered through exploration of the survey responses.

METHODOLOGY

Source of Data

Longitudinal data for the study comes from a secondary data analysis of two representative samples, one of 683 adult residents in Wisconsin (Reynolds and White 1993) and the other of 1016 adult residents of the United States (Curtin 1982). Data had been collected in these two studies through a procedure that starts with a random selection of households, followed by a random selection of an adult member of the household. During the course of a phone interview these randomly selected adults were asked: "Are you, alone or with others, now trying to start a business?" If they answered yes, they were asked if they had "given serious thought to the new business" and whether a number of different activities associated with starting a new firm had been initiated or completed. They were also asked the month and year all reported actions were initiated. Those that reported two or more firm gestation behaviors were considered nascent entrepreneurs. Follow-up interviews were completed on both samples. When the follow-up sample was restricted to autonomous start-ups and franchises, data were available for 71 nascent entrepreneurs. Subsidiaries, branches, or purchases of another business were excluded from the study.

Measures

Precursor Activities

During the phone interviews the nascent entrepreneurs were asked about a series of activities associated with the gestation process. For each activity respondents indicated whether the activity was: (1) not yet initiated; (2) initiated; (3) complete; or (4) not relevant. If the behavior had been initiated or completed they were asked to indicate the month and year of initiation and/or completion. The entrepreneurs also were asked if the new business was included in any of the standard lists of businesses: Dun and Bradstreet files, unemployment insurance files, social security files, or the federal tax return listing. At the time of the second interview the respondents were again asked to indicate the status of the start-up activities and whether they were included on the various standard lists of businesses. We classified 14 of the activities as precursor behaviors that entrepreneurs commonly undertake to establish a new business (e.g., develop a business plan, look for facilities or equipment or location, ask for funding). The activities and their intercorrelations are displayed in Table 1.

Using the dates associated with when the activities were initiated, a time frame of firm development was constructed. An activity was considered initiated if the entrepreneur reported in either of the two interviews that they had initiated or completed the activity. Each activity was categorized according to the length of time separating its initiation or completion from that of the earliest reported activity. The time scale was separated into categories beginning with the first month of activity and progressing by quarter through the fourth year. Thus, for example, a value of 1 corresponded to activities that were initiated during the first month of the firm's development, a value of 2 to activities within the first quarter, and 3 to activities undertaken during the 2 quarter, etc. A value of 17 accordingly, represented activities initiated in the fourth quarter of the fourth year and 18 represented activities corresponding to the 5th year of activity. All activities commencing in the fifth year were grouped together. This measure was used to examine the sequencing of the start-up activities.

We created three measures from the time scale. First, each activity was dummy coded to designate whether the respondent reported initiating or completing the behavior (1 = yes; 0 = no). This information was used to examine what activities entrepreneurs engaged in during their firms' development. Second, a count was made of the total number of activities initiated (range possible; 0 = 14). This measure was used to assess the rate of activity initiation. Third, each category of the time scale was assigned a value designating the time period in which the action was initiated. Values ranged from 1 (corresponding to activities initiated within a month of the first behavior) to 18 (corresponding to the 5th year of activity). Thus, for example, a value of 3 signified activities that were initiated during the second quarter of the first year of the firm's development, whereas a value of 16 represented activities initiated in the third quarter of the fourth year. This measure was used to examine the sequencing of start-up activities.

TABLE 1 Pearson Product Correlation Coefficients for Activities Initiated or Completed within Five Years of Initiating First Start-Up Behavior

	1	2	3	4	5	6	7	8	9	10	11	12	13
1. Organized team													
2. Prepared plan	0.16												
3. Bought facilities/equip	−.13	−.08											
4. Rented facilities/equip	−.06	−.11	−.05										
5. Looked for facilities	.08	.10	.29[a]	.08									
6. Invested own money	−.02	.12	.57[b]	−.02	.38[b]								
7. Ask for funding	−.06	.08	.27[a]	.02	.28[a]	.30[a]							
8. Got financial support	−.07	.05	.34[b]	.07	.30[a]	.26[a]	.61[a]						
9. Developed models	.22	.10	−.05	−.14	.23[a]	−.02	−.05	−.01					
10. Devoted fulltime	.01	−.16	.17	.27[a]	.18	−.11	.15	.22	.12				
11. Applied license/patent	.10	.18	.33[a]	.02	.26[a]	.33[b]	.14	.19	.09	.21			
12. Formed legal entity	.39[b]	.24[a]	.13	−.09	.02	.13	.22	.21	.29[a]	−.01	.22		
13. Hired employees	.12	.13	.29[a]	.18	.22	.14	.12	.25[a]	−.08	.39[b]	.21	.16	
14. Saved money to invest	.23	.10	.07	−.20	.15	.03	.03	.03	.02	−.01	−.15	.09	.07

[a] $p < .05$.
[b] $p < .01$.

Start-up Indicators

During the second interview, the respondents were asked a self-perception measure of the current status of the development of their firm: (1) still working on putting the business in place; (2) given up, do not expect to start that business; (3) the business is now in operation, up and running. Responses to this question were used to group the entrepreneurs into one of three outcome categories that we refer to as "outcome status." Additionally, several other start-up indicators were assessed. Using the same scale as that used to assess the precursor behaviors, respondents were asked to indicate whether their business was included on four standard business listings (i.e., Dun and Bradstreet files, unemployment insurance files, social security files, or the federal tax return listing), whether they had received any money from the sales of goods or services, and if they had achieved a positive cash flow (monthly revenues exceeded the monthly expenses). If they responded "yes," they were asked to indicate the date when the start-up indicator first happened.

Analytical Techniques

Discriminant analysis and one-way analysis of variance were used to test whether there were significant differences among the three outcome categories. Additionally, descriptive statistics were displayed to illustrate sequencing of the start-up activities. The discriminant variables (precursor activities) were entered stepwise according to the Wilks' lambda criterion. Stepwise analysis was appropriate, because the relationship between the discriminant variables and the status outcomes was not known from previous research. The functions were rotated using varimax rotation to aid in the interpretation of the functions' meanings.

RESULTS

Table 2 shows the outcome status of the gestation efforts. Between the first and the second interview, 48% of the nascent entrepreneurs reported they had put a business into operation, up and running. Over 20% had given up and were no longer actively trying to establish the new venture. Almost a third of the respondents reported they were still trying to establish a firm.

Table 3 reports the results of a forward stepwise discriminant analysis used to examine whether the kinds of activities nascent entrepreneurs initiate varies by outcome status. The discriminant analysis revealed that the first discriminant function had an eigenvalue of 0.279 accounting for 62.7% of the variance, with a canonical correlation of 0.467. The second discriminant function had an eigenvalue of 0.166, accounting for 37.3 percent of the variance. Wilks' lambdas prior to extraction of each function were 0.67 and 0.86. Both lambdas were significant at .005 or less.

The first function, which explained the most variance, differentiated the entrepreneurs who were still actively trying to start businesses from the other two groups. These nascent entrepreneurs were least likely to get financial support or to buy facilities or equipment. In

TABLE 2 Outcome Status at Time of Second Interview

Fledgling new firm, started	34 (48%)
Still actively trying to establish firm	21 (30%)
Not actively trying – Gave up	16 (22%)
Total	71

TABLE 3 Results of Discriminant Analysis: Activities Initiated within Five Years of First Behavior

Variable	Function 1	Function 2
Canonical discriminant funcitons evaluated at group means (centroids)		
Started businesses	.658	−.497
Gave up, not actively trying	−.084	.739
Still actively trying	−.720	−.254
Rotated standardized discriminant function coefficients		
Bought facilities/equipment	.658	−.498
Got financial support	.604	.555
Developed models	−.000	.789
Correctly classified 63%		

contrast, nascent entrepreneurs who had started businesses were most likely to have bought facilities or equipment and to have obtained financial support. The second function separated entrepreneurs who gave up and were no longer actively trying to establish a new business from the other two groups. Those who gave up were more likely to get financial support and to have developed models or prototypes.

Table 4 provides further insight into the kinds of activities nascent entrepreneurs in the three outcome status groups initiated. A review of the precursor activities that did not statistically discriminate the groups indicates that a substantial percentage of all entrepreneurs in the study reported having saved and invested their own money in the start-up, having looked for equipment or facilities, and having organized a start-up team.

A review of the start-up indicators shows that over 90% of the entrepreneurs who had

TABLE 4 Percentage of Activities Initiated within Five Years of First Behavior

	Started (n = 34)	Gave Up (n = 16)	Still Trying (n = 21)	Total (n = 71)
Discriminating activities				
Bought facilities, equipment	85	50	43	65
Got financial support	47	44	5	34
Developed models/prototypes	15	44	14	21
Other precursor activities				
Organized start-up team	68	56	48	59
Devoted full time	47	38	14	35
Asked for funding	53	44	10	38
Invested own money	91	81	67	82
Looked for facilities/equipment	82	81	52	73
Applied license/patent	71	56	38	58
Saved money to invest	68	56	67	65
Prepared plan	53	56	43	51
Formed legal entity	49	45	36	28
Hired employees	32	6	10	20
Rented facilities, equipment	24	19	19	21
Start-Up indicators				
Sales	94	50	48	70
Positive cash flow	50	19	19	34
D&B credit listing	6	6	5	5
Unemployment insurance	24	0	0	11
FICA	47	0	0	22
Filed federal tax	71	6	19	41

TABLE 5 Summary of Analysis of Variance for Total Number of Activities Initiated

Source	*df*	MS	F	*p*
Outcome status	2	114.35	9.75	.0002
Error	68	398.89		

a business in operation at the time of the second interview had sales from goods or services, 71% had filed federal income tax returns, and 50% reported having a positive cash flow. These rates far exceed those of the other two groups.

We used a one-way analysis of variance to examine whether the total number of activities entrepreneurs initiate varies across the outcome status groups. The results reported in Table 5 indicate a statistical difference. Pairwise comparisons of the means revealed that the average total number of precursor activities initiated by entrepreneurs who have a business operating (mean = 8.00) are significantly greater than the number initiated by entrepreneurs who gave up (mean = 6.56), or those who are still trying (mean = 5.05).

Figure 1 plots the initiation of activities across the time scale. The trends indicate that entrepreneurs who started businesses initiated more activities at all time periods measured. Entrepreneurs who eventually gave up were similar in their rate of activity to those who got a business started through the first year. However, after the first year, the rate of initiation by those who eventually gave up began to taper off. Those who reported they were still trying to establish a business initiated significantly fewer activities across all time periods than either of the other two groups.

To further analyze the trends we recalculated the scores plotted in Figure 1 as a percentage of total activities initiated by their group. The results indicate that by the end of the first year, almost two-thirds of all activities that would be initiated by each of the groups already had been undertaken. We then sought to determine whether the kinds of activities initiated early in the developmental process varied by outcome status.

The analytic techniques that could be employed to address this issue were limited. The number of activities initiated early in the process resulted in the time scale variable being highly skewed to the left. We relied on median values to examine the sequencing of activities initiated during the first year. The results are displayed in Table 6.

The results from this analysis provide further insight into the apparent passive approach of entrepreneurs still in the gestation process. During the first six months of start-up, these entrepreneurs focused on saving money to invest in the business, preparing a business plan, and organizing a start-up team. In contrast, entrepreneurs who got a business operating looked for and bought facilities or equipment, invested their own money, prepared a business plan, asked for and got financial support, organized a start-up team, formed a legal entity, and devoted full time to the business. Table 7 displays additional information about the sequencing patterns. The data indicates that six months after initiating their first start-up activity, 50% of the entrepreneurs who reported staring a business had received money from sales. Entrepreneurs who had given up and were no longer actively trying to establish a business appear to be somewhat less aggressive than those who started operations. Those who gave up were distinct in their early efforts by developing models or prototypes. By the sixth month, only 25% of this latter group had money from sales.

It should also be noted that we conducted analyses to determine whether the results were affected by industry. There was no industry effect among the three groups of nascent entrepreneurs (i.e., started, gave up, trying to start). For example, developing a model or prototype is an activity that differentiates those nascent entrepreneurs who gave up from those

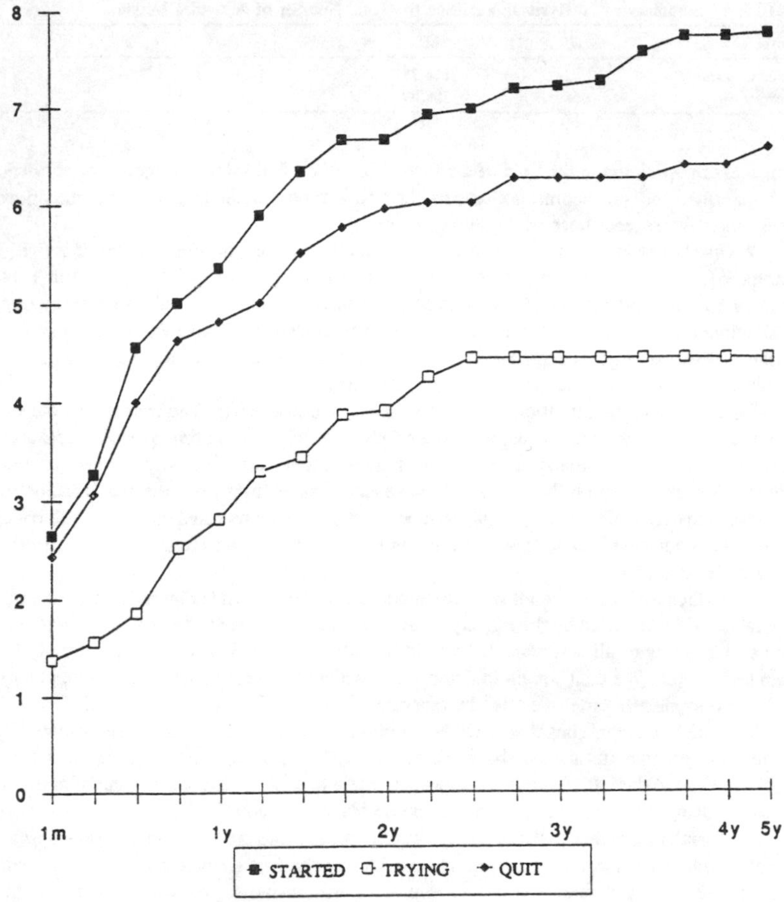

FIGURE 1 Number of activities initiated since first start-up behavior.

nascent entrepreneurs who continued to try and, therefore, it seemed plausible that those entrepreneurs who had developed a model and gave up would likely be in industries that are in manufacturing or other types of industries that might be more capital intensive than service industries. Yet, of the 14 nascent entrepreneurs who indicated they had initiated or completed models or prototypes, nearly seven of these individuals were in the gave up category in such industries as: one in nondurable manufacturing, one in restaurants/bars/clubs, two in consumer services, and three in business services.

DISCUSSION

As way to summarize the results and as a springboard toward some insights into the implications of this research for practice and future research, we developed the following activity profiles

TABLE 6 Sequencing of Startup Activities[a,b]

Year 1	Started (n = 34)	Gave up (n = 16)	Still Trying (n = 21)
1st month	Looked for F + E	Asked for funding Developed models Saved money to invest Organized start-up team	
1st quarter	Invested own money Asked for funding Got financial support Prepared plan	Invested own money Got financial support	Saved money to invest
2nd quarter	Formed legal entity Organized team Bought F + E Devoted full time	Prepared plan Bought F + E	Prepared plan Organized team
3rd quarter	Hired employees	Looked for F + E	Invested own money Looked for F + E Applied for L/P
4th quarter	Saved money Rented F + E Applied for L/P	Devoted full time Applied for L/P	Bought F + E

[a] Categorized by median value of those who had initiated the activity.
[b] Median values reported only if more than five entrepreneurs in the group had initiated activity.

of the three types of nascent entrepreneurs studied. These profiles are offered as a combination of both fact and some intuition about the findings.

Profiles of Types of Nascent Entrepreneurs

Started A Business

Nascent entrepreneurs who were able to start a business were more aggressive in making their businesses real, that is, they undertook activities that made their businesses tangible to others: they looked for facilities and equipment, sought and got financial support, formed a legal entity, organized a team, bought facilities and equipment, and devoted full time to the business. Individuals who started businesses seemed to act with a greater level of intensity. They undertook more activities than those individuals who did not start their businesses. The pattern of activities listed in Table 5 seem to indicate that individuals who started firms put themselves into the day-to-day process of running an ongoing business as quickly as they could and that these activities resulted in starting firms that generated sales (94% of the entrepreneurs) and positive cash flow (50% of the entrepreneurs). What is not known is how successful or profitable these new firms will be over time. For example, the 50% of the firms started that have not reached positive cash flow may be firms started by individuals who were foolhardy and rushed into operation of a business that could not be sustained.

Gave Up

The pattern of activities for the group of entrepreneurs who gave up seems to indicate that these entrepreneurs discovered that their initial idea for their businesses would not lead to

TABLE 7 Percentage of Entrepreneurs Initiating Activity within the First Year of Initial Start-Up Behavior

	Started				Gave Up				Still Trying			
	1mo	3mo	6mo	12mo	1mo	3mo	6mo	12mo	1mo	3mo	6mo	12mo
Discriminating activities												
Bought facilities, equip.	32	38	53	59	19	25	25	31	14	14	14	24
Developed models	0	0	6	6	25	31	38	38	0	0	0	10
Got financial support	21	24	27	32	19	25	38	38	0	0	0	0
Other precursor activities												
Organized start-up team	24	32	44	56	31	31	31	38	19	24	24	33
Devoted full time	15	18	29	29	0	6	19	19	10	10	10	10
Asked for funding	24	27	41	44	25	38	44	44	0	0	0	10
Invested own money	41	53	68	71	31	44	56	63	24	24	29	38
Looked for facilities	44	47	59	65	13	19	38	63	10	14	19	33
Applied license/patent	12	15	27	35	6	13	19	31	10	10	14	24
Saved money to invest	18	24	32	41	38	38	44	50	29	33	38	48
Prepared plan	18	27	32	38	25	25	38	44	19	19	24	33
Formed legal entity	6	9	21	27	6	6	6	13	0	5	10	14
Hired employees	3	6	9	21	0	0	0	0	0	0	0	0
Rented facilities, equip.	9	9	12	12	6	6	6	13	5	5	5	5
Start-up indicators												
Sales	29	35	50	65	13	19	25	31	10	14	14	19
Positive cashflow	15	15	21	32	6	6	13	13	5	10	10	10
D&B credit listing	0	0	3	6	6	6	6	6	5	5	5	5
Unemployment insur.	3	3	12	15	0	0	0	0	0	0	0	0
FICA	15	12	27	32	0	0	0	0	0	0	0	0
Filed federal tax	15	15	27	41	0	6	6	6	5	5	10	14

success. The finding that the activity of developing a model or prototype differentiated individuals who gave up from those who were still trying would suggest that those who gave up had tested their ideas out and found that they would not work according to their expectations. Nascent entrepreneurs who gave up seemed to be similar in their activity patterns compared with those who started their firms, that is, individuals who gave up pursued the activities of creating a business in an aggressive manner at the beginning of the process. But as the business unfolded over time, these entrepreneurs decreased their activities and then ceased start-up activities. This group of individuals might be seen as either having the wisdom to test their ideas out before jumping into something that might lead to failure or lacking the flexibility to find more creative ways to solve the problems that they were confronted with.

Still Trying

It would seem that those who are still trying are not putting enough effort into the start-up process in order to find out whether they should start the business, or give up. The still trying had undertaken fewer activities than individuals in the other two groups. The still trying entrepreneurs were devoting their short-term efforts toward activities internal to the start-up process (e.g., saving money and preparing a plan) and less effort toward activities that would make the business real to others. The still trying entrepreneurs may be all talk and little action. Or, these still trying entrepreneurs might be involved in developing businesses that take longer for these particular opportunities to unfold. (Yet, as noted earlier, there was no industry effect.)

Implications for Practice

In terms of advice to individuals considering starting a business, it would seem that the results provide evidence that nascent entrepreneurs should aggressively pursue opportunities in the short-term, because they will quickly learn that these opportunities will either reveal themselves as worthy of start-up or as poor choices that should be abandoned. Individuals who do not devote the time and effort to undertaking the activities necessary for starting a business may find themselves perennially still trying, rather than succeeding or failing. It would seem that a certain level of effort and activity is necessary to determine success or failure in starting a business.

Consultants, advisors, and investors involved in helping nascent entrepreneurs may find in these results evidence that entrepreneurs are action oriented rather than passive. Individuals who do not begin a business or reach a decision to abandon efforts to start a business within a year are likely to remain in a constant state of abeyance, thereby wasting the valuable time and resources of advisors that could be devoted to helping individuals who will actually undertake the activities to discover whether they can start a business.

These findings may lead to a better diagnostic to help nascent entrepreneurs and entrepreneurship advisors determine whether these nascent entrepreneurs should abandon their efforts at start-up sooner, change their activities, or continue their efforts. The analytical results may also be useful for the development of a set of indicator variables for use in identifying those nascent entrepreneurs who are likely to develop ventures that have the potential for substantial growth in sales and employment.

Implications and Directions for Research

Given that this study was based on an analysis of secondary data, the measures available for analysis were not as comprehensive or as specific as we would have liked. In future longitudinal studies of nascent entrepreneurs, the measures in these studies should capture additional information about various factors and behaviors that might influence the venture start-up process. For example, it would be valuable to explore the expectations of these nascent entrepreneurs regarding their perceptions of the future success of their ventures and their subsequent activities. It would also be valuable to explore whether nascent entrepreneurs expect to start their firms quickly (i.e., in less than six months) compared with other nascent entrepreneurs that may expect the start-up process to take longer. One reason that some firms may take longer to create may involve acquiring substantial financial resources or the procurement of government licenses or regulatory approval. Some nascent entrepreneurs may also expect to start firms that grow more rapidly compared with other nascent entrepreneurs.

A number of start-up behaviors (e.g., gathering marketing information on competitors and customers, acquiring know-how or expertise, seeking advice from mentors and advisors, and the activities involved with selling, marketing, and distribution) were not explored in this research and might have a significant influence on the outcome of the start-up process. It might also be appropriate to develop measures of the activities that reflect estimates of the number of hours the nascent entrepreneur devoted to a particular activity between the date of inception and its completion.

It would also be of value to collect additional information on the types of ventures that nascent entrepreneurs are planning to create. Characteristics of these emerging ventures that would be appropriate to study would include: strategy (e.g., pricing policy, perceived distinctive competence) and industry characteristics (e.g., growth rates, technological change, competition, power of suppliers and buyers, and barriers to entry). In addition, the firms that were started should be studied to find out if they were successful in the long run.

A larger effort at identifying and tracking nascent entrepreneurs is critical to generating a sample size sufficient for the statistical power necessary to identify the nuances inherent in the business start-up process. With a sample of size of 71 cases, a division of these cases into even a few groups quickly eliminates the use of many statistical and analytical tools. We believe there are many factors that are likely to have a significant moderating affect on the activities of nascent entrepreneurs (e.g., previous experience and background of the entrepreneur, the venture's strategy, the venture's industry) that will likely surface when a larger sample size is available for analysis.

Finally, we offer some speculations for future research based on the three profiles that were generated from the quantitative analyses of the data. The differences in the number of activities initiated among the three groups (started a business, gave up, and still trying) might suggest that "enacting" an organization, that is, taking venture creation actions that are visible to others (e.g., buying facilities and equipment, forming a legal entity) is more likely to result in an ongoing business. We believe that future empirical research on nascent entrepreneurs could lead to an operationalization of the actions involved in enactment. Empirical research on entrepreneurship could therefore inform Weick's theory on organizing. The finding that the "still trying" group undertakes fewer activities might suggest that a critical factor for differentiating individuals who get into business from those that do not involves action rather than planning, or "doing" rather than "thinking about it." It might be useful to explore how nascent entrepreneurs undertake planning and whether entrepreneurs who get into business use planning as a springboard for action, compared to those "still trying" who may use planning as a form of procrastination. The finding that those individuals who "gave up" undertook a similar number of activities in the first year compared with those who got into business should be explored through case studies and in-depth interviews. It would be very valuable to uncover how entrepreneurs make judgments about the potential success of a new venture, and whether those who "gave up" were more discerning in their ability to spot fatal flaws in a new business, or whether those who "gave up" were less creative in surmounting perceived potential problems. If, as Gartner, Bird, and Starr (1992) suggest, entrepreneurial action transforms equivocal events into nonequivocal interpretations and interactions, the impact of circumstance on the process and outcomes of business formation is important and deserves careful study. For example, MacMillan and Katz (1992) point out that entrepreneurial events are often idiosyncratic, obscure, and infrequent. In-depth longitudinal case studies are necessary to explore the effects of chance occurrences, such as how the sharing of a limousine ride to the airport with a stranger leads to the formation of a tea company (Ziegler, Rosenzweig, and Ziegler 1992) on the process of organization formation.

CONCLUSIONS

What entrepreneurs do in their day-to-day activities matters. The kinds of activities that nascent entrepreneurs undertake, the number of activities, and the sequence of these activities have a significant influence on the ability of nascent entrepreneurs to successfully create new ventures. This study suggests that the behaviors of nascent entrepreneurs who have successfully started a new venture can be identified and differentiated from the behaviors of nascent entrepreneurs who failed. We believe that future studies will more precisely identify the kinds of behaviors appropriate for certain new venture conditions. If such contingency information can be generated, entrepreneurship research is likely to have significant benefits for entrepreneurship practice, education, and public policy.

REFERENCES

Aldrich, H.E., and Auster, E.R. 1986. Even dwarfs started small: Liabilities of age and size and their strategic implications. *Research in Organizational Behavior* 8:165–198.

Aldrich, H.E., and Fiol, C.M. 1994. Fools rush in? The institutional context of industry creation. *Academy of Management Review* 19(4):645–670.

Birch, D.L. 1987. *Job creation in America.* New York: The Free Press.

Curtin, R. 1982. Indicators of consumer behavior: The University of Michigan Surveys of Consumers. *Public Opinion Quarterly* 46:340–362.

Gartner, W.B. 1985. A conceptual framework for describing the phenomenon of new venture creation. *Academy of Management Review* 10(4):696–706.

Gartner, W.B., Bird, B.J., and Starr, J.A. 1992. Acting as if: Differentiating entrepreneurial from organizational behavior. *Entrepreneurship: Theory and Practice* 16(3):13–31.

Gartner, W.B. and Starr, J.A. 1993. The nature of entrepreneurial work. In S. Birley and I.C. MacMillan, eds., *Entrepreneurship Research: Global Perspectives.* Amsterdam: North-Holland, pp. 35–67.

Gatewood, E.J., Shaver, K.G., and Gartner, W.B. 1995. A longitudinal study of cognitive factors influencing start-up behaviors and success at venture creation. *Journal of Business Venturing* 10(5):371–391.

Hansen, E.L. 1990. Entrepreneurial networks: Their effect on new organization outcomes. Unpublished doctoral dissertation. Knoxville, TN: University of Tennessee.

Hansen, E.L., and Wortman, M.S. 1989. Entrepreneurial networks: The organization in vitro. In F. Hoy, ed., *Best Papers Proceedings.* Washington, DC.: Academy of Management, pp. 69–73.

Katz, J., and Gartner, W.B. 1988. Properties of emerging organizations. *Academy of Management Review* 13(3):429–442.

March, J.G., and Simon, H.A. 1958. *Organizations.* New York: Wiley.

MacMillan, I.C., and Katz, J.A. 1992. Idiosyncratic milieus of entrepreneurial research: The need for comprehensive theories. *Journal of Business Venturing* 7:1–8.

McMullan, W.E., and Long, W.A. 1990. *Developing New Ventures.* San Diego, CA: Harcourt Brace Jovanovich.

Miles, R.H. 1980. *Organizational Behavior.* Glenview, IL: Scott Foresman.

Mintzberg, H. 1979. *The Structuring of Organizations.* Englewood Cliffs, NJ: Prentice-Hall.

Reynolds, P. 1992. Predicting new-firm births: Interactions of organizational and human populations. In D.L. Sexton and J.D. Kasarda, eds., *The State of the Art of Entrepreneurship.* Boston: PWS-Kent, pp. 268–297.

Reynolds, P. 1994. Reducing barriers to understanding new firm gestation: Prevalence and success of nascent entrepreneurs. Paper presented at the Academy of Management Meetings, Dallas, TX (August).

Reynolds, P., and Miller, B. 1992. New firm gestation: Conception, birth, and implications for research. *Journal of Business Venturing* 7:405–417.

Reynolds, P., and White, S. 1993. Wisconsin's entrepreneurial climate study. Milwaukee, WI: Marquette University Center for the Study of Entrepreneurship. Final Report to Wisconsin Housing and Economic Development Authority.

Stinchcombe, A.L. 1965. Social structure and organizations. In J.G. March, ed., *Handbook of Organizations.* Chicago, IL: Rand McNally, pp. 142–193.

Van de Ven, A.H., Angle, H.L., and Poole, M.S. 1989. *Research on the Management of Innovation.* New York: Harper and Row.

Vesper, K.H. 1990. *New Venture Strategies*, 2nd ed. Englewood Cliffs, NJ: Prentice Hall.

Whetten, D.A. 1987. Organizational growth and decline processes. *Annual Review of Sociology* 13: 335–358.

Ziegler, M., Rosenzweig, B., and Ziegler, P.1992. *The Republic of Tea.* New York: Doubleday.

[8]

A COMPARISON OF ASSISTANCE NEEDS OF MALE AND FEMALE PRE-VENTURE ENTREPRENEURS

JAMES J. CHRISMAN
University of South Carolina

ALAN L. CARSRUD
University of California at Los Angeles

JULIO DeCASTRO
University of Colorado

LANNY HERRON
University of Baltimore

EXECUTIVE SUMMARY

In spite of the proliferation of studies of female entrepreneurs, few researchers have attempted to directly compare female and male entrepreneurs in terms of their problems, the assistance received in addressing these problems, the value of outside consulting services, and the number of startups subsequent to counseling. Such studies are needed, not only to determine if there are differences in the problems male and female entrepreneurs face, but more importantly, to determine if any of these differences affect the successful development of new ventures. The fact that the SBA recently established a special training program for women entrepreneurs funded by a new $10 million grant, approved by Congress in 1988 (H.R. 5050), makes the issue even more timely and pertinent.

To address this issue, this article compares samples of aspiring male and female entrepreneurs who received consulting assistance from a state-level Small Business Development Center (SBDC). The two groups were compared in terms of: (1) the strategic, administrative, and operating assistance received; (2) their evaluation of the value of the consulting services; and (3) their propensity to initiate ventures after receiving SBDC assistance. The study was based on the results of two surveys of the entire population of 457 long-term pre-venture clients that received counseling from one SBDC state system between July 1, 1985, and June 30, 1987. All clients were asked to complete a questionnaire concerning the kinds of assistance sought, the quality of the service received, and whether or not they subsequently went into business. We received 162 (35.4%) usable responses, of which 94 were from males (58.0%) and 68 were from females (42.0%). T-tests and chi-square tests of independence and

Address correspondence to James J. Chrisman, College of Business Administration, University of South Carolina, Columbia, SC 29208.

An earlier version of this article was presented at the 34th World Conference of the International Council for Small Business.

Journal of Business Venturing 5, 235–248 0883-9026/90/$3.50

goodness-of-fit were used to test hypotheses pertaining to the assistance needs of aspiring male and female entrepreneurs.

Results indicated that male and female clients of the SBDC are virtually identical in terms of their assistance needs. Females do not appear to need more assistance than males, nor do they appear to require different types of assistance. The virtually identical ratings of service value among males and females also indicates that both genders are equally satisfied with the assistance received.

Taken together, these findings suggest that females suffer no significant entrepreneurial disadvantages compared to males. If they had, it would be logical to assume that females, who received the same types and amounts of assistance as males, would find such levels of service inadequate, and consequently, rate it less favorably. Furthermore, the fact that the proportion of female clients was statistically equal to the proportion of net new businesses operated by women refutes the notion that general-assistance programs such as the SBDC are not equally accessible to both genders. The fact that female client start-ups were significantly higher *than their proportional representation in the region further supports this conclusion.*

The primary implication for public policy makers and outside consultants is that little evidence exists to warrant special treatment or special programs for females, especially at a cost of $10 million. In terms of research implications, our results suggest that it would be better if future studies concentrated on behaviors and strategic factors affecting the performance of new ventures (whether male- or female-owned), rather than merely comparing the characteristics of the entrepreneurs who start them.

INTRODUCTION

The proliferation of women-owned businesses is part of a workplace metamorphosis that began in the 1970s and has continued unabated into the 1980s. This change has been chronicled by a number of recent studies of female entrepreneurs, most of which have focused on personality characteristics or factors affecting the start-up of female-owned firms (Anderson and Anderson 1988; Carsrud and Olm 1986; Harlan and Weiss 1982; Hisrich and Brush 1986: Jacklin and Mccoby 1975; Kanter 1977; Riger and Galligan 1980; Sexton and Bowman-Upton 1990). A few studies have also sought to determine the assistance, training, and information needs of female entrepreneurs. These studies indicate that in addition to a lack of business education and experience, and a need for outside assistance, women have problems in marketing, obtaining financing, and business planning (Aldrich 1989; Aldrich et al. 1989; Carter 1989; Hisrich 1989; Hisrich and Brush 1983, 1984, 1985; Nelson 1987; Pellegrino and Reece 1982). However, these problems do not appear to be much different from the problems faced by male entrepreneurs (Davis et al. 1981; Kazanjian 1988; Vozikis and Glueck 1980).

Unfortunately, despite the studies mentioned above, few researchers have attempted to directly compare female and male entrepreneurs in terms of their problems, the assistance received in addressing these problems, the value of this assistance, and the number or successes of venture start-ups. Even fewer studies have statistically analyzed data to determine if the similarities or differences found apply to populations of male and female entrepreneurs. As Carsrud and Olm (1986) have noted, such studies are needed, not only to determine if differences between male and female entrepreneurs exist, but more importantly, to determine if any of these differences affect the successful development of new ventures. Furthermore, since entrepreneurship is vital to the economic future of the United States (Birch 1987; Reagan 1985) the determinants of the success and failure of male- and female-owned ventures may also have significant public policy implications. The fact that the SBA recently established a special training program for women entrepreneurs funded by a new $10 million grant (H.R. 5050), approved by Congress in 1988, makes the issue even more timely and pertinent (*USA Today*, September 22, 1989, p. 5B).

If aspiring female entrepreneurs, relative to male entrepreneurs, encounter additional obstacles to successful venturing, as a result of discrimination (e.g., in obtaining financing) or a lack of basic business training, special programs and policies may help alleviate these problems. On the other hand, if the principal obstacles that exist are a result of inappropriate strategies, unattractive environments, or lack of business experience, then general programs that already exist (e.g., the SBA, SBDC, SBI, SCORE, ACE) to assist would-be entrepreneurs in formulating strategies, analyzing industry environments, and assessing their personal capabilities, may be sufficient.

To explore these issues, this study compares samples of aspiring male and female entrepreneurs who received consulting assistance from a state-level Small Business Development Center (SBDC) over a two-year period. The two groups were compared in terms of the strategic, administrative, and operating assistance received; their evaluation of the value of the consulting services; and their propensity to initiate ventures after receiving SBDC assistance.

LITERATURE REVIEW

Several studies have focused on the personality and motivational differences between male and female entrepreneurs, as well as the organizational and management issues affecting their businesses. Aside from educational background and experience, few significant sex-related differences have been found (Carsrud and Olm 1986; Chaganti 1986; Cromie 1987; Gomolka 1977; Masters and Meier 1988; Neider 1987; Nelson 1987; Scott 1986; Stevenson 1986). Furthermore, even though females tend to have less *business* education they are well educated (Bowen and Hisrich 1986) and, in fact, more highly educated than men (Mescon et al. 1983/1984). A recent study by Sexton and Bowman-Upton (1990) found that female entrepreneurs scored lower on energy level and risk taking than male entrepreneurs, but higher on traits related to autonomy and change. Sexton and Bowman-Upton (1990, p. 30) concluded, however, that female and male entrepreneurs were more similar than different, and that the differences found, "would not be expected to affect the person's ability to manage a growing company."

In spite of this, several authors have advocated government intervention as a solution for the potential problems of discrimination and inexperience facing female entrepreneurs (Hisrich and O'Brien 1981). For example, Watkins and Watkins (1983) suggest that, in the short term, special programs are necessary to encourage and assist female venturing. These arguments are more prescriptive than empirical, however. While training programs are a good idea, little (if any) evidence has been provided that indicates women (or men) who require special treatment actually possess sufficient potential for success to warrant such encouragement and special help.

In an earlier attempt to address these questions, Birley et al. (1987) compared the backgrounds of, and businesses formed by, male and female entrepreneurs after attending courses on small businesses. One of the most important findings of their study was the extremely high proportion of females who subsequently started businesses. Those authors suggest that the results of their study indicate that while women may have the motivation to begin business ventures, they also need enabling devices, such as training programs to put their ideas into effect. Nonetheless, they concluded that, "no strong evidence emerges to support female-specific programs," (Birley et al. 1987, p. 34).

Another question with particular research importance—and related to the argument that the start-up barriers differ significantly for males and females, is whether the alleged biases in funding for women owned businesses actually exist (see Bowman-Upton et al. 1987; Buttner and Rosen 1988; Carter 1989; Hisrich and Brush 1986; Hisrich and O'Brien 1981, 1982; Olm et al. 1988). Scott (1986) found in her survey that about one-third of her respondents felt it was harder for a woman business owner to raise money than for a man, and a nearly equal number thought that maintaining adequate cash flow was their greatest problem. Furthermore, Schwartz (1976) suggests that many women entrepreneurs have been denied financing for their businesses just because of their sex.

On the other hand, financial institutions attribute women entrepreneurs difficulties in obtaining credit to their lack of previous experience in the financial arena as well as to their lack of self-confidence in presenting their business concepts and plans (Humphreys and McClung 1981). In fact, recent research has suggested that blatant biases against women in lending no longer exist in the United States (Brophy 1989; Buttner and Rosen 1989; Hisrich and Brush 1987; Olm et al. 1988). As both Brophy (1989) and Bowman-Upton et al. (1987) noted, financing is an external barrier to venture initiation regardless of the gender of the entrepreneur. Therefore, it is possible that a significant portion of the bias (if any) that exists on the part of lenders is against certain low-asset, low-profit businesses which also happen to be in female- (and minority-) dominated industries (Bowman-Upton et al. 1987; Brophy 1989; Buttner and Rosen 1989; Chrisman and Carsrud 1990).

CONCEPTUAL FRAMEWORK AND HYPOTHESES

In this study, an entrepreneur was defined as a person who starts a business (Gartner 1988). An aspiring (or pre-venture) entrepreneur was defined as a person who plans to start a firm. In order to expand the knowledge about the differences between male and female entrepreneurs, several hypotheses were formulated. Because it was not possible to specify the direction expected for every hypothesis, they are presented in the null form for the sake of consistency.

H1 There is no difference in the amount of strategic assistance that female and male pre-venture clients receive.

H1a There is no difference in the proportion of female and male pre-venture clients who receive assistance in preparing business plans.

H2 There is no difference in the amount of administrative assistance that female and male pre-venture clients receive.

H2a There is no difference in the proportion of female and male pre-venture clients who receive assistance in finance.

H3 There is no difference in the amount of operating assistance that female and male pre-venture clients receive.

H3a There is no difference in the proportion of female and male pre-venture clients who receive assistance in marketing.

The literature reviewed above suggests that, aside from possible sex discrimination in obtaining financing, aspiring female entrepreneurs are hampered by a lack of business education and experience. Women are also more likely than men to initiate retail and service businesses. Given these differences, one might expect that women require more (and perhaps different types of) assistance than men, particularly in finance, business planning, and marketing where discrimination or lack of experience may be significant obstacles to venture success (e.g., Hisrich and Brush 1983, 1984, 1985).

H4 There is no difference in perceptions of the value of outsider consulting assistance between male and female pre-venture entrepreneurs.

H5 There is no difference in the proportion of business start-ups among female and male pre-venture entrepreneurs after receiving outsider assistance.

Previous studies have indicated that the real and perceived value of outsider services is directly related to the types and amounts of assistance they receive (Chrisman 1989; Chrisman and Carsrud 1989; Chrisman and Carsrud 1990; Chrisman et al. 1987; Robinson 1982). Therefore, *if* the assistance needs of women are greater than the assistance needs of men *and* the amount of assistance received is equal or less, one would expect women to rate outsider services lower than men. In the same vein, if women need extra assistance and do not get it, one might expect the proportion of female start-ups to be lower than the proportion of male start-ups.

H6 There is no difference between the proportion of female pre-venture clients and the proportion of new businesses started by women.

H7 There is no difference between the proportion of female pre-venture clients who started a business and the proportion of new businesses started by women.

The final two hypotheses were formulated to determine if general assistance programs such as the SBDC are sufficiently accessible to females in general, and more importantly, to qualified female entrepreneurs. Even if females and males are equally equipped to start businesses, special programs might be justified if females are underrepresented in the populations of both aspiring entrepreneurs and entrepreneurs who obtained outsider assistance. If the SBDC is not equally accessible to women in general, one would expect the proportion of women pre-venture clients to be substantially lower than the proportion of new businesses started by women.

THE STUDY

The research sample was composed of clients of the Small Business Development Center (SBDC) program in one Southern state. Before discussing the details of the study, it is important to explain why we used SBDC clients, rather than drawing the sample from some other population of aspiring entrepreneurs.

Identifying aspiring entrepreneurs, especially those who never actually initiate a venture, is no easy task. There are no comprehensive directories and few lists of such individuals available. The SBDC, which offers broad-based, in-depth assistance to aspiring entrepreneurs, maintains files on past clients. Therefore, the SBDC is one of the best sources for obtaining information on aspiring entrepreneurs.

In addition, SBDC clients generally have few resources and limited business backgrounds (Flewellen and Bramlett 1978; Robinson 1982), problems that also tend to plague female entrepreneurs (Bowen and Hisrich 1986) as well as most small businesses in general (Bowman-Upton et al. 1987; Carter 1989). By and large, most pre-venture clients start ventures in retail or service industries. These industries also have the highest concentrations of female entrepreneurs (Bowen and Hisrich 1986; Carter 1989; Hisrich and Brush 1984).

Thus, SBDC clients are, in general, representative of aspiring entrepreneurs, with respect to their type of business, assistance needs, and business experience (Lenti 1989).

Study Design

The similarities and differences of male and female pre-venture clients in terms of the types, amounts, and value of the outsider assistance they received were examined by two surveys of the entire population of long-term pre-venture clients (defined by the SBDC as those receiving 12 consulting hours or more) that received counseling from one SBDC state system over a two-year period between July 1, 1985, and June 30, 1987. The 249 clients served in 1985–1986 were contacted in the summer of 1987, and the 208 clients served in 1986–1987 were contacted in the summer of 1988. The two-year population of 457 clients included 261 males (57.1%), 136 females (28.8%) and 60 male/female "teams" (13.1%).

All clients were asked to complete a questionnaire concerning the kinds of assistance sought, the quality of the service received, and whether or not they subsequently went into business. Two mailings and telephone follow-ups were used in both surveys to minimize non-response bias. The two surveys yielded 188 responses (41.1%), of which 162 (35.4%) were used for the analysis. Eighty-four questionnaires (18.4%) were returned undeliverable. Additional data on sex, ethnic background, type of business, military service, and area of counseling were collected from SBDC files.

The 188 respondents included 26 pre-venture teams consisting of both male and female clients. Because the purpose of this study was to compare male and female entrepreneurs, the male/female teams were excluded from the analysis. The sample of 162 pre-ventures included 94 males (58.0%) and 68 females (42.0%). Of these, 100 clients (61.7%) subsequently started a business.

Testing at the 5% level, chi-square goodness-of-fit tests indicated that these respondents were highly representative of the long-term client population in terms of their sex, ethnic background, type of business, and areas of counseling. Furthermore, testing for goodness-of-fit at the 5% level indicated that the types of businesses clients intended to start were also representative of the types of businesses started in the state and in the United States as a whole between 1985 and 1987 (Dun and Bradstreet 1987, 1988). An examination of the SBDC's files on a sub-sample of 19 male and 12 female clients by two independent judges (74.2% agreement) also suggested that the SBDC's female clients were representative of female entrepreneurs, in that they tended to have slightly less business experience than male clients.

Variable Definition and Operationalization

Male and female pre-venture clients of the SBDC were compared with respect to the types and amounts of assistance they received, the perceived value of the assistance, and their propensity to start a venture after receiving outsider assistance. These variables are described in the following sections.

Types and Amounts of Assistance

Clients were asked to indicated the areas in which they received assistance. These areas included (1) developing a business plan, (2) feasibility analysis, (3) pro-forma financial analysis, (4) strategic planning, (5) finance, (6) accounting, (7) personnel, (8) general management, (9) marketing, (10) production, (11) inventory control and purchasing, (12) startup operations, and (13) other. Respondents received assistance in an average of 2.9 problem areas (2.8 for men and 3.0 for women).

To determine if clients' perceptions were reliable indicators of the actual assistance rendered, the consulting files for a sub-sample of 34 pre-venture respondents were analyzed. In 85% of the cases, the consultants' reports describing the assistance rendered were consistent with clients' perceptions of the assistance received.

To condense these areas of assistance into a more manageable set, three broad classes of business problems were identified. According to Ansoff (1965, pp. 5-6), the *strategic problem* is "deciding what businesses the firm is in and what kinds of businesses it will seek to enter." *Administrative problems*, on the other hand, concern the firm's organization (e.g., structuring of authority and responsibility relationships, work flows) and its acquisition and development of resources (e.g., personnel training and development, financing). Finally, *operating problems* involve functional decisions in areas such as marketing, production, and inventory control.

Using Ansoff's definitions, each area of assistance listed above (except the "other" category, which was not included in the analysis) was classified by the lead author as strategic (areas 1–4 from above), administrative (areas 5–8), or operating (areas 9–12) problems. A panel of five judges then independently classified each of the above problems. The judges and the lead author agreed on 72.4% of the classifications (42 of 58 with two non-responses).

The amount of assistance was measured by the number of strategic, administrative, and operating problems in which each client received help. For example, if help was received in business-planning, finance, and personnel, then scores of one, two, and zero would be used to reflect the amount of strategic, administrative, and operating assistance received, respectively.

Perceived Service Value

Clients were also asked to rate the SBDC's consulting services on a seven-point scale, ranging from "worthless" (0) to "vital to success" (6). In general, respondents rated the service quite favorably; the overall average service rating was 4.40/6.00 (S.D. = 1.50).

A subjective assessment of service value was utilized because over one-third of the respondents did not go into business and, therefore, could not provide any performance data. Furthermore, as both surveys were conducted only one year after the end of the SBDC's fiscal years, many respondents had not been in business long enough to provide useful data on sales or profits. To be able to assess the reliability of the service-value rating, we also asked clients whether the service received was beneficial or not. Eighty-five percent of the clients indicated that the service was beneficial. A point biserial correlation showed that the responses to this question were significantly correlated with respondents' ratings of service value ($r = .7308$; $P < .0001$).

Start-up Propensity

Startup propensity was determined by asking clients whether or not they had started a business after receiving outsider assistance from the SBDC.

Data Analysis Procedures

T-tests were used to analyze H1–H4. Hypothesis 5 and the subhypotheses H1a–H3a were analyzed using chi-square tests of independence. Chi-square goodness-of-fit tests were used to test hypotheses 6 and 7. The alphas for rejecting the null hypotheses were set at the .05 level. Assuming a medium effect size (i.e., a difference one can detect through the course of normal experience and observation), a sample of 94 males and 68 females (harmonic mean = 78.91, rounded to 79), nondirectional alternative hypotheses, and an alpha (probability of a Type I error) of .05, the statistical power of the t-tests was approximately .88, that is, there was a 12% chance of a Type II error (Cohen 1988). Furthermore, the statistical power of the chi-square tests (medium effect size; n = 162; alpha = .05) was .98. Both values are well above the traditionally desired power level of .80 (Magid et al. 1987).

Controlling for Industry Effects

Because different types of ventures may have different problems (Storey 1985), it was also necessary to determine if the clients' type of business would have a moderating effect before testing the hypotheses. A chi-square test of independence indicated a significant difference in the types of businesses started by female and male clients ($X^2 = 10.81$; $P < .001$); women were more likely to initiate retail or service businesses than men (89.1% versus 63.4%). This is consistent with the findings of past studies (Carter 1989; Hisrich and Brush 1983, 1984; Neider 1987; Olm et al. 1987; Scott 1986), and again underscores the representativeness of the SBDC client respondents.

One-way ANOVAs, t-tests, and chi-square tests found that the type of business clients intended to start had no significant moderating effect on the relationships between sex and the types of assistance received, its perceived value, or the propensity of clients to start a venture. Therefore, the sample was not divided by type of business for the analyses presented in this article.

RESULTS

Hypotheses 1–3 were tested to determine if female pre-venture clients received different amounts of strategic, administrative, and operating assistance than male pre-venture clients. None of the three null hypotheses could be rejected. Female clients received less strategic (H1) assistance than male clients (1.41 areas vs. 1.52 areas), but a t-test indicated the difference was not statistically significant at the 5% level. With respect to H2 and H3, females received more administrative assistance (0.63 areas vs. 0.60 areas) and operating assistance (0.91 areas vs. 0.69 areas) than males, but again, the differences did not approach statistical significance (see Table 1).

With respect to subhypotheses H1a–H3a, chi-square tests of independence found that aspiring female and male entrepreneurs were equally likely, statistically speaking, to receive assistance in preparing business plans, finance, and marketing (see Table 2). In fact, statistically equal proportions of males and females received assistance in all 12 areas analyzed in this study (see the methodology section above for a description of these 12 areas of assistance). Although the results were not statistically significant at the 5% level, a larger proportion of females than males received help in business planning (58.8% vs. 53.2%) and marketing (29.4% vs. 23.4%). Interestingly, a smaller (but not significantly smaller) proportion of females than males received assistance in finance (26.5% vs. 36.2%).

The above results clearly and consistently indicate that males and females receive the same basic types of assistance in the same basic amounts. Therefore, one would expect to find evidence for rejecting H4 and H5 if women actually need more assistance than men. Nevertheless, the null hypothesis (H4) that male and female pre-venture clients would attach

TABLE 1 Amount of Strategic, Administrative, and Operating Assistance Provided to Male and Female Pre-Venture Clients and Their Ratings of the Value of Outsider Services

	Males (N = 94)		Females (N = 68)				
	Mean	S.D.	Mean	S.D.	t-stat.	2-way sign.	Null Hypothesis
H1 Amount of strategic assistance	1.52	1.04	1.41	1.18	−0.62	$P < .54$	Not rejected
H2 Amount of administrative assistance	0.59	0.91	0.63	0.75	0.27	$P < .79$	Not rejected
H3 Amount of operating assistance	0.69	0.86	0.91	0.84	1.63	$P < .11$	Not rejected
H4 Rating of service value*	4.40	1.51	4.39	1.48	−0.07	$P < .95$	Not rejected

*One female client did not respond to this question.

equal values to the outsider assistance provided could not be rejected (see Table 1). Males rated the services higher, but not significantly higher than females (4.40 versus 4.39). In fact, both their ratings of service value and the standard deviations (1.51 versus 1.48) of these ratings were virtually identical.

A chi-square test of independence also failed to reject hypothesis 5 (see Table 2). Even though the proportion of female clients who eventually started a business was larger than the proportion of male clients who did so (69.1% versus 56.4%), the proportions were statistically equal, testing at the 5% level.

These results clearly suggest that whatever the obstacles these female clients faced, the SBDC effectively helped surmount them. Furthermore, they were certainly no greater than the obstacles faced by the male clients.

To test hypotheses 6 and 7 it was first necessary to estimate the proportions of males and females who started a business. For the purpose of analysis, we assumed that survival rates for male- and female-owned firms were approximately equal. According to data extracted from *The State of Small Business* (1989, p. 115), female-owned firms accounted for approximately 35.6% of the net increase in the number of businesses in Region IV (Region IV, where the studied SBDC operates, includes Alabama, Florida, Georgia, Kentucky,

TABLE 2 Proportion of Male and Female Pre-Venture Clients Who Received Assistance in Business Planning, Finance, and Marketing and the Proportion Who Subsequently Started a Venture

	Males (N = 94)		Females (N = 68)				
	#	%	#	%	Chi-square	Sign.	Null Hypothesis
H1a Assistance in business planning	50	53.2	40	58.8	0.51	$P < .48$	Not rejected
H2a Assistance in finance	34	36.2	18	26.5	1.70	$P < .19$	Not rejected
H3a Assistance in marketing	22	23.4	20	29.4	0.74	$P < .39$	Not rejected
H5 Started a venture	53	56.4	47	69.1	2.70	$P < .11$	Not rejected

TABLE 3 Comparison of the Proportion of Net Surviving Businesses in Region IV of the United States Owned by Females, the Proportion of Female Pre-Venture SBDC Clients, and the Proportion of Female Client Start-ups

	Number of Non-Farm Businesses in Region IV*			
	1980	1986	Net Change	% of Net Change
Female-Owned	370,000	578,000	208,000	35.6%
Male-Owned	1,111,000	1,487,000	376,000	64.4%
Total	1,481,000	2,065,000	584,000	100.0%

	Males #	Males %	Females #	Females %	Chi-square	Sign.	Null Hypothesis
H6 Proportion of pre-venture clients	261	65.7%	136	34.3%	0.22	$P < .65$	Not rejected
H7 Proportion of client starts	53	53.0%	47	47.0%	5.67	$P < .02$	Rejected

*Region IV includes Alabama, Florida, Georgia, Kentucky, Mississippi, North Carolina, South Carolina, and Tennessee.
Source: *The State of Small Business* 1989, p. 115.

Mississippi, North Carolina, South Carolina, and Tennessee) of the United States between 1980 and 1986 (see Table 3). Excluding male/female teams, 34.3% (136 of 397) of the SBDC's clients were female. A chi-square goodness-of-fit test could not reject hypothesis 6; the proportion of female SBDC clients was not significantly less than the proportion of new female businesses started in U.S. Region IV between 1980 and 1986.

H7 was the only null hypothesis rejected, but it was not rejected in the direction one might expect (see Table 3). Female-owned ventures accounted for 47% of the known start-ups among SBDC clients, a proportion that was statistically *greater* than the proportion of female-owned businesses started in Region IV ($X^2 = 5.67$; $P < .02$). Again, these results provide no evidence to support the need for female-specific programs to promote entrepreneurship.

CONCLUSIONS

Male and female clients of the SBDC are virtually identical in terms of their assistance needs. Females do not appear to need more assistance than males, nor do they appear to require different types of assistance. The only possible exception to this conclusion was not in the area of finance, as might have been expected (Brophy 1989; Buttner and Rosen 1988; Scott 1986). Indeed, a larger proportion of males than females received this sort of assistance. Rather, females, relative to males, appeared to need the most assistance in dealing with operating problems, although even this difference was not statistically significant. These results clearly suggest that aspiring female entrepreneurs have few if any substantive disadvantages vis-a-vis males.

Furthermore, the virtually identical ratings of service value among males and females indicates that both sexes are equally satisfied with the assistance received. This again suggests that females suffer no significant entrepreneurial disadvantages. If they had, it would be logical to assume that females, who received the same types and amounts of assistance as males, would find such levels of service inadequate. In the same vein, if the service provided was inadequate, females would be expected to rate it less favorably than males.

The fact that the proportion of female clients was statistically equal to the proportion of net new businesses operated by women also refutes the notion that general assistance programs such as the SBDC are not equally accessible to both sexes. The fact that the proportion of female start-ups was significantly *higher* than the proportional representation in their region further supports this conclusion.

Limitations

Before discussing this study's implications, it is important to discuss its limitations. First, the study was conducted among SBDC clients in a single Southern state over a two-year period. Therefore, the results may not apply to non-SBDC clients or to SBDC clients in other states, other regions, or in other years, even though the analysis suggests they might. Second, there is the matter of possible response bias. The representativeness of respondents was verified to the extent possible, but it was not possible to determine conclusively if response bias existed. Third, aside from a small subsample of cases, no data were collected on the education, business experience, strategy, or resources of the SBDC's clients. Thus, in spite of efforts to ensure that the sample was representative of aspiring entrepreneurs in general, it is possible that the studied females possessed extraordinary knowledge, abilities, or resources.

Implications for Public Policy and Outsider Assistance Programs

The primary implication for public policy makers and outsiders providing assistance to pre-venture clients is that little evidence exists to warrant special treatment or special programs designed exclusively for females, especially those with a price tag of $10 million (*USA Today* 1989). Females need the same sorts of outside assistance as men and have similar perceptions of its value. Furthermore, general programs offering outside assistance appear to be equally accessible to aspiring entrepreneurs of both genders. In fact, this finding, and the finding that female entrepreneurs are overrepresented in the SBDC start-up populations, may indicate that females in general are able to assess their potential (or lack thereof) for entrepreneurial success more quickly or more realistically than males.

However, whether true or not, it does not follow that special programs to encourage even more females to start businesses are appropriate. If special programs "open the door" for more qualified female entrepreneurs, then they may serve a useful purpose. But if they instill unrealistic expectations in participants, then they may do more harm than good. Trying to make up for past injustices by promoting entrepreneurship, without regard to the qualifications of the entrepreneur or the quality of the ventures they wish to start may not be the real answer. Indeed, previous research has suggested that a major role of outsiders in the venture-development process is to *discourage* aspiring entrepreneurs with limited skills and ill-conceived business ideas (Chrisman et al. 1987; Chrisman and Carsrud 1989; Chrisman and Carsrud 1990). Female entrepreneurs should be pleased to note that they can expect such unbiased, objective assistance from the Small Business Development Center program.

In sum, given the need to balance the Federal budget, one must question the logic of spending $10 million to finance a special program with no empirical justification for its existence.

Directions for Future Research

Additional research is needed to verify and build upon these findings. For instance, replication studies of other outside assistance programs would be useful, as would similar studies of aspiring entrepreneurs who do not seek counseling from outsiders. It might also be useful to investigate why the proportion of female start-ups among SBDC clients is higher than the proportion of females who start businesses in general (and why the reverse is true for men). Perhaps, as Birley et al. suggested (1987), women have the motivation to be successful but need enabling devices to get them started. And this need may be greater for women than men. On the other hand, the difference could be due to the types of businesses that men and women usually start, the types of men and women who are attracted to outsider-assistance programs, or a more realistic self-assessment of qualifications and business ideas on the part of women *before* obtaining outside assistance.

Whatever the reason, it appears, based on the results of this study and previous research, that further research concentrating solely on the characteristics of female entrepreneurs is of questionable value. While males and females are obviously not exactly alike, no evidence exists that the determinants of venture success or failure differ according to sex. As Carter (1989) has noted, female entrepreneurs are not a homogeneous group, but neither are male entrepreneurs. Future comparative studies, therefore, would do far better to concentrate on behaviors (Gartner 1988) and strategic factors (Hofer and Sandberg 1987; Sandberg and Hofer 1987) affecting the performance of male- and female-owned ventures, rather than merely comparing the characteristics of the entrepreneurs themselves. However, there is still a need for similar comparative studies of minority and nonminority entrepreneurs. Such studies could help determine if any *meaningful* differences exist between these two groups and perhaps suggest means for correcting those that might exist.

REFERENCES

Aldrich, H. 1989. Networking among women entrepreneurs. In O. Hagan, C. Rivchen, and D.L. Sexton, (eds.), *Women-Owned Businesses*. New York: Praeger, pp. 103–132.

Aldrich, H., Reese, P.R., and Dubini, P. 1989. Women on the verge of a breakthrough: Networking among entrepreneurs in the United States and Italy. *Entrepreneurship and Regional Development* 1(4):339–356.

Anderson, R.L., and Anderson, K.P. 1988. A comparison of women in small and large companies. *American Journal of Small Business* 12(3):23–34.

Ansoff, H.I. 1965. *Corporate Strategy: An Analytical Approach to Business Policy for Growth and Expansion*. New York: McGraw-Hill.

Birch, D. 1987. *Job Creation in America: How our Smallest Companies Put the Most People to Work*. New York: The Free Press.

Birley, S., Moss, C., and Saunders, P. 1987. Do women entrepreneurs require different training? *American Journal of Small Business* 12(1):27–36.

Bowen D.D., and Hisrich, R.D. 1986. The female entrepreneur: A career development perspective. *Academy of Management Review* 11:393–407.

Bowman-Upton, N., Carsrud, A.L., and Olm, K.W. 1987. New venture funding for the female entrepreneur: A preliminary analysis. In N.C. Churchill, J.A. Hornaday, B.A. Kirchhoff, O.J. Krasner, and K.H. Vesper, (eds.), *Frontiers of Entrepreneurship Research*. Wellesley, MA: Babson College, pp. 200–201.

Brophy, D.J. 1989. Financing women-owned entrepreneurial firms. In O. Hagan, C. Rivchen, and D.L. Sexton, (eds.), *Women-Owned Businesses*. New York: Praeger, pp. 55–76.

Buttner, E.H., and Rosen, B. 1988. Bank loan officers' perception of the characteristics of men, women, and successful entrepreneurs. *Journal of Business Venturing* 3:249–258.

Buttner, E.H., and Rosen, B. 1989. Funding new business ventures: Are decision makers biased against women? *Journal of Business Venturing* 4:249–261.

Carsrud, A.L., and Olm, K.W. 1986. The success of male and female entrepreneurs: A comparative analysis of the effects of multidimensional achievement motivation and personality traits. In R.W. Smilor and R.L. Kuhn, (eds.), *Managing Takeoff in Fast-Growth Companies*. New York: Praeger, pp. 147–162.

Carter, S. 1989. The dynamics and performance of female-owned entrepreneurial firms in London, Glasgow, and Nottingham. *Journal of Organizational Change Management* 2(3):54–64.

Chaganti, R. 1986. Management in women-owned enterprises. *Journal of Small Business Management* 24(4):18–29.

Chrisman, J.J. 1989. Strategic, administrative, and operating assistance: The value of outside consulting to pre-venture entrepreneurs. *Journal of Business Venturing* 4:401–418.

Chrisman, J.J., and Carsrud, A.L. 1989. Outsider contributions to the development and change of business ventures. *Journal of Organizational Change Management* 2(3):75–87.

Chrisman, J.J., and Carsrud, A.L. 1990. Outsider assistance needs of pre-venture and established small businesses: A comparison of minority and non-minority clients. *Proceedings of the International Council for Small Business*, pp. 10–16.

Chrisman, J.J., Hoy, F., and Robinson, R.B., Jr. 1987. New venture development: The costs and benefits of public sector assistance. *Journal of Business Venturing* 2:315–328.

Cohen, J. 1988. *Statistical Power Analysis for the Behavioral Sciences*. Hillsdale, NJ: Lawrence Erlbaum Associates, Inc.

Cromie, S. 1987. Similarities and differences between women and men who choose business proprietorship. *International Small Business Journal* 5(3):43–60.

Davis, C.H., Jones, B.M., and Kraft, F.B. 1981. Small business owners/managers information needs: An empirical overview. *Proceedings of the International Council for Small Business*, pp. 45–52.

Dun and Bradstreet. 1987. *Business Start Record: 1985/1986*. New York: Dun and Bradstreet.

Dun and Bradstreet. 1988. *Business Start Record: 1986/1987*. New York: Dun and Bradstreet.

Flewellen, W.C., and Bramlett, L.R. Spring 1978. The Small Business Development Center program in Georgia. *AACSB Bulletin*, 3–10.

Gartner, W.B. 1988. "Who is an entrepreneur?" is the wrong question. *American Journal of Small Business* 12(4):11–32.

Gomolka, E. 1977. Characteristics of minority entrepreneurs and small business enterprises. *American Journal of Small Business* 2(1):12–21.

Harlan, A., and Weiss, C.L. 1982. Sex differences in factors affecting managerial career advancement. In P.A. Wallace, (ed.), *Women in the Workplace*. Boston, MA: Auburn House.

Hisrich, R.D. 1989. Women entrepreneurs: Problems and prescriptions for success in the future. In O. Hagan, C. Rivchen, and D.L. Sexton, (eds.), *Women-Owned Businesses*. New York: Praeger, pp. 3–32.

Hisrich, R.D., and Brush, C. 1983. The woman entrepreneur: Implications of family educational and occupational experience. In J.A. Hornaday, J.A. Timmons, and K.H. Vesper, (eds.), *Frontiers of Entrepreneurship Research*. Wellesley, MA: Babson College, pp. 255–270.

Hisrich, R.D., and Brush, C. 1984. The woman entrepreneur: Management skills and business problems. *Journal of Small Business Management* 22(1):30–37.

Hisrich, R.D., and Brush, C. 1985. Women and minority entrepreneurs: A comparative analysis. In J.A. Hornaday, E.B. Shils, J.A. Timmons, and K.H. Vesper, (eds.), *Frontiers of Entrepreneurship Research*. Wellesley, MA: Babson College, pp. 566–587.

Hisrich, R.D., and Brush, C. 1986. *The Woman Entrepreneur*. Lexington, MA: Lexington Books.

Hisrich, R.D., and Brush, C. 1987. Women entrepreneurs: A longitudinal study. In N.C. Churchill, J.A. Hornaday, B.A. Kirchhoff, O.J. Krashner and K.H. Vesper, (eds.), *Frontiers of Entrepreneurship Research*. Wellesley, MA: Babson College, pp. 187–199.

Hisrich, R.D., and O'Brien, M. 1981. The woman entrepreneur from a business and sociological perspective. In K.H. Vesper, (ed.), *Frontiers of Entrepreneurship Research*. Wellesley, MA: Babson College, pp. 21–39.

Hisrich, R.D., and O'Brien, M. 1982. The woman entrepreneur as a reflection of the type of business.

In K.H. Vesper, (ed.), *Frontiers of Entrepreneurship Research*. Wellesley, MA: Babson College, pp. 54–67.

Hofer, C.W., and Sandberg, W.R. 1987. Improving new venture performance: Some guidelines for success. *American Journal of Small Business* 12(1):11–25.

Humphreys, M.A., and McClung, J.M. 1981. Women entrepreneurs in Oklahoma. *Review of Regional Economics and Business* 6(2):13–21.

Jacklin, C.N., and Mccoby, E.E. 1975. Sex implications for management. In F.E. Gordon and H.M. Strober, (eds.), *Bringing Women Into Management*. New York: McGraw-Hill, pp. 23–38.

Kanter, R.M. 1977. *Men and Women of the Corporation*. New York: Basic Books.

Kazanjian, R.K. 1988. Relation of dominant problems to stages of growth in technology-based new ventures. *Academy of Management Journal* 31:257–279.

Lenti, J. 1989. Interview with the Assistant Director of the state Small Business Development Center.

Magid, A., Mazen, M., Hemmasi, M., and Lewis, M.F. 1987. Assessment of statistical power in contemporary strategy research. *Strategic Management Journal* 8:403–410.

Masters, R., and Meier, R. 1988. Sex differences and risk-taking propensity of entrepreneurs. *Journal of Small Business Management* 26(1):31–35.

Mescon, T.S., Stevens, G., and Vozikis, G.S. 1983/1984. Women as entrepreneurs: An empirical evaluation. *Wisconsin Small Business Forum* 2(2):7–17.

Neider, L. 1987. A preliminary investigation of female entrepreneurs in Florida. *Journal of Small Business Management* 25(3):22–29.

Nelson, G.W. 1987. Information needs of female entrepreneurs. *Journal of Small Business Management* 25(3):38–44.

Olm, K.W., Carsrud, A.L., and Alvey, L. 1988. The role of networks in new venture funding for the female entrepreneur. *Frontiers of Entrepreneurship Research*. Wellesley, MA: Babson College, pp. 658–659.

Pellegrino, E.T., and Reece, B.L. 1982. Perceived formative and operational problems encountered by female entrepreneurs in retail and service firms. *Journal of Small Business Management* 20(2):15–24.

Reagan, R. 1985. Why this is the entrepreneurial age. *Journal of Business Venturing* 1:1–4.

Riger, S., and Galligan, P. 1980. Women in management: An exploration of competing paradigms. *American Psychologist* 35:902–910.

Robinson, R.B., Jr. 1982. The importance of 'outsiders' in small firm planning and performance. *Academy of Management Journal* 25:80–93.

Sandberg, W.R., and Hofer, C.W. 1987. Improving new venture performance: The role of strategy, industry structure, and the entrepreneur. *Journal of Business Venturing* 2:5–28.

Schwartz, E. 1976. Entrepreneurship: A new female frontier. *Journal of Contemporary Business* 53:47–75.

Scott, C.E. 1986. Why more women are becoming entrepreneurs. *Journal of Small Business Management* 24(4):37–44.

Sexton, D.L, and Bowman-Upton, N. 1990. Female and male entrepreneurs: Psychological characteristics and their role in gender-related discrimination. *Journal of Business Venturing* 5:29–36.

Stevenson, L.A. 1986. Against all odds: The entrepreneurship of women. *Journal of Small Business Management* 24(4):30–36.

Storey, D.J. 1985. The problems facing new firms. *Journal of Management Studies* 3:269–291.

The State of Small Business: A Report to the President. 1989. Washington, D.C.: Unites States Government Printing Office.

USA Today. 1989. SBA names head of women's program. September 22: 35.

Vozikis, G.S., and Glueck, W.F. 1980. Small business problems and stages of development. *Proceedings of the Academy of Management*, pp. 373–377.

Watkins, J.M, and Watkins, D.S., 1983. The female entrepreneur: Her background and determinants of business choice—some British data. In J.A. Hornaday, J.A. Timmons, and K.H. Vesper, (eds.), *Frontiers of Entrepreneurship Research*. Wellesley, MA: Babson College, pp. 271–288.

[9]

THE DEVELOPMENT AND INTERPRETATION OF ENTREPRENEURIAL TYPOLOGIES

CAROLYN Y. WOO
ARNOLD C. COOPER
Purdue University

WILLIAM C. DUNKELBERG
Temple University

EXECUTIVE SUMMARY

The impact of the entrepreneur on the development and subsequent success of a new venture has been demonstrated in many studies. Indeed one of the most important judgement calls of professionals assisting entrepreneurs is to evaluate their strengths, limitations, management practices, and likelihood of success. Research has responded to the need for such evaluation with different attempts to identify the relevant characteristics of the entrepreneur that may bear upon the management practices and subsequent success of new ventures.

One direction of this research has led to the identification of different types of entrepreneurs. Entrepreneurs within each typology share common traits but differ significantly from those of other types. Such attempts are useful in that they identify key differences within the larger population of entrepreneurs and do so in a way that yields holistic and meaningful portrayals. More importantly, classifications allow us to make better predictions, based on membership in a specific typology, about the likely behavior, responses, and success of the entrepreneur. These offer a powerful conceptual tool for the evaluation of entrepreneurs during the start-up or early stages of a venture before the track record of the individual involved can be established and observed.

Research studies over the last decade appear to converge on two types of entrepreneurs, craftsmen and opportunists. Craftsmen usually come from a blue collar background with limited education and managerial experience. They prefer technical work to administrative tasks and are generally motivated by needs for personal autonomy rather than the desire for organizational or financial success. In contrast, opportunists are characterized by broader experiences and higher levels of education. They are more likely to be motivated by financial gains and the opportunity for building a successful organization. These two types have been widely accepted and have been found to differ

Address correspondence to Dr. Carolyn Y. Woo, Associate Professor, Krannert Graduate School of Management, Purdue University, West Lafayette, IN 47907.

Earlier parts of this work were presented at the Babson Entrepreneurship Research Conference, 1988.

The authors would like to acknowledge the support provided by the National Federation of Independent Business and American Express Travel Related Services Company, Inc., and the assistance of Ms. Anne McCarthy in the data analysis of this project.

Journal of Business Venturing 6 0883-9026/91/$3.50

in regard to an array of characteristics and behavior. For example, the two types appear to engage in different levels of explicit planning and information gathering in preparation for the start-up of business. The ventures shared by the two types can also be contrasted along such dimensions as size, capital, the presence of partners, and relatedness to prior experience. The two types also manage differently as exhibited in the formality of administrative procedures, allocation of time to different functions, spans of control, and levels of authority. Some evidence suggests that the typology even appears to distinguish entrepreneurs in terms of attitudes toward risk, adaptiveness to change, and cognitive processing of opportunities. Most important, the classification seems to suggest that typologies differ in regard to growth potential and the likelihood that ventures will proceed to the next life cycle stage. The classification consisting of these two types of entrepreneurs represents a critical contribution to the extent that it possesses strong predictive power regarding a range of entrepreneurial behavior and performance.

This study focuses upon the conceptual frameworks used and specific methods applied in developing entrepreneurial typologies. It examines the extent to which different entrepreneurial typologies are consistent. It seeks to alert us to how the methods used in developing typologies affect the results. It suggests that typologies developed to date lack comparability and predictive power.

A close examination of previous studies disclosed major differences in the criteria used to classify entrepreneurs. Thus, craftsmen in one study might have been identified on the basis of two characteristics, whereas another study employed as many as 50 criteria. In some studies, all entrepreneurs are classified into typologies, whereas in others, many entrepreneurs are "in-betweens" and left unclassified. The same labels have often been applied to types derived through divergent methodologies, suggesting a degree of commonality that may be misleading. There is the appearance of a body of consistent and additive knowledge about craftsmen and opportunist entrepreneurs that does not rest upon a careful consideration of the methodologies employed.

Yet, how likely are we to obtain the same groupings of entrepreneurs from different classification schemes as implicitly assumed in the cross-references we have accepted?This study explicitly evaluated the impact of such differences by contrasting the groupings of entrepreneurs obtained through three different classifications. It is, we think, the first empirical examination of the extent to which traditionally defined entrepreneurial typologies are sensitive to the classification criteria used. Patterned after demonstrated practices in the literature, this study grouped entrepreneurs using: (1) goals; (2) goals and background (education and experience); and (3) goals, background, and management style. Within each classification, entrepreneurs were divided into two groups using cluster analysis. The results showed that different classification criteria did result in different groupings. In particular, classification based solely on goal orientation demonstrated the most pronounced differences from the results of the other classifications. Second, we found that none of the three pairs of groups patterned closely the craftsman/opportunist delineation as described in the literature.

The primary conclusion that different groupings result from different classification frameworks should not be surprising, at least from a methodological standpoint. Yet the problem has been totally overlooked in the analysis and interpretation of entrepreneurial types. Very likely, the same labels may have been applied to rather different entities. What then are the implications for the use of this typology as an evaluative tool? First, we note that the definitions of craftsman and opportunist have not been resolved and take on as many variations as the number of studies on the topic. Second, the findings of each study have not really been corroborated by findings in other analyses. As such, the level of generalizability and confidence attached to each must be checked. Third, the cumulative evidence in the body of literature on entrepreneurial typologies cannot be taken as additive knowledge about the wide range of characteristics associated with each type. Hence, the predictive power of the craftsman–opportunist typology cannot be taken for granted. Fourth, it remains to be demonstrated what percentage of the population of entrepreneurs can be represented by the two types. How universal are craftsman and opportunist entrepreneurs or can only some entrepreneurs be classified in this way? Do other types, though yet unidentified, exist? The above reservations lead us to conclude that while the craftsman–opportunist classification appears to serve as a useful yardstick for measuring the potential behavior and likely success of entrepreneurs, its applicability and scope may have been exaggerated to this point. This is not to say that typologies have little value, but rather to demonstrate the need for consistency and careful consideration of the definition of types before integrated and validated portrayals of entrepreneurs can be developed. Without these, the validity of our yardstick remains questionable.

INTRODUCTION

A central theme in entrepreneurial research focuses on the motivations and background characteristics of the entrepreneur. Historically, much of this research has examined how entrepreneurs[1] are similar to or different from the general population (see review by Vesper 1980). Much of the research has also centered upon how characteristics of entrepreneurs may contribute to success and eventual development of the new venture (Cooper et al. 1987; Van de Ven et al. 1984; Low and MacMillan 1988; Kimberley 1979; Mintzberg and Waters 1982). In recent years, increasing attention has been devoted to how groups of entrepreneurs differ from each other. Thus, there is explicit recognition that there is diversity among entrepreneurs and that understanding can be advanced through grouping them according to certain common characteristics (Smith 1967; Braden 1977; Filley and Aldag 1978; Dunkelberg and Cooper 1982; Smith and Miner 1983; Lorraine and Dussault 1987; Davidsson 1988; Lafuente and Salas 1989). The development of typologies represents a middle ground between treating each entrepreneur as unique and representing diverse populations through one set of averages.

This study focuses upon the development of entrepreneurial typologies. We suggest that the evolving stream of research on entrepreneurial typologies is proceeding forward without careful consideration and integration of its underlying premises. Thus, although terms such as "craftsman entrepreneur" or "opportunistic entrepreneur" are frequently encountered, there may be more consistency in the use of terms than in the underlying constructs.

These distinctions are not merely pedantic. If we are to improve our ability to advise entrepreneurs and to appraise their prospects, then we must determine what membership in particular typologies implies. If research on entrepreneurial studies is to make progress, then it is important that we build upon solid ground.

In this paper we first review classification theory and consider reasons for the utilization of typologies in many fields. We then examine the research done to date on entrepreneurial typologies. We note that, although entrepreneurial typologies may bear the same names, they often reflect major differences in the underlying constructs. The paper then tests explicitly, using a large data base, whether these distinctions in the way typologies are developed make a difference. Implications for researchers and for advisors to entrepreneurs are then developed.

CLASSIFICATION AND THEORY DEVELOPMENT

Classification or "systematics" is the science of developing typologies or arranging phenomena into categories (McKelvey 1982; Sneath and Sokal 1973). Typologies are derived either through empirical analysis or conceptual formulation. Typologies offer a way of organizing diversity, so that researchers can see patterns in complex phenomena. By isolating major

[1]Entrepreneurs are defined here as those who assume the risks of becoming owner-managers of firms, regardless of whether they then manage those businesses in innovative ways.

differences, typologies reduce the influences of confounding factors so that relationships can be more clearly detected. Relationships may be found for particular subgroups that do not apply to larger, pooled samples (Miller 1981; Hatten et al. 1978; Pinder and Moore 1979). Well-defined sub-groups enhance the chances for replicating results across studies through increasing the likelihood that samples can be drawn from intended sub-populations.

The process of classifying and labeling members of a population also shapes conceptual thinking in the following ways. Typology derivation begins with the selection of classification dimensions. This entails an explicit assessment of the theoretical and practical significance of the chosen dimensions. Typologies are often defined along multiple dimensions, leading to a more comprehensive or holistic understanding of the subject. Such "gestalts" capture interdependencies among attributes and presumably offer richer portrayals than a series of adhoc descriptions of single variables. Appropriately labeled, typologies facilitate easy recall and identification. Thus, a group of entrepreneurs labeled as "craftsman entrepreneurs" suggests a set of characteristics. Since properly derived typologies are intended to illuminate the essential differences or major sources of variance across subjects, the resulting types thus serve as explanatory or contingency variables in subsequent modeling efforts. As such, they emerge as pivotal concepts around which data interpretation can be undertaken.

Typologies have occupied a central role in the study of strategy (Hambrick 1984; Miller and Friesen 1977; Chrisman et al. 1988), organization (McKelvey 1975; Miller 1981; Pinto and Pinder 1972; Pugh et al. 1969; Gartner et al. 1989), and environment (Hambrick 1983; Dubini 1989; Lawrence and Lorsch 1967). In a review of taxonomies, McKelvey (1982) noted the contribution of classifications to the advancement of such disciplines as Physics, Chemistry, Mineralogy, Zoology, and Botany.

Against this theoretical backdrop, let us consider some of the specific typologies that have been developed and widely utilized in the field of entrepreneurship.

ENTREPRENEURIAL TYPOLOGIES

The study of entrepreneurs would seem to be a logical area of application for classification theory. Those who start businesses could be described by many attributes, including goals, background variables, and management methods. Since entrepreneurs can vary along these dimensions, it may be possible to cluster them into particular types, each consisting of entrepreneurs who have particular combinations of attributes in common. In the tradition of mid-range theory building, entrepreneurial types have been employed to explain a wide array of factors, which include performance of the entrepreneurial venture (Filley and Aldag 1980; Lafuente and Salas 1989), managerial practices (Lorraine and Dussault 1987), structure of the firm (Filley and Aldag 1978), degree of innovation (Davidsson 1988), venture start-up process (Dunkelberg and Cooper 1982), and even the entrepreneur's perception of opportunities (Davidsson 1988). As shown above, entrepreneurial typologies seem to play a central role in the developing literature on venture start-up, management, and subsequent performance.

Research on entrepreneurial typologies is relatively recent, starting with Smith's (1967) study of 52 organizational founders. In recent years, there has been a growing amount of work using the concept, with at least seven studies since 1977 (Braden 1977; Filley and Aldag 1978; Dunkelberg and Cooper 1982; Smith and Miner 1983; Lorraine and Dussault 1987; Davidsson 1988; Lafuente and Salas 1989). As will be noted later, most of the early studies formed typologies based upon a priori conceptual formulation. Some more recent studies have been based upon multi-attribute empirical analysis.

In the work done to date, two predominant entrepreneurial types have emerged, often termed "craftsmen" and "opportunists" (Smith 1967; Smith and Miner 1983; Lorraine and Dussault 1987; Davidsson 1988). The findings suggest that craftsmen usually come from blue-collar backgrounds with narrow educational and managerial experience. They preferred technical work to administrative tasks and generally had primary motivations of "making a comfortable living" (versus "making a lot of money"). They avoided risk-taking and were less likely to seek multiple investors or partners. Businesses led by such individuals were less adaptive to change and experienced lower growth.

By contrast, opportunists were characterized by broader experiences and higher levels of education. They demonstrated a proclivity for managerial challenges and were more oriented towards the future. They seemed more willing to change and exhibited greater confidence in their ability to respond to the environment. Their organizations grew rapidly while drawing on outside sources of funds and pursuing strategies that were diverse and innovative. These entrepreneurs were more likely to be motivated by financial gains and the opportunity for building a successful organization. Though labeled differently, Braden's (1977) "caretakers" and "managers" essentially parallel the craftsmen–opportunists classifications.

A number of other studies have resulted in more than two categories. Filley and Aldag (1978) factor-analyzed the attributes of entrepreneurs and their organizations along three latent dimensions. These dimensions were labeled "craft," "promotion," and "administrative." Managers and organizations with high "craft" scores resembled the craftsman type as defined in earlier studies. Those with high "promotion" scores were formed to exploit temporary opportunities. Growing rapidly, these organizations were loosely structured and were highly oriented towards change. Characterized by higher degrees of task differentiation and layers of hierarchy, organizations demonstrating high "administrative" scores consisted of larger, complex firms led by professional managers who adopted formal planning and control systems.

Respondents in the Dunkelberg and Cooper (1982) study were divided into "craftsmen," "growth-oriented" and "independent" entrepreneurs. The first two types resembled the craftsman–opportunist categories in other studies. "Independents" were mostly driven by a need for personal autonomy. Though the latter experienced the highest growth rate among the three groups, they had the least supervisor and work experience. They also had the highest percentage with graduate school education. In a classification of Spanish entrepreneurs, Lafuente and Salas (1989) identified four types: "craftsman"—motivated by the nature of the work; "family" entrepreneurs who placed a high priority on family welfare and meeting a challenge; "managerial" entrepreneurs who sought prestige and self-development; and "risk" entrepreneurs who demonstrated a strong preference for risk-taking. The first two groups resembled "craftsman" entrepreneurs in earlier studies, whereas the last two demonstrated similar characteristics as "opportunists."

In sum, the literature on entrepreneurial typologies provides consistent support for the two dominant types, craftsmen and opportunists. Other types may exist although the profiles generated thus far do not converge on a clearly defined third category. See "Appendix I" for a summary of these studies.

Despite apparent agreement across studies, we should note that the typologies reported to date reflect the idiosyncracies of particular studies. Differences can be found in the definitions of entrepreneurs, sample characteristics, methodologies, and variables employed. One difference, which may be of fundamental importance, relates to the variables used in the classification of entrepreneurs. None of the studies on entrepreneurial typologies has employed the same set of criteria. There are overlaps and similarities but not full agreement on this important choice. Furthermore, within the entrepreneurship literature, there has been almost no explicit examination of the implications of the choice of divergent classification variables, either for the forming of typologies or for the subsequent interpretation of differences across classifications. Thus, an increasing body of research has utilized entrepreneurial typologies without consideration of whether the methods used are substantially affecting the results.

CLASSIFICATION CRITERIA USED IN PRIOR STUDIES

Braden's (1977) classification of managers and caretakers was based on the entrepreneur's motivations for starting a company. Respondents chose one of four statements that best described their intentions. These were "to provide you with steady employment," "to let you do the kind of work you want to do," "to provide a moderate income for you and your family," and "to make you wealthy." (Braden 1977, p. 54)

Lafuente and Salas (1989) also focused solely on the motivations of entrepreneurs. In this study, entrepreneurs rated the importance of 12 objectives: opportunities to prove oneself; produce something that is perfect; build up something; pursue a challenge; have variety and adventure; allow for improvisation; help relatives; gain security; lead; work in a prestigious company; develop oneself; and have high earnings.

Goal statements similar to those of Braden (1977) were also used in the classification by Dunkelberg and Cooper (1982). In addition to these four goal variables, four additional classification variables tapped the degrees of growth and also of change in the business, the presence of formal controls, and how comfortable the entrepreneur felt with technical versus managerial problems. Lorraine and Dussault (1987), in contrast, employed only two attributes: former education and past experience.

Relative to the above, a second group of analyses incorporated a much larger set of criteria in their classifications. Smith (1967) as well as Smith and Miner (1983) incorporated breadth in education and experience, social orientation (reference group, degree of social involvement, and communication ability), management style, use of formal processes, functional strategies, and nature of competitive environment. Davidsson's (1988) test of Smith's typology examined 17 characteristics similar to those just mentioned. Types derived by Filley and Aldag (1978, 1980) were built on an even broader set of 45 to 55 characteristics. These included goals, presence of formal systems and procedures, managerial style, attitudes toward employees, and degree of anticipated change.

These studies examined above might be thought of as falling into two groups that represent fundamentally different approaches to classification (McKelvey 1982, pp. 15–17). The first group falls into the family of *special classifications*, which is based on a small number of attributes. This type of classification is useful in circumstances in which researchers are interested in the implications of specific factors. Examples would be primary motivations of the entrepreneur or amount of formal education. Thus, if entrepreneurs are classified according to primary motivation, then the research can examine how other variables, such as management style or performance, vary by these types.

The second group, known as *general classifications*, defines types on the basis of a comprehensive set of characteristics. Such classifications would be more suited to the derivation of generic types or representative profiles of the underlying population. General classifications provide the integrated or holistics portrayals we would think of in a gestalt.

These classifications incorporate interdependencies or interactions among all relevant attributes identified in the received theory of the field.

In the process of defining types, general classifications involve the assignment of non-zero weights to all potentially relevant dimensions. The contribution of each attribute to the classification is determined within the empirical analysis. On the other hand, special classifications assign non-zero weights only to a few dimensions. As such, special classifications "predetermine" the contributions of different attributes and "force" differentiation among population members to take place only along a highly restricted set of characteristics. For example, if entrepreneurs are classified according to prior education, then typologies will differ along this dimension. As such, special classifications carry a heavier burden of conceptualization and theoretical assessment of selected and omitted dimensions.

Two related outcomes should be noted. First, when a small number of criteria are used to define groups, within group variances of *these* classification dimensions tend to be low. For instance, if entrepreneurs are classified according to primary motivation, then the entrepreneurs within each group would show little variance along this dimension. In the extreme but not infrequent case, when each value of a categorical variable gives rise to a group (such as having supervisory experience or not), within-group variances of that variable would be zero. As more variables are introduced, tight within-group variances along the classification criteria are harder to achieve. Measured on a multivariate basis, similarity among members of the same group can be higher on some attributes and lower on others. Members are not likely to exhibit identical values on all dimensions. Thus, if entrepreneurs are classified according to several measures, such as primary motivation, education, and management style, they would demonstrate some variance along each of these dimensions within each group. As such, special classifications produce groups with a much higher degree of homogeneity along the classification criteria than general classifications.

Second, we note that in either type of classification, omitted variables are allowed to vary within each group and to do so in both positive and negative directions. Thus, in special classifications, these attributes not used in the classification procedure are allowed to take on diverse values within each group. General classifications, in contrast, seek homogeneity among a large set of classification variables. The tradeoff between the two types of classifications is that tight within-group variances will be achieved on a small number of variables in special classifications, whereas a lesser degree of homogeneity will be obtained with a larger set of variables in general classifications.

Without dispute, each type of classification serves a legitimate purpose. A problem arises, however, when we fail to note the distinction between groups formed using these different approaches. Extant practices associated with the formulation and interpretation of entrepreneurial typologies present such a danger. While both special and general classifications have been used, authors have not explicitly recognized these differences and the implications of utilizing these different approaches. Types obtained in different analyses were often given the common set of "opportunist–craftsman" labels. No recognition was explicitly directed at the conceptual implications of variables omitted from special classifications but incorporated in general classifications.

The magnitude of problems created by such divergent definitions is unclear. Logically, one would expect the problem to be less serious when high correlations exist among all relevant descriptors of entrepreneurs. For instance, if virtually all entrepreneurs classified as craftsmen because of their motivation also tended to have relatively low levels of education, then entrepreneurs would be grouped in about the same way, regardless of which variable was used for classification purposes. If researchers feel intuitively that certain variables tend always to correlate together, they may conclude that the choice of classification variables does not make a material difference. However, entrepreneurship is a young field of study and correlations among all potentially relevant attributes have not been examined extensively. Moreover, we have no means of prescribing "problematically low" levels of correlations nor of predicting their consequences. Considering the evolving role occupied by typologies in the conceptual development of the field of entrepreneurship, it would be helpful to evaluate these differences in an explicit and systematic manner. This study provides such an assessment.

RESEARCH DESIGN

Research Question

In the current study, evaluation of divergent entrepreneurial classification approaches revolves around the central question: How would the use of different sets of classification variables (variables already used in the extant literature) affect the groupings of entrepreneurs? If the grouping of entrepreneurs is robust and not sensitive to the choice of classification variables, then we need not be concerned about the considerable differences in approaches used in prior research. However, if the classification procedures are not robust, then statistical differences across types would vary depending upon what variables are used for classification purposes. The following empirical analysis (which we think is the first of its kind) will examine the statistical behavior of entrepreneurial groups derived under different classifications. These tests will enable us to assess the degree of comparability between different classification attempts and the extent to which findings on the "same" entrepreneurial type can be integrated across studies.

Sample and Variable Definition

This research is based on what we believe to be the largest and most representative samples of small businesses studied to date. A survey focusing on new businesses was administered in May 1985 to members of the National Federation of Independent Businesses who reported that they had recently become owners. Of the 4,814 entrepreneurs who responded, 2,994 had become owners no earlier than 1984, that is during the preceding 17 months. These entrepreneurs, who might be considered as new business owners, had, on the average, been in business for 11 months at the time of the first questionnaire. The sample included a cross-section of industries, geographic areas, and types of businesses. The initial questionnaires solicited information on the entrepreneur's background, motivations, prior training, nature of business, start-up process, and the nature of their environment. A follow-up questionnaire was mailed to the entrepreneurs one year later, in 1986. A total of 1,190 responded, reporting subsequent developments and management practices, including one dimension that may be particularly relevant to the development of entrepreneurial typologies, i.e., how they allocated their time. All of their businesses had achieved a degree of success, in the sense that they survived to the time of the second questionnaire, when the average business was 23 months old.

From the above sample, only businesses from the retail and personal services sectors will be examined. This decision follows established precedence whereby authors either examined one sector (Lorraine and Dussault 1987) or ran separate analyses for such groups as retail and manufacturing firms. Prior analysis of the data in this sample showed clear differences across industries in such important characteristics as start-up size and entrepreneurial background, suggesting that it would be unwise to pool across industries. Retail and personal services are similar, in that both involve selling to consumers, both involve serving local or regional markets, and both involve lower barriers to entry (in terms of capital requirements or professional training) than many of the other industry categories. Statistical tests indicated that these two sectors had similar start-up size and demonstrated similar management practices in terms of time allocated to managing employees, record keeping, maintenance, cash management, and planning for future growth. The pooling of personal services and retail firms was also undertaken in an earlier study by Vozikis and Glueck (1980). The focus is thus upon retail and personal services firms, which made up about 65% of the initial sample. After case-wise deletion of missing values across 2 years of responses, the sample consisted of 510 entrepreneurs, all of whom had responded to both the first- and second-year questionnaires.

In selecting the variables for this analysis, we note that the primary purpose of this research is not to develop new variables by which entrepreneurs might be classified. Rather, it is to determine whether the choice of classification variables makes a difference. Therefore, to the extent possible, we adhered closely to the precedents set by the prior literature in the choice of variables and the questions employed in operationalizing these concepts. The literature review and "Appendix I" showed that criteria used to date in classifying entrepreneurs can be grouped into three categories: (1) goals; (2) background in terms of education and managerial experience; and (3) management style. These will be incorporated in this study. The specific variables, their corresponding measures, and prior literature sources are described below and summarized in Table 1.

Goals at the time of starting the business were based upon the relative rankings of the following four motivations: (1) to let you do the kind of work you wanted to do; (2) to avoid having to work for others; (3) to make more money than you would have otherwise; and (4) to build a successful organization.[2] Education and experience reflected the highest level of formal education and the highest level of supervisory responsibility attained by the entrepreneur.[3] Management style was based in part upon the extent of agreement of the following statements: (1) "In my business, operating controls and methods are in writing," and (2) "I am most comfortable in selling or handling technical problems rather than working on management issues."[4] In addition, management style was based upon responses to the question of how the entrepreneur allocated his or her time.[5]

As we consider the effect of moving from special classifications to more general ones, three classifications (A, B, C) will be performed employing a hierarchical structure of classification dimensions as shown in the following:

	Classification dimensions
Classification A:	Goals
Classification B:	Goals, background (education/experience)
Classification C:	Goals, background (education/experience), management style

[2]These questions are based primarily upon the work of Braden (1977) and Dunkelberg and Cooper (1982).

[3]These questions parallel the work by Smith (1967), Smith and Miner (1983), and Lorraine and Dussault (1987).

[4]These questions are based on those utilized by Filley and Aldag (1978).

[5]Management time was not used as a classification variable in any of the referenced studies. However, it seems to relate closely to some of the variables used by Smith (1967) and Filley and Aldag (1978).

TABLE 1 Variables Definition

Goals[1]

When you went into your business, what were your most important goals? (Indicate with a "1" the most important goal, a "2" the next most important goal, a "3" the third most important goal, and a "4" the fourth most important.)

Do work:	To let you do the kind of work you wanted to do
Avoid:	To avoid having to work for others
Makemon:	To make more money than you would have otherwise
Sucorg:	To build a successful organization

Education[2]

Level of formal education

E1 = 1 if high school or less, otherwise 0

E2 = 2 if enrolled in graduate education, otherwise 0

Experience[3]

S = 1 if supervisory experience, otherwise 0

Own = 1 if managed or owned a prior business, otherwise 0

For each statement, write the number that indicates the extent to which you agree or disagree with each statement:

(1) Agree strongly (2) Agree somewhat (3) Neither agree or disagree (4) Disagree somewhat (5) Disagree strongly

Management Style

Opcontrol:[4] In my business, operating controls and methods are in writing

Techprob: I am most comfortable in selling or handling technical problems rather than working on management issues

Approximately how much of your time is allocated to the following activities: (Please put the approximate percentage of your time spent in these areas over the course of the last 12 months.)

TA1[5]—% Dealing with employees

TA2 —% Record-keeping (financial, government forms, etc.)

TA3 —% Direct selling or customer contact

TA4 —% Actual production or provision of services

TA5 —% Maintenance, upkeep, cleaning of physical plant

TA6 —% Purchasing or dealing with suppliers

TA7 —% Cash management and arranging financing

TA8 —% Planning firm growth/change

TA9 —% Other

[1]Based in modified form upon questions used by Braden (1977) Dunkelberg and Cooper (1982), Filley and Aldag (1978, 1980).

[2]Based on education variables employed by Smith (1967), Smith and Miner (1983), and Davidsson (1988).

[3]Variables measuring prior experience are based on those used by Smith (1967), Smith and Miner (1983), and Davidsson (1987).

[4]Questions upon operating controls and technical problems were based upon the work of Filley and Aldag (1978, 1980) and Dunkelberg and Cooper (1982). Variables pertaining to emphases given to different functional areas were based on survey used by Lorraine and Dussault (1987).

[5]Time allocation priorities were examined in studies by Farmer (1978) and Van de Ven et al. (1984).

These three schemes progress from a narrow set (special classification) to a broad scheme with all three classes of characteristics included (general classification). This structure parallels what we observe in the literature, which yields types defined only on the basis of the entrepreneur's start-up intentions in some studies (Braden 1977; Lafuente and Salas 1988) to types that are formed from diverse characteristics in others (Smith and Miner 1983; Filley and Aldag 1978). Excluded in this analysis are measures of the entrepreneur's social orientation, communication ability, or propensity toward risk-taking. Though these have been used in some prior studies, they were not as frequently employed and have not represented critical points of departure in the definition of typologies. As such, we will examine the impact upon classifications of the three major groups of variables to maintain some degree of focus and keep the task of interpretation at a manageable level of complexity.

Methodology

In the development of each of the classifications, cluster analyses were performed to derive types. Three sets of dimensions as depicted previously in Classifications A, B, and C were used. The analysis employed the Ward method, a common hierarchical clustering algorithm. (Anderberg 1973; Lorr 1983) The Ward method merges two clusters, which results in the smallest increase in the overall sum of squared within-cluster distances. The sum comprises all distances from each case in the cluster to the centroid of the cluster. The implied distance measure employed by this method is the squared Euclidean distance. Variables were first standardized to eliminate the differences in scales of measurement.

Determination of the appropriate number of groups or types is a key but arbitrary decision in cluster analysis. Guidance is provided by the increase in within-cluster distances as groups are merged. Relatively large increases signify the merging of less similar clusters. Despite such indications, the decision is largely subjective in nature (Arnold 1979; Harrigan 1985). No parametric statistics are available to indicate the degree of "significant" increase. Moreover, all increases tend to be quite large when a small number of clusters remains in the final stages of the analyses. This decision must then be made with strong prior theoretical assessment. In this analysis, we select the two-cluster solution as the basis of comparison across the three classification schemes. This choice explicitly builds on the extant literature, which has converged on two major types of entrepreneurs: craftsmen and opportunists. If the population can indeed be classified into these two generic types, then a two-cluster solution should generate groups that mirror the characteristics of each of these types.

Two-cluster solutions were obtained for the three separate classifications, moving from the most "specific" classification scheme (A—based upon goals only) to the most "general" basis of classification (C—based upon multiple criteria). For each pair of clusters obtained under each classification (A, B, and C), cluster means were computed for all variables; *t*-tests were used to compare the variable means between each pair of clusters under each of three classifications (Table 2). Group memberships resulting from the three different classifications are also cross-tabulated in Table 3.

RESULTS

Refer to Table 2 for results on the three classifications.

Classification A: Classification Based on Goals

Under Classification A, the two groups (designated here as Groups 1 and 2) differed in a statistically significant manner along the goal variables, which was the only set of criteria used. All four goal variables were significant at the $\alpha = 0.01$ level. This is not surprising since these variables were used as the basis for classification. The two groups did not differ along any of the education/experience variables. Of the 11 management-type descriptors, only three were significant. Based on the goal characterisitics, Group 1 can be thought of

TABLE 2 The Impact of Classification Criteria on Cluster Characteristics

	(A) Classification by goals		(B) Classification by goals, education/experience		(C) Classification by goals, education/experience, management style	
Variables	"Independents" (Group 1, n = 226)	"Organization builder" (Group 2, n = 284)	"Craftsman" (Group 3, n = 419)	"Administrative" (Group 4, n = 91)	"Craftsman" (Group 5, n = 467)	"Administrative" (Group 6, n = 43)
Goals						
DOWORK	2.77	2.22^{+++}	2.50	2.31	2.47	2.40
AVOID	1.58	3.60^{+++}	2.71	2.68	2.71	2.63
MAKEMON	2.88	2.40^{+++}	2.57	2.83^{++}	2.60	2.74
SUCORG	2.86	1.94^{+++}	2.34	2.31	2.34	2.35
Background						
E1	0.42	0.39	0.46	0.14^{+++}	0.44	0.000^{+++}
E2	0.10	0.08	0.000	0.48^{+++}	0.004	0.98^{+++}
S	0.12	0.11	0.000	0.64^{+++}	0.100	0.28^{++}
OWN	0.23	0.28	0.29	0.09^{+++}	0.27	0.16^{+}
Management Style						
OPCONTRL	2.93	2.73^{++}	2.82	2.80	2.81	2.88
TECHPROB	2.84	2.85	2.75	3.24^{+++}	2.81	3.17^{++}
TA1	9.45	10.80	9.87	11.70	9.88	13.67^{+}
TA2	11.74	12.90	12.23	13.11	12.33	12.99
TA3	30.99	29.85	30.79	28.36	30.39	29.98
TA4	19.46	14.30^{+++}	17.05	14.45	16.92	12.96
TA5	6.83	6.80	6.72	7.23	6.82	6.76
TA6	9.23	10.24	9.93	9.14	9.85	9.21
TA7	5.75	7.88^{+++}	6.94	6.89	6.89	7.37
TA8	5.87	6.70	5.98	7.92^{+}	6.32	6.44
TA9	0.69	0.54	0.48	1.20	0.61	0.63

$^{+}$Significant at α = 0.10.
$^{++}$Significant at α = 0.05.
$^{+++}$Significant at α = 0.01.

TABLE 3 Cross-Tabulation of Group Memberships by Classification

		Classification B		Classification C	
		3 (*n* = 419)	4 (*n* = 91)	5 (*n* = 467)	6 (n = 43)
Classification A	1 (n = 226)	183 (81%)[a]	43 (19%)[a]	203 (90%)	23 (10%)
	2 (n = 284)	236 (83%)	48 (17%)	264 (93%)	20 (7%)
Classification B	3 (n = 419)			419 (100%)	0 (0%)
	4 (n = 91)			48 (53%)	43 (47%)

[a]Of the 226 entrepreneurs originally in Group 1, 81% were then classified into group 3, and 19% in Group 4.

as "independents" who placed a high priority on not having to work for others. In contrast, the second group was motivated by the chance to build a successful organization. These "organization builders" were more likely to adopt formal controls and documentation (opcontrl), to spend less time on direct provision of services (TA4), and to devote more time to cash and financial management (TA7).

Classification B: Classification Based on Goals and Background

When background variables depicting education and management experience were added in this classification, the entrepreneurs were reclassified into two new groups (designated here as Groups 3 and 4). Statistical differences between types did not resemble results obtained under Classification A. All four background indicators now yielded significant differences between the two types. Only one goal variable was significant (makemon). In addition, two management variables were also statistically different between the two groups.

The two groups in Classification B can best be distinguished by education level and prior management experience. None of the Group 3 members reported any form of graduate education or prior supervisory experience. Group 4 members, on the other hand, tended to have reached a higher level of achievement on both counts. Group 3 members, however, were more likely to have owned a prior business. They expressed a stronger preference for technical problem-solving over administrative work (techprob) and spent less time on planning for growth (TA8). The label "craftsman" is given to Group 3 as we consider the education and style characteristics of these entrepreneurs. Note however that Group 3 members did not show particularly high preferences for craftsman-related goals such as autonomy or doing the type of work they like to do. (This point will be discussed later.) Group 4 members resembled the "administrative" type derived by Filley and Aldag (1978). Thus Group 4 is labeled "administrative."

Classification C: Classification Based on Goals, Background, and Management Style

Classification C, involving multiple criteria, resulted in Groups 5 and 6. Group differences changed only moderately as we moved from Classification B to C. All the background variables remained significant. Directions on these differences were also consistent with the prior classification. The two groups still differed in the likelihood of having had graduate training, management experience, and prior ownership of another business. The group with lower education and management background was again characterized by a stronger inclination towards technical problems (techprob). They also spent less time dealing with employees (TA1). Time spent on planning (TA8) was no longer significant. Groups 5 and 6 were given the same respective labels as Groups 3 and 4.

Cross-Tabulation of Group Memberships

In developing typologies, an important question is the extent to which individuals exhibit stable membership across different classifications. We thus examine the membership of individual entrepreneurs within each typology and note how that changes as we move from special to general classifications. If the overlap between classifications is strong, then we should observe a one-on-one mapping, i.e., entrepreneurs who cluster together under classification A would also cluster together under classification B. To illustrate, the majority of Group 1 entrepreneurs (from Classification A) should map onto either Group 3 or Group 4 (from Classification B) but they should not be divided across both. Group 2 should then map onto the remaining group. Similar comparisons would be made between Classifications A and C, and B and C.

Table 3 shows that Classification A failed to show the type of one-on-one mapping described earlier with Classifications B and C. Group 3 from Classification B became the "home" of Groups 1 and 2 (81% and 83%). Similarly, Group 5 from Classification C contained 90% and 93% of Groups 1 and 2 members. (Note that Groups 3 and 5 are both very large, reflecting the fact that most of the entrepreneurs had no graduate education.) Entrepreneurs originally classified into Groups 1 or 2 of Classification A thus showed little tendency to cluster together in the groups formed under Classifications B or C. Classifications B and C showed a high degree of overlap, with 100% of Group 3 members appearing in Group 5. However, Group 4 was almost equally divided between Group 5 (53%) and Group 6 (47%).

DISCUSSION

The analysis showed that different classification criteria produced different groupings of entrepreneurs. Although this may not be surprising from a methodological standpoint, it does raise a number of basic questions about the universality and validity of entrepreneurial types as they have been formulated in the extant literature. The concerns do not pertain to each previous study taken singularly. Rather, they challenge the strong degree of perceived agreement across entrepreneurial classifications. This, in turn, has implications for interpretation of prior research.

First, the results in Table 2 demonstrate that group differences obtained in special classifications did not retain their statistical significance when the number of criteria was expanded. Hence, the derivation of entrepreneurial types does not appear to be robust with respect to the choice of typing criteria. The differences were particularly pronounced when the goal variables were supplemented by background indicators. The addition of management style variables to background indicators did not result in as large a difference. The results in Table 3 show that individual entrepreneurs often shift group membership as classification variables are added.

Note that differences observed in the current analysis would likely be amplified across studies. Our research design retained the same sample, survey instrument, variable definitions, and methodology across classifications. The only variation was in the choice of clustering criteria. The latter were introduced in a hierarchical manner where A was a subset of B, and B a subset of C. Across other studies, differences would exist in sample selection, survey design, data collection, variable operationalization, and methodology. Typing criteria would not be monotonically nested as in the three classifications in this study. These factors strongly raise doubt as to the likelihood of obtaining similar types across studies. Very likely, similar labels may have been attached to divergent entities.

The analysis also yielded an unexpected outcome that pertains to the craftsman–opportunist distinction. Across the three classifications, we did not obtain the clear-cut tradeoffs in goals, which characterize opportunists and craftsmen. As described in the literature, opportunists are motivated by financial success and the chance to build a successful enterprise. Craftsmen, in direct contrast, pursue independence and the chance to work in a problem area of personal interest. If this characterization is correct, we should see one group placing high rankings on success, both financial and organizational, and low rankings on autonomy and doing what they want to do. The reverse would be true for the other group.

This tradeoff should be most observable in Classification A, where goals were the only classification variables. Yet, even in this context, we failed to obtain such a differentiation. (Note that individual respondents were asked to rank the relative importance of the goals, so that they could not place equal importance on more than one goal.) Even so, the average rankings in Group 1 were about the same for three of the four goals: "doing the type of work you wanted," "making more money," and "building a successful organization." In Group 2, the most emphasized goals were those for "doing the type of work you wanted" and "building a successful organization." Neither group showed the clear-cut trade-offs in goals that one might have expected. This pattern was repeated under Classification B and C. Hence, it appeared that financial and personal motivations were *simultaneous* rather than *mutually exclusive* driving forces.

The question raised here is not one of the existence of craftsmen and opportunists types as depicted in the received theory of the field. Rather, we query how representative these may be in describing the population of entrepreneurs. Do these types capture the majority or only a small fraction of entrepreneurs? Are these the only two clusters or two among many clusters? Do these represent perhaps the extremes or the most archtypical groups of entrepreneurs?

Prior studies provide some clues to these questions. A number of authors selected solutions that led to more than two clusters: Filley and Aldag (1978), Dunkelberg and Cooper (1982), and Lafuente and Salas (1989). While only the last of these employed cluster analysis, all three studies demonstrated the same point—that two groups might not be sufficient for describing their samples. Even though Davidsson (1988) supported Smith's two types of entrepreneurs, the author specifically pointed out that a three-group solution would be better. Certain studies assigned points or factor scores to entrepreneurs and classified into groups those that were at the high or low ends of the distributions (Smith 1967; Filley and Aldag 1978). Those in the middle were not labeled or included in further analysis. In these cases, only a portion of the businesses were classified into the two groups. This study showed that, when a two-cluster solution was used to group all entrepreneurs, the resulting profiles of the two groups did not match well with the two generic types (craftsmen and opportunist) described in the literature.

It is clear that there is a great deal of diversity among entrepreneurs. Goals, background variables, and management styles do not cluster as tightly or as consistently as we might have expected. This means that typologies are sensitive to the classification criteria chosen and that the often-used craftsman–opportunist typology may only have limited applicability. There are a number of implications for researchers:

1. Unless care has been used in the choice of classification variables, it may be that hypotheses are being generated from one set of typologies and then tested with data from other typologies that differ in important ways. (Even though the same titles may be used, the typologies may differ because of the classification variables chosen.)
2. Our ability to replicate other researchers' findings may be hampered. This in turn hinders the accumulation and cross-validation of a critical mass of knowledge.
3. Findings may be generalized in inappropriate ways. For example goal differences found in special classifications and in smaller samples have been extended to the population at large and presumed to represent critical universal tradeoffs.
4. As these generalizations become widely accepted, they shape the conceptual frameworks that guide the process of hypothesis development and data collection. To the extent that we do not anticipate any additional categories, survey instruments would not systematically allow for the identification of other types, and model specifications would not unveil the true effects of types.

Noting these concerns, our recommendations to researchers suggest the following:

1. Research focused on the derivation of typologies must offer a strong theoretical framework for the choice of selected as well as omitted entrepreneurial characteristics. If classification of entrepreneurs had been found to be robust, then choices of criteria would not have a pronounced effect on the relationships being examined. A broader range would have been available for experimentation and idiosyncratic preferences. However, it is clear that typologies are very sensitive to the classification criteria chosen. Given the inconsistencies underlying the derivation of types and the absence of strong theoretical priors, we may first have to examine the impact of specific entrepreneurial characteristics on performance, the degrees of variation within the population of entrepreneurs, and the conceptual implications for classification. This procedure lays the foundation for the construction of typologies that may be similar to or different from those developed to this point. In addition to explicit selection of criteria, the number of groups selected as a solution and the observations dropped from classifications should be clearly reported and appraised.
2. With respect to the choice of group structure, researchers would naturally seek to apply constructs used in the past. However, we should recognize the limitations of the widely accepted and seemingly safe two-group solution. Stronger consideration should be given to alternative structures or additional categories even though these have not been clearly identified or consistently supported in the past. Researchers must highlight the decision rules they employ, the percentage of their samples *not* classified, and the nature of these "middle of the road" entrepreneurs.
3. For those who employ the entrepreneurial type as a predictor of strategy and performance in young firms, one must pay close attention to the differences across prior studies and how these may bear on the development of hypotheses. The positive correlations among type, strategy, and performance reported in the past do not necessarily reveal the same relationships. Thus, statements about typology–performance linkages may reflect the relationships between goals and performance, background and performance, or management style and performance.

What are the implications for practice? Entrepreneurial typologies have seemed to be a useful way of thinking about entrepreneurs. Thus, entrepreneurs who engage in self-assessment and those who provide resources and advice to other entrepreneurs need to have ways of anticipating problems and predicting performance. It would be convenient to think of entrepreneurs being classified into two primary types with a predictable set of experiences, problems, strengths, and probabilities of success. An increasing body of literature has certainly encouraged the adoption of such generic profiles. The potential of the existing craftsman–opportunist framework appeared very strong in that it seemed to shed light on a wide range of behavior. However, the work presented here suggests that the world may be more complicated. While the craftsman–opportunist classification appears to serve as a useful dimension, its applicability and predictive capability may have been exaggerated to this point. Thus, in the future, we may be able to develop useful typologies that enable us to see patterns, to anticipate problems, and to predict performance. However, at our present stage of understanding it is better to recognize that there is great diversity, and that only some entrepreneurs fit the idealized "craftsman" and "opportunist" classifications.

LIMITATIONS

This study is limited in execution and focus. While the sample is one of the largest to date, it includes only owner-managers of new firms. In terms of methodology, this study employed only the Ward method of clustering. While Ward is a frequently used method, it would be helpful to examine the impact of classification criteria across other hierarchical and non-hierarchical clustering algorithms. Similarly, the distance measure could be expanded from the squared Euclidean distance to other indicators. The clustering solution chosen was the two-group structure and did not examine the impact of divergent classification criteria in cluster solutions with more than two groups.

In terms of focus, this study examined only one dimension of the classification problem. Other factors also contribute to the validity of typologies. One issue is the temporal stability of types. Do group members retain the same characteristics over time? If they do change, do group members evolve in the same direction? To what degree is that direction predictable from current group membership?

While this study focuses on the influence of divergent classification criteria, it did not provide an appraisal of the appropriateness and relative importance of different criteria. Should goals, background characteristics, and management practices be used in the first place? Another key question pertains to the degree of homogeneity within type. For typologies to be useful, members within one group must demonstrate greater homogeneity with each other than with members in other groups. Yet within each group, members are not completely identical. To what degree can members vary and still be classified as one group? Hence, even though we demonstrated the outcomes of different classification criteria, we have only addressed one part of a much bigger challenge.

SUMMARY

We note that entrepreneurship is a young field of study. As such, the common language that gives rise to pattern recognition, theory building, and hypothesis testing is still developing. Typology constitutes part of this language. In this respect, this study suggests that extreme caution must be exercised as we interpret previous findings on entrepreneurial types. Though significant agreement appears to link different studies, divergencies may be hiding underneath similar labels. Moreover, direct comparisons are often not possible given the different methodologies and instruments employed across studies. Craftsmen–opportunist classifications may be highly convenient ways of anchoring our classifications and descriptions of entrepreneurs, yet the polarity inherent in such a distinction was not supported on a large sample. This analysis does not call into question prior studies on an individual basis. Rather, it challenges the conclusion that, in aggregate, we have succeeded in classifying the population of entrepreneurs into two robust categories with, by and large, consistent differences across categories. Given the central role of classification in the theoretical development of entrepreneurial behavior and performance, it is important that close examination be given to this critical subject.

REFERENCES

Anderberg, M.R. 1973. *Cluster Analysis for Applications*. New York: Academic Press.

Arnold, S.T. November 1979. A test for clusters. *Journal of Marketing Research* pp. 454–551.

Braden, P.L. 1977. *Technological Entrepreneurship*. University of Michigan.

Chrisman, J.J., Hofer, C.W. and Boulton, W.R. July 1988. Toward a system for classifying business strategies. *Academy of Management Review* pp. 413–428.

Cooper, A.C., Dunkelberg, W.C. and Woo, C. 1987. Patterns of survival, growth and change—A large-scale longitudinal study. In R..G. Wyckham, L.N. Meredith, and G.R. Busha, eds, *The Spirit of Entrepreneurship*, 32nd Annual World Conference, International Council for Small Business. Simon Fraser University, pp. 140–155.

Davidsson, P. 1988. Type of man and type of company revisited: A confirmatory cluster analysis approach. In B.A. Kirchoff, W.A. Long, W.E. McMullan, K. Vesper, and W. Wetzel, Jr., eds, *Frontiers of Entrepreneurship Research*. Wellesley, MA: Babson College, pp. 88–105.

Dubini, P. 1989. The influence of motivations and environment on business start-ups: Some hints for public policies. *Journal of Business Venturing* 4(1):11–26.

Dunkelberg, W.C., and Cooper, A.C. 1982. Entrepreneurial typologies: An empirical study. In K.H. Vesper, ed, *Frontiers of Entrepreneurship Research*. Wellesley, MA: Babson College, pp. 1–15.

Farmer, P. 1978. *Managerial Work and the Growth and Development of the Firm*, Ph.D. diss. Purdue University.

Filley, A.C., and Aldag, R.J. 1978. Characteristics and measurement of an organization typology. *Academy of Management Journal* pp. 578–591.

Filley, A.C., and Aldag, R.J. 1980. Organizational growth and types: Lessons from small institutions. In B.M. Shaw, L.L. Cummins, eds, *Research in Organizational Behavior* JAI Press, pp. 279–320.

Gartner, W.B., Mitchell, T.R., and Vesper, K.H. 1989. A taxonomy of new business ventures. *Journal of Business Venturing* 4(3):169–186.

Hambrick, D.C. 1983. An empirical typology of mature industrial-product environments. *Academy of Management Journal* pp. 213–230.

Hambrick, D.C. 1984. Taxonomic approaches to studying strategy: Some conceptual and methodological issues. *Journal of Management* 10(1):27–41.

Harrigan, K.R. 1985. An application of clustering for strategic group analysis. *Strategic Management Journal* 6:55–73.

Hatten, K., Schendel, D., and Cooper, A. 1978. A strategic model of the U.S. brewing industry: 1952–1971. *Academy of Management Journal* 21(4):592–610.

Kimberly, J. 1979. Issues in the creation of organizations: Initiation, innovation and institutionalization. *Academy of Management Journal* 22(3):437–457.

Lafuente, A., and V. Salas, 1989. Types of entrepreneurs and firms: The case of new Spanish firms. *Strategic Management Journal* 10:17–30.

Lawrence, P.R., and Lorsch, J.W. 1967. *Organization and Environment*. Boston: Harvard University Press.

Lorr, M. 1983. *Cluster Analysis for Social Scientists*. San Francisco: Jossey-Bass.

Lorraine, J., and Dussault, L. 1987. Management behaviors and types of entrepreneurs: The case of manufacturing businesses in the survival and establishment stage. In R.G. Wyckham, L.N. Meredith, G.R. Bushe, eds, *Proceedings of the 32nd World Conference, International Council for Small Business*. Simon Fraser University, pp. 77–94.

Low, M., and MacMillan, I. 1988. Entrepreneurship: Past research and future challenges. *Journal of Management* 14(2):139–161.

McKelvey, B. December 1985. Guidelines for the empirical classification of organizations. *Administrative Science Quarterly* 20:509–525.

McKelvey, B. 1982 *Organizational Systematics*. University of California Press.

Miller, D. 1981. Toward a new contingency approach: The search for organizational gestalts. *Journal of Management Studies* pp. 1–26.

Miller, D., and Friesen, P.H. 1977. Strategy-making in context: Ten empirical archetypes. *Journal of Management Studies* pp. 253–280.

Mintzberg, H., and Waters, J. 1982. Tracking strategy in an entrepreneurial firm. *Academy of Management Journal* 25(3):465–499.

Pinder, C., and Moore, L. 1979. The resurrection of taxonomy to aid the development of middle range theories of organizational behavior. *Administrative Science Quarterly* 24(1):99–118.

Pinto, P.R., and Pinder, C.C. 1972. A cluster analytic approach to the study of organizations. *Organizational Behavior and Human Performance* 8:508–522.

Pugh, D.S., Hickson, D.J., and Hinnings, C.R. 1969. An empirical taxonomy of structures of work organizations. *Administrative Science Quarterly* 14:115–126.

Smith, N.R. 1967. *The Entrepreneur and His Firm: The Relationship Between Type of Man and Type of Company*. Michigan State University.

Smith, N.R., and Miner, J.R. 1983. Type of entrepreneur, type of firm, and managerial motivation: Implications for organizational life cycle theory. *Strategic Management Journal* pp. 325–340.

Sneath, P.H.A., and Sokal, R.R. 1973. *Numerical Taxonomy*. San Francisco: Freeman.

Van de Ven, A.R., Hudson, and Schroeder, D. 1984. Designing new business startups: Entrepreneurial, organizational and ecological considerations. *Journal of Management* pp. 87–107.

Vesper, K.H. 1980. *New Venture Strategies* (revised ed.). Englewood Cliffs, NJ.

Vozikis, G. and Glueck, W. 1980. Small business problems and stages of development. *Academy of Management Proceedings* pp. 373–377.

NOVICE, PORTFOLIO, AND SERIAL FOUNDERS: ARE THEY DIFFERENT?

PAUL WESTHEAD
Warwick Business School

MIKE WRIGHT
University of Nottingham

EXECUTIVE SUMMARY

There is growing interest in entrepreneurs who have been involved in more than one venture, yet to date there has been relatively little theoretical development and systematic empirical examination of the topic. In particular, there has been little attention to the potential heterogeneity of habitual entrepreneurship. This study aims to contribute to this emerging area in two ways. First, it outlines a conceptual typology of habitual entrepreneurs who have founded, purchased, or inherited businesses. Second, the empirical part of the study focuses on owner-managers, providing an exploratory analysis of the characteristics and effects of independent business ownership by novice, portfolio, and serial founders. Novice founders are those that have no prior entrepreneurial experience as either a founder, an inheritor, or a purchaser of a business. Portfolio founders retain their original business and inherit, establish, and/or purchase another business. Serial founders are those who sell their original business but at a later date inherit, establish, and/or purchase another business.

The study derives propositions suggesting differences among the three types of founders. At the individual founder level of analysis, similarities as well as differences in the personal background, work experiences, reasons leading to the start-up of businesses, and personal attitudes to entrepreneurship of these three types of entrepreneurs are explored. At the organizational level of analysis, finance, employment and performance differences among the businesses owned by the three types of entrepreneurs are presented.

The issues are examined using a sample of entrepreneurs who were the principal owner-managers of independent businesses in Great Britain. The sample included 389 novice founders (62.6%), 75 portfolio founders (12.1%), and 157 serial founders (25.3%). No statistically significant differences were found among the three groups of entrepreneurs with regard to the main industrial activity, geographical location,

Address correspondence to: Paul Westhead, Department of Entrepreneurship, Faculty of Management, University of Stirling, FK9 4LA, Scotland.

This study was designed in association with Sue Birley and the Society of Associated Researchers on International Entrepreneurship (SARIE). All opinions and errors are the authors alone. Financial support for the Centre for Management Buy-Out Research from BZW Private Equity and Deloitte Touche Corporate Finance is also acknowledged. We would also like to thank Harry Sapienza and the two anonymous referees for their very helpful comments.

Journal of Business Venturing **13**, 173–204

655 Avenue of the Americas, New York, NY 10010

0883-9026/98/$19.00
PII S0883-9026(97)00002-5

and the age of their businesses. Univariate and multivariate tests were used to examine potential differences between the groups.

The results of the study show significant differences between portfolio and serial founders with regard to their parental background, work experience, and their age when they started their first business. Differences were also found with respect to reasons leading to start-up, personal attitudes to entrepreneurship, and sources of funds used during the launch period of the surveyed business. These findings suggest that habitual entrepreneurs cannot be treated as a homogeneous group. The analysis, however, failed to find any significant differences between the performance of the surveyed firms owned by habitual founders and novice founders and between the two types of habitual founders.

The findings of the study indicate for researchers that there is a need to carefully define the unit of analysis in any examination of entrepreneurs. In particular, there is a need to take note of the heterogeneity of types of entrepreneur and to consider the entrepreneur as the appropriate unit of analysis rather than simply the firm. Although this study focused on habitual founders of businesses, the theoretical section of the study also identified other types of habitual entrepreneurs, such as serial corporate entrepreneurs and serial management buy-out and buy-in cases. These other types of habitual entrepreneurs would appear to warrant further analysis.

The findings of this study have a number of implications for practitioners, especially venture capitalists. The absence of significant performance differences between novice and habitual entrepreneurs, which is consistent with the results from other studies, emphasizes the need for venture capitalists screening potential investees not to rely solely on previous experience.

The study also has implications for policy-makers, especially with respect to decisions concerning the allocation of resources to assist nascent entrepreneurs, novice entrepreneurs, and habitual entrepreneurs. The similarities in business performance among novice, serial, and portfolio entrepreneurs suggests that policy-makers need to be careful in targeting scarce resources. Most notably, targeting resources to encourage talented nascent entrepreneurs to become novice entrepreneurs may offer returns which are at least as good as targeting resources to more experienced entrepreneurs.

INTRODUCTION

Starting a new business and/or owning and managing an independent business is an important career option for many people (Scott 1990; Dyer 1994). To encourage innovativeness, competitiveness, wealth creation, job generation and local and regional development (Reynolds et al. 1994), governments in industrialized countries have introduced programs and initiatives (De Koning and Snijders 1992) to increase the willingness and/or opportunity for individuals to become self-employed or establish businesses with employees (Van Praag and Van Ophem 1995). In recent years, many individuals have made the transition from being nascent entrepreneurs, that is in the position of considering starting a business (Carter et al. 1996) and have actually established new businesses. As a result of higher new firm entry rates than firm exit rates (Keeble and Walker 1994; Westhead and Birley 1994), the number (or stock) of businesses in the total United Kingdom economy has increased (Daly 1991). However, this increase in the creation of new businesses is not necessarily a reliable indicator of the development of entrepreneurship in an economy. This study addresses an important part of this issue. In particular, we draw attention to the need to focus on the behavior of individual entrepreneurs in a variety of settings that extend beyond one-time start-ups to include the purchase and inheritance of a firm as well as the ownership of multiple entrepreneurial ventures. Consideration of this broad context of entrepreneurship permits the development of a framework for the analysis of habitual entrepreneurs.

As they are easier to identify and monitor over time, many researchers have explored the nature of entrepreneurship by focusing upon the formation and development of organizations, using a variety of frameworks (Pfeffer and Salancik 1978; Gartner 1985; Van de Ven et al. 1989; Vesper 1990; Hannan and Carroll 1992). Studies focusing on new firm births as the primary dependent variable have implied that the nature of entrepreneurship simply involves getting into business (Reynolds and Miller 1992). Birley and Westhead (1994a, p. 57) during their comparison of novice and habitual founders, however, concluded, "if the business is the sole unit of analysis there is a threat that the value of the new venturing event will be underestimated. It also indicates that future attempts to explain business growth should incorporate the possibility that owner-managers may attempt to resolve their personal materialistic aspirations through the growth of further multiple business operations, which may not be directly related to the single unit of analysis being studied."

Studies of individuals (such as the self-employed and owner-managers) have implied that the nature of entrepreneurship involves issues of ownership and control as the primary dependent variable (Steinmetz and Wright 1989). Gartner and Shane (1995) also suggested that the scale and nature of entrepreneurship in an economy can be influenced by whether the focus is upon individuals or organizations. In doing so they focused upon Hawley's (1907) theory of entrepreneurship, which argued that in order to obtain an income or profits, an entrepreneur must be the owner-manager of the organization; without such rights an entrepreneur would be unable to make decisions about the successful coordination of scarce resources.

Recognition of the importance of ownership emphasizes the potential for entrepreneurship to be extended from start-ups to cases where individuals purchase a firm (Cooper and Dunkelberg 1986; Robbie and Wright 1996) and/or where they have inherited the business from the original founder (Westhead and Cowling 1996). In addition, the introduction of direct equity ownership through stock options and managerial equity holdings in subsidiaries of groups emphasizes the importance of an ownership interest in the firm for corporate entrepreneurship to be enhanced.

In considering individuals, however, many studies have focused upon people in work situations when developing career theory and exploring the nature of entrepreneurship (Schein 1978; Pickles and O'Farrell 1987; Dyer 1994; Katz 1994). Following Smith (1967), Woo et al. (1991) examined the notion that based on their characteristics, entrepreneurs can be broadly divided into craftsmen and opportunists. They concluded that the grouping of entrepreneur types was dependent on the sample of firms involved and the method of analysis used to group entrepreneurs. In contrast, Gartner and Starr (1993) argued that it is specific patterns of interlocked behaviors among individuals that influence the creation of an organization.

Whether analysis focuses on individuals or organizations, there is a need to recognize that entrepreneurship may not be a single-event action. More recently, researchers have focused upon the characteristics of novice and habitual founders. Ronstadt (1982) suggested many entrepreneurs start several businesses before launching a successful business. Survey evidence has revealed approximately a third of owner-managers are habitual founders because they have prior business founding experience (Birley and Westhead 1994a). Habitual founders are, therefore, an important phenomenon. Moreover, there is growing recognition that studying habitual founders may yield important insights into the nature of entrepreneurial characteristics and into the nature of entrepreneurial behavior (Anonymous 1986; Starr and Bygrave 1991). There is, as yet, no evidence to support the hypothesis that habitual founders run more successful businesses than novice founders who have only established/owned only one business. In addition, research surrounding the habitual owner-manager phenomenon has not so far explored systematically the nature of habitual entrepreneurship, nor the consequences of its differing manifestations. It should also be borne in mind that a subset of current novice entrepreneurs will become portfolio or serial entrepreneurs, which may blur the distinction between types.

Starr and Bygrave (1991) have, nevertheless, drawn attention to issues surrounding the assets and liabilities of habitual entrepreneurship, although they do not distinguish different types of habitual entrepreneurship. Dyer's (1994) work on entrepreneurial careers is also couched very much in terms of its development in a growing business over time rather than the shift from one venture to another or the multiple creation or purchase of ventures. Whereas there is a growing literature that appreciates there are different "types" of owner-managed independent firms (Birley and Westhead 1990; Westhead 1990, 1995a) very few studies have, however, been conducted that have explored the behaviors of novice and habitual owner-managers (Birley and Westhead 1994a) and serial and portfolio owner-managers (Wright et al. 1995).

The purpose of this study is to address this research gap. As intimated above, in the theoretical and empirical literature on entrepreneurial behaviour there is a growing recognition of the need to carefully define the terms being used, since these may have a major impact upon the generation of research hypotheses, the interpretation of empirical results, and ultimately to our understanding of the entrepreneurial phenomenon.

As yet, there is no generally accepted definition of a "habitual" entrepreneur (Starr and Bygrave 1991). A variety of definitions have been used which makes comparative analysis difficult. Donckels et al. (1987, p.48) claimed, "Multiple business starters are entrepreneurs who, after having started a first company, set up or participate in the start-up of (an) other firm(s)." Kolvereid and Bullvåg (1993) adopted a narrower and more conservative definition of experienced business founders. They suggested experienced business founders have established more than one business and they still owned the most recent business prior to the start-up of the current new independent venture. A wider definition of habitual founders was, however, used by Birley and Westhead (1994a, p.40) who suggested, "'habitual' founders had established at least one other business prior to the start-up of the current new independent venture." Hall (1995, p.220) has also divided habitual entrepreneurs into serial and portfolio entrepreneurs. Most notably, "There are those owners who own one business after another but effectively only own one business at a time. Previous businesses may have been sold, closed, or had a legal outcome. These owners can be classified as serial owners. There is another category of habitual owner in which the owners own more than one business at a time. These are portfolio owners."

Two types of habitual founder behavior are identified in this study. Serial founders are defined as those who sell their original business but at a later date inherit, establish, and/or purchase another business (Beresford 1996). A portfolio founder, however, retains his/her original business and inherits, establishes, and/or purchases another business. The characteristics of serial and portfolio founders and their independent small firms will be compared with one another in this study. In addition, these two groups of habitual founders will be compared with novice founders who at the time of the survey had established only one independent business. Founders in this novice category may themselves at a later date become serial or portfolio founders.

To focus upon the characteristics of habitual founders, the article is structured as follows. Theoretical frameworks and empirical studies are summarized to identify a

TABLE 1 Categorization of Multiple or Habitual Entrepreneurship

Ownership Status	Multiple Entrepreneurship Involving Existing Firms	Multiple Entrepreneurship Involving New Firms
Ownership change between ventures	Quadrant 1 Inheritors/serial management buy-out/management buy-in	Quadrant 2 Serial start-up
No ownership change between ventures	Quadrant 3 Multiple corporate entre-preneurship	Quadrant 4 Portfolio entrepreneurship

broad conceptual categorization of habitual entrepreneurs, which includes founder, inheritor, and purchaser entrepreneurs as well as corporate entrepreneurs. The analysis is then extended to identify behavioral differences among novice, serial, and portfolio founders as well as differences among their businesses. Propositions are derived suggesting differences between the three types of founders and their businesses. At the individual founder level of analysis, similarities as well as differences in the personal background, work experiences, reasons leading to the start-up of the surveyed business, and personal attitudes to entrepreneurship between the three defined types of founders will be explored. At the organization level of analysis, finance, employment, and performance differences among the three types of businesses will be presented. This latter focus is important "because the quantity of entrepreneurial profit is determined, not by the number of individuals involved in each organization, but by the number of organizations that create the surplus of revenues over costs" (Gartner and Shane 1995, p.294). The subsequent section describes the data collection methodology. Results from the univariate and multivariate analyses are then presented, and derived propositions are formally tested. The final section presents our conclusions and suggestions for further research.

THEORETICAL PERSPECTIVES

Habitual entrepreneurship can be viewed along two broad dimensions, whether entrepreneurship involves a new or existing business and whether or not there is a change of ownership between ventures (Table 1). This framework thus includes habitual entrepreneurs who are founders, inheritors, or purchasers of businesses or who have undertaken multiple actions as corporate entrepreneurs. In our opinion, this framework opens up a broad empirical agenda, but as will be seen below, the empirical part of this study focuses only on founders rather than inheritors/purchasers of businesses.

In discussing habitual or multiple business founders, but not purchasers, Hall (1995) distinguished portfolio owners (quadrant 4 of Table 1), where ownership of the first venture is maintained when a subsequent venture is embarked upon, from serial owners who dispose of one venture before founding another (quadrant 2). Although there is some evidence to show that habitual entrepreneurship is extensive (Birley and Westhead 1994a), little empirical research has distinguished between these two types of owners or embraces other forms of entrepreneurship beyond start-ups. A noteworthy exception is the empirical work conducted by Kolvereid and Bullvåg (1993) who examined portfolio founders who started more than one business. Surprisingly, these researchers explicitly excluded from their analysis businesses where the founder may have sold a business entity before or as well as embarking on another one.

This study argues that it is important to address these issues, because entrepreneurship is a heterogeneous phenomenon, which in turn has implications for expectations about its nature and effects. In the light of the recent developments in the notion of entrepreneurship, these categories can be broadened to include the inheritance and/or purchase of an existing firm after the first business is sold (quadrant 1). Serial entrepreneurs may have exited from an initial business when entrepreneurial opportunities are perceived to have been exhausted. These entrepreneurs have, however, searched for new possibilities through the inheritance, establishment, and/or purchase of another business. There is also, a somewhat erroneous, strand in the literature that suggests that serial entrepreneurship only takes place after the first venture has failed.

Corporate entrepreneurship involves managers creating new combinations of resources in existing firms (Block and MacMillan 1993; Guth and Ginsberg 1990). Multiple corporate entrepreneurship may occur within the same firm with individual managers undertaking repeated entrepreneurial actions (quadrant 3). Managers in such organizations may be remunerated at least in part by direct ownership stakes in the business, either through stock options or through direct ownership in the subsidiary of a larger group where they are employed.

It should also be borne in mind that Table 1 effectively relates to "pure" habitual entrepreneurship cases where entrepreneurs obtain controlling interests in subsequent businesses. Between these four pure types, a range of intermediate types can be identified. Entrepreneurs building a portfolio of ventures may dispose of some of them over time thus introducing a serial element to their behavior. Rather than becoming involved in further ventures as a full/controlling owner, entrepreneurs as individuals may use wealth generated from initial ventures to acquire minority stakes in ventures controlled by other entrepreneurs, so fulfilling a role as habitual or serial business angels. There may also be some blurring of the distinction between portfolio and multiple corporate entrepreneurs. Institutional and legal frameworks may provide entrepreneurs with the incentive to create new legal entities rather than engage in additional entrepreneurial behavior in the existing firm. For example, this may be a means of diversifying into risky ventures while avoiding potentially damaging effects on the initial entity if it fails (Scott and Rosa 1996). Between pure management buy-outs and corporate entrepreneurship is the case where rather than disposing fully of subsidiaries, corporations retain majority equity ownership but remunerate managers with a significant direct minority stake in the subsidiary where there is a clear role for specific entrepreneurial skills. Such actions may then be repeated in other new ventures of this type with the same entrepreneurial individuals.

Clearly, the categories identified in Table 1 suggest a broad research agenda, which is beyond the scope of a single article. The empirical part of this study focuses on entrepreneurs who are founders rather than purchasers of businesses or corporate entrepreneurs. In particular, we examine differences both between novice founders and multiple start-up cases (quadrants 2 and 4) and between serial and portfolio founders. Propositions to be tested in this exploratory article are derived in the following section.

DERIVATION OF PROPOSITIONS

Research on the traits, characteristics, and motivations for entrepreneurship suggests differences between contrasting types of entrepreneurs are to be expected. For example,

Woo et al. (1991) have provided an analysis of the craftsman / opportunist categorization in start-up businesses. In addition, Robbie and Wright (1996) showed that whereas novice buy-out entrepreneurs were more likely to exhibit craftsman type characteristics, buy-in entrepreneurs were more likely to exhibit opportunist characteristics, though both buy-outs and buy-ins entrepreneurs displayed both types of characteristics. There have been suggestions that buy-out and buy-in entrepreneurs (Wright and Coyne 1985; Robbie and Wright 1996) differ in relation to length of managerial career and age at which they started a business from novice entrepreneurs. These differences may, however, be blurred if some current novice entrepreneurs become habitual entrepreneurs in the future.

During their study of novice and habitual independent firm founders, Kolvereid and Bullvåg (1993) noted that very few women become habitual entrepreneurs. Supporting the evidence presented by Donckels et al. (1987) they also found habitual entrepreneurs were more likely to have obtained higher education qualifications. As found elsewhere (Birley and Westhead 1994a), Kolvereid and Bullvåg (1993) noted habitual founders started their first business at a younger age than novice founders. Although a priori it is difficult to identify potential differences between portfolio and serial founders on the grounds of qualifications and age, the greater complexities likely to emerge in managing a portfolio of businesses rather than in selling one and founding another, suggests that portfolio founders may have a background that has greater exposure to managerial issues. The resources required to finance and the complexities involved in running and developing a portfolio of businesses suggests that these founders may require contributions from a greater number of partners than is the case for serial or novice founders. Although serial founders may have created wealth on exit and may seek to found larger businesses, these may not necessarily involve the level of complexity expected in a portfolio of businesses. This evidence yields the following propositions:

P1a: Novice founders were less likely to be as highly educated as habitual founders.

P1b: Novice founders were more likely to be female than habitual founders.

P1c: Novice founders were less likely to be drawn from a managerial and business parental background than habitual founders.

P1d: Portfolio founders were more likely than serial and novice founders to have a greater number of partners in their surveyed businesses.

P1e: Novice founders were more likely to be older when starting their first venture than habitual founders.

As a result of prior business experience, many habitual entrepreneurs have developed skills and competencies, a rolodex of network contacts, a business reputation, and a track record. However, the development of a portfolio of businesses, as in the case of portfolio entrepreneurs, suggests a need for greater managerial skills than might be expected in the case of novice and serial entrepreneurs. Hence, it is expected that these entrepreneurs were more likely to have had a managerial or an executive position immediately prior to start-up (Donckels et al. 1987). As intimated above, because habitual founders are drawn from more resourceful backgrounds they are more likely to have developed contacts and networks with potential partners and sources of resources (such as financiers, suppliers, customers, etc.). Supporting this viewpoint, Kolvereid and Bullvåg (1993) found firms established by portfolio founders generally had two or more partners or shareholders.

Serial entrepreneurs, by definition, move from one specific economic activity to another to achieve personal objectives. This type of habitual founder generally places greater emphasis on achieving a particular goal and receiving recognition for it which is crystallized through the act of disposal. As the serial entrepreneur is expected to grow businesses to a certain stage and then exit them, it is anticipated that such ventures are likely to be smaller than those in which portfolio entrepreneurs are involved. It may also be expected that serial founders have work experience backgrounds involving employment in a larger number of organizations with periods of self-employment. Notions that places of employment often act as incubators for individuals seeking to found a business (Cooper 1985) suggest that novice founders are more likely to start a business in the same sector as their last employer. Drawing upon their previous business founding experience, habitual entrepreneurs may be more likely to perceive opportunities and have the confidence to start businesses in sectors that are not related to the activities of their last employer. This discussion suggests the following propositions:

> *P2a:* Novice founders were more likely to have worked for fewer organizations than portfolio and serial founders prior to the start-up of the surveyed business.
>
> *P2b:* Serial founders were more likely to have worked in a smaller firm prior to founding their latest business than portfolio or novice founders.
>
> *P2c:* Novice founders were more likely than portfolio and serial founders to have founded a business in the same industry as their last employer.

The initial reasons leading to the start-up of a new venture can, in part, influence the development trajectory of a business (O'Farrell and Hitchens 1988). Entrepreneurs who desire to create a successful and large independent organization of their own, rather than pursuing a managerial career in a large organization owned by somebody else, may have motivational characteristics associated with a need for independence, a need for personal development, and a perceived instrumentality of wealth (Scheinberg and MacMillan 1988; Birley and Westhead 1994b).

Drawing upon case study evidence, Wright et al. (1995) found three different categories of serial behavior with individuals having differing objectives for their businesses. Portfolio entrepreneurs may establish a new business for a variety of reasons. Some of these reasons may be concerned with circumventing legislation, for example, labor laws that may only become effective above a certain size level. Strategically, they may create a new business entity as a means of diversifying their activities. Whereas independence is a strong reason for starting a first business, a variety of other more materialistic reasons (for example, to increase market possibilities, diversification, tax reasons, enlarge business property for the family, etc.) come to the fore when a founder establishes a subsequent business (Donckels et al. 1987; Gray 1993).

Following Smith (1967) and Schein (1978), Katz (1994) has also suggested, the prototypical autonomy-oriented individual (or craftsman entrepreneur) will tend to emphasize freedom rather than financial or status achievement when starting a business. Further, issues of market opportunity (exchange) or asset accumulation (resources) are less likely to be the dominant reasons leading to the start-up of a business. Such a person, when employed by others, is less likely to change jobs to increase his or her level of autonomy. When they own a business, they generally limit the size of the business and grow it to a psychologically comfortable level. By adopting this strategy, a consistent living is provided for the owner and it ensures that the venture can be personally managed and controlled. Katz (1994) has suggested if this type of individual has multiple episodes of self-employment, they are handled one-at-a-time. This group of individuals are, therefore, more likely to be novice or serial founders.

Individuals who pursue entrepreneurial careers for greater pay and/or status are more likely to be opportunist entrepreneurs. Further, this type of entrepreneur is more likely to be pulled into entrepreneurship by the external pressures of market (exchange) or wealth (resources) (Katz 1994). Opportunist entrepreneurs own businesses generally for the pursuit of growth and wealth creation, and they are more likely to adopt legal structures that minimize financial growth constraints. Because of the need for greater pay and/or status, opportunist entrepreneurs operate businesses with high levels of sales revenue and employment growth. Katz (1994) has suggested if this type of individual has multiple episodes of self-employment, they generally have more than one business going at the same time. This latter individual is, therefore, more likely to be a portfolio founder. Accordingly, this evidence yields the following propositions:

> *P3a:* Novice founders were more likely to emphasize a need for independence when starting the surveyed business.
>
> *P3b:* Portfolio founders were more likely to emphasize a perceived instrumentality of wealth when starting the surveyed business.
>
> *P3c:* Portfolio founders were more likely to emphasize tax reduction and indirect benefits when starting the surveyed business.

Cultural values can influence the predisposition of individuals to become entrepreneurs (Shapero and Sokol 1982). Four underlying dimensions of culture have been identified by Hofstede (1980) as power distance (management of inequality between people), individualism (relationship between individuals and collectives), uncertainty avoidance (stance toward the future), and masculinity (allocation of roles between the sexes). Using these concepts, McGrath et al., (1992) were able to empirically discriminate between the cultural values of entrepreneurs and nonentrepreneurs. This study, however, failed to distinguish among the cultural values of novice, portfolio, and serial founders.

Nevertheless, with regard to personal attitudes to entrepreneurship, Kolvereid and Bullvåg (1993) have argued that the creation of multiple businesses may arise where opportunities for growth in existing businesses are restricted. Scott and Rosa (1996) have also provided evidence that suggested portfolio entrepreneurs have created new legal entities as a means of testing new products in the knowledge that if a new business fails, its loss could be insulated from the other firms that they own. Portfolio entrepreneurs may, however, focus insufficient attention on each of their individual ventures and experience either uncontrolled or weaker growth. As noted earlier, serial founders placing greater emphasis on achieving a particular goal may be seen as attempting to reduce uncertainty by crystallizing their gains through venture disposal. For these reasons it is proposed:

> *P4:* Serial founders may be more cautious in their approach to entrepreneurship, preferring to seek opportunities with lower degrees of uncertainty.

Different types of entrepreneurs may use contrasting sources of finance during the launch period. As intimated above, habitual founders if successful may be expected to have greater access to funds than novice founders. Serial founders who have successfully exited from their initial venture may have generated sufficient funds to use personal resources to finance their subsequent venture(s). If serial founders are not successful in their first venture, they may still be able to raise funds as evidence suggests that venture capitalists seek evidence of an ability to succeed the next time around and not just previous experience per se (Wright et al. 1997). Hence, we would expect novice founders without an established track record to rely upon personal savings, family, and friends as a source of launch finance. Whereas portfolio founders who have not exited from their earlier venture(s) may be able to lever up resources from the existing business and with their established track record may also make use of finance from existing customers and suppliers.

Habitual entrepreneurs may be expected to become involved in ventures the second time around that are larger than those begun by novices. To achieve ownership of a larger business, serial entrepreneurs may purchase rather than start-up their second venture. In such cases the entrepreneur may be able to leverage his/her personal wealth with funds from venture capitalists, whereas venture capitalists typically (in the United Kingdom at least) have an aversion to funding start-ups. Portfolio founders who by definition retain at least part of their trading activities may also be able to leverage funds from trading partners to develop new ventures. In contrast, serial founders who have relinquished their equity stakes in previously owned businesses currently have no trading partners to leverage-up. This evidence yields the following propositions:

P5a: Serial founders, especially previously successful ones, were more likely to have used personal savings, family, and friends as a source of start-up finance during the launch period of their present venture (which is subsequent to their first venture) than novice and portfolio founders.

P5b: Portfolio founders were more likely to have used banks and financial institutions as a source of start-up finance during the launch period of their present venture (which is subsequent to their first venture) than novice and serial founders.

P5c: Portfolio founders were more likely to have used customers and suppliers as a source of start-up finance during the launch period of their present venture (which is subsequent to their first venture) than novice and serial founders.

Entrepreneural experience may lead to increased performance in subsequent ventures. Enhanced performance may be measured in terms of faster sales and employment growth, greater profitability and greater profitability in relation to competitors. Experience may be expected to bring the skills required, including marketing and financial expertise, to identify and serve market segments that have both growth potential and profit possibilities. Experienced entrepreneurs founding a new business in the same sector as their previous/current venture are also likely to be in a relatively stronger position by virtue of that experience than novice founders. In addition, they may be able to identify more clearly what is required to earn profits in the selected market(s). However, Starr and Bygrave (1991) have suggested experience may bring liabilities as well as assets. These liabilities may retard the performance of subsequent ventures. Subsequent ventures may, therefore, not perform better than the first business. For serial entrepreneurs it may be difficult to find a further successful venture, despite the fact that an earlier venture was a success. If they seek to purchase another venture, they may need to engage in an extensive search process to find a venture that matches their skills and which has the potential to achieve significant returns. Not surprisingly, this process carries with it the dangers of asymmetric information between the vendor and the outside entrepreneur which may still persist even among those with experience (Robbie and Wright 1996). If they seek to found a new venture, experienced entrepreneurs face the problems both of identifying another successful idea and may attempt to repeat actions that were successful in an earlier venture in new circumstances that are quite different. Evidence from venture capitalists' screening of experienced entrepreneurs indicates that failure to find a suitable project the next time around is an important reason why experienced entrepreneurs may not be funded again from this source (Wright et al. 1995). However, such entrepreneurs may fund further ventures themselves in the optimistic but mistaken belief (hubris) that they can repeat their success, yet may attempt to repeat previously successful actions in a changed environment.

Faster business growth and greater profitability may be expected to be associated with experienced entrepreneurs because, as intimated above, they are more likely to be opportunistic type entrepreneurs. Supporting this viewpoint, Donckels et al. (1987) during their study of the first businesses started by novice and multiple business starters found businesses established by multiple business starters were markedly larger in employment size at start-up as well at the time of the survey. In marked contrast, with reference to the last business started by novice and portfolio founders, Kolvereid and Bullvåg (1993) were unable to identify performance differences between the two groups of independent firms. Similarly, Birley and Westhead (1994a) found no evidence that new independent businesses established by habitual founders were particularly advantaged compared to those established by novice founders. At this point, it is acknowledged that in order to fully identify performance and growth differences there is a need to consider all the businesses owned by habitual entrepreneurs rather than just the current business. These findings are consistent both with evidence that there are no significant performance differences between craftsman and opportunist entrepreneurs (Woo et al. 1991). Further, serial entrepreneurs may display heterogeneous characteristics and are not strongly growth or profit maximization oriented. Nevertheless, the following tentative propositions are suggested:

P6: Portfolio and serial founders were more growth oriented than novice founders.

P7: Surveyed firms owned by portfolio and serial founders had performed better than firms owned by novice founders.

DATA COLLECTED

Empirical data presented in this exploratory study were derived from a wider international study of founders of new ventures (Shane et al. 1991, Birley and Westhead 1994a). The data were collected in late 1990 and early 1991. The approach adopted in this study appreciated the differential importance of various social influences at significant points in an individual's life cycle with a consequent effect on the start-up process (Cooper 1981; Gibb and Ritchie 1982). This study was, however, not designed specifically to compare novice, serial, and portfolio founders. Nevertheless, the research instrument presented to the principal founders of responding independent businesses enabled us to identify these three types of firm founders.

Reflecting the increased recognition of the importance of locational considerations in the functioning of the economy and spatial variations in business formation, survival, and growth (Westhead and Moyes 1992; Keeble and Walker 1994; Reynolds et al. 1994), 12 contrasting locations in Great Britain were selected. They included government-designated assisted areas (Birley and Westhead 1992); rural and urban environments (Westhead 1995b); areas associated with specialized declining traditional heavy industries and high concentrations of external ownership, particularly in manufacturing industry; localities with high personal disposable income and high service new firm formation; and areas with strong and varied enterprise promotion through the activities of enterprise agencies and development agencies.

Because there is no comprehensive list of independent firms in Great Britain, a pragmatic approach was taken in the construction of the survey frame. Based on the assumption that local economic development units were most likely to be concerned about the profile of their business population, regional and borough business directories were taken as the primary data source. Lists of potential independent businesses were identified. These lists were cleaned, and community businesses and the subsidiaries and branches of companies were excluded.

After this data cleaning, a list of 4,914 names and addresses of potential independent new and small businesses was identified. Questionnaires were sent by post over a 6-month period (1.10.90 to 31.3.91) to the principal owner-managers of these businesses [a full discussion of the limitations of the methodology have been presented in Birley and Westhead (1992)]. Some 744 questionnaires were returned, of which 621 questionnaire responses covered businesses between 1 and 50 years of age and the respondents had specified their age when they had started their first business. It was not possible to make any sensible calculation regarding response rates or, as noted above, about the representativeness of the sample as a whole. Indeed, as argued in this study, it is difficult to be clear as to whether the characteristics of the owner-manager as opposed to those of the firm should be the appropriate criteria for judging the latter (Westhead and Birley 1995). Nevertheless, at a two-digit Standard Industrial Classification (1980) minimum list heading level (frequently used by government departments in the United Kingdom), no statistically significant response bias was detected between the respondents and nonrespondents. On this criterion, we have no cause to suspect this sample of independent firms was not a representative sample. However, the response rates were generally higher in government-designated assisted areas (Birley and Westhead 1992). Therefore, the results from the questionnaire survey are most appropriately to be seen as suggestive rather than representative (O'Farrell and Hitchens 1989).

In total, 389 businesses (62.6%) involved novice or one-shot founders, that is the business concerned was the first to be established by the key founder. A further 75 businesses (12.1%) involved portfolio founders, where the key founder had owned two or more businesses and still owned the first business. The remaining 157 businesses (25.3%) were serial founders who had owned two or more businesses but who did not now own the first business. Of the serial founders, 61 (9.8%) founders had sold their first business, whereas the remaining 96 founders (15.5%) had either closed it or had other reasons for not still owning it. In comparison, in their study of 248 new firms in Norway, Kolvereid and Bullvåg (1993) found 132 firms were owned by novice founders (53%) whereas a further 77 firms (31%) were owned by multiple business starters (or portfolio founders) who still owned their first business start-up. The level of portfolio business ownership in the Norwegian sample is, therefore, far higher than the level reported in the British sample. Locational, sectoral, and age of business differences in the composition of the two samples may, in part, explain this marked difference. Further, reflecting a common weaknesses of prior research in this area (Donckels et al. 1987; Kolvereid and Bullvåg 1993; Birley and Westhead 1994a), the characteristics of the other businesses owned by portfolio owner-managers were not collected. As a result, the full economic contribution of portfolio owner-managers cannot be assessed by this study.

Tests were carried out on three demographic attributes of the businesses in the sample (their main industrial activity, the location of the businesses primary operational premises, and age of the businesses since they received their first orders) to examine whether there were significant differences that might contaminate the analysis (Gartner 1989). No statistically significant differences were identified among the groups of novice, portfolio, and serial founder firms with regard to these three demographic attributes. Over 52% of firms in each of the groups were engaged in service activities (59.9%, 56.0%, and 52.2% of novice, portfolio, and serial firms, respectively) (χ^2 = 16.44; *df* = 6, significance level = 0.172). A slightly larger proportion of portfolio firms were located in rural areas (those located in an area with less than 10.000 people), although not in a statistically significant direction (26.2%, 32.0%, and 22.9% of novice, portfolio, and serial firms, respectively) (χ^2 = 2.18; *df* = 1, significance level = 0.337). In addition, no marked differences in the age of businesses since they received their first order was recorded (on average 7.3, 6.2, and 6.9 years of age for novice, portfolio, and serial firms, respectively) (F = 1.17, significance level = 0.310).

TESTING THE PROPOSITIONS

Univariate Analysis

Chi-square and one-way analysis of variance (ANOVA) tests were conducted to identify statistically significant differences between founders and firms in the three ownership type groups. Chi-square analysis was used to identify differences among the three types with regard to variables measured at a nominal level, whereas ANOVA was used in relation to variables measured at an interval level. In total, data were collected on 95 variables that characterize the founder and the firm [for a summary description see Birley and Westhead (1992)]. Dichotomizing among the three founder types statistically significant differences were observed for only 25 variables (26%). Statistically significant differences among the three groups of entrepreneurs–novice, portfolio, and serial—are detailed in Tables 2 to 10, with notes to the tables indicating the existence of significant differences between pairwise combinations of these three founder types. Given the exploratory nature of the study, it is the intention to identify issues that may be important in the context of either a fuller replication analysis and/or in another country context. Accordingly, we report significance tests up to the 0.1 level in order to minimize the potential problem that important variables may be overlooked using the more conventional 0.05 level of significance.

Personal Background of the Founder

No statistically significant differences were recorded among the three founder types with regard to the education level of the founder. As a result, proposition P1a cannot be supported.

Whereas over 87% of the founders in each of the groups were male, as expected, a significantly smaller proportion of habitual founders, particularly serial founders, were females (row 1 in Table 2). In addition, a significantly larger proportion of portfolio founders rather than novice and serial founders were drawn from a managerial parental background (row 2). Novice founders, however, were significantly more likely than se-

TABLE 2 Personal Background of the Founder Contrasts by Type of Key Founder

Variable	Novice Founders No.	Novice Founders %	Portfolio Founders No.	Portfolio Founders %	Serial Founders No.	Serial Founders %	χ^2 Statistic	Significance Level
1. Sex of key founder[b]							5.05	0.0801
Male	341	87.9	68	90.7	148	94.3		
Female	47	12.1	7	9.3	9	5.7		
2. Occupational status of key founder's parents (i.e., the main income earner) during childhood—manager[a,c]							10.16	0.0062
No	344	88.4	59	78.7	146	93.0		
Yes	45	11.6	16	21.3	11	7.0		
3. Occupational·status of key founder's parents (i.e., the main income earner) during childhood—unskilled employee[b]							4.63	0.0986
No	344	88.4	69	92.0	148	94.3		
Yes	45	11.6	6	8.0	9	5.7		
4. Number of shareholders or partners in the surveyed small firm[a]							7.64	0.0220
1	155	39.9	18	24.0	52	33.5		
≥2	253	60.1	57	76.0	103	66.5		

[a] Statistically significant difference between novice and portfolio founders at least at the .1 level.
[b] Statistically significant difference between novice and serial founders at least at the .1 level.
[c] Statistically significant difference between portfolio and serial founders at the .1 level.

rial founders to be drawn from an unskilled employee parental background (row 3). Propositions P1b and P1c are, therefore, supported.

Portfolio owners may be able to found and own multiple businesses because they use partners, whereas the novice and serial entrepreneurs found their businesses alone. This team aspect of entrepreneurship may be important in providing the skills and resources needed to maintain ownership of multiple businesses (Slevin and Covin 1992). As expected, habitual founders, particularly portfolio founders, were significantly more likely to have established their new businesses with an additional shareholder or partner (row 4). Additional research needs to clarify whether joint ownership is the key to the ability to ownership of multiple businesses. Nevertheless, proposition P1d is tentatively supported.

As anticipated, portfolio and serial founders were significantly younger than novice founders when they started their first business with little difference found between the average age of two types of habitual founders (row 1 in Table 3). However, at the time of the survey, novice founders were significantly younger than habitual entrepreneurs, with serial founders being markedly older than novice as well as portfolio founders (row 2). Proposition P1e is therefore supported.

Work Experience of the Founder

Founders were asked to report on their work experience before the start of the business being surveyed in this study. The results in some instances relate to lifetime prior work experience. As expected, habitual founders, particularly serial founders, had worked for more organizations before the start-up of the surveyed business (row 3 in Table 3). The differing ages of the types of entrepreneur may, however, be a confounding factor.

TABLE 3 Analysis of Variance Test Differences between Founders and Small Firms by Type of Key Founder

Variable	Novice Founders	Portfolio Founders	Serial Founders	Analysis of Variance F Statistic	Significance Level
1. Age of key founder when started first business[a,b]				31.56	0.000
Mean	35.1	29.6	29.1		
Median	34.0	30.0	29.0		
2. Age of key founder at the time of the survey[b,c]				6.60	0.001
Mean	41.4	42.3	44.9		
Median	41.0	43.0	45.0		
3. Number of different organizations key founder has worked for on a full-time basis[b]				4.73	0.009
Mean	4.1	4.8	5.2		
Median	3.0	4.0	4.0		
4. Number of sources of start-up capital used during the launch period of surveyed small firm[b]				2.67	0.070
Mean	1.6	1.7	1.8		
Median	1.0	2.0	2.0		

[a] Statistically significant difference between novice and portfolio founders at least at the .1 level.
[b] Statistically significant difference between novice and serial founders at least at the .1 level.
[c] Statistically significant difference between portfolio and serial founders at least at the .1 level.

Supporting evidence presented elsewhere, habitual founders, particularly serial founders, were significantly more likely to have been self-employed immediately before start-up (row 1 in Table 4). Novice founders were, however, significantly more likely to have started their business in the same industry as their last employer, with portfolio founders being more likely to have changed their industrial focus (row 2). Habitual founders, particularly serial founders, were significantly more likely to have worked in a small firm with fewer than 100 employees before start-up than was the case for novice founders (row 3). In marked contrast, significantly more novice rather than habitual founders had last worked immediately before start-up in a large firm with 1,000 or more employees (row 4). As a result, propositions P2a, P2b, and P2c are supported.

Reasons Leading to Start-Up

Twenty-three reasons leading to start-up statements were presented to respondents (see Birley and Westhead (1994b) for a complete list). Significant differences among the three types of founders emerged with reference to seven variables (Table 5).

Novice founders were significantly more likely than serial founders to have suggested "it made sense at that time in my life" ("need for independence"). They were also significantly more likely than portfolio founders to have suggested "to achieve something and to get recognition for it" ("need for approval"). In marked contrast, novice founders were significantly less likely than portfolio and serial founders to have reported "to continue a family tradition" ("follow role models").

Habitual founders were, in addition, significantly more likely to have emphasized

TABLE 4 Work Experience of the Founder Contrasts by Type of Key Founder

Variable	Novice Founders No.	Novice Founders %	Portfolio Founders No.	Portfolio Founders %	Serial Founders No.	Serial Founders %	χ^2 Statistic	Significance Level
1. Job title of key founder when left last employer immediately before start up—self-employed[b]							23.14	0.0000
No	371	95.4	68	90.7	130	82.8		
Yes	18	4.6	7	9.3	27	17.2		
2. Key founder started business in the same industry as last employer[a]							6.09	0.0477
No	180	47.5	45	61.6	85	54.8		
Yes	199	52.5	28	38.4	70	45.2		
3. Employment size of establishment key founder last worked in before start-up—small firm (≤99 employees)[b]							6.67	0.0335
No	211	54.2	33	44.0	68	43.3		
Yes	178	45.8	42	56.0	89	56.7		
4. Employment size of establishment key founder last worked in before start-up—large firm (≥1,000 employees)[a,b]							6.40	0.0408
No	288	74.0	63	84.0	129	82.2		
Yes	101	26.0	12	16.0	28	17.8		

[a] Statistically significant difference between novice and portfolio founders at least at the .1 level.
[b] Statistically significant difference between novice and serial founders at least at the .1 level.

"perceived instrumentality of wealth" and "need for personal development" reasons leading to start-up than was the case for novice founders. Portfolio founders were significantly more likely than novice and serial founders to have suggested "to give myself, my spouse, and children security" ("perceived instrumentality of wealth"). A significantly larger proportion of portfolio rather than serial founders also reported "to have access to indirect benefits such as tax exemptions" ("tax reduction and indirect benefits"). Serial founders, however, were significantly more likely than novice founders to have suggested "to develop an idea for a product" ("need for personal development"). In marked contrast, serial founders were significantly less likely than novice and portfolio founders to have reported "to have more influence in my community" ("welfare considerations"). Hence, propositions P3a, P3b, and P3c are supported.

Personal Attitudes to Entrepreneurship

Twenty-one personal attitudes to entrepreneurship statements were presented to founders (see Birley and Westhead (1992) for a complete list). Statistically significant personal attitudes to entrepreneurship statement differences were recorded among the three types of founders, particularly between portfolio and serial founders (Table 6). Portfolio founders were significantly more likely than novice and serial founders to have agreed with the personal attitude to entrepreneurship dimension relating to "individualism—relationship between individuals" ("I have a duty to give clients and customers

TABLE 5 Reasons Leading to Start-Up Contrasts by Type of Key Founder

Variable	Novice Founders		Portfolio Founders		Serial Founders		χ^2 Statistic	Significance Level
	No.	%	No.	%	No.	%		
1. Reason leading to start-up—it made sense at that time in my life ("need for independence")[b]							11.16	0.0038
To no extent	38	9.8	9	12.0	32	20.4		
To some extent	348	90.2	66	88.0	125	79.6		
2. Reason leading to start-up—to achieve something and to get recognition for it ("need for approval")[a]							5.38	0.0678
To no extent	85	22.0	25	33.3	44	28.0		
To some extent	301	78.0	50	66.7	113	72.0		
3. Reason leading to start-up—to continue a family tradition ("follow role models")[a,b]							5.58	0.0615
To no extent	331	85.8	58	77.3	124	79.0		
To some extent	55	14.2	17	22.7	33	21.0		
4. Reason leading to start-up—to give myself. my spouse. and children security ("perceived instrumentality of wealth")[a,c]							8.20	0.0166
To no extent	79	20.5	5	6.7	27	17.2		
To some extent	307	79.5	70	93.3	130	82.8		
5. Reason leading to start-up—to have access to indirect benefits such as tax exemptions ("tax reduction and indirect benefits")[c]							7.22	0.0270
To no extent	205	53.1	32	42.7	96	61.1		
To some extent	181	46.9	43	57.3	61	38.9		
6. Reason leading to start-up—to develop an idea for a product ("need for personal development")[b]							6.98	0.0305
To no extent	214	55.4	36	48.0	68	43.3		
To some extent	172	44.6	39	52.0	89	56.7		
7. Reason leading to start-up—to have more influence in my community ("welfare considerations")[b,c]							6.51	0.0385
To no extent	271	70.2	51	68.0	126	80.3		
To some extent	115	29.8	24	32.0	31	19.7		

[a] Statistically significant difference between novice and portfolio founders at least at the .1 level.
[b] Statistically significant difference between novice and serial founders at least at the .1 level.
[c] Statistically significant difference between portfolio and serial founders at the .1 level.

the same treatment" and "equality is characterized by a stress on rewards based on merit. ability. and skill"). In addition. novice and portfolio founders were significantly more likely than serial founders to have agreed with the personal attitude to entrepreneurship dimension relating to "power distance - management of inequality between

TABLE 6 Personal Attitudes to Entrepreneurship Contrasts by Type of Key Founder

	Novice Founders		Portfolio Founders		Serial Founders			
Variable	No.	%	No.	%	No.	%	χ^2 Statistic	Significance Level
1. Personal attitude to entrepreneurship—I have a duty to give clients and customers the same treatment ("individualism—relationship between individuals")[a,b,c]							15.23	0.0005
Other	93	24.3	10	13.5	57	36.3		
Agree	290	75.7	64	86.5	100	63.7		
2. Personal attitude to entrepreneurship—equality is characterized by a stress on rewards based on merit, ability and skill ("individualism—relationship between individuals")[a,c]							5.08	0.0790
Other	198	51.8	30	40.5	88	56.4		
Agree	184	48.2	44	59.5	68	43.6		
3. Personal attitude to entrepreneurship—equality is everyone's right ("power distance—management of inequality between people)[b,c]							10.91	0.0043
Other	90	23.5	11	14.9	53	33.8		
Agree	293	76.5	63	85.1	104	66.2		
4. Personal attitude to entrepreneurship—starting a business means uncertainty but adds to the excitement of life ("uncertainty avoidance—stance towards the future")[b]							5.18	0.0751
Other	31	8.1	4	5.4	21	13.4		
Agree	353	91.9	70	94.6	136	86.6		

[a] Statistically significant difference between novice and portfolio founders at least at the .1 level.
[b] Statistically significant difference between novice and serial founders at least at the .1 level.
[c] Statistically significant difference between portfolio and serial founders at the .1 level.

people" ("equality is everyone's right"). Serial founders, however, were weakly significantly less likely than novice founders to have agreed with the personal attitude to entrepreneurship statement relating to an "uncertainty avoidance—stance toward the future") ("starting a business means uncertainty but adds to the excitement of life"). As expected, serial founders had taken a more cautious view and had sought to reduce uncertainty by greater control, by focusing on achieving an exit at an appropriate time to realize their gains and putting themselves in a position to focus on their next venture. This seems in contrast to the suggestion made above that portfolio entrepreneurs may start-up new ventures in uncertain areas on the back of their original business, but focus insufficient attention on each of their individual ventures, thereby introducing the scope for greater uncertainty. Proposition P4 is therefore tentatively supported.

Sources of Finance Used During the Launch Period

With regard to the sources of finance used during the launch period of the surveyed businesses, four weakly significant differences were recorded among the three founder types. Habitual founders, particularly serial founders, used significantly more sources of finance than novice founders (row 4 in Table 3). Contrary to expectation, over 51% of

TABLE 7 Sources of Start-Up Finance Contrasts by Type of Key Founder

	Novice Founders		Portfolio Founders		Serial Founders			
Variable	No.	%	No.	%	No.	%	χ^2 Statistic	Significance Level
1. Personal savings. family. and friends used as a source of start-up capital during the launch period of surveyed small firm[a,b]							7.85	0.0197
No	76	19.5	20	26.7	19	21.1		
Yes	313	80.5	55	73.3	138	87.9		
2. Customers and suppliers used as a source of start-up capital during the launch period of surveyed small firm[a]							6.84	0.0327
No	373	95.9	67	89.3	144	91.7		
Yes	16	4.1	8	10.7	13	8.3		
3. "Other" sources of start-up capital used during the launch period of surveyed small firm							5.71	0.0576
No	369	94.9	67	89.3	152	96.8		
Yes	20	5.1	8	10.7	5	3.2		

[a] Statistically significant difference between novice and serial founders at least at the .1 level.
[b] Statistically significant difference between portfolio and serial founders at the .1 level.

founders in each group had used finance from banks and financial institutions. Portfolio founders with established track records were. however. more likely to have obtained finance from this source, although not in a statistically significant direction. Supporting the view that serial founders may have used the funds received on exiting from their last venture to finance the next. this group of founders was significantly more likely than the other founders to have used personal savings. family. and friends as a source of start-up capital in their current business (row 1 in Table 7). Portfolio founders were the least likely to do so. perhaps reflecting notions that they can fund new ventures from the reputation and track record associated with their existing ventures. This is to some extent borne out by the greater incidence of portfolio founders having used customers and suppliers (row 2) and "other" sources of finance (row 3). As a result, P5a and P5c are supported. In marked contrast. P5b cannot be confirmed.

Future of the Business

Approximately. half the founders in each of the three groups considered that their standard of living was better now than when they started the business (row 1 in Table 8). Although not in a statistically significant direction. both types of habitual founders were somewhat more likely than novice founders to be optimistic that their business would expand over the next 2 years (row 2). Moreover. over 91% of founders in each of the groups suggested that they wished to grow their business in the future, with there being no significant difference between the groups (row 3). To a lesser extent founders wanted to increase the total employment sizes of their businesses (row 4). Although not in a statistically significant direction, slightly fewer novice founders reported that they wished to grow employment, whereas both types of habitual founders expressed similar

TABLE 8 Future of the Business Contrasts by Type of Key Founder

Variable	Novice Founders No.	Novice Founders %	Portfolio Founders No.	Portfolio Founders %	Serial Founders No.	Serial Founders %	χ^2 Statistic	Significance Level
1. Standard of living today compared to when the founder started the business							4.73	0.3167
Worse	54	13.9	15	20.0	29	18.6		
About the same	110	28.3	20	26.7	50	32.1		
Better	225	57.8	40	53.3	77	49.4		
2. How the founder believes the future looks for the business in the next two years?							1.91	0.7530
Shrinking/declining business	42	10.8	8	10.7	14	8.9		
Stable/unchanged more or less	97	24.9	16	21.3	33	21.0		
Growing/expanding business	250	64.3	51	68.0	110	70.1		
3. Does the founder want to grow the business in the future?							0.33	0.8489
No	33	8.5	5	6.7	12	7.6		
Yes	356	91.5	70	93.3	145	92.4		
4. Does the founder want to increase the total employment size of the business in the next two years?							4.31	0.1157
No	133	34.3	20	26.7	41	26.1		
Yes	255	65.7	55	73.3	116	73.9		

levels of positive support for increasing the number of employees in their businesses. Consequently, P6 cannot be supported.

Performance of the Business

Business performance was examined on several dimensions covering levels and changes in sales revenues, levels and changes in profitability, the performance of the firm relative to the competition, and the share of sales exported abroad. No significant differences in performance were identified between firms owned and controlled by the three groups of founders (Table 9). However, at a coarse level of analysis, a weakly significantly larger proportion of novice rather than habitual founders operated businesses that were profitable (rather than making a loss or at break-even) at the 0.1 level of significance. Although not in a statistically significant direction, firms owned by portfolio founders were somewhat more likely to have increased their profits in the last year and to rate their businesses favorably in relation to the competition than was the case for firms owned by novice or serial founders.

ANOVA tests were also used to detect levels and changes in employment contrasts among the three groups of firms. Part-time and casual employees were taken into account by scoring full-time, part-time, and casual employees 1, 0.5, and 0.25, respectively (Cooper et al. 1989, pp. 323–324). No statistically significant differences were identified (Table 10). Nevertheless, serial founder firms reported higher levels of current employment and standardized changes in employment (i.e., after adjusting for the effects of

TABLE 9 Performance Contrasts by Type of Key Founder

Variable	Novice Founders No.	Novice Founders %	Portfolio Founders No.	Portfolio Founders %	Serial Founders No.	Serial Founders %	χ^2 Statistic	Significance Level
1. Level of sales for the last financial year (£'s. excluding value-added tax (VAT))							14.48	0.1523
1–99.999	188	48.8	34	47.2	61	39.4		
100.000–249.999	85	22.1	20	27.8	42	27.1		
250.000–499.999	57	14.8	5	6.9	18	11.6		
500.000–999.999	30	7.8	7	9.7	20	12.9		
£1m–£1.99m	11	2.9	5	6.9	7	4.5		
≥£2m	14	3.6	1	1.4	7	4.5		
2. Percentage increase or decrease in sales recorded by the business during the past year							11.53	0.4839
20% or more decrease	32	8.5	7	9.9	13	8.6		
1–19% decrease	38	10.1	7	9.9	14	9.3		
About the same	66	17.6	12	16.9	27	17.9		
1–25% increase	111	29.6	22	31.0	45	29.8		
26–50% increase	70	18.7	9	12.7	26	17.2		
51–100% increase	32	8.5	8	11.3	23	15.2		
More than doubled	26	6.9	6	8.5	3	2.0		
3. Level of profitability for the last financial year							7.02	0.1346
Loss	65	16.8	21	28.4	30	19.5		
Break-even	66	17.1	13	17.6	32	20.8		
Profit	255	66.1	40	54.1	92	59.7		
4. Percentage increase or decrease in pretax loss/profit recorded by the business during the past year							10.29	0.5904
20% or more decrease	30	8.5	7	10.6	11	7.7		
1–19% decrease	51	14.4	9	13.6	19	13.4		
About the same	90	25.4	22	33.3	42	29.6		
1–25% increase	123	34.7	17	25.8	42	29.6		
26–50% increase	26	7.3	3	25.8	17	12.0		
51–100% increase	14	4.0	4	6.1	7	4.9		
More than doubled	20	5.6	4	6.1	4	2.8		
5. How does the business rate its current profit performance relative to competition?							16.03	0.1899
Very poor	7	1.9	3	4.2	2	1.3		
Poor	18	4.8	2	2.8	9	6.0		
Fairly poor	34	9.1	5	6.9	13	8.6		
Average	150	40.1	23	31.9	56	37.1		
Fairly good	93	24.9	20	27.8	29	19.2		
Good	54	14.4	17	23.6	27	17.9		
Very good	18	4.8	2	2.8	15	9.9		
6. Percentage of sales revenue exported abroad							3.17	0.2044
0	302	78.4	51	68.9	121	77.1		
≥1	83	21.6	23	31.1	36	22.9		

TABLE 10 Employment Size and Change Contrasts by Type of Key Founder

Variable	Novice Founders	Portfolio Founders	Serial Founders	Analysis of Variance F Statistic	Significance Level
1. Number of total employees employed when business received its first order				0.46	0.634
Mean	2.7	3.0	2.9		
Median	2.0	2.0	2.0		
2. Number of standardized total employees employed when business received its first order[a]				0.25	0.782
Mean	2.4	2.5	2.6		
Median	1.5	2.0	2.0		
3. Number of total employees presently employed				1.54	0.214
Mean	9.5	9.0	12.5		
Median	5.0	5.0	5.0		
4. Number of standardized total employees presently employed[a]				1.94	0.144
Mean	7.9	7.7	11.1		
Median	3.5	3.5	4.3		
5. Standardized absolute employment change ((present total employment size—total employment size when received first order)/age of the business)				1.65	0.194
Mean	1.4	1.4	2.5		
Median	0.4	0.7	0.5		

[a] Full-time, part-time, and casual employees were taken into account by scoring full-time, part-time, and casual employees 1, 0.5, and 0.25, respectively.

part-time and casual employees), although not in a statistically significant direction. Hence, P7 cannot be confirmed.

Discriminant Analysis

Results discussed above show prima facie evidence for dissimilarities among novice, portfolio, and serial founders. An exploratory discriminant analysis minimizing the Wilks' lambda (Norusis 1988) was used to identify the *combination* of variables that best summarized and dichotomized the three types of founders. A stepwise selection method was used to identify a more parsimonious subset of variables that discriminates nearly as well as, if not better than, the full set (Klecka 1980). The final parsimonious model also provides a means to assign (and classify) any respondent into the ownership category (or type) it most closely resembles. As in previous studies, the predictive accuracy of the final model was not the paramount objective for using this multivariate technique. Consequently, a hold-out sample to test the predictive utility of the final model was not assembled.

The final discriminant analysis model is detailed in Table 11. This parsimonious model includes 15 variables. The discriminant analysis revealed that the first discriminant function had an eigenvalue of 0.25 accounting for 70.6% of the variance, with a canonical correlation of 0.45. The second discriminant function had an eigenvalue of 0.10, accounting for 29.4% of the variance. Wilks' lambda values for functions 1 and

2 were 0.72 and 0.91, respectively. Both lambdas were significant at the .001 level or less. Another indicator of the effectiveness of the discriminant model is the degree of predictive accuracy measured by the percentage of cases (or founders) classified correctly. Overall, 57% of the founders were correctly classified, considerably greater than that could be achieved by chance alone. The final model correctly assigned 58% of novice founders and 57% of serial founders to their correct ownership category. Slightly fewer portfolio founders (51%) were, however, assigned to their correct group.

Standardized canonical discriminant function coefficients in Table 11 indicate the relative importance of the variables included in the model and are used to describe the significant differences between the founder types. The pooled within-groups correlations show how closely a variable and a discriminating function are related, and a discriminating function is described on the basis of the structure matrix.

The first function, which explained most of the variance, differentiated the serial founders from the other two types of founders. Serial founders were drawn from non-managerial parental backgrounds and they established their first business at a very early age. They had gained experience by working in a large number of organizations on a full-time basis. Immediately before the start-up of the surveyed firm, a larger proportion of them had been self-employed. In terms of the reasons leading to start-up of their current venture, "it made sense at that time in my life" ("need for independence") and "to have more influence in my community" ("welfare considerations") were to no extent important. Further, they had obtained start-up capital during the launch period from personal savings, family, and friends.

The second function separated portfolio founders from the other two types of founders. Portfolio founders' parents during childhood mostly held managerial positions. They were young when they started their first business. Because they owned other businesses (with employees), portfolio founders generally had not been self-employed immediately before the start-up of the surveyed business. The managerial, technical and financial resources of at least one additional shareholder or partner were used to develop the surveyed business. In addition, drawing upon prior experience and contacts, customers and suppliers had been used as a source of start-up capital during the launch period of the business. The principal reasons leading to the start-up of the surveyed firms were as follows: "to give self, spouse, and children security" ("perceived instrumentality of wealth") and "to have access to indirect benefits such as tax exemptions" ("tax reduction and indirect benefits"). Interestingly, "to achieve something and get recognition for it" ("need for approval") was to no extent important. However, three personal attitudes to entrepreneurship were important: "I have a duty to give all clients and customers the same treatment" ("individualism—relationship between individuals"), "equality is everyone's right" ("power distance—management of inequality between people"), and "starting a business means uncertainty but adds to the excitement of life" ("uncertainty avoidance—stance toward the future").

CONCLUSIONS AND IMPLICATIONS FOR FUTURE RESEARCH

This study has provided an exploratory analysis of different types of habitual entrepreneurs. The particular focus has been on two types of habitual entrepreneurs, portfolio and serial entrepreneurs, who had established/owned more than one business. This study has identified similarities and differences between novice and habitual founders as well as between the two types of habitual founders. In respect of portfolio and serial

TABLE 11 Discriminant Groups of Independent Owner-Managed Firms in Great Britain

	Function 1		Function 2	
Variable	Standardized Canonical Discriminant Function Coefficients	Pooled Within-Groups Correlations (Structure Matrix)	Standardized Canonical Discriminant Function Coefficients	Pooled Within-Groups Correlations (Structure Matrix)
1. Age of the key founder when starting first business (years)	−0.74	−0.60	−0.28	−0.30
2. Job title of key founder when left last employer immediately before start-up—self-employed (0=no; 1=yes)	0.36	0.39	−0.20	−0.09
3. Reason leading to start-up—it made sense at that time in my life ("need for independence") (0=to some extent; 1=to no extent)	0.27	0.27	−0.08	−0.07
4. Number of organizations worked for on a full-time basis	0.30	0.25	0.16	0.05
5. Reason leading to start-up—to have more influence in my community ("welfare considerations") (0=to some extent; 1=to no extent)	0.23	0.21	−0.14	−0.17
6. Occupational status of founder's parents (i.e., the main income earner) during childhood—manager (0=no; 1=yes)	−0.17	−0.09	0.50	0.44
7. Personal attitude to entrepreneurship—I have a duty to give all clients and customers the same treatment ("individualism—relationship between individuals") (0=other; 1=agree)	−0.12	−0.22	0.36	0.36
8. Personal attitude to entrepreneurship—equality is everyone's right ("power distance—management of inequality between people") (0=other; 1=agree)	−0.19	−0.21	0.27	0.33
9. Reason leading to start-up—to give myself, my spouse and children security ("perceived instrumentality of wealth") (0=to some extent; 1=to no extent)	−0.15	−0.09	−0.26	−0.29
10. Number of shareholders or partners in the business (0=1; 1=≥2)	0.17	0.16	0.22	0.28
11. Personal savings, family, and friends used as a source of start-up capital during the launch period (0=no; 1=yes)	0.21	0.12	−0.14	−0.26
12. Customers and suppliers used as a source of start-up capital during the launch period (0=no; 1=yes)	0.08	0.15	0.26	0.26
13. Reason leading to start-up—to have access to indirect benefits such as tax exemptions ("tax reduction and indirect benefits") (0=to some extent; 1=to no extent)	0.16	0.15	−0.23	−0.24

Continued

TABLE 11 *Continued*

Variable	Function 1: Standardized Canonical Discriminant Function Coefficients	Function 1: Pooled Within-Groups Correlations (Structure Matrix)	Function 2: Standardized Canonical Discriminant Function Coefficients	Function 2: Pooled Within-Groups Correlations (Structure Matrix)
14. Reason leading to start-up—to achieve something and to get recognition for it ("need for approval") (0=to some extent; 1=to no extent)	0.14	0.19	0.44	0.23
15. Personal attitude to entrepreneurship—starting a business means uncertainty but adds to the excitement of life ("uncertainty avoidance—stance toward the future") (0=other; 1=agree)	−0.11	−0.13	0.19	0.13

Function	Eigenvalue	Percentage of Variance	Cumulative Percentage	Canonical Correlation	After Function	Wilks Lambda	χ^2 Statistic	*df*	Significance Level
1*	0.2505	70.62	70.62	0.4476:	0	0.7242	185.88	30	0.0000
2*	0.1042	29.38	100.00	0.3072:	1	0.9056	57.11	14	0.0000

Canonical discriminant functions evaluated at group means (group centroids)

Group	Function 1	Function 2
1. Novice founders	−0.36	−0.09
2. Portfolio founders	0.17	0.90
3. Serial founders	0.79	−0.18

Percentage of cases correctly classified by the model:
1. Novice founders = 225 cases (58%)
2. Portfolio founders = 38 cases (51%)
3. Serial founders = 89 cases (57%)

TOTAL FOUNDERS = 352 cases (57%)

*marks the two canonical discriminant functions remaining in the analysis.

founders, significant differences were identified in terms of the age of the founders when starting their first businesses, parental background, and the work experiences of the founders. Differences between the habitual founders were also noted with regard to reasons leading to start-up, personal attitudes to entrepreneurship, and sources of finance used during the launch period.

Our analysis, therefore, suggests habitual entrepreneurs cannot be treated as a homogeneous group. Birley and Westhead (1994a) during their comparison of novice and habitual new firm founders identified only two significant variables relating to reasons leading to start-up when they compared novices with habituals as a group (i.e., portfolio and serial founders combined). In marked contrast, our finer level of analysis, which distinguished habitual founders into portfolio and serial founders, identified seven significant differences. Birley and Westhead (1994a) found habitual founders were not more likely to stress materialistic reasons for starting their current venture, our more refined analysis interestingly noted portfolio founders were significantly more likely than serial and novice founders to have reported this start-up reason. In addition, Birley and Westhead (1994a) found significant differences between novice and habitual founders with regard to sources of finance used during the launch period. Most notably, they reported novice founders were significantly more likely to have used finance from personal savings, family and friends, and from customers and suppliers. Our analysis, however, shows that when habitual founders are divided into two founder types, serial founders were significantly more likely to have used launch finance from personal sources, whereas portfolio founders were more likely to have used finance from customers and suppliers. Birley and Westhead (1994a) also reported firms owned by habitual founders were more likely to be associated with teams of partners than was the case for novice firms. Further, our more refined analysis suggests this difference was driven by portfolio founders. Birley and Westhead's finding that habitual founders had gained greater previous experience through being self-employed immediately before the start-up of the surveyed business appears to have been driven by serial founders.

Consistent with other studies that have compared novice and habitual founders, our analysis failed to find any significant differences between the performance of firms owned by habitual founders when they were separated into serial and portfolio businesses. This evidence suggests owner-managers with prior business owning experience do not establish/own businesses that outperform those established by founders who have no prior business founding experience. Many habitual entrepreneurs, therefore, bring to their subsequent ventures some liabilities that may impede their performance. Identification of the liabilities and assets brought by habitual entrepreneurs to their subsequent ventures is, therefore, an important area for additional analysis.

When we explored the attributes and reasons leading to business start-up, the individual founder was the unit of analysis. However, when we focused upon performance, the unit of analysis was the organization (or the single surveyed firm). To appreciate fully the economic contribution of the habitual entrepreneurship phenomenon, we must gather information on all the organizations founded/owned by habitual entrepreneurs. Moreover, it will be necessary to distinguish real additional entrepreneurial activity from that which is merely a device to circumvent institutional restrictions, for example, to avoid labor laws which may become effective when a business exceeds a certain number of employees. Future research should focus on the founder/entrepreneur (rather than a particular organization) as the unit of analysis to enable a more detailed assessment of the nature and contribution of entrepreneurship. We believe the organization should not be the sole unit of analysis because some entrepreneurs attempt to resolve their personal materialistic aspirations through the growth of a portfolio of businesses (Birley and Westhead 1994a). It should also be noted that empirical analysis of novice or one-time entrepreneurs is fraught with the potential difficulty that a subset of such entrepreneurs may be future habitual entrepreneurs. As such, attempts to distinguish the characteristics of novice and habitual entrepreneurs may be colored by an absence of strict mutual exclusivity between the groups. As noted earlier, it should be borne in mind that the analysis in this article has focused upon habitual founders of businesses, which is only a subset of the wider phenomenon that includes habitual inheritors/purchasers of businesses and multiple corporate entrepreneurship.

The findings of this study have implications for practitioners, especially venture capitalists. The absence of significant performance differences between novice and habitual entrepreneurs, which is consistent with evidence from other studies, emphasizes the need for venture capitalists screening potential investees not to rely solely on previous experience but to analyze carefully the assets and liabilities of entrepreneurs' earlier background and whether experienced entrepreneurs have the motivation to undertake a subsequent venture. It was beyond the scope of this study to consider the relationships between financiers and types of habitual entrepreneur. Given the differences between serial and portfolio entrepreneurs, venture capitalists need to examine carefully the objectives of potential investees with previous experience. For example, serial entrepreneurs may be more amenable to the notion of venture capitalists' investment time horizons and be more willing to accept the possibility of an exit within a given period. Portfolio entrepreneurs may be more attuned to a more indefinite development of the business, which may be in conflict with venture capitalists' objectives. Our results also raise questions about the growth objectives of different types of habitual entrepreneurs that venture capitalists may need to consider. For example, serial entrepreneurs may be more comfortable with the notion of growing the business to a manageable size, whereas portfolio entrepreneurs may seek greater growth opportunities. These differing perspectives may have implications for the nature of the control processes that venture capitalists may be able to introduce for each type of founder. Further work examining the links between venture capitalists and serial entrepreneurs would seem warranted.

The empirical evidence presented here and elsewhere suggests researchers and policy-makers must appreciate there is a variety of types of entrepreneurs (as well as firms) (Birley and Westhead 1990; Westhead 1995a). Future research attention must, therefore, focus upon developing frameworks and theories that better describe the variety of career options open to entrepreneurs. In addition, future research should increasingly monitor all the businesses established/owned by portfolio and serial founders and inheritors/purchasers of businesses. Cohorts of different types of founders and inheritors/purchasers (and their firms) need to be monitored over considerable time periods to provide the research community and policy-makers with a more accurate assessment of the scale and nature of entrepreneurship.

The finding that prior experience did not lead to significantly higher performance raises a number of issues for researchers. The finding keys into research on the assets and liabilities of entrepreneurial experience (Starr and Bygrave 1991) and suggests that perhaps the former may offset the latter. There would, therefore, appear to be scope for large scale research that examines carefully the relative importance of different assets and liabilities of previous entrepreneurial experience.

One interpretation of the findings of this study is to call into question research on venture capitalists' screening processes that emphasize the importance of prior experience. However, a more attractive approach may be the need to appreciate that prior entrepreneurial experience per se may be a necessary but not a sufficient condition for the enhanced performance of a subsequent venture. A major issue is whether the entrepreneur is able to identify an opportunity the second time around that can achieve greater performance than the first. Evidence from venture capitalists' views of serial entrepreneurs has suggested that this is often the major problem (Wright et al. 1997). This in turn suggests that research that examines trade-offs between the various attributes of entrepreneurs and their business plans (Muzyka et al. 1996) may provide an important approach for understanding the likely prospects for subsequent ventures owned by habitual entrepreneurs.

This study has focused on the characteristics of habitual and novice entrepreneurs and their firms. Future research might usefully examine carefully the different processes used by these different types of entrepreneur in searching for, entering, and growing their first and subsequent ventures. Further, this study has not examined the role of venture capitalists and other financiers in providing governance of entrepreneurial ventures. This may be important in enabling entrepreneurs to profitably extend their ventures beyond the initial more entrepreneurial growth phase.

Habitual entrepreneurs may be sufficiently competent covering less routine areas of entrepreneurship. However, beyond the start-up phase they may be less competent at growing their business above a modest size and scale of development. This suggests there is a need to explore the attributes and behavior of entrepreneurs who have succeeded in growing their businesses to larger sizes and greater performance levels. To identify more closely the learning experience, there is also scope for further academic research that compares both the subsequent experiences of first time successful versus unsuccessful entrepreneurs, and the prior experiences of successful versus unsuccessful habitual entrepreneurs.

Additional research will enable policy-makers to assess the direct and indirect benefits as well as costs of providing assistance to nascent entrepreneurs compared with novice, portfolio, or serial entrepreneurs. Increased information will enable policy-makers more appropriate resource allocation decisions toward potential or different types of practicing entrepreneurs.

To encourage regional and national development, two important policy-led questions need to be addressed. First, should policy-makers target scarce economic resources to nascent entrepreneurs and increase the number of firm owners in an economy to its carrying capacity level? Second, should policy-makers target scarce resources toward the small number of existing founders (of which, a number are habitual entrepreneurs) or the small proportion of owner-managed firms (Storey 1994) that have the inclination as well as the ability to be significant wealth creators and employment generators?

The empirical evidence presented in this article makes a contribution to this important debate. Most notably, we found novice founders established firms that made comparable contributions to wealth creation and job generation as those established by portfolio and serial entrepreneurs. Policy-makers desiring to target scarce economic resources to firms that generate the vast majority of jobs must, therefore, appreciate prior venture experience does not necessarily ensure that this type of founder will subsequently establish/own a high growth venture. Moreover, the existing pool of experienced entrepreneurs may not be the source of high growth potential ventures. Efforts, therefore, may be needed to encourage more talented nascent entrepreneurs to become novice entrepreneurs. Policy-makers, however, must appreciate that the encouragement of more new firm founders (and new firms) in an economy may lead to increased competition, particularly in market niches at their carrying capacity level, and new entrants may displace existing firms. With regard to this important issue of targeting assistance to particular types of founders and firms, Reynolds et al. (1994) have argued:

> ... in regions where economic growth is quite satisfactory, government efforts might be restricted to assisting new firms with high growth potential or a potential for out-of-region exports. In a region with poor economic growth but with a promising economic base, government assistance might emphasize new firms with potential for high growth or out-of-region exports but also provide some assistance for all new firm start-ups. In regions with neither economic growth nor a promising economic base, the only option available may be to provide general assistance to all potential new firm founders.

Before we can conclusively answer the two policy-led research questions stated above, future research must address the following research questions (Dyer 1994, p.16). What are the relative influences of various antecedents on a portfolio or serial career choice? Which factors—individual, social, or economic—have the greatest impact? How do these factors interact with one another to motivate someone to start a portfolio or serial entrepreneurial career? By what processes can these antecedents be changed or influenced? Are there common socialization experiences for all types of entrepreneurs? Do certain types of socialization experiences determine whether particular types of entrepreneurs are more successful? In what industrial sectors/regions/cultures are habitual entrepreneurs over/underrepresented? In addition, it is important to consider a multifaceted approach that covers both the multiple creation and inheritance/purchase of businesses. As well as wealth creation from the founding of businesses, habitual purchasing of businesses followed by restructuring and innovation (especially where such businesses have been underperforming as an unfavored part of a larger group or a potentially strong part of a failing larger organization) also offer such prospects (Wright et al. 1997).

As appreciated elsewhere (Dyer 1994), to address these research questions there is a need for additional research from an objective as well as a subjective stance. There is a need for more in-depth longitudinal research focusing upon different types of potential and practicing entrepreneurs (Van de Ven 1992). Whereas additional quantitative questionnaire studies will bear further fruitful information and confirmatory evidence, there is also the need for more in-depth ethnographic case study research using semi-structured interviews as well as the participant-observation techniques of sociology and anthropology (Churchill 1992).

REFERENCES

Anonymous. 1986. To really learn about entrepreneurship, let's study habitual entrepreneurs. *Journal of Business Venturing* 1:241–243.

Beresford, P. 1996. The men who won't give up. *Director* 49(July):38–44.

Birley, S., and Westhead, P. 1990. Growth and performance contrasts between "types" of small firms. *Strategic Management Journal* 11:535–557.

Birley, S., and Westhead, P. 1992. A comparison of new firms in "assisted" and "nonassisted" areas in Great Britain. *Entrepreneurship and Regional Development* 4:299–338.

Birley, S., and Westhead, P. 1994a. A Comparison of new businesses established by "novice" and "habitual" founders in Great Britain. *International Small Business Journal* 12:38–60.

Birley, S., and Westhead, P. 1994b. A taxonomy of business start-up reasons and their impact on firm growth and size. *Journal of Business Venturing* 9:7–31.

Block, Z., and MacMillan, I.C. 1993. *Corporate Venturing*. Boston, MA: Harvard Business School Press.

Carter, N.M., Gartner, W.B., and Reynolds, P.D. 1996. Exploring start-up event sequences. *Journal of Business Venturing* 11:151–166.

Churchill, N.C. 1992. Research issues in entrepreneurship. In D.L. Sexton and J.D. Kasarda, eds., *The State of the Art of Entrepreneurship*. Boston, MA: PWS-Kent Publishing Co. pp. 579–596.

Cooper, A.C. 1981. Strategic management, new entrants and small business. *Long Range Planning* 14:39–45.

Cooper, A.C. 1985. The role of incubator organizations in the founding of growth-oriented firms. *Journal of Business Venturing*, 1:75–86.

Cooper, A.C., and Dunkelberg, W.C. 1986. Entrepreneurship and paths to business ownership. *Strategic Management Journal* 7:53–68.

Cooper, A.C., Woo, C.Y., and Dunkelberg, W.C. 1989. Entrepreneurship and the initial size of firms. *Journal of Business Venturing* 4:317–332.

Daly, M. 1991. VAT registrations and deregistrations in 1990. *Employment Gazette* November: 579–588.

Donckels, R., Dupont, B., and Michel, P. 1987. Multiple business starters. Who? Why? What? *Journal of Small Business and Entrepreneurship* 5:48–63.

Dyer, W.G. Jr. 1994. Towards a theory of entrepreneurial careers. *Entrepreneurship Theory and Practice* 19:7–21.

Gartner, W.B. 1985. A conceptual framework for describing the phenomenon of new venture creation. *Academy of Management Review* 10:696–706.

Gartner, W.B. 1989. Some suggestions for research on entrepreneurial traits and characteristics. *Entrepreneurship Theory and Practice* 14:27–37.

Gartner, W.B., and Shane, S.A. 1995. Measuring entrepreneurship over time. *Journal of Business Venturing* 10:283–301.

Gartner, W.B., and Starr, J.A. 1993. The nature of entrepreneurial work. In S. Birley, I. MacMillan, and S. Subramony, eds., *Entrepreneurship Research: Global Perspectives*. Amsterdam: Elsevier Science Publishers, pp. 35–67.

Gibb, A. A., and Ritchie, J.R. 1982. Understanding the process of starting small businesses. *European Small Business Journal* 1:26–45.

Gray, C. 1993. Stages of growth and entrepreneurial career motivation. In F. Chittenden, M. Robertson, and I. Marshall, eds., *Small Firms: Recession and Recovery*. London: Paul Chapman Publishing, pp. 149–159.

Guth, W.D., and Ginsberg, A. 1990. Guest editors' introduction: Corporate entrepreneurship. *Strategic Management Journal* 11:5–15.

Hall, P. 1995. Habitual owners of small businesses. In F. Chittenden, M. Robertson, and I. Marshall, eds., *Small Firms: Partnership for Growth*. London: Paul Chapman Publishing, pp. 217–230.

Hannan, M T., and Carroll, G.R. 1992. *Dynamics of Organizational Populations: Density, Legitimation and Competition*. New York: Oxford University Press.

Hawley, F. 1907. *Enterprise and the Production Process*. New York: G.P. Putman.

Hofstede, G. 1980. *Culture's Consequences: International Differences in Work Related Values*. Beverly Hills, CA: Sage.

Katz, J.A. 1994. Modeling entrepreneurial career progressions: Concepts and considerations. *Entrepreneurship Theory and Practice* 19:23–39.

Keeble, D., and Walker, S. 1994. New firms, small firms, and dead firms: Spatial patterns and determinants in the United Kingdom. *Regional Studies* 28:411–427.

Klecka, W.R. 1980. *Discriminant Analysis. Quantitative Applications in the Social Sciences Sage University Paper No. 19*. London: Sage Publications.

Kolvereid. L.. and Bullvåg. E. 1993. Novices versus experienced founders: An exploratory investigation. In S. Birley. I. MacMillan. and S. Subramony. eds.. *Entrepreneurship Reserch: Global perspectives*. Amsterdam: Elsevier Science Publishers. pp. 275–285.

de Koning. A.. and Snijders. J. 1992. Policies on small- and medium-sized enterprises in countries of the European Community. *International Small Business Journal* 10:25–39.

McGrath. R.G.. MacMillan. I.C.. and Scheinberg. S. 1992. Elitists. risk-takers. and rugged individuals? An exploratory analysis of cultural differences between entrepreneurs and non-entrepreneurs. *Journal of Business Venturing* 7:115–135.

Muzyka. D.. Birley. S.. and Leleux. B. 1996. Trade-offs in the investment decisions of European venture capitalists. *Journal of Business Venturing* 11:273–288.

Norusis. M.J. 1988. *SPSS/PC+ Advanced Statistics Guide*. Chicago: McGraw Hill.

O'Farrell, P.N., and Hitchens. D.M.W.N. 1988. Alternative theories of small-firm growth: A critical review. *Environment and Planning A* 20:1365–1382.

O'Farrell, P.N., and Hitchens. D.M.W.N. 1989. The competitiveness and performance of small manufacturing firms: An analysis of matched pairs in Scotland and England. *Environment and Planning A* 21:1241–1263.

Pfeffer. J.. and Salancik. G.R. 1978. *The External Control of Organizations: A Resource Dependence Perspective*. New York: Harper & Row.

Pickles. A.R., and O'Farrell. P.N. 1987. An analysis of entrepreneurial behaviour from male work histories. *Regional Studies* 21:425–444.

Reynolds, P.D., and Miller. B. 1992. New firm gestation: Conception. birth. and implications for research. *Journal of Business Venturing* 7:405–418.

Reynolds. P.. Storey. D.J.. and Westhead. P. 1994. Cross-National comparisons of the variation in new firm formation rates. *Regional Studies* 28:443–456.

Robbie. K., and Wright. M. 1996. *Management Buy-Ins: Entrepreneurship, Active Investors and Corporate Restructuring*. Manchester: Manchester University Press.

Ronstadt, R. 1982. Does entrepreneurial career path really matter? In K.H. Vesper, ed., *Frontiers of Entrepreneurship Research*. Wellesley, MA: Babson College, pp. 540–567.

Schein. E.H. 1978. *Careet Dynamics: Matching Individual and Organizational Needs*. Reading, MA: Addison-Wesley.

Scheinberg, S.. and MacMillan. I.C. 1988. An 11-country study of motivations to start a business. In B.A. Kirchhoff. W.A. Long. W.E. McMullan. K.H. Vesper, and W.E. Wetzel, Jr., eds., *Frontiers of Entrepreneurship Research*. Wellesley. MA: Babson College, pp. 669–687.

Scott. M.G. 1990. The entrepreneurial life cycle: Some preliminary results from a 20-year study of new Scottish independent businesses and their founders. *Proceedings of the Thirteenth United Kingdom Small Firms Policy and Research Conference—Towards the 21st Century*. Leeds, UK: Leeds Business School.

Scott. M.G., and Rosa. P. 1996. Existing businesses as sources of new firms: A missing topic in business formation research. *Paper Presented at Babson Entrepreneurship Conference*. Seattle, Washington.

Shane. S., Kolvereid. L., and Westhead, P. 1991. An exploratory analysis of the reasons leading to new firm formation across country and gender. *Journal of Business Venturing* 6:431–446.

Shapero. A., and Sokol, L. 1982. The social dimensions of entrepreneurship. In C. Kent. D.L. Sexton, and K.H. Vesper. eds., *Enclopedia of Entrepreneurship*. Englewood Cliffs, NJ: Prentice Hall, pp. 72–90.

Slevin. D.P., and Covin. J.G. 1992. Creating and maintaining high-performance teams. In D.L. Sexton and J.D. Kasarda. eds.. *The State of the Art of Entrepreneurship*. Boston, MA: PWS-Kent Publishing Company, pp. 358–386.

Smith. N.R. 1967. *The Entrepreneur and His Firm: The Relationship between Type of Men and Type of Company*. East Lansing, MI: Bureau of Business and Economic Research, Michigan State University.

Starr. J., and Bygrave, W. 1991. The assets and liabilities of prior start-up experience: An exploratory study of multiple venture entrepreneurs. In N.C. Churchill, W.D. Bygrave, J.G. Covin, D.L. Sexton, D.P. Slevin, K.H. Vesper, and W.E. Wetzel, eds., *Frontiers of Entrepreneurship Research 1991*. Wellesley, MA: Babson College, pp. 213–227.

Steinmetz, G., and Wright, E.O. 1989. The fall and the rise of the petty bourgeoisie: Changing patterns of self-employment in the postwar United States. *American Journal of Sociology* 94:973–1018.

Storey, D.J. 1994. *Understanding the Small Business Sector*. London: Routledge.

Van de Ven, A.H. 1992. Longitudinal methods for studying the process of entrepreneurship. In D.L. Sexton and J.D. Kasarda, eds., *The State of the Art of Entrepreneurship*. Boston, MA: PWS-Kent Publishing Company, pp. 214–242.

Van de Ven, A.H., Angle, H.R., and Poole, M.S. 1989. *Research on the Management of Innovation*. New York: Harper and Row.

Van Praag, C.M., and Van Ophem, H. 1995. Determinants of willingness and opportunity to start as an entrepreneur. *Kyklos* 48:513–540.

Vesper, K. 1990. *New Venture Strategies*, 2nd edition. Englewood Cliffs, NJ: Prentice Hall.

Westhead, P. 1990. A typology of new manufacturing firm founders in Wales: Performance measures and public policy implications. *Journal of Business Venturing* 5:103–122.

Westhead, P. 1995a. Survival and employment growth contrasts between types of owner-managed high-technology firms. *Entrepreneurship Theory and Practice* 20:5–27.

Westhead, P. 1995b. New owner-managed businesses in rural and urban areas in Great Britain: A matched pairs comparison. *Regional Studies* 29:367–380.

Westhead, P., and Birley, S. 1994. Environments for business deregistrations in the United Kingdom, 1987–1990. *Entrepreurship and Regional Development* 6:29–62.

Westhead, P., and Birley, S. 1995. Employment growth in new independent owner-managed firms in Great Britain. *International Small Business Journal* 13:11–34.

Westhead, P., and Cowling, M. 1996. *Demographic Contrasts between Family and Non-Family Unquoted Companies in the United Kingdom*. Coventry, U.K.: The University of Warwick, Centre for Small and Medium-Sized Enterprises, Working Paper No.32.

Westhead, P., and Moyes, A. 1992. Reflections on Thatcher's Britain: Evidence from new production firm registrations 1980–88. *Entrepreneurship and Regional Development* 4:21-56.

Woo, C.Y., Cooper, A., and Dunkelberg, W. 1991. The development and interpretation of entrepreneurial typologies. *Journal of Business Venturing* 6:93–114.

Wright, M., and Coyne, J. 1985. *Management Buy-Outs*. Beckenham, UK: Croom-Helm.

Wright, M., Robbie, K., and Ennew, C. 1995. Serial entrepreneurs. In W.D. Bygrave, B. Bird, S. Birley, N.C. Churchill, F. Hoy, R. Keeley, and W.E. Wetzel, eds., *Frontiers of Entrepreneurship Research*, Wellesley, MA: Babson College, pp. 158–171.

Wright, M., Robbie, K., and Ennew, C. 1997. Venture capitalists and serial entrepreneurs. *Journal of Business Venturing*. In press.

Part III
Environments for Venture Creation and Development

[11]

THE JOURNAL OF INDUSTRIAL ECONOMICS
Volume XXXIII December 1984 No. 2

SMALL FIRMS' SEEDBED ROLE AND THE CONCEPT OF TURBULENCE

M. E. Beesley and R. T. Hamilton

I. INTRODUCTION

An important role of independent small firms is often asserted to be to function as the 'seedbed' for new enterprises capable of challenging established businesses. The authors bring original data to bear on this, suggesting a workable definition of what constitutes a seedbed; measuring its industrial incidence; and defining the part played by independent firms in it. The study reveals substantial variation in the level of such activity among manufacturing industries. It is shown that seedbed activity is essentially innovative (the precursor of new industries) rather than a source of increased rivalry within existing industries. Conclusions are drawn about small firms policy, in particular that government aid for small business should be aimed more at reducing death rates among small firms.

II. THE SEEDBED FUNCTION

The notion of a seedbed process influencing industry population over time is implicit in Marshall's analogy with ". . . the young trees of the forest as they struggle upwards through the benumbing shade of their older rivals" [1920, Chapter 8, p. 263]. Marshall describes a continuous process of birth and death in the forest's undergrowth, with few undertakings reaching maturity and surviving, perhaps in perpetuity, as joint-stock companies. Since he was concerned at that point with aggregate industry structure, Marshall did not need to consider the variation of fertility and mortality across industries. The seedbed role was seized upon in 1971 by the Report of the Committee of Inquiry into Small Firms (the Bolton Report [1971]). This inquiry confined itself to small *independent* firms (i.e. those managed by the people who own them) and excluded from its scope the subsidiary units of large companies. To quote from the Report [1971, p. 85, para. 8.5]:

> "We believe that the health of the economy requires the birth of new enterprises in substantial number and the growth of some to a position from which they are able to challenge and supplant the existing leaders of industry. . . . This 'seedbed' function, therefore, appears to be a vital contribution of the small firm sector to the long-run health of the economy. We cannot assume that the ordinary working of market forces will necessarily preserve a small firm sector large enough to perform this function in the future."

The Committee thus expressed its major concern that, if left unattended, the fertile undergrowth may erode to such an extent as to jeopardize the continued propagation of the seedplants. In fact, in the event, the Committee went on to judge that erosion on such a scale was not then a serious prospect but that the situation be subject to "regular monitoring" [1971, p. 90, para. 8.16]. However, the seedbed process has proved more easily grasped as a concept than measured. No doubt due in large part to the lack of relevant data, the situation has not come under close monitoring. Given the public attention and resources now being devoted to the small business sector, it is important to gain some understanding on whether the benefits which it is thought society as a whole derives from the 'seedbed' are likely to exist.

The Bolton Committee perceived the challenge of independent small firms to be on two related fronts. The first emphasised the innovative role of new ventures and the threat to established industry leaders from the emergence of entirely new industries. Second, new firms expanding within established industries would erode the market power of the dominant suppliers, that is the incumbent firm's ability to deter actual entry. The major objectives of this paper are to establish the existence of a seedbed, and to clarify the extent to which the sector's contribution is either to establish new industries or to increase rivalry within well-defined industry orders.

The 'seedbed' can be viewed as the arena in which businesses are born and, judging by the body of evidence on the infant mortality of businesses (Boswell [1971]; Churchill [1955]; Gudgin [1978]; Marcus [1967]), where most will die. It follows that to show the extent and industrial composition of seedbed activity we need data on the birth and death rates of businesses by industry. Seedbed industries will be those with high birth and death rates. In other words, introducing a term which we develop below, the firm population of such industries will be subject to high levels of 'turbulence' because of the contemporaneous impact of these flows. By measuring births and deaths as distinct flows at the industry level we can identify the more active seedbed areas and begin to assess the extent to which this process is likely to lead either to more competitive industries or to more industries.

III. THE DATA

The work reported here is part of a wider study into the dynamics of industry structure. Data on births and deaths of establishments were extracted from the registers of HM Inspector of Factories (HMIF) for Scotland. Births are establishments observed to have opened in Scotland between 1 January 1976 and 31 March 1980. Deaths mean establishments which closed in Scotland between 1 January 1977 and 31 December 1979. A full account of the data collection and validation process is in Hamilton [1982]. The data's characteristic advantage was that they permitted the measurement of gross birth and death rates: almost all previous studies had had to be content with measuring the effect of differences between births or deaths over a period, i.e. the net increase or decrease in the total stock.

Unlike most official information sources, the HMIF registers extend to all sizes of establishment. This is most important in any study of new and small businesses since, at least in numerical terms, it is very small units which are likely to be predominant. However, for the purpose in hand, a measurement difficulty arises because the movement of an establishment to a new location will be recorded as both an opening and a closure. To minimize this distortion all businesses were traced which, in the relevant time period, moved location within Scotland. These businesses (82 in all) were excluded from the birth and death measures. Unfortunately it proved impossible to identify those businesses observed in the act of moving to or from Scotland. Thus, whilst the data are treated as births and deaths, 'births' include establishments which moved into Scotland and 'deaths' encompass units which transferred from the country. This renders the data somewhat imprecise but available statistics[1] do confirm business movement to and from Scotland to be much less frequent than internal movement. We are therefore confident that our measures closely approximate true births and deaths.

As seen earlier, we must distinguish between independent businesses and 'dependent' operations (i.e. subsidiary or associate companies; branch plants; and franchises). This is the dichotomy intended[2] in the Bolton Report. So in a 'birth' or 'death' the distinction must be maintained. Moreover, the processes leading up to the birth (or death) of a dependent unit are likely to be essentially different from those of an independent business. To achieve this distinction between dependence and independence, elements of the database were checked through trade directories and editions of *Who Owns Whom*. Each business was presumed to be independent in the absence of contrary evidence and so a number of dependent units—particularly the smallest—may have been misclassified as independent (rather than vice-versa).

The HMIF registers cover all of manufacturing and register entries (business premises) are classified to a Minimum List Heading (MLH) under the 1968 Standard Industrial Classification. At this stage the database was four absolute flows for each MLH industry: independent births (IB); dependent births (DB); independent deaths (ID); and dependent deaths (DD). The final step in the construction of the database involved transforming the individual flows into industry birth and death rates by dividing each flow by a count of the initial stock of establishments in that industry. The appropriate denominator for this calculation had to meet stringent requirements. Stock figures had to relate to Scotland at the MLH industry level. Enumeration must not have involved either sampling or the imposition of lower cut-off limits in terms of size (otherwise, this would have led to the exclusion of

[1] See *Regional Trends* 1981, Table 10.5, page 115.

[2] The Bolton Committee of Inquiry was not able to make this dichotomy in the quantitative sections of its report because official statistics are not compiled on this basis.

considerable numbers of small units). Finally, stock numbers were required to apply to a point in time before the start of the birth and death flows. These requirements were met by the data produced by the Annual Census of Employment (ACE) for June 1973, and this is the source of the denominators used to obtain industry birth and death rates. Table I aggregates the various flows to convey the size and structure of the database.

TABLE I
BIRTHS AND DEATHS IN MANUFACTURING INDUSTRY

	Births		*Deaths*	
	IB	*DB*	*ID*	*DD*
Employment:	*Period:*	*4½ years*	*Period:*	*3 years*
10 or less	719	163	890	175
11–49	259	88	341	102
50+	29	42	87	90
Unknown	287	104	121	50
TOTAL	1294	397	1439	417
Rates (based on June 1973 stock of 9606 units)				
Total/Stock %	13.5	4.1	15.0	4.3

Upon viewing Table I the reader is reminded that the birth and death flows relate to monitoring periods of different durations. This is a consequence of HMIF rules governing the retention period of register details on businesses which have closed. What information we have on the employment size of these establishments is sufficient to emphasize the extent to which we are indeed dealing with a host of small firms, independent and dependent. The birth and death rates calculated in Table I are global mean values for manufacturing in Scotland. Despite a shorter monitoring period,[3] deaths outnumber births—a result consistent with the general decline in Scottish manufacturing over the years to which our data relate.

IV. THE CONCEPT OF TURBULENCE

The term 'turbulence' is introduced to denote the flux created in an industry's total composition by flows of births and deaths. A few authors have come close to this concept but none appears to have carried through with the analysis. Caves and Porter [1976] suggest that:

> "Firms may go through life cycles, with lifespans varying from industry to industry. If some industries experience higher rates of generational turnover, perhaps due to greater frequency as amplitude of disturbances, they will show (*ceteris paribus*) more deaths and more births than other industries. . . . If industries vary in their rates of turnover, the occurrence

[3] To standardise for the different monitoring periods we presume the HMIF registers to operate with constant lags between birth or death and the monitoring thereof. Hence the annual rate of IB is (13.5 ÷ 4.5)% = 3.0%, cf. ID rate of 5.0% per annum. For DB and DD the annual rates are 0.9% and 1.4% respectively.

> of exit should be positively related to the occurrence of entry, with entry serving as a proxy for the unknown underlying forces that speed the generalizational turnover of settlers."

Caves and Porter go on to claim to have uncovered evidence of systematic differences in industries' rates of generational turnover. This evidence is in the form of a positive though weakly significant association between dummy variables which reflect the occurrence but not the extent of both entry and exit. Gudgin [1978, p. 193] broaches our concept of turbulence thus:

> "There are thus industries characterised by high turnover in firms and establishments and others with low turnover. This situation, which is also described by Wedervang for Norwegian industries, is only part of the story since some industries with high closure rates also have low entry rates."

Gudgin does not appear to have expanded on this casual observation. Our concept of turbulence reflects the same phenomenon which has attracted the attention of these authors. At this juncture it is useful to clarify terminology. A number of industrial economists have developed narrower measures of intra-industry mobility (or turnover). This also expresses the idea of challenge to established positions, in that it considers displacement of top ranking firms in industries by others. Such movements take place over many years. Thus particular studies (see Scherer [1980, pp. 54–56]) have been confined to analyses of changes over long periods of time in the size rankings of none but the largest corporations drawn from widely defined areas (e.g. the whole of manufacturing industry or the population of all non-financial corporations).

According to Boyle and Sorenson [1971] a general weakness of such studies has been their lack of industry specificity. Our turbulence analysis is conducted within narrowly defined (MLH) industries but the time-scale is short. We cannot identify the rank size order in each industry at any point in time. Hence our analysis is not of mobility (or turnover) as these terms have come to be used. Turbulence expresses a different source of challenge—by change in the identity of separate units in particular industries over a shorter period.[4]

V. EXTENT AND NATURE OF TURBULENCE

Drawing on the discussion of section III, our measure of industry turbulence is:

$$T = \frac{(\mathrm{IB} + \mathrm{ID}) + (\mathrm{DB} + \mathrm{DD})}{\mathrm{Stock}}$$

[4] In operating at industry level our measures also avoid a problem which arises with these studies' use of rank correlation coefficients as measures of mobility over time. These coefficients are sensitive to the ranks assigned to new entrants to, and exits from, the sector over the period. This measurement problem becomes more critical if rank correlation is used to reflect mobility within a larger number of more narrowly defined industries.

In the manufacturing industries as a whole, the global mean value of T is 0.37. In calculating T values for individual industries we must guard against the possibility of very small industries generating extreme values. Hence our detailed analysis of turbulence is confined to those MLH industries with a stock of at least 50 establishments. This serves to reduce our sample size to 57 MLH manufacturing industries (from 123).

In Figure 1 we have plotted birth rate against death rate for these 57 industries. The quadrants arise from imposing on to this scatter diagram the global mean rates for the whole of manufacturing (see Table I). The 10 industries in the upper right quadrant have above average rates of birth and death. The lower left quadrant contains the 26 industries with below average birth and death rates. Other quadrants contain industries with either an above average birth or death rate, but not both. The small group of high birth, high death rate industries are turbulent in the fullest sense with an average T value of 0.60. This compares with a mean of 0.21 for the low birth, low death grouping. (The difference between these means is highly significant on a Student's t test.) Remaining industries have an average T score of 0.39, close to the global mean (0.37) for all manufacturing.

Having revealed the extent to which turbulence varies across industries, let us now concentrate on the groups of high and low turbulence industries (upper right and lower left quadrants respectively of Figure 1). When the average turbulence values of these industries are decomposed into their independent and dependent components, the result is set out in Table II.

TABLE II
COMPONENTS OF TURBULENCE IN HIGH AND LOW TURBULENCE INDUSTRIES

Components of turbulence	*High T industries*	*Low T industries*	*All manufacturing*
IB + ID/Stock (mean)	0.49	0.15	0.28
DB + DD/Stock (mean)	0.11	0.06	0.09
Number of industries	10	26	123

It is readily apparent that turbulence is essentially a phenomenon involving independent businesses. In the group of high T industries, the contribution of the dependent component (mean 0.11) is not markedly different from its average over all manufacturing (0.09). It is the very large independent component which renders these industries highly turbulent. In the set of 26 low T industries, whilst both components are much lower, the bulk of the fall in total turbulence is due to the threefold reduction in the independent component. So it is correct to identify the seedbed as involving independent businesses primarily.

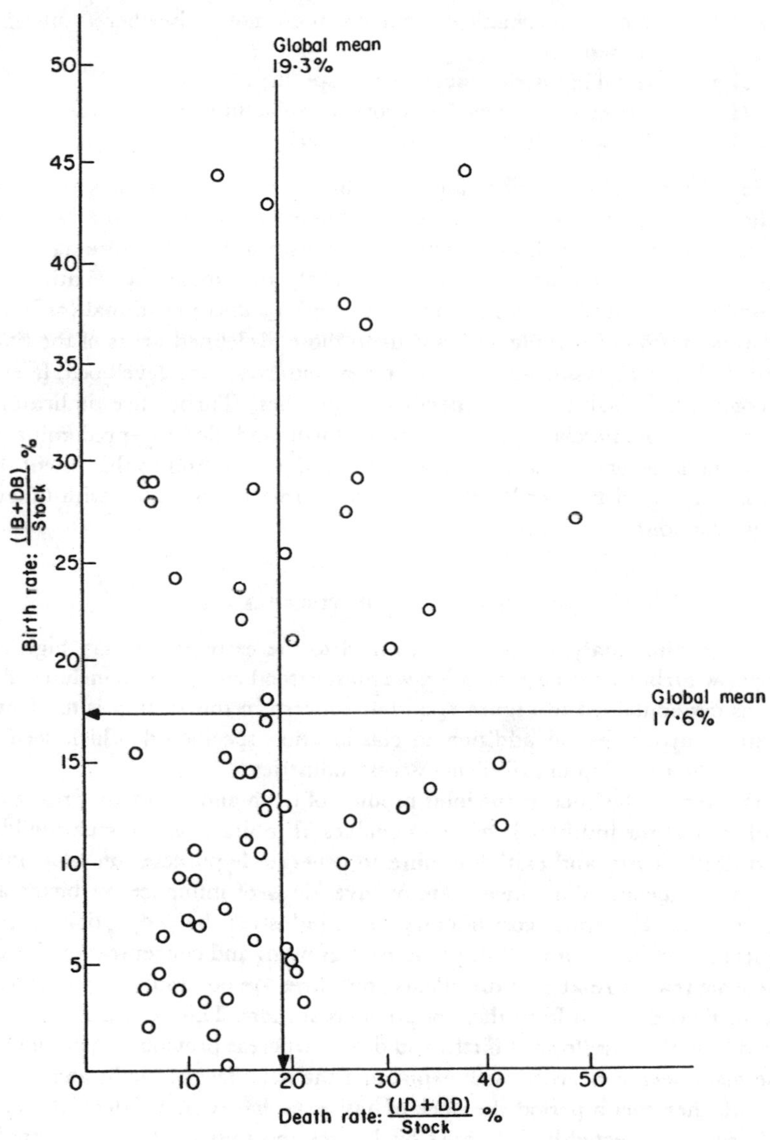

FIGURE 1

Plot of birth rate against death rate for 57 manufacturing industries

To take the analysis further, we note that the very highest levels of turbulence occur in the following industries:

MLH 349 Other mechanical engineering not elsewhere specified ($T = 0.65$)
MLH 399 Metal industries not elsewhere specified ($T = 0.66$)
MLH 479 Miscellaneous wood and cork manufacturers ($T = 0.76$)
MLH 496 Plastic products not elsewhere specified ($T = 0.83$)

These extremely turbulent industries have in common a lack of precise definition. Each is a residual category intended to capture those businesses whose products are such as to defy ready classification into more narrowly-defined MLH industries. It seemed very likely that these classifications are biased towards products which are either novel or unconventional (or both). Thus discussion of turbulence leads us to those ill-defined areas of the Standard Industrial Classification in which new industries are developed, later to become recognisable as independent industries. Turbulence indicates a process of commercial trial and error (birth and death), predominantly involving independent entrepreneurs. It is in this sense and to this extent that we might regard the 'seedbed' role of small firms as correlated with innovatory behaviour.

VI. INFLUENCES ON TURBULENCE

The foregoing analysis has been confined to the extremes of very high and very low turbulence. To generalise, we must extend our scope to include all 57 industries contained in Figure 1. So our concern in this section is to identify industry attributes (in addition to classification specificity) which seem to govern the variation in turbulence across industries.

We treat turbulence as the joint product of birth and death (or gross entry and exit) at the industry level. This enables us to draw on the separate birth and death (entry and exit) literature to generate hypotheses on what influences turbulence. We concentrate on five kinds of influence on births and deaths, viz. the capital cost of entry to an industry; the proportion of small units in it; industry profitability; industry growth; and concentration. Two of these are readily related to turbulence, but three are not and so we must make distinctions different from those of previous authors. This need arises because we deal with gross flows of births and deaths whereas previous studies have in the main been concerned with explaining the net effect of births and deaths, i.e. whether over a period the stock of businesses has risen or fallen. If a given influence is expected both to raise birth rates and raise death rates, there is a straightforward inference for effects on turbulence—it will be higher. The converse applies when the influence is likely to reduce both birth and death rates. But other cases are not clear. For example, if one anticipates a raised birth rate and a lower death rate, the effect on turbulence is unclear.

The higher the capital (and other) costs of entry, the more difficult it is thought to be to enter (Mansfield [1962]; Gorecki [1975]) and exit (Caves and Porter [1976]). Moreover, the greater the share of larger units (or conversely, the smaller the proportion of small units) the greater is inertia inherent in operations. Both these factors, obviously not unrelated themselves, would tend to be clearly related to turbulence—they would lower it. Higher profit is thought to encourage entry and lead to a net increase in units in an industry (Mansfield [1962]; Gorecki [1975]). But with respect to turbulence the effect is uncertain because circumstances favourably affecting profits would simultaneously increase births and decrease deaths (Marcus [1967]). So also for industry growth. Higher concentration would normally be expected to raise profit levels and so encourage entry (Duetsch [1975]). But rising concentration would also discourage births because of associations with entry barriers in general (Orr [1974]). We therefore expect the last three influences to be ambiguous for turbulence. To sum up: the level of industry turbulence (*T*) should be negatively related to the capital cost of entry to the industry; positively related to the proportion of very small units in the employment structure of the industry; but statistically independent of measures of industry profitability; growth; and concentration. In addition to these hypotheses, and drawing on the conclusion of the previous section, we also postulate a strong positive association between turbulence and the lack of specificity in an industry's classification. We now analyse these influences on turbulence. If and when the direction of the ambiguous effects is established, we can attempt further explanations.

Statistical analysis strongly confirms that two of the three ambiguous elements—profitability and concentration—are insignificant concomitants of total turbulence. The results of regression analysis involving the remaining explanatory variables[5] are presented in Table III. In equation (1) the small firm share (SHSM) coefficient is statistically insignificant. This can be attributed in part to the degree of correlation between entry cost (KINT) and SHSM (see correlation matrix). Omitting SHSM (equation (2)) has very little effect on the explanatory power of the regression. Introducing a dummy variable (DMY) reflecting the specificity of industry classification serves (equation (3)) to substantially increase the $\bar{R}^2$ value. In this final equation all the coefficients are highly significant (with no serious multicollinearity) and we explain 40% of the variation in industry levels of turbulence. The KINT and DMY coefficients have the expected signs and the size of the DMY coefficient confirms our earlier observation about the nature of the most turbulent industries. However, the significant positive relationship between turbulence and growth (GTH) is contrary to expectation. The most obvious explanation for this is that growth stimulates births but, even over the short

[5] The reader is referred to the Appendix for definitions and statistical sources of the explanatory variables used in this investigation.

TABLE III
MULTIPLE REGRESSION ANALYSIS OF TURBULENCE

Equation	*Y*	*Constant*	*KINT*	*SHSM*	*GTH*	*DMY*	*N*	$\bar{R}^2$	*F*
(1)	*T*	0.26 (2.07)	−0.004 (−1.75)	0.002 (1.19)	0.002 (2.77)		43	0.26	5.94 (3, 39)
(2)	*T*	0.40 (12.29)	−0.006 (−2.43)		0.003 (3.10)		43	0.25	8.12 (2, 40)
(3)	*T*	0.37 (11.60)	−0.005 (−2.41)		0.002 (2.87)	0.20 (3.30)	43	0.40	10.39 (3,39)

Notes: The figures in brackets are the *t*-values.
N represents the number of observations used.
Serial correlation absent in each estimated equation (Durbin-Watson test).

Correlation matrix

	KINT	*SHSM*	*GTH*	*DMY*
KINT	1.00	−0.40	−0.05	−0.10
SHSM		1.00	0.22	0.43
GTH			1.00	0.17
DMY				1.00

time span covered by this study, high birth rates themselves come to be associated with high death rates. (The simple correlation coefficient between the total birth and death rates plotted in Figure 1 is +0.31.) Death rates could thus be due to factors independent of industry types, but related to the fact that the population is young; seedlings are more vulnerable. To test this hypothesis would require data relating particular births to particular deaths.

VII. TURBULENCE AND INDUSTRY CONCENTRATION

The second aspect of small firms' seedbed challenge involves the erosion of the market power of dominant suppliers. We have just reported total turbulence (*T*) to be independent of the level of industry concentration. However, we can explore further the relationship between total turbulence and concentration by distinguishing the dependent and independent firm components.

The industry concentration ratios used are the percentage of 1973 industry employment in units each employing more than 500 people. Each of the 57 industries was allocated to one of three groups depending on the value of the concentration ratio. Within each grouping, we calculated the mean value of total turbulence (*T*) and the means of the independent and dependent components. This information is contained in Table IV.

The concentration ranges were chosen to ensure a reasonable spread of industry observations across the groups. Noting the mean concentration ratio for each group, we can reasonably regard the data as relating to low; medium; and high levels of concentration.

TABLE IV
TURBULENCE AND INDUSTRY CONCENTRATION

Concentration range *Mean concentration*	*0–15.9%* *4.5%*	*16.0–49.9%* *30.4%*	*50–100%* *65.9%*
T (mean)	0.34	0.34	0.37
IB + ID/Stock	0.28	0.26	0.24
BD + DD/Stock	0.06	0.08	0.13
Number of industries	22	20	15

The slight increase of turbulence (to 0.37) in the most concentrated industries is not statistically significant. The independent component of *T* falls slightly with increased concentration but this decline is more than offset by the large (and statistically significant) increase in the dependent component when we move into the highly concentrated industries. The immediate inference to be drawn is that, whilst dependent businesses are only involved to a minor degree in the overall turbulence of the less concentrated industries, such businesses do make a major contribution to turbulence in highly concentrated industries. We can in fact refine this conclusion because the simple correlation coefficient (r) between dependent birth and death rates is insignificant at +0.02 (between independent birth and death rates, $r = +0.44$). Thus, the high dependent component of turbulence in these industries is very much more likely to be the consequence of a high rate of birth or death, but not both. Table V sets out individual birth and death rates according to the level of industry concentration.

TABLE V
BIRTH AND DEATH RATES OF BUSINESSES AT DIFFERENT CONCENTRATION LEVELS

Concentration range	*0–49.9%*	*50–100%*
IB (%, mean)	11.5	13.0
DB	2.9	8.1
ID	15.8	10.4
DD	4.0	4.7

Of the increases and decreases reported in Table V, only the increase in dependent birth rate is statistically significant (Student's *t* test).

To refine our original inference, the increased contribution of dependent businesses to the turbulence of highly concentrated industries reflects their much higher birth rate in these industries. But why should dependent businesses gravitate so strongly into these areas? The most likely explanation, following Berry [1974], is that only large firms are able to encroach—via the setting up of dependent units—into areas already dominated by other large firms. Less likely, drawing on Brozen [1974], is that concentration is indeed a good proxy for profits and that, in this respect, established companies are more perspicacious than independent entrepreneurs. Thus, the overall level of seedbed activity is not influenced by concentration level but seedbed composition is markedly different in the most concentrated industries. Independent founders do not appear to be significantly repelled by increased concentration. However, the competitive challenge of dependent units is much more selective and directed at the areas of highest concentration. On these grounds we would argue that the more serious competitive threat to dominant suppliers is from the strategic entry moves of other large companies rather than the activities of the archetypal small entrepreneur.

VIII. CONCLUSIONS AND IMPLICATIONS FOR UK SMALL FIRMS POLICY

An essential function of the small business sector is alleged to be the seedbed of the new initiatives from which will emerge the successful businesses and industries of the future. This notion is intuitively plausible but we have so far lacked any measure of the extent or nature of seedbed activity. The concept of a seedbed cannot be disassociated from business trial and error (birth and death). Active seedbed industries will be in continuous flux due to contemporaneous birth and death flows. The usual measures of intra-industry mobility (or turnover) are inappropriate as indicators of this type of flux. We have developed the idea of turbulence into a direct measure of the flux created within individual industries due to the coincidence of birth and death flows.

The first point to emerge on the nature of seedbed activity is to confirm that it does involve independent much more than dependent units. The most turbulent MLH industries, we found, had the least specific definitions. It is to such open-ended industries that one would tend to classify those innovative ventures based on products sufficiently novel or unconventional as to prevent their being recorded in any narrowly-defined industry. Thus, seedbed activity is indeed associated with innovation. We intend to pursue the determinants of inter-industry variation in birth and death rates making up turbulence in subsequent work.

Further, we observed the nature of turbulence to be significantly influenced by industry concentration. Whilst independent founders do appear to be predominantly innovative, we see the major competitive challenge to dominant suppliers as coming from the diversification moves of other established companies.

From the early 1970s—provoked by the recommendations of the Bolton Committee—successive UK governments have contributed to the *ad hoc* development of a small firms policy. Towards the end of the decade the thrust of policy had become more selective in favour of new firms (rather than all small firms). Our evidence suggests that the benefits from such a policy will be in the form of innovation and new industries rather than the erosion of producer surplus in established industries. The more effective attack on this is likely to come from other established firms. In terms of the selectivity of policy instruments, we have traced high seedbed activity to a few ill-defined areas of industry. Our data reveal many independent entrepreneurs prepared to try something out of the ordinary—and that many fail in the attempt.

Initiatives intended to stimulate new business creation must anticipate turbulence and be able to tolerate high death rates. Their lack of industrial definition will make it difficult to channel specific support into such areas. To reduce the anticipated early failure rate of new businesses requires a method of choosing the 'best', *ex ante*, on the basis of formal plans and entrepreneurial skills. Apart from the question of the policy operators' ability to make the judgements, the method would require detailed analyses of 'industry' prospects and trends, when we have indicated that many entrepreneurs focus on ill-defined, and thus necessarily badly documented industries. Such individuals are likely to have extreme difficulty obtaining the data to support their claims. (They might have even greater difficulty accepting the need to reveal and justify their ideas on paper.)

These difficulties of running a policy based on *ex ante* encouragement are as desirable as they are inevitable. The willingness to act in the face of uncertainty is just what we require of entrepreneurs. Hence we are led to suggest that if aid to seedbed activity is to be given, it should be directed more at the problem of helping newly established firms recognise the symptoms of incipient failure in advance, i.e. of reducing the general tendency for young firms to be especially vulnerable. This, in turn, would redirect attention to increasing management skills, opportunities for finding consultancy advice, and like activities; that is, to a policy based on adding to the skills of entrepreneurs whilst engaged in running their business. This shift to a post-entry policy is supported by our finding less variance among death rates than among birth rates when industries are compared. But in general, the instinct to support small business, which has grown remarkably irrespective of government changes since the Bolton Committee reported, has been shown to have rather more solid support in fact than the Committee was itself able to demonstrate.

ACCEPTED NOVEMBER 1983

M. E. Beesley,
London Business School, Sussex Place,
Regent's Park, London NW1 4SA

R. T. Hamilton,
Department of Business Administration,
University of Canterbury, Christchurch 1, New Zealand

APPENDIX

DEFINITIONS AND STATISTICAL SOURCES OF THE EXPLANATORY VARIABLES

Variable	*Definition*	*Statistical sources*
Capital cost of entry (KINT) (£,000)	Net capital expenditure per employee (1975) *times* mid-point of modal employment size band (1975).	Scottish Abstract of Statistics (SAS) 1980, Table 12.7. Annual Census of Employment (ACE) 1975.
Share of small units (SHSM) (%)	Percentage number of units with less than 25 people in June 1974.	ACE 1974 (Scotland).
Industry profitability:		
* NQHD (£,000 per employee)	Net output per person employed (1975).	SAS 1980, Table 12.7.
* MARG (% profit margin)	Net output less wages and salaries, as % of industry sales.	Business Monitor PA1000, Census of Production 1976 (UK data).
Industry growth (GTH) (%)	Percentage change in industry employment between 1970 and 1977.	SAS 1974, Table 118. SAS 1981, Table 12.5.
* Concentration (CONC) (%)	Percentage of 1973 industry employment in units each employing more than 500 people.	ACE 1973 (Scotland).
Industry classification specificity (DMY) (dummy variable)	Value of 1 in following MLH industries: 229, 279, 349, 369, 399, 469, 479, 489, 496, 499.	Based on the 1968 Standard Industrial Classification.

* Statistically insignificant as determinants of the level of industry turbulence.

REFERENCES

BERRY, C. H., 1974, 'Corporate Diversification and Market Structure', *The Bell Journal of Economics*, Vol 5, No 1 (Spring), pp. 196–204.

BOLTON REPORT, 1971, Committee of Inquiry on Small Firms, Cmnd 4811, (HMSO, London).

BOSWELL, J., 1971, *The Rise and Decline of Small Firms*, (George Allen & Unwin, London).

BOYLE, S. E. and SORENSON, R. L. 1971, 'Concentration and Mobility: Alternative Measures of Industry Structure', *The Journal of Industrial Economics*, Vol 19, No 2 (April), pp. 118–32.

BROZEN, G., 1974, 'Concentration and Profits: Does Concentration Matter?', *Antitrust Bulletin*, Vol 19 (Summer), pp. 381–99.

CAVES, R. E. and PORTER, M. E., 1976, 'Barriers to Exit', Chapter 3 in *Essays on Industrial Organisation in Honor of Joe S. Bain*, edited by R. T. Masson and P. D. Qualls, (Ballinger Publishing, Cambridge, Mass.).

CHURCHILL, B. C., 1955, 'Age and Life Expectancy of Business Firms', *Survey of Current Business*, Vol 35, No 12 (December), pp. 15–19, 24.

DEUTSCH, L. L., 1975, 'Structure, Performance and the Net Rate of Entry into Manufacturing Industries', *The Southern Economic Journal*, Vol 41, No 3 (January), pp. 450–56.

GORECKI, P. K., 1975, 'The Determinants of Entry by New and Diversifying Enterprises in the UK Manufacturing Sector 1958–1963: Some Tentative Results', *Applied Economics*, Volume 7, No 2 (June), pp. 139–47.

GUDGIN, G., 1978, *Industrial Location Processes and Regional Employment Growth*, (Saxon House, Farnborough).

HAMILTON, R. T., 1982, *Measures and Determinants of Entry and Exit Rates of Businesses in Scotland*, Unpublished PhD thesis, University of London.

MANSFIELD, 1962, 'Entry, Gibrat's Law, Innovation and the Growth of Firms', *American Economic Review*, Vol 52, No 5 (December), pp. 1023–51.

MARCUS, M., 1967, 'Firms' Exit Rates and their Determinants', *The Journal of Industrial Economics*, Vol 16, No 1, (November), pp. 10–22.

MARSHALL, A., 1920, *Principles of Economics*, (8th edition), (Macmillan & Co Ltd, London).

ORR, D., 1974, 'The Determinants of Entry: A Study of Canadian Manufacturing Industries', *Review of Economics and Statistics*, Vol 56, No 1 (February), pp. 58–66.

SHERER, F. M., 1980, *Industrial Market Structure and Economic Performance* (2nd edition), (Rand McNally, Chicago).

[12]

Regional Studies, Vol. 28.4, pp. 411–427.

New Firms, Small Firms and Dead Firms: Spatial Patterns and Determinants in the United Kingdom

DAVID KEEBLE and SHEILA WALKER

Department of Geography and Small Business Research Centre, University of Cambridge, Downing Place, Cambridge CB2 3EN, UK

(Received April 1993)

KEEBLE D. and WALKER S. (1994) New firms, small firms and dead firms: spatial patterns and determinants in the United Kingdom, *Reg. Studies* **28**, 411–427. The paper analyses marked county-level spatial variations in new enterprise formation, growth in numbers of small businesses, and business failures in the UK 1980–90 as measured by VAT business registration and deregistration statistics. Multivariate econometric models for different periods and sectors are used to identify a range of key determinants, chosen from previous theoretical and survey research, notably previous population growth, capital availability through housing wealth, professional expertise, firm size structures, urban agglomeration advantages and diseconomies, and growing market demand. Some evidence is found for local enterprise culture, local government expenditure and enterprise agency effects, but not for unemployment-push processes. Policy implications are discussed.

New firms   Small firm growth   Firm deaths   Population growth   Urban agglomeration
Enterprise agencies

KEEBLE D. et WALKER S. (1994) La naissance, la petite taille et le décès des entreprises: la distribution géographique et les déterminants au Royaume-Uni, *Reg. Studies* **28**, 411–427. Cet article analyse au niveau des comtés les variations géographiques sensibles dans la création de nouvelles enterprises, la croissance du nombre de petites entreprises, et les dépôts de bilan au Royaume-Uni de 1980 à 1990 à partir des inscriptions et des radiations pour la TVA. On se sert des modèles économétriques à plusieurs variables relatifs à des périodes et à des secteurs différents afin d'identifier toute une gamme de déterminants clés, choisis à partir des recherches théoriques et empiriques antérieures, notamment l'évolution de la population, l'accès au capital par moyen de la propriété foncière, le savoir-faire professionnel, la taille des entreprises, les avantages et les déséconomies des agglomérations urbaines, et la demande porteuse du marché. Ils s'avèrent quelques preuves en faveur des effets de 'l'esprit d'entreprise' local, des dépenses municipales et de la Enterprise Agency (agence pour la création des entreprises), mais non pas du chômage. Les conséquences pour la politique se voient discuter.

Nouvelles entreprises   Croissance des petites entreprises
Décès   Evolution de la population
Agglomération urbaine
Agences pour la création des entreprises

KEEBLE D. und WALKER S. (1994) Neue Firmen, kleine Firmen und stillgelegte Firmen: räumliche Muster und Determinanten im Vereinigten Königreich, *Reg. Studies* **28**, 411–427. Dieser Aufsatz analysiert ausgeprägte räumliche Unterschiede in der Gründung neuer Unternehmen auf Grafschaftsebene, zahlenmäßiges Wachstum kleiner Firmen und Scheitern von Firmen im Vereinigten Königreich im Zeitraum 1980–1990, die in den Schätzungen der Statistiken für Registrierung und Deregistrierung von Firmen zu Mehrwertsteuer (VAT)zwecken erscheinen. Es werden vielfach veränderliche ökonometrische Modelle für verschiedene Zeitabschnitte und Sektoren benutzt, um verschiedene, von früheren theoretischen und Umfragensuntersuchungen ausgewählte Schlüsseldeterminanten zu identifizieren, besonders vorausgegangenes Bevölkerungswachstum, Verfügbarkeit von Kapital dank Hausbesitz, berufliches Fachwissen, Betriebsgrößsenstrukturen, Vorteile und Unwirtschaftlichkeit städtischer Ballung, und wachsende Marktnachfrage. Es werden etliche Beweise für 'Unternehmenskultur' und Verwaltungsausgaben am Orte sowie für die Wirksamkeit von Unternehmensagenturen erstellt, doch nicht für Prozesse, die sich mit dem Druck der Arbeitslosigkeit beschäftigen. Implikationen derartiger Bestrebungen werden diskutiert.

Neue Firmen   Zunahme kleiner Firmen
Stillegung von Firmen   Bevölkerungswachstum
Städtische Ballung   Unternehmensagenturen

INTRODUCTION

Between 1980 and 1990, both the total stock of United Kingdom businesses and the annual number of new business registrations increased substantially, as measured by the Employment Department's (now DTI's) annual VAT business registration databank (DALY, 1991: CENTRAL STATISTICAL OFFICE (CSO), 1993). New registrations rose from 158,000 in 1980 to 256,000 in 1989, before falling back with recession to 239,000 in 1990 and 206,000 in 1991 (CSO, 1993—see Fig. 1). Notwithstanding high and rising rates of business deregistration (142,000 in 1980, 203,000 in 1991), this surge in new firm formation resulted in a marked increase in the total stock of UK businesses, which rose from 1·29 million at the beginning of 1980 to 1·71 million at the end of 1990 (1·72 million at the end of 1991), a growth of 33%. And as DALY, 1991, p. 579, stresses, although these statistics include businesses of all sizes, 'the vast majority of registered businesses are small, so that the figures are a good guide to trends in the size of the UK small business population'.

The VAT business registration data also reveal that this growth of new and small businesses has been sectorally and geographically very uneven (KEEBLE, 1990a, 1990b). Fig. 2 shows that by far the fastest rates of growth in numbers of businesses—and predominantly small businesses—have occurred in 'finance, property and professional services' and 'other services', the latter being dominated by business services such as computer services and management consultancy. These two groups of services alone accounted for 54% of the net growth of the UK's total stock of businesses in the 1980s. The number of production businesses (mainly manufacturing) grew more slowly (but still by 30%), while the number of retailing businesses actually declined. These trends probably reflect different rates of growth of demand for different products and services, together with differences in barriers to entry and large firm competitive pressures in different sectors.

Regional unevenness in new firm formation and small business growth is clearly illustrated by Table 1. This reveals a broad north–south divide in enterprise formation between 1980 and 1990, with the South East, South West and East Anglia recording much higher rates than Northern England, Scotland, the North West and Northern Ireland. The South

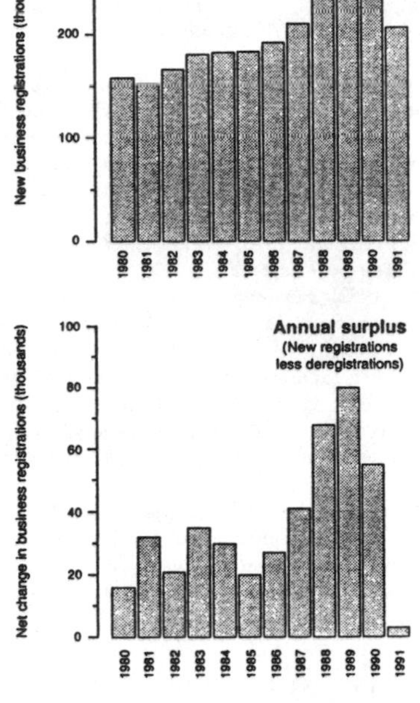

Fig. 1. The growth of new and small businesses in the United Kingdom, 1980–91

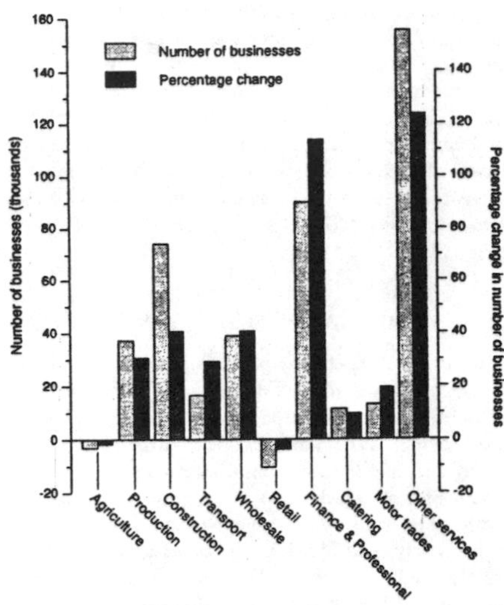

Fig. 2. Sectoral variations in small business growth in the United Kingdom, 1980–91

Table 1. Regional new firm creation rates and small business growth in the United Kingdom, 1980–90

	New firms (000s)	New firm formation rate[1]	Net growth in firms (000s)	Net firm growth rate[1]
South East	850	100·3	193·4	22·8
South West	190	99·7	41·4	21·7
East Anglia	79	95·8	17·9	21·7
East Midlands	140	79·3	28·1	15·9
Wales	93	77·5	16·5	13·8
West Midlands	180	72·1	32·7	13·1
Yorkshire and Humberside	158	70·3	24·3	10·8
North West	207	68·7	23·8	7·9
Northern Ireland	39	61·1	9·3	14·5
Scotland	134	55·4	21·7	9·0
North	77	55·3	11·0	7·9
United Kingdom	2,147	81·4	420·4	15·9

Note: 1. Per 1,000 civilian labour force, 1981.
Source: VAT business statistics from Daly, 1991.

East in particular stands out as the country's leading region for small business growth, with 850,000 new businesses and nearly 200,000 additional (and predominantly small) businesses during this 11-year period. The latter comprises 46% of the UK net national increase. This growth is undoubtedly closely linked to the historic sectoral concentration in South East England of financial, professional and business services, the key new and small business sectors identified above. In contrast, the traditional manufacturing regions of Northern England, Scotland and the North West had net growth rates less than 40% of the South East's, with increases of less than 25,000 firms in each case. These figures of course also illustrate the high death rate of new businesses, with net growth in many regions being less than one-fifth the total number of new registrations during the same period. In 1991, after the period of this study, the intensifying recession boosted deaths (203,000) and reduced births (206,000) to roughly equal levels nationally.

AIMS AND OBJECTIVES

Within this context, this paper reports the results of a series of spatial modelling analyses which attempt to identify the most important influences underpinning spatial variations in new firm formation, growth in numbers of (small) businesses and firm dissolution or death rates, in the UK during the 1980s. The method of investigation is via econometric analysis of VAT business statistics, the most widely used measure of UK business formation and dissolution (Ashcroft *et al.*, 1991), in terms of a set of independent variables deliberately selected on the basis of previous theoretical and empirical work as probable determinants of such spatial variations. These include both demand-side and supply-side influences on entrepreneurship and small business growth, and while focusing primarily on key possible economic, labour market and demographic influences, do also incorporate measures of policies, both national and local, which might have influenced local variations in small firm creation and survival during the 1980s. The analyses are conducted in terms of the 64 UK counties, including Northern Ireland (see Fig. 3).

The study draws on and is greatly indebted to the considerable volume of previous work in this field by UK academics (see, amongst many examples, Cross, 1981; Storey, 1982; Fothergill and Gudgin, 1982; Johnson, 1983; Gould and Keeble, 1984; Storey and Johnson, 1987; Moyes and Westhead, 1990; Keeble, 1990a; Mason, 1991; Ashcroft *et al.*, 1991; Westhead and Moyes, 1992). However, it attempts to break new ground in various ways. It is the first to analyse data for the whole of the 1980s and of the United Kingdom, and to examine within a common framework measures of new firm births, firm deaths and net changes in stock of (small) businesses; and it is the first to investigate and compare spatial trends in the three key sectors of production (dominated by manufacturing), financial, professional and business services, and consumer services. The original full study (Keeble *et al.*, 1993) also combines, for the first time, spatial and temporal modelling within a single common methodology.

DATA AND METHODOLOGY

The VAT data used as the measure of spatial variations in business formation, dissolution and net change in stock of businesses, while possessing certain well-documented limitations (see Daly, 1990), represents the most up-to-date, comprehensive, reas-

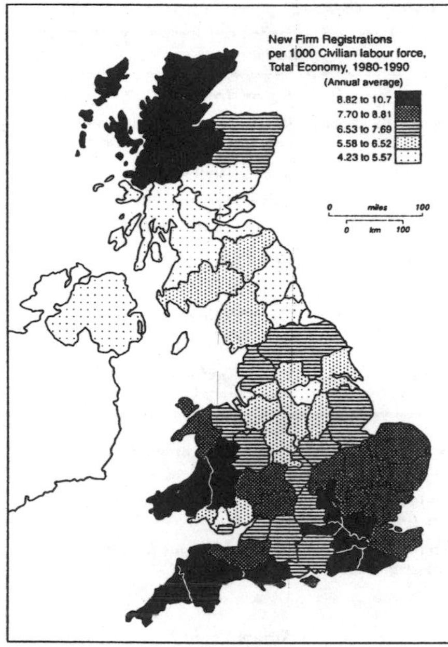

Fig. 3. Spatial variations in new firm formation rates (relative to labour force) in the UK, 1980–90

onably long-term and spatially disaggregated data source currently available for such investigation.[1] Analyses were conducted both for the whole 11-year period (January 1980 to December 1990) for which data were available at the outset of the research, and for two sub-periods (1980–84 and 1985–90) broadly characterized by different trends of recession and economic growth. In addition to total economy analyses, initial investigation of four key sectors revealed that results for 'financial' and 'other' services (see Fig. 2) were virtually identical, and these two overlapping service groups were therefore combined into one category, 'financial, professional and business services', for sectoral analysis, along with 'production' and 'consumer services' (catering, retail and motor trades).

The frequently-discussed problem of choice of denominator for normalization or standardization of the VAT statistics in terms of *rates* (see ASHCROFT *et al.*, 1991; KEEBLE *et al.*, 1993) was resolved by using two different measures, namely total civilian labour force[2] (LF models) and total business stock as measured by the VAT statistics (BS models). The first of these is the favoured normalization measure in this study on conceptual grounds and empirical evidence concerning the labour-market origins of entrepreneurship and successful small business growth. GAROFOLI, 1988, amongst others is in fact severely critical of the use of business stock as a denominator for both theoretical and empirical reasons. In contrast, AUDRETSCH and FRITSCH, 1992, argue that business stock is essential for analysis of firm death rates. Analysis of both measures enables comparison of results, another original feature of this study.

An extensive review of previous theoretical and empirical research (KEEBLE *et al.*, 1993, chapter 3) resulted in identification of the 31 separate independent variables listed in Table 2 for investigation as possible influences on birth, death and business stock change rates. These cover a wide range of demand-side, supply-side and policy variables. On the demand side, much research suggests that new and small businesses tend to serve restricted geographical markets, and are therefore influenced by local variations in level and growth of market demand. These are measured here by county GDP, household disposable income, and resident population statistics, and include levels and rates of change, as well as a measure of geographically-concentrated urban demand (*URBAN*). An important point however is that both the population change (*CHPOP*) and net migration (*MIGRAT*) measures, which are lagged over the five years preceding a particular analysis, undoubtedly incorporate a supply-side as well as demand-side influence. This is because population growth, which often includes selective in-migration, also increases the local pool of potential entrepreneurs; and recent research (KEEBLE, TYLER, BROOM and LEWIS, 1992) has conclusively demonstrated that entrepreneurship and small business creation in Britain's rural areas is strongly associated with previous population in-migration, itself powerfully stimulated by residential amenity and preference considerations.

Equally, the urban demand measure (*URBAN*) is included to measure the degree of spatial concentration of local markets, on the theory that large cities provide greater and more accessible market opportunities via dense concentrations of other firms and consumers (BATSTONE and MANSFIELD, 1992). These advantages may be particularly important for new firms. For existing firms, however, *URBAN* can also—and perhaps should—be interpreted as measuring the wider existence of either agglomeration economies or diseconomies, related to costs of premises, labour and accessibility/congestion, as argued in some earlier studies (KEEBLE, 1980). Specification of this variable uses the square root of population density in order to reduce the overwhelming effect on regression analysis of the very high densities recorded by London and Britain's other big cities.

Wherever possible, the demand-side variables included in subsequent models are specified in dynamic, rather than static, terms, as rates of change

Table 2. Explanatory variables used in modelling

Variable	Definition/description	Source of data
CHOP	Average annual % change in total population	*Regional Trends*
MIGRAT	Average annual net civilian migration per thousand total population	*Regional Trends*, OPCS, General Register Offices (Scotland and NI)
GDPHD	Average annual Gross Domestic Product per head	Central Statistics Office
CHGDPHD	Average annual % change in GDP per head	Central Statistics Office
CHGDP	Average annual % change in GDP	Central Statistics Office
INCHD	Average annual Household Disposable Income per head	Central Statistics Office
CHINCHD	Average annual % change in HDI per head	Central Statistics Office
CHINC	Average annual % change in HDI	Central Statistics Office
URBAN	Population density (square root of persons/sq.km)	*Regional Trends*
HOUSEVAL	Average house purchase price, excluding sales to LA sitting tenants (£000)	Building Society mortgage data from Department of Environment
TENURE	% dwellings owner-occupied or privately rented	*Regional Trends*
NONMAN	% usually resident economically active population >16 in non-manual socio-economic groups	Census of Population, 1981
PROFMAN	% usually resident economically active population >16 in managerial and professional socio-economic groups (SIC Codes 1–4)	Census of Population, 1981
PROFMANF	% usually resident economically active population >16 in managerial and professional socio-economic groups (including farmers-employers and managers) (SIC Codes 1–4 and 13)	Census of Population, 1981
SCHLEAVE	% school leavers with graded results	*Regional Trends*
HIGHEDUC	% employees in employment with higher education qualification	Census of Population, 1981
SIZETURN	% turnover in legal units of less than £500,000	Central Statistics Office
SIZEEMP	% employees in manufacturing units of 11–20 employees (1979); less than 20 employees (1983)	Business Monitor PA1003, 1985
SECTOR	% of employees in industries with low barriers to entry	Census of Employment, 1981
CHRUNEMP	Average annual % change in rate of unemployment	*Regional Trends*, Department of Employment
CHVUNEMP	Average annual % change in volume of unemployment	*Regional Trends*, Department of Employment
UNEMPRAT	Average annual unemployment rate	*Regional Trends*, Department of Employment
CHPUNEMP	Change in percentage point unemployment rate	*Regional Trends*, Department of Employment
COUNCIL	% Labour and Nationalist councillors on local councils	*Municipal Yearbook*, 1979, 1984
ASSAREA	Dummy variable: value of 1 if 50% or more of county comprises an assisted area; 0 if less than 50%	Assisted Areas Map, 1984
ENTERAG	Number of enterprise agencies with direct access to loan and/or grant funds per million civilian labour force	Directory of Enterprise Agencies, Trusts and Community Action Programmes, 1987, Department of Employment
LOCALTAX	Total rates per head collected by local authorities in county	CIPFA, COSLA, NIERC
EXPEND	Expenditure per head on all services by local authorities in county	CIPFA, COSLA, NIERC
WALEDUM	Dummy variable: value of 1 if Welsh county; 0 if not	–
SCOTDUM	Dummy variable: value of 1 if Scottish region; 0 if not	–
NEWREG	Lagged new registrations relative to labour force or business stock as appropriate	Department of Employment

Notes: 1. With the exception of GDP-based variables, average annual rates of change are calculated using all years during the period.
2. *CHOP* and *MIGRAT* are lagged five years; GDP, income and unemployment variables are lagged one year.
3. Unemployment figures are adjusted to take full account of changes in definition during the period.

rather than levels. This also applies to unemployment. This approach is based on the theoretical judgment that, in terms of processes of firm formation or dissolution, it is preceding *changes* in these environmental influences (for example, *growth* of local population, income or unemployment) that are likely to be significant in stimulating new enterprise formation, rather than static levels. In addition, nearly all variables are measured either lagged by an appropriate period (five years for population change, one year for unemployment, for example) or for a year immediately prior to or at the beginning of the study period.

Supply-side variables include measures of personal wealth and asset availability, as indicated by local house values (*HOUSEVAL*) and the extent of home ownership (*TENURE*), of occupational structure, reflecting the argument that professional and managerial staff (*PROFMAN* and *PROFMANF*) and non-manual workers generally (*NONMAN*) are more likely to set up new businesses (this is especially true in business and professional services: Keeble, Bryson and Wood, 1992), and of educational levels. Variations in local industrial structure are measured by indicators of firm size (*SIZETURN*) and sectoral composition (*SECTOR*), the inclusion of the latter being based on the theoretical judgment that possible sectoral impacts are better measured in this way than by adjusting the dependent variable, as earlier studies such as Ashcroft *et al.*, 1991, have done. Its measurement involved identification of low barrier-to-entry industries and their relative importance in each local economy. The impact of firm size is conceptualized here as likely to be sector specific, given the clear empirical evidence of the importance of small firms as 'incubators' for new firm founders in the manufacturing sector (Fothergill and Gudgin, 1982), but of large firms in business and professional services (Keeble *et al.*, 1992). Possible recession-push mechanisms on entrepreneurship are measured by several unemployment-based variables (e.g. *CHRUNEMP*). A local political affiliation measure (*COUNCIL*) attempts to test the thesis that communities traditionally electing a high proportion of Labour (or Nationalist) party councillors exhibit relatively negative socio-cultural attitudes to self-employment and entrepreneurship, the existence of a local enterprise culture being hypothesized as more likely to be associated with Conservative-dominated counties. However, this variable may also be interpreted as a measure of local policies towards small businesses, with Labour-controlled councils perhaps having more interventionist and supportive policies than Conservative-controlled authorities.

Finally, policy variables include levels of local tax burdens and local government expenditure (*LOCALTAX* and *EXPEND*), assisted area status in relation to central government regional policy (*ASSAREA*), and level of enterprise agency activity (*ENTERAG*). Enterprise agencies are independent business-led local partnerships established generally only since 1980 to assist new firm start-ups (Enterprise Dynamics, 1987). The presence of such agencies was found by Ashcroft *et al.* (1991) to be significantly associated with above-average new firm formation rates between 1980 and 1986, notwithstanding the fact that many agencies only began operating in or after 1983. The present study thus affords an opportunity for a more appropriate test of this finding over the whole of the 1980s. As with the Ashcroft *et al.* study, regional dummies for Scotland and Wales are included to capture particular differential regional effects, which could possibly reflect special regional policy initiatives via the Scottish and Welsh Development Agencies.

The methodological approach, using the SHAZAM econometrics package, involved three key steps. First, previous theoretical and empirical research on new firm formation and successful small business development was used to specify a theoretically-preferred model (see below) as the initial basis for investigation. Secondly, this model was tested and modified both to minimize multicollinearity problems by excluding particular severely collinear variables and to identify additional significant variables not initially included.[3] Thirdly, the statistical validity of the preferred models was checked both by the Jarque–Bera asymptotic LM normality test[4] and by calculating the Cliff–Ord *I*-statistic for spatial autocorrelation in regression residuals. The need for the latter test has been ignored in previous econometric work in this area, though recognized by geographers since the 1970s (Cliff and Ord, 1972). In several models tested, the presence of spatial autocorrelation necessitated model respecification to eliminate this autocorrelation by including significant additional independent variables, notably the Scottish and Welsh regional dummies.

NEW FIRMS, SMALL FIRMS AND FIRM DEATHS: THE SPATIAL PATTERNS

The variety and complexity of spatial patterns of new firm formation, small business growth[5] and firm deaths as measured by the VAT statistics are illustrated in Figs. 3–8. Four points about these patterns are particularly noteworthy. First, they reveal how different are the results obtained when the alternative labour force and business stock denominators are used for calculating rates. While Figs. 3 and 4 both reveal a broad north–south divide characterized by low rates in northern and high rates in southern Britain, the former, using labour force, indicates a relatively dispersed pattern of high rate counties whereas the latter, using business stock, yields a highly concentrated London-focused pattern. Differences are

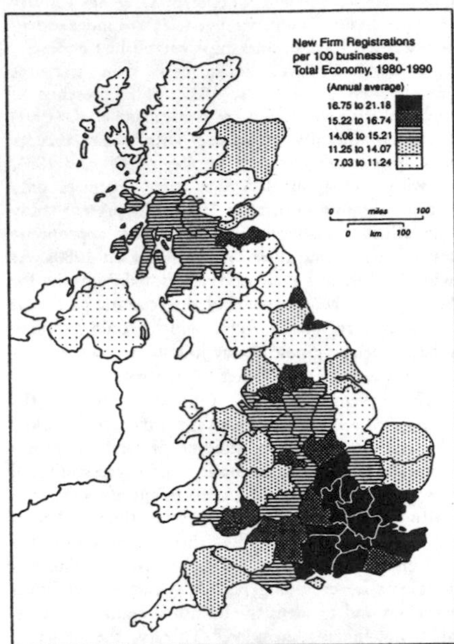

Fig. 4. Spatial variations in new firm formation rates (relative to business stock) in the UK, 1980–90

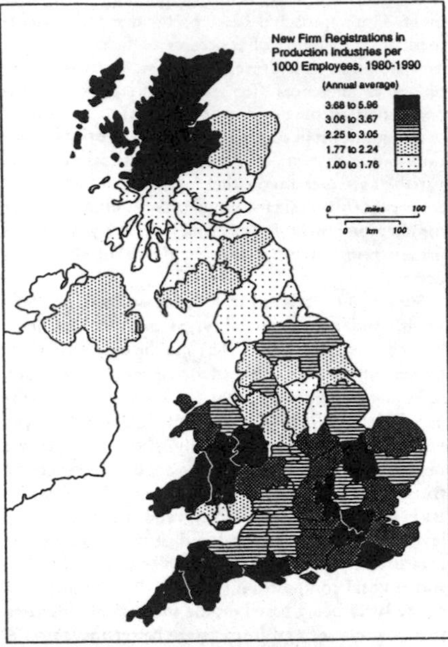

Fig. 5. Spatial variations in new production firm formation rates in the UK, 1980–90

less evident in the small business growth maps, but recur in maps of death rates (where the BS measure strikingly isolates most of Britain's most urbanized areas, not just London). This study thus reveals that choice of denominator is very important in terms of patterns (and results). The greater conceptual logic of using the labour force, rather than the number of businesses, as the source of local entrepreneurship and successful small business growth renders the former the preferred measure in this study.

Differences also however occur between sectors (Figs. 5 and 6), with high manufacturing firm creation rates (LF-based) exhibiting a relatively dispersed pattern (including south west England, central and west Wales, Scottish Highlands), but high financial, professional and business services rates being spatially much more concentrated in southern—and especially south-eastern—England. This difference is fully consistent with trends revealed by other independent studies (Keeble, Tyler, Broom and Lewis, 1992: Keeble *et al.*, 1991). A third area of difference is that between the maps of new firm rates (Fig. 3) and small business growth (Fig. 7). The latter, measuring the positive balance between new registrations and deregistrations during the period, is clearly focused on a Cambridgeshire–Somerset axis which is not evident in the new firm formation case, while the dispersed new firm pattern of Fig. 3 is also somewhat less evident in Fig. 7 (with the exception of Powys, Cornwall and the Highlands). High small firm birth rates in some peripheral counties (south west England, west Wales, Isle of Wight) appear therefore to be accompanied by relatively high subsequent death rates. Finally, and notwithstanding this point, the maps of firm births (Fig. 3) and deaths (Fig. 8) do reveal considerable general similarities. This important point will be considered again later.

NEW FIRM FORMATION: RESULTS

The models identified using this methodology all satisfied the econometric tests referred to above, as well as the Cliff–Ord test for spatial autocorrelation, achieved very significant *F*-test values and yielded high levels of explained variance. The initial model incorporated two demand-side and five supply-side variables, identified by previous work as probable major determinants of local rates of new enterprise formation and small business survival.

On the demand side, previous growth of local income or GDP, and changes in local population,

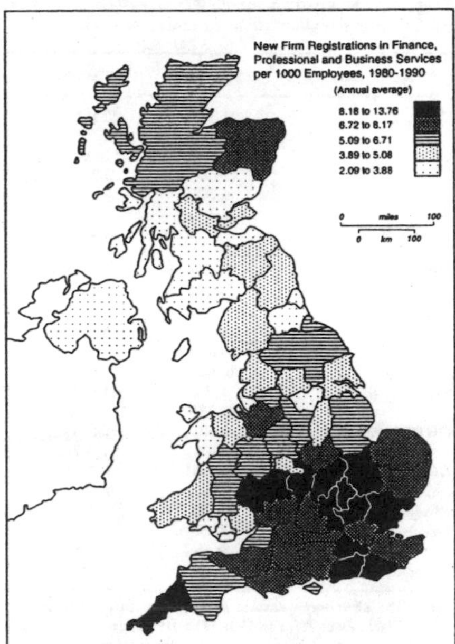

Fig. 6. Spatial variations in new financial, professional and business service firm formation rates in the UK, 1980–90

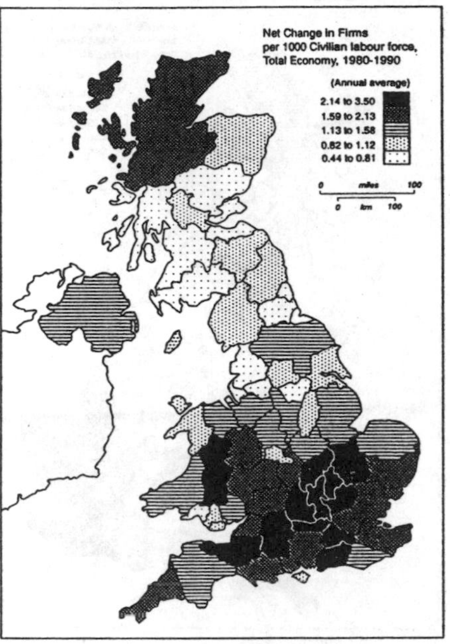

Fig. 7. Spatial variations in small business growth in the UK, 1980–90

were selected as key measures of growing local market demand and hence stimuli for small firm creation. On the supply side, the variables most likely to determine the supply of entrepreneurs, in addition to population change, were identified as local occupational, firm size and sectoral structures, capital availability, and growth in unemployment. The theoretical and empirical justification for this initial model is strong, notwithstanding debate over the relative importance of certain variables, such as firm size compared with occupational structure (GOULD and KEEBLE, 1984: GUDGIN and FOTHERGILL, 1984). Inclusion of both occupational structure (e.g. *PROFMAN* or *NONMAN*) and capital availability (measured in this study as in other previous work by housing wealth in the form of *HOUSEVAL*) does however immediately raise problems of multicollinearity, reflecting the inevitable close spatial relationship between professional and managerial occupations, high incomes and more valuable owner-occupied housing. In several cases this necessitated model re-specification and exclusion of a separate occupational structure measure. In these cases, there is little doubt that the housing wealth variable is measuring simultaneously both local capital availability and professional and managerial expertise. This must be born in mind in interpreting the results of the modelling analyses.

Testing of the initial model resulted in two important changes in the preferred framework. These were the dropping of the sectoral variable (*SECTOR*) because of consistently insignificant statistical results,[6] but the addition in several models of the *URBAN* variable, included as a measure of the influence on new firm formation of geographically-concentrated urban demand. A further interesting result of this evaluation stage was the inclusion in several analyses of the *COUNCIL* variable, adopted as a possible surrogate measure of negative local socio-cultural attitudes to entrepreneurship. For the BS models, however, this relationship was unexpectedly and consistently positive, not negative (see below).

The preferred total economy and sectoral new firm formation models are set out in Tables 3 and 4. Sub-period and consumer service models are omitted for reasons of space, as are BS sectoral models generally.[7] The results reveal high coefficients of determination (between 0·70 and 0·86) and provide strong support for most of the variables included in the initial theoretical framework of demand and supply-

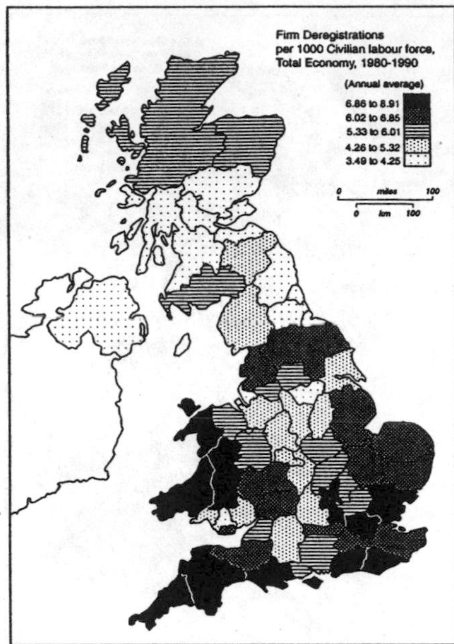

Fig. 8. Spatial variations in business deregistrations in the UK, 1980–90

Table 3. The determinants of spatial variations in new firm formation: total economy, 1980–90

Independent variable	LF model	BS model
Constant	−24·337	30·111
	(−0·992)	(1·702)
CHPOP	16·305***	17·544**
	(5·621)	(3·375)
CHGDPHD	0·782	–
	(1·718)	
CHINCHD	–	4·480*
		(2·187)
URBAN	0·545***	0·934***
	(3·706)	(3·993)
HOUSEVAL	0·538*	1·764***
	(2·582)	(3·669)
NONMAN	0·814**	–
	(2·669)	
SIZETURN	0·602**	−1·153***
	(3·055)	(−4·729)
CHRUNEMP	0·397	−0·995
	(0·634)	(−1·067)
COUNCIL	−0·198*	0·741***
	(−2·285)	(6·298)
R^2 adjusted	0·799	0·768
F-statistic	32·255	30·790
	(8,55)	(7,56)
z (*I*-statistic)	1·628	0·557

Notes: The LF model measures rates of new firm formation per 1,000 labour force in 1981. The BS model measures rates of new firm formation per 100 businesses at end-1979.
t-statistics shown in brackets:
* significant at 5%
** significant at 1%
*** significant at 0·1%

side influences outlined above, with the exception of sectoral structure and unemployment change. Spatial variations in new firm formation in the total United Kingdom economy (Table 3) during the 1980s appear to have been significantly influenced by the impact of earlier population growth or decline, geographically-concentrated urban markets, local availability of capital and of professional or non-manual expertise, inherited local firm size structures, growing local demand as measured by income per head, and by aspects of the local socio-cultural environment as expressed through the surrogate of local political affiliation.

In this total economy case, examination of results for the two subperiods as well as the 1980s as a whole (six models) highlights the leading importance of the rate of population change during the preceding five-year period (*CHPOP*) in influencing spatial variations in new enterprise creation. This arguably reflects both the demand-side pull of growing local market opportunities, and the supply-side push of an increasing pool of potential local entrepreneurs, especially in Britain's less-urbanized and rural counties, by far the chief destinations of recent major migration flows (Keeble, 1993a). This finding is the more interesting in that antecedent population growth is totally ignored as a possible influence by most other recent new firm modelling studies (such as Ashcroft *et al.*, 1991; Fritsch, 1992). These two studies also ignore the influence of concentrated urban demand (*URBAN*), which is significant and positive in five of the six models. This supports the view that notwithstanding substantial population decline in most large cities, the existence of a large local market and agglomeration economies are important in stimulating new enterprise formation in these areas. Large cities do thus appear still to act as nurseries or incubators for new enterprise, following traditional urban incubator theory (Nicholson *et al.*, 1981).

Another variable which appears as a positive stimulus in both the LF and BS models is capital availability as measured by housing wealth and value (*HOUSEVAL*). The local availability of personal financial resources, epitomized and embodied in the value of local owner-occupied housing, thus appears to play an important role in enabling or inhibiting new business creation. Moreover, and strikingly, this finding for spatial variation is powerfully replicated in the project's separate time-series analyses (quarterly, new registrations), which found 'strong effects on the rate of new business formation from . . . the real value of net housing wealth' (ROBSON, 1992: KEEBLE *et al.*, 1993, chapter 7). However, as noted earlier, it must also be stressed that *HOUSEVAL* undoubtedly also captures, in part, the impact of local occupational structures biased towards professional and non-manual workers. *HOUSEVAL* is highly correlated with the *PROFMAN* and, to a lesser extent, *NONMAN* variables, and alternative analyses replacing *HOUSEVAL* with *PROFMAN* yield almost as good results as the preferred model reported here. While *NONMAN* does appear independently, significantly and positively in its own right in the LF models (Table 3), this composite interpretation of *HOUSEVAL* must be borne in mind in interpreting later results.

The total economy new firm models also indicate a strong spatial relationship (five out of six models) with local firm size structures (*SIZETURN*). However, in this case the LF models indicate that it is *small* firm structures which have a positive impact, whereas the BS models suggest the opposite, namely a strong association with *large* firm structures (see Table 3). This is precisely the reversal of association recently also found by AUDRETSCH and FRITSCH, 1992, in the West German case. They suggest that this reflects the fact that in the business stock case, areas where employment is dominated by large firms are, in effect, bound to possess fewer existing firms than other areas relative to their stock of potential new firm founders. As a result, those firms which are founded in such areas will have a relatively large impact on the BS measure of new firm formation, leading to high BS-based firm creation rates in these areas. The opposite will be true for areas characterized by many small firms, and hence inevitably a large business stock base, notwithstanding large numbers of births in these areas. Traditional theory concerning the positive impact of small firm structures on enterprise birth rates thus applies only to the LF measure of new firm formation. The LF results for *SIZETURN* fully support the latter theory at the total economy level (Table 3). The BS results are however likely to be explained by Audretsch and Fritsch's argument, which implies a statistical rather than causal mechanism underpinning the observed relationship.

More difficult to explain is the similar reversal found for the relationship between new firm formation and *COUNCIL*, where a negative relationship is hypothesized as a surrogate index of positive local socio-cultural attitudes to entrepreneurship and the existence of a local enterprise culture. For two of the three LF models (e.g. Table 3), this hypothesis is supported by the results. Relative to its labour force, a local community which elected a high proportion of Labour (or Nationalist) councillors during the 1980s was likely to generate significantly fewer new firms, all else being equal, than one which elected mainly Conservative, Liberal Democrat or Independent councillors. However, this relationship is reversed in the BS models (e.g. Table 3), where *COUNCIL* is significantly positive in all three cases. This counter-intuitive result appears to be associated with high *COUNCIL* values in urban-industrial areas of northern and western Britain, such as Tyne and Wear, Cleveland and Cardiff, which as noted earlier (Fig. 4) do exhibit relatively high BS-based firm formation rates. Whether this association is again in some way statistical rather than causal, or reflects active encouragement of business formation by more interventionist local Labour councils, is very difficult to determine.

Finally, in this total economy case, the models do indicate that growing local market demand stimulates new business formation, especially in periods of rapid national economic growth, with a positive and significant relationship in the 1980–90 BS model and in both the LF and BS 1985–90 models. In contrast, the results do not support the thesis that rising local unemployment is a major influence, with insignificant t-values (Table 3) in all cases except the 1980–84 BS model. In this latter sub-period of severe recession, high percentage increases in unemployment were particularly characteristic of urban areas and the south-east. The latter had low unemployment rates at the beginning of the period, so this finding lends some support to HAMILTON's, 1989, argument that 'recession-push' impacts on new firm formation are greatest below a certain critical unemployment level. In general, however, such impacts are not apparent as a major influence on spatial variations in entrepreneurship, a finding replicated even more powerfully by the time-series analyses reported in ROBSON, 1992. Lastly, a significant Welsh regional effect in the 1980–84 LF model could possibly reflect startup initiatives by agencies such as Mid Wales Development, the Welsh Development Agency, or British Steel Industry (Ltd) during this recessionary period.

Sectoral LF results are presented in Table 4. These reveal very interesting differences between manufacturing and professional and business services in the variables identified as significantly influencing new firm formation. Indeed, the only common—and powerful—influence is previous population growth or decline (*CHPOP*). For production (manufacturing) firms, the other key positive influences identified are geographically-concentrated urban demand (*URBAN*), local occupational structures characterized by non-manual skills (*NONMAN*), and a relative predominance of small firms (*SIZETURN*). *CHPOP*, *URBAN* and *SIZETURN* are also and equally significant in the BS model. These findings are all fully consistent both with the initial theoretical framework adopted, and

Table 4. The determinants of spatial variations in new firm formation: sectors, per 1,000 employees in sector, 1980–90

	Sector	
Independent variable	Production	Finance, professional and business services
Constant	−37·613	−37·822*
	(−1·989)	(−2·466)
CHPOP	8·716**	20·743***
	(3·398)	(7·055)
CHGDPHD	–	1·889**
		(3·162)
URBAN	0·506***	–
	(4·697)	
HOUSEVAL	–	2·046***
		(10·133)
NONMAN	0·848***	–
	(3·528)	
SIZETURN	0·474***	−0·635***
	(3·683)	(−3·564)
CHRUNEMP	−0·395	1·969*
	(−0·977)	(2·578)
COUNCIL	−0·126	–
	(−1·819)	
R^2 adjusted	0·698	0·863
F-statistic	25·306	80·184
	(6,57)	(5,58)
z (*I*-statistic)	1·395	0·638

Notes: *t*-statistics shown in brackets:
* significant at 5%
** significant at 1%
*** significant at 0·1%

with previous empirical and survey research findings. In addition, the local enterprise culture variable (*COUNCIL*) is significant at the 10% level. Rising unemployment is not found to be of any importance. Indeed, in the BS case it acts significantly to depress, not stimulate, manufacturing business formation rates, a finding replicated in the total economy time series models.

Spatial variations in new firm formation in financial, professional and business services are influenced by different forces, apart from the ubiquitous population change factor. Here it is growing local demand (*CHGDPHD*), capital availability through housing wealth (*HOUSEVAL*), rising unemployment (*CHRUNEMP*) and, most interesting of all, a strong relationship with the presence of *large*, not small firms (a *negative SIZETURN* relationship). The latter reversal is, of course, exactly that to be expected from recent survey research on entrepreneurship in business and professional services (Keeble, Bryson and Wood, 1992). These findings thus conclusively establish the powerful but *sectorally-specific* effect of firm size structures on spatial variations in new enterprise formation in the UK. For manufacturing firm formation, a pool of small firms is very important, whereas for the creation of professional and business service firms, it is the local existence of large firms which provide entrepreneurs with essential professional expertise, reputation and client contacts. The importance of local professional expertise is also, of course, suggested by inclusion of the *HOUSEVAL* variable, with its very high correlation with *PROFMAN* (r=0·916).

SMALL BUSINESS GROWTH: RESULTS

Analysis of spatial variations in the growth in numbers of small businesses within the UK during the 1980s focuses attention on the local determinants not just of new enterprise creation but also, and uniquely in this study, of small business survival. In the absence of any separate theory of the spatial distribution of small business survival rates, it seems logical to adopt the same theoretical framework here as for the new firm analyses, on the argument that forces stimulating small firm creation are also in general likely to assist survival and net growth in the small firm population.

The results of these analyses are recorded in Tables 5 and 6. Both the total economy models (Table 5) achieve good levels of explained variance (over 0·75), and reveal that small business growth is consistently

Table 5. The determinants of spatial variations in small business growth: total economy, 1980–90

Independent variable	LF	BS
Constant	−9·613**	11·615
	(−2·677)	(1·291)
CHPOP	6·177***	9·276**
	(5·714)	(3·191)
CHGDPHD	0·297	–
	(1·319)	
URBAN	–	−0·186*
		(−2·479)
HOUSEVAL	0·556***	1·406***
	10·629)	(8·360)
SIZETURN	–	−0·318*
		(−2·554)
SECTOR	–	−0·554**
		(−3·030)
COUNCIL	–	0·237***
		(4·232)
ASSAREA	1·588	–
	(1·700)	
R^2 adjusted	0·792	0·753
F-statistic	61·003	32·956
	(4,59)	(6,57)
z (*I*-statistic)	1·359	1·541

Notes: The LF model measures rates of small business growth per 1,000 labour force in 1981. The BS model measures rates of small business growth per 100 businesses at end-1979.
t-statistics shown in brackets:
* significant at 5%
** significant at 1%
*** significant at 0·1%

and very strongly related to previous local population growth (*CHPOP*) and to capital availability measured by housing wealth (*HOUSEVAL*), the latter also undoubtedly incorporating the impact of local occupational structures characterized by professional and managerial expertise. These results are repeated in the sub-period models as well. The results thus demonstrate that rapid growth in numbers of small firms is most likely in areas where previous population growth has increased local market opportunities and the pool of potential entrepreneurs, and where professional expertise combined with housing wealth provide the human and capital resources necessary for entrepreneurs to establish and operate successful small businesses.

In the LF models, the only other significant variable identified is growth in market demand (*CHGDPHD*) during the 1985–90 subperiod. The assisted area status measure (*ASSAREA*) does however reach the much weaker 10% level (Table 5), perhaps hinting at a weak regional policy effect on small business survival rates. This would at least be in line with recent research which shows significantly greater small firm uptake of DTI Enterprise Initiative consultancy assistance and technology grants in assisted areas of Britain (Mason and Harrison, 1992: Keeble and Bryson, 1993: Keeble, 1993b).

The BS models contain the same counter-intuitive results for *SIZETURN* and *COUNCIL* already discussed in the new firm case, but this time with additional significant *negative* relationships with *URBAN* and *SECTOR*. The latter could possibly imply that new firms established in high barrier-to-entry industries, and the areas in which these are most common, have a higher probability of survival and longer life spans than their counterparts in low barrier-to-entry sectors. The negative *URBAN* relationship is however in striking contrast with the *positive* relationship found in the BS new firm formation model (Table 3). This reversal supports the argument that while urban environments with their concentrated local market opportunities act as new firm incubators or nurseries, agglomeration diseconomies result in above-average urban death or relocation rates, resulting in low rates of growth in numbers of small businesses. Evidence supporting this argument is provided by the recent comparative study by North and Smallbone, 1993, of small firms in London, the outer southeast, and northern rural England, which highlights the significance of small firm relocation, and constraints on small firm growth resulting from labour problems and declining demand, in the London case. Conversely, of course, the BS model result identifies a clear association between rural environments and high rates of growth of small businesses.

As in the new firm case, sectoral differences (Table 6) are considerable, with population change (*CHPOP*) again being the only significant influence common to both manufacturing and business services. For production (manufacturing), there is also a clear small firm size structure effect (*SIZETURN*), but a *negative* unemployment growth impact (*CHRUNEMP*). This result, which is repeated in the BS model, suggests that the environment in areas with rapidly rising unemployment inhibits the chances of small firm survival. However, the most interesting production model result is the finding in the BS case of a significant and positive relationship between small manufacturing firm growth and the activities of local enterprise agencies (*ENTERAG*). This echoes Ashcroft *et al.*'s, 1991, finding for new firms generally, and is supported by survey findings (Enterprise Dynamics, 1987) of significantly greater survival rates (84% after three years) for new startups assisted by enterprise agencies compared with non-assisted startups. The evidence of this and the earlier studies thus does suggest that enterprise agency advice and assistance has aided the survival and viability of new small businesses in particular localities of the UK since the early 1980s.

Table 6. The determinants of spatial variations in small business growth: sectors, per 1,000 employees in sector, 1980–90

	Sector	
Independent variable	Production	Finance, professional and business services
Constant	5·217***	−13·537
	(4·673)	(−1·590)
CHPOP	5·863***	11·091***
	(7·408)	(6·190)
CHGDPHD	–	0·937*
		(2·429)
HOUSEVAL	–	0·777***
		(7·136)
SIZETURN	0·169**	−0·401***
	(2·773)	(−4·560)
CHRUNEMP	−0·342*	0·571
	(−2·265)	(1·652)
R^2 adjusted	0·606	0·846
F-statistic	33·358	70·001
	(3,60)	(5,58)
z (*I*-statistic)	0·933	1·337

Notes: t-statistics shown in brackets:
* significant at 5%
** significant at 1%
*** significant at 0·1%

Spatial variation in small business growth in financial, professional and business services (Table 6) reflects exactly the same significant influences as the pattern of new firms (Table 4), with the one exception of an unemployment effect (*CHRUNEMP*, though positive, is not significant). High rates of growth of small business service enterprises are thus

Table 7. The determinants of spatial variations in firm deregistration: total economy, 1980–90

Independent variable	LF	BS
Constant	−22·901	63·655***
	(−1·421)	(3·979)
CHPOP	7·246**	8·888*
	(2·968)	(2·311)
URBAN	0·555***	1·070***
	(4·580)	(4·522)
HOUSEVAL	–	1·025**
		(3·399)
NONMAN	1·181***	–
	(5·177)	
SIZETURN	0·628***	−0·528*
	(4·691)	(−2·438)
COUNCIL	−0·144*	0·536***
	(−2·376)	(5·907)
ENTERAG	–	−0·635*
		(−2·166)
EXPEND	−0·020**	–
	(−3·100)	
R^2 adjusted	0·751	0·759
F-statistic	32·739	34·027
	(6,57)	(6,57)
z (I-statistic)	1·836	0·399

Notes: The LF model measures rates of firm deregistration per 1,000 labour force in 1981. The BS model measures rates of firm deregistration per 100 businesses at end-1979.
t-statistics shown in brackets:
* significant at 5%
** significant at 1%
*** significant at 0·1%

shown to reflect rapid previous population (*CHPOP*) and market demand (*CHGDPHD*) growth, capital availability and professional expertise (*HOUSEVAL*), and the positive effect of a local predominance of large, not small, firms (*SIZETURN*). The population change and large firm influences are also identified by the BS model for this sector.

FIRM DEATHS: RESULTS

Analysis of spatial variations in VAT deregistration rates, taken as a broad surrogate index of small business deaths and closures,[8] is even less susceptible to *a priori* theoretical specification than net changes in business numbers, given the almost complete lack of theory relating to the location of business failures (KEEBLE *et al.*, 1993, chapter 3). The initial framework already outlined for earlier analyses was therefore adopted again here.

The results of the modelling analyses of small business deaths using the VAT data are presented in Tables 7–9. The first of these is closely and consistently similar to Table 3 with, in each case, five out of six significant variables the same, and possessing the same signs, positive or negative as the case may be. In other words, those variables most strongly associated with high new firm *birth* rates during the 1980s are generally also those most strongly associated with high firm *death* rates.

The reason for this is quite simple, namely that new firms are inherently vulnerable, high-risk and prone to failure. New firm subsequent death rates are thus much higher than those for established firms. Spatially, this translates into a situation in which areas in which supply or demand-side forces stimulate high levels of new business formation will inevitably in due course also exhibit high death rates, simply because there are more new, vulnerable small firms in these areas than elsewhere. This is conclusively demonstrated by Table 8. In this, antecedent new firm formation rates (*NEWREG*: see Table 2) lagged by three years following HUDSON, 1986, are shown to be extremely powerful predictors of subsequent firm deregistration rates. These models yield very high coefficients of determination (0·93–0·94) but contain only a handful of other significant variables.

Table 8. The determinants of spatial variations in firm deregistration: total economy, 1980–90 (using lagged registration rates)

Independent variable	LF	BS
Constant	0·281	26·211***
	(0·130)	(6·228)
NEWREG	1·108***	1·046***
	(27·902)	(18·558)
URBAN	–	0·407***
		(5·504)
HOUSEVAL	–	−0·520***
		(−5·720)
CHRUNEMP	0·511*	–
	(2·194)	
SIZETURN	0·116**	–
	(3·248)	
R^2 adjusted	0·931	0·943
F-statistic	285·453	347·405
	(3,60)	(3,60)
z (I-statistic)	1·543	1·674

Notes: The LF model measures rates of firm deregistration per 1,000 labour force in 1981. The BS model measures rates of firm deregistration per 100 businesses at end-1979.
t-statistics shown in brackets:
* significant at 5%
** significant at 1%
*** significant at 0·1%

The implication of this clear finding for interpretation of the results in Tables 7–9 is that these are only of substantive interest in relation to those few variables which *differ* in their significance between new firm and firm dissolution analyses for the same periods. These differences may be interpreted as indicating influences specifically increasing or reducing firm death rates, over and above those basic relationships determining initially high or low birth rates.

One of the most striking of these is the consistently negative significant relationship between firm deregistration rates and *EXPEND* in all three period/subperiod LF models (Table 7). In other words, high rates of local authority expenditure on goods and services are associated with lower business death rates. Interestingly, a weak (10% significance level only) positive relationship between *EXPEND* and new firm births was also included in the BS 1985–90 model. So these results do suggest that high local authority expenditure encourages local small business activity, primarily through enhanced small firm survival and reduced death rates.

A second important result is the significant and negative BS model relationship (Table 7) between business death rates and the activities of local enterprise agencies (*ENTERAG*). This echoes the earlier finding of a positive relationship between *ENTERAG* and production firm survival rates. In this case, too, it implies that local enterprise agency activities, in providing business advice, loans and grants have helped reduce small firm death rates, this time in the total economy, a finding again in line with survey research (Enterprise Dynamics, 1987). It is also consistent with the recent findings of a national survey of small and medium-sized British businesses conducted by the Small Business Research Centre, 1992, p. 34, where use of enterprise agency advice was found to be particularly common amongst 'new, manufacturing-based and rapidly-growing firms'. This study concluded that 'this could indicate agency counselling is of some help in assisting new firms to grow more rapidly'. The present finding is consistent with this recent judgment.

An alternative approach to identifying additional influences on spatial variations in small business death rates is provided by Table 8, where *NEWREG* in a sense standardizes death rates for earlier birth rate variations. The LF analysis here suggests that rising unemployment (*CHRUNEMP*) and a preponderance of small firms (*SIZETURN*) both enhance the likelihood of local small business failure, while the BS analysis suggests the same for location in large cities (*URBAN*). The last finding of course replicates that of a negative effect of urban areas on small business growth noted earlier (Table 5). High levels of personal financial resources and professional expertise (*HOUSEVAL*), however, appear to reduce the level of business failures. All these findings are intuitively logical.

Sectoral differences (Table 9) involve only a few variables. For the production (manufacturing) sector, these involve *CHPOP* (in both LF and BS models) and the *LOCALTAX* variable (in the BS case). The former is highly significant in the new firm models, but ceases to be significant for firm deaths. This indicates that areas where rapid local population growth stimulates high manufacturing firm birth rates do not necessarily thereafter suffer equally high death rates. This further reinforces the significance of population growth as a factor influencing the changing geography of small businesses in the UK. The *LOCALTAX* finding indicates an association between high local authority tax burdens and increased business deregistrations, either because of failure or relocation. It must be stressed, however, that this finding relates to now-historic rating differences which no longer exist, following the introduction of the Uniform Business Rate in 1990. Finally, for the professional and business services sector, the only significant difference is the additional association between increased death rates and urban location (*URBAN*) in both LF and BS models, in line with a number of earlier analyses.

Table 9. The determinants of spatial variations in firm deregistration: sectors, per 1,000 employees in sector, 1980–90

	Sector	
Independent variable	Production	Finance, professional and business services
Constant	−45·183**	−35·792***
	(−2·969)	(−5·150)
CHPOP	3·137	10·754***
	(1·732)	(4·908)
CHGDPHD	–	1·327***
		(4·185)
URBAN	0·450***	0·259**
	(3·915)	(3·257)
HOUSEVAL	–	1·217***
		(11·206)
NONMAN	0·883***	–
	(4·228)	
SIZETURN	0·276**	–
	(2·684)	
CHRUNEMP	–	1·083
		(1·997)
COUNCIL	−0·089	–
	(−1·785)	
R^2 adjusted	0·674	0·830
F-statistic	27·056	62·400
	(5,58)	(5,58)
z (I-statistic)	0·941	0·279

Notes: t-statistics shown in brackets:
* significant at 5%
** significant at 1%
*** significant at 0·1%

CONCLUSIONS

The modelling results presented in this paper, which are rooted in the findings of previous theoretical and empirical research, indicate that marked spatial variations in new firm formation, small business growth and business deregistrations in the UK reflect a variety of key influences. For new firm formation, the most important of these are previous local population growth, capital availability as indicated by housing wealth, occupational structures focused on professional, managerial, and non-manual expertise, firm size structures, and geographically-concentrated urban demand. Manufacturing firm formation is, however, influenced by the existence of small firms, whereas the creation of business service new firms reflects the presence of large firms. Significant further influences are local enterprise cultures as measured by political affiliation and growing market demand. In the early 1980s, rising unemployment and a Welsh effect appear also to have had some impact.

For small business growth, key positive influences are previous population growth, capital availability through housing wealth, and professional and managerial expertise. Less important are growing local market demand and the negative, not positive, effects of both rising unemployment and urban location. The very interesting reversal in the direction of the last two relationships compared with those for new enterprises suggests that, while rising unemployment and urban agglomeration can stimulate higher start-up rates, they also result in the long run in higher death rates with resultant below-average growth in numbers of small businesses.

Spatial variations in firm death rates unequivocally reflect the dominant influence of earlier creation rates, additional and independent factors including the negative effect of rising unemployment, urban location and small firm size structures. In contrast, above average local government expenditure and enterprise agency assistance appear to help reduce the death rate of small enterprises.

The policy implications of these findings are limited, given the basic conclusion that spatial variations in new firm formation and small business survival and growth appear primarily to be determined by the inherited and historic supply-side characteristics of different areas, and recent demographic and market demand trends. However, two points are noteworthy. First, the analyses suggest that Britain's major cities and conurbations exhibit significant problems in terms, not of new enterprise creation, but of small business survival and death rates. Indeed, in extreme cases such as manufacturing in London, the stock of small businesses is actually declining, despite a high birth rate. This finding suggests that small startups in British cities experience agglomeration diseconomies and constraints on their growth which diminish their chances of survival, relative to their counterparts in less urbanized and rural areas. The implications of this for urban regeneration agencies and Training and Enterprise Councils is that urban economic renewal is not fundamentally a matter of stimulating entrepreneurship. Policy should perhaps rather aim at helping small firms to survive and compete effectively in the context of higher costs and other agglomeration diseconomies.

The second point is the identification of certain limited, weak but measurable policy impacts affecting the geography of small business development in the UK during the 1980s. These are not evident with regard to new enterprise creation, other than perhaps a Welsh effect during the early 1980s. But the analyses do show a significant spatial association between the activities of local enterprise agencies and enhanced survival and reduced death rates of small businesses. This finding is also consistent with recent small business survey research. A further link with government is the strong association between local government expenditure on goods and services and reduced small firm death rates. This finding is logical but novel. So too is the association between manufacturing firm deregistrations and high historic local tax levels. Finally, there is even some hint of a regional policy effect on small business growth, via associations with the Welsh and, weakly, assisted area variables. Policy and local government impacts cannot therefore be discounted as minor influences on spatial variations in small business development in the UK in the 1980s.

Acknowledgements—We gratefully acknowledge the advice and assistance in carrying out this research of David Storey of the SME Centre, University of Warwick; Michael Daly of the Employment Department and John Kerr of the Department of Trade and Industry; Jonathan Thomas, Andrew Cliff and Alan Hughes of the University of Cambridge; and Jenny Wyatt and Ian Agnew of the Department of Geography Drawing Office, University of Cambridge, who drew the maps and diagrams. We also wish to acknowledge the essential financial support of the Employment Department and Directorate-General for Enterprise Policy (DG XXIII) of the European Commission. Any views expressed do not, however, necessarily reflect those of the sponsoring organizations.

NOTES

1. Policy responsibility for small firms and hence VAT registration data was transferred from the Employment Department to the Department of Trade and Industry (DTI) in May 1992. The DTI published estimates of VAT registrations and deregistrations for 1991 in *CSO Bulletin*, issue 5/93.
2. This includes all people resident in the county aged 16 or over who are employed, self-employed, unemployed or on government training programmes, as recorded by the Labour Force Survey. Unemployment is based on ILO/OECD definitions. The sectoral analyses use local sectoral employment rather than labour force, which was available only for the total economy.
3. Model testing was based on the significance of variable *t*-ratios, likelihood ratio tests, and overall adjusted *R*-squared values. SHAZAM automatically corrects for heteroscedasticity.

4. All the models presented here meet the requirements of this test.
5. Throughout this paper, the phrase 'small business growth' is used as short-hand for 'net growth in numbers of businesses' in a given county during the study period. As argued earlier, net growth is dominated by changes in numbers of small businesses.
6. This lack of correlation is surprising. It is possible that the 'barriers-to-entry' approach adopted to measure likely sectoral impacts, though grounded in available economic theory, has resulted in variable mis-specification. Alternatively, it may be that non-sectorally specific forces shaping the spatial pattern of new enterprise creation are sufficiently powerful to swamp the specific effect of sectoral variation.
7. Full results for these models are reported in KEEBLE *et al.*, 1993.
8. In fact, a significant minority—about one-quarter between 1980 and 1986—of VAT deregistrations represent takeovers rather than company failures. Some of these do, however, subsequently cease trading, while the deregistration statistics in general provide the only accessible measure of local variations in small firm deaths currently available.

REFERENCES

ASHCROFT B., LOVE J. H. and MALLOY E. (1991) New firm formation in the UK counties with special reference to Scotland, *Reg. Studies* **25,** 395–410.

AUDRETSCH D. B. and FRITSCH M. (1992) A note on the measurement of entry rates, Wissenschaftszentrum Berlin (mimeo).

BATSTONE S. and MANSFIELD E. (1992) Births, deaths and turbulence in England and Wales, in ROBERTSON M., CHELL E. and MASON C. (Eds) *Towards the Twenty-first Century: The Challenge for Small Business*, pp. 179–208. Nadamal Books, Macclesfield.

CENTRAL STATISTICAL OFFICE (1993) VAT registrations and deregistrations in the UK (1980–1991), *CSO Bulletin* 5/93, 15 January.

CLIFF A. and ORD K. (1972) Testing for spatial autocorrelation among regression residuals, *Geogr. Analysis* **4,** 267–84.

CROSS M. (1981) *New Firm Formation and Regional Development*. Gower, Farnborough, Hants.

DALY M. (1990) The 1980s—a decade of growth in enterprise, *Employment Gazette* November, pp. 553–65.

DALY M. (1991) VAT registrations and deregistrations in 1990, *Employment Gazette*, November, pp. 579–88.

ENTERPRISE DYNAMICS (1987) *Small Firms: Survival and Job Creation; the Contribution of Enterprise Agencies*. Business in the Community and Enterprise Dynamics, Birmingham.

FOTHERGILL S. and GUDGIN G. (1982) *Urban and Regional Employment Change in the UK*. Heinemann, London.

FRITSCH M. (1992) Regional differences in new firm formation: evidence from West Germany, *Reg. Studies* **26,** 233–41.

GAROFOLI G. (1988) New firm formation in Italy, in ANTONELLI C., CAPPELLIN R., GAROFOLI G. and JANNACCONE PAZZI R. (Eds) *Le Politiche di Sviluppo Locale*, pp. 37–93. Franco Angeli, Milan.

GOULD A. and KEEBLE D. (1984) New firms and industrialization in East Anglia, *Reg. Studies* **18,** 189–201.

GUDGIN G. and FOTHERGILL S. (1984) Geographical variation in the rate of formation of new manufacturing firms, *Reg. Studies* **18,** 203–6.

HAMILTON R. T. (1989) Unemployment and business formation rates: reconciling time-series and cross-section evidence, *Environ. Plann. A* **21,** 249–55.

HUDSON J. (1986) An analysis of company liquidations, *Appl. Econ.* **18,** 219–35.

JOHNSON P. S. (1983) New manufacturing firms in the UK regions, *Scot. J. Pol. Econ.* **30,** 75–9.

KEEBLE D. (1980) Industrial decline, regional policy and the urban–rural manufacturing shift in the United Kingdom, *Environ. Plann. A* **12,** 945–62.

KEEBLE D. (1990a) New firms and regional economic development: experience and impact in the 1980s, in CAMERON G., MOORE B., NICHOLLS D., RHODES J. and TYLER P. (Eds) *Cambridge Regional Economic Review*, pp. 62–71. PA Cambridge Economic Consultants/Department of Land Economy, University of Cambridge.

KEEBLE D. (1990b) Small firms, new firms and uneven regional development in the United Kingdom, *Area* **22,** 234–45.

KEEBLE D. (1993a) Small firm creation, innovation and growth and the urban–rural shift, in CURRAN J. and STOREY D. J. (Eds) *Small Firms in Urban and Rural Locations*, pp. 54–78. Routledge, London.

KEEBLE D. (1993b) Regional influences and policy in new technology-based firm creation and growth, Working Paper 34, Small Business Research Centre, University of Cambridge.

KEEBLE D. and BRYSON J. (1993) Small firm creation and growth, regional development and the north–south divide, Working Paper 29, Small Business Research Centre, University of Cambridge.

KEEBLE D., BRYSON J. R. and WOOD P. (1991) Small firms, business services growth and regional development in the United Kingdom: some empirical findings, *Reg. Studies* **25,** 439–57.

KEEBLE D., BRYSON J. and WOOD P. (1992) Entrepreneurship and flexibility in business services: the rise of small management consultancy and market research firms in the UK, in CALEY C., CHELL E., CHITTENDEN F. and MASON C. (Eds) *Small Enterprise Development: Policy and Practice in Action*, pp. 43–58. Paul Chapman, London.

KEEBLE D., TYLER P., BROOM G. and LEWIS J. (1992) *Business Success in the Countryside: the Performance of Rural Enterprise*. Report to the Department of the Environment by PA Cambridge Economic Consultants, HMSO, London.

KEEBLE D., WALKER S. and ROBSON M. (1993) New firm formation and small business growth in the United Kingdom: spatial and temporal variations and determinants, Research Paper 15, Department of Employment.

Mason C. (1991) Spatial variations in enterprise, in Burrows R. (Ed) *Deciphering the Enterprise Culture*, pp. 74–104. Routledge, London.

Mason C. and Harrison R. (1992) The regional take-up of the Enterprise Initiative in Great Britain: the consultancy initiatives programme, in Robertson M., Chell E. and Mason C. (Eds) *Towards the Twenty-first Century: The Challenge for Small Business*, pp. 162–78. Nadamal Books, Macclesfield.

Moyes A. and Westhead P. (1990) Environments for new firm formation in Great Britain, *Reg. Studies* **24**, 123–36.

Nicholson B. M., Brinkley I. and Evans A. W. (1981) The role of the inner city in the development of manufacturing industry, *Urban Studies* **18**, 57–71.

North D. and Smallbone D. (1993) Small firms and the inner city, report for the Department of Trade and Industry, Centre for Enterprise and Economic Development Research, Middlesex University.

Robson M. (1992) Macroeconomic factors in the birth and death of UK firms: evidence from quarterly VAT registrations. Department of Economics, University of Newcastle upon Tyne (mimeo).

Small Business Research Centre. (1992) *The State of British Enterprise: Growth, Innovation and Competitive Advantage in Small and Medium-sized Firms*. Small Business Research Centre, University of Cambridge.

Storey D. J. (1982) *Entrepreneurship and the New Firm*. Croom Helm, London.

Storey D. J. and Johnson S. (1987) Regional variations in entrepreneurship in the UK, *Scot. J. Pol. Econ.* **36**, 161–73.

Westhead P. and Moyes A. (1992) Reflections on Thatcher's Britain: evidence from new production firm registrations 1980–88, *Entrepreneurship & Reg. Develop.* **4**, 21–56.

[13]

Environments for Entrepreneurship Development: Key Dimensions and Research Implications

Devi R. Gnyawali
Daniel S. Fogel

An integrated framework is not available for studying the environmental conditions conducive for entrepreneurship despite their importance for the emergence and growth of enterprises in a country. This paper develops such a framework consisting of five dimensions of entrepreneurial environments and links these dimensions to the core elements of the new venture creation process. Specific emphasis is given to the role of environmental conditions in developing opportunities and in enhancing entrepreneurs' propensity and ability to enterprise. The paper outlines some propositions and research implications of the integrated model and offers initial guidelines for formulating public policies to develop entrepreneurial environments.

While a growing body of literature exists on entrepreneurial environments, the literature is highly fragmented. Some scholars have prepared a list of environmental conditions that may play a role in developing entrepreneurship in a country or region (e.g., Bruno & Tyebjee, 1982; Gartner, 1985; Manning, Birley, & Norburn, 1989; Staley & Morse, 1971). Others have a more descriptive approach to show "what is out there" in a particular country or region (e.g., Dana, 1987, 1990; Davidsson, 1991; Doutriaux, 1988; Hawkins, 1993; Pennings, 1982; Swanson & Webster, 1992; Takyi-Asiedu, 1993). Still others have focused on what governments can do or have done to develop entrepreneurship (e.g., Goodman, Meany, & Pate, 1992; Mokry, 1988; Segura, 1988; Vesper, 1983; Westhead, 1990).

Thus, while the role of environmental conditions in developing entrepreneurship has been recognized, most of these studies have been fragmented, highly descriptive, and focused on only a few aspects of the environment. More importantly, most of the literature has neither paid adequate attention to the needs of the entrepreneur—the main beneficiary of the environment—nor described the environmental conditions in terms of the process of new venture creation.

Gaps are evident in the literature. First, a conceptual framework is lacking to integrate the available literature on entrepreneurial environments. Second, explicit links have not been established between the needs of entrepreneurs and how environments can fulfill entrepreneurs' needs, induce or reinforce their desire to go into business, and thus facilitate the process of new venture creation. Third, limited guidelines exist to conduct empirical research on entrepreneurial environments. Finally, a limited body of literature addresses the needs of policy makers despite the recognition of this group as an important audience for research on entrepreneurship (Hoy, 1989).

In an attempt to bridge these gaps in the literature, we first develop a conceptual framework to integrate existing literature on entrepreneurship environments. Then, we introduce the core elements of the new venture creation process and explicitly link the environmental dimensions to the process of new venture creation and show how environments can help increase people's likelihood to go into business. We draw research implications of the integrated model, develop some propositions to facilitate future empirical research, and offer some guidelines for policy makers in developing entrepreneurship-supportive environments.

LITERATURE ON ENTREPRENEURIAL ENVIRONMENT

In this paper, we refer to an "entrepreneurial environment" as a combination of factors that play a role in the development of entrepreneurship. First, it refers to the overall economic, sociocultural, and political factors that influence people's willingness and ability to undertake entrepreneurial activities. Second, it refers to the availability of assistance and support services that facilitate the start-up process.

One can group the available literature on entrepreneurial environments into three broad streams: (a) general environmental conditions for entrepreneurship; (b) descriptive studies of the environmental conditions of a particular country or region; and (c) the role of public policy in shaping the entrepreneurial environments.

General environmental conditions discussed in the literature include legal and institutional frameworks for efficient functioning of private enterprises, presence of experienced entrepreneurs, presence of skilled labor force, accessibility of suppliers, accessibility of customers or new markets, high degree of competition among firms, favorable government policies, provision of training and support services, and supportive infrastructure (Bruno & Tyebjee, 1982; El-Namaki, 1988; Gartner, 1985; Staley & Morse, 1971). In addition, the literature suggests that the characteristics of people, their skills, experience, and motivation, play important roles in new venture creation (Manning, Birley, & Norburn, 1989).

Empirical studies of entrepreneurial environments of various countries show that countries that keep rules and regulations at a minimum, offer tax and other incentives, and provide training and counselling services to start-up entrepreneurs increase the likelihood of new venture start-ups (Dana, 1987, 1990). Furthermore, factors such as availability of financial resources, large size urban areas, and presence of universities for training and research are found to be very important to increase the rate of new venture creation (Pennings, 1982). Studies also show that entrepreneurs face several obstacles, such as lack of financial assistance, lack of information on various aspects of business, excessive taxation, and high rate of inflation (e.g., Young & Welsch, 1993).

Scholars that focused on the role of public policy (El-Namaki, 1988; Goodman, Meany, & Pate, 1992; Mokry, 1988; Vesper, 1983; Westhead, 1990) suggest several policy options for developing entrepreneurship. These policy options include provision of venture capital funds, tax-based incentives, and government procurement programs; protection of proprietary ideas and innovations; investment in education and research; explicit recognition of, and support for, entrepreneurship by government agencies; fostering of entrepreneurship by educational institutions; and minimization of entry barriers. [See Goodman, Meany, & Pate (1992) for a further review of activities governments have undertaken to stimulate entrepreneurship.]

Some commonalities exist among these streams of literature. First, there is agreement among scholars that the more conducive the business environment, the more likely that new businesses will emerge and grow. People will more likely be encouraged and feel competent to start a business when the social environment values entrepreneurship, when various opportunities are available for entrepreneurs, and when they have sufficient knowledge and skills required to start and manage a business. The willingness and capability to start a business may be further enhanced if potential entrepreneurs do not face hurdles during the start-up process and if they are confident that outside expertise could be obtained easily when necessary. Governments both directly and indirectly affect the development of an environment that could support entrepreneurship.

This literature also suggests that the need for the development of a conducive environment may be greater in emerging market economies and in developing countries because of the low level of entrepreneurial activities and several environmental hostilities operating in these countries (El-Namaki, 1988; Segura, 1988). This is because "there is sufficient evidence that environmental forces ranging from purely cultural and social currents to ingrained government bureaucracy go quite a long way towards restraining the driving force behind entrepreneurs (El-Namaki, 1988, p. 101).

Furthermore, compared to large-scale enterprises, the need for a conducive environment could be greater in the case of small-scale enterprises because such enterprises may have little control over the environment in which they operate (Pfeffer & Salancik, 1978). These enterprises may lack resources and "political clout" that usually are needed to influence an enterprise's environment. However, Brown, Hamilton, and Medoff (1990) have stirred a debate on this issue. They argue that organizations such as the National Federation of Independent Business and National Small Business United have a strong influence on public policy.

While scholars generally agree on the importance of several environmental conditions for entrepreneurship development, the list of environmental conditions is so fragmented that the available literature is of very little help in studying entrepreneurial environments or in developing policies and programs for entrepreneurial development. For example, we know little about the relationship among various elements of the environment and about the relative importance of each element in developing entrepreneurship. Therefore, in the next section we organize various environmental conditions into a framework. In the following sections, we link this framework to the process of new venture creation, develop propositions to show the interrelationships among various elements, and draw further implications for research and public policy.

A FRAMEWORK FOR AN ENTREPRENEURIAL ENVIRONMENT

Three major considerations entered into the development of our framework. First, we have attempted to include major environmental conditions empirically studied or mentioned in the existing literature. Second, we show interrelationships among these conditions. Third, and most importantly, we have attempted to develop a parsimonious framework that captures the richness of an entrepreneurial environment and can be subjected to systematic research.

We grouped the environmental conditions into five dimensions: government policies and procedures, socioeconomic conditions, entrepreneurial and business skills, financial support to businesses, and non-financial support to businesses. Table 1 presents the framework. Key empirical studies cited throughout this section are summarized in Table 2.

Table 1

A Framework for Entrepreneurial Environments

Government Policies and Procedures	*Financial Assistance*
Restrictions on imports and exports	Venture capital
Provision of bankruptcy laws	Alternative sources of financing
Entry barriers	Low-cost loans
Procedural requirements for registration and licensing	Willingness of financial institutions to finance small entrepreneurs
Number of institutions for entrepreneurs to report to	Credit guarantee program for start-up enterprises
Rules and regulations governing entrepreneurial activities	Competition among financial institutions
Laws to protect proprietary rights	
Socioeconomic Conditions	*Non-Financial Assistance*
Public attitude toward entrepreneurship	Counselling and support services
Presence of experienced entrepreneurs	Entrepreneurial networks
Successful role models	Incubator facilities
Existence of persons with entrepreneurial characteristics	Government procurement programs for small businesses
Recognition of exemplary entrepreneurial performance	Government support for research and development
Proportion of small firms in the population of firms	Tax incentives and exemptions
Diversity of economic activities	Local and international information networks
Extent of economic growth	Modern transport and communication facilities
Entrepreneurial and Business Skills	
Technical and vocational education	
Business education	
Entrepreneurial training programs	
Technical and vocational training programs	
Availability of information	

Government Policies and Procedures

Governments can influence the market mechanisms and make them function efficiently by removing conditions that create market imperfections and administrative rigidities. They can also create an ''enterprise culture'' that enables firms to take reasonable risks and seek profits.

Entrepreneurs may be discouraged to start a business if they have to follow many rules and procedural requirements, if they have to report to many institutions, and if they have to spend more time and money in fulfilling the procedural requirements (Dana, 1987, 1990; Young & Welsch, 1993). The Czech and Slovak Republics recently introduced Value Added Taxes (VAT). This intervention was perceived negatively by most entrepreneurs because it has added more confusion to this emerging market economy and increased already cumbersome procedural requirements entrepreneurs needed to follow. For instance, if products were to be exported from Slovakia, VAT would be paid there, to be claimed back at the Slovak border, then paid again on the Czech side and cleared through Prague (*Financial Times*, 1993). Examples of similar types of effects of rules and regulations can be found in many countries.

Socioeconomic Conditions

Entrepreneurship may not prosper if most members of the society view it with suspicion. A favorable attitude of the society toward entrepreneurship and a widespread public support for entrepreneurial activities are both needed to motivate people to start a new business. In fact, social factors may be equally important as availability of loans, technical assistance, physical facilities, and information:

Table 2

Selected Research on the Importance of Environmental Conditions for Entrepreneurship Development

Environmental conditions	Findings	Citation
Government Policies and Procedures	In Cayman Islands, entrepreneurship was facilitated by keeping paperwork and procedural requirements at minimum.	Dana, 1987
	In Malaysia, concentration of power in the business development agency established by the government and too many procedural requirements discouraged entrepreneurship.	Dana, 1990
	In Saint Martin, excessive regulations on businesses suppressed the growth of entrepreneurship; conversely, in Sint Maarten, minimum regulation and procedural requirements encouraged entrepreneurship.	Dana, 1990
	In Mexico, key barriers for start-up included excessive government regulation, high rates of taxes, and increasing inflation.	Young & Welsch, 1993
Socioeconomic Conditions	In Sweden, tax and other incentives had greater impact on persons who were strongly motivated to start a business than on persons who were less motivated.	Davidsson, 1991
	In the Czech and Slovak Republics, negative public attitudes toward entrepreneurs discouraged entrepreneurs.	Swanson & Webster, 1992
	Cities having larger number of economic development programs achieved higher growth in number of new firm establishments than cities having smaller number of such programs.	Feiock, 1987
	The greater the percentage of small firms in a growing sector, the greater the share of jobs created by small firms in that sector.	Phillips, 1993
Entrepreneurial and business skills	In Sweden, both business-related experience and business education were highly correlated with entrepreneurs' ability to start and manage a business.	Davidsson, 1991
	In the region of Sub-Saharan Africa, entrepreneurs suffer from barriers such as the need for following societal stereotypes and traditions, a general lack of realization of the importance of thrift, and lack of perseverance.	Takyi-Asiedu, 1993

Continued overleaf

Table 2

Continued

Environmental conditions	Findings	Citation
	Every 1% increase in a state's college-educated population leads to 1.2% increase in jobs created by small firms.	Phillips, 1993
Financial support	In Cayman Islands, creation of investment companies facilitated entrepreneurship.	Dana, 1987
	In Singapore, provision of low-interest loans and government grants facilitated entrepreneurship development.	Dana, 1987
	In the US, availability of financial resources was an important contributor of organizational birth rate.	Pennings, 1982
	In the State of Michigan, investment by the State Pension Fund in venture capital investment attracted large venture capital companies to invest in small businesses.	Kleiman & Bygrave, 1988
	In Japan, 52 credit guarantee associations exist to guarantee loans to SMEs; local governments have special funds that serve as a reserve for loans to SMEs. Consequently, most entrepreneurs get loans for start-up business.	Hawkins, 1993
	In the United Kingdom, private investors are attracted to invest in new companies because the government provides tax relief for new equity investment by individuals in unquoted companies.	Harrison & Mason, 1988
	In Mexico, key barriers for start-up included lack of working capital, difficulty in obtaining loans, and seasonal fluctuations in cash.	Young & Welsch, 1993
Non-financial support	In Australia, the provision of nationwide management training programs and the supply of textbooks and information materials on business start-up issues encouraged new business start-ups.	Dana, 1987
	In Virgin Islands, tax concession on all businesses for ten years, tax concession for hotels for twenty years, and exemption from custom duty on imports of capital equipment facilitated the development of entrepreneurship.	Dana, 1987
	In Cayman Islands, government guarantee not to tax businesses for 20 years attracts entrepreneurs.	Dana, 1987

Table 2

Continued

Environmental conditions	Findings	Citation
	In the US, entrepreneurs spent nearly half of their time during business start-up in making contacts.	Aldrich, 1986
	In Japan, regional information centers gather, analyze, and disseminate technical and market information and offer free access to computers; local business development centers provide free consulting and training services; government purchases certain quantity of the products of small enterprises every year. All these facilitated entrepreneurship development.	Hawkins, 1993
	In Canada, the government procurement program helped firms to grow faster and to develop competence in marketing and export-related activities.	Doutriaux, 1988
	In the US, large size urban areas and presence of universities for training and research assistance were important factors contributing to the birth of new firms.	Pennings, 1982
	Presence of business development assistance was significantly correlated with the share of jobs created by small firms.	Phillips, 1993

> The more fundamental forces bringing entrepreneurship about, such as family, the presence and effectiveness of social networks, or attitudes supportive of entrepreneurship, receive virtually no serious attention from formal economic development programs. . . . [I]f entrepreneurial development is to be more than a token collection of programs, it is imperative that individuals sympathetic to entrepreneurial thinking be spread throughout community structures and organizations, non-profits, for profits and government bodies (Mokry, 1988, pp. 111, 114).

Mokry (1988) suggests that local communities can play an important role in developing an entrepreneurial environment. For example, close relatives can help entrepreneurs seek out solutions, locate resources, and assemble a team of willing people to address the entrepreneur's problems (Kao, 1993).

The presence of experienced entrepreneurs and successful entrepreneurial role models in a community or country conveys a message to the potential entrepreneurs that business is an attractive career option. Conversely, negative public attitude towards entrepreneurs coupled with the lack of role models may discourage people from going into business. For example, in Central and Eastern Europe there exists a general feeling in the society that those who bid for government-owned shops are black marketers, corrupt former officials, and people backed by foreign investors (Rondinelli, 1991). Thus, small business owners have often become victims of social prejudice against private enterprises and profit making (Swanson & Webster, 1992).

Societies and cultures that value entrepreneurship tend to develop societal systems to encourage it (Vesper, 1983). For example, it is often recognized that among people of Chinese origin, entrepreneurial role models encourage people to go into business supported by close networks of family members and relatives (Kao, 1993; Siu & Martin, 1992).

Government and business development organizations can organize programs in order to develop societal awareness towards entrepreneurship and make people recognize the importance of being entrepreneurs. The US Small Business Administration, for example, recognizes outstanding entrepreneurs through several awards (SBA, 1993). The Czechoslovak Management Center has created a country-wide Entrepreneur-of-the-Year Award, one of the first in the region (Fogel, 1993). The Australian government has eased immigration procedures for foreigners with a business idea, capital, and experience (Dana, 1988). Similar examples can be found in many other countries, suggesting that positive societal factors help attract potential entrepreneurs to start a business. The need for such motivational factors is generally higher in countries where entrepreneurial awareness is low than in countries where such awareness is high (McClelland, 1961). Tax and other start-up incentives have a greater impact when people have greater motivation to go into business (Davidsson, 1991).

Economic factors such as proportion of small firms in the population of firms, extent of economic growth, and diversity of economic activities also influence the rate of new venture creation and growth. Research has shown that the greater the percentage of small firms in growing sectors, the greater the share of jobs created by small firms in the industries operating in those sectors (Phillips, 1993). Firms are more likely to grow if they are in highly innovative industries than if they are in less-innovative industries (Kirchhoff, 1991). Feiock's (1987) research has shown that cities having a larger number of economic development programs achieve a higher rate of growth in new venture establishments than cities having a smaller number of such programs. Factors such as high sophistication of buyers, strong distribution channels, and intense rivalry among existing firms provide an opportunity for entrepreneurs to pursue innovation (Porter, 1990).

Entrepreneurial and Business Skills

A low level of technical and business skills could prevent motivated entrepreneurs from starting a new venture (Davidsson, 1991; Vesper, 1990). Similarly, unless entrepreneurs are well equipped with technical and business skills, they may not be able to overcome various problems they encounter at different stages of their business development. The need for training programs appears greater in countries where very limited external assistance is available, market imperfections exist, large industries dominate the industrial sector, government policies do not support small businesses, and several bureaucratic hurdles have to be overcome to get permission to start a business.

Training and educational services are particularly important in emerging market economies because entrepreneurs lack basic business skills. In one survey, 30% of the entrepreneurs requested training in the areas of business plan preparation, planning, decision making, negotiation, pricing, market penetration, organization and management, management of the workforce, and handling of cash-flow (Swanson & Webster, 1992). Some research evidence has shown that successful entrepreneurs can be developed through educational and short-term training programs (McClelland & Winter, 1969; Management Systems International, 1990). A study of job creation in various states of the US showed that every 1% increase in a state's college-educated population led to 1.2% increase in jobs created by small firms (Phillips, 1993).

Despite the importance of entrepreneurial and business skills, the need for developing such skills is often overlooked. For example, one study of World Bank assistance for small enterprise development shows that 96% of the World Bank lending in developing countries has been for financial assistance and a negligible portion of the remaining four percent has been spent for developing technical and business capability of the entrepreneurs (Gnyawali, 1991).

Financial Support to Businesses

Generally, entrepreneurs require financial assistance for at least one of three purposes: to diversify or spread the start-up risk, to accumulate start-up capital, and to finance growth and expansion. While availability of financial resources appears to be a major predictor of the frequency of new business start-ups, many lenders seem to be unwilling to invest in high-risk projects or tend to withhold support until the firm has been established successfully (Pennings, 1982). One out of three businesses funded by venture capital companies in the US have resulted in financial loss to venture capital firms; consequently, venture capital companies are "simply inappropriate for most start-up firms" (Bhide, 1992, p. 111). In most developing countries and emerging market economies, only a few venture capital companies and commercial banks are available and alternative sources of financing are almost non-existent. Thus, a paradox emerges: entrepreneurs cannot start a business without financial assistance, they do not have access to financial institutions and cannot secure financial assistance if they lack prior business experience.

Most commercial operations such as venture capital firms and commercial banks tend to exhibit greater interest in concentrated, urban areas that usually have a well-developed infrastructure and concentrated demand for funds, in areas where businesses are easier to supervise and monitor, and in businesses that have demonstrated some potential for success (e.g. Fried & Hisrich, 1988). Also, most bankers, especially commercial ones, may hesitate to finance small start-up firms because of the high costs involved in the processing and supervision of loans. Moreover, most bankers lack the kind of experience and capability needed for understanding and responding to the special needs of small entrepreneurs (Vesper, 1983). Research has shown that creation of investment companies, provision of low-interest loans, and availability of credit guarantee schemes for small business financing have all contributed to the establishment of new businesses (Dana, 1987; Harrison & Mason, 1988; Hawkins, 1993).

Non-Financial Support to Businesses

Entrepreneurs need support services in addition to financial assistance. In particular, entrepreneurs need most assistance in conducting market studies, in preparing business plans, and in getting loans. Business incubators can play a major role in providing a variety of services to start-up entrepreneurs (Hoy, Wisnieski, Gatewood, Bryant, & Patel, 1991). As most incubator facilities provide office space, common office facilities, faster and efficient means of communication, and counselling and advisory services to their tenants at low costs, incubators can be very helpful in places where infrastructure is not well developed or where modern physical facilities are costly.

Entrepreneurs spend nearly half of their time during their start-up phase in making contacts and networks with other entrepreneurs and related agencies (Aldrich, 1986). Therefore, networks are useful mechanisms to enhance business capability of entrepreneurs. Networks provide four essential ingredients to entrepreneurship (Manning, Birley, & Norburn, 1989): support and motivation; examples and role models; expert opinion and counselling; and access to opportunities, information, and resources. The forms of network include trade fairs, entrepreneurial fairs, associations and clubs.

Studies have shown the importance of small business assistance programs to developing entrepreneurship. In a study of the growth of jobs created by small firms across various US states, Phillips (1993) found that the presence of business development assistance was significantly correlated with the share of jobs created by small firms. In their study of the Czech and Slovak entrepreneurs, Swanson and Webster (1992, p. 6) found that:

> [m]any entrepreneurs expressed a need for better information services, especially in rural areas, including most of Slovakia. They lacked basic economic information such as forecasts, business directories, legal notices, and data on the foreign sector . . . they also wanted advice on how to become more competitive, deal with banks, and find trade and investment partners abroad.

Government procurement programs and subsidies for research and development are also important for entrepreneurs (Goodman, Meany, & Pate, 1992). Further, research has shown that provision of management and entrepreneurship training programs, various forms of start-up incentives (e.g., tax concession, exemption of custom duty), and provision of consulting services enable a person to start a business (Dana, 1987; Hawkins, 1993).

Certain infrastructural elements seem to make substantial impact on the entrepreneurial environment. These elements include the existence of universities and research and development programs, a well-educated and technically skilled labor force, and modern transport and communication facilities that provide easy access to suppliers and customers (Bruno & Tyebjee, 1982; Gartner, 1985). Galbraith and Noble (1988) show that firms make location decisions based on the community's ability to supply trained and capable workers and on the proximity to research and development institutions.

The foregoing discussion shows that the existence of various environmental conditions increases the chances of emergence and growth of businesses in a country. Though a single factor may have less significant impact, the interaction of various factors may considerably increase the impact on entrepreneurial development in a country. "If a development program improves only one [of these] factors, the results may be quite meager, perhaps not worth the efforts and expense. To improve a properly selected *combination* of factors may, on the other hand, prove highly effective" (Staley & Morse, 1971, p. 361; emphasis in original). For example, without having some business opportunities in the environment, and without having motivated and capable entrepreneurs in starting a business, any amount of financial assistance or government procurement system may not increase entrepreneurial activity. Without having some opportunities in the environment, entrepreneurs will not be able to start a business; and, even if they start, they are likely to fail. Therefore, some conditions appear important only when the conditions of primary importance exist. To understand what conditions are of primary importance or how the factors interact, it is necessary to look at the core elements of new venture creation. The next section discusses these core elements and matches the core elements of new venture creation to environmental conditions in our framework.

CORE ELEMENTS OF A VENTURE CREATION PROCESS

Some key factors may lead to an increase in a person's desire and decision to start a business. Examples of such factors include a person's perception of desirability and feasibility of starting a business (Shapero & Sokol, 1982) or the person's propensity and intention to found a business and his or her sense-making about the environmental forces (Learned, 1992). Vesper (1990) identified four elements in venture creation: a profitable business opportunity, technical know-how of the entrepreneur, business know-how of the entrepreneur, and entrepreneurial initiative. Thus, some literature suggests that for an entrepreneur to start a business, he or she should perceive that a profitable opportunity exists, should feel confident that he or she possess necessary skills to go into business, and should take an initiative for starting a business. This section builds on these factors, especially those articulated by Vesper, by redefining Vesper's term "initiative" as "propensity to enterprise" (El-Namaki, 1988) and combining the "technical know-how" and "business know-how" into "ability to enterprise." Thus, we conceptualize the three key elements of a venture creation process as *opportunity, propensity to enterprise,* and *ability to enterprise.*

Opportunity

Opportunity refers to the extent to which possibilities for new ventures exist and the extent to which entrepreneurs have the leeway to influence their odds for success through their own actions. Entrepreneurial opportunities tend to be higher in economies that are deregulated, where market mechanisms operate freely, and where entrepreneurs have to face very few barriers to entry (El-Namaki, 1988). Thus, government policies and procedures affect the business opportunity. The opportunity will influence an entrepreneur's propensity to enterprise and ability to enterprise.

Propensity to Enterprise

A stream of research on entrepreneurship emphasizes the psychological and behavioral characteristics of entrepreneurs. The most common of these are the high need for achievement (McClelland & Winter, 1969), capacity to innovate (Schumpeter, 1934), internal locus of control (Shapero, 1977), propensity for taking risks (Brockhaus, 1980), and key entrepreneurial characteristics (Management Systems International, 1990).

People that have an urge for excellence, willingness to take moderate risk, and desire to be independent are very likely to become entrepreneurs (McClelland, 1961). A study conducted in various countries (Management Systems International, 1990) found ten behavioral characteristics of successful entrepreneurs. These characteristics are opportunity seeking and initiative, persistence, risk taking, demand for quality and efficiency, commitment to work, goal setting, information seeking, systematic planning and monitoring, persuasion and networking, and independence and self-confidence.

The literature on personal entrepreneurial competencies argues that people with certain behavioral characteristics are able to perceive the opportunities available in the environment, seize such opportunities, and then turn such opportunities into profitable ventures. Yet, a personality or behavioral profile is not a sufficient condition for people to go into business. An individual with high propensity to start a business is more likely to go into business when he or she sees several business opportunities in the environment. Furthermore, the propensity to enterprise will be enhanced when an individual feels confident in his or her ability to enterprise.

Ability to Enterprise

Ability to enterprise refers to the sum of technical and business capabilities required to start and manage a business. While "technical capability" refers to the technical skills, "business capability" refers to the knowledge and skills in various functional aspects of business (Vesper, 1990) such as business planning, product development, marketing, personnel management, general management, accounting, finance, etc. Furthermore, as entrepreneurs face resistance from customers, investors, and several other stakeholders, they require some political and strategic planning skills in order to succeed in their endeavors (MacMillan, 1983). Without having the ability to enterprise, entrepreneurs may not be able to seize the opportunities available to them and successfully go through various start-up activities or manage the on-going business. Individuals with the necessary ability to enterprise, when combined with enhanced propensity to enterprise, will increase their chances of going into business. And, once they are in business, they are most likely to be the winners (Vesper, 1983).

A crucial requirement in the process of new venture creation is a match between the opportunity, the propensity to enterprise, and the ability to enterprise. While the opportunity may enhance one's propensity to enterprise, persons with high propensity to enterprise will perhaps be able to identify the opportunities in the environment. Similarly, ability to enterprise may depend upon the nature of available opportunities. Some people may have high engineering skills but the opportunity for the use of such skills may be low. Persons with a high ability to enterprise may also be more able to locate opportunities than those with lower ability to enterprise. The likelihood to enterprise increases with an increase in the propensity and ability to enterprise and a match with available opportunities. Thus, a high level of opportunity, propensity to enterprise, and ability to enterprise will positively correlate with an individual's *likelihood to enterprise*. A model showing the relationship between opportunity, propensity to enterprise, and ability to enterprise is depicted in Figure 1.

The model shows that the process of developing competent entrepreneurs and increasing their likelihood to enterprise consists of developing plentiful business opportunities in the environment, enhancing people's propensity to enterprise, and developing their capability to enterprise. Competent entrepreneurs will be able to take advantage of most opportunities and respond to the needs of the environments.

A key role of the entrepreneurial environment is to help entrepreneurs develop both propensity to enterprise and ability to enterprise. Persons with low propensity to enterprise lack the necessary motivation and mind-set required to start a business, whereas persons with low ability to enterprise lack the skills needed to manage the start-up and subsequent processes of business operation.

THE INTEGRATED MODEL AND ITS IMPLICATIONS FOR RESEARCH

The foregoing discussion suggests that the importance of each dimension of the environmental factors varies depending upon the availability of opportunities for business start-up and the overall level of propensity and ability of people to start an enterprise. This section integrates the discussion of the environmental conditions and the core elements of new venture creation and develops propositions to facilitate future empirical research. Figure 2 presents the integrated model.

The model shows that each aspect of environmental condition is related to a specific aspect of the core elements of new venture creation. Generally, the availability of opportunities is a primary element for enhancing the propensity and ability to enterprise

Figure 1
Core Elements of New Venture Creation

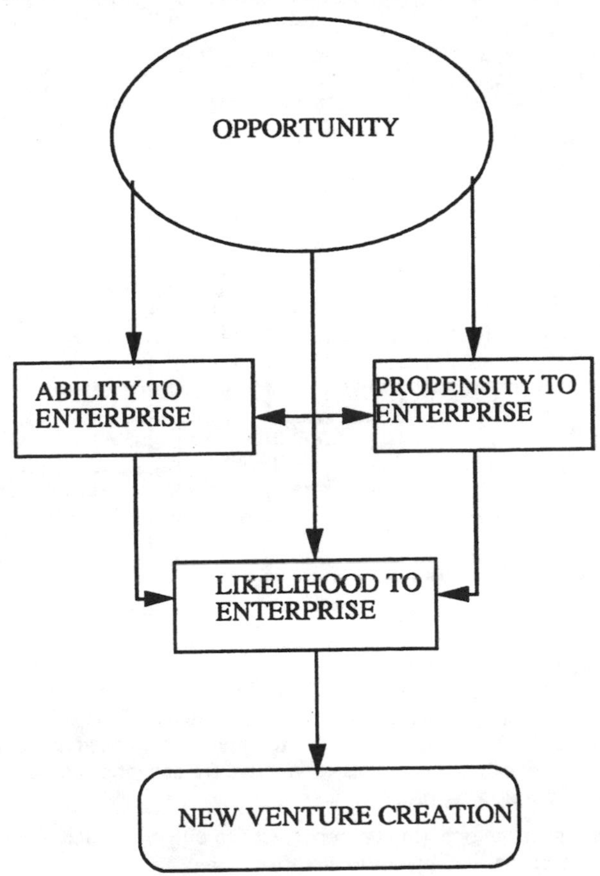

and consequently the likelihood to enterprise. The dimension of the environment that directly relates to the opportunity is macroeconomic policies and procedures. The better the legal and institutional framework for efficient functioning of the markets and the fewer the barriers that constrain people to pursue business opportunities, the greater the likelihood of business start-up.

The dimension of the environment that relates to the propensity to enterprise is socioeconomic factors. The greater the importance placed by the society on entrepreneurial values and behaviors, the larger the proportion of experienced entrepreneurs and role models, and the higher the societal recognition of entrepreneurial performance, the more likely that the propensity to enterprise is high.

The dimension of the environment that relates to the likelihood to enterprise is the level of entrepreneurial and business skills. The greater the availability of technical and business-related training, the greater the ability of the potential entrepreneurs to start and manage a business. Thus, if people have a high propensity to enterprise but a low ability

Figure 2
An Integrative Model of Entrepreneurial Environments

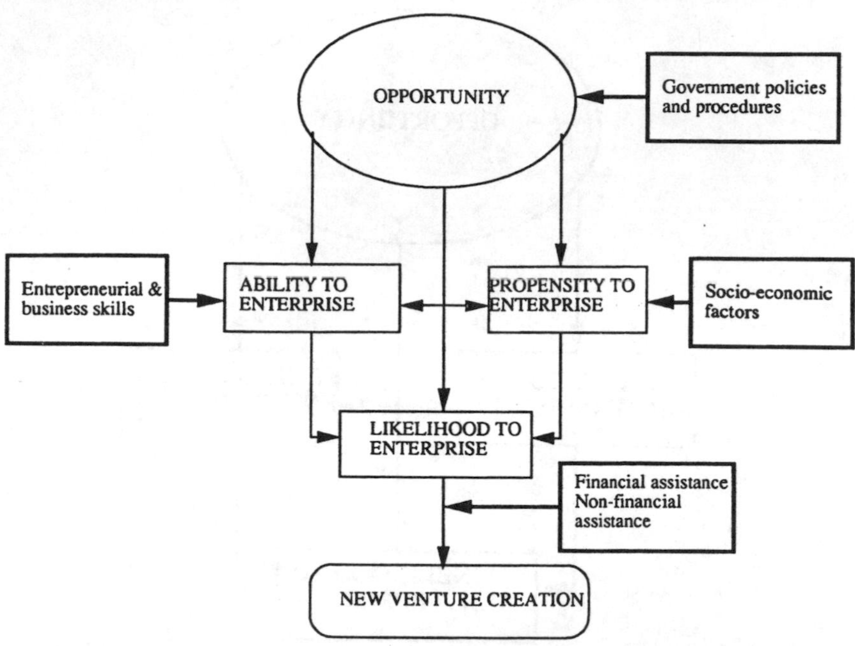

to enterprise, environmental interventions will need to develop the entrepreneurial and business skills of these people. Conversely, if people have high ability to enterprise but a low propensity to enterprise, environmental interventions need to be oriented towards making the socioeconomic conditions conductive for entrepreneurship. The above analysis suggests the following propositions.

P1: The higher the opportunity, propensity to enterprise, and ability to enterprise, the higher the likelihood to enterprise.

P2: The more favorable the socioeconomic factors, the greater the propensity to enterprise.

P3: The greater the entrepreneurial and business skills, the greater the ability to enterprise.

P4: The more favorable the government policies and procedures, the higher the opportunity to enterprise.

As argued earlier, a person with high propensity to enterprise may enter into business; yet the person is likely to fail either at the start-up stage or afterwards if he or she lacks the ability to enterprise. Conversely, a person with high ability to enterprise but low propensity to enterprise lacks adequate motivation to venture into business. Successful entrepreneurship thus requires high levels of propensity and ability to enterprise. Therefore,

P5: The higher the likelihood to enterprise, the higher the new venture creation.

The model (Figure 2) shows that financial and non-financial assistance appear important only if the overall likelihood to enterprise is high. Previous studies (e.g., Davidsson, 1991) have shown that tax and other incentives were important when people had higher motivation to go into business. Therefore,

P6: The higher the likelihood to enterprise and the greater the availability of financial and non-financial assistance, the higher the new venture creation.

Ideally, research aimed at studying entrepreneurial environments should include entrepreneurs, policy makers, entrepreneurship development consultants, and the general public as key informants. This is because it is the perception of entrepreneurs about the environment that shapes their actions; it is the set of policies and actions of the government and the set of programs of the business development organizations that influence the opportunity, propensity to enterprise, and ability to enterprise. And, it is the overall attitude of the general public that influences the propensity to enterprise. Research aimed at studying the opportunity and government policy and procedures should use government officials and entrepreneurs as key informants and include other groups of informants if resources permit. On the other hand, use of the general public is extremely important if the research is aimed at studying the propensity to enterprise and the socioeconomic dimension of the environment. Similarly, business development organizations need to be taken as key informants to study the ability to enterprise and the entrepreneurial and business skills dimension of the environment.

An important agenda for research is to identify the relative importance of each factor in developing entrepreneurship. It would be useful to know the relative importance of each factor as assigned by entrepreneurs, policy makers, and entrepreneurship development agencies working in a country. Also, it might be appropriate to study inter-country differences in the level of ability and propensity to enterprise, especially with reference to the countries that differ in the duration of the free enterprise system. Secondary and unobtrusive sources provide data on current policy frameworks, rules and regulations, the extent of available training and counselling services, and the number of institutions available for financial and non-financial assistance. Interviews and questionnaires will be useful to collect data about societal attitudes towards entrepreneurship and entrepreneurs' perceptions about their ability to enterprise and propensity to enterprise and the overall business environment.

Implications for Public Policy

This paper has important implications for public policy and for the design and implementation of programs to develop entrepreneurship. Generally, the primary role of the government and other agencies is to increase opportunities, to develop the motivation of potential entrepreneurs to go into business, and to enhance potential entrepreneurs' ability to start a business. Government agencies that develop entrepreneurial environments may be efficient in their work if they address the specific elements of our model. The following points summarize the guidelines for formulating public policy that evolve from our model.

1. Governments can contribute to entrepreneurship by adopting policies and procedures that provide a broader scope of opportunities to entrepreneurs. Examples of possible interventions are the provision of laws and regulations to protect entrepreneurial innovation such as patents and copyrights, liberal economic policy to let people freely exercise their entrepreneurial talents, and minimum rules and regulations for entrepreneurs to follow so that the costs of doing business can be minimized.

2. Governments whose countries have low propensity to enterprise but high ability to enterprise could design policies and programs aimed at improving the socioeconomic dimension of the environment. Short-term interventions could include such programs as the best-entrepreneur-of-the-year award, provisions of trade fairs, and similar activities that reward entrepreneurial activities and increase overall societal awareness toward entrepreneurship. A possible long-term policy approach is to introduce entrepreneurial values and thinking in the educational system.
3. Governments whose countries have a low level of ability to enterprise but high level of propensity to enterprise could try to develop policies and programs that enhance the entrepreneurial and business skills of the potential entrepreneurs. Examples of useful interventions are technical and vocational training, and short-term entrepreneurship development courses and workshops aimed at enhancing specific business skills.
4. Some caution is needed in offering broad-based financial assistance to potential entrepreneurs in countries where propensity and ability to enterprise are low. If the propensity and ability to enterprise are low, policies and programs should also be directed to developing the propensity and ability to enterprise. This is because despite the financial assistance, people with low propensity and ability to enterprise may not venture into business or, even if they did, they may not be able to manage the enterprise. The greater the likelihood to enterprise, the greater the role of financial and non-financial assistance in creating new ventures.

Overall, the arguments above suggest that before developing specific policies and programs, governments could focus on analysis of the extent of the opportunity, propensity to enterprise, and ability to enterprise, could identify weak areas, and then formulate policies and programs to strengthen the weaker areas. The framework presented in Table 1 provides useful guidelines to formulate policies and design programs for entrepreneurship development.

CONCLUSION

At the firm level, existing literature has documented the influence of environmental factors on firm performance (Covin & Slevin, 1991; Venkatraman & Prescott, 1990; Zahra, 1993). The arguments developed in this paper suggest that similar relationships may exist between environmental factors and performance of an individual entrepreneur, and that a match between specific requirements of the entrepreneurs and environmental forces would lead to greater likelihood of business start-up and success.

We identified and addressed some gaps in the literature on entrepreneurial environments: (a) lack of a conceptual framework to integrate the available literature on entrepreneurial environments; (b) lack of explicit links between the needs of entrepreneurs and the dimensions of the environments; (c) lack of guidelines to conduct empirical research on entrepreneurial environments; and (d) lack of consideration of the needs of policy makers. A major thesis of this paper is that entrepreneurship can flourish if potential entrepreneurs find opportunities in the environment, if environmental conditions motivate entrepreneurs to take advantage of these opportunities, and if environmental conditions enhance entrepreneurs' ability to start and manage a business. We have shown how the framework of entrepreneurial environments and the model developed in this paper provide a basis for studying entrepreneurial environments, for developing richer theories in entrepreneurship, and for formulating public policy.

The first and most obvious contribution of this model is that it provides a comprehensive and integrated view of the entrepreneurial environments and develops guidelines for conducting future empirical research. The model and propositions developed in this paper provide a starting point for the study of a country's entrepreneurial environment.

This model also provides a basis for formulating public policy on entrepreneurship development. The common areas to be addressed by the public policy are: (a) increasing the opportunity for entrepreneurs and creating a general environment that fosters entrepreneurship; (b) encouraging the establishment of institutions that support entrepreneurs; and (c) providing financial and non-financial assistance once entrepreneurs' likelihood to enterprise has been enhanced. We show how the importance of each dimension of the entrepreneurial environment varies across countries. For example, in countries where opportunities are few, focus should be on improving the macro economic policies and procedures and on developing a legal and institutional framework for the efficient functioning of the private sector (Fogel, 1994; Porter, 1990). The reason is clear: if there are no attractive opportunities in the environment, entrepreneurs will not go into business. Also, the paper argues that not all environmental factors are equally important in all countries or at the same time. The role of each environmental factor varies depending upon the specific aspect of the new venture development process it intends to address.

Finally, as Van de Ven (1993, p. 211) argued, "the study of entrepreneurship is deficient if it focuses exclusively on the characteristics and behaviors of individual entrepreneurs, on the one hand, and if it treats the social, economic, and political factors influencing entrepreneurship as external demographic statistics, on the other hand." We have developed a useful model to advance these arguments. We believe that the model and testable propositions developed in this paper will be useful for researchers interested in studying entrepreneurial environments and for practitioners involved in designing and improving policies and programs for entrepreneurship development.

REFERENCES

Aldrich, H. (1986). Social behavior and entrepreneurial networks. In R. Ronstadt, J. A. Hornaday, R. Peterson, & K. H. Vesper (Eds.), *Frontiers of entrepreneurship research*, pp. 239-240. Wellesley, MA: Babson College.

Bhide, A. (1992). Bootstrap finance: The art of start-ups. *Harvard Business Review*, Nov-Dec, 109-117.

Brockhaus, R. H. (1980). Risk taking propensity of entrepreneurs. *Academy of Management Journal, 23*, 509-520.

Brown, C., Hamilton, J., & Medoff, J. (1990). *Employers large and small*. Cambridge, MA: Harvard University Press.

Bruno, A. V., & Tyebjee, T. T. (1982). The environment for entrepreneurship. In C. A. Kent, D. L. Sexton, & K. H. Vesper (Eds.), *Encyclopedia of entrepreneurship*, pp. 288-307. Englewood Cliffs, NJ: Prentice Hall.

Covin, J. G., & Slevin, D. P. (1991). A conceptual model of entrepreneurship as firm behavior. *Entrepreneurship Theory and Practice, 16*(1), 7-25.

Dana, L. P. (1987). Entrepreneurship and venture creation—An international comparison of five commonwealth nations. In N. C. Churchill, J. A. Hornaday, B. A. Kirchhoff, O. J. Krasner, & K. H. Vesper (Eds.), *Frontiers of entrepreneurship research*, pp. 573-583. Wellesley, MA: Babson College.

Dana, L. P. (1988). The spirit of entrepreneurship and the commonwealth government of Australia. *Journal of Small Business Management, 26*(1), 63-65.

Dana, L. P. (1990). Saint Martin/Sint Maarten: A case study of the effects of culture on economic development. *Journal of Small Business Management, 28*(4), 91-98.

Davidsson, P. (1991). Continued entrepreneurship: Ability, need, and opportunity as determinants of small firm growth. *Journal of Business Venturing, 6,* 405-429.

Doutriaux, J. A. (1988). Government procurement and research contracts at start-up and success of Canadian high-tech entrepreneurial firms. In B. A. Kirchhoff, W. A. Long, W. E. McMullan, K. H. Vesper, & W. E. Wetzel (Eds.), *Frontiers of entrepreneurship research,* pp. 582-594. Wellesley, MA: Babson College.

El-Namaki, M. S. S. (1988). Encouraging entrepreneurship in developing countries. *Long Range Planning, 21*(4), 98-106.

Feiock, R. (1987). Urban economic development: Local government strategies and their effects. In S. Nagel (Ed.), *Research in public policy analysis and management*. London: JAI Press.

Financial Times. (1993). Week 2, Number 31, p. 960.

Fogel, D. S. (1993). *Entrepreneurship in the Czech Republic*. Working Paper, Center for International Enterprise Development, University of Pittsburgh.

Fogel, D. S. (1994). Lessens learned. In D. S. Fogel (Ed.), *Managing in emerging market economies,* pp. 225-233. Boulder, CO: Westview Press.

Fried, V. H., & Hisrich, R. D. (1988). Venture capital research: Past, present and future. *Entrepreneurship Theory and Practice, 13*(1), 15-28.

Galbraith, C., & Noble, A. F. (1988). Location decisions by high technology firms: A comparison of firm size, industry type, and institutional form. *Entrepreneurship Theory and Practice, 13*(2), 31-47.

Gartner, W. B. (1985). A conceptual framework for describing the phenomenon of new venture creation. *Academy of Management Review, 10*(4), 696-706.

Gnyawali, D. (1991). *Promoting small businesses through entrepreneurship development*. Washington, DC: The World Bank, Asia Technical Department.

Goodman, J. P., Meany, J. W., & Pate, L. E. (1992). The government as entrepreneur: Industrial development and the creation of new ventures. In D. L. Sexton & J. D. Kasarda (Eds.), *The state of the art on entrepreneurship*. Boston: PWS-Kent.

Harper, M. (1991). Enterprise development in poorer nations. *Entrepreneurship Theory and Practice, 15*(4), 7-11.

Harrison, R. T., & Mason, C. M. (1988). Risk finance, the equity gap, and new venture formation in the United Kingdom: The impact of business expansion scheme. In B. A. Kirchhoff, W. A. Long, W. E. McMullan, K. H. Vesper, & W. E. Wetzel (Eds.), *Frontiers of entrepreneurship research*. Wellesley, MA: Babson College.

Hawkins, D. L. (1993). New business entrepreneurship in the Japanese economy. *Journal of Business Venturing, 8,* 137-150.

Hoy, F. (1989). Editorial: Audiences for entrepreneurship research. *Entrepreneurship Theory and Practice, 13*(3), 5-6.

Hoy, F., Wisnieski, J., Gatewood, E., Bryant, L., & Patel, V. (1991). An incubator within an incubator: A case study of biotechnology venturing. In N. C. Churchill, W. D. Bygrave, J. G. Covin, D. L. Sexton, D. P. Slevin, K. H. Vesper, & W. E. Wetzel (Eds.), *Frontiers of entrepreneurship research,* pp. 391-405. Wellesley, MA: Babson College.

Kao, J. (1993). The worldwide web of Chinese business. *Harvard Business Review,* March-April, 24-36.

Kirchhoff, B. A. (1991). Entrepreneurship's contribution to economics. *Entrepreneurship Theory and Practice, 16*(2), 93-112.

Kleiman, R. T., & Bygrave, W. D. (1988). Public sector involvement in venture capital finance: The case of Michigan. In B. A. Kirchhoff, W. A. Long, W. E. McMullan, K. H. Vesper, W. E. Wetzel (Eds.), *Frontiers of entrepreneurship research*, pp. 610-611. Wellesley, MA: Babson College.

Learned, K. E. (1992). What happened before the organization? A model of organization formation. *Entrepreneurship Theory and Practice, 17*(1), 39-48.

Management Systems International (1990). *Entrepreneurship training and strengthening entrepreneurial performance*. Report submitted to the USAID.

Manning, K., Birley, S., & Norburn, D. (1989). Developing new ventures strategy. *Entrepreneurship Theory and Practice, 14*(1), 69-76.

McClelland, D. C. (1961). *The achieving society*. Princeton, NJ: Van Nostrand Publishing Company.

McClelland, D. C., & Winter, D. G. (1969). *Motivating economic achievement*. New York: Free Press.

MacMillan, I. C. (1983). The politics of new venture management. *Harvard Business Review*, Nov-Dec, 8-16.

Mokry, B. W. (1988). *Entrepreneurship and public policy: Can government stimulate start ups?* New York: Quorum Books.

Pennings, J. M. (1982). Organizational birth frequencies: An empirical investigation. *Administrative Science Quarterly, 27*, 120-144.

Pfeffer, J., & Salancik, G. J. (1978). *The external control of organizations: A resource dependence view*. New York: Harper and Row.

Phillips, B. D. (1993). The growth of small firm jobs by state, 1984-1988. *Business Economics*, April, 48-53.

Porter, M. (1990). *Competitive advantage of nations*. New York: Free Press.

Rondinelli, D. A. (1991). Developing private enterprises in the Czech and Slovak Republic: The challenges of economic reform. *Columbia Journal of World Business, 16*(3), 26-36.

Schumpeter, J. A. (1934). *The theory of economic development*. Cambridge, MA: Harvard University Press.

Segura, E. (1988). Industrial, trade and financial sector policies to foster private enterprises in developing countries. *Columbia Journal of World Business, 23*(1), 19-27.

Shapero, A. (1977). *The role of entrepreneurship in economic development at the less than national level*. Washington, DC: US Department of Commerce.

Shapero, A., & Sokol, L. (1982). The social dimensions of entrepreneurship. In C. A. Kent, D. L. Sexton, & K. H. Vesper (Eds.), *Encyclopedia of entrepreneurship*, pp. 72-90. Englewood Cliffs, NJ: Prentice Hall.

Small Business Administration. (1993). *1993 guidelines for small business award nominations*. Washington, DC: US Small Business Administration.

Siu, W., & Martin, R. G. (1992). Successful entrepreneurship in Hong Kong. *Long Range Planning, 25*(6), 87-93.

Staley, E., & Morse, R. (1971). Developing entrepreneurship: Elements for a program. In P. Kilby (Ed.), *Entrepreneurship and economic development*, pp. 357-384. New York: Free Press.

Swanson, D., & Webster, L. (1992). *Private sector manufacturing in the Czech and Slovak Republic: A survey of firms*. Washington, DC: The World Bank.

Takyi-Asiedu, S. (1993). Some socio-cultural factors retarding entrepreneurial activity in sub-Saharan Africa. *Journal of Business Venturing, 8*, 91-98.

Van de Ven, A. (1993). The development of an infrastructure for entrepreneurship. *Journal of Business Venturing, 8*, 211-230.

Venkatraman, N., & Prescott, J. E. (1990). Environment-strategy coalignment: An empirical test of its performance implications. *Strategic Management Journal, 11*, 1-23.

Vesper, K. H. (1983). *Entrepreneurship and national policy*. Chicago: Walter E. Heller International Corporation Institute for Small Business.

Vesper, K. H. (1990). *New venture strategies*. Englewood Cliffs, NJ: Prentice Hall.

Wall Street Journal. (1993). January 7, A10.

Westhead, P. (1990). A typology of new manufacturing firms in Wales: Performance measures and public policy implications. *Journal of Business Venturing, 5*, 103-122.

Young, E. C., & Welsch, H. P. (1993). Major elements in entrepreneurial development in central Mexico. *Journal of Small Business Management*, October, 80-85.

Zahra, S. A. (1993). A conceptual model of entrepreneurship as firm behavior: A critique and extension. *Entrepreneurship Theory and Practice, 17*(4), 5-21.

Devi R. Gnyawali is a PhD student and teaching Assistant at the University of Pittsburgh.

Daniel S. Fogel is Associate Dean & Professor of Business Administration at the Katz Graduate School of Business, University of Pittsburgh.

We appreciate the support of the Andrew W. Mellon Foundation for Business Development in Central and Eastern Europe awarded to the University of Pittsburgh and FORMAPER of the Milan, Italy, Chamber of Commerce and their support in Central and Eastern Europe. We would like to thank Usha Ganesh, John Grant, Ravindranath Madhavan, John Naman, Dennis Slevin, and three anonymous reviewers for their helpful comments on earlier drafts of this paper.

[14]

THE ROLE OF INCUBATOR ORGANIZATIONS IN THE FOUNDING OF GROWTH-ORIENTED FIRMS*

ARNOLD C. COOPER
Purdue University

EXECUTIVE SUMMARY

The role of incubator organizations, those organizations where entrepreneurs work before starting their own firms, is examined. Using a sample of 161 new, growth-oriented firms, the relationships of the new companies to their incubator organizations are considered, as well as the characteristics of the incubator organizations. ¶The findings have implications for prospective entrepreneurs. Entrepreneurs in most industry categories do not change geographic location and, in most technical industries, usually start businesses related to what they did before. An individual's decision to join a particular organization results in a particular geographic location and in knowledge about a particular industry. The would-be founder located in an unpromising geographic area and getting experience in an industry offering few opportunities for company start-ups is unlikely to be able to start a growth-oriented technical firm, regardless of personal motivation. However, the prospective founder of a nontechnical firm appears to be less tied to the experience gained in an incubator organization.

There are also implications for regional economic development. Because technically oriented start-ups are tied closely to the business of their incubator organizations and because most entrepreneurs don't move when starting, the possibilities for high-technology start-ups may be very limited in many geographic regions. There have been no studies, to date, on why some founders move when starting. Programs to attract entrepreneurs at the time of start-up may have promise, but, at least to date, there is not much evidence of entrepreneurs being mobile at this stage of their careers.

Local and regional programs to attract branch facilities of larger corportions have a long history. The emphasis is usually upon attracting facilities that will offer the maximum number of blue-collar jobs. In contrast to this traditional approach, it might be beneficial to shift the emphasis to those facilities most

*Earlier parts of this research were presented at the National Meetings of the Entrepreneurship Interest Group, The Academy of Management, San Diego, CA, August 12–14, 1985, and at the Babson Research Conference, Atlanta, GA, April 24, 1984.

Address reprint requests to Arnold C. Cooper, Krannert Graduate School of Management, Purdue University, West Lafayette, IN 47907.

Journal of Business Venturing 1, 75–86 (1985) 0883-9026/85/$03.30

likely to function as incubators. The greatest benefits might come from laboratories or divisions that would "seed" a region with people learning about promising technologies or industries.

The role of universities in this process appears to be less direct than is often assumed. Based upon our sample, it appears that software and biotechnology/medical firms often have spun-off from universities or hospitals. However, in other industry categories, it is business firms that have primarily served as incubators. There are currently many experiments underway to create university-affiliated innovation centers or incubator centers intended to help aspiring entrepreneurs. Whether these will enable universities to function more effectively as incubators, spinning off students and faculty who start growth-oriented firms, remains to be seen.

THIS ARTICLE FOCUSES UPON THE ORGANIZATIONS WHERE ENTREPRENEURS WORK before they start their own firms. These organizations, which might be termed incubators, appear to influence the processes by which entrepreneurs, at particular times and places, leave to start new firms. In this sense, every organization might be viewed as a potential incubator, influencing its members by making them more or less prepared and more or less motivated to start new firms.

In this article, I shall do the following: 1) review prior research on the ways in which incubator organizations appear to influence entrepreneurship; 2) present the findings from a current study that examines the incubator phenomenon for a cross section of visible growth-oriented firms; and 3) consider the implications, both for prospective entrepreneurs and for those concerned with regional economic development.

PREVIOUS RESEARCH

Every organization might be viewed as a potential incubator, influencing its employees in a variety of ways that make them more or less likely to leave and start new firms. The characteristics of the incubator organizations also appear to influence the nature of the new firms that might be started and, to some degree, their subsequent patterns of success. Previous research has identified a number of factors relating incubator organizations to the entrepreneurial process. These are discussed below, although our primary concern in this paper is with the first four factors, those concerned with location, nature of business, type of incubator organization, and size of incubator organization.

Location

The incubator organizations affect the locations of new firms. Even though founders may have been geographically mobile at earlier stages of their careers, they usually do not move when they found new firms. The percentage of new companies started that involved at least one founder who was already working in the area ranged from 97.5% in Palo Alto, to 90% in Austin and in England, to 75% in a broad study of 890 founders across the United States (Cooper 1970, p. 18; Susbauer 1972, p. 37; Watkins 1973, p. 66; Cooper and Dunkelberg 1981, p. 10).

By starting in the same geographic region, the entrepreneur can utilize first-hand knowledge of markets and suppliers. It may thereby also be possible to start a new business on a parttime basis while maintaining a fulltime job. The full energies of the founder also can be focused on the start-up, without the diversions associated with moving a family and without his or her spouse having to give up a job. One implication is that regional entrepreneurship is largely dependent on the pool of people already living in an area.

Nature of the Business

Established organizations also influence the nature of the new businesses established. This is particularly the case with high-technology firms, in which current knowledge of technologies and markets is essential for success. Interpretation of prior studies is difficult because of differences in terminology used. However, it appears that previous studies have found new businesses closely related to the technologies or markets of the incubator organizations for 70% of 890 founders from a cross section of industries and for 85% of 250 technical entrepreneurs (Cooper and Dunkelberg 1981; Cooper 1970, p. 19). Founders had experience in similar businesses in about 70% of low technology manufacturing firms in Michigan, and about 60% of service enterprises in Rhode Island (Hoad and Rosko 1964, p. 92; Mayer and Goldstein 1961, p. 104).

The new firm typically depends upon what the founder knows and can do. That is often related to what the founder learned to do in the incubator organization. One implication is that the nature of new firms started in an area is likely to be related to the nature of organizations already there. Another implication is that organizations may vary widely in the extent to which their employees acquire the skills and knowledge that could easily be applied to starting a new firm.

Type of Incubator Organization

The extent to which universities and nonprofit organizations function as incubators appears to vary widely. In Boston, Austin, and Ann Arbor, substantial percentages of the new firms studied were direct spin-offs from a university or one of its laboratories (Roberts 1972, p. 127; Susbauer 1972, p. 33; Lamont 1972, p. 151). However, a variety of other patterns exist. In Silicon Valley, only six of 243 firms founded in the 1960s had one or more fulltime founders who came directly from a university (Cooper 1970, p. 32). In the same study, other nonprofit organizations also had low spin-off rates. In both England and the U. S. there are universities strong in science and engineering that have been associated with very little entrepreneurship. One study of 22 technical complexes found that only seven had major university affiliation and several had no colleges involved when the technical company was forming (Shapero 1972, p. 71).

Universities and other nonprofit organizations often do state-of-the-art technical work that provides their members with knowledge of technical opportunities. However, the extent to which the students, faculty, or members of nonprofit organizations are prepared and motivated to become business founders probably varies widely. In particular, they may lack knowledge of market opportunities and may not have much experience in selling or in building an organization.

Size of Incubator Organization

Spin-off rates appear to vary widely, even among firms in the same industry. One factor that seems to have a bearing is the size of the incubator organization. Several studies have indicated that small firms tend to have higher spin-off rates than large firms. In England, small firms considered as a class (fewer than 250 employees) had spin-off rates six times as high as large firms considered as a class (Johnson and Cathcart 1979, pp. 219–224). In Palo Alto, incubator firms with fewer than 500 employees had spin-off rates ten times as high as large firms considered as a class (Cooper 1970, p. 31).

In small companies, employees learn about technologies or markets that can be exploited by small firms. They also develop broad experience and can see what is involved in managing a small firm. There is also probably some self-selection, with those choosing to work for smaller firms probably being more entrepreneurial.

Motivation

The established organization also appears to influence the motivation of the entrepreneur. People who are frustrated because they cannot get along with their bosses or because their ideas are turned down, or who have lost jobs because of plant closings are ready to consider a change.

Findings from previous research vary widely (possibly due to differences in research methodology), but it appears that substantial numbers of founders studied left their previous jobs because of strong negative "pushes" (Shapero and Sokol 1982, pp. 80–81). Furthermore, some organizations that have spun off many entrepreneurs seem to have done so most often during times of internal troubles and change. One implication is that organizations that are good at recruiting ambitious people, but are then afflicted with internal mismanagement or turmoil, may be most likely to spin off entrepreneurs.

Team Formation

Incubator organizations also provide the setting within which founding teams can be formed. New firms, particularly growth-oriented firms, are often founded by teams of two or more founders. A study of 890 foundings indicated that 31% involved teams (Cooper and Dunkelberg 1981, p. 10); in another study of 955 high-technology foundings 59% involved teams (Shapero 1971, p. 22). (Other research has indicated that companies started by teams tend to be more successful.)

Teams permit the assembly of a broader range of skills; for instance, a founder strong in manufacturing can work with another founder strong in marketing. Members of founding teams often meet each other in the incubator organization. If the incubator organization includes, at a given site, all of the key functional activities, such as engineering, manufacturing, and marketing, then it is more likely that balanced founding teams can be formed.

Previous research suggests that incubator organizations influence not only the nature of new firms, but also whether spin-offs actually occur. Existing organizations, even within the same industry, vary widely in the extent to which their employees leave to start new firms (Cooper 1973, p. 61). Table 1 indicates the characteristics of firms and the industries in which they operate that may be associated with high or low birth-rates of new firms.

Implications

The implications of this prior research are the following.

1) Young people making career decisions to join particular organizations may be determining, in part, whether they will ever be in a position to become entrepreneurs. Any organization might be viewed as an educational institution, in which its employees acquire skills and knowledge to make them more or less prepared to become entrepreneurs. In addition, the extent to which particular organizations may locate potential entrepreneurs in promising geographical areas or motivate them to undertake the forbidding step of entrepreneurship may vary widely.

TABLE 1 Industry and Organizational Attributes Related to the Birth-Rate of New Firms

Low birth-rate	High birth-rate
Characteristics of industry	
Slow industry growth	Rapid industry growth
Homogeneous markets	Opportunities to segment markets
Heavy capital investment required	Low capital investment required
Substantial economies of scale	Minor economies of scale
Characteristics of established incubator organizations	
Large number of employees	Small number of employees
Organized by function	Product-decentralized organization
Recruit average people	Recruit very capable, ambitious people
Relatively well-managed	Afflicted with periodic crises
Located in geographic areas of little entrepreneurship	Located in geographic areas of high entrepreneurship

All of the attributes in a given column are not necessarily found together nor are they required to bring about a given spin-off rate. Various combinations may exist.

2) Geographic regions seeking to encourage entrepreneurial activity may find the possibilities shaped by the nature of established organizations already there. Because founders tend to start firms where they are already living and working, there must be organizations that will hire, bring into the area, and train the engineers and managers who may some day become entrepreneurs. However, the nature of these organizations is critical in determining whether spin-offs will actually occur as well as the nature of the new businesses that might be started. If existing businesses are involved primarily in mature industries offering few growth opportunities, it is unlikely that their employees will be in a position to start new firms in growth industries. Unless promising incubator organizations are present or can be created or attracted, the prospects for the founding of high-potential firms may be limited.

The Incubator Phenomenon and Recent Start-Ups

The extent of previous research into the incubator phenomenon is quite limited. Most of the referenced studies concern high-technology firms, particularly electronics companies. There has been no systematic examination or even speculation on whether the influence of incubator organizations varies across industries. In addition, many of the cited studies were done in the 1960s or early 1970s. We wonder whether the climate for entrepreneurship has changed in material ways, ways that would affect the role of the incubator in entrepreneurial activity. In particular, the following factors may have a bearing.

1) The technologies that seem fertile for entrepreneurship may have changed. Some technologies previously very attractive for new firms seem to have developed in ways that make start-ups more difficult. For instance, capital requirements for semiconductor manufacture have increased substantially and new areas have evolved that offer attractive opportunities for company formation, such as computer software and biotechnology. For non-technical growth-oriented firms, opportunities have undoubtedly changed. However, it is not clear how all of these changes may relate to the role of incubator organizations in the entrepreneurial process.

2) The role of new firms in local and regional economic development has become

widely recognized. Many local and state agencies have begun to offer financial and other incentives to targeted firms. The extent to which these incentives may have altered the entrepreneurial process, including lowering the barriers to entry or causing entrepreneurs to move when starting, is unknown.

3) A national climate more favorable to entrepreneurs appears to have evolved. Magazines oriented toward entrepreneurs and a growing number of university courses and weekend seminars on entrepreneurship may have raised consciousness about the entrepreneurial process. Increasing pools of venture capital have become available. Universities have started innovation centers, small business development centers, and other sources of assistance and encouragement. This may have made entrepreneurs more sophisticated as they develop new business strategies and search for needed resources. A more favorable entrepreneurial climate may also have led founders to emerge from some organizations that normally would not have served as incubators.

The limited number and scope of previous studies raise questions about how broadly the incubator concept might apply. The changing environment and the emergence of new technical and market opportunities may mean that earlier findings are no longer broadly applicable.

THE SAMPLE

This study examines new firms that have been the subject of feature stories in national magazines. It includes those appearing in *Inc.* magazine from January 1981 through November 1984 and in *Venture* magazine (most issues) from January 1980 through June 1984. They are primarily growth-oriented firms that have had, or give promise of having, substantial economic impact. Many, but by no means all, are high-technology firms.

This is a biased sample in the sense that it in no way is reflective of the broad cross section of new businesses. The criteria used by reporters and editors in choosing these firms for feature articles are unknown and may reflect geographic or industry biases. However, if the focus is upon entrepreneurial processes leading to growth-oriented firms, the sample should be of particular interest. These are exactly the kinds of new firms sought by economic development commissions and venture capitalists; they are the kinds of firms that many entrepreneurs would like to start.

A total of 161 firms was identified, although complete data were not available for all. In many cases, the primary data were obtained from the feature magazine article, with supplementary data on the incubator organization from other sources. The sample was divided into five industry categories. These categories and the number of firms in each are indicated below:

Industry	Number of firms
Electronics/Computers	55
Software	24
Biotechnology/Medical	20
Other technical	19
Nontechnical	43
Total sample	161

FINDINGS

This research was focused upon four of the factors previously discussed that might be expected to relate incubator organizations to the entrepreneurial process: 1) the location of the new firm, relative to the incubator organization; 2) the nature of the business of the new firm, relative to the incubator organization; 3) the type of incubator organization, whether an industrial firm, or a university or hospital; and 4) the size of the incubator organization.

The findings on location, given in Table 2, show that most of these new firms (84% of the total sample) were started in the same geographic location as their incubator organizations. (The "same location" was defined as within commuting distance of where the founders worked before.) The same pattern existed in all of the industry groups, except for biotechnology, where 47% of the small sample of new firms studied moved when starting up.

Those 21 new firms whose founders moved at the time of founding were examined separately. (Patterns of geographic mobility for entrepreneurs have received almost no attention in the literature to date.) Their patterns of movement were examined to determine whether there was a tendency to move toward high "quality of life" states, toward or away from larger metropolitan areas, or toward states with "more attractive" economic climates. These findings are summarized in Table 3. Because only 16% of the total sample moved, sample sizes are small. Differences are not statistically significant at the 0.05 level, but the patterns may be of interest. In general, there seems to be only a slight pattern of movement toward quality of life states, a more pronounced movement away from larger metropolitan areas, and a slight movement toward those states ranked economically most attractive by *Inc.* magazine. These findings should, of course, be regarded as only suggestive, both because of the small sample size and the subjective nature of quality of life and economic climate ratings.

There are a number of complications in examining the relationship between the nature of the business of the new firm and of the incubator organization. A new semiconductor firm whose founders previously worked for another semiconductor firm is related; by contrast, the solid waste disposal firm whose founder previously worked for a public accounting firm is unrelated. But how should we view the software firm, with an initial strategy of custom software programs, whose founder previously did systems analysis consulting for an accounting firm? Clearly, there can be degrees of relatedness, particularly to the functional activities performed by an entrepreneur within an apparently unrelated incubator organization. In this analysis, reflected in Table 4, a conservative approach was taken in determining

TABLE 2 Location of New Firm Relative to Incubator Organization

	Same location[a]	Different location	Unknown
Electronics/Computers	41 (97.6%)[b]	1 (2.4%)	13
Software	19 (86.4%)	3 (13.6%)	2
Biotechnology/Medical	9 (52.9%)	8 (47.1%)	3
Other technical	9 (81.8%)	2 (18.2%)	8
Nontechnical	30 (81.1%)	7 (18.9%)	6
Total sample	108 (83.7%)	21 (16.3%)	32

[a]Same location is defined as within commuting distance of the incubator organization.
[b]Percentage of new firms within an industry classification for which the location relationship is known.

TABLE 3 Patterns of Movement for Entrepreneurs Moving at the Time of Founding

"Quality of life" states	
Toward "quality of life" states[a]	10 (47.6%)
Away from "quality of life" states	7 (33.3%)
No change	4 (19.0%)
Metropolitan areas	
Toward larger cities	6 (30.0%)
Away from larger cities	14 (70.0%)
Unknown	1 —
Economic climate[b]	
Toward "more attractive" economic climate	10 (58.8%)
Away from "more attractive" economic climate	7 (41.2%)
Involving foreign countries	2 —

[a]Quality of life states included California, Colorado, Florida, North Carolina, Oregon, and Texas.
[b]Attractiveness of economic climate was based upon *Inc.* magazine rankings, October 1984.

relatedness. Unless the incubator organization and the new firm were closely related, e.g., both making word processors or software, they were classified as unrelated. Problems also arise in analyzing these relationships for spin-offs from universities or hospitals. There may be close relationships between the technology utilized in the new firm and research performed in the university; however, universities are in a different "business" than industrial firms. For purposes of this analysis, spin-offs from universities and hospitals are excluded, as are firms started by independent professionals or housewives. (They are considered explicitly later in the paper.)

Most of the new businesses in this sample were related to their incubator organizations in nature of business. As shown in Table 4, about 64% of the new firms showed this relationship. These patterns were particularly pronounced for electronics/computers. Interestingly, for nontechnical firms, the majority (54%) were unrelated to the incubator organization, suggesting that the requisite technical and market knowledge for these industries may be more easily learned or available from suppliers or other sources. Sample sizes for the other groups are so small (particularly with university or hospital spin-offs excluded)

TABLE 4 Relationship Between Nature of Business of New Firm and of Incubator Organization

	Related business	Unrelated business	Unknown
Electronics/Computers	36 (78.3%)[a]	10 (21.7%)	5
Software	9 (56.3%)	7 (43.7%)	1
Biotechnology/Medical	4 (57.1%)	3 (42.9%)	1
Other technical	10 (76.9%)	3 (23.1%)	4
Nontechnical	17 (45.9%)	20 (54.1%)	1
Total sample[b]	76 (63.9%)	43 (36.1%)	12

[a]Percentage of new firms within an industry classification for which the type of incubator is known.
[b]Thirty firms that were spin-offs from universities or hospitals or which involved other backgrounds were excluded.

TABLE 5 Type of Incubator Organization

	Business firm	University or hospital[a]	Other	Unknown
Electronics/Computers	47 (85.5%)[b]	6 (10.9%)	2 (3.6%)	3
Software	17 (70.8%)	7 (29.2%)	—	—
Biotechnology/Medical	7 (41.2%)	10 (58.8%)	—	1
Other technical	16 (88.9%)	1 (5.6%)	1 (5.6%)	1
Nontechnical	33 (80.5%)	3 (7.3%)	5 (12.2%)	1
Total sample	120 (77.4%)	27 (17.4%)	8 (5.2%)	6

[a]Only biotechnology firms were spin-offs from hospitals.
[b]Percentage of new firms within an industry classification for which the type of incubator is known.

that it is difficult to draw conclusions; it does appear that "other technical" firms tended to be related to their incubator organizations.

In regard to type of incubator organization, industrial firms were the incubator organizations for 77% of the new firms, while universities and hospitals considered together accounted for 17% (see Table 5). The industry breakdown is revealing. Electronic/computer firms, other technical firms, and nontechnical firms were primarily spin-offs from businesses (86%, 89%, and 81%, respectively). However, universities or hospitals were an important source of software firms (29%), and particularly of biotechnology/medical firms (59%).

The sizes of the incubator organizations were determined by classifying them according to whether they were in the 1984 *Fortune* magazine compilation of the 500 largest industrial firms or 500 largest service firms. Of the 125 new firms that were spin-offs from business organizations, the size of the incubator could be determined for 119. Of these, 49 or 41% were from these 1000 largest firms. (An additional three or 3% were from "Big Eight" accounting firms, see Table 6.) In 1983, these 1000 corporations had total employment of 23.5 million, about 32% of U.S. private sector nonagriculatural employment. This difference, statistically significant at the 0.05 level, suggests that large firms served as incubators for somewhat more than their share of these new companies. This contrasts sharply with most of the previous research on this subject, which indicated that large firms are likely to have lower spin-off rates. (However, one previous study found founders of high-growth firms to be more likely to come from large corporations (Cooper and Bruno 1977, p. 22). Bearing in mind that the companies in this sample tend to be high-growth

TABLE 6 Size of Incubator Organization

	Number of new firms	Number of employees
Total new firms	161	—
New firms from business organizations	125 (100%)	73.8 million[c] (100%)
New firms from "*Fortune* 500"[a]	49 (41%)[b]	23.5 million[d] (32%)

[a]Fortune 500 industrial firms or Fortune 500 service firms, *Fortune* April 30, 1984, pp. 274–295, and *Fortune* June 11, 1984, pp. 170–191.
[b]Calculated as a percentage of the 119 firms whose size could be determined.
[c]Number of employees in nonagricultural industries less government employees (*Statistical Abstract of the United States, 1984* 1983, pp. 427–429).
[d]Calculated from employment data provided in *Fortune* 500 lists.

firms, the substantial percentage of entrepreneurs from large corporations appears consistent with this earlier study.)

DISCUSSION

Considering the entire sample of growth-oriented firms, the incubator phenomenon seems to have played an important role. Most new firms did start geographically close to their incubator organizations. This reinforces the concept that entrepreneurship within a region is largely dependent upon the pool of people already there. Furthermore, almost two-thirds of the new firms were closely related to their incubator organizations in nature of business. Most of the founders of these growth-oriented firms came from business organizations, with somewhat more from large businesses than expected.

There were variations across industries. The expected relationships were most pronounced for electronics/computer firms and for "other technical" firms. In both categories, more than 80% of the companies were spin-offs from industrial firms located in the same geographic area. In more than 75% of the cases in both industry categories, they were engaged in closely related businesses.

The software and biotechnology firms displayed somewhat different patterns. Software firms located close to their incubators, but were less likely to be engaged in a closely related business. (Note, however, that some entrepreneurs came from accounting firms or from data-processing departments in "unrelated" incubator firms.) Software firms were more likely than the total sample to be spin-offs from universities. Biotechnology/medical firms were distinctive in being most likely to move and most likely to come from universities or hospitals. Examination of the relationship between the business of these firms and their incubator organizations was made difficult by the small sample size and the large number of spin-offs from universities or hospitals.

Field research involving interviews with entrepreneurs in these industries is needed to understand more fully the factors at work. However, we speculate that to some extent for software, but particularly for biotechnology, state-of-the-art technology is found primarily in universities and hospitals. The perception of enormous commercial potential for biotechnology has led to large amounts of money being made available to entrepreneurs, probably giving them unusual flexibility in location decisions. In computer software, many of the entrepreneurial opportunities during the time studied are related to personal computers. Many of the computer specialists in industry were skilled in developing software for mainframes and minicomputers, but were not positioned to take advantage of the developing opportunities in personal computers.

For the nontechnical firms, more than 80% were spin-offs from business firms located in the same area. However, more than 50% of these companies were not engaged in a business closely related to that of the incubator organization. In this type of venture, it was apparently often possible to develop the technical and market familiarity needed without fulltime experience in the industry.

These findings have implications for prospective entrepreneurs. Entrepreneurs in most industry categories do not move geographically and, in most technical industries, usually start businesses related to what they did before. An individual's decision to join a particular organization results in being located in a particular geographic area and in being immersed in knowledge about a particular industry. The would-be founder located in an unpromising geographic area and getting experience in an industry offering few opportunities for company start-ups is unlikely to be able to start a growth-oriented technical firm, regardless of personal motivation. However, the prospective founder of a nontechnical firm appears to be less tied to the experience gained in an incubator organization.

The implications for regional economic development seem clear. Because technically oriented start-ups are tied closely to the business of their incubator organizations and because most entrepreneurs don't move when starting, the possibilities for high-technology start-ups may be very limited in many geographic regions. There have been no studies on why some founders move when starting. Programs to attract entrepreneurs at the time of start-up may have promise, but, at least to date, there is not much evidence of entrepreneurs being mobile at this stage of their careers.

Local and regional programs to attract branch facilities of larger corporations have a long history. The emphasis is usually upon attracting a facility that will offer the maximum number of blue-collar jobs. In contrast to this traditional approach, it might be beneficial to shift the emphasis to those facilities most likely to function as incubators. The greatest benefits might come from laboratories or divisions that would "seed" a region with people learning about promising technologies or industries.

The role of universities in this process appears to be less direct than is often assumed. Based upon this sample, it appears that software and biotechnology/medical firms have often spun off from universities or hospitals. However, in other industry categories, it is business firms that have served primarily as incubators. There are currently many experiments underway to create university-affiliated innovation centers or incubator centers intended to help aspiring entrepreneurs. Whether these will enable universities to function more effectively as incubators, spinning off students and faculty who start growth-oriented firms remains to be seen.

The study presented here is limited in scope and may suffer from biases in the generation of the sample. However, the findings seem to be generally consistent with prior research and suggest that incubator organizations play an important role in the founding of growth-oriented firms.

REFERENCES

Cooper, A.C. 1970. *The Founding of Technologically-Based Firms*. Milwaukee, WI: The Center for Venture Management.

Cooper, A.C. February 1973. Technical entrepreneurship: What do we know? *R&D Management* 3(2).

Cooper, A.C., and Bruno, A.V. March 1977. Success among high-technology firms. *Business Horizons* 20(2).

Cooper, A.C., and Dunkelberg, W.C. 1981. A new look at business entry: Experiences of 1805 entrepreneurs. In K. Vesper, ed., *Frontiers of Entrepreneurship Research*. Wellesley, MA: Babson Center for Entrepreneurial Studies.

Cooper, A.C., and Dunkelberg, W.C. August 4, 1981. Influences upon entrepreneurship—A large scale study. San Diego, CA: Academy of Management Meetings.

The Fortune directory of the largest U.S. industrial corporations. April 30, 1984. *Fortune*.

The Fortune directory of the largest U.S. non-industrial corporations. June 11, 1984. *Fortune*.

Hoad, W.M., and Rosko, P. 1964. *Management Factors Contributing to the Success or Failure of New Small Manufacturers*. Ann Arbor, MI: The University of Michigan.

Johnson, P.S., and Cathcart, D.G. December 1979. The founders of new manufacturing firms: A note on the size of their incubator plants. *The Journal of Industrial Economics* 28(2).

Lamont, L.M. 1972. The role of marketing in technical entrepreneurship. In A. Cooper and J. Komives, eds., *Technical Entrepreneurship: A Symposium*. Milwaukee, WI: The Center for Venture Management.

Mayer, K.B., and Goldstein, S. 1961. *The First Two Years: Problems of Small Firm Growth and Survival*. Washington, DC: US Government Printing Office.

Roberts, E.B. 1972. Influences upon performance of new technical enterprises. In A. Cooper and J. Komives, eds., *Technical Entrepreneurship: A Symposium*. Milwaukee, WI: The Center for Venture Management.

Shapero, A. 1971. *An Action Program for Entrepreneurship*. Austin, TX: Multidisciplinary Research, Inc.

Shapero, A. 1972. The process of technical company formation in a local area. In A. Cooper and J. Komives, eds., *Technical Entrepreneurship: A Symposium*. Milwaukee, WI: The Center for Venture Management.

Shapero, A., and Sokol, L. 1982. The social dimensions of entrepreneurship. In C. Kent, D. Sexton, and K. Vesper, eds., *Encyclopedia of Entrepreneurship*. Englewood Cliffs, NJ: Prentice-Hall, Inc.

Statistical Abstract of the United States, 1984. 1983. Washington, DC: US Government Printing Office.

Susbauer, J.C. 1972. The technical entrepreneurship process in Austin, Texas. In A. Cooper and J. Komives, eds., *Technical Entrepreneurship: A Symposium*. Milwaukee, WI: The Center for Venture Management.

Watkins, D.S. February 1973. Technical entrepreneurship: A cis-Atlantic view. *R&D Management* 3(2).

[15]

Academy of Management Review, 1985, Vol. 10, No. 4, 696-706.

A Conceptual Framework for Describing the Phenomenon of New Venture Creation

WILLIAM B. GARTNER
Georgetown University

A review of the entrepreneurship literature suggests that differences among entrepreneurs and among their ventures are as great as the variation between entrepreneurs and nonentrepreneurs and between new firms and established firms. A framework for describing new venture creation integrates four major perspectives in entrepreneurship: characteristics of the individual(s) who start the venture, the organization which they create, the environment surrounding the new venture, and the process by which the new venture is started.

The major thrust of most entrepreneurship research has been to prove that entrepreneurs are different from nonentrepreneurs (Brockhaus, 1980a, 1980b; Carland, Hoy, Boulton, & Carland, 1984; Collins & Moore, 1964; DeCarlo & Lyons, 1979; Hornaday & Aboud, 1971; Howell, 1972; Komives, 1972; Litzinger, 1965; McClelland, 1961; McClelland & Winter, 1969; Palmer, 1971; Schrier, 1975; Shapero, 1975) and that entrepreneurial firms are different from nonentrepreneurial firms (Collins & Moore, 1970; Cooper, 1979; Smith, 1967; Thorne & Ball, 1981). The basic assumption underlying this research is that all entrepreneurs and their new ventures are much the same. The present paper suggests that the differences among entrepreneurs and among their ventures are much greater than one might expect; in fact, the diversity may be larger than the differences between entrepreneurs and nonentrepreneurs and between entrepreneurial firms and nonentrepreneurial firms. Once the diversity among entrepreneurs and their ventures is recognized, the necessity for finding a way to classify them becomes apparent. Groups sharing similar characteristics must exist within the universe of entrepreneurs and their ventures. How are these groups revealed? Many different characteristics have been employed in past research to describe entrepreneurs and their ventures. Do the characteristics themselves fall into groups? In other words, does one subset of characteristics describe a single aspect of new venture creation, such as the environment surrounding the new venture, or the features of the organization that results?

This paper attempts to organize the many variables that have been used in past research to describe entrepreneurs and their ventures into a comprehensive framework. Far from being reductive, this new view of the entrepreneurship literature should provide valuable insights into the process of new venture creation by showing it to be a complex and multidimensional phenomenon. Once a clear retrospective analysis of the literature is provided, future research can proceed on more solid footing. Instead of many different researchers palpating different parts of the elephant and reaching reductive conclusions, at least all will know the name, if not the nature, of the beast with which they are dealing.

Much past research has been unidimensional, focusing on a single aspect of new venture creation, and its main purpose has been to show how entrepreneurs or their firms differ from nonentrepreneurs or nonentrepreneurial firms. (In fact, it might be said that unidimensional research goes

The research leading to this paper was supported in part by a grant from the National Science Foundation and is based on the author's doctoral dissertation. Additional support was provided by the Center for Entrepreneurial Studies, University of Virginia.

Requests for reprints should be sent to William B. Gartner, Center for Entrepreneurship Studies, School of Business Administration, Georgetown University, Washington, D.C. 20057.

hand in hand with the attitude that all entrepreneurs and their firms are alike, the task of the unidimensional research being to prove how all things entrepreneurial differ from all things nonentrepreneurial.) It has been consistently pointed out, however, in reviews of literature on entrepreneurs, for example, (Brockhaus, 1982; Glueck & Mescon, 1980; McCain & Smith, 1981) that variables that are assumed to differentiate entrepreneurs from nonentrepreneurs (managers, for instance) frequently do not bear up under close scrutiny. Yet the search for these elusive variables continues, and entrepreneurs and prospective entrepreneurs are subjected to batteries of psychological tests in attempts to isolate the single spring that makes them tick differently from others. As with other aspects of new venture creation, attempts are made to isolate key variables that separate entrepreneurial situations from nonentrepreneurial ones. Pennings (1980, 1982a, 1982b) has explored environments that support new venture creation; Van de Ven (1980) and Kimberly (1979) have focused on the process of venture creation.

This search for key variables is a motivation for research only if the task of entrepreneurial research is taken to be the distinction of entrepreneurs and things entrepreneurial from nonentrepreneurs and nonentrepreneurial situations. If a much different perspective is taken, the perspective that there are many different kinds of entrepreneur and many ways to be one and that the firms they create vary enormously as do the environments they create them in, then the burden shifts. How is each new venture creation different from another? Researchers need to think in terms of a combination of variables that make up each new venture creation (Van de Ven, Hudson, & Schroeder, 1984). The creation of a new venture is a multidimensional phenomenon; each variable describes only a single dimension of the phenomenon and cannot be taken alone. There is a growing awareness that the process of starting a business is not a single well-worn route marched along again and again by identical entrepreneurs (Hartman, 1983). New venture creation is a complex phenomenon: entrepreneurs and their firms vary widely; the actions they take or do not take and the environments they operate in and respond to are equally diverse — and all these elements form complex and unique combinations in the creation of each new venture. It is not enough for researchers to seek out and focus on some concept of the "average" entrepreneur and the "typical" venture creation. New organizational forms evolve through variation, and this variation in new venture creation needs to be studied (Aldrich, 1979; Hannan & Freeman, 1977; Pfeffer & Salancik, 1978; Weick, 1979). This insistence on variation can be seen, for example, in Vesper (1979), who posits 11 different kinds of entrepreneur, and in a recent study by Cooper and Dunkelberg (1981), which reveals that entrepreneurs in certain industries can be very different from those in other industries.

Once the variation and complexity in new venture creation is recognized, it then is necessary to find a framework for systematically discovering and evaluating the similarities and differences among new ventures (McKelvey, 1982). Once it is no longer assumed that all entrepreneurs and their ventures present a homogeneous population, then other homogeneous subsets within the entrepreneurial universe must be sought out in order that entrepreneurial research can produce meaningful results. A primary value of the framework for describing new venture creation presented here is that it provides a systematic means of comparing and contrasting complex ventures; it provides a way to conceptualize variation and complexity.

A Framework for Describing New Venture Creation

Definitions of key words such as entrepreneur are often various and always a problem in the study of entrepreneurship (Brockhaus, 1980b; Komives, 1969; Long, 1983). Because the entrepreneur is only one dimension of this framework, it seems more important in this paper to define the term "new venture creation." Such a definition can be outlined here with less trepidation, if only because there is less precedent.

New venture creation is the organizing (in the Weickian sense) *of new organizations.* "To organize is to assemble ongoing interdependent actions into sensible sequences that generate sensible outcomes" (Weick, 1979, p. 3). The definition of new venture creation is synonymous with the definition of the new organization developed by the Strategic Planning Institute (1978, p. 1-2):

> a new business venture launched as one of the following:
> 1. an independent entity
> 2. a new profit center within a company which has other established businesses, or
> 3. a joint venture which satisfies the following criteria:
> 1. Its founders must acquire expertise in products, process, market and/or technology.
> 2. Results are expected beyond the year in which the investment is made.
> 3. It is considered a new market entrant by its competitors.
> 4. It is regarded as a new source of supply by its potential customers.

The importance of this definition should not be overlooked, because it recognizes the multidimensional aspects of new venture creation. First, it emphasizes that individuals with expertise are a key element of the new venture. At the same time that it recognizes the new venture as an organizational entity, it stresses that the new venture is not instantaneously produced, but evolves over time (beyond a year). The new venture is seen further within the context of its environment: it is forced to seek out resources, and it competes in the market place. All these aspects of the new venture must be kept in mind if it is to be adequately described and classified.

Figure 1 presents a framework for describing the creation of a new venture across four dimensions: (a) individual(s)—the person(s) involved in starting a new organization; (b) organization—the kind of firm that is started; (c) environment—the situation surrounding and influencing the new organization; and (d) new venture process—the actions undertaken by the individual(s) to start the venture.

Any new venture is a gestalt (Miller, 1981) of variables from the four dimensions. No new venture creation can be comprehensively described, nor can its complexity be adequately accounted for, unless all of its four dimensions are investigated and an attempt is made to discover how variables from each dimension interact with variables from other dimensions.

This framework is the first to combine the four dimensions of venture creation, though other researchers have sought to combine two or more of the dimensions. This "thinking across dimensions" is especially apparent in the work of those theorists and researchers who have developed entrepreneurial classification schemes. Classifications of entrepreneurs themselves are often based on two dimensions: individual characteristics plus new venture process considerations — the word often used is "style." Danhoff (1949) based his scheme on the entrepreneur's openness to innovation; Cole (1959) on the sophistication of the entrepreneur's decision making tools; and Dailey (1971) according to bureaucratic or entrepreneurial style. Smith (1967) divided entrepreneurs by a stylistic orientation — craftsman or opportunistic. Filley and Aldag (1980) used management orientation. Vesper (1979, 1980) in two similar classifications differentiated among entrepreneurs by the activities involved in business formation and operation, and in another scheme (1980) by competitive strategy. In Cooper (1979) entrepreneurs are linked to particular environments, and, as cited previously, Cooper and Dunkelberg's (1981) study matches different entrepreneurs and their characteristics to the types of firms they are likely to start. In Vesper's (1979) classification the entrepreneur's type of firm is also a factor, as it is in several other classification studies (Braden, 1977; Filley & Aldag, 1980; Smith, 1967). Recently, Van de Ven et al.'s (1984) empirical study examined educational software firms on the basis of three dimen-

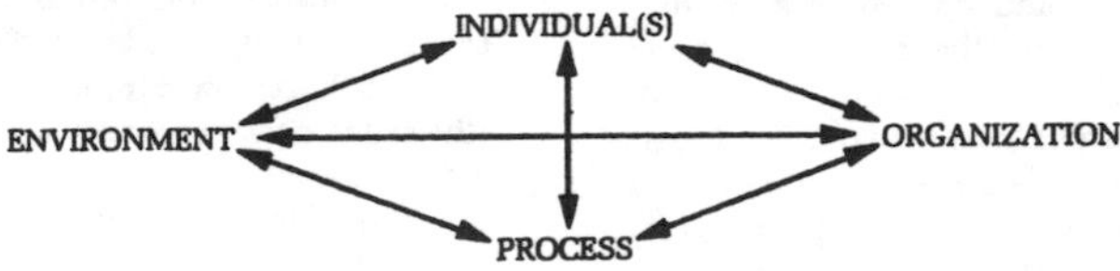

Figure 1. A framework for describing new venture creation.

sions: entrepreneurial—background characteristics and psychological attributes of the founding entrepreneurs; organizational—planning and organizational activities undertaken before and after company startup; and ecological—support and resources made available to influence the development of the industry. These classification schemes and frameworks are ways of stepping back to get an overall picture, a process like model-building, which involves integration and synthesis.

Individual(s)

Whether an entrepreneur is viewed as a "captain of industry," a hard-headed risk bearer (Mill, 1848), risk taker (Palmer, 1971) or a "rapacious risk avoider" (Webster, 1976); whether he merely metamorphoses into an entrepreneur at certain moments and is something else the rest of the time (Danhoff, 1949), or whether his need for achievement (McClelland, 1961) and capacity for innovation (Schumpeter, 1934) are always ticking away; whether he is a "displaced person" (Shapero, 1975), something close to a juvenile delinquent (Gould, 1969), or a "man apart" (Liles, 1974) with an absolutely clear-headed (veridical) perception of reality (Schrage, 1965), an aberrant "artist" with an "innate sense of impending change" (Hill, 1982); or whether he is, indeed, that completely political animal, a community builder (Schell & Davig, 1981), the entrepreneur is overwhelmingly perceived to be different in important ways from the nonentrepreneur, and many researchers have believed these differences to lie in the background and personality of the entrepreneur.

One often pursued avenue has been the attempt to develop a psychological profile of the entrepreneur and to measure such psychological characteristics as need for achievement (DeCarlo & Lyons, 1979; Hornaday & Aboud, 1971; McClelland, 1961; McClelland & Winter, 1969; Schwartz, 1976). However, other researchers have not found need for achievement useful in describing entrepreneurs (Brockhaus, 1980b; Litzinger, 1965; Schrage, 1965); still others have questioned the value and validity of using psychological characteristics of any kind to describe entrepreneurs (Brockhaus, 1982; Glueck & Mescon, 1980; Jenks, 1965; Kilby, 1971; McCain & Smith, 1981; Van de Ven, 1980). However, the following psychological characteristics have been used in many studies and may have some validity in differentiating among types of entrepreneurs (Brockhaus, 1982):

1. Need for achievement
2. Locus of control
3. Risk taking propensity

Some researchers have found it fruitful to look at the entrepreneur's background, experience, and attitudes. Some individual characteristics that may be of value in describing entrepreneurs are:

1. Job satisfaction (Collins & Moore, 1970; Komives, 1972)
2. Previous work experience (Cooper, 1970; Lamont, 1972; Susbauer, 1972)
3. Entrepreneurial parents (Collins & Moore, 1970; Roberts & Wainer, 1968; Schrier, 1975; Secrest, 1975; Shapero, 1972; Susbauer, 1972)
4. Age (Komives, 1972; Liles, 1974; Roberts & Wainer, 1968; Secrest, 1975; Thorne & Ball, 1981)
5. Education (Brockhaus & Nord, 1979; Collins & Moore, 1964; Howell, 1972; Roberts, 1969; Susbauer, 1969)

Process

In 1949 Danhoff wrote, "Entrepreneurship is an activity or function and not a specific individual or occupation . . . the specific personal entrepreneur is an unrealistic abstraction" (p. 21). Other theorists have pursued this idea of function and have tried to differentiate the entrepreneurial function from other more routine functions such as the managerial function (Baumol, 1968; Cole, 1965; Hartmann, 1959; Leibenstein, 1968; Schumpeter, 1934). This "dynamic" aspect of the entrepreneur has been acknowledged in the work of eight researchers who have enumerated certain actions that an entrepreneur performs in order to create a new venture. Except for Peterson and Berger (1971), who described the entrepreneurial activities of record producers, these studies were theoretical, that is, based on general observation rather than systematic research. The similarities in their views are summarized here; six common behaviors are listed (the order does not imply a sequence of actions):

1. The entrepreneur locates a business opportunity (Cole, 1965; Kilby, 1971; Maidique, 1980; Schumpeter, 1934; Vesper, 1980).
2. The entrepreneur accumulates resources (Cole, 1965; Kilby, 1971; Leibenstein, 1968; Peterson & Berger, 1971; Schumpeter, 1934; Vesper, 1980).

3. The entrepreneur markets products and services (Cole, 1965; Kilby, 1971; Leibenstein, 1968; Maidique, 1980; Peterson & Berger, 1971; Schumpeter, 1934; Vesper, 1980).
4. The entrepreneur produces the product (Kilby, 1971; Maidique, 1980; Peterson & Berger, 1971; Schumpeter, 1934; Vesper, 1980).
5. The entrepreneur builds an organization (Cole, 1965; Kilby, 1971; Leibenstein, 1968; Schumpeter, 1934).
6. The entrepreneur responds to government and society (Cole, 1965; Kilby, 1971).

Environment

Much of the current concern (Peters & Waterman, 1982) over how to design organizations that keep and encourage innovative individuals is an indirect acknowledgment that entrepreneurs do not operate in vacuums — they respond to their environments. The existence of highly supportive regional entrepreneurial environments (Cooper, 1970; Draheim, 1972; Pennings, 1982b; Susbauer, 1972) — including "incubator organizations" — can, from one perspective, be said actually to *create* entrepreneurs. The idea of "pushes" and "pulls" from the environment has found its way into many studies of entrepreneurship (Shapero & Sokol, 1982).

In organization theory literature, two different views of the environment have been developed. One perspective, environmental determinism, sees the environment as an outside set of conditions to which the organization must adapt (Aldrich, 1979; Aldrich & Pfeffer, 1976; Hannan & Freeman, 1977). The other perspective, strategic choice, sees the environment as a "reality" that organizations create via the selectivity of their own perceptions (Child, 1972; Starbuck, 1976; Weick, 1979). In the entrepreneurship literature, both perspectives on the environment have been taken. In the present paper those characteristics that are viewed as relatively fixed conditions imposed on the new venture from without are called environmental variables. Variables over which the organization has more control (strategic choice variables) are more readily viewed as characteristics of the organization itself and are treated as such.

In an overview of 17 research papers on environmental variables that influenced new venture creation, Bruno and Tyebjee (1982) found 12 factors that they judged stimulated entrepreneurship:

1. Venture capital availability
2. Presence of experienced entrepreneurs
3. Technically skilled labor force
4. Accessibility of suppliers
5. Accessibility of customers or new markets
6. Governmental influences
7. Proximity of universities
8. Availability of land or facilities
9. Accessiblity of transportation
10. Attitude of the area population
11. Availability of supporting services
12. Living conditions

Another study of environmental influences on new venture creation was Pennings' studies of organization birth frequencies (1980, 1982a, 1982b). Pennings found that organization birth rates were high in areas with: high occupational and industrial differentiation; high percentages of recent immigrants in the population; a large industrial base; larger size urban areas; and availability of financial resources.

Another field of research has taken the deterministic perspective regarding the environment and new ventures: industrial economics. Oliver Williamson (1975) explored the process by which the failure of markets to coordinate efficiently the production and distribution of goods and services often resulted in the start-up of organizations to coordinate the production function through administration. Porter (1980) focused on the competitive environment that confronts firms in a particular industry. Porter's work provides five environmental influences on organizations: barriers to entry, rivalry among existing competitors, pressure from substitute products, bargaining power of buyers, and bargaining power of suppliers.

Organization

Despite a bold early attempt by Stauss (1944) to direct the focus away from the entrepreneur and toward his created organization (by claiming, somewhat tortuously, that the firm *is* the entrepreneur), most subsequent studies of new venture creation have neglected to comment on or even communicate certain characteristics of the organizations on which they focused. The assumption behind this seems to derive from two other assumptions: (a) if all entrepreneurs are virtually alike and (b) they all go through the same process to create their ventures, then (c) the organizations they create must, like widgets, not be of any interest in themselves.

Many research samples in entrepreneurship studies are selected, for example, without regard to type of firm (i.e., manufacturing, service, retail, wholesale). Of the studies that have indicated the type of firm, Smith (1967), Cooper (1970), Collins and Moore (1970), Susbauer (1972), and Braden (1977) studied manufacturing firms, and most focused on high technology manufacturing firms. Litzinger (1965) studied motel firms, and Mescon and Montanari (1981) studied real estate firms. However, researchers in these studies made no attempts to compare the type of firm studied to other types of firm to determine what difference type of firm might make in the process of new venture creation. Cooper and Dunkelberg (1981), Gartner (1982), and Van de Ven et al. (1984) have begun to link type of firm across other dimensions, such as entrepreneurial background and response to environment.

The presence of partners is another firm characteristic suggested by Timmons, Smollen, and Dingee (1977) as a vital factor in starting certain types of firm, and some research has mentioned partners as a characteristic of the firms studied (Cooper, 1970; DeCarlo & Lyons, 1979).

Strategic choice variables are treated here as characteristics of the organization. Porter (1980) identified three generic competitive strategies that firms may "choose": (a) overall cost leadership, (b) differentiation, and (c) focus. Vesper (1980) identified 14 competitive entry wedges: the new product or service, parallel competition, franchise entry, geographical transfer, supply shortage, tapping unutilized resources, customer contract, becoming a second source, joint ventures, licensing, market relinquishment, sell off of division, favored purchasing by government, and governmental rule changes.

Conclusion

Listing each variable of new venture creation under the appropriate dimension of the framework illustrates the potential for a high degree of complexity in the interaction of these variables within the multidimensional phenomenon of venture creation (Figure 2).

The four dimensional conceptual framework can be seen as a kaleidoscope, as an instrument through which to view the enormously varying patterns of new venture creation. Past attempts to differentiate the typical entrepreneur and his/her typical creation from all nonentrepreneurs and all nonnew ventures have, whether intentionally or not, advanced the notion that all entrepreneurs are alike and all new venture creation is the same. However, there clearly is a wide variation in the kinds of new ventures that are started. For example, are there similarities between the creation of a waterbed store by a 20-year old college student and the creation of a personal computer company by three engineers? Are the differences between them more important than the similarities? What is the value of comparing the creation of a pet store by two unemployed physical therapists to the creation of a 5,000-acre business park by four real estate developers? The goal is not to smooth over any differences that might exist among these new ventures or to throw these very different individuals into the same pot in order to extract the typical qualities of the typical entrepreneur. The goal is to identify the specific variables that describe how each new venture was created, in order that meaningful contrasts and comparisons among new ventures can be made.

First must come careful description with an eye to variation. The search for key variables, for general principles, for universally applicable laws of entrepreneurship that has characterized much of the entrepreneurship literature betrays an impatience with the slow methodical process of description. Attention to careful observation and description is the basis of good scientific research (McKelvey, 1982). In what does all this careful description of new ventures result? A collection of uniquely described ventures, each different from all the others? Once good description is achieved, then good comparisons and contrasts can be made, and subsets of similar ventures can be established. These homogeneous populations are needed before any general rules or theories of new venture creation can be postulated. The lack of such homogeneous samples in the past has led to conflicts in the results of research studies.

The conceptual framework presented here provides a way of analyzing past research studies. Each study can be broken down into the types of individuals, organizations, environments, and processes that were investigated. One way in which the framework can be useful is in identify-

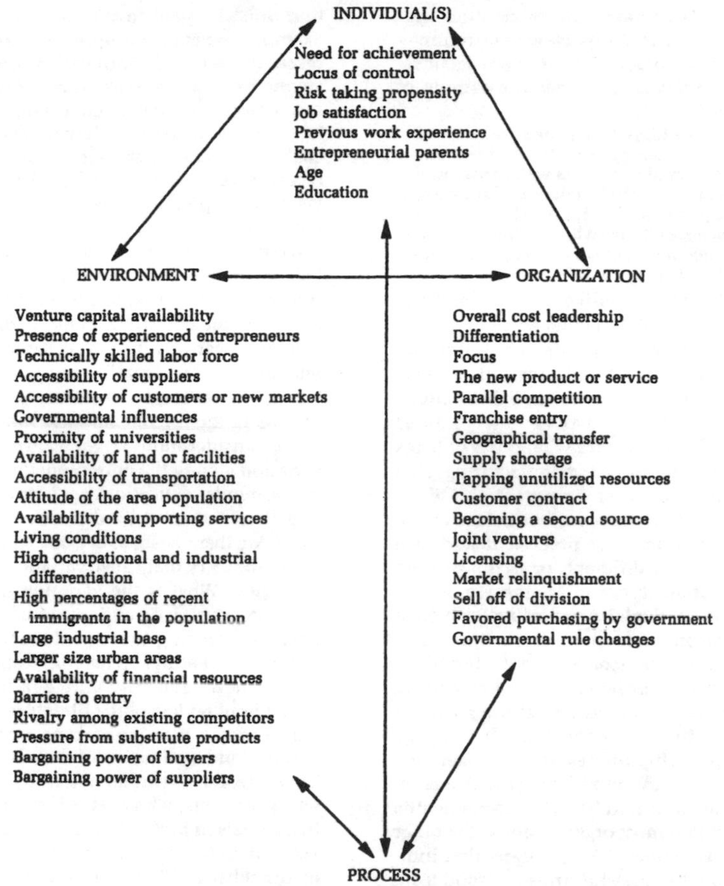

Figure 2. Variables in new venture creation.

ing those aspects of new venture creation neglected by a particular study. New research may then be designed to account for these lacunae. For example, Brockhaus defines his sample of entrepreneurs as:

> Individuals who within three months prior to the study had ceased working for their employers and at the time of the study owned as well as managed business ventures. . . . The businesses whose owners served as participants were selected from the listing of businesses licensed by St. Louis County, Missouri during the months of August and September, 1975 (1980a, p. 39).

Although Brockhaus, unlike other researchers, attempts to close in on the actual entrepreneurial function by interviewing his entrepreneurs within a few months of the creation of their ventures, useful and necessary distinctions among the individuals and their new ventures are not made. One is not sure what types of firms were studied (retail, service, manufacturing, etc.) or whether the St. Louis environment was likely to influence certain types of individuals to create certain types of firms. Is the process of starting a venture in St. Louis different, or is the process different for certain types of businesses or certain kinds of individuals? Accounting for type of firm, environment, and process in this study would enhance comparison among the individuals in the study and individuals in other studies.

In analyzing results of research studies, a focus on differences in one of the four dimensions might explain conflicting results. For example, studies such as Collins and Moore (1970) suggest that individuals who start firms are social misfits who do not fit into most organizations. Yet other studies such as Cooper (1970) suggest that individuals who start successful firms are good team players. On closer examination it is seen that Collins and Moore studied manufacturing firms that were more like job shops in the 1950s, and Cooper studied high technology firms in the 1960s. High technology industries might require more skills than one individual would be likely to have, necessitating that individuals combine their abilities in teams in order to start an organization successfully.

In addition to providing a means by which past research can be analyzed, the framework outlines a format for future research methodologies and for reporting such research. More careful attention must be paid to the research sample. For example, women entrepreneurs are a popular research topic. If similarities are discovered among women who start firms, are these similarities a result of similar environments? Can differences be attributed solely to psychological or background characteristics? What is the value of research results that are based on such unexamined and possibly heterogeneous sample populations?

Even in a narrowly selected research sample, the framework might be useful in drawing the researcher's attention to considerations inherent in each of the four dimensions, in order that conclusions regarding the virtual sameness of all the members of the sample may not be made too hastily. For example, in a sample of new organizations in the micro-computer industry, a number of considerations might be made. What is the variation among the entrepreneurs in their work backgrounds, education, age? How do competitive strategies used by these new organizations vary? Are there regional or other subenvironments in the industry that cause variations in firms and strategies? What is the variation in the venture creation process: do all individuals devote equal time to financing the organization, hiring personnel, marketing? What differences exist between "new" and "old" firms in this industry?

The brief review of the literature provided earlier is only a running start at a comprehensive analysis and evaluation of the entrepreneurship literature. For example, in a study of individuals who start firms, who are the individuals? Are the individuals in McClelland's samples (McCelland, 1961; McCelland & Winter, 1969) similar to those in Brockhaus (1980a) or Schrage (1965)? More about the similarities and differences within and among past research samples needs to be known. There are many dimensions and variables across which these samples may be compared.

The framework also points up the importance of interactions of variables among dimensions in understanding new venture creation. How does an individual's background influence the type of activities undertaken to start an organization? Does the marketing individual devote his time to marketing instead of manufacturing, and are there some environments or firms that require more marketing? Is the process of starting a retail store similar to that of starting a steel mill? Are entry strategies used by new organizations in the robotics industry similar to those used in the brewery industry?

The framework for describing new venture creation provides the possibility of describing subsets within the unwieldy set of all entrepreneurs and all new ventures. Newly created ventures that display meaningful similarities across the four dimensions could be described and classified together (Gartner, 1982). Significant generalizations regarding some or all new venture creations might emerge, generalizations that do not, however, attempt to mask the variation in new venture creation.

This paper does not purport to answer specific questions about how new ventures are started or provide specific developmental models for new venture creation. No claim is made that the framework or the list of variables is comprehensive; the claim is only that the description of new ventures needs to be more comprehensive than it is at present. A great many more questions are asked here than are answered. However, the paper provides a means of making a fundamental shift in the perspective on entrepreneurship: away from viewing entrepreneurs and their ventures as an unvarying, homogeneous population, and towards a recognition and appreciation of the complexity and variation that abounds in the phenomenon of new venture creation.

References

Aldrich, H. E. (1979) *Organizations and environments*. Englewood Cliffs, NJ: Prentice-Hall.

Aldrich, H. E., & Pfeffer, J. (1976) Environments of organizations. *Annual Review of Sociology*, 76-105.

Baumol, W. J. (1968) Entrepreneurship in economic theory. *American Economic Review*, 58(2), 64-71.

Braden, P. (1977) *Technological entrepreneurship* (Michigan Business Reports, No. 62). Ann Arbor: University of Michigan.

Brockhaus, R. H. (1980a) The effect of job dissatisfaction on the decision to start a business. *Journal of Small Business Management*, 18(1), 37-43.

Brockhaus, R. H. (1980b) Risk taking propensity of entrepreneurs. *Academy of Management Journal*, 23, 509-520.

Brockhaus, R. H. (1982) The psychology of the entrepreneur. In C. A. Kent, D. L. Sexton, & K. H. Vesper (Eds.), *Encyclopedia of entrepreneurship* (pp. 39-56). Englewood Cliffs NJ: Prentice-Hall.

Brockhaus, R. H., & Nord, W. R. (1979) An exploration of factors affecting the entrepreneurial decision: Personal characteristics vs. environmental conditions. *Proceedings of the National Academy of Management*, 364-368.

Bruno, A. V., & Tyebjee, T. T. (1982) The environment for entrepreneurship. In C. A. Kent, D. L. Sexton, & K. H. Vesper (Eds.), *Encylopedia of entrepreneurship* (pp. 288-307). Englewood Cliffs, NJ: Prentice-Hall.

Carland, J. W., Hoy, F., Boulton, W. R., & Carland, J.A.C. (1984) Differentiating entrepreneurs from small business owners: A conceptualization. *Academy of Management Review*, 9, 354-359.

Child, J. (1972) Organizational structure, environment and performance: The role of strategic choice. *Sociology*, 6, 1-22.

Cole, A. H. (1959) *Business enterprise in its social setting*. Cambridge, MA: Harvard University Press.

Cole, A. H. (1965) An approach to the study of entrepreneurship: A tribute to Edwin F. Gay. In H.G.J. Aitken (Ed.), *Explorations in enterprise* (pp. 30-44). Cambridge, MA: Harvard University Press.

Collins, O. F., & Moore, D. G. (1964) *The enterprising man*. East Lansing: Michigan State University.

Collins, O. F., & Moore, D. G. (1970) *The organization makers*. New York: Appleton-Century-Crofts.

Cooper, A. C. (1970) The Palo Alto experience. *Industrial Research*, 12(5), 58-61.

Cooper, A. C. (1979) Strategic management: New ventures and small business. In D. E. Schendel & C. W. Hofer (Eds.), *Strategic management* (pp. 316-327). Boston: Little, Brown.

Cooper, A. C., & Dunkelberg, W. C. (1981) A new look at business entry: Experiences of 1,805 entrepreneurs. In K. H. Vesper (Ed.), *Frontiers of entrepreneurship research* (pp. 1-20). Wellesley, MA: Babson College.

Daily, C. A. (1971) *Entrepreneurial management: Going all out for results*. New York: McGraw-Hill.

Danhoff, C. H. (1949) Observations on entrepreneurship in agriculture. In A. H. Cole (Ed.), *Change and the entrepreneur* (pp. 20-24). Cambridge, MA: Harvard University Press.

DeCarlo, J. F., & Lyons, P. R. (1979) A comparison of selected personal characteristics of minority and non-minority female entrepreneurs. *Journal of Small Business Management*, 17(4), 22-29.

Draheim, K. P. (1972) Factors influencing the rate of formation of technical companies. In A. C. Cooper & J. L. Komives (Eds.), *Technical entrepreneurship: A symposium* (pp. 3-27). Milwaukee, WI: Center for Venture Management.

Filley, A. C., & Aldag, R. J. (1980) Organizational growth and types: Lessons from small institutions. In B. Staw & L. Cummings (Eds.), *Research in organizational behavior* (Vol. 2, pp. 279-320). Greenwich, CT: JAI Press.

Gartner, W. B. (1982) *An empirical model of the business startup, and eight entrepreneurial archetypes.* Unpublished doctoral dissertation, University of Washington, Seattle.

Glueck, W., & Mescon, T. (1980) *Entrepreneurship: A literature analysis of concepts.* Paper presented at the annual meeting of the Academy of Management, Detroit, MI.

Gould, L. C. (1969) Juvenile entrepreneurs. *American Journal of Sociology*, 74, 710-719.

Hannan, M. T., & Freeman, J. (1977) The population ecology model of organizations. *American Journal of Sociology*, 82, 929-964.

Hartman, C. (1983) Who's running America's fastest growing companies? *Inc.*, 5(8), 41-47.

Hartmann, H. (1959) Managers and entrepreneurs: A useful distinction? *Administrative Science Quarterly*, 3, 429-457.

Hill, R. (1982) The entrepreneur: An artist masquerading as a businessman? *International Management*, 37(2), 21-22, 26.

Hornaday, J., & Aboud, J. (1971) Characteristics of successful entrepreneurs. *Personnel Psychology*, 24(2), 141-153.

Howell, R. P. (1972) Comparative profiles—Entrepreneurs versus the hired executive: San Francisco Peninsula semiconductor industry. In A. C. Cooper & J. L. Komives (Eds.), *Technical entrepreneurship: A symposium* (pp. 47-62). Milwaukee, WI: Center for Venture Management.

Jenks, L. (1965) Approaches to entrepreneurial personality. In H. G. J. Aitken (Ed.), *Explorations in enterprise* (pp. 80-92). Cambridge, MA: Harvard University Press.

Kilby, P. (1971) Hunting the heffalump. In P. Kilby (Ed.), *Entrepreneurship and economic development* (pp. 1-40). New York: Free Press.

Kimberly, J. R. (1979) Issues in the creation of organizations: Initiation, innovation, and institutionalization. *Academy of Management Journal*, 22, 437-457.

Komives, J. L. (Ed.). (1969) *Karl A. Bostrum seminar in the study of enterprise.* Milwaukee, WI: Center for Venture Management.

Komives, J. L. (1972) A preliminary study of the personal values of high technology entrepreneurs. In A. C. Cooper & J. L. Komives (Eds.), *Technical entrepreneurship: A symposium* (pp. 231-242). Milwaukee, WI: Center for Venture Management.

Lamont, L. M. (1972) The role of marketing in technical entrepreneurship. In A. C. Cooper & J. L. Komives (Eds.), *Technical entrepreneurship: A symposium* (pp. 150-164). Milwaukee, WI: Center for Venture Management.

Leibenstein, H. (1968) Entrepreneurship and development. *American Economic Review*, 58(2), 72-83.

Liles, P. R. (1974) *New business ventures and the entrepreneur.* Homewood, IL: Irwin.

Litzinger, W. D. (1965) The motel entrepreneur and the motel manager. *Academy of Management Journal*, 8, 268-281.

Long, W. (1983) The meaning of entrepreneurship. *American Journal of Small Business*, 8(2), 47-59.

Maidique, M. A. (1980) Entrepreneurs, champions and technological innovation. *Sloan Management Review*, 21(2), 59-76.

McCain G., & Smith, N. (1981, Summer) A contemporary model of entrepreneurial style. *Small Business Institute Review*, 40-45.

McClelland, D. (1961) *The achieving society.* Princeton, NJ: Van Nostrand.

McClelland, D., & Winter, D. G. (1969) *Motivating economic achievement.* New York: Free Press.

McKelvey, B. (1982) *Organizational systematics—Taxonomy, evolution, classification.* Berkeley: University of California Press.

Mescon, T., & Montanari, J. (1981) The personalities of independent and franchise entrepreneurs: An empirical analysis of concepts. *Journal of Enterprise Management*, 3(2), 149-159.

Mill, J. S. (1848) *Principles of political economy with some of their applications to social philosophy.* London: J. W. Parker.

Miller, D. (1981) Toward a new contingency approach: The search for organization gestalts. *Journal of Management Studies*, 18, 1-26.

Palmer, M. (1971) The application of psychological testing to entrepreneurial potential. *California Management Review*, 13(3), 32-39.

Pennings, J. M. (1980) Environmental influences on the creation process. In J. R. Kimberly & R. Miles (Eds.), *The organization life cycle* (pp. 135-160). San Francisco: Jossey Bass.

Pennings, J. M. (1982a) Organizational birth frequencies. *Administrative Science Quarterly*, 27, 120-144.

Pennings, J. M. (1982b) The urban quality of life and entrepreneurship. *Academy of Management Journal*, 25, 63-79.

Peters T. J., & Waterman, R. H. (1982) *In search of excellence.* New York: Harper & Row.

Peterson, R. A., & Berger, D. G. (1971) Entrepreneurship in organizations: Evidence from the popular music industry. *Administrative Science Quarterly*, 16, 97-107.

Pfeffer, J., & Salancik, G. R. (1978) *The external control of organizations.* New York: Harper & Row.

Porter, M. E. (1980) *Competitive strategy: Techniques for analyzing industries and competitors.* New York: Fress Press.

Roberts, E. B. (1969) Entrepreneurship and technology. In W. Gruber & D. Marquis (Eds.), *Factors in the transfer of technology* (pp. 219-237). Cambridge, MA: M.I.T. Press.

Roberts, E. B., & Wainer, H. A. (1968) New enterprise on Rte. 128. *Science Journal*, 4(12), 78-83.

Schell, D. W., & Davig, W. (1981) The community infrastructure of entrepreneurship. In K. H. Vesper (Ed.), *Frontiers of entrepreneurship research* (pp. 563-590). Wellesley, MA: Babson College.

Schrage, H. (1965) The R & D entrepreneur: Profile of success. *Harvard Business Review*, 43(6), 56-69.

Schrier, J. W. (1975) Entrepreneurial characteristics of women. In J. W. Schrier & J. Susbauer (Eds.), *Entrepreneurship and enterprise development: A worldwide perspective* (pp. 66-70). Milwaukee, WI: Center for Venture Management.

Schumpeter, J. A. (1934) *The theory of economic development* (R. Opie, Trans.). Cambridge, MA: Harvard University Press.

Schwartz, E. B. (1976) Entrepreneurship: A new female frontier. *Journal of Contemporary Business*. 5, 47-76.

Secrest, L. (1975) Texas entrepreneurship. In J. W. Schrier & J. Susbauer (Eds.), *Entrepreneurship and enterprise development: A worldwide perspective* (pp. 51-65). Milwaukee, WI: Center for Venture Management.

Shapero, A. (1972) The process of technical company formation in a local area. In A. C. Cooper & J. L. Komives (Eds.), *Technical entrepreneurship: A symposium* (pp. 63-95). Milwaukee, WI: Center for Venture Management.

Shapero, A. (1975) The displaced, uncomfortable entrepreneur. *Psychology Today*, 9(6), 83-88.

Shapero, A., & Sokol, L. (1982) The social dimensions of entrepreneurship. In C. A. Kent, D. L. Sexton, & K. H. Vesper (Eds.), *Encylclopedia of entrepreneurship* (pp. 72-90). Englewood Cliffs, NJ: Prentice-Hall.

Smith, N. (1967) *The entrepreneur and his firm: The relationship between type of man and type of company*. East Lansing: Michigan State University.

Starbuck, W. H. (1976) Organizations and their environments. In M. Dunnette (Ed.), *Handbook of industrial and organizational psychology* (pp. 1069-1123). Chicago: Rand McNally.

Stauss, J. H. (1944) The entrepreneur: The firm. *Journal of Political Economy*, 52(2), 112-127.

Strategic Planning Institute. (1978) *The startup data manual*. Unpublished manuscript. Cambridge, MA: Strategic Planning Institute.

Susbauer, J. C. (1969) *The technical company formation process: A particular aspect of entrepreneurship*. Unpublished doctoral dissertation, University of Texas, Austin.

Susbauer, J. C. (1972) The technical entrepreneurship process in Austin, Texas. In A. C. Cooper & J. L. Komives (Eds.), *Technical entrepreneurship: A symposium* (pp. 28-46). Milwaukee, WI: Center for Venture Management.

Thorne, J. R., & Ball, J. G. (1981) Entrepreneurs and their companies: Smaller industrial firms. In K. H. Vesper (Ed.), *Frontiers of entrepreneurship research* (pp. 65-83). Wellesley, MA: Babson College.

Timmons, J. A., Smollen, E, & Dingee, A. L. M. (1977) *New venture creation*. Homewood, IL: Irwin.

Van de Ven, A. H. (1980) Early planning, implementation and performance of new organizations. In J. R. Kimberly & R. Miles (Eds.), *The organization life cycle* (pp. 83-134). San Francisco: Jossey Bass.

Van de Ven, A. H., Hudson, R., & Schroeder, D. M. (1984) Designing new business startups: Entrepreneurial, organizational, and ecological considerations. *Journal of Management*, 10(1), 87-107.

Vesper, K. H. (1979) Commentary. In D. E. Schendel & C. W. Hofer (Eds.), *Strategic management* (pp. 332-338). Boston: Little, Brown.

Vesper, K. H. (1980) *New venture strategies*. Englewood Cliffs, NJ: Prentice-Hall.

Vesper, K. H. (1981) Scanning the frontier of entrepreneurship research. In K. H. Vesper (Ed.), *Frontiers of entrepreneurship research* (pp. vii-xiv). Wellesley, MA: Babson College.

Vesper, K. H. (1982a) Expanding entrepreneurship research. In K. H. Vesper (Ed.), *Frontiers of entrepreneurship research* (pp. vii-xx). Wellesley, MA: Babson College.

Vesper, K. H. (1982b) Introduction and summary of entrepreneurship research. In C. A. Kent, D. L. Sexton, & K. H. Vesper (Eds.), *Encyclopedia of entrepreneurship* (pp. xxxi-xxxviii).

Webster, F. A. (1976) A model for new venture initiation: A disclosure on rapacity and the independent entrepreneur. *Academy of Management Review*, 1(1), 26-37.

Weick, K. E. (1979) *The social psychology of organizing* (2nd ed.). Reading, MA: Addison-Wesley.

Williamson, O. E. (1975) *Markets and hierarchies, analysis and antitrust implications*. New York: Free Press.

William B. Gartner is Assistant Professor of Business and Director of the Center for Entrepreneurship Studies in the School of Business Administration, Georgetown University.

Strategic Management Journal, Vol. 10, 75–87 (1989)

STRATEGIC MANAGEMENT OF SMALL FIRMS IN HOSTILE AND BENIGN ENVIRONMENTS

JEFFREY G. COVIN
College of Management, Georgia Institute of Management, Atlanta, Georgia, U.S.A.

DENNIS P. SLEVIN
Katz Graduate School of Business, University of Pittsburgh, Pittsburgh, Pennsylvania, U.S.A.

This paper reports the results of a study designed to investigate the effective strategic responses to environmental hostility among small manufacturing firms. Data on environmental hostility, organization structure, strategic posture, competitive tactics, and financial performance were collected from 161 small manufacturers. Findings indicate that performance among small firms in hostile environments was positively related to an organic structure, an entrepreneurial strategic posture, and a competitive profile characterized by a long-term orientation, high product prices, and a concern for predicting industry trends. In benign environments, on the other hand, performance was positively related to a mechanistic structure, a conservative strategic posture, and a competitive profile characterized by conservative financial management and a short-term financial orientation, an emphasis on product refinement, and a willingness to rely heavily on single customers.

While the performance levels of small firms have traditionally been attributed to managerial factors (Albert, 1981; Stegall, Steinmetz and Kline, 1976), external environmental factors may have a strong impact on small firm viability and growth. General economic conditions as well as fiscal and regulatory influences are commonly acknowledged as determinants of small firm creation and success (Cooper, 1979; Boskin, 1984; Chilton, 1984). Recent research has shown that industry structure may have a powerful effect on the performance of new business ventures (Sandberg, 1986). More general environmental dimensions such as level of industry stagnation and dynamism may also affect small firm performance (Peterson, 1985; Miller and Toulouse, 1986).

An environmental dimension which, by definition, serves as a threat to small firm viability and performance is hostility. Hostile environments are characterized by precarious industry settings, intense competition, harsh, overwhelming business climates, and the relative lack of exploitable opportunities. Non-hostile or benign environments, on the other hand, provide a safe setting for business operations due to their overall level of munificence and richness in investment and marketing opportunities (Khandwalla, 1976/77; Miller and Friesen, 1983). Surviving and competitively flourishing in a hostile environment is difficult for large, established firms (Hall, 1980). The adverse impact of environmental hostility probably presents an even greater threat to small firms due to their limited resource bases and relative inabilities to survive the consequences of poor managerial decisions. Because of the continuing trend toward greater environmental hostility in many domestic manufacturing industries, learning to compete effectively in hostile environments will become a top priority for increasing numbers of small manufacturing firms.

This paper reports the results of a study in which the overall strategic orientation, the competitive tactics, and the organizational attributes of small manufacturing firms in hostile and benign environments were examined. The purpose of this study was to identify and contrast

0143–2095/89/010075–13$06.50

Received 15 March 1987
Revised 17 March 1988

the strategic postures and organization structures associated with high performance in both hostile and benign environments.

HYPOTHESES

Organization structure and environmental hostility

Although references to the concept of environmental hostility have been scattered throughout the organization theory literature for 30 years (March and Simon (1958) were perhaps the first theorists to refer to this concept), empirical research that broadly addresses the relationship between organization structure and environmental hostility is limited to a small number of studies.

Hall (1980) conducted an in-depth investigation of the 'survival strategies' of 64 large manufacturing firms in eight industries which were experiencing adverse, 'hostile' trends. In addition to drawing a number of conclusions concerning the effective business strategies of firms in such environments, Hall briefly addressed organization structure issues. Specifically, he noted that high-performing firms typically reacted to increased hostility by creating internal administrative structures which allowed them effectively and efficiently to manage any necessary strategic repositioning. The example of General Motors' organizational restructuring efforts in response to the need to 'down-size' their products was cited. Since structural issues were not the principal focus of Hall's study, he did not elaborate on the organizational implications of a hostile environmental context.

In an unpublished manuscript cited in Lawrence and Lorsch (1967: 191–195), Fouraker described a series of experiments he had conducted on the impact of threatening environmental contexts on several dimensions of organizational structure. His findings suggest that threatening environments, operationally defined in terms of resource scarcity and competitive intensity, cause organizations to place more emphasis on discipline and authority (i.e. control issues) and to become more hierarchical. Research conducted by Pfeffer and Leblebici (1973) on 38 small manufacturing firms supports Fouraker's findings. Pfeffer and Leblebici studied the effect of competitive intensity on organization structure. Their findings suggest that 'the extent of competition in the environment is positively associated with frequency of reporting, the extent to which decision procedures are specified in advance and weakly associated with a relatively taller organizational structure' (1973: 268).

Mintzberg wrote:

> Hostility affects structure through the intermediate variables of the predictability of work, in that hostile environments are unpredictable ones. But of greater interest is its relationship with the intermediate variable of speed of response, since very hostile environments generally demand fast reactions by the organization (1979: 269).

Considerable evidence suggests that 'organic' structures permit rapid organizational response to changing external forces in unpredictable environments, while 'mechanistic' structures are better suited to predictable environments where rapid organizational responses are not typically required (Burns and Stalker, 1961; Lawrence and Lorsch, 1967). As such, one would expect that organic structures will be effective for firms operating in hostile environments, whereas mechanistic structures will be relatively more effective for firms in benign environments. This expectation is supported by research conducted by Khandwalla (1977).

Khandwalla (1977) examined the relationship between organization structure, environmental context, and firm performance in 103 large Canadian firms. He found that high-performing firms in industries characterized by intense, diverse, and shifting competitive pressures (i.e. hostile industries) adopted organic structures, while high-performing firms in industries with minimal competitive pressure (i.e. benign industries) adopted more mechanistic structures. Although caution must be exercised when generalizing to small firm settings the findings of research studies based on samples of large firms, Khandwalla's results in combination with Mintzberg's theory-based assertions support the following hypothesis:

H1: An organic structure will be more positively related to firm performance for small firms in hostile environments than small firms in benign environments.

Strategic posture and environmental hostility

Strategic posture can be broadly defined as a firm's overall competitive orientation. A firm's entrepreneurial-conservation orientation is indicative of its strategic posture. The entrepreneurial-conservation orientation of a firm is demonstrated by the extent to which the top managers are inclined to take business-related risks, to favor change and innovation in order to obtain a competitive advantage for their firm, and to compete aggressively with other firms (Miller, 1983). Entrepreneurial firms are those in which the top managers have entrepreneurial top management styles, as evidenced by the firms' strategic decisions and operating management philosophy. The strategic orientations of these firms are roughly similar to those of Miles and Snow's (1978) prospector firms and Mintzberg's (1973) entrepreneurial organizations. Conservative firms are those in which the top management style is decidedly risk-averse, non-innovative, and reactive. The strategic orientations of these firms approximate those of Miles and Snow's (1978) defender firms and Mintzberg's (1973) adaptive organizations.

An entrepreneurial strategic posture may be particularly beneficial to small firms in hostile environments. These environments, as previously noted, contain fewer opportunities and are more competitive than benign environments. Accordingly, it might be expected that successful firms in hostile environments will gear their competitive efforts to the prevailing conditions by aggressively trying to gain or maintain a competitive advantage. Such an advantage will more likely result from the proactive, innovative, and risk-taking efforts of entrepreneurial firms than the passive and reactive efforts of conservative firms.

In benign environments, on the other hand, the relationship between an entrepreneurial strategic posture and small firm performance may be much weaker and possibly negative. Entrepreneurial behaviors entail more risk than conservative behaviors. The assumption of this risk may be necessary for survival in hostile environments. In benign environments firms are faced with a much greater level of munificence, and consequently are not typically forced to engage in uncertain, resource-consuming endeavors in order to maintain viability. Thus, while an entrepreneurial posture may just as easily result in a sustainable competitive advantage in a benign environment as in a hostile environment, such a posture may not be essential for superior performance, and could possibly represent an unwarranted risk for smaller firms.

A small number of studies have focused on the relationship between environmental hostility and firms' entrepreneurial-conservative orientations. Miller (1983) studied the correlates of entrepreneurial behavior in a sample of 52 large, diverse Canadian firms. He operationally defined entrepreneurial orientation in terms of innovation, proactiveness and risk-taking. He hypothesized that environmental hostility requires enterpreneurial efforts because only through such efforts can firms effectively cope with the adverse forces prevalent in such environments. Miller found a positive, significant correlation ($r = 0.26$, $p < 0.10$) between environmental hostility and entrepreneurial orientation.

In a separate study, Miller and Friesen examined the performance consequences of the relationship between environmental hostility and entrepreneurial behavior. Their sample consisted of 50 large Canadian firms and 88 large U.S. firms. They argued that 'extensive risk taking, forceful proactiveness and a strong emphasis on novelty can be very hazardous when competitive or economic conditions are becoming more taxing [i.e. hostile]' (1983: 233). Contrary to the arguments made here, Miller and Friesen hypothesized that 'relative to samples of poor performers, samples of successful firms will shows . . . more *negative* [emphasis added] correlations between increases in environmental hostility and increases in innovation' (1983: 223). Innovation was operationally defined in terms of the entrepreneurial attributes of product and technological innovation, top management risk-taking, and proactiveness. The results of their data analysis differed for the U.S. and Canadian samples, with the Canadian sample largely supporting their hypothesis while the U.S. sample contradicted their hypothesis.

In Khandwalla's (1977) study of 103 large Canadian firms, the relationship between top management style, environmental context, and firm performance was examined. Among other things, Khandwalla found that a conservative top management style is effective for smaller firms in benign environments, while an entrepreneurial style is effective for smaller firms in hostile environments. These findings, while appearing to bear directly on the current discussion, must be interpreted with caution because of the way Khandwalla operationally defined entrepreneurial and conservative style. Specifically, he clustered together 5 management style dimensions, then labeled two of the resulting clusters entrepreneurial style and conservative style. Therefore, Khandwalla's measures of entrepreneurial and conservative style encompass more than just risk-taking, innovation, and proactiveness.

Collectively, these findings seem to warrant the following hypothesis:

H2: An entrepreneurial strategic posture will be more positively related to firm performance for small firms in hostile environments than small firms in benign environments.

METHODS

The sample

A research questionnaire was mailed to the senior-most managers of 1225 single-industry, indepently owned firms. A follow-up letter was sent to all nonresponding firms, resulting in a sample of 344 firms, a response rate of 28.1 percent. All of the firms are either clients, members, or affiliates of three Pittsburgh-based organizations which share the purpose of promoting entrepreneurship and economic development in the western Pennsylvania area. A comparison of the early-responding firms (those that responded before the follow-up letter was sent) with the late-responding firms (those that responded after the follow-up letter was sent) showed that these groups did not differ in terms of number of employees, sales revenue, years in business, or any of the key variables in this study (i.e. environmental hostility, strategic posture, organization structure, and firm performance).

From the sample of 344 firms, 161 were chosen for this study. The average number of employees for these firms is 73. The average annual sales revenue is $8.2 million. Approximately 25 different industries are represented in this subsample.

The 161 firms included in this study were selected on the basis of three criteria. First, all of these firms are primarily involved in manufacturing activities. Most of the studies cited in the preceding literature review investigated manufacturing-type firms. This same type of firm was chosen for this study in order to increase the probability that any inconsistent findings are primarily attributable to differences in the sizes rather than types of firms in the samples. Second, all of these firms have between 5 and 500 employees. As such, they can all be classified as small firms. Finally, all of these firms have been in business for at least 5 years. Therefore, they have all survived the most critical years for small firms (Pickle and Abrahamson, 1976) and their business practices presumably approximate those of established firms rather than new ventures.

The great majority of the 183 firms excluded from this study were omitted because they are either the wrong type of firm (e.g. service, wholesale) or too young to be considered 'established'. Very few of the excluded firms have more than 500 employees, and none of these firms would generally be regarded as large.

The measures

Measures of environmental hostility, organization structure, strategic posture, and financial performance were employed in this research. With the exception of the financial performance measure, which is described in detail below, all of these measures are included in the Appendix.

Environmental hostility

A three-item scale, developed by Khandwalla (1976/77), was used to measure environmental hostility. The respondents' ratings on these three items were averaged to arrive at a single environmental hostility index for each firm. The higher the index, the more hostile the firm's environment. This scale has a mean of 4.13, a standard deviation of 1.32, a range of 1.0 to 7.0, and an inter-item reliability coefficient of 0.73.

Organization structure

Organization structure was limited to a seven-item scale which measures organicity—that is, the extent to which organizations are structured in organic versus mechanistic manners. This scale was also developed by Khandwalla (1976/77). The respondents were asked to indicate on seven-point Likert-type scales the extent to which each item of the measure characterizes the structure of their firms. Each firm's mean rating on these seven items was used as that firm's organicity index. The higher the index, the more organic the firm's structure. This scale has a mean value of 5.07, a standard deviation of 1.10, a range of 1.29 to 7.0, and an inter-item reliability coefficient of 0.80.

Strategic posture

A nine-item scale was used to measure strategic posture. This scale contains items that focus on innovation, proactiveness, and risk-taking. As previously noted, an entrepreneurial strategic posture is characterized by frequent and extensive technological and product innovation, an aggressive competitive orientation, and a strong risk-taking propensity by top management. A conservative strategic posture is characterized by minimal technological and product innovation, a cautious competitive orientation, and a weak risk-taking propensity by top management. These three components of strategic posture (innovation, proactiveness, and risk-taking) were argued by Miller to comprise a basic, unidimensional strategic orientation:

> In general, theorists would not call a firm entrepreneurial if it changed its technology or product-line ('innovated' according to our terminology) simply by directly imitating competitors while refusing to take any risks. Some proactiveness would be essential as well. By the same token, risk-taking firms that are highly leveraged financially are not necessarily entrepreneurial. They must also engage in product-market or technological innovation (1983: 780).

Therefore a scale was developed to assess strategic posture in terms of the firm's reliance on these three activities (see Appendix). The first three items of this scale assess the firm's tendency toward innovation; the second three items assess the firm's proactive orientation; the third three items assess the firm's risk-taking propensity. The specific items of this scale were either adapted from existing instruments (items 1, 2, 3, 7 and 8 are adapted from Miller and Friesen, 1982 and Khandwalla, 1976/77) or are original items (items 4, 5, 6 and 9). The respondents were asked to characterize their firms' strategic posture in terms of these nine items. The mean ratings on these items were used as the firms' strategic posture scores. The higher the score, the more entrepreneurial the strategic posture.

Because the items of this scale focus on different aspects of strategic posture (i.e. innovation, proactiveness, and risk-taking), they were factor-analyzed in order to assess their dimensionality or 'factorial validity'. As noted by Allen and Yen (1979), factorial validity is a form of construct validity. High loadings on a single factor would suggest that, although the items focus on different aspects of strategic posture, they are empirically related and constitute a distinct, unidimensional strategic orientation. All of the items loaded above 0.5 on a single-factor (average loading = 0.66), indicating that it is appropriate to combine these items in a single scale. This scale has a mean of 4.33, a standard deviation of 1.23, a range of 1.22 to 6.78, and an inter-item reliability coefficient of 0.87.

Financial performance

Financial performance was measured with a modified version of an instrument developed by Gupta and Govindarajan (1984). The respondents were first asked to indicate on a five-point Likert-type scale, ranging from 'of little importance' to 'extremely important', the degree of importance their firm attaches to each of the following financial performance criteria: sales level, sales growth rate, cash flow, return on shareholder equity, gross profit margin, net profit from operations, profit to sales ratio, return on investment, and ability to fund business growth from profits. The respondents were then asked to indicate on another five-point Likert-type scale, ranging from 'highly dissatisfied' to 'highly satisfied', the extent to which their firm's top managers are currently satisfied with their firm's performance on each of these same financial performance criteria. These 'satisfaction' scores were multiplied by the 'importance' scores in order to compute a weighted average performance index for each firm. This scale has a mean value of 11.57, a standard deviation of 4.06, a range of 3.78 to 23.33, and an inter-item reliability coefficient of 0.88.

This subjective measure of performance was chosen over objective data for several reasons. First, small firms are 'notorious for their inability and unwillingness to provide desired information' (Fiorito and LaForge, 1986: 11). It was therefore felt that more complete financial information could be obtained with a subjective measure. Furthermore, objective financial data on the sampled firms were not publicly available, making it impossible to check the accuracy of any reported financial performance figures. Second, assuming that accurate financial data were reported, such data on small firms are difficult to interpret. Cooper (1979: 326), for example, noted that operating losses or low profits in small, growth-oriented firms may not be indicative of poor management if the reason for this apparent poor performance is heavy investment in product and market development. Third, absolute scores on financial performance criteria are affected by industry-related factors (Miller and Toulouse, 1986). As such, directly comparing the objective financial data obtained for small firms in different industries would be misleading.

The analytical technique

The hypotheses suggest that the relationships between the independent variables (organization structure and strategic posture) and firm performance are contingent upon the level of hostility in the environment. According to Schoonhoven (1981), Darrow and Kahl (1982) and others, moderate regression analysis is an appropriate technique for testing hypothesized contingency relationships since it allows interaction terms, which are implied in all contingency relationships, to be directly examined.

Although other analytical techniques, such as analysis of variance or dummy variable regression, could have been used to test the hypotheses, moderated regression analysis was chosen for two reasons. First, moderated regression analysis, according to Arnold (1982: 170), 'provides the most straightforward and the most general method for testing [contingency hypotheses in which an interaction is implied]'. Second, moderated regression analysis is regarded as a conservative method for identifying interaction effects in the sense that interaction terms are tested for significance only after other independent variables are entered into the regression equation. As such, interaction effects are found to be significant only if they explain a significantly greater portion of the variance in the dependent variable than that portion already explained by the other independent variables.

In moderated regression analysis the statistical significance of interaction effects is tested by regressing the dependent variable on two (or more) main variables (one being the independent variable, the other the hypothesized moderator variable) and the cross-product of those main variables (Sharma, Durand, and Gur-Arie, 1981). The form of the moderated regression equation employed in this research was $Y = a + bX + cZ + dXZ$, where Y is the dependent variable (financial performance), X is the theoretically defined independent variable (either organization structure or strategic posture), Z is the theoretically defined moderator variable (environmental hostility), and XZ is the interaction term. If the addition of the interaction term significantly increases the power of the regression equation to explain the variance in the dependent variable, then an interaction or contingency effect can be said to exist. Furthermore, a positive and significant interaction term coefficient (d) would imply that the positive influence of X on Y is greater when Z is large than when Z is small. A negative and significant interaction term coefficient would imply the opposite.

RESULTS

Table 1 presents the results of the moderated regression analysis. This table shows that the interactive influence of organization structure and environmental hostility on firm performance is significant at the $p < 0.05$ level, and the interactive influence of strategic posture and environmental hostility on firm performance is significant at the $p < 0.005$ level. Furthermore, the interaction term regression coefficients have positive signs, implying that the relationships are consistent with the hypotheses. Specifically, the data suggest that:

1. Small firms with high organicity indices (i.e. organic structures) generally perform best in hostile environments, whereas small firms with low organicity indices (i.e. mechanistic

Table 1. Moderated regression analysis of organization structure, strategic posture, and environmental hostility with firm performance as the dependent variable[a] (n = 161)

Variables included	Cumulative R-squared	Unstandardized regression coefficients[b]	F-ratio for individual variables	df
Organic structure	0.0000	0.0120	0.0015	1,159
Organic structure	0.1323	0.0794	0.0760	1,158
Environmental hostility		−1.1190	21.6494***	1,158
Organic structure		−1.3329	3.7015	1,157
Environmental hostility	0.1620	−2.9837	11.8354	1,157
OS × EH		0.3772	4.9967*	1,157
Strategic posture	0.0134	0.3814	1.9349	1,159
Strategic posture	0.1450	0.3782	2.1800	1,158
Environmental hostility		−1.1146	21.8575***	1,158
Strategic posture		−1.8255	5.3087	1,157
Environmental hostility	0.1941	−3.3406	17.6887	1,157
SP × EH		0.5375	8.5884**	1,157

[a] Organization structure and environmental hostility are not significantly correlated (r = 0.050, $p > 0.1$), nor are strategic posture and environmental hostility (r = −0.003, $p > 0.1$).

[b] Unstandardized regression coefficients are reported because, unlike standardized regression coefficients, they are not affected by changes in the points of origin of the main variables (organization structure, strategic posture, and environmental hostility). See Southwood (1978) for details.

* $p < 0.05$; ** $p < 0.005$; *** $p < 0.001$.

structures) generally perform best in more benign environments.

2. Small firms with high strategic posture indices (i.e. entrepreneurial firms) generally perform best in hostile environments, whereas small firms with low strategic posture indices (i.e. conservative firms) generally perform best in more benign environments.

Table 1 also shows that neither organization structure (i.e. organicity) nor strategic posture are significant independent predictors of firm performance. Organization structure explains less than 1 percent of the variance in firm performance, while strategic posture explains only slightly more than 1 percent of the variance in performance. Environmental hostility, on the other hand, is a highly significant ($p < 0.001$) predictor of performance, explaining about 13 percent of the variance in performance. The negative regression coefficient for environmental hostility implies, as might be expected, that this factor has a negative impact on performance. Collectively, the figures shown in Table 1 suggest that while organization structure and strategic posture may not have strong independent effects on performance, the fit between these variables and the level of hostility in the environment may contribute to the performance differences of higher- and lower-performing firms.

Because of the modest amount of performance variance explained by the regression equations in general, and interaction terms in particular, a reliability analysis was performed on the data. Specifically, the sample was randomly split in half and the same analyses were run for these subsamples as for the entire sample. This was performed ten times. In each case the overall regression equation remained statistically significant ($p < 0.05$ or less) and, consistent with the hypotheses, the interaction terms had positive regression coefficients. Using a simple nonparametric sign test, the probability that 20 positive interaction term coefficients (10 for the organicity–hostility interaction and 10 for the strategic posture–hostility interaction) would appear in the 10 regression runs if the data did not generally support the hypotheses is less than 0.001. Therefore, the findings presented in Table 1 hold consistently throughout the data.

The data anlysis results do not warrant the conclusion that small, high-performing firms in hostile and benign environments necessarily have distinct structural and strategic posture attributes. However, the findings do suggest general differences in the effective strategic management of small firms in these environments. This conclusion was corroborated through an examination of several other variables examined in this study.

A measure was included in the research questionnaire which assessed the firms' reliance on various business practices and competitive tactics. The respondents were asked to rate the extent to which they agreed or disagreed that various statements were descriptive of their firms' current overall business strategy. The rating scales for these statements ranged from 'strongly disagree' (= 1) to 'strongly agree' (= 5). The zero-order correlations between performance and the ratings given to several of these statements differed for small firms in hostile and benign environments. For example, the statements in Table 2 were significantly correlated with performance for small firms in hostile environments (those with hostility indices greater than the mean value of 4.13, n = 77), but not small firms in benign environments (those with hostility indices less than the mean, n = 84). The statements in Table 3 were significantly correlated with performance for small firms in benign environments, but not small firms in hostile environments.

Each of these correlation analysis findings is theoretically defensible. The positive correlations between performance and emphasizing long-term profitability, capital investments, and high product prices in hostile environments are consistent with Hall's (1980) research findings. Hall observed that high-performing firms in hostile environments frequently adopt clearly defined, long-term orientations coupled with high product prices.

The utility of adopting a long-range orientation and high product prices may not be as great for small firms in more benign environments. Digman (1986: 338) asserted that 'small firms should strive to excel in short-term, not long-term planning'. Similarly, Cohn and Lindberg (1972: 2) argued that 'the smaller quantities of goods purchased, fewer salesmen, lower inventory levels, smaller outlays for advertising and promotion, and similar characteristics of small businesses seldom justify the risk or costs imposed by long-range plans'. Many small-firm management theorists have also argued that there are no generally superior price setting strategies for small firms (e.g. Baumback, Lawyer and Kelley, 1973; Pickle and Abrahamson, 1976). Accordingly, it is understandable that emphasizing the short-term goal of immediate profitability was significantly correlated with performance in benign environments while emphasizing high prices was not.

Miller and Friesen's (1982, 1983), as well as

Table 2. Performance-Policy Correlations: Small Firms in Hostile Environments

	Correlation coefficient	Significance level
We emphasize long-term capital investments	0.22	0.05
We emphasize long-term profitability	0.28	0.01
We offer our products/services at a high price relative to our competitors	0.30	0.01
We actively attempt to predict industry trends	0.21	0.05

Table 3. Performance-Policy Correlations: Small Firms in Benign Environments

	Correlation coefficient	Significance level
We have a highly leveraged financial position	−0.23	0.05
We emphasize immediate profitability	0.19	0.05
We emphasize the development and refinement of existing products/services	0.31	0.01
We actively attempt to minimize our dependence on any single customer	−0.22	0.05

Khandwalla's (1977), studies strongly suggest that environmental scanning efforts aimed at forecasting the industry environment are particularly critical to firms facing hostile environments. However, actively attempting to predict industry trends may be of lesser importance to firms in more benign environments. These environments are, by definition, characterized by less competitive intensity and are frquently less dynamic than hostile environments. Therefore, industry monitoring efforts may not be as strongly associated with performance in benign environments as they would arguably be in more hostile environments. Indeed, this is suggested by the fact that the forecasting of industry trends was significantly correlated with performance only in more hostile environments.

The importance of conservative financial management is generally acknowledged in the small-firm management literature. Most successful small firms have low to moderate debt positions, while poorer-performing small firms are often forced to assume riskier, more leveraged financial positions (Cohn and Lindberg, 1974). The same may not be true of small firms in hostile environments. It is possible that a conservative, risk-averse financial posture may cause small firms in hostile environments to shy away from making the capital investments needed to develop or maintain a competitive advantage. This reasoning could account for the presence of a significant (negative) correlation between performance and financial leverage in benign environments and the absence of a significant correlation between these variables in more hostile environments.

The significant correlation between performance and emphasizing the development and refinement of existing products in benign environments is consistent with Cohn and Lindberg's assertion regarding effective small firm innovation and product R&D practices:

> Because the risks of failure of original products is great and can cause more serious losses for small companies than large companies, small firms should lean more toward evolution than invention in product development (1972: 3).

In hostile environments, on the other hand, the absence of a significant correlation between these variables may be attributable to the possibility that a more aggressive emphasis on innovation is warranted in these settings. Consistent with this point, Hall (1980) found that heavy investment in new product (vs existing product) research and development was characteristic of many high-performing firms in hostile environments.

Finally, research by Gardner (1983) may provide a clue to why attempting to minimize dependence on any single customer was significantly (and negatively) correlated with performance in benign environments, but not hostile environments. In a study of small manufacturing firms, Gardner found that it was common for these firms to 'survive by having a close relationship with a relatively small number of customers who account for a very large portion of their sales volume' (1983: 61). Such strong dependence on a few large accounts would represent a particularly substantial risk for small firms in hostile environments given the inherent uncertainties of these environments. Therefore, it is not too surprising that the correlations between performance and dependency on single customers differed for small firms in hostile and benign environments.

Collectively, these findings concerning the individual business practices and competitive tactics further suggest that diverse and dissimilar strategic management practices appear to be characteristic of small, high-performing firms in hostile and benign environments.

DISCUSSION AND CONCLUSION

The data indicate that the business practices and organizational responses of effective small firms in hostile and benign environments may differ in many ways. The attributes which appear to contribute to high performance among small firms in hostile environments are an organic structure, an entrepreneurial strategic posture, and a competitive profile characterized by a long-term, goal-oriented approach to management, high product/service prices, and a concern for maintaining an awareness of industry trends. In benign environments, on the other hand, the attributes which appear to promote performance include a more mechanistic structure, a more conservative strategic posture, and a competitive profile characterized by conservative, risk-averse financial management, an emphasis on immediate profitability and the development and refinement of existing products and services, and a strong dependence, if necessary, on individual customers for the firm's sales revenues.

The apparent managerial implication of these findings is that small firms in hostile and benign environments should strive to adopt the attributes associated with high performance in those settings. However, the drawing of any such strong implication from this research must be done with caution in light of three important considerations.

First, the data analysis merely shows that certain strategic management practices are more strongly related to performance among small firms in hostile environments than among small firms in benign environments (or vice-versa). The analysis does not suggest that poorer-performing firms will never engage in the practices typically associated with better performance in a given environmental setting. Likewise, it is certainly possible for small firms to perform well in hostile or benign environments without engaging in the practices identified in this study as associated with high performance in those environments.

Second, there is no objective basis for determining when a benign environment becomes a hostile environment. As such, the use of a mean split of the environmental hostility scale as the basis for operationally defining hostile and benign environments was largely arbitrary. Although the results of the correlation analysis were easily explained using existing theory and research, it must be recognized that these results may have been influenced by this imprecise methodological decision.

Third, while the results of the moderated regression analysis were statistically significant and consistent with the hypotheses, neither complete regression equation explained more than 20 percent of the variance in firm performance. The purpose of this analysis was to determine whether environmental hostility has a moderating influence on the organization structure–performance and strategic posture–performance relationships, rather than to identify the best predictors of performance for the sampled firms. However, the fact that the regression equations did not explain large portions of the variance in performance suggests that other organizational context variables (e.g. organization culture, industry structure) may be equally or more important than organization structure and strategic posture in predicting small firm performance in hostile and benign environments.

The finding that several of the correlations between performance and specific business practices differed in magnitude in hostile and benign environments raises an interesting possibility concerning the inability of organization structure and strategic posture to explain large variations in performance. Performance is, presumably, a function not only of a firm's organization structure and strategic posture, but also of the fit between these variables and the firm's business practices and competitive tactics. Furthermore, the interrelationships between the business practices and competitive tactics themselves would arguably have an impact on performance. As such, it seems reasonable to suggest that the internal cohesiveness and consistency of a firm's strategic management practices, assessed in terms of the aforementioned relationships, would be more strongly linked to performance than would any small number of independently observed variables. While clearly beyond the intended scope of this paper, research along these lines would seem to be a step in the right direction.

In conclusion, the body of literature on small-firm management offers many valuable suggestions on how to effectively conduct business operations. These suggestions are frequently based on empirical research, wisdom gained through years of trial-and-error experience, and sound theorizing. Nonetheless, these *general* prescriptions, by definition, do not consider variations in the environmental setting which can moderate their effectiveness. As such, adhering too closely to general prescriptions can lead to poor performance and missed opportunities. This argument was recently made by Cooper, Willard and Woo (1986), who showed that, in certain industries, direct competition with larger competitors can be a more effective strategy for a small firm than the usually recommended niche strategy.

The findings of this study suggest that different organizational responses and business practices are appropriate for firms in hostile and benign environments. This is most likely true for large as well as small firms. However, a perusal of the literature on small-firm management can lead one to assume that small firms can effectively compete by adhering to business principles which are offered without regard for the individual firm's environmental context. The folly of this assumption is highlighted by the finding that different strategic management practices were associated with high performance in different environmental settings. Clearly a critical analysis of environmental factors is central to the effective strategic management of firms of all sizes.

Given these conclusions, future research on small-firm management might fruitfully focus on differentiating effective and ineffective management practices in various organizational and environmental contexts. The findings of this study suggest that a particularly promising line of research may be an investigation into the impact on small firm performance of the relationships between individual business practices and overall structural and strategic postures. Hopefully, such efforts will increase the level of sophistication and practical utility of the small firm strategic management paradigm.

ACKNOWLEDGEMENTS

The authors would like to thank the two anonymous reviewers for their many helpful insights and suggestions.

APPENDIX

The environmental hostility scale

How would you characterize the external environment within which your firm operates?

Very safe, little threat to the survival and well-being of my firm	1 to 7	Very risky, a false step can mean my firm's undoing
Rich in investment and marketing opportunities	1 to 7	Very stressful, exacting, hostile; very hard to keep afloat
An environment that my firm can control and manipulate to its own advantage, such as a dominant firm has in an industry with little competition and few hindrances	1 to 7	A dominating environment in which my firm's initiatives count for very little against the tremendous competitive, political, or technological forces

The organization structure scale

In general, the operating management philosophy in my firm favors . . .

Highly structured channels of communication and a highly restricted access to important financial and operating information	1 to 7	Open channels of communication with important financial and operating information flowing quite freely throughout the organization
A strong insistence on a uniform managerial style throughout the firm	1 to 7	Managers' operating styles allowed to range freely from the very formal to the very informal
A strong emphasis on giving the most to say in decision-making to formal line managers	1 to 7	A strong tendency to let the expert in a given situation have the most say in decision-making, even if this means temporary bypassing of formal line authority
A strong emphasis on holding fast to tied and true management principles despite any changes in business conditions	1 to 7	A strong emphasis on holding fast to tried changing circumstances without too much concern for past practice
A strong emphasis on always getting personnel to follow the formally laid down procedures	1 to 7	A strong emphasis on getting things done even if this means disregarding formal procedures

Tight formal control of most operations by means of sophisticated control and information systems	1 to 7	Loose, informal control; heavy dependence on informal relationships and norm of cooperation for getting work done
A strong emphasis on getting line and staff personnel to adhere closely to formal job descriptions	1 to 7	A strong tendency to let the requirements of the situation and the individual's personality define proper on-job behavior

The strategic posture scale

In general, the top managers of my firm favor . . .

A strong emphasis on the marketing of tried and true products or services	1 to 7	A strong emphasis on R&D, technological leadership, and innovations

How many new lines of products or services has your firm marketed in the past 5 years?

No new lines of products or services	1 to 7	Very many new lines of products or services
Changes in product or service lines have been mostly of a minor nature	1 to 7	Changes in product or service lines have usually been quite dramatic

In dealing with its competitors, my firm . . .

Typically responds to actions which competitors initiate	1 to 7	Typically initiates actions which competitors then respond to
Is very seldom the first business to introduce new products/services, administrative techniques, operating technologies, etc.	1 to 7	Is very often the first business to introduce new products/services, administrative techniques, operating technologies, etc.
Typically seeks to avoid competitive clashes, preferring a 'live-and-let-live' posture	1 to 7	Typically adopts a very competitive, 'undo-the-competitors' posture

In general, the top managers of my firm have . . .

A strong proclivity for low-risk projects (with normal and certain rates of return)	1 to 7	A strong proclivity for high-risk projects (with chances of very high returns)

In general, the top managers of my firm believe that . . .

Owing to the nature of the environment, it is best to explore it gradually via timid, incremental behavior	1 to 7	Owing to the nature of the environment, bold, wide-ranging acts are necessary to achieve the firm's objectives

When confronted with decision-making situations involving uncertainty, my firm. . .

Typically adopts a cautious, 'wait-and-see' posture in order to minimize the probability of making costly decisions	1 to 7	Typically adopts a bold, aggressive posture in order to maximize the probability of exploiting potential opportunities

REFERENCES

Albert, K. J. *Straight Talk about Small Business*, McGraw-Hill, New York, 1981.

Allen, M. J. and W. M. Yen. *Introduction to Measurement Theory*, Brooks/Cole, Monterey, CA, 1979.

Arnold, H. J. 'Moderator variables: a clarification of conceptual, analytic, and psychometric issues', *Organizational Behavior and Human Performance*, **29**(2), 1982, pp. 143–174.

Baumback, C. M., K. Lawyer and P. C. Kelley. *How to Organize and Operate a Small Business*, 5th edition, Prentice-Hall, Englewood Cliffs, NJ, 1973.

Boskin, M. J. 'The fiscal environment for entrepreneurship'. In Kent, C. A. (ed.), *The Environment for Entrepreneurship*, Lexington Books, Lexington, MA, 1984, pp. 59–68.

Burns, T. and G. M. Stalker. *The Management of Innovation*, Tavistock, London, 1961.

Chilton, K. W. 'Regulation and the entrepreneurial environment'. In Kent, C. A. (ed.), *The Environment for Entrepreneurship*, Lexington Books, Lexington, MA, 1984, pp. 91–116.

Cohn, T. and R. A. Lindberg. *How Management Is Different in Small Companies*, AMA, Inc., New York, 1972.

Cohn, T. and R. A. Lindberg. *Survival & Growth: Management Strategies for the Small Firm*, AMACOM, New York, 1974.

Cooper, A. C. 'Strategic management: New ventures and small business'. In Schendel, D. E. and C. W. Hofer (eds), *Strategic Management: A New View of Business Policy and Planning*, Little, Brown and Company, Boston, 1979, pp. 316–327.

Cooper, A. C., G. E. Willard and C. Y. Woo. 'Strategies of high-performing new and small firms: A reexamination of the niche concept', *Journal of Business Venturing*, **1**, 1986, pp. 247–260.

Darrow, A. L. and D. R. Kahl. 'A comparison of moderated regression techniques considering strength of effect', *Journal of Management*, **8**, 1982, pp. 35–47.

Digman, L. A. *Strategic Management: Concepts, Decisions, Cases*, Business Publications, Inc., Plano, TX, 1986.

Fiorito, S. S. and R. W. LaForge. 'A marketing strategy analysis of small retailers', *American Journal of Small Business*, **10**(4), 1986, pp. 7–17.

Gardner, D. M. 'The marketing concept: its dimensions for the "big" small firm'. In Hills, G. E., D. J. Barnaby and L. R. Duffus (eds), *Marketing and Small Business/Entrepreneurship*, International Council for Small Business, Washington, DC, 1983, pp. 51–62.

Gupta, A. K. and V. Govindarajan. 'Business unit strategy, managerial characteristics, and business unit effectiveness at strategy implementation', *Academy of Management Journal*, **27**, 1984, pp. 25–41.

Hall, W. K. 'Survival strategies in a hostile environment', *Harvard Business Review*, **58**(5), September–October 1980, pp. 75–85.

Khandwalla, P. N. 'Some top management styles, their context and performance', *Organization and Administrative Sciences*, **7**(4), Winter 1976/77, pp. 21–51.

Khandwalla, P. N. *The Design of Organizations*, Harcourt, Brace, Jovanovich, New York, 1977.

Lawrence, P. R. and J. W. Lorsch. *Organization and Environment*, Richard D. Irwin, Homewood, Ill., 1967.

March, J. G. and H. A. Simon. *Organizations*, John Wiley & Sons, New York, 1958.

Miles, R. E. and C. C. Snow. *Organization Strategy, Structure and Process*, McGraw-Hill, New York, 1978.

Miller, D. 'The correlates of entrepreneurship in three types of firms', *Management Science*, **29**, 1983, pp. 770–791.

Miller, D. and P. H. Friesen. 'Innovation in conservative and entrepreneurial firms: two models of strategic momentum', *Strategic Management Journal*, **3**, 1982, pp. 1–25.

Miller, D. and P. H. Friesen. 'Strategy-making and environment: the third link', *Strategic Management Journal*, **4**, 1983, pp. 221–235.

Miller, D. and J. M. Tolouse. 'Strategy, structure, CEO personality and performance in small firms', *American Journal of Small Business*, **10**(3), 1986, pp. 47–62.

Mintzberg, H. 'Strategy-making in three modes', *California Management Review*, **16**(2), 1973, pp. 44–53.

Mintzberg, H. *The Structuring of Organizations*, Prentice-Hall, Englewood Cliffs, NJ, 1979.

Peterson, R. 'Creating contexts for new ventures in stagnating environments'. In Hornaday, J. A., E. B. Shils, J. A. Timmons and K. H. Vesper (eds), *Frontiers of Entrepreneurship Research*, Babson College Center for Entrepreneurial Studies, Wellesley, MA, 1985, pp. 258–283.

Pfeffer, J. and H. Leblebici. 'The effect of competition on some dimensions of organizational structure', *Social Forces*, **52**, 1973, pp. 268–279.

Pickle, H. B. and R. L. Abrahamson. *Small Business Management*, John Wiley and Sons, New York, 1976.

Sandberg, W. R. *New Venture Performance: The Role of Strategy and Industry Structure*, Lexington Books, Lexington, MA, 1986.

Schoonhoven, C. B. 'Problems with contingency theory: Testing assumptions hidden within the language of contingency "theory"', *Administrative Science Quarterly*, **26**, 1981, pp. 349–377.

Sharma, S., R. M. Durand and O. Gur-Arie. 'Identification and analysis of moderator variables', *Journal of Marketing Research*, **18**, 1981, pp. 291–300.

Southwood, K. E. 'Substantive theory and statistical interaction: five models', *American Journal of Sociology*, **83**, 1978, pp. 1154–1203.

Stegall, D. P., L. L. Steinmetz and J. B. Kline. *Managing the Small Business*, Richard D. Irwin, Homewood, Ill., 1976.

[17]

The Population Ecology of Organizations[1]

Michael T. Hannan
Stanford University

John Freeman
University of California, Berkeley

A population ecology perspective on organization-environment relations is proposed as an alternative to the dominant adaptation perspective. The strength of inertial pressures on organizational structure suggests the application of models that depend on competition and selection in populations of organizations. Several such models as well as issues that arise in attempts to apply them to the organization-environment problem are discussed.

I. INTRODUCTION

Analysis of the effects of environment on organizational structure has moved to a central place in organizations theory and research in recent years. This shift has opened a number of exciting possibilities. As yet nothing like the full promise of the shift has been realized. We believe that the lack of development is due in part to a failure to bring ecological models to bear on questions that are preeminently ecological. We argue for a reformulation of the problem in population ecology terms.

Although there is a wide variety of ecological perspectives, they all focus on selection. That is, they attribute patterns in nature to the action of selection processes. The bulk of the literature on organizations subscribes to a different view, which we call the adaptation pespective.[2] According

[1] This research was supported in part by grants from the National Science Foundation (GS-32065) and the Spencer Foundation. Helpful comments were provided by Amos Hawley, Francois Nielsen, John Meyer, Marshall Meyer, Jeffrey Pfeffer, and Howard Aldrich.

[2] There is a subtle relationship between selection and adaptation. Adaptive learning for individuals usually consists of selection among behavioral responses. Adaptation for a population involves selection among types of members. More generally, processes involving selection can usually be recast at a higher level of analysis as adaptation processes. However, once the unit of analysis is chosen there is no ambiguity in distinguishing selection from adaptation. Organizations often adapt to environmental conditions in concert and this suggests a systems effect. Though few theorists would deny the existence of such systems effects, most do not make them a subject of central concern. It is important to notice that, from the point of view embraced by sociologists whose interests focus on the broader social system, selection in favor of organizations with one set of properties to the disfavor of those with others is often an adaptive process. Societies and communities which consist in part of formal organizations adapt partly through processes that adjust the mixture of

to the adaptation perspective, subunits of the organization, usually managers or dominant coalitions, scan the relevant environment for opportunities and threats, formulate strategic responses, and adjust organizational structure appropriately.

The adaptation perspective is seen most clearly in the literature on management. Contributors to it usually assume a hierarchy of authority and control that locates decisions concerning the organiation as a whole at the top. It follows, then, that organizations are affected by their environments according to the ways in which managers or leaders formulate strategies, make decisions, and implement them. Particularly successful managers are able either to buffer their organizations from environmental disturbances or to arrange smooth adjustments that require minimal disruption of organizational structure.

A similar perspective, often worded differently, dominates the sociological literature on the subject. It plays a central role in Parsons's (1956) functional analysis of organization-environment relations and it is found in the more strictly Weberian tradition (see Selznick 1957). It is interesting to note that, while functionalists have been interested in system effects and have based much of the logic of their approach on survival imperatives, they have not dealt with selection phenomena. This is probably a reaction against organization theory which reflects social Darwinism.

Exchange theorists have also embraced the adaptation perspective (Levine and White 1961). And it is natural that theories emphasizing decision making take the adaptation view (March and Simon 1958; Cyert and March 1963). Even Thompson's (1967) celebrated marriage of open-systems and closed-systems thinking embraced the adaptation perspective explicitly (see particularly the second half of Thompson's book).

Clearly, leaders of organizations do formulate strategies and organizations do adapt to environmental contingencies. As a result at least some of the relationship between structure and environment must reflect adaptive behavior or learning. But there is no reason to presume that the great structural variability among organizations reflects only or even primarily adaptation.

There are a number of obvious limitations on the ability of organizations to adapt. That is, there are a number of processes that generate structural inertia. The stronger the pressures, the lower the organizations'

---

various kinds of organizations found within them. Whereas a complete theory of organization and environment would have to consider both adaptation and selection, recognizing that they are complementary processes, our purpose here is to show what can be learned from studying selection alone (see Aldrich and Pfeffer [1976] for a synthetic review of the literature focusing on these different perspectives).

adaptive flexibility and the more likely that the logic of environmental selection is appropriate. As a consequence, the issue of structural inertia is central to the choice between adaptation and selection models.

The possibility that organization structure contains a large inertial component was suggested by Burns and Stalker (1961) and Stinchcombe (1965). But, on the whole the subject has been ignored. A number of relevant propositions can be found in the organizations literature, however.

Inertial pressures arise from both internal structural arrangements and environmental constraints. A minimal list of the constraints arising from internal considerations follows.

1. An organization's investment in plant, equipment, and specialized personnel constitutes assets that are not easily transferable to other tasks or functions. The ways in which such sunk costs constrain adaptation options are so obvious that they need not be discussed further.

2. Organizational decision makers also face constraints on the information they receive. Much of what we know about the flow of information through organizational structures tells us that leaders do not obtain anything close to full information on activities within the organization and environmental contingencies facing the subunits.

3. Internal political constraints are even more important. When organizations alter structure, political equilibria are disturbed. As long as the pool of resources is fixed, structural change almost always involves redistribution of resources across subunits. Such redistribution upsets the prevailing system of exchange among subunits (or subunit leaders). So at least some subunits are likely to resist any proposed reorganization. Moreover, the benefits of structural reorganization are likely to be both generalized (designed to benefit the organization as a whole) and long-run. Any negative political response will tend to generate short-run costs that are high enough that organizational leaders will forego the planned reorganization. (For a more extensive discussion of the ways in which the internal political economy of organizations impedes change or adaptation, see Downs [1967] and Zald [1970].)

4. Finally, organizations face constraints generated by their own history. Once standards of procedure and the allocation of tasks and authority have become the subject of normative agreement, the costs of change are greatly increased. Normative agreements constrain adaptation in at least two ways. First, they provide a justification and an organizing principle for those elements that wish to resist reorganization (i.e., they can resist in terms of a shared principle). Second, normative agreements preclude the serious consideration of many alternative responses. For example, few research-oriented universities seriously consider adapting to

declining enrollments by eliminating the teaching function. To entertain this option would be to challenge central organizational norms.[3]

The external pressures toward inertia seem to be at least as strong. They include at least the following factors.

1. Legal and fiscal barriers to entry and exit from markets (broadly defined) are numerous. Discussions of organizational behavior typically emphasize barriers to entry (state licensed monopoly positions, etc.). Barriers to exit are equally interesting. There are an increasing number of instances in which political decisions prevent firms from abandoning certain activities. All such constraints on entry and exit limit the breadth of adaptation possibilities.

2. Internal constraints upon the availability of information are paralleled by external constraints. The acquisition of information about relevant environments is costly particularly in turbulent situations where the information is most essential. In addition, the type of specialists employed by the organization constrains both the nature of the information it is likely to obtain (see Granovetter 1973) and the kind of specialized information it can process and utilize.

3. Legitimacy constraints also emanate from the environment. Any legitimacy an organization has been able to generate constitutes an asset in manipulating the environment. To the extent that adaptation (e.g., eliminating undergraduate instruction in public universities) violates the legitimacy claims, it incurs considerable costs. So external legitimacy considerations also tend to limit adaptation.

4. Finally, there is the collective rationality problem. One of the most difficult issues in contemporary economics concerns general equilibria. If one can find an optimal strategy for some individual buyer or seller in a competitive market, it does not necessarily follow that there is a general equilibrium once all players start trading. More generally, it is difficult to establish that a strategy that is rational for a single decision maker will be rational if adopted by a large number of decision makers. A number of solutions to this problem have been proposed in competitive market theory, but we know of no treatment of the problem for organizations generally. Until such a treatment is established we should not presume that a course of action that is adaptive for a single organization facing some changing environment will be adaptive for many competing organizations adopting a similar strategy.

A number of these inertial pressures can be accommodated within the adaptation framework. That is, one can modify and limit the perspective in order to consider choices within the constrained set of alternatives. But

[3] Meyer's (1970) discussion of an organization's charter adds further support to the argument that normative agreements arrived at early in an organization's history constrain greatly the organization's range of adaptation to environmental constraints.

to do so greatly limits the scope of one's investigation. We argue that in order to deal with the various inertial pressures the adaptation perspective must be supplemented with a selection orientation.

We consider first two broad issues that are preliminary to ecological modeling. The first concerns appropriate units of analysis. Typical analyses of the relation of organizations to environments take the point of view of a single organization facing an environment. We argue for an explicit focus on populations of organizations. The second broad issue concerns the applicability of population ecology models to the study of human social organization. Our substantive proposal begins with Hawley's (1950, 1968) classic statement on human ecology. We seek to extend Hawley's work in two ways: by using explicit competition models to specify the process producing isomorphism between organizational structure and environmental demands, and by using niche theory to extend the problem to dynamic environments. We argue that Hawley's perspective, modified and extended in these ways, serves as a useful starting point for population ecology theories of organizations.

II. POPULATION THINKING IN THE STUDY OF ORGANIZATION-ENVIRONMENT RELATIONS

Little attention is paid in the organizations literature to issues concerning proper units of analysis (Freeman 1975). In fact, choice of unit is treated so casually as to suggest that it is not an issue. We suspect that the opposite is true—that the choice of unit involves subtle issues and has far-reaching consequences for research activity. For instance, in the case at hand, it determines which of several ecological literatures can be brought to bear on the study of organization-environment relations.

The comparison of unit choice facing the organizational analyst with that facing the bioecologist is instructive. To oversimplify somewhat, ecological analysis is conducted at three levels: individual, population, and community. Events at one level almost always have consequences at other levels. Despite this interdependence, population events cannot be reduced to individual events (since individuals do not reflect the full genetic variability of the population) and community events cannot be simply reduced to population events. Both the latter employ a population perspective which is not appropriate at the individual level.

The situation faced by the organizations analyst is more complex. Instead of three levels of analysis, he faces at least five: (1) members, (2) subunits, (3) individual organizations, (4) populations of organizations, and (5) communities of (populations of) organizations. Levels 3–5 can be seen as corresponding to the three levels discussed for general ecology, with the individual organization taking the place of the individual organism. The added complexity arises because organizations are more nearly decomposable into constituent parts than are organisms. Individual members and subunits may move from organization to organization in a manner which has no parallel in nonhuman organization.

Instances of theory and research dealing with the effects of environments on organizations are found at all five levels. For example, Crozier's well-known analysis of the effects of culture on bureaucracy focuses on the cultural materials members bring to organizations (1964). At the other end of the continuum we find analyses of "organizational fields" (Turk 1970; Aldrich and Reiss 1976). But, the most common focus is on *the* organization and *its* environment. In fact, this choice is so widespread that there appears to be a tacit understanding that individual organizations are the appropriate units for the study of organization-environment relations.

We argue for a parallel development of theory and research at the population (and, ultimately, the community) level. Because of the differing opinions about levels of analysis, "population" has at least two referents. Conventional treatments of human ecology suggest that the populations relevant to the study of organization-environment relations are those aggregates of members attached to the organization or, perhaps, served by the organization. In this sense, the organization is viewed as analogue to a community: it has collective means of adapting to environmental situations. The unit character of a population so defined depends on shared fate. All members share to some extent in the consequences of organizational success or failure.

We use the term population in a second sense: to refer to aggregates of organizations rather than members. Populations of organizations must be alike in some respect, that is, they must have some unit character. Unfortunately, identifying a population of organizations is no simple matter. The ecological approach suggests that one focus on common fate with respect to environmental variations. Since all organizations are distinctive, no two are affected identically by any given exogenous shock. Nevertheless, we can identify classes of organizations which are relatively homogeneous in terms of environmental vulnerability. Notice that the populations of interest may change somewhat from investigation to investigation depending on the analyst's concern. Populations of organizations referred to are not immutable objects in nature but are abstractions useful for theoretical purposes.

If we are to follow the lead of population biologists, we must identify an analogue to the biologist's notion of species. Various species are defined ultimately in terms of genetic structure. As Monod (1971) indicates, it is useful to think of the genetic content of any species as a blueprint. The blueprint contains the rules for transforming energy into structure.

Consequently all of the adaptive capacity of a species is summarized in the blueprint. If we are to identify a species analogue for organizations, we must search for such blueprints. These will consist of rules or procedures for obtaining and acting upon inputs in order to produce an organizational product or response.

The type of blueprint one identifies depends on substantive concerns. For example, Marschak and Radner (1972) employ the term "organizational form"[4] to characterize the key elements of the blueprint as seen within a decision-making framework. For them the blueprint or form has two functions: an information function that describes the rules used in obtaining, processing, and transmitting information about the states of external environments, and an activity function that states the rules used in acting on received information so as to produce an organizational response. To the extent that one can identify classes of organizations that differ with regard to these two functions, one can establish classes or forms of organization.

Since our concerns extend beyond decision making, however, we find Marschak and Radner's definition of forms too limiting. In fact, there is no reason to limit a priori the variety of rules or functions that may define relevant blueprints. So for us, an organizational form is a blueprint for organizational action, for transforming inputs into outputs. The blueprint can usually be inferred, albeit in somewhat different ways, by examining any of the following: (1) the formal structure of the organization in the narrow sense—tables of organization, written rules of operation, etc.; (2) the patterns of activity within the organization—what actually gets done by whom; or (3) the normative order—the ways of organizing that are defined as right and proper by both members and relevant sectors of the environment.

To complete the species analogue, we must search for qualitative differences among forms. It seems most likely that we will find such differences in the first and third areas listed above, formal structure and normative order. The latter offers particularly intriguing possibilities. Whenever the history of an organization, its politics, and its social structure are encoded in a normative claim (e.g., professionalization and collegial authority), one can use these claims to identify forms and define populations for research.

Having defined the organizational form, we can provide a more precise definition of a population of organizations. Just as the organizational analyst must choose a unit of analysis, so must he choose a system for study. Systems relevant to the study of organization-environment relations are

[4] The term "organizational form" is used widely in the sociological literature (see Stinchcombe 1965).

usually defined by geography, by political boundaries, by market or product considerations, etc. Given a systems definition, a population of organizations consists of all the organizations within a particular boundary that have a common form. That is, the population is the form as it exists or is realized within a specified system.

Both uses of the term population (and the ecological theories implied thereby) are likely to prove beneficial to the study of organizational structure. The first, more common, view suggests that organizational structure ought to be viewed as an outcome of a collective adaptive process. According to this view, structure and change ought to depend on the adaptiveness of subunits and on the differential access of subunits to environmental resources. The second view ignores the adaptive activities of elements within the organization except as they constitute organizational structure. It focuses on the organization as an adapting unit. Certainly both perspectives are needed. We are concerned here only with the latter, however.

Finally, we would like to identify the properties of populations most interesting to population ecologists. The main concern in this regard was expressed clearly by Elton (1927): "In solving ecological problems we are concerned with *what animals do* in their capacity as whole, living animals, not as dead animals or as a series of parts of animals. We have next to study the circumstances under which they do those things, and, most important of all, the limiting factors which prevent them from doing certain other things. By solving these questions it is possible to discover the reasons for *the distribution and numbers of animals in nature*." Hutchinson (1959) in the subtitle to his famous essay, "Homage to Santa Rosalia," expressed the main focus even more succinctly: "Why Are There So Many Kinds of Animals?" Taking our lead from these distinguished ecologists, we suggest that a population ecology of organizations must seek to understand the distributions of organizations across environmental conditions and the limitations on organizational structures in different environments, and more generally seek to answer the question, Why are there so many kinds of organizations?

III. DISCONTINUITIES IN ECOLOGICAL ANALYSIS

Utilization of models from ecology in the study of organizations poses a number of analytic challenges involving differences between human and nonhuman organizations with regard to their essential ingredients. Consider, first, the nongenetic transmission of information. Biological analyses are greatly simplified by the fact that most useful information concerning adaptation to the environment (which information we call structure) is transmitted genetically. Genetic processes are so nearly invariant that extreme continuity in structure is the rule. The small number of imperfections generates structural changes, which, if accepted by the environment, will be transmitted with near invariance. The extreme structural invariance of species greatly simplifies the problem of delimiting and identifying populations. More important, the adaptiveness of structure can be unambiguously identified with net reproduction rates. When a population with given properties increases its net reproduction rate following an environmental change, it follows that it is being selected for. This is why modern biologists have narrowed the definition of fitness to the net reproductive rate of population.

Human social organization presumably reflects a greater degree of learning or adaptation. As a result it is more difficult to define fitness in a precise way. Under at least some conditions, organizations may undergo such extreme structural change that they shift from one form to another. As a result, extreme adaptation may give rise to observed changes that mimic selection. This is particularly problematic when the various organizational forms are similar on many dimensions.

We have argued previously (Hannan and Freeman 1974) for a composite measure of fitness that includes both selection (actual loss of organizations) and mobility among forms (extreme adaptation). Fitness would then be defined as the probability that a given form of organization would persist in a certain environment. We continue to believe that such an approach has value, but we now believe that it is premature to combine adaptation and selection processes. The first order of business is to study selection processes for those situations in which inertial pressures are sufficiently strong that mobility among forms is unlikely.

Furthermore, it is worth noting that the capacity to adapt is itself subject to evolution (i.e., to systematic selection). As we argue below, organizations develop the capacity to adapt at the cost of lowered performance levels in stable environments. Whether or not such adaptable organizational forms will survive (i.e., resist selection) depends on the nature of the environment and the competitive situation. Therefore, a selection point of view treats high levels of adaptability as particular evolutionary outcomes.

There is a second sense in which human ecology appears to differ from bioecology. Blau and Scott (1962) point out that, unlike the usual biological situation, individual organizations (and populations of organizations) have the potential to expand almost without limit. The expandability of primitive elements is a problem because of our focus on the distribution of organizational forms over environments. A given form (e.g., formal bureaucracy) can expand throughout some system, market, or activity, either because one bureaucracy grows or because many bureaucracies are founded. Either process will generate an increase in the prevalence of bureaucratic organizational activity. A literal application of population ecology theory to the problem of organizational change would involve simply counting relative numbers in populations. Such a procedure may miss a phenomenon of central interest to the organizational analyst. Winter (1964), in discussing the analytic problem raised here, suggests distinguishing between survival, which describes the fate of individual organizations, and viability, which describes the "share of market" of a given organizational form.

We find at least as much merit in another perspective on the issue of size. Many theorists have asserted that structural change attends growth; in other words, a single organization cannot grow indefinitely and still maintain its original form. For instance, a mouse could not possibly maintain the same proportion of body weight to skeletal structure while growing as big as a house. It would neither look like a mouse nor operate physiologically like a mouse. Boulding (1953) and Haire (1959) argue that the same is true for organizations. Caplow (1957), building on work by Graicunas (1933) and others, argues that the ability of each member of an organization to carry on face-to-face interactions with each of the others declines with the number of organizational participants. This creates a shift in the nature of interactions such that they assume a more impersonal, formal style. Blau and a number of coauthors have argued for similar causal effects of size on structure (Blau and Scott 1962, pp. 223–42; Blau and Schoenherr 1971; Blau 1972). If it is true that organizational form changes with size, selection mechanisms may indeed operate with regard to the size distribution. When big organizations prevail it may be useful to view this as a special case of selection, in which the movement from "small form" to "large form" is theoretically indistinguishable from the dissolution ("death") of small organizations and their replacement by (the "birth" of) large organizations.

In sum, we have identified a number of challenges. The first concerns the two sources of change, selection and adaptive learning. We feel that the organizations literature has overemphasized the latter at the expense of the former. Much more is known about decision-making practices, forecasting, and the like than about selection in populations of organizations. The second challenge involves the distinction between selection and viability. Whether such a distinction is necessary depends on the results of research on size which is currently being pursued by many organization researchers.

IV. THE PRINCIPLE OF ISOMORPHISM

In the best developed statement of the principles of human ecology, Hawley (1968) answers the question of why there are so many kinds of organizations. According to Hawley, the diversity of organizational forms is isomorphic to the diversity of environments. In each distinguishable environmental configuration one finds, in equilibrium, only that organizational form optimally adapted to the demands of the environment. Each unit experiences constraints which force it to resemble other units with the same set of constraints. Hawley's explanation places heavy emphasis on communication patterns and structural complements of those patterns: "[organization units] must submit to standard terms of communication and to standard procedures in consequence of which they develop similar internal arrangements within limits imposed by their respective sizes" (1968, p. 334).

While the proposition seems completely sound from an ecological perspective, it does not address a number of interesting considerations. There are at least two respects in which the isomorphism formulation must be modified and extended if it is to provide satisfactory answers to the question posed. The first modification concerns the mechanism or mechanisms responsible for equilibrium. In this respect, the principle of isomorphism must be supplemented by a criterion of selection and a competition theory. The second modification deals with the fact that the principle of isomorphism neither speaks to issues of optimum adaptation to changing environments nor recognizes that populations of organizations often face multiple environments which impose somewhat inconsistent demands. An understanding of the constraints on organizational forms seems to require modeling of multiple, dynamic environments. Of course, we cannot fully extend Hawley's principle here. We attempt only to outline the main issues and suggest particular extensions.

V. COMPETITION THEORY

The first of the needed extensions is a specification of the optimization process responsible for isomorphism. We have already discussed two mechanisms: selection and adaptive learning. Isomorphism can result either because nonoptimal forms are selected out of a community of organizations or because organizational decision makers learn optimal responses and adjust organizational behavior accordingly. We continue to focus on the first of these processes: selection.

Consideration of optimization raises two issues: Who is optimizing, and what is being optimized? It is quite commonly held, as in the theory of the firm, that organizational decision makers optimize profit over sets of organizational actions. From a population ecology perspective, it is the environment which optimizes.[5] Whether or not individual organiza-

[5] In biological applications, one assumes that power (in the physical sense) is optimized by natural selection in accordance with the so-called Darwin-Lotka law.

tions are consicously adapting, the environment selects out optimal combinations of organizations. So if there is a rationality involved, it is the "rationality" of natural selection. Organizational rationality and environmental rationality may coincide in the instance of firms in competitive markets. In this case, the optimal behavior of each firm is to maximize profit and the rule used by the environment (market, in this case) is to select out profit maximizers. Friedman (1953) makes use of this observation to propose a justification of the theory of the firm in terms of the principles of evolution. However, Winter (1964) has argued convincingly that the actual situation is much more complicated than this and that it is most unusual for individual rationality and environmental or market rationality to lead to the same optima. When the two rationalities do not agree, we are concerned with the optimizing behavior of the environment.

A focus on selection invites an emphasis on competition. Organizational forms presumably fail to flourish in certain environmental circumstances because other forms successfully compete with them for essential resources. As long as the resources which sustain organizations are finite and populations have unlimited capacity to expand, competition must ensue.

Hawley (1950, pp. 201–3) following Durkheim (1947) among others, places a heavy emphasis on competition as a determinant of patterns of social organization. The distinctive feature of his model is the emphasis on the indirect nature of the process: "The action of all on the common supply gives rise to a reciprocal relation between each unit and all the others, if only from the fact that what one gets reduces by that amount what the others can obtain . . . without this element of indirection, that is, unless units affect one another through affecting a common limited supply, competition does not exist" (Hawley 1950, p. 202). In Hawley's model, competition processes typically involve four stages: (1) demand for resources exceeds supply; (2) competitors become more similar as standard conditions of competition bring forth a uniform response; (3) selection eliminates the weakest competitors; and (4) deposed competitors differentiate either territorially or functionally, yielding a more complex division of labor.

It is surprising that there is almost no reliance on competitive mechanisms in Hawley's later work. In particular, as we noted above, the rationale given for the isomorphism principle uses an adaptation logic. We propose to balance that treatment by adding an explicit focus on competition as a mechanism producing isomorphism.[6] In so doing, we can bring a rich set of formal models to bear on the problem.

For the case of human social organization, one might argue that selection optimizes the utilization of a specific set of resources including but not restricted to the power and the time of members.

[6] We include only the first and third of Hawley's stages in our model of competi-

The first step in constructing an ecological model of competition is to state the nature of the population growth process. At a minimum we wish the model to incorporate the idea that resources available at any moment for each form of organization are finite and fixed. This corresponds with Hawley's notion of limited supply and Stinchcombe's (1965) argument that human communities have limited "capacities for organizing." We also wish to incorporate the view that the rate at which units are added to populations of organizations depends on how much of the fixed capacity has already been exhausted. The greater the unexhausted capacity in an environment, the faster should be the rate of growth of populations of organizations. But the rate at which populations of organizations can expand into unused capacity varies among forms of organization. So there are two distinctive ecological considerations: the capacity of the environment to support forms of organization and the rate at which the populations grow (or decline) when the environmental support changes.

In order to state the model formally, it is helpful to begin with the control function that Hummon, Doreian, and Teuter (1975) use to add dynamic considerations to Blau's theory of size and differentiation. The control model states that the rate of change in the size of any unit (here a population of organizations) varies proportionately with the difference between existing size, X, and the equilibrium level of size, X^*, permitted in that environment. Then one possible representation would be

$$\frac{dX}{dt} = f(X^* - X) = r(X^* - X). \tag{1}$$

In (1) X^* and r represent the limited supply or environmental capacity and the structural ability of the population of organizations to respond to changes in the environment, respectively.

A particular form of the general growth model in (1) underlies most population ecology work on competition. This is the logistic growth model (for per capita growth):

$$\frac{dX_1}{dt} = r_1 X_1 \left(\frac{k_1 - X_1}{k_1}\right) \tag{2}$$

where X_1 denotes population size, k_1 is the capacity of the environment to support X_1 (this parameter is usually called the carrying capacity), and r_1 is the so-called natural rate of increase of the population or the rate at which the population grows when it is far below the carrying capacity.

As we indicated above, both k and r are ecological parameters of funda-

tion. We prefer to treat uniformity of response and community diversity as consequences of combinations of certain competitive processes and environmental features.

mental importance. Our research group has begun to compare various forms of organization by estimating the parameters of models like (2) for each form of organization. We have been successful to date in relating structural features of organizations such as complexity of core activity to variations in r and k (Nielsen and Hannan 1977; Freeman and Brittain 1977). This work, together with that of Hummon et al. (1975), gives us confidence that the model in (1) and/or (2) gives a good approximation of the growth of populations of organizations.

Up to this point we have presumed that the limits on growth reflect the finite nature of the environment (e.g., community wealth and mix of occupational skills). It is now time to reintroduce competition. According to Hawley, competition enters indirectly when the competitors lower the fixed supply. We can model this by following the lead of bioecologists and extending the logistic growth model. For example, consider a second population of organizations whose size is denoted by X_2. The two populations are said to compete if the addition of units of either decreases the rate of growth of the other. This will be the case when both populations are sustained by the same types of resources. Then the appropriate model is represented in the following system of growth equations (known as the Lotka-Volterra equations for competing populations):

$$\frac{dX_1}{dt} = r_1 X_1 \left(\frac{k_1 - X_1 - \alpha_{12} X_2}{k_1} \right)$$
$$\frac{dX_2}{dt} = r_2 X_2 \left(\frac{k_2 - X_2 - \alpha_{21} X_1}{k_2} \right). \quad (3)$$

The coefficients α_{12} and α_{21}, called competition coefficients, denote the magnitude of the effect of increases in one population on the growth of the other. In this simple formulation, the only consequence of competition is to lower the carrying capacity of the environment for a population of organizations.

Analysis of (3) produces interesting qualitative results. It is not difficult to show that a stable two-population equilibrium exists for the system in (3) only if

$$\frac{1}{\alpha_{21}} < \frac{k_2}{k_1} < \alpha_{12}. \quad (4)$$

Therefore, very similar populations (i.e., populations with competition coefficients near unity) can coexist only under a very precise k_2/k_1 ratio. As a result, when $\alpha_{12} = \alpha_{21} = 1$, no two-population equilibrium can be stable; any exogenous shock will result in the elimination of one of the populations. This result supports the generality of the widely cited "principle of competitive exclusion" (Gause 1934).[7] According to this principle, no two populations can continuously occupy the same niche. Populations are said to occupy the same niche to the extent that they depend on identical environmental resources. If they are identical, then the addition of an element to X_2 has the same consequences for growth in X_1 as does the addition of an element to X_1; in other words, the competition coefficients are unity. The broad conclusion is that the greater the similarity of two resource-limited competitors, the less feasible is it that a single environment can support both of them in equilibrium.

If two populations of organizations sustained by identical environmental resources differ in some organizational characteristic, that population with the characteristic less fit to environmental contingencies will tend to be eliminated. The stable equilibrium will then contain only one population which can be said to be isomorphic to the environment.

In order to see the implications of the model for organizational diversity, we extend the Lotka-Volterra system to include M competitors:

$$\frac{dX_i}{dt} = r_i X_i \,(k_i - X_i - \Sigma\alpha_{ij}X_j)/k_i \quad (i = 1, \ldots, M). \tag{5}$$

The general system (5) has a community equilibrium:

$$k_i = X_i + \Sigma\alpha_{ij}X_j \qquad (i = 1, \ldots, M). \tag{6}$$

These equations can be expressed in matrix form:

$$k = A\,x, \tag{7}$$

where x and k are $(M \times 1)$ column vectors and A is the community matrix:

$$A = \begin{pmatrix} 1 & \alpha_{12} & \cdot & \cdot & \alpha_{1m} \\ \alpha_{21} & 1 & & & \cdot \\ \cdot & & & & \cdot \\ \cdot & & & & \cdot \\ \cdot & & & & \cdot \\ \alpha_{m1} & \cdot & \cdot & \cdot & 1 \end{pmatrix}$$

whose elements are the competition coefficients.

The so-called theory of community structure entails the analysis of the equilibrium behavior of the system of equation (7) from the perspective of postulated competition processes.[8] The results, though stated in

[7] This so-called principle has mostly suggestive value (see MacArthur [1972, pp. 43–46] for a penetrating critique of attempts to derive quantitative implications from Gause's principle; most of these criticisms do not apply to the qualitative inferences we consider).

[8] We restrict attention to the case in which all entries of A are nonnegative. Nega-

terms of species diversity, are quite general. In particular, one can show that when growth in population is constrained only by resource availability, the number of distinct resources sets an upper bound on diversity in the system.[9] Even more generally, the upper bound on diversity is equal to the number of distinct resources plus the number of additional constraints on growth (Levin 1970).

It is difficult to apply either result directly in order to calculate the upper bound on diversity even in the nonhuman context. The chief difficulty is that of identifying distinct constraints. A good deal of empirical work is required if one is to judge how different two constraints must be in order to have distinct consequences for community equilibria. The theorems do, however, imply useful qualitative results. If one can identify environmental changes which add constraints to a system or eliminate them, one can conclude that the upper bound of diversity is increased or decreased.

This broad qualitative result has a number of potential applications to the research problems of interest. For example, the expansion of markets and of state control mechanisms through social systems tends to have the consequence of eliminating or reducing the number of constraints which are idiosyncratic to local environments. Viewed from the perspective of the larger system, the process of expansion of the economic and political center should, then, tend to replace some local constraints with more uniform ones. As long as the local environments were heterogeneous at the outset, expansion of the center ought to reduce the number of constraints on organization in the whole system.

The theory just discussed implies on the one hand that the change in constraint structure ought to lower organizational diversity through the elimination of some population.[10] One can imagine, on the other hand, that in some local environments, the combination of unaltered local constraints and new larger system constraints might increase the total number of constraints in the local system. In that case, organizational diversity in those local environments should increase. Such an increase would result in the creation or adoption of new organizational forms.

The increasingly important role of the state in regulating economic and social action provides numerous opportunities for analyzing the impact of changes in constraint structures on the diversity of organizational

---

tive entries are appropriate for predator/prey (or more generally, host/parasite) relations. The typical result for this case is cyclical population growth.

[9] A more precise statement of the theorem is that no stable equilibrium exists for a system of M competitors and $N < M$ resources (MacArthur and Levins 1964).

[10] For a more comprehensive statement of this argument with reference to ethnic organization, see Hannan (1975).

forms. Consider the impact of licensing laws, minimum wage, health, and safety legislation, affirmative action, and other regulations on organizational action. When such regulations are applied to the full range of organizations in broad areas of activity they undoubtedly alter the size distributions of organizations. Most often they select out the smallest organizations. But it is not difficult to imagine situations in which medium-sized organizations (more precisely, those with some minimum level of complexity) would be more adversely affected. Besides altering size distributions, such regulations undoubtedly affect the diversity of organizational arrangements in other ways. Here one could analyze the impact of state action on the diversity of accounting systems within industries, curricula within universities, departmental structures within hospitals, etc. In each case it would be essential to determine whether the newly imposed constraint replaced lower level constraints, in which case diversity should decline, or whether the constraint cumulated with the existing constraints, in which case organizational diversity would be likely to increase.

To indicate the richness of the simple competition theory we have proposed we will briefly discuss another sort of empirical test. We noted above that research on regulation might concern itself with impacts on distributions of organizations by size. The classical model of organizational size distributions (Simon and Bonini 1958) proposes the following simple process. A number of organizations begin with the same small size. Some fraction are able to make or borrow some useful technical or organizational innovation that permits them to grow to some larger size. During some specified time period the process repeats itself with the same fraction making the innovation required to attain a larger size. Such a growth process eventually yields the lognormal distribution that characterizes so many size distributions.

Competition theory suggests a refinement of this classical model. If, as we argued earlier, large changes in organizational size are accompanied by structural changes (changes in form), organizations of very different size in the same area of activity will tend to exhibit different forms. As a consequence of these structural differences, they will tend to depend on different sets of environmental resource (and constraints). That is, within any area of activity, patterns of resource use will tend to be specialized to segments of the size distribution. This being the case, organizations will compete most intensely with similar size organizations. Also, competition between pairs of organizations within an activity will be a decreasing function of the distance separating them on the size gradient. For example, small local banks compete most with other small banks, to a lesser extent with medium-scale regional banks, and hardly at all with international banks. Under these conditions, significant alterations in the size distribution indicate selection for and against certain organizational forms closely associated with regard to size.

Now let us return to the classical model. When large-sized organizations emerge they pose a competitive threat to medium-sized but hardly any threat to small organizations. In fact, the rise of large organizations may increase the survival chances of small ones in a manner not anticipated in the classical model. When the large organizations enter, those in the middle of the size distribution are trapped. Whatever strategy they adopt to fight off the challenge of the larger form makes them more vulnerable in competition with small organizations and vice versa. That is, at least in a stable environment the two ends of the size distribution ought to outcompete the middle (see below). So in a longitudinal analysis of organizational size distributions we would expect to see the number of medium-sized organizations decline upon the entry of larger organizations. Also, we would expect the fortunes of small organizations to improve as their competitors are removed from the environment. This reasoning holds generally for competition along a single gradient: those in the middle will be eliminated in stable environments (MacArthur 1972, pp. 43–46).

VI. NICHE THEORY

The principle of isomorphism implies that social organizations in equilibrium will exhibit structural features that are specialized to salient features of the resource environment. As long as the environment is stable and certain, we see no difficulty with this proposition. But does it hold when the environment shifts either predictably or unpredictably among several alternative configurations? Though the issues raised by attempting to answer this question are complex, doing so is crucial to developing adequate models of organizational-environment relations.

Intuition suggests that isomorphism holds as a good approximation only in stable environments. Faced with unstable environments, organizations ought to develop a generalist structure that is not optimally adapted to any single environmental configuration but is optimal over an entire set of configurations. In other words, we ought to find specialized organizations in stable and certain environments and generalist organizations is unstable and uncertain environments. Whether or not this simple proposition holds for social organizations, only empirical research will tell. However, a variety of population ecology models suggests that it is too simplistic. We cannot hope in one paper to develop fully the arguments involved. Instead we indicate the main lines of development with reference to one rather evocative perspective developed by Levins (1962, 1968): the theory of niche width.

The concept of "niche," initially borrowed by biologists from early social science, plays a central role in ecological theory. This is not the place for an extended discussion of the multiple uses of the concept (see Whittaker and Levin 1976). The model which follows uses Hutchinson's (1957) formulation. From this point of view the (realized) niche of a population is defined as that area in constraint space (the space whose dimensions are levels of resources, etc.) in which the population outcompetes all other local populations. The niche, then, consists of all those combinations of resource levels at which the population can survive and reproduce itself.

Each population occupies a distinct niche. For present purposes it suffices to consider cases where pairs of populations differ with respect to a single environmental dimension, *E*, and are alike with respect to all others. Then relative competitive positions can be simply summarized as in figure 1. As we have drawn this figure, one population, *A*, occupies a

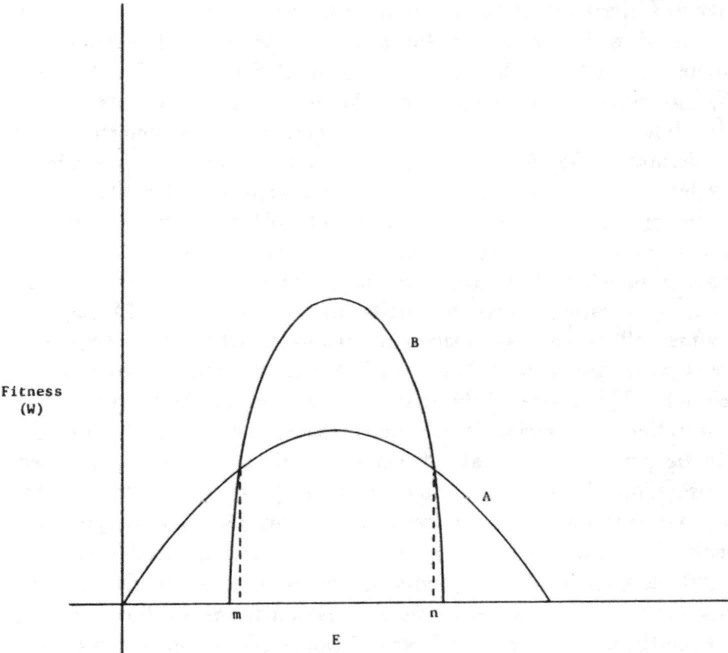

FIG. 1.—Fitness functions (niches) for specialists and generalists

very broad niche, whereas the other, *B*, has concentrated its fitness, denoted *W*, on a very narrow band of environmental variation. This distinction, which is usually referred to as generalism versus specialism, is crucial to biological ecology and to a population ecology of organizations.

In essence, the distinction between specialism and generalism refers to whether a population of organizations flourishes because it maximizes its exploitation of the environment and accepts the risk of having that environment change or because it accepts a lower level of exploitation in return for greater security. Whether or not the equilibrium distribution of organizational forms is dominated by the specialist depends, as we will see, on the shape of the fitness sets and on properties of the environment.

Part of the efficiency resulting from specialism is derived from the lower requirements for excess capacity. Given some uncertainty, most organizations maintain some excess capacity to insure the reliability of performance. In a rapidly changing environment, the definition of excess capacity is likely to change frequently. What is used today may become excess tomorrow, and what is excess today may be crucial tomorrow. Organizations operating in environments where the transition from state to state is less frequent will (in equilibrium) have to maintain excess capacity in a given allocational pattern for longer periods of time. Whereas those charged with assessing performance will be tempted to view such allocations as wasteful, they may be essential for survival. Thompson (1967) has argued that organizations allocate resources to units charged with the function of insulating core technology from environmentally induced disruption. So, for example, manufacturing firms may retain or employ legal staffs even when they are not currently facing litigation.

The importance of excess capacity is not completely bound up with the issue of how much excess capacity will be maintained. It also involves the manner in which it is used. Organizations may insure reliable performance by creating specialized units, as Thompson (1967) suggests, or they may allocate excess capacity to organizational roles, by employing personnel with skills and abilities which exceed the routine requirements of their jobs. This is one of the important reasons for using professionals in organizations. Professionals use more resources not only because they tend to be paid more, but also because organizations must allow them more discretion (including the freedom to respond to outside reference groups). Organizations, in turn, become more flexible by employing professionals. They increase their capacity to deal with a variable environment and the contingencies it produces. For example, hospitals and their patients often employ obstetricians and pediatricians in their delivery rooms even though the normal delivery of babies can be performed equally well, and perhaps even better, by midwives. The skills of the medical doctor represent excess capacity to insure reliable performance should delivery not be normal. Usually, the pediatrician examines the infant immediately after birth to see if there is any abnormality requiring immediate action. If the mother is suffering dangerous consequences from giving birth, and the child is also in need of attention, the presence of the pediatrician insures that the obstetrician will not have to choose between them in allocating his attention.

Excess capacity may also be allocated to the development and maintenance of procedural systems. When the certainty of a given environmental state is high, organizational operations should be routine, and coordination can be accomplished by formalized rules and the investment of resources in training incumbents to follow those formalized procedures. If in fact the environment were unchanging ($p = 1$), all participants were procedurally skilled, and the procedures were perfectly tuned, there would be no need for any control structure at all, except to monitor behavior. However, when certainty is low, organizational operations are less routine. Under these circumstances, a greater allocation of resources to develop and maintain procedural systems is counterproductive and optimal organizational forms will allocate resources to less formalized systems capable of more innovative responses (e.g., committees and teams). In this case, excess capacity is represented by the increased time it takes such structures to make decisions and by increased coordination costs.

The point here is that populations of organizational forms will be selected for or against depending upon the amount of excess capacity they maintain and how they allocate it. It may or may not be rational for any particular organization to adopt one pattern or another. What would seem like waste to anyone assessing performance at one time may be the difference between survival and failure later. Similarly, organizations may survive because high levels of professionalization produce coordination by mutual adjustment despite a somewhat chaotic appearance. Others, in which everyone seems to know precisely what he is doing at all times, may fail. Under a given set of environmental circumstances the fundamental ecological question is: which forms thrive and which forms disappear.

Generalism may be observed in a population of organizations, then, either in its reliance upon a wide variety of resources simultaneously or in its maintenance of excess capacity at any given time. This excess capacity allows such organizations to change in order to take advantage of resources which become more readily available. Corporations which maintain an unusually large proportion of their total assets in fluid form ("slack," in terms of theory of the firm; Penrose 1959; Cyert and March 1963) are generalizing. In either case, generalism is costly. Under stable environmental circumstances, generalists will be outcompeted by specialists. And at any given point in time, a static analysis will reveal excess capacity. An implication—shifting our focus to individual generalists—is that outside agents will often mistake excess capacity for waste.

We can investigate the evolution of niche width if we make the assumption that areas under the fitness curve are equal, and that specialists differ from generalists in how they distribute the fixed quantity of fitness over environmental outcomes. Specialists outcompete generalists over the range of outcomes to which they have specialized (because of the fixed level of fitness assumption). As long as the environmental variation remains within that interval (the interval $[m,n]$ in fig. 1), generalists have no adaptive advantage and will be selected against. Alternatively, if the environment is only occasionally within the interval, specialists will fare less well than generalists. These brief comments make clear the importance of environmental variation for the evolution of niche width.

To simplify further, consider an environment which can take on only two states and in every period falls in state one with probability p and in state two with probability $q = (1 - p)$. Assume further that variations in environmental states are Bernoulli trials (independent from period to period). For this situation Levins (1962, 1968) has shown that optimal niche width depends on p and the "distance" between the two states of the environment.

To see this, we change focus slightly. Since each organization faces two environments, its fitness depends on fitness in the pair. We can summarize the adaptive potential of each organization by plotting these pairs of values (fitness in state 1 and in state 2) in a new space whose axes are fitness in each of the states, as in figure 2. In this representation, each point denotes the fitness of a distinct organizational form. The cloud of points is termed the "fitness set." We presume that all of the naturally possible adaptations are represented in the fitness set.

Our interest is in determining which points in the fitness set will be favored by natural selection. Notice first that all points interior to the set are inferior in terms of fitness to at least some point on the boundary of the set. In this sense the boundary, drawn as a continuous line, represents the optimal possibilities. Since natural selection maximizes fitness, it must choose points on the boundary. This narrows our search to seeking which form(s) on the boundary will be favored.

As figure *2b* is drawn, no organizational form does particularly well in both states of the environment—no form has high levels of fitness in both. This will be the case when the two states are "far apart" in the sense that they impose very different adaptive contingencies on organizations. In such cases (see Levins 1968), the fitness set will be concave. When the "distance" between states is small, there is no reason why certain organizational forms cannot do well in both environments. In such cases, the finess set will be convex, as in figure *2a*.

The fitness functions in figures *2a* and *2b* describe different adaptive situations. The next step is to model the optimization process. To do so,

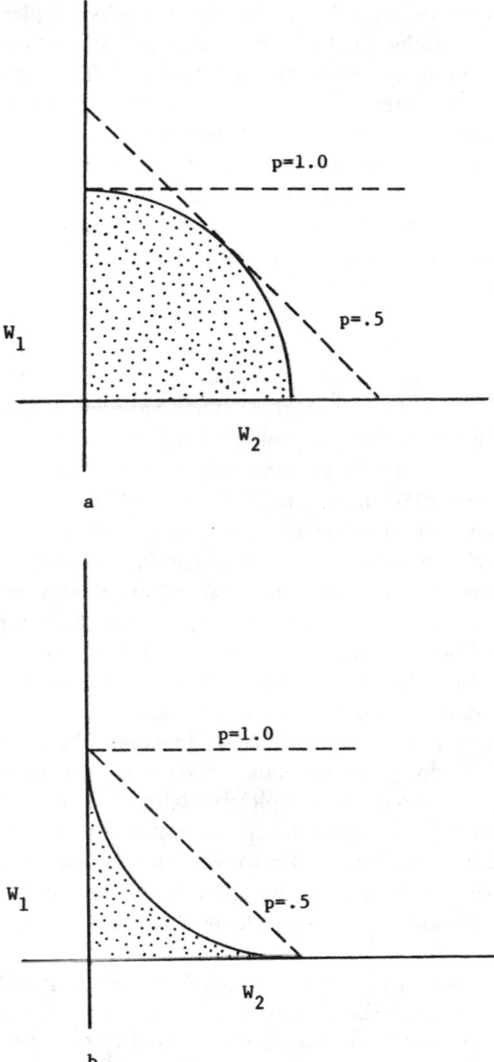

FIG. 2.—Optimal adaptation in fine-grained environment; *a*, convex fitness set; *b*, concave fitness set.

we introduce a further distinction. Ecologists have found it useful to distinguish both spatial and temporal environmental variation according to grain. Environmental variation is said to be fine-grained when a typical element (organization) encounters many units or replications. From a temporal perspective, variation is fine-grained when typical durations in states are short relative to the lifetime of organizations. Otherwise, the environment is said to be coarse-grained. Demand for products or services is often characterized by fine-grained variation whereas changes in legal structures are more typically coarse-grained.

The essential difference between the two types of environmental variation is the cost of suboptimal strategies. The problem of ecological adaptation can be considered a game of chance in which the population chooses a strategy (specialism or generalism) and then the environment chooses an outcome (by, say, flipping a coin). If the environment "comes up" in a state favorable to the organizational form, it prospers; otherwise, it declines. However, if the variation is fine-grained (durations are short), each population of organizations experiences a great many trials and environment is experienced as an average. When variation is coarse-grained, however, the period of decline stemming from a wrong choice may exceed the organizational capacity to sustain itself under unfavorable conditions.

To capture these differences, Levins introduced an adaptive function to represent how natural selection would weight fitness in each state under the different conditions. In discussing fine-grained variation, we suggested that the environment is experienced as an average.[11] The appropriate adaptive function, then, simply weights fitness in the two states (W_1 and W_2) according to frequency of occurrence: $A(W_1,W_2) = pW_1 + qW_2$. In order to consider optimal adaptation we merely superimpose the adaptive function on the fitness set and find points of tangency of adaptive function and fitness functions. Points of tangency are optimal adaptations. The solutions for various cases are presented in figure 2. If the environment is completely stable (i.e., $p = 1$), then specialism is optimal. If the environment is maximally uncertain (i.e., $p = .5$), generalism is optimal in the convex case (when the demands of the different environments are not too dissimilar) but not in the concave case. In fact, as the model is developed, specialism always wins out in the concave case.

Consider first the cases in which the environment is stable (i.e., $p = 1$). Not surprisingly, specialism is optimal. The results for unstable environments diverge. When the fitness set is convex (i.e., the demands of the different environmental states are similar and/or complementary), generalism is optimal. But when the environmental demands differ (and the fitness set is concave), specialism is optimal. This is not as strange

[11] That selection depends on average outcomes is only one hypothesis. Templeton and Rothman (1974) argue that selection depends not on average outcomes but on some minimum level of fitness. Whether average outcomes or some other criterion guides selection in populations of organizations is open to question. We follow Levins in order to keep the exposition simple.

a result as it first appears. When the environment changes rapidly among quite different states, the cost of generalism is high. Since the demands in the different states are dissimilar, considerable structural management is required of generalists. But since the environment changes rapidly, these organizations will spend most of their time and energies adjusting structure. It is apparently better under such conditions to adopt a specialized structure and "ride out" the adverse environments.

The case of coarse-grained environments is somewhat more complex. Our intuitive understanding is that since the duration of an environmental state is long, maladaptation ought to be given greater weight. That is, the costs of maladaptation greatly outweigh any advantage incurred by the correct choice. One adaptive function which gives this result is the log-linear model used by Levins: $A(W_1,W_2) = W_1^pW_2^q$. The method of finding optimal adaptations is the same. The results are found in figure 3. Only one case differs from what we found for fine-grained environments: the combination of uncertain and coarse-grained variation with concave fitness sets. We saw above that when such variation is fine-grained, it is better to specialize. When the duration of environmental states is long, however, the costs of this strategy are great. Long periods of nonadaptation will threaten the survival of the organization. In addition, the fact that the environment changes less often means that generalists need not spend most of their time and energies altering structure. Thus generalism is the optimal strategy in this case as we see in figure 3*b*.

The combination of coarse-grained environmental variation and concave fitness sets raises a further possibility. The optimal adaptation in the face of environmental uncertainty possesses fairly low levels of fitness in either state. It seems clear that there must be a better solution. Levins discusses this case in depth and concludes that for the biological case with genetic transmission of structure "polymorphism" or genetically maintained population heterogeneity will be selected for. The suggestion is that populations combine types (differing, say, in color, blood type, etc.) some of which are specialized to state 1 and some to state 2. With such a combination at least a portion of the population will always flourish and maintain the genetic diversity which allows it to continue to flourish when the environment changes state. The set of all such heterogeneous populations (composed of proportions of specialists to each of the two environments) can be represented in the fitness diagrams as a straight line joining the most extreme points with all combinations falling within this line.

Coarse-grained and uncertain variation favors a distinct form of generalism: polymorphism. We do not have to search very far to find an analogous outcome. Organizations may federate in such a way that supra-organizations consisting of heterogeneous collections of specialist organi-

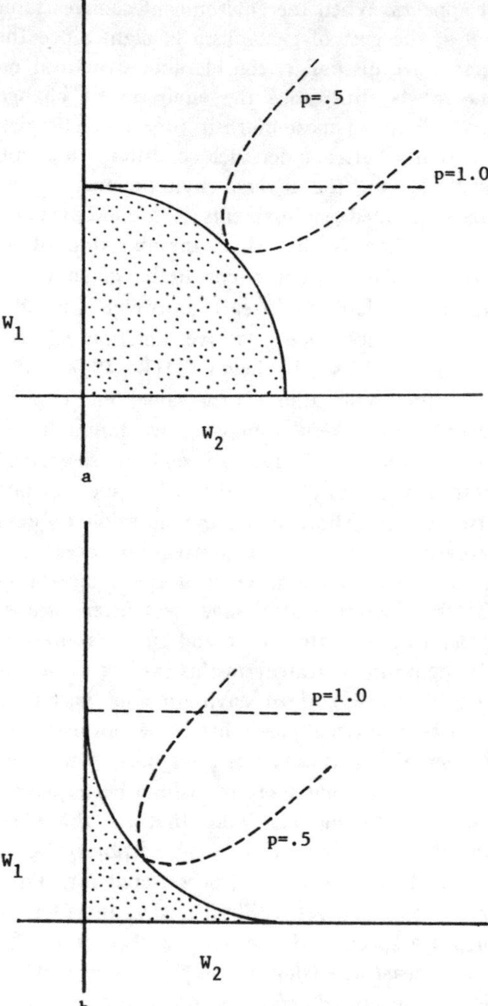

FIG. 3.—Optimal adaptation in coarse-grained environments; *a*, convex fitness set; *b*, concave fitness set.

zations pool resources. When the environment is uncertain and coarse-grained and subunits difficult to set up and tear down, the costs of maintaining the unwieldy structure imposed by federation may be more than offset by the fact that at least a portion of the amalgamated organization will do well no matter what the state of the environment. In terms of the model suggested above there are no other situations in which such federated organizations have a competitive advantage. And even in this case, the only time during which they have such an advantage is when coarse-grained variation is uncertain.

Such an amalgamated "holding company" pattern may be observed in modern universities. Enrollment and research support wax and wane over time as do the yield on invested endowment securities and the beneficence of legislatures. Some of these resources follow predictable cycles. Others do not. But it is extremely expensive to build up and dismantle academic units. It is costly not only in money but also in the energies consumed by political conflict. Consequently, universities are constantly "taxing" subunits with plentiful environments to subsidize less fortunate subunits. It is common, for instance, for universities to allocate faculty positions according to some fixed master plan, undersupporting the rapidly growing departments and maintaining excess faculty in others. This partial explanation of the unwieldly structures that encompass liberal arts departments, professional schools, research laboratories, etc., is at least as persuasive as explanations that emphasize intellectual interdependence among units.

Much more can be said concerning applications of niche theory to organization-environment relations. We have focused on a simple version highlighting the interplay between competition and environmental variation in the determination of optimal adaptive structure in order to show that the principle of isomorphism needs considerable expansion to deal with multiple environmental outcomes and their associated uncertainty. The literature in ecology to which we have made reference is growing exponentially at the moment and new results and models are appearing monthly. The products of these developments provide students of organizations with a rich potential for the study of organization-environment relations.

Consider an example. In his analysis of bureaucratic and craft administration or production, Stinchcombe (1959) argued that construction firms do not rely upon bureaucratically organized administrative staffs because of seasonal fluctuations in demand. Administrative staffs constitute an overhead cost which remains roughly constant over the year. The advantage of the otherwise costly (in terms of salaries) craft administration is that coordination of work is accomplished through a reliance upon prior socialization of craftsmen and upon organization. Since employment levels can more easily be increased or decreased with demand under a craft system, administrative costs are more easily altered to meet demand.

The fundamental source of this pattern is the seasonal variation in construction. In ecological terms, the demand environment is coarse-grained. In addition, the two states defined by season are quite different, resulting in a concave fitness curve. Craft-administered housing construction firms are probably quite inefficient when demand is at its peak and when the kind of housing under construction is standardized. In such situations, we would expect this form of organization to face stiff competition from other firms. For instance, in regions where housing construction is less seasonal, modular housing, mobile homes, and prefabricated housing are more likely to flourish and we would expect the construction business to be more highly bureaucratized.

Another variation in demand is to be found in the business cycle. While seasonal fluctuations are stable (uncertainty is low), interest rates, labor relations, and materials costs are more difficult to predict. Variations of this sort should favor a generalist mode of adaptation. That is, when environments are coarse-grained, characterized by concave fitness curves, and uncertain, populations of organizations will be more likely to survive if they hedge their bets by seeking a wider variety of resource bases. For this reason, we think, craft-administered construction organizations are frequently general contractors who not only build houses but engage in other kinds of construction as well (shopping plazas, office buildings, etc.). In comparison, modular housing is cheaper and the units are installed on rented space. Consequently, interest rates are less important. Since organizations producing this kind of housing do not employ craftsmen but use the cheapest and least skilled labor they can obtain, labor relations are less problematical. It may also be that their reliance on different materials (e.g., sheet aluminum) contributes to a lower level of uncertainty. In consequence, we would expect this form of organization to be more highly specialized in its adaptation (of course there are technical factors which also contribute to this as well).

Craft-administered construction firms are set up in such a way that they can adapt rapidly to changes in demand, and they can adapt to different construction problems by varying the mix of skills represented in their work force. Bureaucratically administered construction firms are more specialized and as a result they are efficient only when demand is high, and very inefficient when it is low. We also believe that they tend to be more specialized with regard to type of construction. Craft-administered organizations sacrifice efficient exploitation of their niche for flexibility. Bureaucratic organizations choose the opposite strategy. This formulation is an extension of Stinchcombe's and serves to show that his argument is essentially ecological.

VII. DISCUSSION

Our aim in this paper has been to move toward an application of modern population ecology theory to the study of organization-environment relations. For us, the central question is, why are there so many kinds of organizations? Phrasing the question in this way opens the possibility of applying a rich variety of formal models to the analysis of the effects of environmental variations on organizational structure.

We begin with Hawley's classic formulation of human ecology. However, we recognize that ecological theory has progressed enormously since sociologists last systematically applied ideas from bioecology to social organization. Nonetheless, Hawley's theoretical perspective remains a very useful point of departure. In particular we concentrate on the principle of isomorphism. This principle asserts that there is a one-to-one correspondence between structural elements of social organization and those units that mediate flows of essential resources into the system. It explains the variations in organizational forms in equilibrium. But any observed isomorphism can arise from purposeful adaptation of organizations to the common constraints they face or because nonisomorphic organizations are selected against. Surely both processes are at work in most social systems. We believe that the organizations literature has emphasized the former to the exclusion of the latter.

We suspect that careful empirical research will reveal that for wide classes of organizations there are very strong inertial pressures on structure arising both from internal arrangements (e.g., internal politics) and the environment (e.g., public legitimation of organizational activity). To claim otherwise is to ignore the most obvious feature of organizational life. Failing churches do not become retail stores; nor do firms transform themselves into churches. Even within broad areas of organizational action, such as higher education and labor union activity, there appear to be substantial obstacles to fundamental structural change. Research is needed on this issue. But until we see evidence to the contrary, we will continue to doubt that the major features of the world of organizations arise through learning or adaptation. Given these doubts, it is important to explore an evolutionary explanation of the principle of isomorphism. That is, we wish to embed the principle of isomorphism within an explicit selection framework.

In order to add selection processes we propose a competition theory using Lotka-Volterra models. This theory relies on growth models that appear suitable for representing both organizational development and the growth of populations of organizations. Recent work by bioecologists on Lotka-Volterra systems yields propositions that have immediate relevance for the study of organization-environment relations. These results concern the effects of changes in the number and mixture of constraints upon systems with regard to the upper bound of the diversity of forms of organization. We propose that such propositions can be tested by examining the impact of varieties of state regulation both on size distributions and on the diversity of organizational forms within broadly defined areas of activity (e.g., medical care, higher education, and newspaper publishing).

A more important extension of Hawley's work introduces dynamic considerations. The fundamental issue here concerns the meaning of isomorphism in situations in which the environment to which units are adapted is changing and uncertain. Should "rational" organizations attempt to develop specialized isomorphic structural relations with one of the possible environmental states? Or should they adopt a more plastic strategy and institute more generalized structural features? The isomorphism principle does not speak to these issues.

We suggest that the concrete implication of generalism for organizations is the accumulation and retention of varieties of excess capacity. To retain the flexibility of structure required for adaptation to different environmental outcomes requires that some capacities be held in reserve and not committed to action. Generalists will always be outperformed by specialists who, with the same levels of resources, happen to have hit upon their optimal environment. Consequently, in any cross-section the generalists will appear inefficient because excess capacity will often be judged waste. Nonetheless, organizational slack is a pervasive feature of many types of organizations. The question then arises: what types of environments favor generalists? Answering this question comprehensively takes one a long way toward understanding the dynamic of organization-environment relations.

We begin addressing this question in the suggestive framework of Levins's (1962, 1968) fitness-set theory. This is one of a class of recent theories that relates the nature of environmental uncertainty to optimal levels of structural specialism. Levins argues that along with uncertainty one must consider the grain of the environment or the lumpiness of environmental outcomes. The theory indicates that specialism is always favored in stable or certain environments. This is no surprise. But contrary to the view widely held in the organizations literature, the theory also indicates that generalism is not always optimal in uncertain environments. When the environment shifts uncertainly among states that place very different demands on the organization, and the duration of environmental states is short relative to the life of the organization (variation is fine-grained), populations of organizations that specialize will be favored over those that generalize. This is because organizations that attempt to adapt to each environmental outcome will spend most of their time adjusting structure and very little time in organizational action directed at other ends.

Stated in these terms, the proposition appears obvious. However, when one reads the literature on organization-environment relations, one finds that it was not so obvious. Most important, the proposition follows from a simple explicit model that has the capacity to unify a wide variety of propositions relating environmental variations to organizational structure.

We have identified some of the leading conceptual and methodological obstacles to applying population ecology models to the study of organization-environment relations. We pointed to differences between human and nonhuman social organization in terms of mechanisms of structural invariance and structural change, associated problems of delimiting populations of organizations, and difficulties in defining fitness for populations of expandable units. In each case we have merely sketched the issues and proposed short-run simplifications which would facilitate the application of existing models. Clearly, each issue deserves careful scrutiny.

At the moment we are frustrated at least as much by the lack of empirical information on rates of selection in populations of organizations as by the unresolved issues just mentioned. Census data are presented in a manner that renders the calculation of failure rates impossible; and little longitudinal research on populations of organizations has been reported. We do, however, have some information on rates of selection. We know, for example, that failure rates for small businesses are high. By recent estimates upwards of 8% of small business firms in the United States fail each year (Hollander 1967; Bolton 1971; see also Churchill 1955).

In part this high failure rate reflects what Stinchcombe (1965) called the liability of newness. Many new organizations attempt to enter niches that have already been filled by organizations that have amassed social, economic, and political resources that make them difficult to dislodge. It is important to determine whether there is any selective disadvantage of smallness not of newness.

We doubt that many readers will dispute the contention that failure rates are high for new and/or small organizations. However, much of the sociological literature and virtually all of the critical literature on large organizations tacitly accepts the view that such organizations are not subject to strong selection pressures. While we do not yet have the empirical data to judge this hypothesis, we can make several comments. First, we do not dispute that the largest organizations individually and collectively exercise strong dominance over most of the organizations that constitute their environments. But it does not follow from the observation that such organizations are strong in any one period that they will be strong in every period. Thus, it is interesting to know how firmly embedded are the largest and most powerful organizations. Consider the so-called Fortune 500, the largest publicly owned industrial firms in the United States. We contrasted the lists for 1955 and 1975 (adjusting for pure name changes). Of those on the list in 1955, only 268 (53.6%) were still listed in 1975. One hundred twenty-two had disappeared through merger, 109 had slipped off the "500," and one (a firm specializing in Cuban sugar!) had been liquidated. The number whose relative sales growth caused them to be dropped from the list is quite impressive in that the large number of mergers had opened many slots on the list. So we see that, whereas actual liquidation was rare for the largest industrial firms in the United States over a 20-year period, there was a good deal of volatility with regard to position in this pseudodominance structure because of both mergers and slipping sales.[12]

Second, the choice of time perspective is important. Even the largest and most powerful organizations fail to survive over long periods. For example, of the thousands of firms in business in the United States during the Revolution, only 13 survive as autonomous firms and seven as recognizable divisions of firms (*Nation's Business* 1976). Presumably one needs a longer time perspective to study the population ecology of the largest and most dominant organizations.

Third, studying small organizations is not such a bad idea. The sociological literature has concentrated on the largest organizations for obvious design reasons. But, if inertial pressures on certain aspects of structure are strong enough, intense selection among small organizations may greatly constrain the variety observable among large organizations. At least some elements of structure change with size (as we argued in Section III) and the pressure toward inertia should not be overemphasized. Nonetheless we see much value in studies of the organizational life cycle that would inform us as to which aspects of structure get locked in during which phases of the cycle. For example, we conjecture that a critical period is that during which the organization grows beyond the control of a single owner/manager. At this time the manner in which authority is delegated, if at all, seems likely to have a lasting impact on organizational structure. This is the period during which an organization becomes less an extension of one or a few dominant individuals and more an organization per se with a life of its own. If the selection pressures at this point are as intense as anecdotal evidence suggests they are, selection models will prove very useful in accounting for the varieties of forms among the whole range of organizations.

The optimism of the previous paragraph should be tempered by the realization that when one examines the largest and most dominant organizations, one is usually considering only a small number of organizations. The smaller the number, the less useful are models that depend on the type of random mechanisms that underlie population ecology models.

Fourth, we must consider what one anonymous reader, caught up in the spirit of our paper, called the anti-eugenic actions of the state in

12 From at least some perspectives, mergers can be viewed as changes in form. This will almost certainly be the case when the organizations merged have very different structures. These data also indicate a strong selective advantage for a conglomerate form of industrial organization.

saving firms such as Lockheed from failure. This is a dramatic instance of the way in which large dominant organizations can create linkages with other large and powerful ones so as to reduce selection pressures. If such moves are effective, they alter the pattern of selection. In our view the selection pressure is bumped up to a higher level. So instead of individual organizations failing, entire networks fail. The general consequence of a large number of linkages of this sort is an increase in the instability of the entire system (Simon 1962, 1973; May 1973), and therefore we should see boom and bust cycles of organizational outcomes. Selection models retain relevance, then, even when the systems of organizations are tightly coupled (see Hannan 1976).

Finally, some readers of earlier drafts have (some approvingly, some disapprovingly) treated our arguments as metaphoric. This is not what we intend. In a fundamental sense all theoretical activity involves metaphoric activity (although admittedly the term "analogue" comes closer than does "metaphor"). The use of metaphors or analogues enters into the formulation of "if . . . then" statements. For example, certain molecular genetic models draw an analogy between DNA surfaces and crystal structures. The latter have simple well-behaved geometric structures amenable to strong topological (mathematical) analysis. No one argues that DNA proteins are crystals; but to the extent that their surfaces have certain crystal-like properties, the mathematical model used to analyze crystals will shed light on the genetic structure. This is, as we understand it, the general strategy of model building.

We have, for example, used results that rely on the application of certain logistic differential equations, the Lotka-Volterra equations. No known population (of animals, or of organizations) grows in exactly the manner specified by this mathematic model (and this fact has caused numerous naturalists to argue that the model is biologically meaningless). What the equations do is to model the growth path of populations that exist on finite resources in a closed system (where population growth in the absence of competition is logistic and the presence of competing populations lowers carrying capacities in that system). To the extent that the interactions of populations of *Paramecium aureilia* and *P. caudatum* (Gause's experiment) meet the conditions of the model, the model explains certain key features of population dynamics and the relationship of environmental variations to structure. To the extent that the interactions of populations of rational-legal bureaucracies and populations of patrimonial bureaucracies also meet the conditions of the model, the model explains the same important phenomena. Neither the protozoa nor the bureaucracies behave exactly as the model stipulates. The model is an abstraction that will lead to insight whenever the stated conditions are approximated.

American Journal of Sociology

Throughout we make a strong continuity-of-nature hypothesis. We propose that, whenever the stated conditions hold, the models lead to valuable insights regardless of whether the populations under study are composed of protozoans or organizations. We do not argue "metaphorically." That is, we do *not* argue as follows: an empirical regularity is found to hold for certain protozoans; because we hypothesize that populations of organizations are like populations of protozoans in essential ways, we propose that the generalizations derived from the latter will hold for organizations as well. This is the kind of reasoning by which biological propositions have most often entered sociological arguments (e.g., the famous—or infamous—organismic analogy advanced by Spencer).

Instead of applying biological laws to human social organization, we advocate the application of population ecology theories. As we have indicated at a number of points, these theories are quite general and must be modified for any concrete application (sociological *or* biological). Our purpose has been twofold. First, we sketched some of the alterations in perspective required if population ecology theories are to be applied to the study of organizations. Second, we wished to stimulate a reopening of the lines of communication between sociology and ecology. It is ironic that Hawley's (1944, p. 399) diagnosis of some 30 years ago remains apt today: "Probably most of the difficulties which beset human ecology may be traced to the isolation of the subject from the mainstream of ecological thought."

REFERENCES

Aldrich, Howard E., and Jeffrey Pfeffer. 1976. "Environments of Organizations." *Annual Review of Sociology* 2:79–105.

Aldrich, Howard E., and Albert J. Reiss. 1976. "Continuities in the Study of Ecological Succession: Changes in the Race Composition of Neighborhoods and Their Businesses." *American Journal of Sociology* 81 (January): 846–66.

Blau, Peter M. 1972. "Interdependence and Hierarchy in Organizations." *Social Science Research* 1 (April): 1–24.

Blau, Peter M., and Richard A. Schoenherr. 1971. *The Structure of Organizations*. New York: Basic.

Blau, Peter M., and W. Richard Scott. 1962. *Formal Organizations*. San Francisco: Chandler.

Bolton, J. E. 1971. *Small Firms*. Report of the Committee of Inquiry on Small Firms. London: Her Majesty's Stationery Office.

Boulding, Kenneth. 1953. "Toward a General Theory of Growth." *Canadian Journal of Economics and Political Science* 19:326–40.

Burns, Tom, and G. M. Stalker. 1961. *The Management of Innovation*. London: Tavistock.

Caplow, Theodore. 1957. "Organizational Size." *Administrative Science Quarterly* 1 (March): 484–505.

Churchill, Betty C. 1955. "Age and Life Expectancy of Business Firms." *Survey of Current Business* 35 (December): 15–19.

Crozier, Michel. 1964. *The Bureaucratic Phenomenon*. Chicago: University of Chicago Press.

Cyert, Richard M., and James G. March. 1963. *A Behavioral Theory of the Firm.* Englewood Cliffs, N.J.: Prentice-Hall.

Downs, Anthony. 1967. *Inside Bureaucracy.* Boston: Little, Brown.

Durkheim, É. 1947. *The Division of Labor in Society.* Translated by G. Simpson. Glencoe, Ill.: Free Press.

Elton, C. 1927. *Animal Ecology.* London: Sidgwick & Jackson.

Freeman, John. 1975. "The Unit Problem in Organizational Research." Presented at the annual meeting of the American Sociological Association, San Francisco.

Freeman, John, and Jack Brittain. 1977. "Union Merger Processes and Industrial Environments." *Industrial Relations,* in press.

Friedman, Milton. 1953. *Essays on Positive Economics.* Chicago: University of Chicago Press.

Gause, G. F. 1934. *The Struggle for Existence.* Baltimore: Williams & Wilkins.

Graicunas, V. A. 1933. "Relationship in Organizations." *Bulletin of the International Management Institute* (March), pp. 183–87.

Granovetter, Mark S. 1973. "The Strength of Weak Ties." *American Journal of Sociology* 78 (May): 1360–80.

Haire, Mason. 1959. "Biological Models and Empirical Histories of the Growth of Organizations." Pp. 272–306 in *Modern Organization Theory,* edited by Mason Haire. New York: Wiley.

Hannan, Michael T. 1975. "The Dynamics of Ethnic Boundaries." Unpublished.

———. 1976. "Modeling Stability and Complexity in Networks of Organizations." Presented at the annual meeting of the American Sociological Association, New York.

Hannan, Michael T., and John Freeman. 1974. "Environment and the Structure of Organizations." Presented at the annual meeting of the American Sociological Association, Montreal.

Hawley, Amos H. 1944. "Ecology and Human Ecology." *Social Forces* 22 (May): 398–405.

———. 1950. *Human Ecology: A Theory of Community Structure.* New York: Ronald.

———. 1968. "Human Ecology." Pp. 328–37 in *International Encyclopedia of the Social Sciences,* edited by David L. Sills. New York: Macmillan.

Hollander, Edward O., ed. 1967. *The Future of Small Business.* New York: Praeger.

Hummon, Norman P., Patrick Doreian, and Klaus Teuter. 1975. "A Structural Control Model of Organizational Change." *American Sociological Review* 40 (December): 812–24.

Hutchinson, G. Evelyn. 1957. "Concluding Remarks." *Cold Spring Harbor Symposium on Quantitative Biology* 22:415–27.

———. 1959. "Homage to Santa Rosalia, or Why Are There So Many Kinds of Animals?" *American Naturalist* 93:145–59.

Levin, Simon A. 1970. "Community Equilibrium and Stability: An Extension of the Competitive Exclusion Principle." *American Naturalist* 104 (September–October): 413–23.

Levine, Sol, and Paul E. White. 1961. "Exchange as a Framework for the Study of Interorganizational Relationships." *Administrative Science Quarterly* 5 (March): 583–601.

Levins, Richard. 1962. "Theory of Fitness in a Heterogeneous Environment. I. The Fitness Set and Adaptive Function." *American Naturalist* 96 (November–December): 361–78.

———. 1968. *Evolution in Changing Environments.* Princeton, N.J.: Princeton University Press.

MacArthur, Robert H. 1972. *Geographical Ecology: Patterns in the Distribution of Species.* Princeton, N.J.: Princeton University Press.

MacArthur, Robert H., and Richard Levins. 1964. "Competition, Habitat Selection and Character Displacement in Patchy Environment." *Proceedings of the National Academy of Sciences* 51:1207–10.

March, James G., and Herbert Simon. 1958. *Organizations.* New York: Wiley.
Marschak, Jacob, and Roy Radner. 1972. *Economic Theory of Teams.* New Haven, Conn.: Yale University Press.
May, Robert M. 1973. *Stability and Complexity in Model Ecosystems.* Princeton, N.J.: Princeton University Press.
Meyer, John W. 1970. "The Charter: Conditions of Diffuse Socialization in Schools." Pp. 564–78 in *Social Processes and Social Structures,* edited by W. Richard Scott. New York: Holt, Rinehart & Winston.
Monod, Jacques. 1971. *Chance and Necessity.* New York: Vintage.
Nation's Business. 1976. "America's Oldest Companies." 64 (July): 36–37.
Nielsen, François, and Michael T. Hannan. 1977. "The Expansion of National Educational Systems: Tests of a Population Ecology Model." *American Sociological Review,* in press.
Parsons, Talcott. 1956. "Suggestions for a Sociological Approach to the Theory of Organizations, I." *Administrative Science Quarterly* 1 (March): 63–85.
Penrose, Edith T. 1959. *The Theory of the Growth of the Firm.* New York: Wiley.
Selznick, Philip. 1957. *Leadership in Administration.* New York: Row, Peterson.
Simon, Herbert A. 1962. "The Architecture of Complexity." *Proceedings of the American Philosophical Society* 106 (December): 467–82.
———. 1973. "The Organization of Complex Systems." Pp. 1–28 in *Hierarchy Theory: The Challenge of Complex Systems,* edited by H. Patee. New York: Braziller.
Simon, Herbert A., and C. P. Bonini. 1958. "The Size Distribution of Business Firms." *American Economic Review* 48 (September): 607–17.
Stinchcombe, Arthur L. 1959. "Bureaucratic and Craft Administration of Production." *Administrative Science Quarterly* 4 (June): 168–87.
———. 1965. "Social Structure and Organizations." Pp. 153–93 in *Handbook of Organizations,* edited by James G. March. Chicago: Rand McNally.
Templeton, Alan R., and Edward A. Rothman. 1974. "Evolution in Heterogenous Environments." *American Naturalist* 108 (July–August): 409–28.
Thompson, James D. 1967. *Organizations in Action.* New York: McGraw-Hill.
Turk, Herman. 1970. "Interorganizational Networks in Urban Society: Initial Perspectives and Comparative Research." *American Sociological Review* 35 (February): 1–19.
Whittaker, Robert N., and Simon Levin, eds. 1976. *Niche: Theory and Application.* Stroudsberg, Pa.: Dowden, Hutchinson & Ross.
Winter, Sidney G., Jr. 1964. "Economic 'Natural Selection' and the Theory of the Firm." *Yale Economic Essays* 4:224–72.
Zald, Mayer. 1970. "Political Economy: A Framework for Analysis." Pp. 221–61 in *Power in Organizations,* edited by M. N. Zald. Nashville, Tenn.: Vanderbilt University Press.

[18]

Munificence and Carrying Capacity of the Environment and Organization Formation

Pamela Hammers Specht

Two streams of research and theory development, resource dependence and population ecology, are combined to develop a model of the relationship between organization formation and environmental munificence and carrying capacity. An interactive and curvilinear relationship is predicted. Munificence is reflected in social, economic, political, market, and infrastructural resources. Carrying capacity involves density and prior births and deaths in an organization's population. Propositions and research recommendations are presented.

Theory development and research on the relationship between the environment and the rate of organization formation are in their early stages. The majority of studies on the relationship have been conducted in the last decade. (For a thorough review of the research, see Specht, 1991.) Past literature has concentrated, instead, on the importance of founders' characteristics to organization formation rates. (See, for example, literature reviews by Gartner, 1985; Wortman, 1987; Aldrich, 1990.) Theorists have indicated that this traits or supply perspective has reached a dead end (e.g., Aldrich, 1990) and has not substantially contributed to the understanding of new firm foundings. The study of the role of the environment, the rates or demand perspective (Peterson, 1980), is seen as a more viable approach.

Proponents of the demand perspective indicate that characteristics of the environment determine rates of new business foundings. Given sufficient availability of resources, founders will emerge (Romanelli, 1989b). While not denying the role played by founders' characteristics, the demand perspective proposes that the environment is more important to understanding organization formation (Cross, 1981; McCarthy, Wolfson, Baker, & Mosakowski, 1988; Staber, 1989).

Theoretical development lags behind empirical research on the relationship between the environment and formation (Fombrun, 1988). Few models exist. (For a thorough review of model development, see Specht, 1991.) Relationships among the variables presented in the models are usually not completely explained. For example, propositions usually do not accompany the models. Two major theoretical frameworks, population ecology and resource dependence, are used to guide research and to provide explanations on how the environment affects formation rates. Theorists and researchers often write from only one orientation, ignoring the valid contributions of the other framework.

This presentation addresses weaknesses of past theory development efforts. A comprehensive model combining, for the first time, the ecological and resource dependence frameworks, is developed. Variable relationships are clearly defined. First, the meaning of organization formation is discussed, followed by a description of the resource dependence and population ecology frameworks. Then the model and propositions are presented with research recommendations.

ORGANIZATION FORMATION

Organization formation models are difficult to test because, among a number of problems, formation does not have a universally accepted meaning, nor is it easily operationalized. Mason (1983) indicates that the definition of a new firm is not an unambiguous issue. The main definitional difficulties concern four aspects of formation:

1. Start-up date: The definition of the start-up date is arbitrary. Approaches in the literature have included the date the company registers or incorporates and the date the first employee is hired. Obviously, firms can "start-up" before either of these events takes place.
2. Changes in activity: If a company starts as a service firm and then switches to manufacturing, is it a new firm?
3. Independence: Independence usually means the firm has no obvious parent. Under this definition, new franchises are not new firms.
4. Newness: Newness is related to the "changes in activity" aspect listed above. Is the company new if the owner bought an existing company and changed some of its activities?

Katz and Gartner (1988) address some of these definitional difficulties with a compromise. They indicate that an organization has four properties as it comes into existence. These are intentionality (distinct goals), resources, boundary (similar to Mason's "independence"), and exchange. When studying organization creation, they suggest using at least one of these properties as a sampling frame.

The Katz and Gartner properties are recommended when testing the model developed here. Researchers need to be aware that most published lists of new firms will contain inaccuracies and omissions because of Mason's four definitional problems. Interviews and detective work will have to supplement published lists. Published accounts of the research must detail the operationalization of formation to facilitate comparisons and conclusions across studies. (The review of the literature for this presentation revealed that such detail is lacking in most studies.)

ENVIRONMENTAL CHARACTERISTICS

Environmental Munificence

Resource dependence theory proposes that the need for external resources and information determines the degree of dependence on the environment (Boyd, 1990). Firms face different levels of dependence. The environment is seen as a pool of resources, and the degree of resource abundance is called environmental munificence (Dess & Beard, 1984; Castrogiovanni, 1991).

Table 1 presents the environmental resources cited in the organization formation literature. A thorough literature review was conducted using several on-line databases. The relationship between environmental munificence and the rate of organization formation assumed in the literature is direct.

Populations of new firms studied reflect a worldwide interest in new firm foundings. Several studies addressed a large number of environmental resources (Wilken, 1979; Cross, 1981; Moyes & Westhead, 1990). Such studies are valuable for determining which resources are most significant in facilitating organization formation.

Research results are sometimes conflicting. For example, support of the government was found to be significant in some studies (e.g., Young & Francis, 1989) and insignificant in others (Del Monte & De Luzenberger, 1989; Mason, 1989). Some resources were found not to be linearly related to organization formation (e.g., unemployment). Relationships were tested without much of a theory base. Overall, research on the relationship of munificence to organization formation is in its infancy and in need of theory development.

Environmental Carrying Capacity

Population ecology theory also emphasizes the importance of environmental resources. Central to the theory is the niche concept, defined as resource space and regarded as a variable property of the environment (Hawley, 1988, p. xiv). According to Brittain and Freeman (1980, p. 293), a niche is any particular combination, or set of combinations, of resource utilization that distinguishes one organizational population from another. Niches may overlap on various resource dimensions.

Another important concept in ecology theory is the environment's carrying capacity. Ecologists have a theoretical objective of explaining foundings by studying the relationship between foundings and rates of prior founding and failing (Staber, 1989). Carrying capacity is related to the density or number of organizations competing for the same resources in a niche. Density is determined by prior births and deaths in an organization's population.

Carrying capacity affects founding rates by several processes. According to Hannan and Freeman (1988, p. 21):

> existing organizations are the only training grounds for knowledgeable organization-builders. . . . The number of foundings depends on the number of jobs in existing organizations that give requisite training. Marrett (1980) argued that high density increases the founding rate by widening and strengthening the networks that connect persons with the inclination and skills to succeed in creating a certain kind of organization. . . . However, as density grows, supplies of potential organizers, members, patrons, and resources become exhausted. Moreover, existing organizations respond to increasing competitive pressures by opposing attempts at creating still more organizations.

Hannan and Freeman (1988) found in their study of national labor unions and manufacturers of semiconductor electronics devices that founding rates are proportional to the legitimacy of the population and inversely proportional to the level of competition. Both relationships are nonlinear: the legitimacy process dominates when N is small; the competition process dominates when N is large.

The effects of prior organization births and deaths on founding rates have also been studied for voluntary social service organizations in the U.S. (Tucker et al., 1988), newspapers in Argentina and Ireland (Delacroix & Carroll, 1983), in the San Francisco area (Carroll & Huo, 1986), and for U.S. banks and life insurance companies (Ranger-Moore, Banaszak-Holl, & Hannan, 1991). Evidence indicates an inverted U-shaped relationship because of the legitimacy and competition processes.

Table 1

Environmental Munificence Factors from the Organization Formation Literature[a,b]

Social
- networks(+)
  - (Wilken, 1979; *Marrett, 1980; Langton, 1984; Robben, 1984;* Gartner, 1985; Aldrich & Zimmer, 1986; Rock, 1988; Manning, Birley, & Norburn, 1989)
- support of sociopolitical elites(+), cultural acceptance(+)
  - (*Schell & Davig, 1981;* Gartner, 1985; *Bull & Winter, 1991*)

Economic
- capital availability(+)
  - (Cross, 1981; *Pennings, 1982a;* Gartner, 1985; *McCarthy, Wolfson, Baker, & Mosakowski, 1988*)
- aggregate economic indicators (mostly +)
  - productivity, household income, industrialization (Walton, 1977)
- economic recessions (+,O)
  - (*Delacroix & Carroll, 1983*(+); Gould & Keeble, 1984(+); Shutt & Whittington, 1987(+); *Mason, 1989*(O); *Staber, 1989*(+)
- unemployment(∩);
  - (*Johnson & Cathcart, 1979; Pennings, 1982a;* Gould & Keeble, 1984; *Whittington, 1984; Hamilton, 1989*)

Political
- support of government (+,O)
  - (Leff, 1979(+); Wilken, 1979(+); Pennings, 1980(+); *Delacroix & Carroll, 1983*(+); Gartner, 1985(+); *McCarthy, Wolfson, Baker, & Mosakowski, 1988*(+); *Tucker, Singh, Meinhard, & House, 1988*(+); Del Monte & Deluzenberger, 1989(O); *Gripaios, Bishop, Gripaios, & Herbert, 1989*(O); *Mason, 1989*(O); *Staber, 1989*(+); Young & Francis, 1989(+); *Walker & Greenstreet, 1991*(+))

Infrastructure Development
- quality of life(+, −,O)
  - housing & urban services, health, income distribution, local control
    - (Walton, 1977(+), *Pennings, 1982a,b*(+, −,O); Gartner, 1985(+); *Bull & Winter, 1991*(−))
- education system, level of education (+,O)
  - (*Pennings, 1982a*(+); Gould & Keeble, 1984(+); *Robben, 1984*(+); Gartner, 1985(+); Romanelli, 1989b(+); *Gripaios, Bishop, Gripaois, & Herbert, 1989*(O); *Bar-El & Felsenstein, 1989*(+); *Bull & Winter, 1991*(+))
- transportation and distribution systems(+)
  - (Langton, 1984; *Robben, 1984;* Gartner, 1985)
- communication systems, including media(+)
  - (Langton, 1984; Romanelli, 1989b)
- nature of local labor market(+, −,O)
  - (*Johnson & Cathcart, 1979*(+, −,O); *Pennings, 1982a*(+,O); *Gudgin & Fothergill, 1984*(O, −); Gould & Keeble, 1984(+); *Lloyd & Mason, 1984*(+, −); *O'Farrell & Crouchley, 1984*(+, −); *Whittington, 1984*(O); Gartner, 1985(+); *Bar-El & Felsenstein, 1989*(+); *Mason, 1989*(+, −))
- incubator organizations(+)
  - (*Johnson & Cathcart, 1979;* Cross, 1981; Gartner, 1985; *Hannan & Freeman,* 1986, *1987;* Young & Francis, 1989; Angel, 1990; Westhead, 1990)
- community size (∩, +)
  - (*Pennings, 1982b*(∩); Gartner, 1985(+))
- information accessibility(+)
  - (Romanelli, 1989b)
- accessibility of suppliers and customers(+)
  - (Gartner, 1985)
- availability of premises (mostly +)
  - (Gartner, 1985(+); *Mason, 1989*(+); *Gripaios, Bishop, Gripaios, & Herbert, 1989*(+); *Turok & Richardson,* 1991(O)

Market Emergence
- niche emergence(+)
  - (Leff, 1979; *Langton, 1984;* Boeker, 1988; *Delacroix & Solt, 1988;* Romanelli, 1989a; Young & Francis, 1989)
- technological innovation(+)
  - (Cross, 1981; Gould & Keeble, 1984; *Tushman & Anderson, 1986; Brittain & Wholey, 1988; Mason, 1989;* Romanelli, 1989a)

[a] Research studies are in italics.

[b] Direction of relationship with firm formation: O: none; +: positive; −: negative; ∩: curvilinear.

Much stronger evidence and more studies exist on the relationship between carrying capacity and formation rate than on the relationship between munificence and formation rate. Because of the number of studies supporting the inverted U-shaped relationship and the lack of contrary findings, further research on the relationship of carrying capacity to formation rate would be unnecessarily duplicative.

MODEL

As stated earlier, research results are mixed on the relationship between munificence and rates of formation. The reason may be that the relationship is complex and dynamic, rather than direct. Environmental munificence may interact with carrying capacity to affect formation rate. There may be a positive relationship between environmental munificence and environmental carrying capacity (Pennings, 1982b, p. 77). As resources are made available for new firm foundings, carrying capacity for new organizations may increase followed by a formation rate increase. But as the resources are used, their availability decreases, causing a decrease in carrying capacity and, subsequently, in the formation rate. These relationships are formally stated in the following propositions:

Proposition 1: Environmental munificence is positively related to environmental carrying capacity.

Proposition 2: As environmental munificence and carrying capacity increase, rate of organization formation increases.

Proposition 3: As the rate of organization formation increases, environmental munificence, then carrying capacity, will decrease, eventually resulting in a decrease in the formation rate.

Figure 1 presents a model depicting the proposed relationships among environmental munificence, carrying capacity, and organization formation. According to Propositions 1 and 2, munificence and carrying capacity interact to determine rate of formation. The relationship can be expressed as the equation:

Rate of Organization Formation =
(a + [b × Carrying Capacity]) Social Munificence +
(a + [b × Carrying Capacity]) Economic Munificence +
(a + [b × Carrying Capacity]) Political Munificence +
(a + [b × Carrying Capacity]) Infrasturcture Munificence +
(a + [b × Carrying Capacity]) Market Munificence +
(a + [b × Carrying Capacity]).

According to Proposition 3, the relationship of munificence and carrying capacity to rate of formation is curvilinear (inverted U-shaped) over time with munificence always having a greater value than carrying capacity.

RESEARCH RECOMMENDATIONS

The proposed relationships require testing. Research is needed that provides greater detail on how changes in the environment influence formation rates (e.g., Wholey & Brittain, 1986). Carroll and Hannan (1989, p. 426) speculate on whether the delayed effect of density at time of founding is best explained by resource scarcity or niche packing: "While the two explanations do not conflict, research that distinguishes the two will clarify the fundamental dynamics." The propositions and model in this presentation

Figure 1
Relationship of Environmental Munificence and Carrying Capacity to Organization Formation

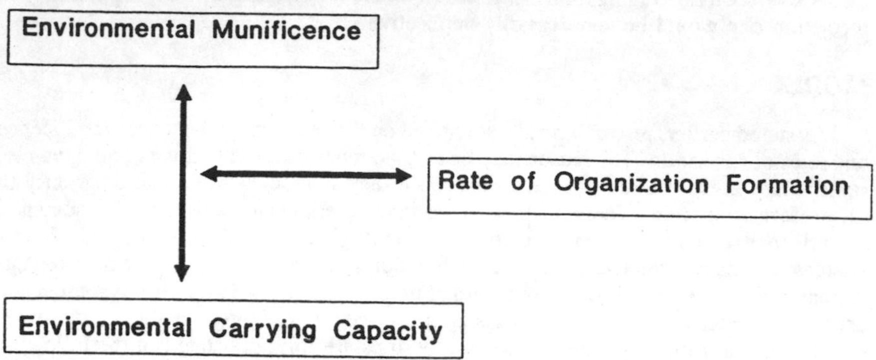

specify the impact of resource scarcity. Additional models and research are required on niche packing or how competition affects formation rates.

A critical window probably exists between the time munificence declines and the time carrying capacity declines. This time period represents instability in a population of organizations and high environmental uncertainty for new firm owners and would-be entrepreneurs. Intervention methods to increase formation rates when munificence and carrying capacity are declining should be studied. An infusion of additional resources before carrying capacity decreases could slow down or cease the formation rate decline. If no infusion of resources occurs, a new firm owner could change to a new niche rather than face possible firm death. However, if the problem is niche packing, instead of resource scarcity, increasing resources may not stop formation rate decline, and a firm owner should switch niches regardless of resource abundance.

Additional research will also reveal whether some resources more than others significantly interact with carrying capacity to affect formation rates. The significant resources may vary by industry (e.g., Castrogiovanni, 1991) or by location (Bull & Winter, 1991). Regional differences in founding rates have already been shown in studies by Gudgin and Fothergill (1984) and Cross (1981). Significant variables may also differ depending on whether new organizations that represent first members of a new class or new organizations that are joining an existing population are being studied (Pennings, 1980).

Research results regarding the relationship between the environment and formation rates have obvious policy implications. For example, Walker and Greenstreet (1990) found that government incentives and assistance were decisive to the location decision for a manufacturing plant, but had little impact on in situ expansion. Further efforts to develop and test organization formation models are, therefore, valuable.

REFERENCES

Aldrich, H. (1990). Using an ecological perspective to study organizational founding rates. *Entrepreneurship Theory and Practice, 14*(3), 7-24.

Aldrich, H., & Zimmer, C. (1986). Entrepreneurship through social networks. In D. Sexton & R. Smilor (Eds.), *The art & science of entrepreneurship*, pp. 3-23. Cambridge, MA: Ballinger.

Angel, D. P. (1990). New firm formation in the semiconductor industry: Elements of a flexible manufacturing system. *Regional Studies, 24*(3), 211-221.

Bar-El. R., & Felsenstein, D. (1988). Technological profile and industrial structure: Implications for the development of sophisticated industry in peripheral areas. *Regional Studies, 23*(3), 253-266.

Boeker, W. P. (1988). Organizational origins: Entrepreneurial and environmental imprinting at the time of founding. In G. R. Carroll (Ed.), *Ecological models of organizations*, pp. 33-51. Cambridge, MA: Ballinger.

Boyd, B. (1990). Corporate linkages and organizational environment: A test of the resource dependence model. *Strategic Management Journal, 11*, 419-430.

Brittain, J. W., & Freeman, J. H. (1980). Organizational proliferation and density dependent selection. In J. Kimberly, R. Miles, & Associates (Eds.), *The organizational life cycle*, pp. 291-338. San Francisco: Jossey-Bass.

Brittain. J. W., & Wholey, D. R. (1988). Competition and coexistence in organizational communities: Population dynamics in electronic components manufacturing. In G. R. Carroll (Ed.), *Ecological models of organizations*, pp. 195-222. Cambridge, MA: Ballinger.

Bull. I., & Winter, F. (1991). Community differences in business births and business growths. *Journal of Business Venturing, 6*, 29-43.

Carroll, G. R., & Hannan, M. T. (1989). Density delay in the evolution of organizational populations: A model and five empirical tests. *Administrative Science Quarterly, 34*, 411-430.

Carroll, G. R., & Huo, Y. P. (1986). Organizational task and institutional environments in ecological perspective: Findings from the local newspaper industry. *American Journal of Sociology, 91*(4), 838-873.

Castrogiovanni, G. J. (1991). Environmental munificence: A theoretical assessment. *Academy of Management Review, 16*(3), 542-565.

Cross, M. (1981). *New firm formation and regional development*. Westmead, Farnborough, Hants., England: Gower Publishing Company.

Delacroix, J., & Carroll, G. R. (1983). Organizational foundings: An ecological study of the newspaper industries of Argentina and Ireland. *Administrative Science Quarterly, 28*, 274-291.

Delacroix, J., & Solt, M. E. (1988). Niche formation and foundings in the California wine industry, 1941–84. In G. R. Carroll (Ed.), *Ecological models of organizations*, pp. 53-70. Cambridge, MA: Ballinger.

Del Monte, A., & De Luzenberger, R. (1989). The effect of regional policy on new firm formation in southern Italy. *Regional Studies, 23*(3), 219-230.

Dess, G., & Beard, D. (1984). Dimensions of organizational task environments. *Administrative Science Quarterly, 29*, 52-73.

Fombrun, C. J. (1988). Crafting an institutionally informed ecology of organizations. In G. R. Carroll (Ed.), *Ecological models of organizations*, pp. 223-239. Cambridge, MA: Ballinger.

Gartner, W. B. (1985). A conceptual framework for describing the phenomenon of new venture creation. *Academy of Management Review, 10*(4), 696-706.

Gould, A., & Keeble, D. (1984). New firms and rural industrialization in East Anglia. *Regional Studies, 18*(3), 189-201.

Gripaios, P., Bishop, P., Gripaios, R., & Herbert, C. (1988). High technology industry in a peripheral area: The case of Plymouth. *Regional Studies, 23*(2), 151-157.

Gudgin, G., & Fothergill, S. (1984). Geographical variation in the rate of formation of new manufacturing firms. *Regional Studies, 18*(3), 203-206.

Hamilton, R. T. (1989). Unemployment and business formation rates: Reconciling time-series and cross-section evidence. *Environment and Planning A, 21*, 249-255.

Hannan, M. T., & Freeman, J. (1986). Where do organizational forms come from? *Sociological Forum, 1*(1), 50-72.

Hannan, M. R., & Freeman, J. (1987). The ecology of organizational founding: American labor unions, 1836–1985. *American Journal of Sociology, 92*(4), 910-943.

Hannan, M. R., & Freeman, J. (1988). Density dependence in the growth of organizational populations. In G. R. Carroll (Ed.), *Ecological models of organizations*, pp. 8-31. Cambridge, MA: Ballinger.

Hawley, A. H. (1988). Foreword. In G. R. Carroll (Ed.), *Ecological models of organizations*. Cambridge, MA: Ballinger.

Johnson, P. S., & Cathcart, D. G. (1979). New manufacturing firms and regional development: Some evidence from the northern region. *Regional Studies, 13*(3), 269-280.

Katz, J., & Gartner, W. B. (1988). Properties of emerging organizations. *Academy of Management Review, 13*(3), 429-441.

Langton, J. (1984). The ecological theory of bureaucracy: The case of Josiah Wedgwood and the British pottery industry. *Administrative Science Quarterly, 29*, 330-354.

Leff, N. H. (1979). Entrepreneurship and economic development: The problems revisited. *Journal of Economic Literature, 17*, 46-64.

Lloyd, P. E., & Mason, C. M. (1984). Spatial variations in new firm formation in the United Kingdom: Comparative evidence from Merseyside, Greater Manchester and South Hampshire. *Regional Studies, 18*(3), 207-220.

Manning, K., Birley, S., & Norburn, D. (1989). Developing a new ventures strategy. *Entrepreneurship Theory and Practice, 14*(1), 68-76.

Marrett, C. B. (1980). Influences on the rise of new organizations: The formation of women's medical societies. *Administrative Science Quarterly, 25*, 185-199.

Mason, C. (1983). Some definitional difficulties in new firms research. *Area, 15*(1), 53-60.

Mason, C. M. (1989). Explaining recent trends in new firm formation in the U.K.: Some evidence from South Hampshire. *Regional Studies, 23*(4), 331-346.

McCarthy, J. D., Wolfson, M., Baker, D. P., & Mosakowski, E. (1988). The founding of social movement organizations: Local citizens' groups opposing drunken driving. In G. R. Carroll (Ed.), *Ecological models of organizations*, pp. 71-84. Cambridge, MA: Ballinger.

Moyes, A., & Westhead, P. (1990). Environments for new firm formation in Great Britain. *Regional Studies, 24*(2), 123-136.

O'Farrell, P. N., & Crouchley, R. (1984). An industrial and spatial analysis of new firm formation in Ireland. *Regional Studies, 18*(3), 221-236.

Pennings, J. M. (1980). Environmental influences on the creation process. In J. Kimberly, R. Miles, & Associates (Eds.), *The organizational life cycle*, pp. 135-160. San Francisco: Jossey-Bass.

Pennings, J. M. (1982a). Organizational birth frequencies: An empirical investigation. *Administrative Science Quarterly*, *27*, 120-144.

Pennings, J. M. (1982b). The urban quality of life and entrepreneurship. *Academy of Management Journal*, *25*(1), 63-79.

Peterson, R. A. (1980). Entrepreneurship and organization. In P. C. Nystrom & W. H. Starbuck (Eds.), *Handbook of organization design*. New York: Oxford University Press.

Ranger-Moore, J., Banaszak-Holl, J., & Hannan, M. T. (1991). Density-dependent dynamics in regulated industries: Founding rates of banks and life insurance companies. *Administrative Science Quarterly*, *36*, 36-65.

Robben, A. C. G. M. (1984). Entrepreneurs and scale: Interactional and institutional constraints on the growth of small-scale enterprises in Brazil. *Anthropological Quarterly*, *57*(3), 125-138.

Rock, P. (1988). On the birth of organizations. *Canadian Journal of Sociology*, *13*(4), 359-384.

Romanelli, E. (1989a). Environments and strategies of organization start-up: Effects on early survival. *Administrative Science Quarterly*, *34*, 369-387.

Romanelli, E. (1989b). Organization birth and population variety: A community perspective on origins. In L. L. Cummings & B. M. Staw (Eds.), *Research in organizational behavior*, vol. 11, pp. 211-246. Greenwich, CT: JAI Press.

Schell, D. W., & Davig, W. (1981). The community infrastructure of entrepreneurship: A sociopolitical analysis. *Proceedings of the 1981 Babson College Entrepreneurship Research Conference*, 563-590.

Shutt, J., & Whittington, R. (1987). Fragmentation strategies and the rise of small units: Cases from the north west. *Regional Studies*, *21*(1), 13-23.

Specht, P. H. (1991). Enhancing the entrepreneurial environment in the EEC. *Proceedings of the Eastern Academy of Management*, 43-46.

Staber, U. (1989). Organizational foundings in the cooperative sector of Atlantic Canada: An ecological perspective. *Organization Studies*, *10*(3), 381-403.

Tucker, D. J., Singh, J. V., Meinhard, A. G., & House, R. J. (1988). Ecological and institutional sources of changes in organizational populations. In G. R. Carroll (Ed.), *Ecological models of organizations*, pp. 127-151. Cambridge, MA: Ballinger.

Turok, I., & Richardson, P. (1991). New firms and local economic development: Evidence from West Lothian. *Regional Studies*, *25*(1), 71-86.

Tushman, M. L., & Anderson, P. (1986). Technological discontinuities and organizational environments. *Administrative Science Quarterly*, *31*, 439-465.

Walker, R., & Greenstreet, D. (1990). The effect of government incentives and assistance on location and job growth in manufacturing. *Regional Studies*, *25*(1), 13-30.

Walton, J. (1977). *Elites and economic development: Comparative studies on the political economy of Latin American cities*. Austin: University of Texas Press.

Westhead, P. (1990). A typology of new manufacturing firm founders in Wales: Performance measures and public policy implications. *Journal of Business Venturing*, *5*(2), 103-122.

Whittington, R. C. (1984). Regional bias in new firm formation in the UK. *Regional Studies*, *18*(3), 253-256.

Wholey, D. R., & Brittain, J. W. (1986). Organizational ecology: Findings and implications. *Academy of Management Review*, *11*(3), 513-533.

Wilken, P. H. (1979). Entrepreneurship: A comparative and historical study. In G. M. Platt (Ed.), *Modern sociology: A series of monographs, treatises, and texts*. Norwood, N.J.: Ablex Publishing Corporation.

Wortman, M. S., Jr. (1987). Entrepreneurship: An integrating typology and evaluation of the empirical research in the field. *Journal of Management, 13*(2), 259-279.

Young, R. C., & Francis, J. D. (1989). Who helps small manufacturing firms get started? *Rural Development Perspectives, 6*(1), 21-25.

Pamela Hammers Specht is Associate Dean and Associate Professor in The College of Business Administration, University of Nebraska-Omaha.

We are very pleased to present this paper by Howard Aldrich concerning the use of a population-ecology approach to the study of entrepreneurship as the first offering in our Interdisciplinary Forum. It is hoped that the introduction of the Forum will stimulate and facilitate the contribution of other papers drawing upon knowledge and methodology from a variety of disciplines that may be useful to advance study in the field.

You are encouraged to submit comments or rebuttals to Forum pieces for publication consideration. Such responses should be limited to no more than 2,000 words. The author will have the opportunity to respond in the same issue in which such a response is published. A dialogue is encouraged to enhance the value of the Forum as a vehicle for the exchange of ideas. Obviously, it will not be possible to publish all of the responses submitted. Selections will be made by the Editors and only one response per person will be considered.

Using an Ecological Perspective to Study Organizational Founding Rates

Howard E. Aldrich

Moving away from a "traits" approach to a "rates" approach, using an ecological perspective, highlights the salience of organizations as the key component of environments. Foundings of new organizations are highly dependent upon the experiences of already existing organizations, both in a particular population and in the larger community of populations. Intra-population processes—prior foundings, dissolutions, density, and factors associated with density—structure the environment into which foundings are born. Inter-population processes—the nature of relations between populations, whether competing or cooperating, and actions by dominant organizations—affect the distribution of resources in the environment and the terms on which they are available to entrepreneurs. Institutional factors—government policies, political events, cultural norms, and so on—shape the macro-context within which other processes occur.

Entrepreneurship involves mobilizing resources in pursuit of opportunities, resulting in the founding of a new business. Researchers have traditionally looked at the personal attributes of founders, asking what makes them different from other people. Gartner (1989) called this the "traits" approach. Other researchers have taken a different path, focusing on the environmental conditions generating variations in the number of foundings over time. Ecologists call this the "rates" approach. The approaches are complementary, as each draws on different research traditions in the social sciences. I take an ecological perspective and concentrate on the rates approach.

Ecologists work at four levels of analysis—group, organization, population, community—and take a longer-term view than is typical of the social-psychological perspective behind the traits approach. Using an ecological approach (Aldrich, 1979), I consider three processes affecting founding rates: intra-population, inter-population, and institutional. I conclude by discussing the implications of adopting an ecological approach to explaining founding rates.

BACKGROUND

In preparation for this paper, I conducted a wide-ranging literature search, with the help of Kristin Park, a graduate student in sociology at UNC-CH. We used five primary strategies. First, we searched the *Sociological Abstracts* from 1981 through 1989, looking for references under bureaucratic structure, organizational sociology, voluntary associations, and the sociology of business. Second, we picked a set of key exemplar articles in entrepreneurship, and used the *Social Sciences Citation Index* for the past decade to see which books and articles had cited them. Third, we checked the sources cited in the papers appearing in the Babson College entrepreneurship conference proceedings, *Frontiers of Entrepreneurial Research,* going back to 1981. Fourth, we searched ABI-INFORM, an index on disk of abstracts for over 800 business and trade journals, using the most recent 5-year period. We used the key words "foundings," "creations and organizational," "startups and organizational," and "startups." Fifth, we searched our library's on-line computerized catalog, using the following key words: business foundings, business creations, business startups, organizations, new business, entrepreneurship, entrepreneurs, and entrepreneur. As might be expected, the bulk of the literature generated by this search process was useless for my purposes. Nonetheless, I satisfied myself that the empirical literature using a rates approach is quite thin.

Traditionally, entrepreneurship studies examined the personal traits and attributes of entrepreneurs who found organizations.[1] Gartner (1989) recently reviewed such studies, and pointed out that they focused on individual entrepreneurs' personality traits, parents' occupations, the stages of development of a business, etc. (See Gartner's [1989] paper for a comprehensive review.) Much of this research has hit a dead end, however.[2]

By concentrating on the traits of individual entrepreneurs, rather than on founding rates, the classical tradition deflected attention away from the very volatile and even turbulent nature of the business population in the United States and elsewhere. For example, most articles in the JSBM and the AJSB from 1976 to 1985 focused on going concerns, not new businesses (Ireland & Van Auken, 1987).

An ecological perspective on foundings is well suited to the new approach of examining rates of founding, rather than the traits of founders. It is inherently dynamic in focus, emphasizes the many scales at which social action occurs, and leads to interesting research hypotheses.

THREE EXPLANATIONS FOR VARIATIONS IN FOUNDING RATES

I focus on founding rates at the population level, examining what conditions affect

1. Romanelli (1989) noted that traditional perspectives on entrepreneurship examined either the characteristics of entrepreneurs or the conditions of environments that created opportunities for entrepreneurial activity.
2. Most of the "traits" studies are based on small samples, drawn from unknown populations whose generality is not clear, and limited to cross-sectional designs, thus rendering any causal implications suspect. Many do not use multivariate analysis, which controls for age, education, sex, work experience, etc., thus raising doubts about the significance of personality variables that occasionally appear significant.

the rate at which organizations are added to an existing population. Studying the origins of totally *new* populations requires analysis at the community/instutitional level, a topic addressed in other papers (Aldrich & Mueller, 1982; Astley, 1985). Typically, we cannot "see" a new organizational population until it has begun to establish itself, at which point the population processes discussed in this paper become relevant. Thus, for all practical purposes, most of what we study in the entrepreneurship field today is covered in this paper.

I examine three processes: those occurring within populations, those occurring between populations (at what can be called the community level), and those occurring in the institutional environment. Throughout, I emphasize the time-dependent nature of organizational foundings—knowing *when* something occurs is as important as knowing *why* it occurred. I mostly ignore *what* types of organizations are founded, because that question would require a more detailed examination of how information is disseminated about entrepreneurial opportunities (Romanelli, 1989).

Intra-population Processes

Environmental resources, or an environment's carrying capacity, set a limit on population density—the number of organizations competing for the same resources. If we make some simple assumptions about the intrinsic rate of increase (called **r** by ecologists) of a population and about how carrying capacity (called **K**) affects intra-population competition, we can generate an expected pattern for population growth (Aldrich, 1979, pp. 63-66). Typically, ecologists assume growth is rapid at first, proceeding exponentially, but then tapering off, as a population approaches its carrying capacity.

An S-shaped pattern results, combining the effects of two changing processes: increasing dissolution rates and decreasing founding rates. Together, these processes lead to fewer net additions to a population as it approaches the carrying capacity of its environment. Thus, an analysis of intra-population processes must include foundings, dissolutions, and changes in density over time, as well as the changes that accompany variations in density.[3]

Prior Deaths

Founding rates are constrained by death rates in two ways. First, existing organizations tie up resources, so that foundings only have access to them when they dissolve. Thus, many foundings are a replacement phenomenon, because dissolutions create openings for new organizations. A large proportion of foundings are "lucky" in that they simply replace dissolved organizations, so that high death rates may lead to subsequent high birth rates.

Second, potential founders may be frightened by relatively high or increasing death rates. High numbers of dissolutions might be a signal that a population has exceeded its carrying capacity. Halliday, Powell, and Granfors (1987, p. 460) argued that "an unsuccessful founding will depress subsequent foundings, as members of [an organization] become discouraged and hesitate to try again."

So far, these ecological hypotheses have received mixed support in empirical research, with support stronger for the negative than the positive effect of prior deaths on

3. The ecological model of how populations change over time is very similar to product or industry life cycle theories used in the business strategy literature (Murray, 1984). One difference lies in the uses to which the model is put. Unlike strategists, ecologists treat the life cycle idea not as a predictive tool for designing strategies, but as a useful analytic tool.

subsequent foundings. The strongest support is from Delacroix and Carroll (1983), who studied newspaper foundings in Ireland and Argentina. As newspaper deaths in the previous year increased, newspaper foundings increased up to a point, but then as deaths increased further, the number of foundings declined. They argued that first, the dissolution of newspapers freed resources that could subsequently be used by other entrepreneurs to found their own papers. But, second, as the number of dissolutions increased, potential entrepreneurs received an increasingly negative message about the wisdom of founding a paper. Eventually potential entrepreneurs' negative interpretations of prior deaths more than offset the positive effect of available resources.

Delacroix and Carroll's results were only partially replicated, however, by Carroll and Hannan (1989) in their study of nine newspaper populations, some of which were previously studied by Delacroix and Carroll (1983) and Carroll and Huo (1986). They found the expected curvilinear relationship between prior deaths and foundings in only two populations, and it was only statistically significant in one of them.

Barnett and Amburgey (1990) also only partially replicated Delacroix and Carroll's results. They found that prior deaths were negatively related to subsequent foundings of telephone companies in Pennsylvania from 1877 to 1933. They argued that this may have been the result of first-order autocorrelation, if unobserved factors that increased failures also reduced foundings. (They did not test for a curvilinear relationship between prior deaths and foundings.) Halliday, Powell, and Granfors (1987) also found that prior deaths had a negative effect on the subsequent founding rate of state bar associations.

The importance of prior deaths probably differs by where a population is in its life cycle. In the early growth stage, deaths are not so important in freeing resources. In the later stage, when carrying capacity is approached or reached, prior deaths are very important in freeing resources for new organizations. Though empirical support for the effect of prior deaths on foundings is mixed, it deserves further attention in studies of other populations.

Prior Births

If potential entrepreneurs learn from their environments by imitating what others are doing, then high levels of foundings might be read as a signal that opportunities are growing in a population. Thus, we would expect a positive relationship between prior and subsequent foundings. However, there are probably diminishing returns to the positive effect of prior foundings, as resources and the pool of potential entrepreneurs are exhausted by very high levels of foundings. Thus, researchers have looked for a curvilinear relationship between prior and subsequent foundings.[4]

Support for this prediction has been found in five different studies. Delacroix and Carroll (1983) reported a curvilinear relationship between prior organizational births and subsequent foundings for newspapers, as did Hannan and Freeman (1987) for unions. Staber (1989) reported significant curvilinear effects for two of the three populations of cooperatives he examined in Atlantic Canada. Carroll and Hannan (1989) found support for a curvilinear relationship in five of the eight newspaper populations they tested, but not in three others. Barnett and Amburgey (1990) found that prior foundings of telephone companies were positively associated with subsequent foundings, but they attributed their results to first-order autocorrelation, and they did not test for a curvilinear relationship.[5]

4. Empirically, this means a quadratic specification of the effects of prior foundings, with expectations of a positive linear and negative squared term if the hypothesis is correct.

5. A first-order autocorrelation could arise if some underlying factor, common to both time periods, was left

Foundings also tie up resources, many of which cannot be replenished quickly. We would expect the resource-consuming effect of prior foundings to be insignificant at low levels of foundings, but then to become stronger until at some level it exerts a strong negative effect on subsequent foundings. Untangling the two interpretations of prior foundings—as a symbol to entrepreneurs of potential opportunities and as an indication of already-committed resources—is not an easy task, and prior research has not done so. The net effect of both should be a curvilinear association between levels of prior foundings and current foundings.

Density Dependence

Density dependence refers to the dependence of population processes on the size of the population itself. Density is usually defined simply as the number of organizations within a population. Increasing organizational density has several consequences, some increasing and some inhibiting foundings. Factors increasing foundings include: rising legitimacy and institutionalization of an organizational form; spreading availability of knowledge and skills necessary to generate organizations; and, the possibility of collective action. Factors inhibiting foundings include: diminishing returns and smaller potential gains realized from foundings as competitors become more numerous; and, increasing concentration in some populations, as barriers to entry emerge.

In early ecological studies, density was measured *only* by the number of organizations in a population. Subsequently, ecologists took a more expansive view and defined density more broadly to include the aggregate size of all organizations, as well as the size distribution of organizations within the population. Barnett and Amburgey (1990) have so far been the only ecologists to measure population mass—the aggregate size of all organizations in a population.[6]

Positive effects of increasing density. Some forms of organization must fight for *legitimacy* when they first appear, because they challenge established organizations or institutions: the first newspaper editor in the United States was jailed, and early labor unions were crushed by aggressive employers. Early forms of trade associations were tainted with the anti-competitive aura of their predecessors (cartels and other collectivities that attempted to restrict competition) and had to prove themselves to skeptical potential members as well (Aldrich & Staber, 1988). Early life insurance companies were seen as illegitimate in the United States, because they transformed the sacred event of death into a vulgar commodity (Zelizer, 1978). As the prevalence of these forms increased, however, they gradually assumed a taken-for-granted nature, characteristic of all institutions, and successive cohorts of founders had an easier time (Zucker, 1986).

Support for the density dependence argument was assembled by Carroll and Hannan (1989, p. 535) in their study of nine populations of newspapers: "For all nine populations, density has the predicted nonmonotonic effect . . . the estimated coefficients of the first-order terms are positive and those of the second-order terms negative." These

out of the statistical model. For example, resource availability may have been high in both periods but not measured properly in the model. Statistically, of course, we may observe an association between prior and current births because some third, unmeasured force, such as a change in economic values, is stimulating entrepreneurs into action. In this case, entrepreneurs are not responding to prior births, but rather to the common sensibility underlying their own and the earlier time period.

6. They studied telephone companies, and measured total mass by the number of subscribers of all existing companies in a given year. By including total number of competitors in the same equation with this measure of mass, they thus controlled for the average size of organizations in the population.

results held when other intra-population processes—prior foundings and dissolutions—were controlled. Halliday, Powell, and Granfors (1987) did not have density explicitly in their model of bar association foundings, but they did include a variable for year, and discovered a very strong upward trend in founding rates as the population grew. Founding rates in 1900 were ten times those of 1880, for example, and the trend was not explained by increases in the population of lawyers.

Barnett and Amburgey (1990) measured density in their study of telephone company foundings in Pennsylvania in two ways: number of companies and aggregate size (measured by total subscribers) of all companies. The net effect of number of companies was negative throughout the observed range in their population, indicating only competitive, not cooperative, effects. However, the net effect of aggregate size was positive, indicating that larger organizations increased the founding rate of new organizations, and the effect was especially high during years when the founding rate was higher.

Some theorists have argued that legitimacy is *not* a major problem for new forms of business in capitalist societies because that issue was settled when private property rights were institutionalized (Delacroix, Swaminathan, & Solt, 1989). Zucker (1989) speculated that legitimacy for many new forms of organization should be thought of as "yes or no" rather than "more or less," with the legitimacy issue confronted and dealt with early in a population's history. Either argument suggests that founding rates of many, if not most, organizations are *not* density dependent (or at least, that density itself is not the crucial factor in founding rate changes over time), implying that introducing the proper control variables should eliminate the effect of density.

Entrepreneurial work settings. Many workers in an industry leave to start their own business, and firms spawning such new firms have been called "incubators" by Hart and Denison (1987). Freeman (1983) called the process "organizationally induced entrepreneurship," and Romanelli (1989) has written of the importance of entrepreneurial work settings in spawning foundings (cf. Garvin, 1983).

Knowledge of effective forms is limited in a population's history. Potential entrepreneurs may hesitate to found an organization if they are uncertain of how to construct it: "In such situations, existing organizations are the only training grounds for organization builders" (Hannan & Freeman, 1987, p. 918). The greater the number of organizations of a given form, the more potential entrepreneurs trained. Thus, as populations grow, founding rates ought to increase.

Another source of split-offs from established firms arises from relations between employees and lead users, who may alert employees to bottlenecks, gaps, or other problems with effective uses of firm's products or services (Von Hippel, 1986). Employees can either report these problems to the firm, or use the information to strike out on their own. For this reason, Garvin (1983) argued that spin-offs are more common in the early stages of an industry.

The knowledge gained and contacts made in their previous job provide opportunities for employees to capitalize on, but also constrain their search for opportunities and the strategies of organizations they found (Boeker, 1987; Freeman, 1983; Romanelli, 1989). Some research shows that owners tend to set up businesses in product or service lines similar to those in which they previously worked, and to serve some of the same customers they dealt with as employees (Cooper & Dunkelberg, 1987; Johannisson, 1988).

As density increases, contacts between organizations and outsiders become more frequent, causing *social networks* to change in ways that facilitate some entrepreneurs' breaking through scale barriers that previously blocked their entry into the population (Robben, 1984). If learning is contact contingent, then more learning should occur in dense environments, up to a point.[7] Therefore, we would expect the number of organizations formed by persons *not* employed in the form to also increase with increasing density.

Collective action in some populations involves attempts to stabilize and dampen competitive forces, through tactics such as price leadership and design standards. Hannan and Freeman (1989) noted that small numbers of population members hamper attempts at coordinated action, whereas a larger population produces economies of scale necessary for political and legal action. Aggressive collective actions by small groups of owners may smooth the way for subsequent founders. For example, a small group of business owners succeeded in expanding the use of coal as a fuel in the Northwest in the late 19th century (Albrow, 1976, p. 179). To the extent that potential entrepreneurs read such conditions as raising their chances of successfully copying an effective form, they may be encouraged to found a new organization.

Negative effects of increasing density. Increasing density eventually exacerbates competitive forces and depresses founding rates. "The more numerous the competitors, the smaller the potential gains from founding an organization (and the bigger the cost to potential competitors) at a given level of demand for products and services" (Hannan & Freeman, 1987, p. 918). When a population approaches carrying capacity, several negative effects become apparent, including investors' reluctance to fund new organizations, and a dwindling supply of potential organizers, customers, and suppliers.

Collective action by competitors may also inhibit potential entrepreneurs from attempting foundings. Classic industrial organization writings identify numerous barriers to entry in mature industries that depress founding rates. For examples, tacit agreements on market sharing, price leadership that keeps profits too low to encourage outsiders, and other oligopolistic practices may discourage potential entrepreneurs.

Density effects and favored forms. Foundings have often been treated as a homogeneous, unvarying population, whereas close observation shows a great deal of complexity and variation (Gartner, 1985). The kinds of organizations that are founded and prosper vary by where a population is in its life cycle. Ecologists have identified two dimensions of forms that vary with density: r versus K strategists, and specialists versus generalists (Brittain & Freeman, 1980; Lambkin & Day, 1989).

The r versus K distinction is based on the kinds of organizations that do well in the early as opposed to the late stages of population density, with r-strategists favored early and K-strategists favored late. Organizations following an r-strategy reproduce rapidly and move quickly to obtain the resources available when carrying capacity is underexploited, exploiting their "first-mover" advantage. K-strategists, by contrast, do well when a population is near its carrying capacity, and selection is based on efficient use of resources, rather than quickness (Brittain & Freeman, 1980). K-strategists outcompete r-strategists if they are in the same niche, and so r-strategists are typically replaced by K-strategists as a population matures.

The specialist versus generalist distinction is based on the breadth of the niche occupied by organizations, assuming that organizations sacrifice some degree of competitive edge when they spread their fitness over a wide as opposed to a narrow niche. Specialists concentrate their fitness in a narrow band, and do exceptionally well when the environment is within that band, outcompeting generalists. Generalists, by contrast, spread their fitness over a wider range of their environments, doing better than specialists when environments vary across diverse states with some degree of uncertainty. To

7. I am indebted to Jerome Katz for this observation, taken from statistical learning theory.

the extent that widely differing states of the environment pose very different demands on organizations, specialists will lose out to the generalists that maintain the capacity to compete in several different environmental states, as opposed to the specialist's single state.

The two dimensions of r versus K and specialist versus generalist may be cross-tabulated to produce 4 distinct form types: r-specialists, r-generalists, K-specialists, and K-generalists. Lambkin and Day (1989) elaborated upon Brittain and Freeman (1980) and Brittain and Wholey (1988) in proposing a generic developmental pattern of forms within different population densities. Early in the life of a population, when a niche is first open, the pioneers are likely to be r-specialists which multiply and move quickly. After an early period of development, so-called "early followers" can gain a large market share by being more efficient (and powerful) than r-specialists. Such early followers are likely to be K-generalists: divisions, subsidiaries, or other dependent units of established firms, as well as new firms. Later, K-specialists, with small market shares, can survive on the stable, narrow niches left to them by the K-generalists. Boeker's (1987) study of merchant semiconductor firms confirmed some of these predictions.

Carroll (1984, p. 131) argued that "generalism and specialism not only coexist, but are fundamentally interrelated." Successful generalists create the conditions that promote successful specialists, because the generalists' broad appeal to multiple market segments leaves open many small, specialized niches. Generalists also stabilize markets by their visibility and fairly predictable actions. Carroll illustrated his argument with examples from the brewing, newspaper, music recording, and book publishing industries.

Density-independent Processes

Some intra-population forces affect foundings throughout the life cycle of populations, and are thus independent of population density. *Job-changing* and *technological innovation* are not dependent upon a population's life cycle, and may have an effect on founding rates.

Rates of *job changing* and movement of workers between different employers in the U.S. are very high. For example, "55 percent of all jobs held in the United States [between 1965 and 1970] had new workers in this five year period" (Stewman, 1988, p. 192-193). This aggregate figure included workers who had changed into a new job plus workers entering the labor force for the first time. Such a high level of turnover opens up many opportunities for workers to explore the prospects of self-employment.

Innovation, especially technology-based innovation, is often linked to entrepreneurship and business foundings. Most innovations are competence-enhancing rather than competence-destroying (Schmookler, 1962; Tushman & Anderson, 1986), and can thus be adopted by existing organizations. Competence-enhancing innovations are order of magnitude improvements in price/performance that build on existing know-how within a product/service class, and they do not make old skills obsolete. The change from mechanical to electrical typewriters is an example. Readily transferable technologies, not needing costly adaptations, probably make it easier for workers with entrepreneurial ambitions to capitalize on competence-enhancing discontinuities and leave to found their own businesses.

By contrast, competence-destroying innovations require new skills, abilities, and knowledge in the development and production of a product or service, and they fundamentally alter the set of relevant competencies required of an organization. An example is the transformation from machine tools operated by skilled craftsmen to numerically controlled machine tools. Truly competence-destroying discontinuities probably require, by definition, new populations of organizations to produce or implement the new product, service, or process. We need many more large-scale studies, of diverse industries, to observe how frequently such discontinuities affect founding rates in established populations.

Summary

Prior foundings and dissolutions, rising density, and other intra-population processes are key events in the history of an organizational population. Some events free resources, whereas others stimulate entrepreneurial imaginations. Other events, such as job changing, simply shuffle resources in quasi-random ways, creating the possibilities that resources will be combined in novel ways.

Inter-population Processes

Hawley's (1950) classic statement on human ecology emphasized community succession, achieved as inter-dependent populations are sorted out by processes of competition, domination, and differentiation (Astley & Fombrun, 1987). Within populations, competition pushes organizations toward adopting similar forms, eventually resulting in greater homogeneity. Some organizations may be driven from a population and into adopting another form, but recent population ecology writings have emphasized selection rather than adaptation (Hannan & Freeman, 1977). Within communities, dominant populations drive others into positions of subordination and ancillary roles, resulting in community-level differentiation.

Types of Relations between Populations

Ecologists distinguish between six forms of interaction between populations (Brittain & Wholey, 1988; cf. Astley & Fombrun, 1987). The impact one population has on another may be positive, negative, or insignificant. For ease of illustration, consider a community with two populations, A and B, and the six possible relations between them:

(−,−) Full competition: the presence of A or B suppresses the other's growth. E.g., competition for land between incompatible uses, such as salvage yards and shopping malls.

(−,0) Partial competition: A's growth rate is decreased in the presence of B but B's is unaffected. E.g., corner store grocery specialists versus full-line supermarkets.

(+,−) Predatory competition: A expands at the expense of B. E.g., video stores versus cinemas.

(0,0) Neutrality: A and B do not affect one another, and growth in one has no effect on growth in the other.

(+,0) Commensalism: A benefits from the presence of B, but B is unaffected by the presence of A. Population B supplements population A, but not vice-versa. E.g., fast food restaurants in the vicinity of an auto plant.

(+,+) Symbiosis: Both A and B benefit the from the presence of each other, as two populations complement one another. E.g., hardware stores and lumber yards.

This rich range of possible interactions between populations is only beginning to be recognized by organization theorists (Astley & Fombrun, 1987). Ecological theorists have mostly focused on competition, although that emphasis is now changing. By contrast, institutional theory, in focusing on taken-for-granted aspects of reality and conformity to them, has emphasized mutualism or cooperation, rather than competition. Zucker (1986), for example, presented an extremely detailed historical account of the transformation of the U.S. economic system, in which she stressed the creation of an active market for institutionally based trust. She stressed the spread of institutional mechanisms and organizational populations—such as credit bureaus and stock exchanges—that generated trust, and the extent to which modern economic life takes such mechanisms for granted.

In the section on intra-population processes, I discussed the direct competition and cooperation that occurs between organizations in the same population. In the above listing of relations, indirect, or diffuse, competition occurs between organizations in different populations. Some indirect competition is between populations that are struggling for the same niche, but other forms are more diffuse. For example, many organizations in different populations seek college graduates as white collar workers, and are thus competing with thousands of other organizations.

In this sense, every organization added to the community of populations has a small, perhaps almost infinitesimal, effect on every other organization.[8] Some effects are negative, such as competition for workers, capital, or members. Other effects are positive, such as the creation of technological breakthroughs benefiting others, or the training of workers who subsequently disperse to other sites. Such positive interdependencies are a link between ecology and the institutional perspective (Aldrich, 1989).

Several recent empirical studies have examined inter-population relations affecting organizational foundings. Marrett (1980) examined the organizational context within which medical societies composed of women physicians were founded between 1890 and 1900 in the United States. Only the effect of local regular medical societies was significant; she found no commensalistic or symbiotic relations with other populations. By contrast, Halliday, Powell, and Granfors (1987) found that employment in *all* kinds of professional services raised the founding rate of state bar associations. They speculated that widespread employment in professional services makes professional associations more "available for emulation and encourages the diffusion of experience about the pragmatics of organizational methods and strategies" (Halliday, Powell, & Granfors, 1987, p. 466).

Hannan and Freeman (1987), in their study of labor union foundings, discovered a relation of partial competition between industrial and craft unions. Once industrial unions became numerous in the United States (around 50 or so), they suppressed the rate of formation of craft unions. However, craft union density had no apparent effect on industrial union foundings. Staber (1989) examined relations between three forms of cooperatives in Atlantic Canada, and found some commensalistic and some symbiotic effects, but no significant competitive effects. Two ecological studies of inter-population processes have measured niche overlap between populations, but neither examined its effect on foundings (McPherson, 1983; Dimmick & Rothenbuhler, 1984).

Sources of Capital

Capital obtained from formal sources, such as banks and venture capitalists, repre-

8. I am indebted to Michael Hannan for this idea.

sents an inter-population relationship. Studies show that formal sources are not very important in explaining founding rates, even for technology-based organizations (Hart & Denison, 1987). Most entrepreneurs use more informal sources of funding, especially their own savings and funding from their families (Zimmer & Aldrich, 1987). However, formal sources of capital are important for explaining *growth* rates.

Venture capitalists, and other investors, are probably as important for the mediating role they play in spreading knowledge of effective forms as for their role in funding start-ups (Larsen & Rogers, 1988). "Venture capital firms invest their money largely on the basis of the potential value of an entrepreneur's idea, a collateral that conventional bankers consider worthless" (Larsen & Rogers, 1988, p. 108). With this commitment to a very risky idea, venture capitalists have a stake in making sure a young firm has excellent managerial, marketing, and financial talent, as well as innovative researchers.

Community Succession

Succession in organizational populations may take decades before its effects are visible, and even then, contemporary observers may ignore a community's past. Botkin's (1988) description of the various populations occupying the Route 128 region of Massachusetts over three centuries is an important lesson for people infatuated with only its recent history. Populations have come and gone with regularity. "New England's ice economy, for example, lasted from 1620 to nearly 1870, whaling and the China trade from 1720 to 1880, and textiles and shoes from 1840 to 1940" (Botkin, 1988, p. 118). High technology blossomed in 1957, with the founding of Digital Equipment Corporation, and the bloom may soon be off the rose, according to Jay Forrester.

Botkin (1988) argued that three lessons could be drawn from the history of Route 128. First, while business populations rose and fell (The Boston Ice Company, Waltham Watch, and United Shoe Machinery), the financial institutions, banks, and universities (State Street Bank, Harvard, MIT) of the region remained. Second, the succession process took years, unfolding on a different time scale from transitory government policies. Third, "high tech is no more stable or unstable than ice, whaling, or shoes" (Botkin, 1988, p. 123). Institutional processes dominated the evolution of Route 128, a topic that is taken up in the next section.

Summary

Competitive relations between populations may depress founding rates, but full competition is only one of at least six possible inter-population relations. Some populations actually facilitate foundings in other populations, a phenomenon deserving more study than it has heretofore received in the entrepreneurship literature. Some populations serve as information channels between populations, such as the role played by venture capitalists in Silicon Valley, whereas others train workers who then disperse to other populations.

Institutional Processes

In addition to the processes occurring within and between populations of organizations, many time-dependent processes that affect foundings take place in institutional environments. Some are dramatic, one-of-a-kind historical events, whereas others are mundane, repetitive events that no one notices but whose cumulative effects are substantial. Institutional factors include: politics and governmental policies, spatial location, culture, and other events specific to particular periods in history.

Political Factors and State Policies

Political turbulence is important because it may disrupt established ties between organizations and resources, freeing resources for use by new organizations (Stinchcombe, 1965). For example, the final step in the economic unification of the European Economic Community in 1992 will have major effects on firms' life chances, removing the last major barriers to trans-European marketing of goods and services. Reports from South Africa indicate that entrepreneurship within the black population has increased as a result of foreign governments' economic boycott of South Africa.

Newspaper foundings increase during periods of political turmoil, and not only because more politically oriented newspapers are formed then (Delacroix & Carroll, 1983). Turmoil seems to increase the foundings of *all* types of newspapers. Carroll and Huo (1986) replicated this finding in their study of newspaper foundings in the San Francisco Bay Area. They found that political turmoil had a substantial effect on the foundings of all types of papers, not just political ones.[9]

Government policies may encourage, through enhanced legitimacy, demand stimulation, or even direct subsidies, the formation of new forms of organization. Singh, Tucker, and House (1989) found that the foundings of voluntary social service organizations in the Toronto area increased during the period when the provincial government provided additional funding to that sector. Hannan and Freeman (1987), in their study of unions, discovered that union founding rates dropped sharply after the merger of the AFL and CIO in 1955.

Staber (1989) found that favorable government tax policies had a strong positive effect on foundings of three different types of cooperatives in Atlantic Canada. By contrast, economic recessions had no significant effect on foundings. Similarly, Delacroix and Carroll (1983) discovered that economic variables had no significant effects on newspaper foundings, and neither did regularly scheduled national elections. Carroll and Huo (1986) also found that economic conditions (recessions, number of business failures) were not related to newspaper foundings.

Spatial Location

The most aggressive claims about the importance of location have come from researchers studying technology-based organizations. Such claims have been in evidence since at least the 1960s, as in Mahar and Coddington's (1965) advice to communities wishing to promote "scientific complexes" (cf. Bruno & Tyebjee, 1982). Recent research has produced a more balanced view of location's importance.

Most new businesses are homegrown, rather than founded by migrants. Summarizing their own research and that of others, Cooper and Dunkelberg (1987) noted that people usually start businesses where they already reside. Pennings (1982) found little support for the hypothesis that quality of life factors affected firm foundings in 70 metropolitan areas; only 4 of 15 tested coefficients were significant in the hypothesized direction.

Local educational institutions are often identified as sources of ideas and entrepre-

9. Regional labor unrest, by contrast, decreased foundings, perhaps by raising barriers to entry for new firms (Carroll & Huo, 1986, p. 851).

neurs. Some writers emphasize the spin-offs that occur as scientists leave universities to found their own firms, but careful study shows the rate is quite low (McQueen & Wallmark, 1982). For the three universities McQueen and Wallmark examined, only about 1 percent of the universities' scientists left to form companies each year (cf. Rogers, 1986).

Other important features of local environments often cited as affecting founding rates or the success of new ventures are the number of private, public, or nonprofit research laboratories; supportive attitudes by local elites, politicians, and workers; a good transportation infrastructure (highways, airports, trains, buses, etc.); and the structure of social networks (Aldrich & Zimmer, 1986). Clearly, some communities respond differently to historical trends than others. Youngstown, Ohio, which was economically devastated by the closing of its steel mills, has not recovered, whereas Provo, Utah, which had steel and copper firm closings, has bounced back. However, we have few comparative large-scale studies that have documented the extent to which community characteristics affect foundings.

Culture

Research focusing on how persons interpret their environments may provide a link between research on *rates* of founding and research on *processes* of founding (Aldrich, 1989). Processes of founding depend on how actors *interpret* the macro-level, external conditions. More research is needed on how societal norms affecting potential entrepreneurs' interpretations of economic opportunities change over time.

In Japan, the nature of economic activity had to be re-defined before entrepreneurial activity became legitimate in the eyes of the public. Merchants and capitalists struggled for legitimacy and public respect after the Meiji restoration in the mid-19th century. They finally succeeded by identifying the interests of big business with those of the nation (Hirschmeier, 1970).

In 19th-century America, early life insurance companies' attempts to place a financial value on human life were rejected (Zelizer, 1978). Life was defined as sacred and above financial relationships. However, a host of social and economic changes—especially the spread of notions of economic risk and speculation—led people to a growing awareness of the economic value of life and death, and legitimated the life insurance industry. The commercialization of death did not remove all the rituals associated with death. The sacred symbols associated with disposal of the dead were exploited by the funeral home industry to secure its niche (Torres, 1988).

Other Institutional Factors

In her examination of forces promoting diversity within organization populations and communities, Romanelli (1989) identified several institutional factors that may influence founding rates, as well as the creation of new forms of organizations. *Educational institutions* create and help spread information about dominant competencies. Universities, research institutes, and associated programs not only conduct research but also train persons who are able to exploit the latest research products. Educational institutions also "formalize and centralize information by establishing courses and degree programs that train students in basic competences. Once technologies are understood, and stabilized and identifiable jobs (e.g. computer engineer) emerge in industry, colleges and universities take over much of the training of skilled personnel" (Romanelli, 1989, p. 230).

To the extent that a generalized competency underlies organizational foundings, the growth of national educational systems spurs founding rates. To the extent that specific competencies underlie particular populations, the spread of educational institutions may increase the diversity of organizational communities.

Mass and specialized media—television, magazines, journals, newsletters, and newspapers—disseminate information within and between populations. Information diffusion increases the likelihood that potential entrepreneurs will recognize opportunities for combining old resources in new ways, or at least recognize opportunities in already existing populations.

Summary

Institutional forces probably have their greatest impact when a new form of organization is emerging, constraining and imprinting the new form in distinctive ways (Stinchcombe, 1965). Once established, foundings within an organizational population respond more to intra- and inter-population processes than to institutional forces. Institutional processes, however, are what give shape to organizational forms, transforming initial differences that may have emerged by chance into differences with significant social consequences (Hannan & Freeman, 1986).

IMPLICATIONS AND CONCLUSIONS

Moving away from a "traits" approach to a "rates" approach, using an ecological perspective, highlights the salience of organizations as the key component of environments. Foundings of new organizations are highly dependent upon the events experienced by already existing organizations, both in a population and in the larger community of populations. Intra-population processes—prior foundings, dissolutions, density, and factors associated with density—structure the environment into which foundings are born. Inter-population processes—the nature of relations between populations, whether competing or cooperating, and actions by dominant organizations—affect the distribution of resources in the environment and the terms on which they are available to entrepreneurs. Institutional factors—government policies, political events, cultural norms, and so on—shape the macro-context within which other processes occur.

Implications for Theory

Although the number of empirical ecological studies of foundings is not large, a common finding is evident: intra-population processes have had the most consistently significant effects on foundings of all processes studied. Three implications follow. First, we must pay more attention to conceptualizing (and measuring) the carrying capacity for diverse populations, because carrying capacities set the context within which intra-population processes are played out. Second, traditional theorizing about "organization-environment" relations has taken much too global a view of environments, and thus missed the significant effects that other organizations have on population processes. Third, more effort has been devoted to conceptualizing intra-population processes than inter-population processes, and more effort should be devoted to tracing out the processes linking all populations into a community of organizations.

A rates approach also highlights the time-dependent nature of organizational foundings. Foundings occur within a space-time context in which the order of events is a critical part of the process. History matters, at the community as well as the population level. The traits approach, while telling us about the social-psychological features of the founding process, has blurred the environmental context within which entrepreneurs must interpret and make sense of their actions. Adding an historical, substantive context to our theorizing provides a more comprehensive understanding of why entrepreneurs behave as they do.

Implications for Research

Linking organizational forms to stages in population growth reveals a bias in much of the current literature on entrepreneurship. The ecological model implies that most foundings will be r-specialists, but much of the literature—especially that on entrepreneurial strategy—deals with K-generalists and K-specialists. The bias arises because investigators have not taken account of where the organizations they study fall in a population's life cycle, and because researchers have concentrated on large, successful firms. We need more studies of r-specialists during their formative years, early in a population's life cycle.

Modelling community-level change is notoriously difficult, and most analyses are either confined to two-population interactions or qualitative descriptions. Doing such analyses well will require team work between multiple investigators, and a long-term commitment to building a database.

The methodological demands of the rates approach are daunting: not only must we collect comprehensive data on founding events, but also on other major events in the society *and* on their ordering in time. Our dependence on cross-sectional sample surveys will be difficult to break, but it will be worth it.

Implications for Practice

For practitioners, an ecological approach provides a rich set of concepts for organizing knowledge about the environment of foundings. Knowing how appropriate forms—r, K, specialist, generalist—vary over a population's life cycle, and how they are linked to population density, adds one more guideline that entrepreneurs can use in making decisions about foundings.

Knowledge of population dynamics would also make potential entrepreneurs more informed consumers of writing and research on business foundings. Many claims about causal relationships ignore the environmental context within which the relations hold, and entrepreneurs follow such advice at their peril. We may not make entrepreneurs' lives much easier, but we certainly don't want to make them more difficult!

REFERENCES

Albrow, M. (1976). James J. Hill and the first energy revolution: A study in entrepreneurship, 1865-1878. *Business History Review, 50*(2), 179-197.

Aldrich, H. (1979). *Organizations and environments*. Englewood Cliffs, NJ: Prentice Hall.

Aldrich, H. (1989). Dead theorists' society? Vital signs from three perspectives on organizations. Paper presented at the Lancaster University Conference on New Directions in Organizational Theory, Lancaster, PA, September.

Aldrich, H., & Mueller, S. (1982). The origins of new organizational forms: Coordination, control, and technology. In L.L. Cummings & B. Staw (Eds.), *Research in organizational behavior*, vol. 2, pp. 33-87. Greenwich, CT: JAI.

Aldrich, H., & Staber, U. H. (1988). Organizing business interests: Patterns of trade association foundings, transformations, and deaths. In G. R. Carroll (Ed.), *Ecological models of organization*, pp. 111-126. Cambridge, MA: Ballinger.

Aldrich, H., & Zimmer, C. (1986). Entrepreneurship through social networks. In D. Sexton & R. Smilor (Eds.), *The art and science of entrepreneurship*, pp. 3-23. Cambridge, MA: Ballinger.

Astley, W. G. (1985). The two ecologies: Population and community perspectives on organizational evolution. *Administrative Science Quarterly*, *30*(2), 224-241.

Astley, W. G., & Fombrun, C. J. (1987). Organizational communities: An ecological perspective. In S. B. Bacharach (Ed.), *Research in the sociology of organizations*, vol. 5, pp. 163-185. Greenwich, CT: JAI.

Barnett, W. P., & Amburgey, T. L. (1990). Do larger organizations generate stronger competition? In J. Singh (Ed.), *Organizational evolution*, forthcoming. Beverly Hills, CA: Sage.

Boeker, W. (1987). Organizational origins: Entrepreneurial and environmental imprinting at the time of founding. In G. R. Carroll (Ed.), *Ecological models of organization*, pp. 33-51. Cambridge, MA: Ballinger.

Botkin, J. W. (1988). Route 128: Its history and destiny. In R. W. Smilor, G. Kozmetsky, & D. V. Gibson (Eds.), *Creating the technopolis: Linking technology, commercialization, and economic development*, pp. 117-124. Cambridge, MA: Ballinger.

Brittain, J., & Freeman, J. H. (1980). Organizational proliferation and density dependent selection. In J. Kimberly & R. Miles (Eds.), *Organizational life cycles*, pp. 291-338. San Francisco: Jossey-Bass.

Brittain, J., & Wholey, D. (1988). Competition and coexistence in organizational communities: Population dynamics in electronic components manufacturing. In G. R. Carroll (Ed.), *Ecological models of organization*, pp. 195-222. Cambridge, MA: Ballinger.

Bruno, A. J., & Tyebjee, T. (1982). The environment for entrepreneurship. In C. A. Kent, et al. *Encyclopedia of entrepreneurship*, pp. 288-307. Englewood Cliffs, NJ: Prentice Hall.

Carroll, G. R. (1984). Organizational ecology. *Annual Review of Sociology*, *10*, 71-93.

Carroll, G., & Hannan, M. (1989). On using institutional theory in studying organizational populations. *American Sociological Review*, *54*(August), 545-548.

Carroll, G. R., & Huo, Y. P. (1986). Organizational and institutional environments in ecological perspective: Findings from the local newspaper industry. *American Journal of Sociology*, *91*(4), 838-873.

Cooper, A. C., & Dunkelberg, W. C. (1987). Entrepreneurial research: Old questions, new answers, and methodological issues. *American Journal of Small Business*, *11*(Winter), 11-23.

Delacroix, J., & Carroll, G. R. (1983). Organizational foundings: An ecological study of the newspaper industries of Argentina and Ireland. *Administrative Science Quarterly*, *28*(2), 274-291.

Delacroix, J., Swaminathan, A., & Solt, M. (1989). Density dependence versus population dynamics: An ecological study of failings in the California wine industry. *American Sociological Review*, *54*(2), 245-262.

Dimmick, J., & Rothenbuhler, E. (1984). Competitive displacement in the communication industries: New media in old environments. In R. E. Rice & Associates, *The new media: Communication, research, and technology*, pp. 287-304. Beverly Hills, CA: Sage.

Freeman, J. H. (1983). Entrepreneurs as organizational products: Semiconductor firms and venture capital firms. In G. Libecap (Ed.), *Advances in the study of entrepreneurship, innovation, and economic growth*, vol. 1, pp. 33-52. Greenwich, CT: JAI.

Gartner, W. (1985). A conceptual framework for describing the phenomenon of new venture creation. *Academy of Management Review, 10*(4), 696-706.

Gartner, W. B. (1989). Who is an entrepreneur? is the wrong question. *Entrepreneurship Theory and Practice, 13*(4), 47-68.

Garvin, D. A. (1983). Spin-offs and the new firm formation process. *California Management Review, 25*(2), 3-20.

Halliday, T., Powell, M. J., & Granfors, M. W. (1987). Minimalist organizations: Vital events in state bar associations, 1870-1930. *American Sociological Review, 52*(4), 456-471.

Hannan, M. T., & Freeman, J. H. (1986). Where do organizational forms come from? *Sociological Forum, 1*, 50-72.

Hannan, M. T., & Freeman, J. H. (1987). The ecology of organizational founding: American labor unions, 1836-1975. *American Journal of Sociology, 92*(4), 910-943.

Hannan, M. T., & Freeman, J. H. (1989). *Organizational ecology*. Cambridge, MA: Harvard.

Hart, S., & Denison, D. R. (1987). Creating new technology-based organizations: A system dynamics model. *Policy Studies Review, 6*(3), 512-528.

Hawley, A. (1950). *Human ecology*. New York: Roland.

Hirschmeier, J. (1970). The Japanese spirit of enterprise, 1867-1970. *Business History Review, 54*,(1), 13-38.

Ireland, R. D., & Van Auken, P. M. (1987). Entrepreneurship and small business research: An historical typology and directions for future research. *American Journal of Small Business, 11*(Spring), 9-20.

Johannisson, B. (1988). Emerging female entrepreneurship: Network building characteristics. Paper prepared for the 18th European Samll Business Seminar, Gent-Brussels, Belgium.

Katz, J., & Gartner, W. B. (1988). Properties of emerging organizations. *Academy of Management Review, 13*(3), 429-441.

Lambkin, M., & Day, G. (1989). Evolutionary processes in competitive markets. *Journal of Marketing, 53*, 4-20.

Larsen, J. K., & Rogers, E. M. (1988). Silicon Valley: The rise and falling off of entrepreneurial fever. In R. W. Smilor, G. Kozmetsky, & D. V. Gibson (Eds.), *Creating the technopolis: Linking technology, commercialization, and economic development*, pp. 99-115. Cambridge, MA: Ballinger.

Mahar, J. F., & Coddington, D. C. (1965). The scientific complex—Proceed with caution. *Harvard Business Review, 43*(1), 140-163.

Marrett, C. B. (1980). Influences on the rise of new organizations: The formation of women's medical societies. *Administrative Science Quarterly, 25*(2), 185-199.

McPherson, J. M. (1983). The ecology of affiliation. *American Sociological Review, 48*(4), 519-532.

McQueen, D. H., & Wallmark, J. T. (1982). Spin-off companies from Chalmers University of Technology. *Technovation, 1*(4), 305-315.

Murray, J. (1984). A concept of entrepreneurial strategy. *Strategic Management Journal, 5*(1), 1-13.

Pennings, J. M. (1982). The urban quality of life and entrepreneurship. *Academy of Management Journal, 25*(1), 63-79.

Robben, A. C. G. M. (1984). Entrepreneurs and scale: Interactional and institutional constraints on the growth of small-scale enterprises in Brazil. *Anthropological Quarterly, 57*(3), 125-138.

Rogers, E. M. (1986). The role of the research university in the spin-off of high-technology companies. *Technovation, 4*, 169-181.

Romanelli, E. (1989). Organization birth and population variety: A community perspective on origins. In B. Staw & L. L. Cummings (Eds.), *Research in organizational behavior*, vol. 11, pp. 211-246. Greenwich CT: JAI.

Schmookler, J. (1962). Economic sources of inventive activity. *Journal of Economic History, 22*, 1-20.

Singh, J., Tucker, D., & House, R. (1989). Institutional factors in organizational foundings. Unpublished paper.

Staber, U. H. (1989). Organizational foundings in the cooperative sector in Atlantic Canada: An ecological perspective. *Organization Studies, 10*, 383-405.

Stewman, S. (1988). Organizational demography. *Annual Review of Sociology, 14*, 173-202.

Stinchcombe, A. (1965). Social structure and organizations. In J. G. March (Ed.), *Handbook of organizations*, pp. 142-193. Chicago: Rand McNally.

Torres, D. L. (1988). Professionalism, variation, and organizational survival. *American Sociological Review, 53*(3), 380-394.

Tushman, M., & Anderson P. (1986). Technological discontinuities and organizational environments. *Administrative Science Quarterly, 31*(3), 439-465.

Von Hippel, E. (1986). Lead users: A source of novel product concepts. *Management Science, 32* (July), 791-805.

Zelizer, V. A. (1978). Human values and the market: The case of life insurance and death in 19th-century America. *American Journal of Sociology, 84*(3), 591-610.

Zimmer, C., & Aldrich, H. (1987). Resource mobilization through ethnic networks: Kinship and friendship ties of shopkeepers in England. *Sociological Perspectives, 30*(4), 422-455.

Zucker, L. G. (1986). Production of trust: Institutional sources of economic structure, 1840-1920. In B. M. Staw & L. Cummings (Eds.), *Research in organizational behavior*, vol. 8, pp. 53-112. Greenwich, CT: JAI.

Zucker, L. G. (1989). Combining institutional theory and population ecology: No legitimacy, no history. *American Sociological Review, 54* (August), 542-545.

Howard Aldrich is Professor of Sociology at the University of North Carolina, Chapel Hill.

A longer version of this paper was presented at the 1989 Gateway Conference on Entrepreneurship, St. Louis University, St. Louis, Missouri, and will be published in a forthcoming book. Helpful hints from Jerome Katz were very useful, as was the research assistance of Kristin Park. Deborah Tilley shaped the manuscript into its final form.

[20]

A Critical Exploration of Sponsorship, Infrastructure, and New Organizations

David M. Flynn

ABSTRACT. This research focuses on the effects of public sponsorship, and regional infrastructure on the emergence and survival of new organizations. Propositions are tested regarding the joint effects of sponsorship and infrastructure on industrial development in a randomly selected sample of fourteen regions. The data include six measures of infrastructure, sponsorship as measured by the total dollars spent for economic development and their individual and joint effects on the number of firms and employees in "high technology" industries for the years 1965, 1970, 1975, 1980 and 1984. This preliminary analysis suggests that variation in the infrastructure and level of sponsorship within a region is related to the birth and survival of new organizations.

I. Introduction

Various analyses have been undertaken to determine the potential effects that local resources have on the birth, location, and expansion of firms. These analyses can be classified according to different perspectives. For example, certain studies attempted to determine the effects of property and other taxes on the location and expansion decision of new and existing firms (see e.g., Carlton, 1983; Charney, 1983; Chicago Fed Letter, 1988; Gyourko, 1987; Newman and Sullivan, 1988; and Schmenner, Huber, and Cook, 1987). Among the other variables considered were wage rates and other factors often classified as hedonic factors that include pollution levels, energy costs, crime and unemployment rates, the existence of hospitals, local sports teams, symphony orchestras, theatres, museums, newspapers, as well as climate variables such as temperature, rain, wind, and sun (see especially, Smith, 1983, p. 301; Blomquist *et al.*, 1988; and Boyer and Savageau, 1985).

As suggested by Blomquist *et al.* (1988) different urban locations offer different sets of wages, rents, and amenities, defined herein as infrastructure. Households then attempt to maximize well-being and firms attempt to minimize costs by their location decisions (pp. 89–90). One could also argue that firms seek to similarly maximize value or minimize their costs through their location decisions. For example, firms in high technology industries may seek a highly educated workforce and be less concerned with costs, especially taxes. Carlton (1983), for example, suggests that available technical expertise is important for highly sophisticated industries, e.g., high technology. Further it has been discovered that the availability of labor was more important than its cost in the first stage of a location decision. It was in the second stage that cost became a significant factor (Schmenner *et al.*, 1987).

These studies provide some valuable empirical evidence of the importance of infrastructure on the location decision of new or existing firms. However, there is a paucity of studies on the effect of increasing an area's attractiveness through incentives and their interaction with the existing infrastructure. These incentives, defined as sponsorship (Flynn, 1988), involve intervention by government agencies, business firms, and universities to create an environment conducive to the birth and survival of organizations. Sponsorship is a deliberate attempt to make available a significantly higher and more stable level of resources to selected firms.

The objectives of this paper are to (1) present a framework for describing types of initiatives undertaken to promote the birth of new organiza-

Final version accepted on February 21, 1992

Department of Management
School of Business
049 Weller Hall
Hofstra University
Hempstead, N.Y. 11550, USA

Small Business Economics 5: 129–156, 1993.

tions, (2) pose propositions regarding the joint effects of initiatives and infrastructure on the establishment of new organizations in fourteen urban areas, and (3) provide a preliminary empirical test of the effects of both infrastructure and sponsorship on the existence and emergence of new organizations in these regions.

II. Sponsorship: concept and examples

New organizations contribute to a sense of vitality within a region. This perception is enhanced by the collaboration of public and private organizations in attempting to enhance or design an environment that is more conducive to new business formation and expansion. One could identify this process as the concept of sponsorship. Sponsorship has been previously used to describe idea champions in the innovation process (Daft and Becker, 1978) and relationships associated with business startups (Van de Ven *et al.*, 1984). Sponsorship is also readily used in the popular press, e.g., *The New York Times* and *Financial Times*, to describe the philanthropic support of artistic and cultural organizations. Herein, the concept is extended to the more general notion of a sponsored environment. Sponsorship involves planned environmental change by government agencies, business firms and universities to create new organizations and increase the likelihood of their survival. Sponsorship is a deliberate attempt to provide a significantly higher and more stable level of resources for new organizations.

Many different types of programs have been undertaken to foster startups and encourage the growth of new organizations. Activities range from universities providing physical facilities for new organizations through incubators at universities to changes in the federal or state tax structure that make a location attractive for the start-up of new organizations.

Sponsorship generally requires cooperation between the public and private sectors to be effective. Cooperative efforts are said to increase the number of startups (Premus, 1982), foster the development of high technology industries (Gruenstein, 1984), promote new regional centers of industrial activity (Brody, 1985) and aid in the revitalization of older industrial areas (Harr, 1984).

Examples of sponsorship include (consider also Premus, 1984 and Soete and Freeman, 1985 for other e.g.s):

- The University City Science Center in Philadelphia, a facility for technology oriented companies, established through the cooperation of state and city government agencies, universities and private organizations.
- Efforts at the state level, including special tax rates and subsidized mortgages, were important factors in attracting the Microelectronics and Computer Technology Corporation (MCC) and SEMATECH, two computer consortia, to Austin, Texas.
- Forty states allocated venture capital funds for direct business financing (Livingston, 1989).

In addition, the National Science Foundation (NSF) provides a form of sponsorship by funding engineering research centers at selected universities. These centers may serve as the focal point for new ideas that will contribute to the start-up of new organizations.

Underlying the current interest in sponsorship of new organizations is evidence that small organizations contribute significantly to scientific and technological innovation (U.S. Small Business Administration, 1988). Sponsorship fosters innovation directly through funding research and development and establishing incubator centers. Sponsorship provides indirect support for innovation by providing services, e.g., information networks that new organizations require for early survival. For example, small organizations are often at risk from undercapitalization, but sponsorship lowers the risk by developing links between startups and public and private venture capital organizations.

Sponsorship is also important as a means of rebuilding depressed regional areas since small firms with less than 100 employees provide the highest proportion of new jobs generated each year (U.S. Small Business Administration, 1988), even though the bulk of new employment may not come until the 4th year of the firm's existence (Phillips and Kirchhoff, 1989). Furthermore, the majority of new jobs generated by small organizations tend to be concentrated in a relatively few industries (Birch and McCracken, 1982).

Although there may be support for the notion

of sponsorship, questions are raised in a number of areas: the potential of sponsorship for long term versus short term effects (Luger, 1984), the interaction effect of sponsorship with the existing local infrastructure (Thomas, 1987; Malecki, 1984), and the relationship between patterns of cooperation and the efficient use of resources (Wiewel *et al.*, 1984). Also, there is concern over the extent to which federal and state governments should be involved in local development versus the more important role of financier (Kirlin, 1984; Nelson and Langlois, 1983). Some of these issues are addressed herein, in the attempt to provide policy guidance to governmental organizations — federal, state and local — in sponsoring new, free-standing organizations. The primary focus is to empirically establish if a region's infrastructure and the level of sponsorship has any effect, positive or negative, on the emergence of new organizations in high technology firms in particular.

III. Theoretical perspectives of sponsorship and infrastructure

A theoretical framework has been lacking to explain the phenomenon of organizational birth and death in the context of a focal environment. However, the emergence of the population ecology (Aldrich, 1979; Hannan and Freeman, 1977) and community ecology model (Astley, 1985), and the life-cycle framework (Kimberly and Miles, 1980) has provided some explanation for the emergence, growth, and decline of organizations and populations of organizations.

Ecological studies of the relationship between sponsorship, infrastructure, and the emergence of new organizations are however, relatively rare. There have been few attempts to extend organization theory to the recent efforts by private and public organizations and universities to foster new organizations. This is especially surprising in light of the important role of environmental selection in organizational theory and the deliberate attempt to increase the resource levels of environments in targeted areas, i.e., sponsorship, as it may affect the selection processes of particular organizations for survival.

A. *Theoretical perspectives of sponsorship*

The concept of sponsorship has been employed to describe a range of activities including the encouragement of new ideas and entrepreneurial behavior, and interorganizational relationships. As described earlier, sponsorship describes an environment of planned initiatives by public and private organizations at national, state, and local levels to facilitate the emergence of new organizations. Sponsorship touches on a number of important issues, discussed below, including the assumptions of selection processes in a competitive environment and arguments regarding the liability of newness and the persistence of founding characteristics over time (Stinchcombe, 1965).

1. *Population ecology*

The population ecology model of organization studies, adopted from ecological models, "explains the relationship of the organizational forms to their niches and environments, detailing the rise and fall of populations relative to specific environmental conditions and events" (Aldrich, *et al.*, 1984). Variation in organizational form within populations, along with the factors of selection and retention, are employed to analyze organizational birth and survival.

When organizations are sponsored, their environment is enriched, providing legitimacy (Stinchcombe, 1965) to their birth and early survival. This legitimacy has been shown to affect early survival in the newspaper (Carroll and Hannan, 1989a), and education software industries (Venkataram *et al.*, 1990) as well as in voluntary organizations (Singh *et al.*, 1986). However, in the later stages of the sponsored organization's life cycle, the ability to effectively compete for scarce resources is severely undermined by the previously buoyant, sponsored environment. As Brittain and Freeman (1980, p. 304) suggest, conditions that create environmental richness may very well limit the viability of some populations.

With regard to organizational form, the general munificience of the environmental affecting the semi-conductor industry, a high technology industry, has contributed to a diversity of organization forms (Brittain and Freeman, 1980, p. 303). A sponsored environment would be expected to also create a diversity of organizational forms within populations because it is a munificient environment, by definition.

If, however, the pattern of resource availability over time for new resources matches the pattern of utilization of current populations, then it is very unlikely that a new organizational form will have any competitive advantages, especially considering the disadvantages posed by the liability of newness (Stinchcombe, 1965). Furthermore, from the perspective of niche theory this means that the potential new form's niche is included and subordinate to that of the existing form and is expected to fail (Brittain and Freeman, 1980, p. 320). The process of intervention by public and private organizations into communities may actually create new organizational forms through alteration of the existing ecology of the community. These new forms may be quite different from the requisite form of the relevant population, thus contributing to a lower level of later stage survival. Furthermore, as recently suggested, there is some evidence to suggest a later stage threat to survival, so called the liability of adolescence (Bruderl and Shussler, 1990).

Because the entry of new organizations increases the density of the relevant population, there is an increase in competition among firms for later stage survival. One could argue that the new sponsored organization may in fact be, illegitimate, because its incubating environment was artificially inflated with resources. As the density of the population increases, these new, sponsored firms would have a higher mortality rate versus unsponsored organizations. Sponsored organizations may have difficulty understanding survival in a high density environment where firms compete for limited resources. Greater population density has been shown to effect higher death rates due to the difficulty of competing firms procurring resources, especially new firms (Carroll and Delacroix, 1982). Very recently, however, Shan *et al.* (1991) has shown that density had a positive effect on biotechnology firms, opposite that which is predicted by ecological theory. In particular, higher population density had a negative effect on founding rates in the early years but the effects were positive in the later years. One explanation posed by these authors was that there may have been a limited supply of Ph.D.'s during the early study period, e.g., 1970's. Also plausible and complementary, is the potential effect of low legitimacy of the biotechnology field in the early study period. Therefore, although these results are potentially interesting, there is a need for a more fully specified model, as was also suggested by the authors.

Smilor and Feeser (1991) lends some support to the contention that sponsorship that is targeted to particular companies is doomed to failure because of the chaotic process of formation and subsequent survival of new firms. More importantly, they suggest that small differences in input can quickly become overwhelming differences in output (Smilor and Feeser, 1991, p. 168). Therefore, in the context of population ecology, sponsored organizations may have significantly different later stage success due to the "artificial" incubation process when extra resources are supplied in an attempt to achieve later stage organizational viability.

The population ecology work of Hannan and Freeman has recently come under serious criticism by Young (1988). She astutely points out some serious problems with the model as it has been defined and empirically tested. Even though she suggests that the theory has not contributed to the understanding of organizations (p. 23), she implies that with a more precise definition of the various concepts of birth, death, change, and inertia, their work may provide some insight into the sociology of organizations. Hannan and Freeman (1988) have answered some of the criticisms in their study of the ecology of labor unions for a period of 150 years. In this study, they support the liability of newness contention of Stinchcombe (1965) when they found a higher mortality rate for new unions versus those established through the merger of established unions. Also relevant to our discussion herein, is their finding that a high density of unions affected their disbanding rate, i.e., mortality. In other words, the local environment had a carrying capacity for some relatively fixed number of unions or more generally, organizations within a specific population and community. Population density was also shown to have a positive effect on the mortality rate of new organizations in American labor unions, Argentinean and Irish newspapers, San Francisco newspaper publishers, and American brewers (Carroll and Hannan, 1989b).

2. *Resource dependence*

The resource dependence model of organizations examines the proactive and reactive strategies organizations undertake to reduce the difficulty and variability they experience in obtaining resources (Pfeffer and Salancik, 1978). Since no organization is self-sufficient, the need to acquire resources creates dependencies between organizations. The importance and scarcity of the resources determines the extent of dependency. Interorganizational actions (e.g., joint ventures, interlocking directorates, etc.) are established as an attempt to adapt to environmental change (Pfeffer and Salancik, 1978). The focus of the resource dependence approach is different than population ecology in that the organization is looked upon as more active in attempting to adapt to the environment.

Organizations, in seeking to reduce their dependence on the environment, may attempt to develop loosely coupled systems. One of the most often recommended organizational responses is through the differentiation of the various sub-units to increase their independence both internally and externally. This differentiation necessarily implies diversification of activities to achieve loose coupling (Pfeffer and Salancik, 1978, p. 275).

The resource dependence model highlights the importance of strategies new organizations and their sponsors take to deliberately increase the level of resources available. When sponsorship takes place, the provision of resources and the conditions accompanying their acceptance increases the dependence of new organizations on the environment. However, the dependence may be characterized as benevolent since the sponsors(s) provides support for survival, especially in the short term. Sponsored organizations accept this dependence as a means of increasing their chances of survival. New organizations can make use of benevolent dependence to direct organizational energy, at least temporarily, to meet internal organizational needs. Since competitive interdependence is reduced, it is easier to focus on process or product development rather than on mapping competitive strategies for survival. Sponsorship provides resources and often acts as an intermediary to reconcile some of the incompatible demands that organizations generally face. However, there are costs associated with dependence. For example, at the interorganizational level, the linkages with the sponsoring organizations contribute to the potential for survival (Aiken and Hage, 1968). These linkages, however, may add a degree of bureaucracy that is cumbersome to a new organization. The bureaucratic element requires management control systems that are either not yet developed or require a diversion of resources to fulfill the demands associated with the sponsorship process.

Although, the resource dependence model may emphasize the use of differentiation and diversification for increased survival, "Neither the differentiation of the organization into subunits nor the diversification of activities reduces the organization's dependence on the environment" (Pfeffer and Salancik, 1978, p. 275). This also implies that undifferentiated organizations, especially new small organizations that tend to have simple structures associated with a single product or service, may be vulnerable to their dependence on the environment for resources. Therefore, an effective option available to even these undifferentiated organizations for coping with this constraint, would be through loose coupling.

Population ecology and resource dependence models have been proposed as competing perspectives for studying organization and environmental relations. More recent work points out the potentially complementary nature of the two approaches (Ulrich and Barney, 1984; Wholey and Brittain, 1986). Also, Romanelli's (1989) recent study on the minicomputer industry considered the effects of the strategic orientation of firms, i.e., generalist and specialist organizations as suggested by Brittain and Freeman (1980), on early stage mortality in the mini-computer industry. Her results support the notion that specialist organizations are more likely to survive their early years than generalists. However, as suggested by both the population ecology and resource dependence models, the mortality of young organizations is predominantly influenced by the relative abundance of resources in the environment, independent of competitive conditions (Romanelli, 1989, pp. 385—386).

In consideration of both population ecology and resource dependence models, outcomes of different types of sponsorship need to be assessed at the organizational and population levels. Sponsorship creates new organizations and also has effects, intended and unintended, on existing populations of organizations.

1. *Sponsorship and organizational birth*
Although stable and simple environments exist in some industries (Daft, 1983), environments appear to be evolving toward a turbulent state that involves greater complexity and instability (Aldrich *et al.*, 1984; Huber, 1984; 1990). Sponsorship is often directed toward the creation of new organizations in high technology industries that operate in turbulent environments (e.g., University Science City, Philadelphia; Microelectronics Computer Technology Corporation (MCC), Austin). Since resource acquisition is a major source of uncertainty for organizations, sponsorship provides an increased amount of available resources and lowers the level of environmental uncertainty experienced. Clearly, the expectation is that sponsorship will contribute to a higher rate of new firm births than in unsponsored environments.

2. *Sponsorship: implications for survival*
New organizations have a low probability for long term survival. This observation is supported by statistics on business failures among new organizations (U.S. Small Business Administration, 1988). Part of the tendency to fail is associated with their small size (Freeman *et al.*, 1983), competition (Aldrich, 1979), and environmental shocks (Hall, 1987).

Sponsorship, by reducing competitive disturbances and constraining organizational learning, may produce unintended consequences by aiding the survival of organizations with potential weaknesses. In the population ecology model, negative selection is discussed as a process whereby "some members of a population fail and take with them ineffective attributes, leaving a narrower set of survival-enhancing attributes" (Aldrich *et al.*, 1984). Sponsorship intervenes in this selection process so that sponsored organizations are favored regardless of the effectiveness of their attributes. Therefore, one would expect a higher rate of mortality among sponsored organizations when sponsorship either stops or is no longer effective at buffering organizations from environmental and competitive shocks.

Furthermore, models of organization-environment relations suggest that a higher level of organizational flexibility is necessary for adaptation to complex and unstable environments. Organizations incubated in sponsored and stable environments may be inhibited in their ability to devise effective strategies for survival beyond the period of sponsorship because of their lack of experience in coping with more uncertain environments. The literature on enactive learning indicates that the capacity to adapt depends on organizational skills learned early in organizational life (Miles and Randolph, 1980). As a function of dependence, sponsorship constrains early learning and this effect is reinforced by the structural inertia of organizations (Hannan and Freeman, 1984).

B. *The effects of infrastructure*

The notion of a sponsored environment adds another dimension to research that explored an ecological model of organizational birth rates. Pennings (1982a & b) found that certain environmental elements, i.e., the infrastructure of metropolitan areas, including occupational and industrial differentiation, size of urban areas, availability of venture capital, percentage of immigrants in the labor force and the presence of universities were positively associated with higher than expected rates of organizational birth. Furthermore, the associations were stronger in high technology industries. Other research focused on high technology firms in particular include the availability of skilled and low cost labor, a supportive tax structure, quality educational institutions, and low cost housing (Brody, 1985). Additionally, existing organizations, along with the presence of a high technology workforce, will contribute to the birth of new organizations. Premus (1982; 1984) and Carlton (1983) supported this conclusion indicating that the availability of skilled labor (e.g., percentage of workforce college educated) along with the low labor costs were most significant in influencing the location decision of high technology firms. The tax structure of a state and local community may be especially important to small expanding organizations. A fit with infrastructure is particularly important to meet the location objectives. High technology organizations require a supply of technically trained employees and a high quality educational system. Without these elements of infrastructure, high technology start-ups will relocate to other areas in later stages of the organizational life cycle. Sponsorship that fails to consider the existing infrastructure may crowd out more effective usage of local resources. Browne (1983a) has emphasized the importance of a region's infrastructure in selecting initiatives for rebuilding communities' industrial structure. These findings should caution state and local authorities against being overly zealous in trying to create new organizations without sufficient understanding of the existing physical, industrial, and socioeconomic infrastructure.

C. *A model of the interaction of sponsorship and infrastructure*

The effect of sponsorship, infrastructure and environmental disturbances on the birth and survival of organizations is presented in Figure 1. The model describes public sponsorship at the local level, i.e., some degree of local implementation is assumed by local governmental organizations. The model illustrates changes in the relative magnitude of the three influences at different stages of the life cycle of sponsored organizations. At the time of organizational birth, sponsorship, by definition, exerts the strongest influence. Following birth, the local infrastructure becomes increasingly more important to organizational survival. This is particularly true for organizations with special infrastructure requirements, e.g., a highly skilled labor force. At stage one expansion, the effects of sponsorship and infrastructure are assumed to be about equally important. By the time second stage expansion is reached assuming that sponsorship is withdrawn, infrastructure is the major external influence on organizational survival.

The model also illustrates the role of sponsor-

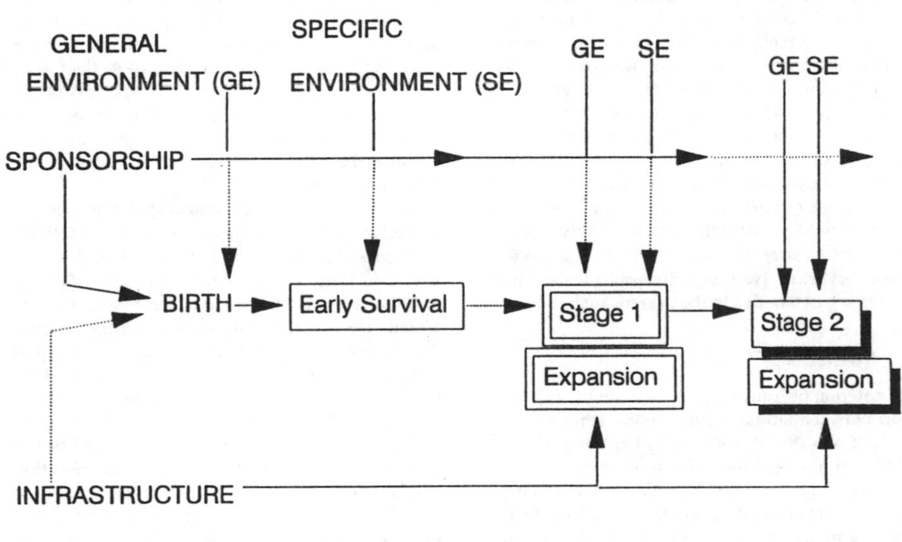

Fig. 1. The effect of environment, infrastructure, and sponsorship on organizational birth and survival

ship as a buffer against competitive and environmental disturbances over the life cycle of the organization. Sponsorship acts as a strong buffer at the time of organizational birth against both types of disturbances. The model illustrates how the buffering role of sponsorship diminishes over the life cycle of the organization. This is indicated in the model by a modest increase in the strength of environmental effects from organizational birth to stage one. By stage two, the organization is directly affected by the environment. The model shows the strong effect of the environment the organization experiences in stage 2. Disturbances from the general environment appear stronger than those of the competition because of the importance of infrastructure in the model. An appropriate fit with infrastructure, i.e., an infrastructure rich enough to meet industry requirements, will help to reduce disturbances from competition at stage two.

The ideas presented in the paper suggest that organizations incubated through sponsorship will exhibit a different pattern of survival than nonsponsored organizations. At stage one, sponsorship enables organizations to overcome the liability of newness and small size. At stage two as sponsorship is withdrawn, a higher mortality rate is expected for sponsored organizations. The strength of the relationships presented in the model indicate that the decrease in the survival rate at stage two may not be as strong if there is a good fit with infrastructure. The effectiveness of sponsorship over the longer term is a critical theoretical issue. However, the available data limit the testing of this idea in the present analysis.

IV. Methodology

As noted above, attempts to measure the relationship between infrastructure, sponsorship and the birth of new organizations have been limited. One of the primary reasons is due to the inadequacy of data available to undertake the analysis. These data are often limited in detail, e.g., distinctions for SIC members, and the years included, e.g., pre-1980 data are often not included. Some of the better data on the births and deaths of firms are available through the Office of Advocacy at the Small Business Administration, e.g., the USEEM and USELM data bases (see e.g., Phillips and Kirchhoff, 1989). However, these data do not include pre-1976 information. Therefore, data included in this analysis were taken from *County Business Patterns* and the U.S. Department of Labor, *Employment and Earnings*. Other data are taken from the *U.S. Statistical Abstracts* and other miscellaneous sources. These sources provided the data for the infrastructure variables, employee, and firm data.

The selection of the five year time frames for measuring the infrastructure, employee and firm data are posited to represent the strategic period during which the effects interaction between the infrastructure and firm births, expansions or contractions would occur. Yearly measures would not be expected to show any significant change. Furthermore, as suggested earlier, small businesses are most vulnerable to failure during the first five years of their existence. Since the analysis is considering high technology industries, i.e., firms and employees, and infrastructure factors that affect them, we are assuming, with some support from the literature, that they tend to be small firms. Small firms are considered to have fewer than 500 employees as defined by the Office of Advocacy of the Small Business Administration in the United States Federal Government. A minor note is that the 1984 year was included because the 1985 year was not available at the time of data collection.

Information for the sponsorship variable included the U.S. Department of Commerce (1988), Bartsch *et al.* (1988), and the National Association of State Development Agencies (1986). Additional information was provided by the Commerce Departments of the fourteen states. The theoretical foundation provided above would suggest the importance of a longitudinal analysis of the sponsorship variable. However, as stated earlier, the data on this variable have not been collected over time by any of the state or Federal agencies associated with economic data collection and analysis. Therefore, the empirical testing of the effect of sponsorship is grossly limited. However, a preliminary analysis has been undertaken to enlighten the one the potential significance of sponsorship.

The choice of the fourteen regions was achieved through a random selection from the Rand McNally's *Places Rated Almanac* (see Boyer and Savageau, 1985). The only criterium used was that the city had to be rated in the top 100 of the 329 urban areas included in the sample. Selected sample characteristics are included in Appendix I and II. Appendix I includes the relative ranking of the fourteen regions for the infrastructure variabies. Appendix II lists the relative rank of each region for the number of firms in the high technology industries included in this study. These data served as the basis for the summary Table IV.

A. *Propositions and results*

The following propositions are presented as a preliminary framework for analysis of the data. These propositions were developed in consideration of the theoretical material discussed above and the available data.

1. *Propositions*

Proposition 1: a) Infrastructure is related to the number of existing firms in high technology industries; and b) infrastructure is related to the number of employees in high technology industries.

Proposition 2: a) Infrastructure is related to the change in the number of firms over two periods in high technology industries; and b) infrastructure is related to the change in the number of employees over two periods in high technology industries.

Proposition 3: Regions with a rich versus a weak infrastructure will have to maintain a higher relative position for the number of firms in high technology over the five time periods. The following values for the infrastructure variables are defined as rich versus weak relative to the fourteen regions (Premus, 1982 & 1984): (Number in parentheses indicates the relative rank of the variable in the research conducted by Premus (1982, p. 23; 1984, p. 49). The variable may represent a close substitute and not the exact variable because of data inavailability.)

1) low relative hourly cost of manufacturing labor (rank of 2);
2) high relative per pupil expenditure on education (rank of 4);
3) high relative number of persons over 25 with four or more years of college education (rank of 1);
4) low relative taxes per capita (rank of 3);
5) high relative income per capita (rank of 7); and
6) low relative cost of housing per capita (rank of 5 & 9).

Proposition 4: Regions with high levels of sponsorship will exhibit higher relative number of firms over time than regions with low levels of sponsorship. This will be evident in the high relative dollars spent by the state for regional economic development and the high relative number of firms in high technology industries.

Proposition 5: The existence of a rich infrastructure and a high level of sponsorship, the higher the relative number of organizations in high technology manufacturing and service industries.

2. *Results*

Proposition #1a & #1b is tested by the significance of the Pearson correlation coefficients (P) for the high technology manufacturing and service industries with the factors representing the six infrastructure variables for each of the five periods. The factor analysis for the aggregate infrastructure variables, i.e., fourteen region values, resulted in two factor solution in four of the five periods with one varimax rotation using Kaiser normalization (see Table I). The fourth period (1980) resulted in a three factor solution. The emergence of per capita tax costs on a single factor may account for the three versus two factor solution. It is difficult to generalize what the factors actually may mean over the five periods. However, it is interesting to note that the per pupil education expenditure generally loads on the other factor from the variable measuring the number of people with 4 or more years of college (standardized for population).

Table II includes the Pearson correlation coefficients for the infrastructure factors and the firm and employee data.

It is evident from the above data that there is preliminary, albeit partial, support for the Proposition #1a & #1b. Specifically, significant correlations exist between infrastructure, and the employee and firm data. However, consideration must be given for both industry, period, and the employee or firm data. Not all high technology industries and not all periods indicate a significant relationship between infrastructure and the number of firms or employees in high technology industries. However, a previous analysis that excluded the employee data minimized the significance of the infrastructure to the existence of firms and employees in high technology industries (Flynn, 1988).

The following data in Table III are presented as a test for Proposition #2a & #2b that the infrastructure variables for period T-1 are related

TABLE I
Factor analysis for infrastructure variables over the 5 periods

Period 1 (1965)	Factor 1	Factor 2	
Per Pupil Expenditure For Education (PPUPEXP)	0.92	0.00	
Housing Costs (HOUPOP)	−0.07	0.98	
Hourly Cost of Labor (COSTLAB)	0.68	−0.39	
Tax Costs, Per Capita (TAXSTRU)	0.39	−0.37	
Income, Per Capita (PERCAP)	0.96	0.04	
Number of People with 4 or more Years of College (COLPOP)	−0.02	0.99	
Eigenvalue	2.81	1.86	
Percent of Variance Explained	46.9	31.1	
Period 2 (1970)	Factor 1	Factor 2	
Per Pupil Expenditure for Education (PPUPEXP)	0.51	0.52	
Housing Cost (HOUPOP)	0.94	−0.11	
Hourly Cost of Labor (COSTLAB)	−0.21	0.81	
Tax Costs, Per Capita (TAXSTRU)	−0.45	0.51	
Income, Per Capita (PERCAP)	0.10	0.91	
Number of People with 4 or more Years of College (COLPOP)	0.96	−0.02	
Eigenvalue	2.42	1.97	
Percent of Variance Explained	40.3	32.9	
Period 3 (1975)	Factor 1	Factor 2	
Per Pupil Expenditure for Education (PPUPEXP)	0.87	−0.27	
Housing Cost (HOUPOP)	−0.33	0.89	
Hourly Cost of Labor (COSTLAB)	0.83	−0.25	
Tax Costs, Per Capita (TAXSTRU)	−0.03	−0.57	
Income, Per Capita (PERCAP)	0.87	0.11	
Number of People with 4 or more Years of College (COLPOP)	−0.17	0.93	
Eigenvalue	3.06	1.46	
Percent of Variance Explained	51.1	24.5	
Period 4 (1980)	Factor 1	Factor 2	Factor 3
Per Pupil Expenditure for Education (PPUPEXP)	−0.05	0.88	0.33
Housing Cost (HOUPOP)	0.95	−0.22	−0.01
Hourly Cost of Labor (COSTLAB)	−0.54	−0.19	0.76
Tax Costs, Per Capita (TAXSTRU)	−0.25	0.83	−0.12
Income, per Capita (PERCAP)	0.24	0.29	0.91
Number of People with 4 or more Years of College (COLPOP)	0.98	−0.14	0.02
Eigenvalue	2.62	1.64	1.26
Percent of Variance Explained	43.7	27.4	21.2
Period 5 (1984)	Factor 1	Factor 2	
Per Pupil Expenditure for Education (PPUPEXP)	−0.31	0.75	
Housing Cost (HOUPOP)	0.97	−0.09	
Hourly Cost of Labor (COSTLAB)	−0.00	0.60	
Tax Costs, Per Capita (TAXSTRU)	−0.55	0.50	
Income, Per Capita (PERCAP)	0.25	0.88	
Number of People with 4 or more Years of College (COLPOP)	0.95	0.16	
Eigenvalue	2.45	1.88	
Percent of Variance Explained	40.9	31.4	

TABLE II

Pearson Correlation Coefficients for Infrastructure Factors with Firm and Employee Values in Fourteen Regions in Aggregate (significance level of variables in parentheses)

Period 1 (1965) Infrastructure Factors with Firm Data (Period 1) in High Technology Industries, Manufacturing & Services.**

Manufacturing	Drugs	Ordac	Compmc	Elec	Missl	Transp	Instru
Factor 1	(0.22)	(0.08)*	(0.06)*	---	---	(0.05)*	
Factor 2	(0.19)	(0.12)	(0.06)*	---	---	(0.10)*	

Services	Services	DataPr	BusSer	Consul
Factor 1	(0.07)*	---	(0.07)*	(0.08)*
Factor 2	(0.05)*	---	(0.04)*	(0.05)*

Period 1 (1965) Infranstructure Factors with Employee Data (Period 1) in High Technology Industries, Manufacturing & Services.

Manufacturing	Drugs	Ordac	Compmc	Elec	Missl	Transp	Instru
Factor 1	(0.40	(0.38)	(0.49)	(0.01)*	---	---	(0.34)
Factor 2	(0.12)	(0.24)	(0.26)	(0.17)	---	---	(0.10)*

Services	Services	DataPr	BurSer	Consul
Factor 1	(0.04)*	---	(0.08)*	(0.11)
Factor 2	(0.05)*	---	(0.06)	(0.04)

** The high technology industries included in this analysis are listed below.

Manufacturing
Drugs (SIC: 283)
Ordnance & Accessories (SIC: 348) (ORDAC)
Office Computers & Accessories (SIC: 357) (COMPMC)
Electrical & Electrical Machinery (SIC: 36) (ELEC)
Guided Misseles, Space Vehicles & Parts (SIC: 376) (MISSL)
Miscellaneous Transportation Equipment (SIC: 379) (TRANSP)
Instruments & Related Products (SIC: 38) (INSTRU)

Services
Services (all)
Business Services (SIC: 73) (BUSSERV)
Data Processing (SIC: 737) (DATAPR)
Consulting & Public Relations (SIC: 739) (CONSUL)

Period 2 (1970) Infrastructure Factors with Firm Data (Period 2) in High Technology Industries, Manufacturing & Services.

Manufacturing	Drugs	Ordac	Compmc	Elec	Missl	Transp	Instru
Factor 1	(0.22)	(0.15)	(0.09)*	(0.05)*	---	(0.16)	(0.03)*
Factor 2	(0.18)	(0.16)	(0.27)	(0.03)*	---	(0.18)	(0.03)*

Services	Services	DataPr	BusSer	Consul
Factor 1	(0.03)*	---	(0.01)*	(0.03)*
Factor 2	(0.05)*	---	(0.16)	(0.12)

* Level of Significance at least 0.10

Continued overleaf

Table II (Continued)

Period 2 (1970) Infrastructure Factors with Employee Data (Period 2) in High Technology Industries, Manfuacturing & Services.

Manufacturing

	Drugs	Ordac	Compmc	Elec	Missl	Transp	Instru
Factor 1	(0.21)	(0.43)	(0.06)*	(0.40)	---	(0.00)*	(0.21)
Factor 2	(0.11)	(0.25)	(0.38)	(0.00)*	---	(0.04)*	(0.03)*

Services

	Services	DataPr	BusSer	Consul
Factor 1	(0.05)*	---	(0.06)*	(0.05)*
Factor 2	(0.04)*	---	(0.15)	(0.13)

Period 3 (1975) Infrastructure Factors with Firm Data (Period 3) in High Technology Industries, Manufacturing & Services.

Manufacturing

	Drugs	Ordac	CompMc	Elec	Missl	Transp	Instru
Factor 1	(0.24)	(0.41)	(0.36)	(0.28)	(0.45)	(0.24)	(0.29)
Factor 2	(0.24)	(0.07)*	(0.07)*	(0.03)*	(0.43)	(0.32)	(0.03)*

Services

	Services	DataPr	BusSer	Consul
Factor 1	(0.16)	(0.43)	(0.26)	(0.37)
Factor 2	(0.01)*	(0.02)*	(0.000)*	(0.02)*

Period 3 (1975) Infrastructure Factors with Employee Data (Period 3) in High Technology Industries, Manufacturing & Services.

Manufacturing

	Drugs	Ordac	Compmc	Elec	Missl	Transp	Instru
Factor 1	(0.07)*	(0.48)	(0.33)	(0.18)	(0.08)*	(0.45)	(0.28)
Factor 2	(0.18)	(0.38)	(0.26)	(0.49)	(0.05)*	(0.03)*	(0.18)

Services

	Services	DataPr	BusSer	Consul
Factor 1	(0.16)	(0.40)	(0.26)	(0.39)
Factor 2	(0.04)*	(0.26)	(0.04)*	(0.04)*

Period 4 (1980) Infrastructure Factors with Firm Data (Period 4) in High Technology Industries Manufacturing & Services.

Manufacturing

	Drugs	Ordac	Compmc	Elec	Missl	Transp	Instru
Factor 1	(0.35)	---	(0.27)	(0.32)	(0.14)	(0.04)*	(0.33)
Factor 2	(0.007)	---	(0.00)*	(0.00)*	(0.35)	(0.45)	(0.03)*
Factor 3	(0.17)	---	(0.43)	(0.42)	(0.02)*	(0.08)*	(0.40)

Services

	Services	DataPr	BusSer	Consul
Factor 1	(0.07)*	(0.32)	(0.04)*	(0.17)
Factor 2	(0.01)*	(0.001)*	(0.01)*	(0.004)*
Factor 3	(0.25)	(0.42)	(0.44)	(0.45)

* Level of Significance at least 0.10

Table II (Continued)

Period 4 (1980) Infrastructure Factors with Employee Data (Period 4) in High Technology Industries, Manufacturing & Services.

Manufacturing

	Drugs	Ordac	CompMc	Elec	Missl	Transp	Instru
Factor 1	(0.05)*	(0.49)	(0.32)	(0.08)*	(0.01)*	(0.07)*	(0.42)
Factor 2	(0.30)	(0.31)	(0.04)*	(0.01)*	(0.42)	(0.30)	(0.00)*
Factor 3	(0.05)*	(0.43)	(0.13)	(0.21)	(0.00)*	(0.09)*	(0.29)

Services

	Services	DataPr	BusSer	Consul
Factor 1	(0.30)	(0.32)	(0.45)	(0.45)
Factor 2	(0.00)*	(0.00)*	(0.00)*	(0.00)*
Factor 3	(0.16)	(0.47)	(0.33)	(0.45)

Period 5 (1984) Infrastructure Factors with Firm Data (Period 5) in High Technology Industries, Manufacturing & Services.

Manufacturing

	Drugs	Ordac	CompMc	Elec	Missl	Transp	Instru
Factor 1	(0.41)	(0.25)	(0.16)	(0.10)*	---	(0.09)*	(0.27)
Factor 2	(0.16)	(0.36)	(0.05)*	(0.01)*	—	(0.08)*	(0.11)

Services

	Services	DataPr	BusSer	Consul
Factor 1	(0.03)*	(0.34)	(0.07)*	(0.11)
Factor 2	(0.08)*	(0.26)	(0.19)	(0.23)

Period 5 (1984) Infrastructure Factors with Employee Data (Period 5) in High Technology Industries, Manufacturing & Services.

Manufacturing

	Drugs	Ordac	CompMc	Elec	Missl	Transp	Instru
Factor 1	(0.07)*	(0.39)	(0.26)	(0.02)*	(0.04)*	(0.30)	(0.41)
Factor 2	(0.18)	(0.16)	(0.02)*	(0.03)*	(0.27)	(0.09)*	(0.01)*

Services

	Services	DataPr	BusSer	Consul
Factor 1	(0.36)	(0.41)	(0.34)	(0.30)
Factor 2	(0.00)*	(0.03)*	(0.01)*	(0.00)*

* Level of Significance at least 0.10

to the subsequent periods net change in firms or employees, respectively. One could tentatively suggest that this measure for net change indicates the births and deaths in forms over the previous four or five year period. However, the data included in the data base do not distinguish for organizational size.

There is some support for the proposition that the net change in firm births and deaths is affected by the infrastructure of the previous period, especially if employee data are included. The significant correlations tend to be in the later periods, i.e., 1970—1975, 1975—1980, & 1980—1984 for a few manufacturing and service industries. The following results for inter-regional differences in infrastructure and firm data may provide some insight to the above results.

The remaining Propositions 3, 4, and 5 are measured by the relative ranking of the number of firms, infrastructure factors in aggregate and dollars allocated for sponsorship and amount of university funding from Federal sources. These data are summarized in Table IV.

The data in columns A1—A2 and B are

TABLE III

Pearson Correlation Coefficients For Infrastructure and the Net Change in Firm Values for Fourteen Regions in Aggregate (significance level of variables in parentheses)

Period 1 (1965) Infrastructure Factors with Firm Data (Period 2-1) in High Technology Industries, Manufacturing & Services.

Manufacturing

	Drugs	Ordac	Compmc	Elec	Missl	Transp	Instru
Factor 1	(0.13)	(0.42)	(0.40)	(0.16)	---	---	(0.13)
Factor 2	(0.12)	(0.48)	(0.20)	(0.26)	---	---	(0.29)

Services

	Services	DataPr	BusSer	Consul
Factor 1	(0.13)	---	(0.44)	(0.20)
Factor 2	(0.29)	---	(0.14)	(0.14)

Period 1 (1965) Infrastructure Factors with Employee Data (Period 2.1) in High Technology Industries, Manufacturing & Services.

Manufacturing

	Drugs	Ordac	Compmc	Elec	Missl	Transp	Instru
Factor 1	(0.20)	(0.26)	(0.41)	(0.30)	---	---	(0.08)*
Factor 2	(0.41)	(0.36)	(0.35)	(0.09)*	---	---	(0.48)

Services

	Services	DataPr	BusSer	Consul
Factor 1	(0.05)*	---	(0.21)	(0.20)
Factor 2	(0.14)	---	(0.10)*	(0.12)

Period 2 (1970) Infrastructure Factors with Firm Data (Period 3-2) in High Technology Industries, Manufacturing & Services.

Manufacturing

	Drugs	Ordac	CompMc	Elec	Missl	Transp	Instru
Factor 1	(0.13)	(0.42)	(0.27)	(0.10)*	---	(0.10)*	(0.19)
Factor 2	(0.21)	(0.43)	(0.34)	(0.20)	---	(0.18)	(0.12)

Services

	Services	DataPr	BusSer	Consul
Factor 1	(0.27)	---	(0.26)	(0.23)
Factor 2	(0.43)	—	(0.42)	(0.21)

Period 2 (1970) Infrastructure Factors with Employee Data (Period 3-2) in High Technology Industries, Manufacturing & Services.

Manufacturing

	Drugs	Ordac	CompMc	Elec	Missl	Transp	Instru
Factor 1	(0.07)*	---	(0.13)	(0.13)	---	(0.04)*	(0.21)
Factor 2	(0.24)	---	(0.07)*	(0.02)*	---	(0.26)	(0.03)*

Services

	Services	DataPr	BusSer	Consul
Factor 1	(0.34)	---	(0.25)	(0.22)
Factor 2	(0.20)	---	(0.48)	(0.22)

* Level of Significance at least 0.10

Table III (Continued)

Period 3 (1975) Infrastructure Factors with Firm Data (Period 4-3) in High Technology Industries, Manufacturing & Services

Manufacturing

	Drugs	Ordac	CompMc	Elec	Missl	Transp	Instru
Factor 1	(0.46)	—	(0.13)	(0.14)	(0.18)	(0.39)	(0.29)
Factor 2	(0.04)*	---	(0.39)	(0.30)	(0.31)	(0.12)	(0.18)

Services

	Services	DataPr	BusSer	Consul
Factor 1	(0.29)	(0.44)	(0.37)	(0.26)
Factor 2	(0.47)	(0.09)*	(0.02)*	(0.02)*

Period 3 (1975) Infrastructure Factors with Employee Data (Period 4-3) in High Technology Industries, Manufacturing & Services.

Manufacturing

	Drugs	Ordac	CompMc	Elec	Missl	Transp	Instru
Factor 1	(0.50)	---	(0.46)	(0.27)	(0.20)	(0.33)	(0.32)
Factor 2	(0.01)*	---	(0.18)	(0.08)*	(0.01)*	(0.01)*	(0.20)

Services

	Services	DataPr	BusSer	Consul
Factor 1	(0.30)	(0.30)	(0.41)	(0.34)
Factor 2	(0.44)	(0.28)	(0.46)	(0.46)

Period 4 (1980) Infrastructure Factors with Firm Data (Period 5-4) in High Technology Industries, Manufacturing & Services.

Manufacturing

	Drugs	Ordac	CompMc	Elec	Missl	Transp	Instru
Factor 1	(0.30)	---	(0.44)	(0.01)*	---	(0.18)	(0.40)
Factor 2	(0.36)	---	(0.004)*	(0.31)	---	(0.43)	(0.000)*
Factor 3	(0.18)	---	(0.42)	(0.14)	---	(0.03)*	(0.37)

Services

	Services	DataPr	BusSer	Consul
Factor 1	(0.03)*	(0.05)*	(0.008)*	(0.03)*
Factor 2	(0.17)	(0.33)	(0.45)	(0.42)
Factor 3	(0.15)	(0.18)	(0.46)	(0.46)

Period 4 (1980) Infrastructure Factors with Employee Data (Period 5-4) in High Technology Industries, Manufacturing & Services.

Manufacturing

	Drugs	Ordac	CompMc	Elec	Missl	Transp	Instru
Factor 1	(0.12)	(0.29)	(0.29)	(0.38)	(0.29)	(0.30)	(0.20)
Factor 2	(0.37)	(0.29)	(0.09)	(0.31)	(0.13)	(0.20)	(0.30)
Factor 3	(0.12)	(0.48)	(0.28)	(0.18)	(0.22)	(0.35)	(0.07)*

Services

	Services	DataPr	BusSer	Consul
Factor 1	(0.14)	(0.20)	(0.09)*	(0.11)
Factor 2	(0.00)*	(0.02)*	(0.23)	(0.30)
Factor 3	(0.37)	(0.19)	(0.46)	(0.06)*

* Level of Significance at least 0.10

TABLE IV
Summary of Relative Rankings for High Technology Firms, Employees, Infrastructure, Sponsorship, and University Factors

Relative	Firm[1]	Employee	Infrastructure[2]	Sponsorship[3]	University[4]
	A(1)	A(2)	B	C	D
Anaheim	27 (9&10)	54 (2)	288 (1)	297 (9)	1.10 (2)
Atlanta	35 (6)	53 (3)	217 (10)	154 (11)	0.28 (6)
Austin	27 (9&10)	42 (10)	242 (5)	952.9 (4)	0.24 (7)
Birmingham	26 (11&12)	32 (13)	148.5 (13)	1235 (3)	0.14 (8)
Boston	83 (1)	47 (7&8)	261 (2)	534 (6)	1.54 (1)
Cincinnatti	35 (5)	44 (9)	247 (4)	1554.5 (2)	0.10 (10)
Charlotte	28 (8)	36 (12)	213 (12)	402.2 (8)	(14)
Detroit	55 (3)	48 (6)	252.5 (3)	163.8 (10)	0.33 (5)
Honolulu	16 (14)	27 (14)	220 (9)	2.2 (14)	0.11 (9)
Minneapolis	48 (4)	47 (7&8)	240 (6)	951 (5)	0.38 (4)
New Orleans	25 (13)	49 (5)	170.5 (14)	43 (13)	(14)
Philadelphia	56 (2)	56 (1)	233 (7)	1974 (1)	0.75 (3)
Portland	34 (7)	39 (11)	214.5 (11)	73 (12)	(14)
Wichita	26 (11&12)	27 (14)	225 (8)	494 (7)	(14)

[1] Firm value based on award of 1 for having firms listed and 2 for being first in the particular period. These values are then summed over the five periods. Rank for all four factors is based on scale of 1—14, i.e. best to worst.
[2] Infrastructure based on ranking of each region over the five periods as included in Appendix # 1.
[3] Sponsorship measured by total spend for state economic development in millions of dollars.
[4] University variable measured by Federal Obligations for research and development to the 100 universities receiving the largest amounts in billions of dollars.

regarded as a test for the significance of infrastructure to the relative ranking of the fourteen regions for the number of firms in the different high technology industries. Although Anaheim has the richest infrastructure, i.e., relative rank of 1, it only ranked 9-10th in firm rankings with Austin. However, Boston which had the second riches infrastructure, has the highest relative rank for the firm data. Detroit ranked third in both infrastructure and firm data. Cincinnati ranked fourth in infrastructure and fifth for firm data. Some consistency between the firm and infrastructure data also include Birmingham and Minneapolis. When we consider the relative ranking of employee data in the same high technology industries, the results are somewhat different. Anaheim, Birmingham, Charlotte, Minneapolis, and Portland emerge as areas in which the relative rankings of infrastructure and employee data are similar (i.e., + or − 2 ranks). These examples suggest that their is some support for Proposition # 3, that a rich infrastructure will facilitate the existence of high technology firms.

Proposition # 4 is measured by the relative ranking of sponsorship, measured in millions of dollars allocated for industrial revenue bonds, direct loans, development corporations, industrial training and venture capital (Column C). These rankings are compared with the firm rankings in Column A1. Evidence to support this proposition include Philadelphia, Minneapolis, Charlotte, Anaheim, New Orleans and Honolulu. When we consider the data in Column A2, even fewer regions show these relationships. These regions are Honolulu, Philadelphia and Portland. Although not all regions show some consistency between sponsorship and the existence of high technology employees and firms, there is some evidence to support the proposition that sponsorship may be important.

The final Proposition # 5, that there is a relationship between a rich infrastructure, a high level of dollars allocated for sponsorship and the stence of high technology includes the relative rankings in Columns B, C, and A1—A2, respectively. There is little evidence that supports this proposition. Minneapolis and New Orleans are the only regions that have relatively equivalent rankings for all four variables. New Orleans does however, have a significantly higher ranking in number of employees in the high technology regions.

A final measure includes the potential role university funding from Federal sources may have in spawning high technology firms. Mitton (1990) has suggested that institutional effects, e.g., university research centers, are important to the "begetting" process in the biotechnology industry in the San Diego area. These effects were hypothesized to be more significant in the early years of firm formation. In the later years, the spawned firms take over as the prime mover for further formation of new firms. Although little research into this issue is available, it is expected that universities serve a critical role as "incubators" of new products and processes. Recently, Louis *et al.* (1989, p. 128) found evidence that communities where universities received larger grants had more significant levels of entrepreneurial activity than those receiving smaller grants. Such grants could be seen as a form of general sponsorship, reducing inconsistencies between the community infrastructure and the need of new firms for an environment with technical and scientific research to provide necessary vitality. Furthermore, the U.S. Department of Education has recently reported that other than tuition, Federal monies account for the largest source of revenue for doctoral degree-granting universities.

Although an operational means for measuring the university variable is problematic, data are aggregated from the National Science Foundation's (NSF) Bulletin Board (an on-line data service), and the Resources, Community, and Economic Development Division of the United States General Accounting Office. Data were gleaned from the NSF for Federal obligations to universities within a fifty mile radius of the relevant region for the 1979—1984 period. These data are not available on the university level prior to the 1979 period.

The data presented in Column D in Table IV suggest that university funding may have some relationship to the prominence of certain areas in the high technology arena. In particular, there is some commonality between the relative rank of firms in Column A and the university funding data in Column D. For example, Atlanta, Boston, Detroit, and Philadelphia rank closely on these two factors (Columns A1 and D). A notable exception is Anaheim with the rank of 11 & 12, and 2 on the firm and university measures, respectively. However, when we include the number of employees as the measure for high technology the results are consistent with the expectation that universities contribute to employment in high technology industries in Anaheim, Cincinnati, Detroit, and Philadelphia.

Although no causality is suggested, there may be some support for the critical role of universities in high technology firm formation and survival. More rigorous data analyses need to be undertaken as better data are procurred from institutions such as the NSF.

In summary, there are data to support the idea that either a rich infrastructure or high relative dollars allocated for sponsorship will support the existence of high technology manufacturing and service firms. Also, there is some evidence that suggests infrastructure will effect a net change in the number of firms in the subsequent period as measured in Proposition #2a & #2b. Further analyses are necessary to more rigorously test the Propositions. This would be facilitated by access to a more detailed data base, especially including sponsorship data over all five periods, i.e., 1965—1984.

Implications

Preliminary analysis of the existing data base suggests that either a rich infrastructure or high relative dollars allocated for sponsorship will support the existence of high technology manufacturing and service firms. However, further analyses are necessary to more rigorously test the propositions. This would be facilitated by access to better data.

The preliminary analysis suggests, however, that sponsorship: (1) support the initial development of industries compatible with the local infrastructure; (2) enrich the local infrastructure through direct and indirect support; and, (3) require firms to include mechanisms for organizational learning to overcome the effects of benevolent dependence resulting from sponsorship.

The matching of the local infrastructure with industry requirements may be problematic given the dynamic aspects of most emerging technologies. However, there are various typologies for classifying organizational technology (Perrow, 1967; Scott, 1981; Thompson, 1967) and organizational environments (Dess and Beard, 1984). This suggests a means for sponsoring organizations to identify technologies that are compatible with the local infrastructure. For example, the infrastructure necessary to support biotechnology research requires a highly educated workforce supported through a local university with graduate programs to maintain the necessary level of basic and applied research.

Although the university was included as a part of the empirical analysis, it does not represent a "best" measure. It is recommended that a region specific analysis be undertaken to assess the contribution of the university to the formation of firms and the expansion of employment. The university is an important element of the local infrastructure and as a vehicle of sponsorship. The university serves critical roles as a part of the local infrastructure and also, as a vehicle of sponsorship, i.e., through the use of Federal grants and contracts and industry sponsored research.

As noted earlier, state and local planners have been favorably biased toward high-technology industries to promote rapid employment growth. However, Browne (1983b) has shown that there may be more employment opportunities in other industries. For example, business services often grow at a higher rate than the populations of high technology firms they support.

Sponsorship can enrich the local infrastructure by various programs aimed at increasing the attractiveness of a region for organizational births and survival through increased educational funding, technical training for displaced workers, and technical and managerial assistance to innovative firms, and improving the quality of life.

Public policy formulation and implementation for sponsorship appears to be more effective at a local versus the state or federal level as indicated by research on decentralization of sponsorship (Joglekar and Hamburg, 1983a & b). Similarly, Kirlin (1984) and Nelson and Langlois (1983) concluded that governmental policy aimed at increasing the innovative output of organizations is more effective with low levels of control, i.e., decentralization. Controlling for level of resources, local sponsorship is the most effective in meeting local needs. However, the initial impact of local sponsorship cannot be maintained if environmental disturbances are considerable. This suggests that multiple sources of sponsorship, i.e., cooperative efforts with decentralization of implementation will be effective over the longer term.

References

Aiken, M. and J. Hage, 1968, 'Organizational Interdependence and Intraorganizational Structure', *American Sociological Review* **33**, 912–930.

Aldrich, H., 1979, *Organizations and Environments*, Englewood Cliffs, N.J.: Prentice Hall.

Aldrich, H., B. McKelvey and D. Ulrich, 1984, 'Design Strategy from the Population Perspective', *Journal of Management* **10**(1), 67–86.

Astley, G., 1985, 'The Two Ecologies: Population and Community Perspectives on Organizational Evolution', *Administrative Science Quarterly* **30**(2), 224–241.

Bartsch, C., M. Basrber and M. Quan, (eds.), 1988, *The Guide to State and Federal Resources for Economic Development*, Washington, D.C.: Northeast-Midwest Institute.

Birch, D. and S. McCracken, 1982, *The Small Business Share of Job Creation: Lessons Learned from the Use of Longitudinal File*, Washington, D.C.: The Small Business Administration.

Blau, J. and K. L. Lieben, 1983, 'Growth, Decline and Death: A Panel Study of Architectual Firms', in J. R. Blau, M. E. LaGoug and J. S. Pipkin (eds.), *Professionals and Urban Form*, Albany: State University of New York Press, pp. 224–250.

Blomquist, G. C., M. C. Berger and J. P. Hoehn, 1988, 'New Estimates of Life in Urban Areas', *American Economic Review* **78**(1), 89–107.

Boyer, R. and D. Savageau, 1985, *Places Rated Almanac*, Chicago: Rand-McNally.

Brittain, J. W. and J. Freeman, 1980, 'Organizational Proliferation and Density Dependant Selection', in J. R. Kimberly and R. H. Miles (eds.), *The Organizational Life Cycle*, San Francisco: Jossey-Bass, pp. 291–338.

Brody, H., 1985, 'States vie for a Slice of the Pie', *High Technology* **5**(1), 16–28.

Browne, L. E., 1983a, 'Can High Tech Save the Great Lake States?', *New England Economic Review*, Nov/Dec, 19–33.

Browne, L. E., 1983b, 'High Technology and Business Services', *New England Economic Review*, July/August, 5–17.

Bruderl, J. and R. Schussler, 1990, 'Organizational Mortality: The Liability of Newness and Adolescence', *Administrative Science Quarterly* **35**(3), 530–547.

Carlton, D. W., 1983, 'The Location and Employment Choices of New Firms: An Econometric Model with

Discrete and Continuous Endogenous Variables', *Review of Economics and Statistics* **65**(4), 440—449.

Carroll, G. R. and J. Delacroix, 1982, 'Organization Mortality in the Newspaper Industries of Argentina and Ireland: An Ecological Approach', *Administrative Science Quarterly* **27**(2), 169—198.

Carroll, G. R. and M. T. Hannan, 1989a, 'Density Dependence in the Evolution of Populations', *American Sociological Review* **54**, 524—541.

Carroll, G. R. and M. T. Hannan, 1989b, 'Density Delay in the Evolution of Organizational Populations: A Model and Five Empirical Tests', *Administrative Science Quarterly* **34**, 411—430.

Charney, A. H., 1983, 'Intraurban Manufacturing Location Decisions and Local Tax Differentials', *Journal of Urban Economics* **14**(2), 184—205.

Chicago Fed Letter, 1989, 'Bidding for Business.' Essays on Issues, *The Federal Reserve Bank of Chicago* **16**, December, 1—3.

Daft, R., 1983, *Organization Theory and Design*, St. Paul: West.

Daft, R. and S. Becker, 1978, *Innovation in Organizations*, New York: Elsevier.

Dess, G. G. and D. W. Beard, 1984, 'Dimensions of Organizational Task Environments', *Administrative Science Quarterly* **29**, 52—73.

Evans, J., 1985, 'Public Employment through Public Infrastructure Investment', in *Organization for Economic Co-Operation and Economic Development (OECD), Employment Growth and Structural Change*, Paris: OECD, pp. 158—171.

Flynn, D. M., 1988, 'Sponsorship, Infrastructure and New Organizations: Exploration of an Ecological Model into Fourteen Regions', *Frontiers of Entrepreneurship*, 238—253.

Freeman, J., G. Carroll and M. Hannan, 1983, 'The Liability of Newness: Age Dependence in Organizational Death Rates', *American Sociological Review* **48**(5), 692—710.

Gomory, R. E., 1983, 'Technology Development', *Science* **220**, 576—580.

Gruenstein, J. M., 1984, 'Targeting High Tech in the Delaware Valley', *Business Review*, May/June, 3—14.

Gyourko, J., 1987, 'Effects of Local Tax Structure on the Factor Intensity Composition of Manufacturing Across Cities', *Journal of Urban Economics* **22**(1), 151—164.

Hall, R., 1987, *Organizations: Structure and Process*, Englewood Cliffs, N.J.: Prentice-Hall.

Hannan, M. and J. Freeman, 1988, 'The Ecology of Organizational Mortality: American Labor Unions, 1836—1985', *American Journal of Sociology* **94**(1), 25—52.

Hannan, M. and J. Freeman, 1986, 'Where Do Organizational Forms Come From?', *Sociological Forum* **1**, 50—72.

Hannan, M. and J. Freeman, 1984, 'Structural Inertia and Organizational Change', *American Sociological Review* **49**(2), 149—164.

Hannan, M. and J. Freeman, 1977, 'The Population Ecology of Organizations', *American Journal of Sociology* **82**, 929—964.

Harr, C. M., 1984, 'The Joint Venture Approach to Urban Renewal: from Model Cities to Enterprise Zones', in H. Brooks, L. Liebman and C. S. Schellings (eds.), *Public-Private Partnership*, Cambridge, MA.: Ballinger, pp. 63—87.

Harris, Louis and Associates Inc., 1984, *Entrepreneurship in America, A Sentry Study*, New York.

Hekman, J. S., 1980, 'Can New England hold onto its High Technology Industry?', *New England Economic Review*, March/April, 35—44.

Huber, G., 1990, 'A Theory of the Effects of Advanced Information Processing Technologies of Organizational Design, Intelligence, and Decision Making', *Academy of Management Review* **15**(1), 47—71.

Huber, G., 1984, 'The Nature and Design of Post-Industrial Organizations', *Management Science* **30**(8), 928—951.

Joglekar, P. and M. Hamburg, 1983a, 'An Evaluation of Federal Policy Instruments to Stimulate Basic Research in Industry', *Management Science* **29**, 997—1015.

Joglekar, P. and M. Hamburg, 1983b, 'An Evaluation of Federal Policies Concerning Joint Ventures for Applied Research and Development', *Management Science* **9**, 1016—1026.

Kimberly, J. and R. Miles (eds.), 1980, *The Organizational Life Cycle*, San Francisco: Jossey-Bass.

Kirlin, J., 1984, 'A Political Perspective', in T. Miller (ed.), *Public Sector Performance*, Baltimore: Johns Hopkins, pp. 161—192.

Livingston, A., 1989, 'State Capital', *Venture*, May, 57—63.

Louis, K. S., D. Blumenthal, M. E. Gluck and M. A. Stoto, 1989, 'Entrepreneurs in Academe: An Exploration of Behaviors among Life Scientists', *Administrative Science Quarterly* **34**(1), 110—131.

Luger, M. I., 1984, 'Does North Carolina's High-Tech Development Program Work?', *Journal of the American Planning Association* **50**(3), 280—289.

Malecki, E. J., 1984, 'High Technology and Local Economic Development', *Journal of the American Planning Association* **50**(3), 262—269.

Miles, R. and W. Randolph, 1980, 'Influence of Organizational Learning Styles on Early Development', in J. Kimberly and R. Miles (eds.), *The Organizational Life Cycle*, San Francisco: Jossey-Bass.

Mitton, D. G., 1990, 'Research Institutions Influence on Technology Transfer: The San Diego Biotech Industry', *USASBE Conference*, October, Orlando: Florida.

National Association of State Development Agencies, 1986, *Directory of Incentives for Business Investment and Development in the U.S.: A State By State Guide*, Washington, D.C.: The Urban Institute.

Nelson, R. G. and R. N. Langlois, 1983, 'Industrial Innovation Policy: Lessons from American History', *Science* **219**, 814—818.

Newman, R. J. and D. H. Sullivan, 1988, 'Econometric Analysis of Business Tax Impacts on Industrial Location: What Do We Know, and How Do We Know It?', *Journal of Urban Economics* **23**, 215—234.

Pennings, J. M., 1982a, 'Organizational Birth Frequencies: An Empirical Investigation', *Administrative Science Quarterly* **27**, 120—144.

Pennings, J. M. 1982b, 'The Urban Quality of Life and Entrepreneurship', *Academy of Management Journal* **25**, 63—79.

Perrow, C., 1967, 'A Framework for the Comparative Analysis of Organizations', *American Sociological Review* **32**, 194—208.

Pfeffer, J., 1982, *Organizations and Organizational Theory*, Boston: Pitman, 1982.

Pfeffer, J. and G. Salancik, 1978, *The External Control of Organizations: A Resource Dependence Approach*, New York: Harper and Row.

Phillips, B. D. and B. A. Kirchhoff, 1989, 'Formation, Growth, and Survival: Small Firm Dynamics in the U.S. Economy', *Small Business Economics* **1** (1), 65—74.

Premus, R., 1984, 'Urban Growth and Technological Innovation', in R. D. and J. P. Blair (eds.), *Urban Economic Development*, Berkeley: Sage, pp. 47—61.

Premus, R., 1982, *Location of High Technology Firms and Regional Economic Development*, Joint Economic Committee of Congress, Washington, D.C.: Government Printing Office.

Romanelli, E., 1989, 'Environment and Strategies of Organization Start-Up: Effects on Early Survival', *Administrative Science Quarterly* **34**, 369—387.

Rosenberg, R., 1985, 'What Companies Look For', *High Technology* **5** (1), 31—37.

Schmenner, R. W., J. C. Huber, and R. L. Cook, 1987, 'Geographic Differences and the Location of New Manufacturing Facilities', *Journal of Urban Economics* **21**, 83—104.

Schmitt, R. W., 1984, 'National R&D Policy: An Industrial Perspective', *Science* **224**, 1206—1209.

Scott, W. R., 1981, *Organizations*, Englewood Cliffs, N.J.: Prentice-Hall.

Shan, W., J. V. Singh and T. L. Aburey, 1991, 'Modelling the Creation of New Biotechnology, 1973—1987', *Proceedings of the Academy of Management* **97**, 78—82.

Singh, J. V., D. J. Tucker and R. J. House, 1986, 'Organizational Legitimacy and the Liability of Newness', *Administrative Science Quarterly* **31**, 171—193.

Smilor, R. W. and H. R. Feeser, 1991, 'Chaos and the Entrepreneurial Process: Patterns and Policy Implications in Technology Research', *Journal of Business Venturing* **6**, 165—172.

Smith, V. K., 1983, 'The Role of Site and Job Characteristics in Hedonic Wage Models', *Journal of Urban Economics* **13**, 296—321.

Soete, L. and C. Freeman, 1985, 'New Technologies, Investment and Employment Growth', in Organization for Economic Co-Operation and Economic Development (OECD), *Employment Growth and Structural Change*, Paris: OECD, pp. 52—82.

Stinchcombe, A. L., 1965, 'Social Structure and Organizations', in J. G. March (ed.), *Handbook of Organizations*, Chicago: Rand McNally.

Thomas, M. D., 1987, 'The Innovation Factor in the Process of Microeconomic Industrial Change: Conceptual Explorations', in G. A. van der Knapp, and E. Wever, *New Technology and Regional Development*, pp. 21—44.

Thompson, J., 1967, *Organizations in Action*, New York: McGraw-Hill, 1967.

Ulrich, D. and J. B. Barney, 1984, 'Perspectives in Organizations: Resource Dependence, Efficiency, and Population', *Academy of Management Review* **9** (3), 471—481.

U.S. Department of Commerce, 1988, *Directory of Federal & State Assistance: A Guide for New and Growing Companies*, Springfield, VA.: National Technical Information Service.

United States General Accounting Office, 1987, *University Funding: Patterns of Distribution of Federal Research Funds to Universities*, GAO/RCED-87-67BR.

United States General Accounting Office, 1988, *Engineering Research Centers: NSF Program Management and Industry Sponsorship*, GAO/RCED-88-177.

U.S. Small Business Administration, 1988, *The Annual Report on Small Business and Competition*, Washington, D.C.: Government Printing Office.

Van de Ven, A. H., R. Hudson and D. M. Schroeder, 1984, 'Designing New Business Startups: Entrepreneurial, Organizational, and Ecological Considerations', *Journal of Management* **10** (1), 87—107.

Venkataram, S., A. H. Van de Ven, J. Buckeye and R. Hudson, 1990, 'Starting Up in a Turbulent Environment: A Process Model of Failure among Firms with High Customer Dependence', *Journal of Business Venturing* **5**, 277—295.

Wholey, D. R. and J. W. Brittain, 1986, 'Organizational Ecology: Findings and Implications', *Academy of Management Review* **11** (3), 513—533.

Weiwel, W., J. S. deBettencourt and R. Mier, 1984, 'Planners, Technology and Economic Growth', *Journal of the American Planning Association* **50** (3), 290—296.

Young, R. C., 1988, 'Is Population Ecology a Useful Paradigm for the Study of Organizations?', *American Journal of Sociology* **94** (1), 1—24.

Appendix I. Rankings of Regions by Infrastructure Variables over Five Periods

Hourly Cost of Manufacturing Labor: COSTLAB
(Mean Rank: lowest to highest)

	1965	1970	1975	1980	1984
Anaheim	13	12	6	5	11
Atlanta	3	1	3	3	5
Austin	2	3	2	2	2
Birmingham	10	6	9.5	6	3
Boston	5	8	5	4	7
Cincinnatti	8	10	7	10	13
Charlotte	1	2	1	1	1
Detroit	14	14	13	13	14
Honolulu	4	4	14	14	4
Minneapolis	11	11	9.5	9	9.5
New Orleans	6	5	4	8	9.5
Philadelphia	7	9	8	7	6
Portland	12	13	11	12	12
Wichita	9	7	12	11	8

State Per Pupil Educational Expenditure: PPUPEXP
(Mean Rank: lowest to highest)

	1965	1970	1975	1980	1984
Anaheim	13	14	8	12	4
Atlanta	3	1	1	7	2
Austin	4	2	3	1	5
Birmingham	1	3	2	3	1
Boston	11	5	6	14	12
Cincinnatti	7	7	7	6	7.5
Charlotte	2	6	5	2	6
Detroit	10	13	14	9.5	7.5
Honolulu	9	8	9	5	14
Minneapolis	6	11	10	8	10
New Orleans	5	4	4	4	3
Philadelphia	12	10	13	13	11
Portland	14	9	11	9.5	13
Wichita	8	12	12	11	9

Persons over Age 25 with Four or more Years of College divided by Population: COLPOP
(Mean Rank: lowest to highest)

	1965	1970	1975	1980	1984
Anaheim	14	14	14	14	14
Atlanta	6	5	7	8	8
Austin	12	13	13	13	13
Birmingham	3	4	4	3	3
Boston	9	9	9	9	9
Cincinnatti	11	11	11	11	10
Charlotte	8	8	8	7	7
Detroit	10	10	10	10	11
Honolulu	1	1	1	1	1
Minneapolis	7	7	6	6	6
New Orleans	5	6	5	5	5
Philadelphia	13	12	12	12	12
Portland	2	2	3	4	4
Wichita	4	3	2	2	2

Appendix I (Continued)

Taxes Paid Per Capita: TAXSTRU
(Mean Rank: lowest to highest)

	1965	1970	1975	1980	1984
Anaheim	3	4	3	1	4
Atlanta	6	1	9	10	9
Austin	2	2	2	3	2
Birmingham	4	3	8	8	3
Boston	14	14	14	14	14
Cincinnatti	10	10	11.5	12	10
Charlotte	5	6	5	4	5
Detroit	12	12	11.5	11	12
Honolulu	11	11	10	7	8
Minneapolis	8	7	6	5	6
New Orleans	9	9	7	9	11
Philadelphia	13	13	13	13	13
Portland	7	8	4	6	7
Wichita	1	5	1	2	1

Income Per Capita: PERCAP
(Mean Rank: lowest to highest)

	1965	1970	1975	1980	1984
Anaheim	14	13	13	14	14
Atlanta	4	1	4	4	4
Austin	5	5	5	6	9
Birmingham	1	2	1	1	1
Boston	13	12	12	10	13
Cincinnati	10	10	7	8	7
Charlotte	2	3	2	2	2
Detroit	12	11	11	12	8
Honolulu	11	14	14	13	12
Minneapolis	6	8	8	7	11
New Orleans	3	4	3	3	3
Philadelphia	8	9	9	5	6
Portland	9	6	6	9	5
Wichita	7	7	10	11	10

Cost of Single Family Home Per Capita: HOUPOP
(lowest to the highest)

	1965	1970.	1975	1980	1984
Anaheim	13	13	12	13	13
Atlanta	1	1	6	6	9
Austin	14	14	14	14	14
Birmingham	10	10	13	9	7
Boston	6	6	2	3	1
Cincinnati	11	11	10	10	10
Charlotte	12	12	11	12	12
Detroit	4	4	3	2	2
Honolulu	7	7	7	8	3
Minneapolis	3	3	4	4	6
New Orleans	8	8	8	7	8
Philadelphia	2	2	1	1	4
Portland	5	5	5	5	5
Wichita	9	9	9	11	11

Appendix II. Firm Data for Counties in High Technology Industries over Five Periods [Source: County Business Patterns 1965, 1970, 1980, & 1984]

Manufacturing
Drugs (SIC: 283)
(Mean Rank: ranked lowest to highest)

	1965	1970	1975	1980	1984
Atlanta	1	2	1	1.5	8
Boston				8	6
Cincinatti	3	3	4	5.5	4.5
Charlotte				1.5	1
Detroit	4	4	5	4	3
Minneapolis			2.5	3	2
Philadelphia	5	5	6	7	7
Portland	2	1	2.5	5.5	4.5

Summary Statistics for Each Period

	1965	1970	1975	1980	1984
Number of Regions	5	5	6	8	8
Mean	15.4	11.8	8.8	7.6	14.1
Std. Dev.	11.5	8.9	4.4	3.8	16.9
Minimum	6	4	5	3	3
Maximum	15	25	17	13	55

Ordac. & Accessories (SIC: 348)
(Mean Rank: ranked lowest to highest)

	1965	1970	1975	1980	1984
Birmingham	3	2			
Boston	4.5	4	5	1	1.5
Cincinatti	2	1	3		
Charlotte	1				
Detroit	7	5	4		
Minneapolis			1.5	2	3
Philadelphia	6	6	1.5		
Portland	4.5	3			1.5

Summary Statistics for Each Period

	1965	1970	1975	1980	1984
Number of Regions	7	6	5	2	3
Mean	14.8	14.5	3.8	1.5	1.3
Std. Dev.	11.4	9.3	3.5	0.7	0.5
Minimum	3	5	1	1	1
Maximum	33	28	9	2	2

Office Computers & Accessories (SIC: 357)
(Mean Rank: ranked lowest to highest)

Appendix II (Continued)

	1965	1970	1975	1980	1984
Anaheim		1.5	3	5	6
Atlanta			5	5	3
Austin		1.5	3	5	6
Boston	4	7	9	10	10
Cincinatti	1	3.5	6	7	6
Charlotte				3	4
Detroit	3	5	7	8	8
Minneapolis	2	6	8	9	9
Philadelphia		3.5	3	2	1.5
Wichita			1	1	1.5

Summary Statistics for Each Period

	1965	1970	1975	1980	1984
Number of Regions	4	7	9	10	10
Mean	10.5	15	12.3	13.9	15.9
Std. Dev.	5.4	19.2	17.2	18.5	23.8
Minimum	5	2	2	2	3
Maximum	18	56	55	62	80

Electrical & Electrical Machinery (SIC: 36)
(Mean Rank: ranked lowest to highest)

	1965	1970	1975	1980	1984
Anaheim	2.5	3.5	4.5	4.5	6.5
Atlanta	6	7	6	6	5
Austin	2.5	3.5	4.5	4.5	6.5
Birmingham	4	5	3	7.5	4
Boston	12	13	13	14	14
Cincinatti	8	9	9	10	10
Charlotte	5	6	7	7.5	8
Detroit	10	11	10	11	11
Honolulu				3	2
Minneapolis	9	10	12	13	13
New Orleans		2	1.5	2	1
Philadelphia	11	12	11	12	12
Portland	7	8	8	9	9
Wichita	1	1	1.5	1	3

Summary Statistics for Each Period

	1965	1970	1975	1980	1984
Number of Regions	12	13	13	14	14
Mean	57.2	64.9	61.3	60.4	63.0
Std. Dev.	64.1	76.3	69.5	74.0	73.5
Minimum	6	9	14	1	8
Maximum	188	266	261	284	288

Guided Missles, Space Vehicles & Parts (SIC: 376)
(Mean Rank: ranked lowest to highest)

Appendix II (Continued)

	1965	1970	1975	1980	1984
Boston			1.5	1.5	
Cincinatti			1.5	1.5	
New Orleans			3.5	3	1
Philadelphia			3.5	4	2

Summary Statistics for Each Period

	1965	1970	1975	1980	1984
Number of Regions			4	4	2
Mean			1.5	1.7	1.5
Std. Dev.			0.5	0.9	0.7
Minimum			1	1	1
Maximum			2	3	2

Miscellaneous Transportation Equipment (SIC: 379)
(Mean Rank: ranked lowest to highest)

	1965	1970	1975	1980	1984
Atlanta				1.5	1
Boston			1.5	3.5	
Charlotte		1			
Detroit		2.5	4	6	3
Minneapolis	5	3	5	2	
Philadelphia	2.5	1.5	3.5		
Portland	4	1.5	1.5		

Summary Statistics for Each Period

	1965	1970	1975	1980	1984
Number of Regions		5	4	6	3
Mean		5.8	3.7	3.1	5
Std. Dev.		3.6	0.9	2.2	4
Minimum		1	3	1	1
Maximum		11	5	7	9

Instruments & Related Products (SIC: 38)
(Mean Rank: ranked lowest to highest)

	1965	1970	1975	1980	1984
Anaheim	5	3.5	5.5	6.5	9.5
Atlanta	5	5	7	4.5	6
Austin	5	3.5	5.5	6.5	9.5
Birmingham	1.5	1.5	1	1	4
Boston	11	13	13	13	7
Cincinnatti	8	9	9	9	11
Charlotte	1.5	1.5	3	4.5	5
Detroit	10	10	10	10	12
Honolulu					2
Minneapolis	9	11	11	12	14
New Orleans		6	2	2	1

Appendix II (Continued)

Philadelphia	12	12	12	11	13
Portland	7	8	8	8	8
Wichita	3	7	4	3	3

Summary Statistics for Each Period

	1965	1970	1975	1980	1984
Number of Regions	12	13	13	13	14
Mean	30.5	32.0	41.5	42.3	28.75
Std. Dev.	30.5	33.7	49.5	51.0	20.9
Minimum	5	7	9	7	9
Maximum	97	111	187	196	80

Services
(Mean Rank: ranked lowest to highest)

	1965	1970	1975	1980	1984
Anaheim	1.5	1.5	2.5	2.5	3.5
Atlanta	9	10	9	10	10
Austin	1.5	1.5	2.5	2.5	3.5
Birmingham	6	6	5	5	6
Boston	12	12	12	12	14
Cincinnatti	10	9	10	9	9
Charlotte	3	4	4	4	2
Detroit	14	14	14	14	13
Honolulu	5	5	7	7	7
Minneapolis	11	11	11	11	11
New Orleans	7	7	6	5	5
Philadelphia	13	13	13	13	12
Portland	8	8	8	8	8
Wichita	4	3	1	1	1

Summary Statistics for Each Period

	1965	1970	1975	1980	1984
Number of Regions	14	14	14	14	14
Mean	4583.0	4695.5	4959.9	5469.3	5868.3
Std. Dev.	3408.9	3064.5	2633.8	2482.0	2775.5
Minimum	1746	1958	2219	2561	2666
Maximum	13317.0	11851	10932	10387	11350

Business Services (SIC: 73)
(Mean Rank: ranked lowest to highest)

	1965	1970	1975	1980	1984
Anaheim	1.5	2	3	3	5
Atlanta	10	10	10	12	12
Austin	1.5	2	2	1	1

Appendix II (Continued)

Birmingham	4	4	4	4	3
Boston	11	11	11	13	14
Cincinnatti	8	9	9	9	9
Charlotte	5	5	5	6	6
Detroit	14	14	14	11	11
Honolulu	6	6	7	7	7
Minneapolis	12	12	12	14	13
New Orleans	7	7	6	5	4
Philadelphia	13	13	13	10	10
Portland	9	8	8	8	8
Wichita	3	2	1	2	2

Summary Statistics for Each Period

	1965	1970	1975	1980	1984
Number of Regions	14	14	14	14	14
Mean	437.7	541.2	682.0	821.1	932.2
Std. Dev.	315.9	339.4	359.8	434.9	567.1
Minimum	148	210	270	219	334
Maximum	1181	1218	1232	1571	2372

Data Processing (SIC: 737)
(Mean Rank: ranked lowest to highest)

	1965*	1970*	1975	1980	1984
Anaheim			3.5	5	7.5
Atlanta			12	12	12
Austin			3.5	5	7.5
Birmingham			6	2	3
Boston			14	14	14
Cincinnatti			8	11	10
Charlotte			7	5	3
Detroit			10	10	11
Honolulu			5	7	5
Minneapolis			13	13	13
New Orleans			2	1	1
Philadelphia			11	8	6
Portland			9	9	9
Wichita			1	3	3

Summary Statistics for Each Period

	1965	1970	1975	1980	1984
Number of Regions			14	14	14
Mean			42.8	81.1	106
Std. Dev.			34.0	65.9	123
Minimum			10	28	29
Maximum			139	276	512

Consulting & Public Relations (SIC: 739)
(Mean Rank: ranked lowest to highest)

Appendix II (Continued)

	1965	1970	1975	1980	1984
Anaheim	2.5	5	5.5	4	7.5
Atlanta	10	10	11	12	12
Austin	2.5	5	5.5	4	7.5
Birmingham	1	2	3	2	3
Boston	12	13	14	14	14
Cincinnatti	9	9	9	9	10
Charlotte	5	5	4	4	3
Detroit	14	12	10	10	11
Honolulu	6	7.5	8	7	5
Minneapolis	11	11	13	13	13
New Orleans	8	3	2	6	1
Philadelphia	13	14	12	11	6
Portland	7	7.5	7	8	9
Wichita	4	1	1	1	3

Summary Statistics for Each Period

	1965	1970	1975	1980	1984
Number of Regions	14	14	14	14	
Mean	69.5	119.2	105.9	143.0	200.0
Std. Dev.	52.1	79.4	69.0	94.9	238.5
Minimum	23	42	33	45	46
Maximum	194	265	248	345	984

[21]

THE DEVELOPMENT OF AN INFRASTRUCTURE FOR ENTREPRENEURSHIP

ANDREW H. VAN DE VEN
Carlson School of Management, University of Minnesota

EXECUTIVE SUMMARY

This paper takes a macroperspective of entrepreneurship, and focuses on the issues and events involved in constructing an industrial infrastructure that facilitates and constrains entrepreneurship. This infrastructure includes: (1) institutional arrangements to legitimate, regulate, and standardize a new technology, (2) public resource endowments of basic scientific knowledge, financing mechanisms, and a pool of competent labor, as well as (3) proprietary R&D, manufacturing, marketing, and distribution functions by private entrepreneurial firms to commercialize the innovation for profit. Although extensive research substantiates the importance of these infrastructure components, they have been treated as externalities to entrepreneurship. By incorporating these components within a single framework, one can systematically examine how various actors and functions interact to facilitate and constrain entrepreneurship.

The paper makes three contributions to understanding entrepreneurship. First, I believe that the study of entrepreneurship is deficient if it focuses exclusively on the characteristics and behaviors of individual entrepreneurs, on the one hand, and if it treats the social, economic, and political factors influencing entrepreneurship as external demographic statistics, on the other hand. Popular folklore notwithstanding, the process of entrepreneurship is a collective achievement requiring key roles from numerous entrepreneurs in both the public and private sectors.

Second, the paper examines how and why this infrastructure for entrepreneurship emerges. I argue that while this infrastructure facilitates and constrains individual entrepreneurs, it is the latter who construct and change the industrial infrastructure. This infrastructure does not emerge and change all

Address correspondence to Professor Andrew H. Van de Ven, University of Minnesota, Curtis L. Carlson School, 271 19th Avenue South, Minneapolis, MN 55455.

An earlier draft of this paper was presented at a conference organized by Ivan Bull on Theories of Entrepreneurship at the University of Illinois, October 18, 1991. Substantive sections in this paper were previously published in Van de Ven (1993). I gratefully appreciate useful suggestions in preparing this paper from Philip Anderson, Avner Ben-Ner, Ivan Bull, Joseph Galaskiewicz, Michael Levenhagen, and Richard Nelson. Support for research underlying this paper has been provided (in part) by a grant to the Strategic Management Research Center at the University of Minnesota from the Program on Organization Effectiveness, Office of Naval Research, under contract No. N00014-84-K-0016.

Journal of Business Venturing 8, 211–230 0883-9026/93/$6.00

at once by the actions of one or even a few key entrepreneurs. Instead, it emerges through the accretion of numerous institutional, resource, and proprietary events that co-produce each other over an extended period. Moreover, the very institutional arrangements and resource endowments created to facilitate industry emergence can become inertial forces that hinder subsequent technological development and adaptation by proprietary firms. This generative process has a dynamic history that is itself important to study systematically if one is to understand how novel forms of technologies, organizations, and institutions emerge.

Finally, the paper emphasizes that the process of entrepreneurship is not limited to the for-profit sector; numerous entrepreneurial actors in the public and not-for-profit sectors play crucial roles. It motivates one to examine the different roles played by these actors, and how their joint contributions interact to develop and commercialize a new technology. This in turn makes it possible to understand how the risk, time, and cost to an individual entrepreneur are significantly influenced by developments in the overall infrastructure for entrepreneurship. It also explains why the entrepreneurs who run in packs will be more successful than those that go it alone to develop their innovations.

I. APPROACHES TO STUDYING ENTREPRENEURSHIP

Schumpeter's (1942) seminal ideas about entrepreneurship, the source of innovation, and economic development are very relevant for assessing alternative approaches to contemporary entrepreneurship scholarship. Schumpeter used entrepreneurship as the engine for his dynamic theory of economic development, and personified this engine in the entrepreneur—an ideal-type theoretical construct. This ideal-type actor possessed the creative labor, vision of a business idea, antagonism of noninnovative administrators, investment seduction skills to lure capitalists, and risk-taking capacities to strike out into the unknown, carrying out a wide variety of innovations—be they new products or processes, product differentiation, new markets, diversifications, new raw materials, or new market structures (Hagedoorn 1989, p. 31).

Unwittingly or erroneously, this ideal-type personification of the entrepreneurship process was subsequently interpreted by many scholars and in places by Schumpeter, himself, as a real-world individual who embodied all these entrepreneurial characteristics. This may explain why, until recently, a search for the traits, personalities, and individual difference characteristics of entrepreneurs (as distinct from nonentrepreneurs) has been almost the exclusive focus of entrepreneurship theories and research. Mixed results have been obtained from an extensive and exhaustive set of studies on entrepreneurial traits. Cooper and Gascon (1992) and Roberts (1991) constructively separate "the wheat from the chaff" in this mixed body of research by summarizing the empirically reliable characteristics of entrepreneurs.

Kimberly (1980) exemplifies this traditional emphasis on the personal characteristics of the entrepreneur as being responsible for organizational innovations.

> Whether one chooses to call him an entrepreneur, a leader, or a guru, the fact is that his personality, his dreams, his flaws, and his talents were largely responsible for the school's early structure and results (Kimberly 1979, p. 454).

We do not disagree with the importance of entrepreneurship in explaining innovation. What is problematic are the misdirected inferences associated with this approach. A common bias in Western culture is to attribute innovations to a particular individual entrepreneur, who at a particular date and place came up with the innovation through a stroke of genius or fortune. Although examples exist to support this bias, historical studies clearly show that most innovations are collective achievements of the efforts of many actors working over an extended period, often in parallel and independent locations (Usher 1954; Jewkes, Sawers, and Stillerman 1958; Constant 1980; Rosenberg 1983). Thus, most innovations are a product of many—not one or even a few—entrepreneurs.

Furthermore, a misdirected causal inference can and has been drawn from the methodological individualism in this approach. It might be inferred that if one could accurately describe the personality, dreams, flaws, and talents of entrepreneurs, an understanding of the entrepreneurship process would be achieved. In other words, one might conclude that from the attributes of the founder one can understand the development and early results of an innovation. But, such a conclusion does not take into consideration the processes that go on before an innovation assumes a recognizable proprietary form, and often before the entrepreneur who claims the credit enters the scene. Kimberly (1980) recognizes this problem in his observation that while change in existing organizations occurs in the context of an established culture and an institutionalized set of norms, values, and procedures, this entire context must be created before an organization can be born. Unfortunately, scholars studying individual entrepreneurs have largely ignored the historical evidence about the numerous actors and events involved in developing an infrastructure for entrepreneurship. A macroperspective on individual entrepreneurs is necessary to gain a collective appreciation of the individual entrepreneurship process.

In the past decade an *ecological approach* (Aldrich 1979; Hannan and Freeman 1977, 1989) to entrepreneurship scholarship has emerged that uses the population of organizations as its unit of analysis to examine organizational birth and death rates as the workings of evolutionary variation and selection mechanisms. Based on Stinchcombe's (1965) liabilities of newness and small size arguments, Hannan and Freeman (1984) propose that organizational death rates should decline monotonically with age because organizational learning and inertia gradually increase with age. Many subsequent studies have provided empirical evidence for this basic proposition (Carroll and Delacroix 1982; Freeman, Carroll and Hannan 1983; Carroll 1983, 1984, 1987; Singh, House, and Tucker 1986; Halliday, Powell, and Granfors 1987). More recently, Fichman and Levinthal (1988) and Bruderl and Schussler (1990) have proposed and provided evidence for a "liability of adolescence" model that introduces two stages in an organizational life cycle. In the first "adolescent" stage, death rates are low because new companies are not expected to be successful immediately after start-up, and venture capital represents an initial stock of assets that entrepreneurs can live on. In the later stage, the "honeymoon" (Fichman and Levinthal 1988) is over; organizations are subjected to the usual risks of failure, producing an age-dependent, monotonic decline in organizational hazard rates.

This stream of ecological research is providing valuable insights into the time-dependent patterns of organization demography, particularly of new small businesses (which represent the organizational population of greatest interest to entrepreneurship scholars, although entrepreneurship in other organizational settings has also received attention). In comparison with the microentrepreneurship "traits" approach, this ecological perspective is stimulating entrepreneurship scholars to examine macro questions regarding the factors that influence "rates" of organizational births and deaths. As Aldrich (1990) points out, the ecological perspective emphasizes that new company start-ups are highly dependent upon macro-processes both within and between organizational populations. Intra-population processes (such as prior foundings, dissolutions, and organizational density) structure the environment into which foundings are born. Cooperative and competitive relationships between populations of organizations affect the distribution of resources available to entrepreneurs in the environment. Finally, institutional factors (government policies, political events, cultural norms, and so on) shape the macro-context within which these population processes occur (Aldrich 1990, p. 7).

But how is this macro-infrastructure for innovation and entrepreneurship created? What are the key components of this infrastructure? The ecological perspective does not address these specific questions, because it does not examine the microscopic events and behaviors of entrepreneurs (either as independent individuals or as employees of a large company). Population ecology models average over these details when they aggregate data and use differential equations to explain the changing demographic characteristics of the population of firms inhabiting a niche. As a consequence, Allen (1988, p. 105) argues that it is not possible to explain how the entrepreneurial process unfolds, and whether innovations emerge as a result of random variations or purposeful entrepreneurial activities.

To understand questions about the process and components of an infrastructure for entrepreneurship requires historical study of the temporal sequence of events and activities that occur to create and transform basic scientific knowledge into a commercially viable set of products delivered to customers. Numerous case histories demonstrated that new technologies are seldom if ever developed by a single firm alone in the vacuum of an institutional environment (e.g., Usher 1954; Jewkes, Sawers, and Stillerman 1958; Constant 1980; Nelson 1982; and Chandler 1990). Many complementary innovations in technical and organizational arrangements are usually required before a particular technology is suitable for commercial application (Binswanger and Ruttan 1978; Hughes 1983; Rosenberg and Birdzell 1986). Research reviews by Mowery (1985), Thirtle and Ruttan (1986), Freeman (1986), and Dosi (1982) show that the commercial success or failure of a technological innovation is in great measure a reflection of institutional innovations that embody the social, economic, and political infrastructure that any community needs to sustain its members.

The social system framework proposed by Van de Ven and Garud (1989) articulates the components of such an industrial infrastructure for entrepreneurship. This framework, outlined in Table 1, adopts the interorganizational community or field as the unit of analysis, and focuses on the core activities necessary to develop and commercialize a technological innovation. This interorganizational community not only includes an industry, commonly defined as the set of firms producing similar or substitute products (Porter 1980), but also many other public- and private-sector actors who perform critical functions to develop and commercialize a new technology. To organization theorists, the emergence of this social system represents the creation of a new environmental niche, which is "a population's way of earning a living" (Hannan and Freeman 1989, p. 95). These environmental niches do not pre-exist, waiting to be filled (McKelvey 1982, p. 109); they are socially constructed through the opportunistic and collective efforts of interdependent actors in common pursuit of a technological innovation.

The relevance of each component of the infrastructure for entrepreneurship will now be discussed. This will be followed in Part II with a set of propositions on how these components of the industrial system emerge and interact over time to facilitate and constrain the development of innovations.

1. Proprietary Functions

The proprietary component of the system incorporates the traditional industrial economic definition of an industry (Porter 1980), which consists of the entrepreneurial firms commercializing innovations that are close substitutes for one another. The focus here is on the actions of individual entrepreneurs and firms who typically appropriate basic knowledge from the public domain and transform it into proprietary knowledge through applied R&D work in areas related to a technological innovation. If they persist in developing the

TABLE 1 Components of an Industrial Infrastructure for Entrepreneurship

- Institutional Arrangements
  — legitimation (creation of trust)
  — governance (norms, rules, regulations, laws)
  — technology standards
- Resource Endowments
  — scientific/technological research
  — financing and insurance arrangements
  — human competence pool (training and accreditation)
- Proprietary Functions
  — technological development functions: R&D, testing, manufacturing, marketing
  — innovation network/resource channel activities: appropriation of common goods (science, financing, labor) vendor–supplier–distributor channels
  — market creation and consumer demand

Source: Adapted from Van de Ven, A., and R. Garud, 1989. A framework for understanding the emergence of new industries. In R. Rosenbloom and R. Burgelman, eds., Research on Technological Innovation, Management and Policy, Vol. 4. *Greenwich, CT: JAI Press, pp. 195–225.*

innovation, they subsequently develop a line of products and gain access to the complementary assets or functions (e.g., manufacturing, marketing, distribution, etc.) necessary to establish an economically viable business.

Williamson's (1975, 1985) and Teece's (1987) transactions costs theory is useful for understanding how firms organize to perform these proprietary functions. They emphasize that the boundaries of the firm are an important strategic variable for innovation (Teece 1987, p. 217). They propose that those functions or complementary assets that are difficult to protect from imitators (i.e., have weak appropriability regimes), require specialized investments, or are highly uncertain to execute, should be integrated and performed within the innovating firm, whereas those that have a strong appropriability regime, entail nonspecialized investments, and for which there are a number of supply sources, should be licensed or contracted by firms with outside suppliers and vendors. From a system perspective, these make or buy decisions by individual firms produce the aggregate industry channels of raw materials, manufacturing, marketing and distribution flows (Stern and El-Ansery 1982; Hakansson 1988).

2. Resource Endowments

Three kinds of resources are critical to the development of most every technology and industry: (1) basic scientific or technological research; (2) financing mechanisms; and (3) a pool of competent human resources (Mowery and Rosenberg 1979). Whereas private entrepreneurial firms do engage in the development of these resources, typically, public organizations (often viewed as external to an industry) play a major role in creating and providing these public goods.

Basic scientific or technological research provides the foundation of knowledge that underlies technological innovations and makes the commercial birth of most industries possible. This basic knowledge is very costly to produce relative to its cost of diffusion and imitation (Mansfield 1985). In addition, it builds in a cumulative fashion, and its generation is inherently an indivisible activity (Metcalfe and Soete 1983). For these reasons, Nelson (1959) and Arrow (1962) argued that the social returns to research investment exceed the private returns to entrepreneurs; a condition leading to underinvestment by the firm (from the social point of view) in research. As a consequence, a variety of studies have shown that firms rely upon outside sources of knowledge and technical inventions for the vast majority of their commercially significant new products (Rosenbloom 1966; Mueller 1962; Utterback 1974; Freeman 1986; Nelson 1982; Stobaugh 1985).

Financing is another key resource endowment for the development and commercialization of an innovation. Although public institutions, such as the National Science Foundation, tend to play the major role in financing the development of basic scientific or technological knowledge, venture capital, either within a corporation or in the market, tends to be the key financial source that supports private firms in transforming basic knowledge into proprietary and commercial applications. In addition, the commercialization of many technological innovations requires unique industry-wide financing arrangements. For example, few biomedical innovations would be commercially viable without the health care insurance industry and the creation of third-party payment reimbursement systems. Without such a financial infrastructure for a broad array of biomedical and health care innovations, most patients would be unable to pay for many biomedical devices and treatments. But because these insurance systems limit coverage to specifically designated medical devices and treatments, the firms competing to commercialize a specific biomedical device must cooperate to both educate and influence third-party payors to include the innovation in their payment reimbursement systems.

A pool of competent human resources is another essential resource necessary for the emergence of a new industry. New technologies mean that new competencies are required to perform essential tasks, be they related to research, manufacturing, or marketing. This pool of competence emerges in various ways, including: (1) the establishment of educational training programs and accredited degrees at colleges and universities; (2) the recruitment and training of people in specific skills related to the innovation, and the diffusion of these skilled people through job transfers and mobility between institutes and firms in the industry (Rappa and Debackere 1990; Garud 1990); and (3) the sharing of knowledge among industry participants at conferences, technical committees, and informal communication networks (Allen 1988; von Hippel 1986), as well as through trade publications and technical journals (Nelson 1982).

3. Institutional Arrangements

The ultimate authorities governing and legitimizing collective action are the rules and norms of the society in which organizations function (Galaskiewicz 1985; Scott 1987). It is widely recognized that a variety of governmental regulations and institutional arrangements facilitate and inhibit the emergence of new technologies and industries. Mowery (1985) and Nelson (1982) for example, discuss how government funding, by broadening the industry-wide knowledge base, can encourage new industry entrance, and thereby support a more competitive environment. So also, a more permissive antitrust policy permitting certain kinds of joint research ventures among competitors speeds the diffusion of innovation (Teece 1987). However as Ouchi and Bolton (1987) discuss, institutional policies encouraging rapid knowledge diffusion, if pursued too eagerly, may undermine the return to the knowledge producer, and thus the incentive to invest in information-producing activities. But here another institutional mechanism has been devised; the patent system grants monopoly rights to the use of knowledge for a limited period. Although these institutional arrangements are often highly imperfect, research shows they often exert a profound effect on technological and industry development (Nelson 1982).

Institutional legitimation of a new technology is fundamental to efficient operation of the market mechanism. When there is high uncertainty about the quality or safeness of an innovation, "lemons" (inferior products) often drive high quality products out of the market because of the bad reputation they create for all other industry products. Consequently, customers require greater assurances to purchase a product in the event it is found, after the purchase, that the product is a lemon (Akerlof 1970). The creation of trust represents a particularly significant entry barrier for product innovations that are costly, technologically sophisticated, and whose purchase entails irreversible health or welfare situations for customers. Numerous mechanisms are often established to counteract this quality uncertainty entry barrier, including guarantees, licensing practices, industry regulations, as well as endorsements by other trusted institutions.

One of the concrete manifestations of industry legitimation is the setting of technical standards pertaining to component specifications, processes, and performance criteria that designs of a new technology are expected to achieve. Such technical standards are powerful institutional mechanisms for selecting dominant designs from among competing technological possibilities, and reducing many uncertainties of technological development by channeling the directions of resource investments and technological change. Besen and Saloner (1989, p. 178) and Tushman and Rosenkopf (1990) describe various ways in which standards develop. In some cases standards are mandated by governmental regulatory agencies. In others, voluntary standards are established cooperatively, with information being exchanged, technologies being altered, or side payments being made to achieve a consensus among firms in an industry. Finally, the setting of standards may be left to the market of the de facto standards imposed by a dominant producer.

Whatever means are used, the typical process for setting standards is influenced more by social and political dynamics than by technical considerations (David 1987; Tushman and Rosenkopf 1990). These socio-political dynamics vary with the relative benefits to public and private parties of promoting a standard, the extent to which interested parties (producers, consumers, regulators) have different views about the standards that are chosen (Besen and Saloner 1989), as well as the evaluation complexity of a new technology (Tushman and Rosenkopf 1990).

II. PROPOSITIONS ON INNOVATION EMERGENCE

Van de Ven and Garud's (1989) system framework maps a conceptual territory of the essential components of an infrastructure for entrepreneurship at the interorganizational level of analysis. Perhaps more than anything else, it helps one get a handle on the key components or functions of the infrastructure. An extensive body of research indicates that these components are necessary (not sufficient) conditions that need to be put in place to foster the development and commercialization of technological innovations. Although many of these components have been studied in varying degrees by different disciplines, they have been treated as "externalities" (Porter 1980) to the system under investigation. But by doing so, one is not likely to study or understand how these components are interdependent in time and space. By incorporating these components within an overall conceptual framework, one can begin to undertake a research agenda designed to understand how various actors and components interact over time to create an infrastructure that can both facilitate and constrain entrepreneurship and innovation.

One way to undertake this research agenda is to observe the development process of a few innovations over time from their inception to their implementation or termination in their natural field settings. As historians have done, process is defined here as a developmental sequence of events (Van de Ven 1992a). This means that the datum, or unit of observation, is an event, and the central task of longitudinal field work is to observe and record the events pertaining to each system component that occurs over time during the emergence of an innovation. Events are defined as incidents actors engage in that develop or change at least one of the system functions listed in Table 2. Following the procedures suggested by Van de Ven (1992b), a chronological recording of these events as they occur can then be analyzed to determine when system functions emerged, the networks of actors involved in developing each function, and how these functions and networks of actors interacted over time to facilitate and constrain innovation development.

Emergence of the Community System

The basic argument underlying the framework is that while the industrial infrastructure facilitates and constrains efforts of individual entrepreneurs, it is the entrepreneur who constructs and changes the infrastructure. Thus, we view the infrastructure at the macro-community level as grounded in a theory of action at the micro-level of individual entrepreneurs in private firms, government bureaus, research institutes, or various trade associations. This infrastructure does not emerge through a few discrete events or by the actions of one or even a few key entrepreneurs. Instead, detailed historical studies show that the process of innovation and entrepreneurship consists of an accretion of numerous institutional, resource, and proprietary events involving many actors who transcend boundaries of many public and private sector organizations.

Usher (1954, p. 60) insisted that the history of mechanical invention is not the history of single inventors nor of random chance events. Gilfillan (1935, p. 5) observed "a perpetual accretion of little details ... probably having neither beginning, completion nor definable limits" in the gradual evolution of shipbuilding. Constant (1980) found that advances in aircraft propulsion emerged not from flashes of disembodied inspiration but from many incremental changes and recombinations of existing technology and organization arrangements, which add up to what might be called a technological revolution.

Moreover, there is a systemic nature to technological advances, as demonstrated in studies by Hughes (1983) of electrical power, Ruttan and Hayami (1984) of agricultural innovations, and by Kuhn (1982) and Hull (1988) of science in general. Developments in other complementary technologies, institutions, and resource endowments often explain bottlenecks and breakthroughs in the development of a given technology. Thus, as Rosenberg (1983, p. 49) states, "What is really involved is a process of cumulative accretion of useful knowledge, to which many people make essential contributions, even though the prizes and recognition are usually accorded to the one actor who happens to have been on the stage at a critical moment."

Discontinuities are inherent to the numerous events in developing the institutional arrangements, resource endowments, and proprietary functions, particularly because they require the involvement of many actors from public and private organizations over an extended period. Individual events are often not made known to others, and various acts of insights pertaining to technical, resource, and institutional capabilities are often required to overcome bottlenecks. These acts or events accumulate probabilistically; they do not proceed deterministically under the stress of necessity or progress (Rosenberg 1983). They are possible for only a limited number of individuals and organizations who, by virtue of their different roles, competencies, and available resources, become exposed to conditions that bring both awareness of problems and elements of solutions within their frame of reference. Thus, Usher (1954, p. 67) stated that "emergent novelty becomes truly significant only

TABLE 2 Event Tracks for Studying the Development of an Infrastructure for Entrepreneurship

Institutional Arrangements	
• Legitimation events	⟶
• Regulation events	⟶
• Technology standards events	⟶
Resource Endowments	
• Basic research events	⟶
• Financing events	⟶
• Education and training events	⟶
Proprietary Functions	
• Applied R&D events	⟶
• Testing and evaluation events	⟶
• Manufacturing and sourcing events	⟶
• Marketing and distribution events	⟶
	Events Occurring Over Time

RESEARCH APPROACH

- Datum—Event: an incident when change occurred in each track above
- Observe—date, actor, action, and outcome of each event
- Analyze—sequence of events in development of each track and temporal relationships between system tracks

through accumulation" of many discontinuous events of technical and institutional change.

These historical studies suggest the following basic proposition on the emergent process of an infrastructure for entrepreneurship.

> *Proposition 1:* An infrastructure for entrepreneurship does not emerge by a few discrete events involving a few key entrepreneurs. Instead, it emerges through the accretion of numerous institutional, resource, and proprietary events involving many entrepreneurs located in the public and private sectors over an extended period.

This process can begin any number of ways and varies by the technology being developed. For example, it can begin with purposeful intentions and inventive ideas of entrepreneurs, who undertake a stream of activities to gain the resources, competence, and endorsements necessary to develop an economically viable enterprise. As they undertake these activities, the paths of independent entrepreneurs—acting out their own diverse intentions and ideas—intersect. These intersections provide occasions for interaction and for recognizing areas for establishing cooperative and competitive relationships. Cooperative relationships emerge among the actors who can achieve complementary benefits by integrating their functional specializations. Competitive relationships emerge as alternative technological paths become evident and as different entrepreneurs or firms pursue alternative paths. It must be emphasized that, during the initial period, applied R&D is highly uncertain and often dependent on basic science and technology. Depending upon the technological alternative chosen by an entrepreneur, s/he becomes highly dependent upon different clusters of basic research institutions that have been producing and directing the accumulation of basic knowledge, techniques, and experience associated with a given technological alternative.

By engaging in cooperative and competitive relationships in the development of alternative technological possibilities, groups of entrepreneurs in both the public and private sectors increasingly isolate themselves from traditional industries by virtue of their interdependencies, growing commitments to, and unique know-how of a new technology. Isolation frees the actors from institutional constraints of existing technologies and industries

(Astley 1985), and permits them to develop their own distinctive structural forms (Rappa 1987). Coordination among actors takes place not so much by a central plan or organization hierarchy, nor through the price mechanism, but mostly through interactions (Mattsson 1987) and partisan mutual adjustments among actors (Astley and Van de Ven 1983).

As the number of entrepreneurs gains a critical mass, a complex network of cooperative and competitive relationships begins to accumulate. This network itself becomes recognized as a new industrial sector, and takes on the form of a hierarchical, loosely coupled system.[1] I view this emerging system as consisting of the entrepreneurial network that governs, integrates, and performs all of the functions required to transform a technological innovation into a commercially viable line of products or services delivered to customers. The structure of this system, when fully developed, consists of the institutional arrangements, resource endowments, and proprietary functions illustrated in Table 1.

Interactions Between System Components

It is generally recognized that resource endowments precede the development of proprietary and institutional system functions, because basic research, which is the search for a fundamental understanding of natural phenomena, provides the foundation of knowledge that makes possible the commercial birth of a technology (Abernathy 1978; Rosenberg 1983; Mowery 1985). What is less well understood is the process by which a common pool of basic scientific or technological knowledge is appropriated and transformed by private firms into proprietary innovations that can become commercial monopolies.

Success at creating a monopoly by commercializing a new technology does not rest on a unique command of basic research, nor on the control of all the competencies and resources relevant to innovation. Instead, as Stobaugh (1985, p. 107) and Mowery (1985) discuss, it rests on orchestrating a highly uncertain journey by linking with numerous organizations and actors and appropriating the competencies and resources relevant to developing and commercializing the innovation. This journey consists of an interactive search process involving parallel developments in building resource endowments of basic research, financing, and competence capabilities, creating institutional legitimation, regulations, and standards, as well as proprietary appropriation and commercialization of new technological products for new markets.

Different search and linking patterns should be expected for innovations in different industrial sectors. As Nelson and Winter (1977, p. 51) discuss, in many sectors there are many R&D organizations, some profit-oriented, some governmental, some academic, doing different things, but interacting in a synergistic way. In particular, in medicine, agriculture, and several other sectors, private for-profit organizations do the bulk of R&D that leads to

[1]Of course, hierarchy in an industry system is a matter of degree, and some industry systems may be only minimally, if at all, hierarchical. Hierarchy is often a consequence of institutional constraints imposed by political and governmental regulatory bodies. Hierarchy also emerges in relationships with key linking-pin organizations who either become dominant industry leaders or control access to critical resources (money, competence, technology) needed by other firms in the industry.

Loose coupling promotes both flexibility and stability to the structure of an industry. Links between subsystems are only as rich or tight as is necessary to ensure the survival of the system (Aldrich and Whetten 1981, p. 388). Based on Simon's (1962) architecture of complexity, Aldrich and Whetten discuss how a loosely joined system provides short-run independence of subsystems and long-run dependence only in an aggregate way. The overall social system can be fairly stable, due to the absence of strong ties or links between elements and subsystems, but individual subsystems can be free to adapt quickly to local environmental conditions. Thus, in a complex, heterogeneous, and changing environment, a loosely joined system is highly adaptive.

marketing products, but academic institutions play a major role in creating basic knowledge and data used in the more applied work.

Relatedly, most people understand that R&D is an uncertain business. Uncertainty resides at the level of an entrepreneurial firm, where the best way to proceed is seldom apparent and the individuals involved have to be satisfied with finding a potentially promising technological path. Less often understood is that the source of much of this uncertainty confronting individual entrepreneurs and investors resides at the system or community level. As the system framework highlights, if institutional arrangements and resource endowments have not yet emerged for an innovation, proprietary entrepreneurs are exposed to high uncertainties and risks in not knowing what kinds of institutional regulations, technical standards, financing arrangements and specialized competencies will emerge for the innovation. Uncertainties are reduced as these institutional arrangements and resource endowments become established and embodied in a dominant technological design for the innovation. This leads to our second proposition on interactions between proprietary, resource, and institutional components of the system framework.

> *Proposition 2:* The time, cost, and risk incurred by proprietary entrepreneurs in developing an innovation are inversely related to the progress of building institutional arrangements and resource endowments for the new technology.

A concrete example of this proposition emerged from a longitudinal study in which Michael Rappa and I tracked the development of gallium arsenide integrated circuits in the United States, Japan, and Western Europe from 1983 to 1987 (see Rappa 1987). While many more firms and scientists were engaged in the development of this technology in the United States than in Japan, by 1985 Japan was judged to be several years ahead of the United States in commercial development and application of the technology. One possible reason for the more rapid advancement of the technology with fewer scientists and engineers is that, in Japan, a system infrastructure was already well established through the Ministry of Industry and Trade (MITI), which encouraged firms that were competing on proprietary technical developments to cooperate with one another and many other actors in various industry and trade committees. They were meeting to develop commercial applications for the technology, influence industrial governance policies, and create a competence pool through training programs and informal information sharing. In the United States no comparable industry infrastructure was in place in 1985. Instead, it appeared that many United States firms, while investing heavily in their own proprietary R&D projects, were "sitting on the fence" waiting for others to build the industry infrastructure for collective advancement.

Of course, the degree of system change varies with the novelty of the technology being developed and commercialized. Some innovations change the entire order of things, making the old ways obsolete and perhaps sending entire businesses the way of the slide rule or the buggy whip. Others simply build upon what is already there, requiring only modest modification in existing system functions and practices. We expect that innovations of different levels of novelty will require differing degrees of change in the industrial infrastructure. For new technologies within established industries, some of the functions, such as governance institutions, may be already established and may change only in subtle, nearly invisible ways. That, however, does not deny their importance. It largely explains why radical new-to-the-world innovations are far more difficult to develop and commercialize than incremental innovations within established industries. Specifically, we propose the following.

> *Proposition 3*: The more novel the innovation, the greater the changes required in all

> components of the infrastructure; and hence, the greater the time and chance of failure incurred in developing the innovation.

Radical or revolutionary innovations not only represent new-to-the-world technologies, they also represent vast departures from existing industrial systems. Development and commercialization of these radical innovations typically entail starting from scratch to construct a new system infrastructure. These system functions do not emerge independent of one another; they are highly interdependent, as witnessed by many convergent and divergent events which become bottlenecks that delay the overall development of the infrastructure. For example, in the development of cochlear implants, a biomedical innovation that provides hearing to profoundly deaf people, Garud and Van de Ven (1989, p. 516) identified numerous temporal interdependencies in the creation of different system functions:

> Basic scientific knowledge had to first ensure safety/efficacy of the technology for use in humans before business firms would become involved. The presence of firms wanting to commercialize cochlear implants was necessary as a thrust for the creation of the FDA (Food and Drug Administration) panel for cochlear devices. FDA's approval of cochlear devices was necessary for Medicare to extend its coverage for cochlear implants, which in turn is necessary for accessing a wider patient base.

The rate of success for entrepreneurial firms is significantly influenced by the length of time it takes for the system to become established. For an individual entrepreneur, start-up funding for a venture represents an initial stock of assets that provides the entrepreneurial unit a period in which to develop and commercialize its innovation (Fichman and Levinthal 1988). These assets reduce the risk of terminating the innovation during its introductory period when setbacks arise and when initial outcomes are judged unfavorable. The likelihood of replenishing these assets is highly influenced by the duration of the change process; interest and commitment wane with time. Thus, after the honeymoon period, proprietary entrepreneurial ventures terminate at disproportionately higher rates, in proportion to the time needed to develop institutional arrangements and resource endowments for the innovation.

Innovation uncertainty decreases over time as system functions emerge. These functions define key technical and institutional parameters for the innovation. Correspondingly, transitions from development to commercialization activities often entail shifts from radical to incremental and from divergent to convergent progressions in the development of system functions. Analogous patterns have been observed of innovation processes within organizations, which become more highly structured and stabilized in their patterns and less differentiated from other organizational arrangements when innovations are implemented (Tornatzky and Fleischer 1990; Zaltman, Duncan, and Holbeck 1973). Thus, at different periods of technological development, we should expect to find that different functional arrangements are needed to foster entrepreneurship, and that different components of the system become the limiting factors that serve as bottlenecks to sustained innovation development.

This developmental pattern often culminates in the selection of a dominant design for the technology from among competing alternatives. As Van de Ven and Garud (1992) observed in cochlear implants, this selection process is largely produced by a convergence in developments of institutional, resource endowments, and proprietary system functions that emerged to embody preferences for the dominant design. As this dominant design emerges, there is a leveling off in further developments of system functions. Once largely established, the infrastructure systematically channels and constrains further technological advances in the direction of the dominant design. This leads to our proposition on the temporal dynamics of system development.

Proposition 4: The very institutional mechanisms and resource endowments that initially are developed to facilitate proprietary entrepreneurship become inertial forces that constrain subsequent development in the direction of a chosen dominant design.

An examination of these propositions on the interactions between system components as they develop over time should lead one to examine if and how learning occurs between functional events, which could provide guidance as to the next paths taken by actors to develop other parts of the system. By examining the outcomes of alternative paths, one could also identify the feasible sets of paths available in the emergence of an industry. While great inter-industry differences should be expected (Mowery 1985), only by cumulative longitudinal studies of these developmental progressions between system functions will we come to appreciate how industry infrastructures emerge for innovation and entrepreneurship (Dosi 1982).

Roles of Individual Entrepreneurial Firms

The social system framework emphasizes that any given entrepreneurial firm is but one actor, able to perform only a limited set of roles, and dependent upon many other actors to accomplish all the functions needed for an industry to emerge and survive. As a consequence, an individual firm must make strategic choices concerning the kinds of proprietary, resource endowments, and institutional functions in which it will engage, and what other actors it will transact with to achieve self-interest and collective objectives. These strategic choices amplify the arguments by Coase (1972) and Williamson (1985) that the transactions in which a firm chooses to engage define its boundaries, and that this boundary is not the same for different innovation activities. Different networks of public and private actors tend to emerge in the development of each component of the industry infrastructure. As a result, entrepreneurial firms competing with each other to develop proprietary products may simultaneously cooperate with each other to develop institutional arrangements and resource endowments. The actors engaged in these networks, and the firm boundaries of these actors, change frequently as different components of the infrastructure emerge. These choices and transaction boundaries evolve, not only as a result of individual firm behavior, but just as importantly by the interdependencies that accumulate among firms engaged in numerous components of the emerging industry.

Pragmatically, therefore, entrepreneurs should be concerned not only with their own immediate proprietary tasks and transaction modes but also with those of other firms in their resource distribution channel and with the overall social system. Switching involvements between different system functions and proprietary distribution channels is not inexpensive. Influencing one's own existing channel may be more efficient than switching channels or creating new channels. Also, there is an ongoing tension for each industry participant to organize its own proprietary functions and distribution channels as opposed to contributing to the creation of the industry's resources and institutional arrangements. Although the former may advance the firm's position as a first mover in the short run, the latter provides the infrastructure that ultimately influences the collective survival of the emerging industry. There is an important counter-intuitive implication of these decisions for individual entrepreneurs, which is captured in the following proposition.

Proposition 5: Entrepreneurial firms that run in packs will be more successful than those that go it alone to develop their innovations.

Conventional wisdom is that entrepreneurs act independently and compete to be the first into the market with their new product or service. There are many technologies and industries in which this may lead to successful monopoly profits. However, this practice may lead to unsuccessful results when the innovation involves a new technology for a new industry. Running in packs means that entrepreneurs coordinate, i.e., simultaneously cooperate and compete, with others as they develop and commercialize their innovation. Running in packs is analogous to bicycle racers who cue their pace to one another and take turns breaking wind resistance until the ending sprint.

The argument for running in packs is similar to that developed by Ben-Ner (1992) for understanding the problem of organization design, where the interests of various participants with a stake in the enterprise are both intertwined and divergent. Participants seek both to maximize the total return from their common transactions and to maximize their respective shares in the surplus. The desire to maximize total surplus amounts to creating an industrial infrastructure that makes it collectively possible for participants to develop and commercialize a new technology for a new market. This draws participants together and drives them to cooperate, since no one actor has sufficient resources, competence, or legitimacy to do it alone. The goal of maximizing individual shares propels participants to conflict with one another. The maximum individual share is obtained by reaping monopoly profits that derive from introducing the dominant design for a new technology or product. Three corollary propositions will be offered to elaborate this overall proposition on the self-interested and collective behavior of entrepreneurial firms.

Contrary to industrial economists' stress on competitive inter-firm relations, the social system perspective emphasizes that cooperative and competitive elements exist in each relationship (Van de Ven, Emmett, and Koenig 1984). For example, it is easy to understand that a firm needs to establish cooperative relationships with suppliers, distributors, and customers in order to make its own activities meaningful. It is also easy to see that other firms who pursue competing technological routes carry out conflicting activities. However, as Mattsson (1987) discusses, there are also important elements of conflict in the relations between cooperating firms that have to do with the negotiation and administration of business transactions and adaptation processes. Between proprietary competitors, there are also elements of complementarity, not only when they cooperate to share resources or develop industry institutional functions, but also when they are complementary suppliers to the same customers.

Indeed, because firms in an emerging industry are often engaged in multiple issues simultaneously, they create a multiplexity of ties (Galaskiewicz 1985, p. 296). Thus, Aldrich and Whetten (1981, p. 392) point out that it is misleading to think of single relations among most firms in an industry. Common forms of multiple linkages between a given set of firms include: exchanging multiple resources, communicating with other firm representatives on industry and trade committees, sharing common pools of knowledge, acquiring personnel trained and socialized in a common pool of competence, friendship and kinship ties, and overlapping board memberships.

> *Proposition 6:* The greater the number of cooperative and competitive ties between firms, the more stable the inter-firm relationships and the more flexible the overall system.

A rupture in one aspect of a relationship does not sever the other ties, and the latter are often used to correct or smooth over the severed link. From an industry perspective, stability through redundance of functions and activities among actors minimizes the negative impact of the loss of services provided by one industry member on the performance of the total system.

Multiple ties among firms emerge over time, and often produce unintended consequences. Prior relationships and transactions among firms in the pursuit of an industry activity are remembered, and thereby become the infrastructure upon which subsequent relations are based (Van de Ven and Walker 1984). Galaskiewicz (1985, p. 299) nicely summarizes some of these temporal dimensions.

> The networks of resource exchange that already existed among organizations are the infrastructure upon which political coalitions are built. In all likelihood, these resource networks were created out of competitive struggle for survival by self-seeking and self-centered actors who were seeking to minimize their dependencies upon one another. Now these networks are the infrastructure upon which coalitions to achieve collective goals are built. In turn, as political coalitions become institutionalized, they impinge on the struggle for dominance in the resource procurement/allocation arena.

An appreciation of the temporal dimension of inter-firm relationships also provides important insight on how competitors emerge in an industry. Generally, the literature tends to assume that competitors are profit-seeking entrepreneurs who somehow recognize and seize commercial opportunities by entering lucrative markets. Based on their longitudinal study of the emergence of the cochlear implant industry, Garud and Van de Ven (1989) provide quite a different proposition to explain how industrial competitors emerged.

> *Proposition 7:* Aborted efforts at establishing cooperative relationships turn out to become competitive relationships.

In studying the development of cochlear implants, Garud and Van de Ven (1989) observed two instances in which the efforts of the first mover to initiate cooperative relationships or joint ventures with other research clinics failed, leading to the birth of the firm's competitors. Initial negotiations of possible relationships with a foreign university and a domestic university did not materialize. Otological scientists and clinicians in each of these two universities subsequently entered into licensing arrangements with two other firms—one a new company start-up, the other a subsidiary of a large manufacturer—who two years later became the first-mover's major competitors.

The proposition that aborted cooperative relationships lead to competitive relationships applies primarily to conditions when a small number of organizations, perhaps the size of an oligopoly, exist with the requisite unique competence or assets necessary for innovation development. Such conditions tend to exist during the early emergence of new-to-the-world technologies, where one can often count on one hand the pioneering firms and inventors world-wide who are pursuing the development of a complementary set of basic research ideas or technological designs. These pioneers make themselves known to one another in a variety of ways: by reporting results of their inventions through patents, professional publications, and association meetings (Dosi 1982). They thereby come to recognize opportunities for obtaining unique competencies or components needed to advance their own work. If efforts to obtain the needed resources go unconsummated because a cooperative relationship could not be established, then the negotiating parties will go their separate ways by entering into cooperative relationships with other parties in this limited set of pioneers who possess the unique competencies or resources. As Ring and Van de Ven (1989) discuss, this implies a shift to a competitive orientation between the parties who disconfirmed one another's initial efforts at cooperation.

Through this and related processes, key first-mover organizations emerge that have extensive and overlapping ties to different components of the emerging technological community, and play the key role of integrating the system. Because they have ties to more than one subsystem of a community, these first movers are the nodes through which a network is loosely joined (Aldrich and Whetten 1981). They serve as communication channels between industry participants, and link third parties by transferring resources, information, or specialties within and outside of the industry. By being linked into multiple components of the infrastructure, these first movers accumulate a broad base of power for ascending to a dominant position in the industry, which permits them to survive at the expense of peripheral participants.

But these first movers also experience the greatest conflicts of interest in emerging industry, because they tend also to have the greatest amount of visibility, which limits their abilities to capture significant proprietary advantages. This is because their dominance serves as a model that is imitated by others and diffused throughout the industrial community. Thus, the leading firm that chooses to "go it alone" must bear significant first mover burdens that permit free-riding by other industry participants. In return for these burdens, first movers are generally believed to have the greatest degrees of freedom to shape industry rules, technology standards, and product perceptions in the directions that benefit them the most (Porter 1985).

However, these first-mover benefits do not appear to be empirically substantiated for technologies with weak appropriability regimes, i.e., those that are easy to imitate, reverse engineer, or substitute. Based on research by Teece (1987), we propose a caveat.

> *Proposition 8:* The technological design of the first mover often turns out not to become the dominant design that ultimately yields the greatest profits.

This is because while striking out to be the first to introduce a new technology, the first mover will inevitably make mistakes. And the followers, who are observing the practice of the first mover, can make adjustments in their own technologies. As a result, after the first mover has introduced the product in the market, then the second, third, and fourth movers, who have been carefully following the leader, can often and rapidly introduce a more significant, advanced, and better product or service. In short, there are strong economic motives for first movers to run in packs, not alone.

CONCLUSION

The social system perspective and its associated propositions make three contributions to understanding entrepreneurship. First, we believe that the study of entrepreneurship is deficient if it focuses exclusively on the characteristics and behaviors of individual entrepreneurs, on the one hand, and if it treats the social, economic, and political infrastructure for entrepreneurship as externalities on the other hand. Popular folklore notwithstanding, the process of entrepreneurship is a collective achievement requiring key roles from numerous entrepreneurs in both the public and private sectors. By taking the interorganizational community or network as the relevant unit of analysis, the framework provides a more inclusive perspective of an industry than does the traditional industrial economics definition of a group of firms competing to produce similar or substitute products. In addition to these proprietary functions, the framework emphasizes that an infrastructure for entrepreneurship includes the development of resource endowments of basic knowledge, financing mechanisms, and competent labor, as well as an institutional governance structure that legitimizes, regulates, and standardizes the activities of industry members. Although extensive research substantiates the importance of these component functions of a community infrastructure, they have been treated as "externalities" (Porter 1980). By incorporating these functions within a conceptual framework, one can undertake a systematic research agenda aimed at understanding how various actors and functions interact to create an infrastructure that both facilitates and constrains entrepreneurship.

Second, this research agenda has the objective of developing a theory on the infrastructure for entrepreneurship at the macro-industry level that is grounded in a micro-theory of action of numerous individual entrepreneurs. We proposed that the odds of a firm successfully developing an innovation are largely a function of the extent to which this infrastructure is developed at the industrial community level. Whereas this community infrastructure facilitates and constrains entrepreneurs, it is the latter who construct and change the infrastructure. This infrastructure does not emerge and change all at once by the actions of one or even a few key individuals. Instead, we proposed that this infrastructure emerges through the accretion of numerous institutional, resource, and proprietary events that co-produce each other through the actions of many public and private sector actors over an extended period. Furthermore, the very institutional arrangements and resource endowments created to facilitate industry emergence can become inertial forces that hinder subsequent technological development and adaptation by proprietary firms. This generative process has a dynamic history that itself is important to study systematically if one is to understand how novel forms of technologies, organizations, and institutions emerge.

Finally, the social system perspective emphasizes that the process of entrepreneurship is not limited to the for-profit sector; numerous entrepreneurial actors in the public and not-for-profit sectors play crucial roles. It motivates one to examine the different roles played by these actors, and how their joint contributions interact to develop and commercialize a new technology. This in turn makes it possible to understand how the risk, time, and cost to an individual entrepreneur are significantly influenced by developments in the overall infrastructure for entrepreneurship. It also explains why the entrepreneurs that run in packs will be more successful than those that go it alone to develop their innovations.

REFERENCES

Abernathy, W.J. 1978. *The Productivity Dilemma: Roadblock to Innovations in the Automobile Industry*. Baltimore: Johns Hopkins University Press.

Akerlof, G.A. 1970. The market for "lemons": quality, uncertainty and the market mechanism." *Quarterly Journal of Economics* 84:488–500.

Aldrich, H. 1979. *Organizations and Environments*. Englewood Cliffs, NJ: Prentice Hall.

Aldrich, H. 1990. Using an Ecological Perspective to Study Organizational Founding Rates. *Entrepreneurship Theory and Practice* 14(3):7–24.

Aldrich, H., and Whetten, D. 1981. Organization-sets, action sets, and networks: making the most of simplicity," In P.C. Nystrom and W.H. Starbuck, eds., *Handbook of Organizational Design*. Oxford: Oxford University Press, pp. 385–407.

Allen, P.M. 1988. Evolution, innovation, and economics. Chapter 5. In G. Dosi, C. Freeman, R. Nelson, G. Silverberg, and L. Soete, eds., *Technical Change and Economic Theory*. London: Pinter Publishers, pp. 95–119.

Allen, T.J. 1977. *Managing the Flow of Technology*. Cambridge: MIT Press.

Arrow, K.J. 1962. Economic welfare and the allocation of resources for innovative activity. In R.R. Nelson, eds., *The Rate and Direction of Inventive Activity*. Princeton, NJ: Princeton University Press.

Astley, W.G. 1985. The two ecologies: population and community perspectives on organizational evolution. *Administrative Science Quarterly* 30:224–241.

Astley, W.G. and Van de Ven, A.H. 1983. Central perspectives and debates in organization theory. *Administrative Science Quarterly* 28:245–273.

Ben-Ner, A. 1992. Cooperation, conflict, and control in organizations. Forthcoming in S. Bowles, H. Gintis, and B. Gustafson, eds., *Democracy and Markets: Participation, Accountability, and Efficiency*. Cambridge: Cambridge University Press.

Besen, S.M., and Saloner, G. 1989. The economics of telecommunications standards. In R.W. Crandall and K. Flamm, eds., *Changing the Rules: Technological Change, International Competition, and Regulation in Communication.* Washington DC: The Brookings Institute.

Binswanger, H.P. and Ruttan, V.W. 1978. *Induced Innovation.* Baltimore: Johns Hopkins University Press.

Bruderl, J., and Schussler, R. 1990. Organizational mortality: the liabilities of newness and adolescence. *Administrative Science Quarterly* 35:530–547.

Carroll, G.R. 1983. A stochastic model of organizational mortality. *Social Science Research* 12:303–329.

Carroll, G.R. 1984. Dynamics of publisher succession in newspaper organizations. *Administrative Science Quarterly* 29:93–113.

Carroll, G.R. 1987. *Publish and Perish.* Greenwich, CT: JAI Press.

Carroll. G.R., and Delacroix, J. 1982. Organizational mortality in the newspaper industries of Argentina and Ireland: an ecological approach. *Administrative Science Quarterly* 27:169–198.

Chandler, Jr., A.D., 1990. *Scale and Scope: The Dynamics of Industrial Capitalism.* Cambridge, MA: Harvard University Press.

Coase, R.H. 1972. Industrial organization: a proposal for research. In V.R. Fuchs, ed., *Policy Issues and Research Opportunities in Industrial Organization.* New York: National Bureau of Economic Research, pp. 59–73.

Cooper, A.C., and Gascon, F.J.G. 1992. Entrepreneurs, processes of founding, and new-firm performance. Chapter 12. In D. Sexton and J. Kasarda, eds., *The State of the Art of Entrepreneurship.* Boston: PWS-Kent Publishers, pp. 301–340.

Constant, E.W. 1980. *The Origins of the Turbojet Revolution.* Baltimore: Johns Hopkins University Press.

David, P. 1987. Some new standards for the economics of standardization in the information age. In P. Dasgupta and P. Stoneman, eds., *Economic Policy and Technological Performance.* Cambridge: Cambridge University Press, pp. 206–239.

Dosi, G. 1982. Technological paradigms and technological trajectories. *Research Policy* 11:147–162.

Fichman, M.A., and Levinthal, D.A. 1988. Honeymoons and the liability of adolescence: a new perspective on duration dependence in social and organizational relationships. Working Paper, GSIA, Carnegie Mellon University, Pittsburgh, PA.

Freeman, C. 1986. *The Economics of Industrial Innovation.* Cambridge, MA: MIT Press.

Freeman, J., Carroll, G., and Hannan, M.T. 1983. The liability of newness: age dependence in organizational death rates. *American Sociological Review* 48:692–710.

Galaskiewicz, J. 1985. Interorganizational relations. *Annual Review of Sociology.* 11:281–304.

Garud, R. 1990. Roles of researcher sub-committee in the development of a new technology: The case of cochlear implants. Working Paper Draft, Stern School of Business, New York University, New York, NY.

Garud, R. and Van de Ven, A.H. 1989. Innovation and the emergence of industries. In A.H. Van de Ven, H. Angle, and M.S. Poole, eds., *Research on the Management of Innovation.* New York: Harper Collins, Ballinger Division.

Gilfillan, S.G. 1935. *The Sociology of Invention.* Cambridge, MA: MIT Press.

Hagedoorn, J. 1989. *The Dynamic Analysis of Innovation and Diffusion: A Study in Process Control.* London and New York: Pinter Publishers.

Hakansson, H. 1988. *Industrial Technological Development: A Network Approach.* London: Croom Heim.

Halliday, T.C., Powell, M.J., and Granfors, M.W. 1987. Minimalist organizations: vital events in state bar associations, 1870–1930. *American Sociological Review* 52:456–471.

Hannan, M.T., and Freeman, J. 1977. The population ecology of organizations. *American Journal of Sociology* 82:929–964.

Hannan, M.T., and Freeman, J. 1984. Structural inertia and organizational change. *American Sociological Review* 49:149–164.

Hannan, M.T., and Freeman, J. 1989. *Organizational Ecology.* Cambridge, MA: Harvard University Press.

Hughes, T.P. 1983. *Networks of Power: Electrification in Western Society, 1880–1930*. Baltimore: Johns Hopkins University Press.

Hull, D.L. 1988. *Science as a Process: An Evolutionary Account of the Social and Conceptual Development of Science*. Chicago, IL: The University of Chicago Press.

Jewkes, J., Sawers, D., and Stillerman, R. 1958. *The Sources of Invention*. New York: Macmillan & Co., Ltd.

Kimberly, J.R. 1980. Initiation, innovation, and institutionalization in the creation process. Chapter 2. In J.R. Kimberly, R.H. Miles, and Associates, eds., *The Organizational Life Cycle*. San Francisco: Jossey-Bass.

Kuhn, T.S. 1982. *The Structure of Scientific Revolutions*. Homewood, IL: Richard Irwin.

Mansfield, E. 1985. How rapidly does new industrial technology leak out? *Journal of Industrial Economics* 34(2) (December):217–223.

Mattsson, L.G. 1987. Management of strategic change in a "markets-as-networks" perspective. In A. Pettigrew, ed., *The Strategic Management of Change*. London: Basil Blackwell.

McKelvey, B. 1982. *Organizational Systematics: Taxonomy, Evolution, Classification*. Berkeley: University of California Press.

Metcalfe, J.S., and Soete, L. 1983. Notes on the evolution of technology and international competition. Paper presented at the workshop on Science and Technology Policy, University of Manchester, (April).

Mowery, D.C. May 1985. Market structure and innovation: a critical survey. Paper presented at the conference, "New Technology as Organizational Innovation," at the Netherlands Institute for Advanced Studies in Humanities, Wasenaar.

Mowery, D.C., and Rosenberg, N. April 1979. The influence of market demand upon innovation: a critical review of some recent empirical studies. *Research Policy*.

Mueller, W.F. 1962. The origins of the basic inventions underlying DuPont's major product and process innovations, 1920–1950. In R.R. Nelson, ed., *The Rate and Direction of Inventive Activity*. Princeton, NJ: Princeton University Press.

Nelson, R.N. 1959. The simple economics of basic scientific research. *Journal of Political Economy* 67:297–306.

Nelson, R.N. 1982. *Government and Technical Progress: A Cross-industry Analysis*. New York: Pergamon Press.

Nelson, R.N., and Winter, S.G. 1977. In search of a useful theory of innovation. *Research Policy* 6:36–76.

Ouchi, W.G., and Bolton, M.K. 1987. The logic of joint research and development. Working paper, Graduate School of Management, University of Southern California-Los Angeles.

Porter, M.E. 1980. *Competitive Strategy: Techniques for Analyzing Industries and Competitors*. New York: The Free Press.

Porter, M.E. 1985. *Competitive Advantage: Creating and Sustaining Superior Performance*. New York: The Free Press.

Rappa, M. 1987. The structure of technological revolutions: An empirical study of the development of III-V compound semiconductor technology. Unpublished Dissertation, University of Minnesota, Carlson School of Management, Minneapolis.

Rappa, M.A. and Debackere, K. 1990. A comparative study of the development of two chemical technologies: polypropylene and EPDM rubber. Paper presented the TIMS/ORSA Joint National Meeting, Las Vegas, NV, (May 7–9).

Ring, P.S., and Van de Ven, A.H. 1989. Formal and informal dimensions of transactions. Chapter 6. In A.H. Van de Ven, H.L. Angle, and M.S. Poole, eds., *Research on the Management of Innovation: The Minnesota Studies*. New York: Ballinger/Harper & Row, pp. 171–192.

Roberts, E.B. 1991. *Entrepreneurs and High-Technology: Lessons from M.I.T. and Beyond*. Cambridge: Oxford University Press.

Rosenberg, N. 1983. *Inside the Black Box. Technology and Economics*. Cambridge: Cambridge University Press.

Rosenberg, N., and Birdzell, Jr., L.E. 1986. *How the West Grew Rich*. Berkeley, CA: University of California Press.

Rosenbloom, R.S. 1966. Product innovation in a scientific age, new ideas for successful marketing. Proceedings of the 1966 World Congress, American Marketing Association, Chapter 23. Chicago: IL.

Ruttan, V.W., and Hayami, Y. 1984. Toward a theory of induced institutional innovation. *The Journal of Development Studies* 20(4):203–223.

Schumpeter, J.A. 1942. *Capitalism, Socialism, and Democracy*. New York: Harper and Row.

Scott, W.R. 1987. The adolescence of institutional theory. *Administrative Science Quarterly* 32:493–511.

Simon, H.A. 1962. The architecture of complexity. *Proceedings of the American Philosophical Society* 106:467–482.

Singh, J.V., House, R.J., and Tucker, D.J. 1986. Organizational Change and Organizational Mortality. *Administrative Science Quarterly* 31:587–611.

Stern, N., and El-Ansery, A.I. 1982. *Marketing Channels*. New Jersey: Prentice Hall.

Stinchcombe, A.L. 1965. Social structures and organizations. In J.G. March, ed., *Handbook of Organizations*. Chicago: Rand McNally, pp. 142–193.

Stobaugh, R. 1985. Creating a monopoly: product innovation in petrochemicals. In R. Rosenbloom, ed., *Research on Technological, Innovation, Management, and Policy*. New York: JAI Press, 2:81–112.

Teece, D.J. 1987. Profiting from technological innovation: implications for integration, collaboration, licensing, and public policy. In D.J. Teece, ed., *The Competitive Challenge*. New York: Harper Collins, Ballinger Division.

Thirtle, C.G., and Ruttan, V.W. 1986. The role of demand and supply in the generation and diffusion of technical change, Bulletin No. 86-5. University of Minnesota Economic Development Center, Minneapolis, MN.

Tornatzky, L.G., and Fleischer, M. 1990. *The Processes of Technological Innovation*. Lexington, MA: D.C. Heath and Company.

Tushman, M.L., and Rosenkopf, L. 1990. On the organizational determinants of technological evolution: towards a sociology of technology. Graduate School of Business, Columbia University, New York, NY.

Usher, A.P. 1954. *A History of Mechanical Inventions*. Cambridge, MA: Harvard University Press.

Utterback, J.M. 1974. Innovation in industry and the diffusion of technology. *Science* 183:620–626.

Van de Ven, A.H. 1992a. Suggestions for studying strategy process: a research note. *Strategic Management Journal* 13:169–188.

Van de Ven, A.H. 1992b. Longitudinal methods for studying the process of entrepreneurship. Chapter 9. In D.L. Sexton and J.D. Kasarda, eds., *The State of the Art of Entrepreneurship*. Boston: PWS-Kent Publishers, pp. 214–242.

Van de Ven, A.H. June 1993. The emergence of an industrial infrastructure for technological innovation. *Journal of Comparative Economics*. 17:2.

Van de Ven, A.H., Emmett, D., and Koenig, R. 1974. Alternative frameworks for interorganizational analysis. *Organization and Administrative Sciences* 5(1):113–129.

Van de Ven, A.H., and Garud, R. 1989. A framework for understanding the emergence of new industries. *Research on Technological Innovation Management and Policy* 4:295–225.

Van de Ven, A.H., and Garud, R. 1992. Innovation and industry development: the case of cochlear implants. Discussion Paper, University of Minnesota, Strategic Management Research Center, Minneapolis, MN. (April).

Van de Ven, A.H., and Walker, G. 1984. The dynamics of interorganizational coordination. *Administrative Science Quarterly* 29:598–621.

von Hippel, E. 1986. Cooperation between rivals: informal know-how trading. Working paper #1759-86, Sloan School of Management, Massachusetts Institute of Technology, Cambridge, MA.

Williamson, O.E. 1975. *Markets and Hierarchies*. New York: Free Press.

Williamson, O.E. 1985. *The Economic Institution of Capitalism*. New York: Free Press.

Zaltman, G., Duncan, R., and Holbek, J. 1973. *Innovations and Organizations*. New York: Wiley.

Part IV
Venture Growth and Performance

[22]

CHALLENGES IN PREDICTING NEW FIRM PERFORMANCE

ARNOLD C. COOPER
Purdue University

EXECUTIVE SUMMARY

Research examining predictors of new firm performance is clearly of interest to entrepreneurs and to those who provide advice and funds for their ventures. A growing body of research has examined the influence upon performance of such variables as entrepreneurs' characteristics, processes of founding, venture attributes, and environmental characteristics. However, considered as a whole, this research has shown mixed results and limited findings to date.

This paper considers some of the challenges that arise in attempting to predict new firm performance. A key factor is the heavy dependence of new ventures upon environmental developments, many of which may be very difficult to predict. All firms are impacted by the environment, but new ventures have a concentration of risk upon a few products or services, narrow markets, and a few key resources. Thus, well-conceived ventures can fail because of unforeseen environmental shocks and the lack of "deep pockets" to ride out hard times. These same factors can cause new firm performance to swing widely, confounding attempts to identify predictors of good or poor performance.

There are also challenges because many entrepreneurs pursue personal goals, some of which are noneconomic in nature. Thus, decisions about whether to found ventures, about how vigorously to grow them, or about whether or not to close down marginal businesses are all influenced by the personal values of entrepreneurs.

The diversity of ventures, encompassing firms that differ greatly in scale and potential, complicates the task of determining predictors of performance. It may be that the influence of a particular variable, such as management experience, varies by type of venture. Previous research has also used a variety of performance measures, making comparisons across studies more difficult. Little has been done to determine whether the factors that enhance one measure of performance, such as survival, are the same as those that lead to others, such as growth or profitability.

Previous research has been hampered by inadequate theoretical frameworks and, in some cases, by

Address correspondence to Arnold C. Cooper, Krannert Graduate School of Management, Purdue University, West Lafayette, IN 47907.

Earlier versions of this paper were presented at the Conference on Theory in Entrepreneurship at the University of Illinois in October 1991, and at the Gateway Conference in Victoria, B.C. in November 1991.

Journal of Business Venturing 8, 241–253 0883-9026/93/$6.00

inappropriate methods of analysis. In addition, past research often could have been characterized by a tendency to examine variables that were easy to study, rather than those that were important.

Despite limited success to date, we should not forsake research on predictors of new venture performance. The challenges discussed probably put limits on our ability to predict performance of individual ventures. However, the field of study is young and there is much that can be done to add to our understanding. The paper then develops recommendations for future research, noting that each of the challenges considered raises specific research opportunities.

INTRODUCTION

One of the central questions in entrepreneurship is why some new firms succeed and others fail. If we can determine what factors influence new firm performance, this has implications for prospective entrepreneurs, as well as their advisors and investors. If certain factors increase the probability of success, then entrepreneurs can appraise their ventures accordingly, possibly modifying their plans or deciding not to start at that time.

Thus a number of reviews of the field have called for attention to the cues distinguishing start-up firms with high-growth potential from those with low-growth potential (Bull 1991), the development of causal models of new venture performance (Low and MacMillan 1988; VanderWerf 1989), and increased understanding of the conditions that promote new venture survival and success (Kalleberg and Leicht 1991).

This paper examines some of the challenges in trying to predict new firm performance. Some of these problems may require care and systematic attention in conducting and interpreting research in this field. Others may relate to fundamental limitations in our ability to predict new venture performance.

My thinking in this area has been sensitized by research now underway at Purdue. My colleagues and I have been studying almost 3000 young firms and following these firms through a three-year period (Cooper et al. 1990). We have been successful in tracking the survival or discontinuance of every one of these firms and the growth or decline of a great many of them. One of the focal points of our research has been to try to predict performance, based upon variables that can be studied at the time the new firm is established. The frustrations and successes we have encountered have made us well aware of the problems in doing this. I shall be making reference to this ongoing work to illustrate some of the problems we shall be considering.

There are, of course, challenges in forecasting performance for any new undertaking, whether an independent start-up or a venture within an established corporation. We shall consider how attempts to forecast performance in independent new ventures may encounter particular and distinctive problems. Such attempts may be complicated by the diversity among independent new firms. Thus, "mom and pop" businesses, stable high-payoff firms, and high-growth ventures (to use Vesper's classification—Vesper 1990) reflect such differences in resource bases, typical environments, and strategies that the problems of trying to predict performance may vary substantially across them.

EXISTING THEORETICAL FRAMEWORKS AND RESEARCH FINDINGS

Theoretical frameworks for analyzing influences upon new firm performance are not well developed. However, one approach is to consider four sets of variables that can be studied at start-up: entrepreneurs' characteristics, founding processes, environmental conditions, and initial firm attributes—all of which appear to influence venture performance. (Other factors, such as changes in the environment and subsequent operating and strategic decisions clearly

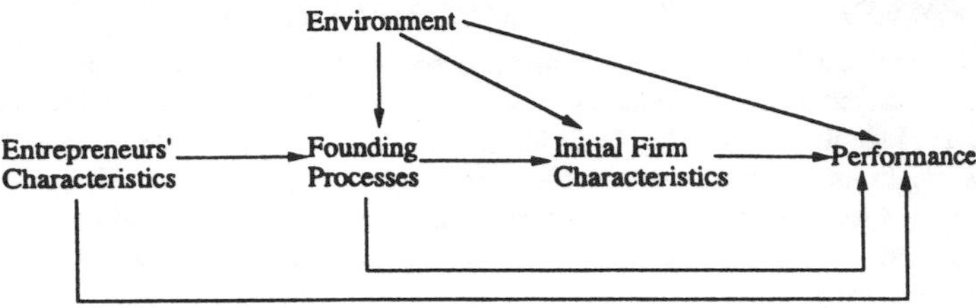

FIGURE 1 Framework for analysis.

influence performance also, but the focus here is upon those variables that can be studied at start-up.) Figure 1 presents these four sets of variables in the framework of a path analysis, in which variables such as entrepreneurs' characteristics and founding processes have both direct and indirect effects upon performance. The interrelationships may be examined in other ways as well. For instance, initial firm attributes might be considered as a moderating variable, in which the influence of particular entrepreneurial characteristics (such as industry experience) varies according to type of organization (Venkatraman 1989). Analysis might also focus upon whether gestalts exist in which particular entrepreneurial characteristics, founding processes, environmental conditions, and firm attributes tend to cluster together (Miller and Friesen 1978).

Using this framework, we see that different streams of research have emphasized different variables. Thus, the work in population ecology has examined such firm characteristics as newness, smallness, and generalist vs. specialist strategies and the dominant role of the environment in determining which firms survive (Aldrich 1979; Astley and Van de Ven 1983; Hannan and Freeman 1984).

Research in organization theory and in strategic management has focused upon environmental characteristics and initial venture characteristics, particularly strategies. Thus, the extent to which subsequent growth is related to initial market focus and to the characteristics of founding teams has been examined (Eisenhardt and Schoonhoven 1990), as has the existence of "archetypes" of new firm strategies and environmental characteristics (McDougall and Robinson 1990).

Research in entrepreneurship has particularly emphasized characteristics of entrepreneurs, such as gender, need for achievement, education, management experience, and goals. These have been examined in regard to whether or not certain attributes of entrepreneurs may be related to greater chances for success. This research stream has also examined founding processes, such as planning, risk management, use of information sources and networking, team formation, and financing. The relationship between venture performance and initial characteristics of firms has also been analyzed, including relatedness to the prior organization of the entrepreneur (Feeser and Willard 1988).

A central theme in much of the research has been to examine influences upon performance. However, the consideration of these relationships is relatively recent, with most of the research having been done in the last dozen years. There were some important antecedents, notably the longitudinal studies by Hoad and Rosko (1964), Mayer and Goldstein (1961), Roberts (1972), and Cooper and Bruno (1977). However, the number and sophistication of studies have increased substantially in recent years.

PROBLEMS IN INTERPRETING PRIOR RESEARCH

There are several problems in comparing and interpreting the work done to date. There is great variation in research methods, including case-based inductive studies, cross-sectional survey research, and longitudinal studies. These longitudinal studies seem particularly promising in giving us insight into founding variables that influence later performance. (Representative of recent longitudinal research is the $5^1/_2$-year follow-up study of technical entrepreneurs by Miner et al. 1991 and the 4-year study of Minnesota entrepreneurs by Reynolds and Miller 1989).

For all studies, a central problem has been the lack of well-developed theories of causal relationships (VanderWerf 1989; Hisrich 1988). This makes it difficult to interpret the spotty and sometimes inconsistent findings to date. Much of the work that has been done might be criticized for being weak at the front end, for lacking theoretical frameworks to drive the research.

There is also great variation in samples. Among the 1.3 million ventures starting in the United States each year, there is, in fact, great diversity. Gartner (1985) noted that the differences among entrepreneurs and across their ventures are as great as the variation between entrepreneurs and nonentrepreneurs and between new firms and established firms. Most empirical studies have been based upon focused samples, such as technical firms in Silicon Valley, manufacturing businesses in Pittsburgh, or companies started in Minnesota in 1979 or 1982. Findings from such studies may reflect those particular samples, but may or may not be broadly applicable. Furthermore, at this stage in the development of the field, we do not know whether or not there are contingent relationships. Thus, the presence of teams of founders and close relationships to prior organization, variables that seem to relate to success for high-technology firms, may or may not be equally important for small retail and service businesses. As we consider how sample selection may have affected research that has been done to date, we should note that studies may reflect the kinds of firms that are easiest to study. Thus, very young firms and those that die quickly are often difficult to identify and so are often not included in samples. (In passing, it should be recognized that the question of when a firm is started is by no means clear-cut (Reynolds and Miller 1989)). At any rate, as we seek to develop better theoretical frameworks, the diversity among entrepreneurial firms should be kept in mind.

Another problem relates to the variety of performance measures that have been utilized. Survival versus discontinuance has often been used, particularly in population ecology studies. However, firms may "survive" with different levels of performance, some being marginal and others outstanding. Growth measures, considering sales or employee growth, have often been used. Some studies have used absolute size as a performance measure, without necessarily measuring growth rate. Subjective assessments of performance or indices of performance have also been utilized. These depend, of course, upon how the index was weighted or the expectations of the entrepreneur. Sapienza, Smith, and Gannon (1988) examined whether or not subjective assessments of sales growth and return on sales were related to objective measures; they found no significant correlations. This variety of performance measures that has been used makes comparisons across studies difficult.

There are also problems relating to the ways in which data have been analyzed. Earlier studies used cross-tabulations or univariate analysis. It is only recently that an increasing number of studies have utilized multivariate methods. In general, analytical methods used to date have been less sophisticated than those characterizing many of the older fields of management.

As we seek to interpret prior studies and build theoretical frameworks, we should recognize the lack of comparability and, in some cases, the weaknesses of much of the empirical work to date. This awareness should help us to understand the mixed patterns of findings reported. They should also guide us as we plan research for the future.

There have been several articles that review the extant literature and consider the extent to which there seem to be clear predictors of success for new firms (Low and MacMillan 1988; VanderWerf 1989; Woo, Daellenbach, and Nicholls-Nixon 1990; Cooper and Gimeno-Gascon 1992). There are some consistent findings, but there are also many differences across studies. Thus, one review reported upon seven previous studies in which the relationship between new firm performance and prior experience in the same industry for the entrepreneur was examined. Three studies found positive relationships, one found mixed relationships, and three found no significant relationships (Cooper and Gimeno-Gascon 1992). These diverse patterns seem to have been typical for a number of variables that have been studied. Furthermore, research seeking to build models to explain new firm performance has often reported large amounts of unexplained variance (Woo et al. 1990). It is clear that predicting new firm performance is challenging. In this paper, I examine some of the reasons for the limited success to date.

The growing body of empirical studies may offer opportunities for meta analysis. This methodology, which takes into account both the strength of relationships in prior studies and sample sizes, has not received much attention in the entrepreneurship field to date. It has been applied to a number of fields where there is a body of research studies to interpret. For instance, it has been applied to such questions as the relationship between strategic planning and financial performance (Boyd 1991) and the various influences upon organizational innovation (Damanpour 1991).

STOCHASTIC PROCESSES AND UNSTABLE PERFORMANCE

The work in population ecology, organization theory, and strategy all call our attention to the dominant role environment plays in influencing firm performance. Factors outside the direct control of the entrepreneur, such as the carrying capacity of an industry, may affect the number of existing firms that are able to survive (Aldrich 1990). Major environmental change may select out many existing firms because they are no longer suited to a changed environment (Hannan and Freeman 1984). The upshot is that the performance of firms may depend, in part, upon whether or not they are in the right place at the right time. Of course, one of the central responsibilities of managers and of entrepreneurs is to evaluate the attractiveness of industries they contemplate entering and to formulate strategies that take into account both their resources and the environment (Vesper 1990). However, the point goes beyond that. Firms that were originally well-conceived and managed may fail because of subsequent unforeseen changes in the environment. Furthermore, many new firms are positioned in developing and turbulent markets, where the challenges of adaptation are particularly severe.

Such events can impact all firms, including new ventures within established corporations. However, independent new firms may be particularly vulnerable. New firms have strategies characterized by limited lines of products or services offered to very particular markets. (For our sample of 2994 new firms, 64% estimated that at least 80% of their customers were located within 25 miles of the business.) These focused strategies can lead to superior performance. If things go well, there is no averaging effect in which other product lines or older facilities or less-effective employees pull performance down. However, the concentration of risk upon a narrow resource base and the dependence upon narrow markets means that performance often is not stable. Thus, the opening of a strong competitor, such as a Walmart in the neighborhood, the closing of access streets due to construction, or the lessening of local purchasing power due to plant closings or strikes—all can have devastating impacts upon new and not very well-established firms. In new firms, the challenge of adapting to a changing environment is compounded by a reliance upon a narrow resource base—a particular facility and a few key employees and suppliers. Thus, a fire or accident or the departure of a key employee may make it difficult to keep the new firm going. Because the new business is built around the entrepreneur, key events in that person's life may impact the firm. Fights with partners, serious illness, or the realization that business ownership is less satisfying than expected may lead to failure or simply to giving up. The independent start-up may find it particularly difficult to deal with the many shocks and unanticipated problems that can arise.

Another source of instability in new ventures is internal change, which can reflect attempts to adjust to turbulent environments. Change also can result from experimentation and learning as the entrepreneur tries to determine how to compete most effectively. In addition, changes can result from rapid growth. Writers in population ecology have argued persuasively that established organizations have substantial inertia so that it is difficult for them to change, particularly with regard to core features of the organization (Hannan and Freeman 1984). They suggest that small organizations may be less subject to inertial forces and be more likely to change; however, they argue that these firms are also more likely to die in the process.

Notwithstanding the presence of inertia and the risks of change, we have found, in our sample of 2994 firms, that many of these firms seem to have changed along a variety of dimensions. Thus, of the 877 firms reporting in the third year, 43% reported that they had added products or services in the previous year and 20% indicated that they had dropped products or services. Ten percent reported that they had lost full-time partners, a change that would seem to affect a core feature of a young firm. Furthermore, 13% had changed locations and 5% had even changed company names. These firms seem to be changing in a number of ways, which may complicate the task of predicting their performance. A very successful small firm may become a mediocre or even failing firm as it outgrows the entrepreneurs or the management methods that accounted for its earlier success. Thus, rapidly growing new firms may find that their very success leads to changes that make their performance unstable.

All of this means that performance in new firms is often erratic. Consider the "*INC.* 500," a set of privately held companies that have experienced phenomenal growth (average compound annual growth rate of sales over the previous four years of 97% for the 500 firms listed in December 1989). In some years *INC.* reports what happened to the firms that made the list in the previous year. They usually report that some of those amazingly successful firms subsequently failed. One of the early studies in entrepreneurship sought to determine factors associated with success and failure in small manufacturing firms. In the midst of the study, the researchers found that some of the firms changed performance categories, i.e., successful firms became unsuccessful (Woodruff and Alexander 1958).

The success of independent start-ups in dealing with unexpected events may depend upon whether or not there are insulating or coping mechanisms (Woo et al. 1990). Low and MacMillan (1988) suggested that ventures can shape their own luck in part by being parsimonious in the use of resources, locating in protected markets, moving incrementally, and building networks. New firms usually have little slack, but may, under some circumstances, have substantial flexibility (Woo, Nicholls-Nixon, and Cooper 1991). This may enable some new ventures to respond more effectively than others to unexpected events. The degree of insulation from environmental shock or the ability to cope with an uncertain environment appear to be important concepts that have yet to be incorporated in our research designs. The stochastic nature of the processes impacting new firms may impose real limits upon our ability to predict performance; however, to date little has been done to explore the factors bearing upon the ability to cope with unexpected change.

The authors of three articles have suggested that chaos theory may be applicable to entrepreneurial processes. They argue that entrepreneurship inevitably focuses upon change. Relationships across variables may be changing rather than stable and the sequence by which events occur may affect outcomes (Stevenson and Harmeling 1990). Furthermore, outcomes such as the formation or performance of firms may be enormously sensitive to slight differences in beginning conditions. "Nonlinear systems, such as we might expect to find in entrepreneurship, are potentially fraught with problems if we try to make predictions about their future behavior" (Bygrave 1989, p. 28). This suggests that efforts "to target selected companies for support—that is, that seek to pick winners and losers—is doomed to failure" (Smilor and Feeser 1991, p. 171). To the extent that these observations apply, entrepreneurial performance may be extremely difficult to predict because of the unstable discontinuous relationships that may exist between initial conditions and subsequent performance.

GOALS—NONECONOMIC AND MIXED MOTIVE

Research on occupational choices suggests that a number of factors interact as people make career choices (Lawler 1973). Entrepreneurs also appear to vary in their primary motivations, as revealed in the numerous research studies that have examined differences in primary goals of entrepreneurs. One study classified organizations as "craft," "promotion," and "administrative" types, with the primary objectives of the chief executive being "comfort-survival," "personal achievement," and "market adaptation," respectively (Filley and Aldag 1978). Another developed an entrepreneurial typology of "caretakers" and "managers," with the former particularly seeking "to let you do the kind of work you want to do" and the latter emphasizing primarily financial goals (Braden 1977). Others have emphasized that business owners may vary substantially in their orientation toward innovation and growth (Carland et al. 1984).

The primary motivations of the entrepreneur bear upon not only the decision to start but also upon decisions about how to manage, including whether or not to grow the firm aggressively. The success level attained by a young firm may depend upon whether or not other competent managers are added (and authority is shared), whether or not outside investors are brought in (and ownership is diffused), and whether or not investments in the future are made (and current income levels are risked). Whether a business stabilizes at a low level or grows may also depend upon the entrepreneur's desire for current compensation and a comfortable lifestyle versus sacrifices to build for the future. If the philosophy is "life is uncertain, eat dessert first," then the young firm is not very likely to achieve high growth. All of these decisions depend upon the values of the entrepreneur. Davidsson (1989) investigated the willingness of entrepreneurs to pursue growth and found that many were not motivated to pursue substantial growth, in part because of fear of reduced control and concern about heavier personal workloads. Thus, firms started with great promise may not realize their potential, and firms that may appear to have modest prospects show growth because of the drive of the founder.

A substantial body of research done to date has treated survival versus discontinuance as categorical measures of performance. The assumption is that one represents a degree of success and the other of failure. However, we should recognize that the decision to continue or close down may be an intensely personal decision, one influenced by the values and perceived alternatives of the individual entrepreneur. Thus, entrepreneurs who are well-prepared, with strong educations, management experience, and high needs for achievement, may be dissatisfied with marginal performance because they think they can do better. Their counterparts with weak preparation may demonstrate great tenacity because they perceive no alternatives. For a firm with marginal performance, the continuance or discontinuance of the business may depend upon the entrepreneur's required threshold levels of performance. Thus, we have the dilemma that strong preparation may increase the probability of venture success, but that same strong preparation may impose a higher minimum level of performance required by the entrepreneur to keep the business going. Likewise, a business that appears to satisfy highly valued noneconomic goals of the entrepreneur (such as being independent) may have low threshold levels of performance required to stay in that business. Econometricians have developed methods to estimate unobserved, stochastic thresholds. Such models have been applied in fields such as labor economics, looking at threshold levels of wages required for housewives to enter or stay out of the labor market (Nelson 1977). In that research, the threshold level was affected by such variables as the number and ages of children and education of the housewife and her husband. We are currently using data from our study of 2994 entrepreneurs to determine whether or not minimum threshold levels differ for entrepreneurs whose backgrounds make it likely that they will have different perceived opportunities. However, as noted above, whether or not they stay in business and their patterns of development may depend greatly upon the goals of the founder.

DO PREDICTORS OF SUCCESS VARY BY TYPE OF VENTURE OR BY LEVEL OF PERFORMANCE?

The diversity of new enterprises raises questions about the ways in which "type of venture" may influence performance. Thus, there may be some differences in the critical variables leading to success for mom-and-pop businesses, stable high pay-off firms, and high potential ventures. These kinds of firms clearly vary in their probable scale and need for the managerial skills associated with building and directing an organization. They probably differ in their degree of reliance upon the entrepreneur's technical or operating skills. Thus, a mom-and-pop business, such as an auto repair shop, may depend greatly upon the founder's mechanical skills, while a high-growth venture may require substantial financial resources and the ability to develop an organization.

One reason why prior research shows such spotty results may be because we have not examined systematically how venture type may exert direct or indirect effects or how it may moderate other relationships being studied (Venkatraman 1989). Thus, industry experience may be critical in high-technology firms or in those fields in which operating knowledge is not widely diffused. In other fields, such as restaurants, it may be possible to acquire many of the needed skills through franchise arrangements or from suppliers.

The clear conclusion is that we must use care in pooling samples and in interpreting prior research. Also needed are better theoretical frameworks that enable us to think about the variables directly or indirectly affecting new venture performance. This kind of understanding should permit us to think about what factors are of general importance across all new firms. They should also help us to consider meaningful ways in which firms may differ and thus help us to develop typologies that illuminate differences across types of firms.

As we seek to predict success in new firms, it should be recognized that drivers of performance may differ according to the performance level achieved. Thus, factors increasing the probability of marginal survival may differ from those bearing upon the probability of high growth. As an example, age of the entrepreneur may be related to performance, but in ways that differ by measure of performance considered. One review of prior research noted that three studies had found that older entrepreneurs were more likely to survive or have higher income, and three other studies found that the firms of older entrepreneurs were less likely to grow (Cooper and Gimeno-Gascon 1992). Although these differences have not been systematically explored, it may be that older entrepreneurs are less likely to invest (and risk) the time and money needed to grow. However, they may be less inclined to close down marginal businesses because they perceive fewer employment alternatives.

These distinctions have received little attention to date. We have found in our research on 2994 young firms that there do seem to be some differences in the factors bearing upon different levels of performance. Thus, we found that having parents who owned a business appeared to increase the probability of marginal survival, but not of growth. However, gender (being male), having full-time partners, and not being in retailing or personal services increased the probability of high growth, but not the probability of marginal survival (Cooper, Gimeno-Gascon, and Woo 1991). We can speculate about, although we do not fully understand, the reasons for these differences. Future research might profitably explore the extent to which the predictors of performance vary according to different dimensions or levels of performance and the reasons for these differences.

STUDIED VARIABLES VERSUS VARIABLES THAT ARE IMPORTANT

Research to date has tended to focus upon variables that are relatively easy to gather information about or to measure. This may not be the same as focusing upon the variables that most bear upon performance. Many studies have examined entrepreneurial attributes, such as age, gender, education, and whether the entrepreneur had experience in the same industry. These offer the advantage of being accessible through questionnaires. Many of these variables presumably are proxies for the underlying knowledge, skills, or drive that really contribute to performance differences; however, the underlying variables usually are not studied. Our models may leave much unexplained variance because we are not measuring the right things.

Some of the variables that we need to study may be relatively obscure, sometimes because the entrepreneurs wish to keep a low profile or because of the strategic information advantages of obscurity. Other variables may relate to unique events and thus be overlooked (MacMillan and Katz 1992).

Behavioral characteristics, such as commitment and determination and the ability to enlist the assistance of others, may deserve more attention than they have received to date. Research reporting the criteria applied by venture capitalists as they evaluate new ventures suggest that these professional investors focus upon factors that have not received much attention in academic research. For instance, some of the factors that they weigh most heavily include whether or not the entrepreneur is "capable of sustained intense effort" and is "able to evaluate and react to risk well" (MacMillan et al. 1985).

What VanderWerf (1989) has termed the "How" variables could be studied much more aggressively than has been done to this point. Research might focus upon the processes followed, such as how relationships were developed with key employees and suppliers or how information was gained about consumer preferences. There is some evidence that many independent entrepreneurs are able to assemble resources at very low cost. They may be able to co-opt these resources more easily than their corporate counterparts because they are not constrained by corporate mindsets and are not required to abide by corporate rules (Starr and MacMillan 1990).

Block and MacMillan (1985) suggested that a new venture is an experiment with implicit hypotheses. Woo and co-authors (1990) emphasized that entrepreneurship is a process of experimentation and learning. Entrepreneurs must assess the environment as they search for opportunities, and they must interpret feedback from the marketplace as their ventures unfold. The cognitive processes followed by entrepreneurs, including those who are successful and those who are not, have received very little attention.

We might expect that independent start-ups, with their limited resources and need to establish a foot-hold where they had no presence before, would be heavily dependent upon decisions about strategy. There has been some examination of relationships between market characteristics, competitive strategy variables, and the performance of young firms (Sandberg and Hofer 1987; Feeser and Willard 1990; McDougall and Robinson 1990). Probably most has been done in considering venture strategies within the corporate context and utilizing the PIMS database. However, research on strategies of independent ventures has been limited, with many unexploited opportunities to apply some of the conceptual frameworks that have been developed in the field of strategic management.

These kinds of research probably require departure from the survey research so common in the field. They may also call for different theoretical frameworks and deeper involvement with the entrepreneurial ventures. There may be trade-offs between sample size and the research methods appropriate for these questions. The criticisms raised here could certainly be posed in regard to the work my colleagues and I have been doing as we followed 2994 entrepreneurs through time. We designed questionnaires that could be self-administered and completed in about 15 minutes. As we work with this large data-base, we are often reminded that we are dealing with variables that lend themselves to surveys, rather than examining the underlying factors that may be driving performance.

CONCLUSIONS

At this time our ability to predict performance of new firms is limited. It may be that some of the factors reviewed here, particularly the stochastic nature of the processes, the importance of noneconomic goals, and the instability of performance levels, place limits on what can be done. Corporate ventures are also uncertain, and their prospects depend upon many contextual variables relating to the strategy and structure of the corporation. However, some of the problems of forecasting venture performance may be particularly challenging for independent start-ups.

Nevertheless, we should recognize that this is a young field. It is only in the last decade or two that researchers have begun to study systematically the factors bearing upon the birth of new firms and their subsequent performance. Prior to 1980, there were no journals and no regularly scheduled conferences dedicated to entrepreneurship. Now, there are about 14 journals and, in some years, over a dozen conferences (Katz 1992, p. 28). A growing cohort of researchers is working in the field, including young faculty with solid training in research methodology and the drive associated with trying to "make their careers" in the field.

Attempts to predict the performance of new firms are likely to continue to be central to the study of entrepreneurship. Despite the inherent problems mentioned above, my view is that we can do better. The challenges discussed here suggest a number of opportunities for future research:

1. We need better theoretical frameworks and more theory-driven empirical research. In some cases our understanding may be advanced by borrowing constructs and theoretical frameworks from other fields (MacMillan and Katz 1992). In doing this we

should ensure that our usage reflects a real understanding of the best current thinking in these fields. For instance, Carsrud and his associates have noted that the failure to use contemporary concepts in the behavioral sciences has been one reason for disappointing research on the role of personality traits of entrepreneurs (Carsrud, Gaglio, and Olm 1987).

2. The influence of environmental uncertainty may limit our ability to predict individual firm performance. However, the strong influence of the environment may also present opportunities for research. We might examine more explicitly the factors influencing the ability of new ventures to function in turbulent environments. Research might also examine the nature and effectiveness of insulating mechanisms or the factors bearing upon the ability of ventures to bring about successful change.
3. Although entrepreneurs' differing goals complicate the task of predicting performance, they also present research opportunities. More could be done in examining entrepreneurs' goals (as measured at different times) and their career alternatives (as perceived at different times) and how these bear upon decisions about starting, growing, and terminating ventures.
4. The diversity among entrepreneurs and ventures presents challenges in planning and interpreting research. However, this diversity raises opportunities in that we need to learn more about how type of entrepreneur or type of venture acts as a moderator in influencing relationships between predictors and performance. We also need to understand more fully the effects of different performance measures and whether the factors that enhance performance vary according to the measure used.
5. We should examine the variables that seem to be important, even if they are not easy to study. Exploratory research and a variety of research methodologies may be needed as we seek to understand processes that have not been studied much to this point.

It is easy to be critical of a young developing field, implicitly applying the standards of more mature fields that represent the fruits of decades of scholarship. However, this is an exciting field that continues to develop, a field not constrained by a required adherence to an established orthodoxy. One of the strengths of the field of entrepreneurship has been its openness to a variety of approaches. This has led to many very interesting questions being posed, even though they may not have been pursued in great depth. My hope is that we can continue this creativity and this openness, even as we work toward more rigor.

Although there are major challenges in predicting new firm performance, progress has been made. I would suggest that we need to be sensitive to the special problems discussed here as we seek to build upon what has been done and to increase our understanding of the factors bearing upon new firm performance.

REFERENCES

Aldrich, H. 1979. *Organizations and Environments*. Englewood Cliffs, NJ: Prentice-Hall.

Aldrich, H. 1990. Using an ecological perspective to study organizational founding rates. *Entrepreneurship: Theory and Practice* 14(3):7–24.

Astley, W.G. and Van de Ven, A. 1983. Central perspectives and debates in organization theory. *Administrative Science Quarterly* 28:245–273.

Block, Z., and MacMillan, I.C. 1985. Milestones for successful venture planning. *Harvard Business Review* 85(5):184–188.

Boyd, Brian K. 1991. Strategic planning and financial performance: A meta-analytic review. *Journal of Management Studies* 28(4):353–374.

Braden, P.L. 1977. *Technological Entrepreneurship*. Ann Arbor, MI: Graduate School of Business Administration, The University of Michigan.

Bull, I. 1991. Towards a theory of entrepreneurship. Faculty Working Paper 91-0107, College of Commerce and Business Administration, University of Illinois at Urbana-Champaign.

Bygrave, W.D., 1989. The entrepreneurship paradigm (II): chaos and catastrophes among quantum jumps? *Entrepreneurship: Theory and Practice* 14(92):7–30.

Carland, J.W., Hoy, F., Boulton, W.R., and Carland, J.A. 1984. Differentiating entrepreneurs from small business owners: A conceptualization. *Academy of Management Review* 9(2):354–359.

Carsrud, A.L., Gaglio, C.M., and Olm, K.W. 1987. Entrepreneurs—mentors, networks, and successful new venture development: an exploratory study. *American Journal of Small Business 12(2):13–18.*

Cooper, A.C., and Bruno, A.V. 1977. Success among high-technology firms. Business Horizons 20(2):16–22.

Cooper, A.C., Dunkelberg, W.C., Woo, C.Y., and Dennis, Jr., W.J. 1990. *New Business in America*. Washington, D.C.: The NFIB Foundation.

Cooper, A.C., and Gimeno-Gascon, F.J. 1992. Entrepreneurs, processes of founding, and new firm performance. In D. Sexton, ed., *The State of the Art in Entrepreneurship*. Boston, MA: PWS Kent Publishing Co.

Cooper, A.C., and Gimeno-Gascon, F.J., and Woo, C.Y. 1991. A resource-based prediction of new venture survival and growth. *Academy of Management Best Paper Proceedings, 1991*. Miami Beach, FL: Academy of Management.

Damanpour, Fariborz. 1991. Organizational innovation: A meta-analysis of effects of determinants and moderators. *Academy of Management Journal* 34(3):555–590.

Davidsson, Per. 1989. Entrepreneurship—and after? A study of growth willingness in small firms. *Journal of Business Venturing* 4(3):211–226.

Eisenhardt, K.M., and Schoonhoven, C.B., 1990. Organizational growth: linking founding team, strategy, environment, and growth among U.S. semiconductor ventures, 1978–1988. *Administrative Science Quarterly* 35: 504–529.

Feeser, H.R., and Willard, G.E. 1988. Incubators and performance: a comparison of high and low growth high tech firms. *Journal of Business Venturing* 4(6):429–442.

Feeser, H.R., and Willard, G.E. 1990. Founding strategy and performance: a comparison of high and low growth high tech firms. *Strategic Management Journal* 11(2):87–98.

Filley, A.C., and Aldag, R.J. 1978. Characteristics and measurement of an organization typology. *Academy of Management Journal* 21(4):578–591.

Gartner, W.B. 1985. A conceptual framework for describing the phenomenon of new venture creation. *Academy of Management Review* 10(4):696–706.

Hannan, M.T., and Freeman, J. 1984. Structural inertia and organizational change. *American Sociological Review* 49: 149–164.

Hisrich, R.D. 1988. Entrepreneurship: past, present and future. *Journal of Small Business Management* 26(4):1–4.

Hoad, W., and Rosko, P. 1964. *Management Factors Contributing to the Success or Failure of New Small Manufacturers*. Ann Arbor, MI: University of Michigan.

Kalleberg, A.L., and Leicht, K.T. 1991. Gender and organizational performance: determinants of small business survival and success. *The Academy of Management Journal* 34(1):136–161.

Katz, J.A. 1992. *Five-Year Review of the Entrepreneurship Division of the Academy of Management*. Saint Louis, MO: Jefferson Smurfit Center for Entrepreneurial Studies, St. Louis University.

Lawler, E.E. 1973. *Motivation in Work Organizations*. Monterey, CA: Brooks/Cole Publishing Co.

Low, M.B., and MacMillan, I.C. 1988. Entrepreneurship: past research and future challenges. *Journal of Management* 14(2):139–161.

MacMillan, I.C. and Katz, J.A. 1992. Idiosyncratic milieus of entrepreneurial research: the need for comprehensive theories. *Journal of Business Venturing* 7(1):1–8.

MacMillan, I.C., Siegel, R., Narasimha, P.N.S. 1985. Criteria used by venture capitalists to evaluate new venture proposals. *Journal of Business Venturing* 1(1):119–128.

Mayer, K., and Goldstein, S. 1961. *The First Two Years: Problems of Small Firm Growth and Survival*. Washington, D.C.: U.S. Government Printing Office.

McDougall, P., and Robinson, R.B. 1990. New venture strategies: an empirical identification of eight "archetypes" of competitive strategies for entry. *Strategic Management Journal* 11(6):447–467.

Miller, D., and Friesen, P.H. 1978. Archetypes of strategy formulation. *Management Science* 24(9):921–933.

Miner, J.B., Smith, N.R., and Bracker, J.S. 1991. Entrepreneur motivation and firm survival among technologically innovative companies: A five and a half year follow-up. 1991 Babson Entrepreneurship Conference. University of Pittsburgh, April 16–20, 1991.

Nelson, F.D. 1977. Censored regression models with unobserved, stochastic censoring thresholds. *Journal of Econometrics* 6: 309–327.

Reynolds, P., and Miller, B. 1989. New firm survival: analysis of a panel's fourth year. In R. Brockhaus, N. Churchill, J. Katz, B. Kirchhoff, K. Vesper and W. Wetzel, Jr., eds., *Frontiers of Entrepreneurship Research*. Wellesley, MA: Babson College.

Roberts, E. 1972. Influences upon performance of new technical enterprises. In A. Cooper and J. Komives, eds., *Technical Entrepreneurship: A Symposium*. Milwaukee, WI: The Center for Venture Management.

Sandberg, W.R., and Hofer, C.W. 1987. Improving new venture performance: the role of strategy, industry structure, and the entrepreneur. *Journal of Business Venturing* 2(1):5–28.

Sapienza, H.J., Smith, K.G., and Gannon, M.J. 1988. Using subjective evaluations of organizational performance in small business research. *American Journal of Small Business* 12(3):45–53.

Smilor, R.W., and Feeser, H.R. 1991. Chaos and the entrepreneurial process: patterns and policy implications for technology entrepreneurship. *Journal of Business Venturing* 6(3):165–172.

Starr, J.A. and MacMillan, I.C. 1990. Resource cooptation via social contracting: resource acquisition strategies for new ventures. *Strategic Management Journal* 11(special summer):79–90.

Stevenson, H. and Harmeling, S. 1990. Entrepreneurial management's need for a more 'chaotic' theory. *Journal of Business Venturing* 5(1):1–14.

VanderWerf, P.A. 1989. Achieving empirical progress in an undefined field. *Entrepreneurship: Theory and Practice* 14(2):45–58.

Venkatraman, N. 1989. The concept of fit in strategy research: toward verbal and statistical correspondence. *The Academy of Management Review* 14(3):423–444.

Vesper, K.H. 1990. *New Venture Strategies*. Englewood Cliffs, NJ: Prentice Hall.

Woo, C.Y., Daellenbach, U., and Nicholls-Nixon, C. 1990. Theory building in the presence of randomness: the case of venture creation and performance. Working Paper, Krannert Graduate School of Management, Purdue University.

Woo, C.Y., Nicholls-Nixon, C.L., and Cooper, A.C. 1991. Experimentation and performance in start-up firms. 1991 Babson Entrepreneurship Conference, University of Pittsburgh, April 16–20, 1991.

Woodruff, A.M., and Alexander, T.G. 1958. *Success and Failure in Small Manufacturing*. Pittsburgh, PA: University of Pittsburgh Press.

[23]

NEW FIRMS: SOCIETAL CONTRIBUTION VERSUS SURVIVAL POTENTIAL[1]

PAUL D. REYNOLDS
University of Minnesota and The Wharton School, University of Pennsylvania

EXECUTIVE SUMMARY

New business firms are now considered a major source of new jobs, economic growth, technical innovation, and economic flexibility. They may provide a major strategic advantage for the United States in world competition. A more complete, precise understanding of the dynamics of new firm development, their societal contributions, and factors affecting their survival has considerable policy and managerial significance. A study of new firm contributions and survival was completed to determine whether the same factors would account for both. They do not.

The research began with a substantial body of descriptive information on 551 new firms initiated in Minnesota between 1978 and 1984. The initial data were collected in the summer of 1984; a one-year follow-up was completed in 1985 to determine new firm survival. The sample was representative of all major industry sectors and all regions of the state; about 60% were located in the Minneapolis–St. Paul urban area.

Attempts to predict current (1984) contributions indicated that age was not a significant factor; older new firms did not contribute more than younger new firms. The developmental pattern, primarily the average annual growth rate, was highly related to sales or jobs provided in 1984. Next most significant was the industry of the new firm; manufacturing, distributive services, and business (producer) service new firms provided more significant contributions.

The one-year follow-up was able to determine the survival status of 548 of the 551 firms; slightly less than 10% (48) had not survived. Major factors related to survival appeared to be age (high death rates at 2–3 years) and attention to financial matters.

Address correspondence to Paul D. Reynolds, Department of Sociology, 909 Social Sciences Building, 267 19th Avenue South, University of Minnesota, Minneapolis, MN 55455-0412.

[1]The research was supported by the University of Minnesota Center for Urban and Regional Affairs, Dr. Tom Scott, Director. Additional support was received from McKnight Research Funds of the University of Minnesota School of Management and the University of Minnesota Computation Center. Much of the data was collected under the supervision of Steve West and Mike O'Neal. Professors Bruce Erickson, William Rudelius, and Al Wickesberg provided helpful comments as the initial project was designed.

Journal of Business Venturing 2, 231–246 (1987) 0883-9026/87/$3.50

For public policy, the most significant implication is that a small percentage of new firms (30%) are providing the majority (60%–80%) of the jobs and sales. Public programs may be more effective if assistance is provided to the high growth firms that are the major sources of contributions. For those starting new firms, the results suggests that risk is minimized when either a modest–low startup, low growth—or major—high initial sales, high growth—firm is developed; and an emphasis on financial issues helps contribute to new firm survival.

INTRODUCTION

New business firms are now considered a major source of new jobs (Armington and Odle 1982; Birch 1979; Teitz et al. 1981), technical innovation (Kamien and Schwartz 1982), and economic flexibility and growth in the economy (Swain 1985).[2] Perhaps the greatest attention has been given to the creation of jobs provided by new "small" firms. This is now considered to be at least as great as the proportion of "old" jobs provided by small firms, perhaps substantially more. Despite this agreement, the dynamics of the processes by which new firms provide these jobs is not well understood.

The most common assumption is that all new firms—or all new organizations, for that matter—have a common pattern of development or life course (Churchill and Lewis 1983; Greiner 1972; Freeman 1982; Kimberly and Miles 1980). Attempts to predict contributions (new firm employment) would then be based on assumptions regarding the timing and nature of different stages of the life course. For example, multiple regression techniques might be used to predict contributions; this would reflect the assumption that all new firms should be treated as having very similar development patterns and equal potential for major contributions.

This is a critical issue for those concerned with public policy, for if *all* new firms are equivalent in their potential for creating jobs, then public policies to encourage their development should be broad and uniform—improve the "business climate." However, if a small percentage of new firms are the major source of most contributions (jobs, sales, exports), then programs targeted to high-potential new firms may be the most efficient and effective public strategy for promoting economic development.

A second issue of major concern regarding new firms (here there is no confusion with small) is their survival. It is widely believed that the death rates of new firms are extremely high; yet the data are often confusing and misleading. To find that 40% of failed firms are less than a year old does not suggest a high initial death rate, for it is unrelated to the number of new firms initiated. Further, identifying the "birth date" and final disposition and actual time over which "life" occurred is both complex and treated unsystematically (Timmons 1985, pp. 3–7).

One systematic study of a complete statewide cohort of all new establishments "born" in 1977 found that about 90% survived each of the first three years (Tauzell 1982); over a five-year period 59% could be expected to survive. One could describe this as an annual survival rate of 90% or a death rate of 40% in five years.

Equally important are attempts to predict the survival of new business firms. An ability to identify those factors associated with survival—and nonsurvival—is of great interest to those starting new firms, investors, potential employees, and public policy makers concerned with economic development.

[2]Unfortunately, much of the discussion fails to make a clear distinction between new and small businesses.

It would be most convenient if the new firms with the greatest potential for social contributions (jobs, sales, and exports) were the same firms with the greatest tendency to survive. Recommendations and public policies would be the same for both objectives—contributions and survival. This is the basis for the issues emphasized in the following discussion:

1. What factors are related to the societal contributions (jobs, sales, and exports) provided by new firms?
2. What factors are related to the survival of new firms?
3. Are the same factors related to contributions and survival?

The analysis is based on an industry-wide representative sample of Minnesota new firms initially studied in 1984 and contacted 12 months later, in 1985, to determine survival.

METHODOLOGY

Initial Sample

An initial sample of 2,000 establishments was purchased from Dun's Marketing Services as a random sample of all establishments with two "year start" dates; 1,000 for 1979 and 1,000 for 1982 (no intervening years were included). Of these 2,000 establishments, 235 were dropped since Dun's data indicated they were subsidiaries or headquarters. Because a large proportion of the listings were retail or consumer services establishments, only one third of these firms were retained for the next stage of the project, which involved 1,245 establishments. All firms were then screened in a brief phone interview; 2% were found to be subsidiaries; 16% had a recent change of ownership; 16% could not be contacted; and 8% were over 8 years old in June of 1984. In the end, 58% (724) of the initial sample of 1,245 firms were determined to be autonomous, operating new firms. This procedure, and the implications, are described in Reynolds, West and Finch (1985).

The phone screening provided the name of a current manager who was active in the start-up of the firm. These managers were sent an individualized initial letter with a 10-page questionnaire; all received a follow-up postcard. Those that failed to return the questionnaire were sent a second individualized letter with the questionnaire; those that still failed to respond were sent a third individualized letter and questionnaire by registered mail. Of the 724 firms that survived the phone screening, 56% returned the questionnaire. Those that did not return the questionnaire were contacted by phone for a truncated interview; about half provided responses to the key items. The overall response rate was 76%.

The questionnaire covered the firm's products and services; choice of location for start-up; an inventory of start-up problems; date and sources of initial, informal financial support; management emphasis; employment policy; history of sales growth; exports; asset growth; profitability; number and types of employees; and structure of the firm. Except for items related to profitability, over 90% of all relevant items were answered. The questionnaire can be obtained from the author.

First Year Follow-Up

Approximately one year later attempts were made to complete phone interviews with the same individuals regarding the current status of the firm; current sales and employment; sources of formal financing; source of major resources used by the firm; and the socioeconomic background and interests of the start-up team.

The entire follow-up interview was completed with 80% of the 1984 sample of 551 new firms; 3% refused to be interviewed; and for 17% there was no completed interview because the firm could not be found or the principal continued to reschedule and delay the interviewer. A determination of survival or nonsurvival in 1985 could be made for 548 of the 551 firms in the 1984 sample.

RESULTS

Factors Accounting for Societal Contributions: (Sales, Exports, Jobs)

Three types of societal contributions were considered: gross sales revenue, out-of-state or "domestic" exports (out-of-the-country exports were almost nonexistent), and job creation.

Table 1 summarizes the major features of these three types of contributions and the relations to urbanity and industry sector. There is a substantial difference among industry sectors. Industries with the highest average contributions (manufacturing, distributive service, and producer service) are concentrated in urban, not rural areas.

Age of firm as a predictor of contributions

The simple Pearson correlations between age and the logarithms of each of the societal contributions is presented in Table 2. Note that despite the wide range in contributions and firm ages (from 0 to 6 years), there is absolutely no relationship between the two—none are statistically significant. Biological (life cycle) analogies abound for describing the development patterns of new businesses (Churchill and Lewis 1983; Greiner 1972; Kimberly and Miles 1980), all of which reflect an implicit assumption that all firms start with equal potential for growth (the equipotential assumption). They are expected to develop through

TABLE 1 Social Contributions in Relation to Selected Factors

		Sales ($1,000)	Domestic exports ($1,000)	Jobs
All firms				
Mean (average)		980	318	10.1
Mode	100	100	0	2
Median	150	150	0	5.4
Highest value	25,000	25,000	22,500	130
Industry sector (averge)				
Agriculture	(n = 3)	340	0	5.0
Construction	(n = 107)	688	0	7.6
Manufacturing	(n = 105)	1,125	630	15.4
Distribution Service	(n = 123)	1,252	238	7.4
Production Service	(n = 102)	1,468	763	12.4
Retail	(n = 84)	351	24	9.4
Consumer Service	(n = 24)	137	1	4.5
Urbancity (average)				
Urban	(n = 375)	1,162	410	10.8
Rural	(n = 176)	569	102	8.6

TABLE 2 Correlation of Age with Societal Contribution

	Sales	Domestic exports	Jobs
Age (in 1984)	0.00	0.00	0.04

similar stages—infancy, adolescent growth spurt, maturity, and decline. Variations in size and longevity are assumed to reflect environmental factors (industry competition, general economic trends). The most fundamental hypothesis associated with this perspective is an expected positive relationship between age and size (sales, employees), particularly in the early years.

The absence of any relationship between age and contributions suggests that firms do *not* start with the same potential for development. This led us to an alternative classification of firms, based on initial performance and rate of development: (measured as first year's sales and subsequent sales growth rates, respectively). First year sales were dichotomized based on initial sales above or below $250,000. Growth rates were divided into above or below $100,000 per year in subsequent years. The result was four types of firms: Low Start, Low Growth (61% of all firms); Low Start, High Growth (15%) High Start, Low Growth (8%); and High Start, High Growth (16%). This analysis was done using the average growth rate in sales from inception to 1984, which increases the collinearity of the start-up of sales and growth rate dimension.

The difference among firms in sales development over time is presented in Figure 1. As one would expect, the largest proportion of new firms start small and stay small. (See also Birely 1986). Only a minority expand rapidly, yet these two groups of high-growth

FIGURE 1 Development patterns.

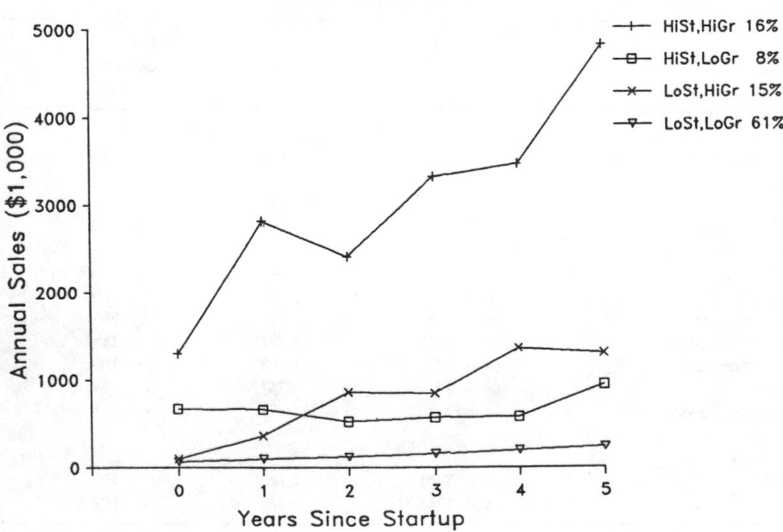

firms (only 31% of firms) accounted for over two-thirds of aggregate sales, exports, and jobs provided by the new firms in the sample. Essentially the same results are obtained if firms are classified on the basis of first year's employment and employment growth rate. The same results also occur if the first year's sales growth is used for prediction rather than the four-year growth (but the sample size is reduced owing to the absence of a year-by-year sales history for one-third of the firms).

Table 3 reports the results of simple linear regressions by industry sector for the log contribution of sales and jobs. It can be seen from the results that the initial development pattern is a highly significant predictor of sales and of job creation—far more so than firm age.

From Table 4 we see that there are a number of variables with statistically significant correlations with 1984 sales and 1984 jobs. In addition to the two characteristics used to identify the development pattern of the firms (first-year status and annual growth rate), the major start-up problem dimensions and dimensions associated with current (summer of 1984) management emphasis are presented. These two sets of dimensions were developed from a factor analysis of the 31 start-up problems dimensions and 25 current emphasis items. See Reynolds and West (1985) for details.

The greater the current sales and jobs, reflecting higher growth rates, the more start-up problems were reported and the greater the attention of management to the firm. The confounding of growth rates with start-up problems and management dimensions immediately suggested a multivariate analysis. This could be used to identify the impact of the start-up problem and management emphasis over and above the relationship to initial size and annual growth.

The major results are summarized in Table 5 (sales) and Table 6 (jobs). Order of entry was forced in the stepwise regression to ensure comparisons across industries. The larger number in each row is the total variance explained as additional factors are entered into the regression equation. Below them, in columns 2 to 4, are the incremental contributions to explained variance. For all industry sectors the majority of the explained variance is provided

TABLE 3 Percentage of Variance in Sales and Job Creation Explained by Development Pattern[a]

Social Contributions	1986 Sales	1986 Jobs
Indepenent variables	First year sales Average annual sales growth	First year jobs Average annual job growth
Variance Explained by Multiple Regressions		
Total sample	32%	46%
Construction	49%	70%
Manufacturing	34	55
Distribution service	29	52
Producer service	42	52
Retail	57	61
Consumer service	45	79

[a]Note: Initial status (in sales, jobs) and average annual growth rates (for sales, jobs) are the two variables used to classify firms into four development types.

TABLE 4 Correlation of Societal Contribution with Selected Factors

	Sales		Jobs	
	Correlations[a]	Stat. Sign.[b]	Correlations[a]	Stat. Sign.[b]
First-year contributions	0.47	.001	0.59	.001
Average growth rate (Start year to 1984)	0.50	.001	0.53	.001
Start-up problems[c]				
Personnel	0.38	.001	0.52	.001
Organizational, coordination, planning	0.17	.001	0.30	.001
Marketing, sales	0.18	.001	0.10	.06
Financial	0.14	.009	0.18	.002
Management emphasis in 1984[d]				
Strategic focus	0.29	.001	0.23	.001
Strategic implementation	0.20	.001	0.22	.001
Marketing, sales, promotion	0.20	.001	0.14	.008
Financial management	0.26	.001	0.17	.001

[a]The log produces a normal distribution and is used in all corrleation analyses.
[b]All reported are two-tailed.
[c]Developed from a factor analysis of 35 start-up problem items.
[d]Developed from a factor analysis of 25 current management focus items.

TABLE 5 Percentages Sales Variance Explained by Regression Analyses

	Variable added to forced regression			
Management focus	First variable: First-year growth	Second variable: Age of firm	Third variable: Initial personnel problems	Fourth variable: Management focus on financial problems
Full sample	32%	34%	43%	48%
Incremental variance		2%	9%	5%
Construction	49%	52%	62%	62%
Incremental variance		3%	10%	0%
Manufacturing	36%	35%	46%	51%
Incremental variance		1%	9%	5%
Distribution service	29%	36%	42%	42%
Incremental variance		5%	8%	0%
Producer service	42%	48%	46%	59%
Incremental variance		6%	−2%	13%
Retailing	57%	60%	57%	66%
Incremental variance		3%	−3%	13%
Consumer service	45%	46%	42%	67%
Incremental variance		−1%	−2%	15%

TABLE 6 Percentage Job Creation Variance Explained by Regression Analyses

	Variable added to forced regression			
	First variable: First-year growth	Second variable: Age of firm	Third variable: Initial personnel problems	Fourth variable: Management focus on financial problems
Full sample	46%	48%	61%	64%
Incremental variance		2%	3%	3%
Construction	70%	71%	76%	75%
Incremental variance		1%	3%	1%
Manufacturing	55%	55%	68%	67%
Incremental variance		0%	13%	−1%
Distribution service	52%	57%	66%	67%
Incremental variance		5%	9%	1%
Producer service	52%	55%	63%	68%
Incremental variance		3%	8%	5%
Retailing	61%	61%	57%	61%
Incremental variance		0%	−6%	4%
Consumer service	79%	86%	84%	99%
Incremental variance		7%	02%	15%

by the two variables used to identify development types: first-year status and annual growth rate. Small, though statistically significant, increments are added by other variables: age, initial problems with personnel, and current management emphases.

These consistent results bring into severe question public policies that take a blanket approach to supporting small business development on the argument that it will "create jobs"—only a limited number of firms create large numbers of jobs. The rest start small and stay small. We see from the first row of Table 5 that for the full sample a regression of sales revenues in the first year explains 32% of variance; as we add firm age to the

TABLE 7 Development Patterns and Average Contributions[a]

		Development type			
Start of year sales		Low	High	Low	High
Average yearly growth rate		Low	Low	High	High
1984 Contributions					
Sales	(n = 483)	$165	$720	$1,158	$4,123
Exports	(n = 408)	24	84	439	1,404
Jobs	(n = 483)	5.4	8.2	16.7	31.4
1985 Contributions					
Sales	(n = 307)	$600	$1,028	$1,880	$5,425
Exports	(n = 303)	106	164	875	2,236
Jobs	(n = 374)	5.4	9.8	19.6	29.8

[a]Note: The substantial increase in average sales and exports for low start, low growth new firms from 1984 to 1985 is primarily due to a bias in the responses to the 1985 follow-up. A larger percentage of low start, low growth firms failed to provide information, even though they appeared to be in operation.

regression this rises a mere 2% to 34%; as we then add initial personnel problems the explanation of variance rises to 43%. The same pattern occurs by sector, and the same pattern occurs for job creation in Table 6.

Not surprisingly, growth rate is a major predictor of both sales and jobs. On the other hand there is little question that firm age contributes very little to explained variance. Depending on the industry, we get far better explanations of variance from start-up problems and subsequent management focus than firm age.

The significance of the growth patterns of these firms is apparent when the average contributions (sales, exports, jobs) of the four types are compared. This is presented in Table 7 for both 1984 and, for those firms with available data, 1985. The 1985 information is independent of the calculations of 1981–1984 annual growth rates and thus provides a measure of societal contributions that are independent of the data used to classify the firms into the four growth pattern categories.

The results are unequivocal—high-start-up, high-growth new firms provide contributions that are 6–20 times greater than low-starting, low-growth new firms.

Factors Accounting for Survival

"Nonsurvival" of the firms in the one-year follow-up was determined in two ways. Most direct was a report in the phone interview that the firm was out of business. This occurred for 22 of the firms. An inference of "nonsurvival" was made for another 27 firms where no phone contact could be made with any individual that seemed to represent the firm. The majority were disconnected phone numbers where no new or replacement phone number could be located. (Repeated "call backs" and broken appointments with a respondent were not counted as "nonsurvival.") Firms that changed ownership were considered as survivors.

Four hundred and ninety-nine firms appeared to continue in the same business and 49 were classed as "nonsurvivors." This gave an overall survival rate of 91%, or a nonsurvival/death rate of 9%.

A number of factors related to new firm survival were explored. Comparison of the surviving and nonsurviving firms on these dimensions is presented in Table 8. For very few variables is the difference statistically significant; for none is the difference dramatic in substantive terms.

Those variables that correlated best with 1985 survival were: being an older firm; not being in the retail sector; a strong pattern of initial sales and sales growth; lower job growth rate; and an emphasis by management (in 1984) on financial issues and on the implementation of strategy.

Age of the Firm as a Predictor of Survival

As many have suggested, there is clearly a "Liability of Newness" (Freeman, Carrol, and Hannon 1983). However, the magnitude of this liability is not as great as might be expected. Liability of newness can be presented more precisely as the "hazard rate"—the probability that firms of a given age will *not* survive one more year. This is presented in graphic form, for firms in each of the six major industry sectors, in Figure 2.

The most striking feature of this presentation is the low level of the hazard rate itself, not greater than 0.10 for any given year. It is also consistent with a 10% annual loss for all industry sectors found in a careful analysis of new firm survival based on entry and attribution from state unemployment insurance files (Tauzell 1982).

TABLE 8 Factors Related to Firm Survival

			Survival (n = 499)	Nonsurvival (n = 49)	Statistical significance[a]
All firms			91%	9%	
Age (in 1985)	1–2 years	(n = 102)	85%	15%	
	34	(n = 160)	89	11	
	5–6	(n = 194)	97	3	
	7–8	(n = 30)	93	7	
	Average age in 1985		4.2	3.3	0.0012
Urbanicity	Urban	(n = 373)	92%	8%	
	Rural	(n = 175)	90	10	
Industry sector	Agriculture	(n = 3)	100%	0%	
	Construction	(n = 107)	94	6	
	Manufacturing	(n = 105)	93	7	
	Distributive service	(n = 123)	88	12	
	Producer service	(n = 102)	94	6	
	Retail	(n = 84)	83	17	0.01[b]
	Consumer service	(n = 24)	96	4	
Growth patterns	Low start, low growth	(n = 297)	92%	8%	
	Low start, high growth	(n = 71)	90	10	
	High start, low growth	(n = 37)	92	8	
	High start, high growth	(n = 76)	99	1	0.05[b]
First year	Sales, average ($1,000)		$ 325	$ 303	
	Jobs, average		6.1	5.0	
1984 contributions	Sales, average ($1,000)		$1015	$ 572	
	Jobs, average		10.2	8.8	
Annual growth (first year to 1984)	Sales, average ($1,000)		$ 304	$ 287	
	Jobs, average		$ 1.5	$ 3.8	0.016
1984–1985 Growth	Sales, average ($1,000)		$ 223	$−572	0.0003
	Jobs, average		1.5	− 8.8	0.0000
Start-up problem dimensions	Personnel		1.25	1.19	
	Organizational/coordination/planning		1.36	1.31	
	Marketing sales		1.60	1.56	
	Financial		1.54	1.61	
Management emphasis dimensions (in 1984)	Strategic focus		4.13	4.13	
	Strategic implementation		3.04	2.69	0.09
	Marketing, sales, promotion		3.85	3.86	
	Financial management		3.57	2.97	0.0003

[a]Unless indicated as otherwise, indicates simple t-test.
[b]Correct chi-square; compared to all others, combined categories.

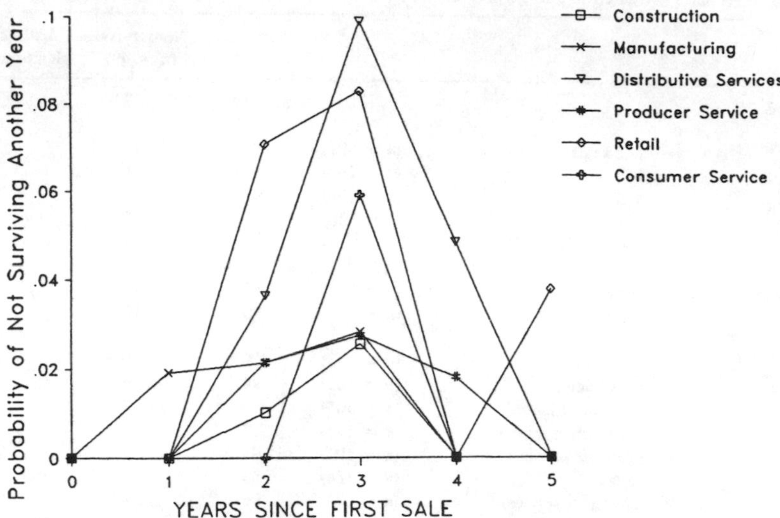

FIGURE 2 Hazard rates by industry sectors.

The curvilinear relation between hazard rate and age is obvious from the graphic presentation, and supported by tests of statistical significance. Firms 2–3 years old are more likely to "not survive" than either brand new firms or those four years or older. This may reflect the time required to exhaust the resources and optimism of those starting new firms. Most probably start a new firm with the expectation that success will require some time; it is only at the end of the second and during the third year that nonviability becomes apparent and resources are exhausted.

The only industry that is consistently more hazardous across all years is retail. It should be noted that restaurants—referred to as the "fruit flies" of organizational research—were classified as retail.

A comparison based on sales development patterns is presented in Figure 3. The lowest hazard rate (statistically significant) is found for the high-initial-sales, high-growth-rate firms. Remarkably, the firms with the next lowest hazard rate are the low-start-up, low-growth firms—small operations that appear to have been started by those with modest, conservative aspirations. Both these findings have significant public policy implications.

It is clear from this preliminary review that further analysis is needed. However, the unexpectedly low death rates pose a considerable research problem—the sample of nonsurvivors is small. Although a complete analysis will require a substantially larger sample of nonsurvivors, a tentative exploration has been attempted.

Discriminant Analysis: Survivors versus Nonsurvivors

Discriminant analysis was used to predict survival or nonsurvival. Those factors that had a statistically significant relationship to survival from the comparison of means tests reported in Table 8—age; average annual job growth; retail sector; high start, high growth; manage-

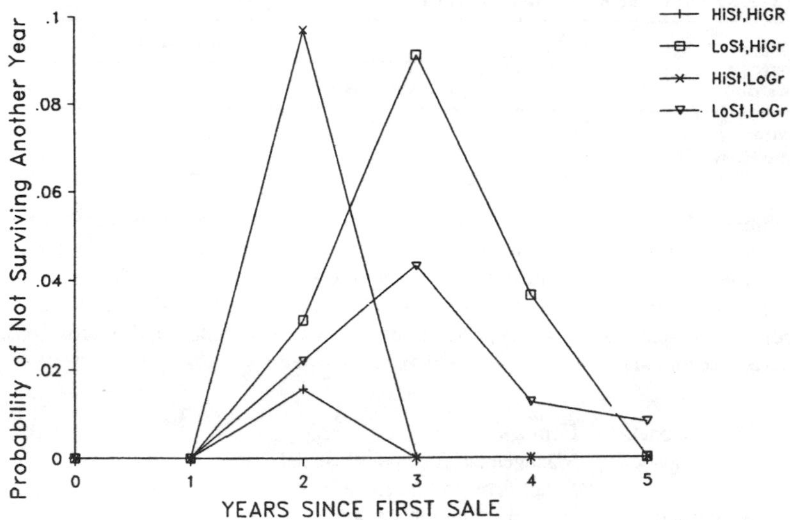

FIGURE 3 Hazard rates by development pattern.

ment focus on finances; management focus on strategy implementation—were obvious candidates as predictors. However, with 91% (499 of 548) of the new firms surviving, the discriminant analysis merely predicts that all firms will survive! This is not very enlightening. An alternative procedure was developed.

The 499 survivors were randomly sorted into ten groups. A discriminant analysis was run for each group of survivors, comparing each group with the same small sample of nonsurvivors. In seven of the analyses, the predictive equation was statistically significant (*P* levels of 0.0005, 0.0045, 0.0030, 0.0045, 0.0193, 0.0011, 0.0006). The average results across these seven analyses were computed. (These are clearly not independent analyses, but the overall results provide some additional information, no matter how tentative.) The major results are summarized in Table 9, while Table 10 reports the hit rates for the

TABLE 9 Predicting Survival with Discriminant Analysis

Independent variable	No. of analyses (out of 7) Significance at: *P* (0.10)	Value of *P* (0.05)	Average coefficient in predictive equation
Years since first sale		5	+0.37308
Management focus on finances in 1984	6	6	+0.58122
Retail firm	4	3	−0.2190
High start, high growth	2	—	+0.17107
No. of jobs added	—	—	−0.36264
Implementation strategy in 1984	—	—	−0.01072

TABLE 10 Hit Rate for Discriminant Analysis

Predictions (averge for 7 analyses)	Actual status	
	Survivors	Nonsurvivors
Survivor	86%	14%
Nonsurvivors	41%	59%

discriminant forecast. Correct predictions were much higher for surviving firms; the average percentage of correct predictions was 86%. Average correct prediction for nonsurvivors was 59%. The original subsamples had an average of 60% survivors and 40% nonsurvivors.

A major purpose of this analysis was to estimate the relative significance of selected predictive variables. The six independent variables could be considered in terms of impact in three categories:

Major impact: Firm age.
Some impact: Management focus on financial matters.
Retail firm (failure more likely).
No impact: High absolute job growth.
Absence of attention to implementation of strategy.

Societal Contributions versus Survival: A Comparison

The major factors associated with these two different outcomes—societal contributions and survival—are presented in Table 11.

Given the small sample size for nonsurvivors, the conclusions must be tentative but the results are provacative. It appears that very different factors are associated with survival as opposed to factors associated with societal contributions.

1. Age predominates as a critical predictor of survival, while age has no role in predicting societal contributions.

TABLE 11 New Firm Contributions and Survival: Comparison of Independent Variables

Importance of independent variables	Predictions of	
	Societal contributions	Survival
Dominant	1. Development pattern	1. Age 2. Management emphasis on financial matters
Highly significant	1. Industry sector	1. Sector significant (not retail) 2. Development pattern (high start, high growth)
Significant	1. Age 2. Personnel problems at start	1. Job growth rate 2. Management emphasis on strategy implementation
Clearly not significant		Start-up problems

2. Management attention to financial matters is significant for survival; but not for societal contributions.
3. The development pattern of new firms (obvious within 18 months of start-up) is the overwhelming factor associated with societal contributions; it is also a significant predictor of survival.
4. As for the industry sector, nonsurvival is associated with retailing while social contributions are associated with manufacturing, distributive services, and business services.
5. Start-up personnel problems have strong correlative association with societal contributions (perhaps because rapidly growing firms are in a constant search for personnel), whereas there is no correlation with survival.
6. Management emphasis on implementing strategy is correlated with firm survival, but not with societal contributions.

IMPLICATIONS

The implications from this study, the first of a series of projects in a continuous longitudinal program of research on new firms, are related to public policy, start-up strategies, management emphasis, and organizational research.

Public Policy

Substantial discussions are now occurring over the extent to which public agencies should encourage new firms. Most commentaries reflect an undifferentiated image of new firms—treating them as equal in their potential for social contributions. In turn, most forms of assistance are envisioned as blanket programs that will assist all eligible new firms. Given the substantial number of new firms born each year, such unfocused programs may have little impact on the high growth new firms with the greatest potential for contributing sales on jobs.

The alternative is to focus on the small percent of new firms that provide the large majority of job sales, and exports. This is likely to be a substantially more effective and efficient use of public resources. However, two problems must be confronted. First, it is currently difficult to identify specific new firms, much less select those that may have high growth rates. However, if they can be identified and followed for 18–24 months after their first sales, predictions of growth and social contributions can be quite good. Public support for new firms can be restricted to the first two years—to ensure the high growth firms get a good start—or it can be delayed until firms are two years old—to ensure that only high-growth firms will receive the assistance.

Second, regardless of which strategy is used, it will be politically insensitive to emphasize the high-growth firms and ignore the two-thirds of new firms that form the majority of start-ups but have low potential for social contributions. Those that initiate low-start, low-growth—or lifestyle—new firms can be significant as a political group. Strong rationale will be needed to respond to them.

Start-Up Strategies

It is clear that the teams that start new firms and hope to survive can choose one of two strategies. If their initial resources, and perhaps skills, are modest, a low-growth strategy seems safest. If the initial resources are substantial (perhaps because a number of experienced individuals have chosen to cooperate in initiating the new firm) the safest route is to plan and manage for "relatively" high growth. The greatest hazards await those that initiate a firm with modest initial sales yet strive for high growth. The small group that start strong but have little or no growth are difficult to advise; perhaps they are "lifestyle" firms in wholesale or specific retail areas that need large sales to reach the minimum level needed for success.

Management of New Firms

The evidence that is available is unequivocal on one point: watch the money. There is a very strong relationship between emphasis on financial management and new firm survival. Less substantial is a relationship between an emphasis on implementing strategy (actually running the business) and survival. Even more marginal is a relationship between the growth rate in employees and survival; firms quick to add employees may have a poorer chance of survival. If supported in additional research, this would recommend substantial care in adding employees, perhaps reflecting substantial care in all management activities.

Organizational Research

For organizational scholars, these results are revealing; they suggest a reexamination of the basic conception of organizations as similar in potential and development patterns. This research suggest that such a biological conceptualization is too simplistic. The low-start, low-growth new firms might be considered more like marriages; they are created and survive—without growth—or they do not.

The high-start, high-growth firms do not seem to have an infant, child stage in their development. They move immediately into an adolescent "growth spurt"—when the growth begins to moderate and the new firm stabilizes is not known. It is clear that the dramatic entrepreneurial model—modest start up, fast growth—encompasses only a small percentage of new firms; and they are the riskiest group.

One major challenge for additional research is predicting the trajectory a firm will take using characteristics present before "birth." This is equivalent to predicting which of four development patterns a new firm will follow. Predicting firm growth is of major interest to a number of groups: public policy makers, investors, and potential employees. A second major challenge is to describe and predict the eventual history of the firms—survival, stable size, decline, etc.

Both of these suggest longitudinal studies of new firms sampled from diverse industries, rather than intensive case studies.

REFERENCES

Armington, C., and Odle, M. Winter 1982. Small business—how many jobs? *The Brookings Review* 1(2):14–17.

Birch, D.L. 1979. *The Job Generation Process*. Cambridge, MA: M.I.T. Program on Neighborhood and Regional Change.

Birely, S. 1986. The small firm—Set at the start. *Frontiers of Entrepreneurship Studies: 1986*. Wellesley, MA: Babson College Center for Entrepreneurial Studies, pp. 267–280.

Churchill, N.C., and Lewis, V.L. March–April 1983. The five stages of small business growth. *Harvard Business Review* 83(2):30–32, 34, 38, 40, 42, 44, 48, 50.

Freeman, J. 1982. Organizational life cycles and natural selection processes. *Research in Organizational Behavior* 4:1–32.

Freeman, J. Carroll, G.R., and Hannan, M.T. October 1983. The liability of newness: Age dependence in organizational death rates. *American Sociological Review* 48:692–710.

Greiner, L.E. July–August 1972. Evolution and revolution as organizations grow. *Harvard Business Review* 37–46.

Hannan, M.T., and Freeman, J. 1977. The population ecology of organizations. *The American Journal of Sociology* 82(5):929–964.

Kamien, M., and Schwartz, N.L. 1982. *Market Structure and Innovation*. Cambridge, England: Cambridge University Press.

Kimberly, J.R., and Miles, R.H. 1980. *The Organizational Life Cycle*. San Francisco, CA: Jossey-Bass.

Reynolds, P.D., and West, S. 1985. *New Firms in Minnesota: Their Contributions to Employment and Exports. Their Startup Problems and Current Status*. Minneapolis, MN: University of Minnesota Center for Urban and Regional Affairs.

Reynolds, P.D., West, S., and Finch, M.D. 1985. Estimating new firms and new jobs: Considerations in using the Dun and Bradstreet files. *Frontiers or Entrepreneurship Research: 1985*. Wellesley, MA: Babson College Center for Entrepreneurial Studies, pp. 383–399.

Swain, F.S. 1985. The 'new entrepreneur': An old answer for today's marketplace. *Frontiers of Entrepreneurship Research: 1985* Wellesley, MA: Babson College Center for Entrepreneurial Studies, pp. 400–408.

Tauzell, J. 1982. Survival of Minnesota new businesses: 1977–1980. *Review of Labor and Economic Conditions*. (Research and Statistical Offices, Minnesota Department of Economic Security) 9(2):10–17.

Teitz, M.B., Glasmeier, A., and Svensson, D. March 1981. *Small Business and Employment Growth in California*. Berkeley, CA: Institute of Urban and Regional Development, Working Paper No. 348.

Timmons, J.A. 1985. *New Venture Creation*. Homewood, IL: Richard D. Irwin.

Strategic Management Journal, Vol. 11, 535–557 (1990)

GROWTH AND PERFORMANCE CONTRASTS BETWEEN 'TYPES' OF SMALL FIRMS

SUE BIRLEY
The Management School, Imperial College, London, U.K.

PAUL WESTHEAD
Cranfield Entrepreneurship Research Centre, Cranfield School of Management, Cranfield Institute of Technology, Cranfield, U.K.

This paper studies the interrelationships in the strategic profile of a sample of small firms, and, by using cross-sectional analysis, attempts to identify any evidence to support the 'stages of growth' theories. Three surrogates for comparative growth were used in the analysis: number of employees, sales turnover, and profitability. A cluster analysis identified eight different 'types' of small firms characterized by 'internal' variables of ownership, management, and product structure; and by 'external' variables of product/market positioning. Analysis of variance tests found no significant differences between the clusters with regard to size. The results suggest that firms do change, but not necessarily in any prescribed sequence. Indeed, the evidence presented in this paper suggests that future research should be focused on developing theories which better describe the heterogeneity of the sector by analyzing the development within clusters of firms rather than seeking generalized over-arching theories.

INTRODUCTION

Over the past 10 years new and small firms have been identified by most western governments as significant components of economic strategies for job and wealth creation. Implicit in these strategies has been the search for policies which will increase the supply of new firms, and will encourage established firms to grow. Yet significant growth is very much the exception; the majority of firms spend the whole of their economic life within the small firm sector. Nevertheless, it may take some time, and whilst the ultimate size may remain small, firms do grow.

O'Farrell and Hitchens (1988a) have provided the most recent analysis of the 'alternative theories of small firm growth'. They suggest that there are four main groups of theory—the industrial economics approach, the stochastic model, stage models, and the strategic management perspective. Each of these they find open to criticism, and conclude that it may be 'easier to provide a critique of contemporary theories than to present a definitive new conceptual framework within which to study small firm growth' (O'Farrell and Hitchins, 1988a: 1379). We believe that the key to this conundrum lies in the underlying assumption, found most clearly in the stage models, that growth is linear, always follows both the same events and the same sequence of events. The aim of this paper is to suggest a multi-dimensional approach to the understanding of the development of the small firm by providing empirical evidence as to the kaleidoscope of factors which describes firms of different sizes.

PREVIOUS RESEARCH

Previous studies have explored the relationship between the origins, personal characteristics

0143–2095/90/070535–23$11.50

Received 12 October 1989
Revised 28 March 1990

(Khan, 1986; Westhead, 1988; Lafuente and Salas, 1989) and traits of owner-managers (Hornaday and Aboud, 1971; England, 1975; Kets de Vries, 1977; Brockhaus, 1982) and small business growth (Perry *et al.*, 1988; Storey *et al.*, 1987, 1989); the role of the 'incubator' organization in the founding of growth-orientated firms (Cooper, 1985); managerial characteristics and the financial performance of small business (Hornaday and Wheatley, 1986; Filley and Aldag, 1988); the prediction of initial success in start-up ventures (Stuart and Abetti, 1987); and the business strategies and performance levels of new ventures which operate in different industry life cycle stages (Covin and Slevin, 1988). However, Milne and Thompson (1982) consider that the growth and development of a small business can be viewed, quite simply, in terms of how quickly the owner-manager can adapt and learn from the experience of dealing with the two environments within which the firm does its business (Hjern *et al.*, 1980). The '*internal environment*' consists of the resources of the firm itself and includes, for example, the personal and leadership characteristics of the owner-manager (Gibb and Scott, 1985), the owner-manager's age and its effect on his attitudes to growth (Deeks, 1976), occupational background, personal objectives, management style and decision-making, the level of the owners' education and training, and personal values and attitudes. Internal managerial factors influencing growth also include the extent of the division of management labour and the proportion of highly qualified personnel; the control system and the extent to which planning is built into it (Gibb and Scott, 1985); the human potential of the organization in terms of skills and flexibility of the workforce; the financial situation of the company; the physical asset base of the company in terms of age and quality of machinery and equipment; availability of management time for coping with change; and awareness of the wider 'macro' environment and of the task environment. The '*external environment*' includes, for example, suppliers; buyers; the strength of competition; potential entrants; interest rates; company taxation; degree of dependency upon a small number of customers; extent of complexity and uncertainty in the market served; sectoral trends; government policies; trends in exchange rates; and social, legal, and political conditions.

The internal environment

The owner-manager

It is generally agreed that, for the small business, the objectives of the firm are synonymous with those of the owner (O'Farrell and Hitchins, 1988a: 1373). Thus his value systems will influence whether a firm pursues the objective of growth or is content to pursue a 'survival' policy. Indeed, one reason for firms wishing to stay small is that the ownership and the management reside in the same person and so future company goals are determined not only by commercial considerations but also by personal lifestyles.

The problem with the studies which accept the thesis described above is that it automatically includes two basic assumptions. First, there is only one individual involved in the business or, if there is more than one, they all have the same concept of the business; and second, that all small firms are run by their founders. Both of these assumptions are clearly invalid. Indeed, some firms do not begin to grow significantly until second or third generations take control (Calori and Bonamy, 1989). These may, however, be the exceptions. In their study of the financial performance of small firms in New England, Begley and Boyd (1986: 12) found that companies run by the founder grew more rapidly than those run by a successor, and longevity of the business was negatively associated with growth rate—older companies grew more slowly than younger companies.

Management

In any organization, management collects and evaluates only a portion of the information concerning characteristics, processes, opportunities, and constraints in both the 'internal task environment' and the 'external macro environment' (O'Farrell and Hitchens, 1988a). For the owner-manager, his ability to manage the business will be a function of the systems and structures which he creates as the business grows. However, in their study of 95 small firms which had experienced a 5-year surge in growth, Fombrun and Wally (1989: 120) found that 'rapid growth may induce managers to design systems that may work at odds with each other'.

At the simplest level, some writers have asserted that there is an association between long-range planning and small firm development (Kudla, 1980). In a study of manufacturing firms in several northeastern states of the USA, O'Neill *et al*. (1987: 40) found the relationships between planning and performance were complex, and that planning did not improve performance in all environments. Interestingly, they found that in the dynamic environments, analysis depressed performance whilst control encouraged performance and that 'the planning function, then, is the ticket to the post-entrepreneurial stage, but it is no guarantee of a strong performance in that stage'. O'Neill and his colleagues also found that age, a surrogate for experience, had a positive effect on performance in dynamic environments. Bamberger (1983) has argued that 'we can assume that there is a positive relationship between the existence of a more or less formal strategic planning system and the firm's growth'. There is, however, by no means universal agreement that planning is either necessary or desirable (Karger and Malik, 1975).

Production

O'Farrell and Hitchins (1988b: 400) argue that production issues (such as design, quality control, correct use of machinery) in small maufacturing firms should be taken into account when considering competitiveness and small firms' growth because 'getting production right is always a necessary condition of growth in all firms. Other factors may also be necessary conditions for companies in certain sectors such as: after-sales service; customer liaison; selling; shortage of working capital and so on. However, although they may be necessary conditions, they are not sufficient.' In their study of the competitive performance of small manufacturing firms in Scotland and the mid-west of Ireland, O'Farrell and Hitchins (1988b: 409) also considered the influence of the comparative cost and quality of the firms' major physical assets—buildings and machinery (in terms of age and the level of introduction of computer numerically controlled (CNC) machines). Interestingly, Irish firms had a substantially higher proportion of equipment less than 5 years old, whilst a higher percentage of Scottish firms had adopted CNC machines. However, there was no relationship between CNC machines per person and the quality and price competitiveness of Scottish engineering companies.

External factors

Product/market structure

In the case of firms engaged in clothing and knitwear, O'Farrell and Hitchens (1988b) found that the most common mechanism of growth in both Scotland and the mid-west of Ireland was by increasing sales to existing customers. They also found that the poor quality of the supplier base in the mid-west of Ireland was a factor which affected growth strategies. The majority of firms in Ireland which purchased inputs locally reported problems of quality, design, delivery, or some other dimension of supply performance.

Accepting that small firms are generally dependent upon one or a few products Wilson and Gorb (1983) examined the extent and nature of dependence in the London Borough of Camden. Their analysis highlighted three findings. First, many of the small firms studied were found to be dependent on a narrow range of industry or customer types. Second, dependence on a small number of customers was not necessarily harmful since it may reflect a symbiotic relationship between the small and large firm with mutual benefits to both buyer and seller. For example, by reducing the costs of marketing, dependence lowers the general overheads in the new small firm, thus reducing barriers to entry brought about by high unit costs and an absence of economies of scale. Third, Wilson and Gorb (1983: 22) found that the youngest small firms were generally dependent on local and regional markets but that as they matured, they lost some of their dependence as their markets became more distant.

Porter (1980, 1985) has argued that the fundamental basis of above-average performance in the long run is sustainable competitive advantage. He identified five groups whose actions (or threats of action) may limit a firm's profitability: competitors, customers, suppliers, potential competitors, and suppliers of substitute products. Of particular importance to small firm growth he suggests are competitor strength and customer concentration. Whilst competitor strength is expected to diminish new venture performance, customer concentration may be a nonlinear influence on performance with a medium value leading to the best result. When concentration is high so is customers' bargaining power. Low concentration implies a lack of power by customers but a start-up with a limited sales force may have difficulty establishing close contact with its customer base. This leaves it vulnerable to late-entering competition from established firms. This view is supported in an empirical study of 34 investments in start-up companies in the U.S.A. (Roure and Keeley, 1989: 214) which showed that 'buyer concentration' was a major factor explaining the success of technological start-ups. The level of competition in market segments also significantly influenced small firm growth with successful start-ups targeting market segments which have a relatively low level of competition. Roure and Keeley do, however, suggest that firms in Europe have a greater tendency to have attacked market segments with a higher level of competition.

Location

Mason and Harrison (1985) conclude that the local environment may be an important influence upon the prospects for small firm growth and expansion, and the characteristics of the region in which small firms are located will have a significant impact on their relative performance (Hitchins and O'Farrell, 1987, 1988; O'Farrell and Hitchins, 1988b; Sweeney, 1987). This is not a view which is confined to the United Kingdom. Lorenzoni and Ornati (1988) stress the importance of 'constellations of firms' and of a contrasting 'environmental texture', factors which they conclude have contributed to the growth of the small firm sector in areas such Route 128 and Silicon Valley in the U.S.A. and the Prato district in Italy. This growth is made possible due to the availability of suppliers who thereby create an 'environmental texture' of opportunities not fully characterizable by a physical or a geographic boundary.

A key assumption in the creation of 'outsider' advisory organizations such as Enterprise Agencies, Development Boards, the Scottish Development Agency (SDA) in Scotland, and the Welsh Development Agency (WDA) in Wales is that they should be able to play a significant role in improving the effectiveness of strategic planning in small firms. O'Farrell and Hitchins (1988a: 1378) suggest that this structuring of the 'external' environment in the peripheral regions is based upon the view that small firm growth may be constrained by the lower quantity and quality of public and private services available. There is some evidence to support the view of a range of impediments to growth in peripheral regions. For example:

1. venture capital availability is more limited in peripheral areas owing to the centralization of the lending institutions and the distorted perception of risk by banks (Mason, 1987);
2. lower rates of economic growth and lower levels of income in peripheral locations inhibit the opportunities for small firm expansion based upon local and regional markets (O'Farrell and Hitchins, 1988a: 1378);
3. small firms in peripheral regions suffer technical impediments to growth, as reflected in the lower rates of innovation compared with similar sized firms in core regions (Oakey *et al.*, 1980);
4. labor supply bottlenecks vary between regional and subregional markets (Hitchins and O'Farrell, 1987);
5. peripheral economies dominated by large firms may not provide an ideal source of labor for small firms—skilled personnel recruited from such enterprises tend to be more narrowly specialized, and to lack the flexibility necessary for working in a small firm environment (Hitchins and O'Farrell, 1988);
6. in peripheral regions there is a restricted supply of managerial and organizational skills (Del Monte and Giannola, 1986: 282) and the shortage of middle-management staff has impeded the growth of some small firms (Hitchins and O'Farrell, 1988);
7. firms in less prosperous areas will be more vertically integrated than those in developed regions and this lack of specialization reduces the competitiveness and the rate of growth of local firms (Del Monte and Giannola, 1986: 282).

LIMITATIONS OF PREVIOUS RESEARCH

The research outlined above presents an apparently coherent and comprehensive picture of the factors influencing the growth of the small firm. However, despite the fact that it is generally agreed that the pressures upon the firm are complex and interrelated, most of the studies discuss only one or two aspects of the firm's profile. Moreover, almost all are based on firms in the manufacturing sector. Indeed, this assumption is so clearly built into most research analyses that O'Farrell and Hitchins (1988a) do not even provide an appropriate caveat in their survey of the literature.

An even more surprising omission in most of the literature is a complete absence of any discussion of an *appropriate* measure of growth. Again, the studies have been uni-dimensional, covering employment, profits, value-added, sales turnover, and assets; in some cases the parameters have not been defined at all. Underlying all these studies, however, is the assumption that performance and growth are not only interlinked, but one can be used as a surrogate for the other. This generally presumed correlation between size and performance is certainly not supported in the literature.

The studies in which measures of small firm performance are used are limited, mainly because the data are both difficult to obtain and notoriously unreliable. Moreover, and for the same reasons, there is very little which relates performance to that of competing firms in the market. For example, recognizing the inherent difficulties both of collecting accurate company data and comparative market data, O'Neill *et al.* (1987) simply asked owner-managers to rate their firm's performance relative to the previous 5 years using verbal anchors such as 'worse', 'same' or 'better'.

THIS RESEARCH

Most of the literature on the stages of growth of the firm attempts to describe a predictable set of characteristics at each stage (Steinmetz, 1969; Churchill and Lewis, 1983; Kimberley *et al.*, 1980). These researchers agree with Devine (1979), Taylor and Thrift (1982), and Fombrun and Wally (1989: 108) that this is too simplistic. It is more likely that all firms do not go through all stages, but rather that they go through different stages, at different times, in different sequences, and that the *total* set of inputs to the business will shape and characterize the development pattern.

This research analysed the strategic profile of a cross-section of 249 small firms in an attempt to reduce the data set to clusters of firms with similar characteristics, and to compare these characteristics with both size and performance.

Data for the analysis were derived from the Cranfield Small Firms Data Base (CSFDB). Firms in the sample are drawn from a wide variety of industries and locations. They range in size from one to 181 employees, and from less than £99,999 to over £10 million sales turnover. In all, 113 firms were engaged in manufacturing activities (45.6 percent), 103 firms were service firms (41.5 percent), and a further 29 firms were engaged in construction (11.1%). The average age of the surveyed firms was 26.6 years, and ranged from 1 year to 240 years. Forty-five percent of firms were established in the last decade, whilst 16.8 percent were established more than 50 years ago. In terms of the legal entity of the independent small firms, 80.6 percent were incorporated, 6.9 percent of firms were sole proprietorships, whilst a further 12.1 percent were a partnership. In total, 7901 people were employed in the 245 firms providing employment data, and each firm employed on average 32 people. A full description of the data collection process, and of the sample characteristics is found in Birley and Westhead (1988).

In the absence of longitudinal data for the firms in the sample, three measures of size are used as surrogates for presumed growth—sales turnover, trading profit, and total number of employees. Performance is measured by the owner-manager's scoring of his firm's profit performance against the market.

Based upon the available literature, preliminary hypotheses were constructed to identify those individual factors which correlated significantly with size and performance, and to test the direction of the correlation. The significant variables were then subjected to cluster analysis in order to reduce the 222 firms to a small number of mutually exclusive groups (Hair *et al.*, 1979).

PRELIMINARY HYPOTHESES

Age and ownership

Ownership structure

Firms with a diluted ownership structure, as reflected by a large number of shareholders, will be positively associated with a high level of growth and performance (SHAREHOLDERS).

Firms without either current first generation majority owners (OWNERS) or current first generation senior executives (EXECUTIVES) will be associated negatively with growth and performance.

Firms in which a large number of original founders who are still partners or shareholders (FOUNDERS) will be positively associated with high performance.

Age of the business

Mature firms (AGE) will be more securely established and will be positively associated with levels of growth and performance (for a dissenting view see Begley and Boyd, 1986: 12).

Management

Managerial and organizational structure

Firms with a diverse range of managerial functions currently operated (MAN) will be positively associated with small firm performance.

Firms which have a high proportion of managerial functions which are the sole responsibility of one person (SOLE) will also be positively associated with growth and performance.

Firms with high levels of delegation of managerial functions to individuals (MANINDEX) will be positively associated with high performance.

Planning

Firms which hold regular and frequent board meetings and management meetings (PLANMAN) will be positively associated with size and performance.

Firms which hold regular and frequent meetings with their professional advisors—banker, accountant and lawyer—(PLANPROF) will be positively associated with size and performance.

Firms which hold regular and frequent meetings with their customers and suppliers (PLANBUS) will be positively associated with size and performance.

Management training

Firms in which management has undergone some form of management training (MANTRAIN) will be positively associated with growth and high performance.

Financial resource base

Firms which have received financial investment from a large number of sources (not including overdraft facilities from banks) (FINANCE) will be positively associated with size and performance.

Production

Manufacturing production technology

Manufacturing firms with non-manual control technology for the major manufactured product lines (PRODUCTION) will be associated with high levels of growth and high performance.

Firms with relatively 'mature' pieces of production equipment (AGEPROD) will be negatively related to small firm performance.

Firms which use sophisticated technology in the control of the administration base (CSADMIN) will be positively associated with size and performance.

Positioning—industry and location

Industrial structure

The direction of the relationship between the industry of the firm and its financial performance varies tremendously from one sector to another within any broad industrial categories such as 'manufacturing' and 'services' (Chaganti, 1986). Consequently at this broad level of analysis the direction of association between the industry of the firm (INDUSTRY) and the level of performance is ambiguous and remains unclear.

Location

Firms located in the prosperous and buoyant markets of the 'south' of England (the standard regions of East Anglia, the South East and the South West) (LOCATION) will be positively associated with high rates of small business growth and performance.

Firms which have taken advantage of government training schemes (TRAINING) will be negatively associated with size and performance.

Firms which have taken advantage of government grants (GRANTS) will be negatively associated with size and performance.

Product/market profile

Diversity of the product base

Firms with a wide number of major product lines or major service groups (PRODUCT) will be positively associated with size and performance.

Firms which have introduced a large number of new major product lines or major service groups (NEWPRODUCT) during the previous year will be positively associated with size and performance.

Sales revenue dependency

Firms with a high percentage of sales revenue accounted for by the major product line or service group (REVENUE) will be negatively associated with growth and performance.

Diversity and location of the customer and supplier base

Firms with diverse customer bases (CUSTOMERS) and which have added significant numbers of new customers over the previous year (NEWCUSTOMERS) will be positively associated with size and performance.

Firms which purchase goods and services from a wide number of suppliers (SUPPLIERS) which are becoming more diverse and wider in scale (NEWSUPPLIERS) will also be associated positively with high performance.

Firms which are less dependent on trends and business demands in immediate 'local' (within a radius of 20 miles from the business's operational premises) or 'regional' (between 20 and 100 miles) markets will be positively associated with small firm growth. Therefore, firms which sell the majority of their products and services in nationwide or overseas markets (DISTCUSTOMERS) will be positively related to high performance, and those firms not exclusively supplied by 'local' suppliers (DISTSUPPLIERS) will also be positively associated with high performance.

Diversity and size of competition

Firms with a small number of direct competitors (COMPETITION) will be positively associated with size and performance.

The level of growth and performance, and the employment size of the major competitor (SIZECOMP) can be either positive or negative.

CORRELATION ANALYSIS

In this section each of the variables hypothesized to be associated with small firm growth and high performance is tested using bivariate and multivariate correlation and regression analysis. These variables are discussed in the previous section, and defined in the Appendix. These variable names will be used in the rest of the paper. The objective of the analysis is to seek guidance and to delimit the level of importance of specified measurable factors presumed to be associated with small firm performance.

Bivariate correlation analysis

Table 1 shows the Pearson product–moment correlation coefficients between total employment size (Y_1) and each of the 31 surrogate variables. Fourteen of the surrogate variables were associated with total employment size at the 0.01 level of significance and a further two (EXECUTIVES and CSADMIN) at the 0.05 level of significance. Three variables (OWNERS, EXECUTIVES, and AGEPROD) were not in the direction hypothesized. The eight surrogate variables found to be highly statistically

Table 1. Correlation coefficients between the total number of employees employed (Y_1) in the small firms and small firm characteristics

Independent variables	Hypothesized direction of relationship	Pearson correlation coefficient (r)	Coefficient of determination (r^2)	Level of significance of 'r'	Number of observations (n)
SHAREHOLDERS	+	0.27	0.07	*0.000*	232
OWNERS	–	0.16	0.03	*0.009*	216
EXECUTIVES	–	0.15	0.02	*0.022*	188
FOUNDERS	+	−0.01	0.00	0.450	167
AGE	+	0.36	0.13	*0.000*	242
MAN	+	0.21	0.04	*0.001*	243
SOLE	+	0.05	0.00	0.228	242
MANINDEX	+	−0.04	0.00	0.271	241
PLANMAN	+	0.17	0.03	*0.002*	247
PLANPROF	+	0.00	0.00	0.473	247
PLANBUS	+	−0.05	0.00	0.234	247
MANTRAIN	+	0.29	0.08	*0.000*	228
FINANCE	+	0.06	0.00	0.179	245
PRODUCTION	+	0.05	0.00	0.316	92
AGEPROD	–	0.46	0.21	*0.000*	95
CSADMIN	+	0.11	0.01	*0.039*	244
INDUSTRY	±	0.01	0.00	0.453	245
LOCATION	+	0.08	0.01	0.099	241
TRAINING	–	−0.18	0.03	*0.002*	239
GRANTS	–	−0.03	0.00	0.311	244
PRODUCT	+	−0.03	0.00	0.349	227
NEWPRODUCT	+	−0.04	0.00	0.299	204
REVENUE	–	−0.09	0.01	0.099	218
CUSTOMERS	+	0.32	0.10	*0.000*	243
NEWCUSTOMERS	+	0.24	0.06	*0.000*	236
SUPPLIERS	+	0.30	0.09	*0.000*	238
NEWSUPPLIERS	+	0.18	0.03	*0.003*	225
DISTCUSTOMERS	+	0.16	0.03	*0.006*	243
DISTSUPPLIERS	+	0.03	0.00	0.350	238
COMPETITION	–	0.01	0.00	0.454	230
SIZECOMP	±	0.33	0.11	*0.000*	190

Note: 'r' value has a level of significance of 0.05 or less.

associated (at the 0.000 level of significance) with the dependent variable (Y_1) were SHAREHOLDERS, AGE, MANTRAIN, AGEPROD, CUSTOMERS, NEWCUSTOMERS, SUPPLIERS, and SIZECOMP.

Table 2 shows that 13 of the surrogate variables were associated at the 0.01 level of significance with the level of sales for the last financial year, and a further one (MAN) at the 0.05 level of significance. The eight surrogate variables found to be highly statistically associated (at the 0.000 level of significance) with the dependent variable (Y_2) were AGE, AGEPROD, PLANMAN, MANTRAIN, LOCATION, CUSTOMERS, SUPPLIERS, and SIZECOMP. The same three variables as above were not in the direction hypothesised.

Table 3 indicates that nine surrogate variables were associated with the third dependent performance measure—level of profitability for the last financial year (Y_3) at the 0.01 level of significance and a further five (SHAREHOLDERS, PLANPROF, NEWCUSTOMERS, SUPPLIERS, and SIZECOMP) at the 0.05 level of significance. The five surrogate variables found to be highly statistically associated (at the 0.000 level of significance) with the dependent variable (Y_3) were OWNERS, AGE, AGEPROD, MANTRAIN, and CUSTOMERS. Six of the significant correlations were not in the direction hypothesized.

Multivariate correlation and regression analysis

In order to explore the multivariate relationships between the performance measures and the

Table 2. Correlation coefficients between the level of sales for the last financial year (Y_2) in the small firms and small firm characteristics

Independent variables	Hypothesized direction of relationship	Pearson correlation coefficient (r)	Coefficient of determination (r^2)	Level of significance of 'r'	Number of observations (n)
SHAREHOLDERS	+	0.07	0.01	0.143	227
OWNERS	−	0.21	0.04	*0.001*	210
EXECUTIVES	−	0.17	0.03	*0.010*	183
FOUNDERS	+	−0.02	0.00	0.381	163
AGE	+	0.38	0.15	*0.000*	236
MAN	+	0.14	0.02	*0.018*	236
SOLE	+	0.01	0.00	0.432	235
MANINDEX	+	−0.06	0.00	0.187	234
PLANMAN	+	0.22	0.05	*0.000*	240
PLANPROF	+	−0.04	0.00	0.278	240
PLANBUS	+	−0.01	0.00	0.467	240
MANTRAIN	+	0.27	0.07	*0.000*	222
FINANCE	+	0.06	0.00	0.183	240
PRODUCTION	+	−0.00	0.00	0.487	89
AGEPROD	−	0.36	0.13	*0.000*	92
CSADMIN	+	0.07	0.01	0.136	238
INDUSTRY	±	0.08	0.01	0.104	239
LOCATION	+	0.22	0.05	*0.000*	235
TRAINING	−	−0.06	0.00	0.181	233
GRANTS	−	0.06	0.00	0.160	238
PRODUCT	+	−0.09	0.01	0.093	220
NEWPRODUCT	+	−0.03	0.00	0.352	198
REVENUE	−	−0.80	0.01	0.117	218
CUSTOMERS	+	0.39	0.15	*0.000*	238
NEWCUSTOMERS	+	0.18	0.03	*0.003*	230
SUPPLIERS	+	0.33	0.11	*0.000*	233
NEWSUPPLIERS	+	0.17	0.03	*0.007*	219
DISTCUSTOMERS	+	0.16	0.03	*0.006*	238
DISTSUPPLIERS	+	0.09	0.01	0.097	233
COMPETITION	−	0.07	0.01	0.137	224
SIZECOMP	±	0.35	0.12	*0.000*	184

Note: 'r' value has a level of significance of 0.05 or less.

surrogate variables, and to test hypotheses detailed in the research literature, the data were further subjected to multiple correlation and regression analysis. This statistical technique allows the *association* of each independent variable with the performance indicator to be examined while controlling for the effects of the other independent variables. The multivariate regression equations presented below were calculated using the 'forward inclusion method', and the technique starts by regressing the variable with the highest zero-order correlation against the dependent variable. A new independent variable is added at each step in order that the null hypothesis of no explanation can be rejected. The 0.05 level of significance was the selected level for the inclusion of significant independent surrogate variables. Relative profitability was not used in this analysis since the categorical data were not sufficiently robust.

Total employment size of the small firms (Y_1)

Equation 1, below, is based on the 15 surrogate variables found to be statistically associated with total employment size at the 0.05 level of significance in Table 1. The AGEPROD variable has been omitted from Equation 1 and the following equations because over 54 percent of firms were engaged in non-manufacturing activities. Equation 1,—which contains the six independent surrogate variables SUPPLIERS, CUSTOMERS, DISTCUSTOMERS, AGE, MANTRAIN, and NEWSUPPLIERS—is statistically significant and has a high adjusted R^2 value of +0.49. It can be inferred from Equation 1 that firms which are mature in age, have diverse customer and supplier bases, customers in nationwide locations, with the management having undertaken management training, and with a limited propensity to acquire new suppliers will record the highest rates of total employment.

In order to calculate a more refined multiple regression equation only those seven surrogate variables found to be statistically associated with (Y_1) at the 0.000 level of significance were selected for inclusion in Equation 2. This refined model is based on 163 observations and has a larger standard error of 0.81 compared to 0.74 in Equation 1. Five independent surrogate variables are stated in Equation 2: SUPPLIERS, AGE, SIZECOMP, CUSTOMERS, and MAN. The equation is significant and it has an adjusted R^2 of +0.39. Again, it can be inferred that mature firms, with diverse supplier and customer bases currently operating a wide range of managerial functions, and whose major competitor is large in employment size, will record the highest levels of total employment (Y_1).

Level of sales

Equation 3 is based on the 13 surrogate variables found to be statistically associated with level of sales for the last financial year (Y_2) at the 0.05 level of significance. This equation is statistically significant, has a high adjusted R^2 value of +0.46, and a standard error value of 0.60. It can be inferred from Equation 3 that mature firms with diverse customer and supplier bases, whose management has frequent management meetings and has undertaken management training with a large employment-sized major competitor will record the highest level of sales.

A more refined model was calculated based on the seven surrogate variables found to be statistically associated with the dependent variable (Y_2) at the 0.000 level of significance. Equation 4 is based on 160 observations and it has a standard error of 0.65. The equation is statistically significant, has a slightly lower adjusted R^2 value of +0.37, and the six independent variables (SUPPLIERS, MANTRAIN, AGE, SIZECOMP, PLANMAN, and LOCATION) are found to be positively associated with the dependent variable. It can be inferred from Equation 4 that mature firms located in 'southern' markets with diverse supplier bases, very large major competitors, whose management has undertaken management training, who hold frequent management meetings, and have a large employment-sized major competitor will record the highest level of sales.

Equation 1. Total employment by surrogate variables (all 15 significant variables at $p = 0.05$)

$$\begin{aligned} Y_1 = {} & \underset{(-0.21)}{-0.07} + \underset{(3.72)^{**}}{0.29}\,(\text{SUPPLIERS}) + \underset{(4.07)^{***}}{0.20}\,(\text{CUSTOMERS}) + \underset{(3.81)^{***}}{0.19}\,(\text{DISTCUSTOMERS}) + \\ & \underset{(2.77)^{**}}{0.01}\,(\text{AGE}) + \underset{(2.75)^{**}}{0.42}\,(\text{MANTRAIN}) - \underset{(-2.03)^{*}}{0.31}\,(\text{NEWSUPPLIERS}) \end{aligned}$$

Multiple $R = 0.72$ Adjusted $R^2 = 0.49$
Standard error of the estimate = 0.74 $n = 110$

Note: For the equations the figures in parentheses are 't' values.
* Significant at the 0.05 level of significance.
** Significant at the 0.01 level of significance.
*** Significant at the 0.001 level of significance.

Equation 2. Total employment by surrogate variables (7 variables at $p = 0.000$)

$$Y_1 = \underset{(1.43)}{0.36} + \underset{(3.31)^{**}}{0.21} \, (\text{SUPPLIERS}) + \underset{(4.17)^{***}}{0.08} \, (\text{AGE}) + \underset{(3.81)^{***}}{0.12} \, (\text{SIZECOMP}) + \underset{(2.87)^{**}}{0.13} \, (\text{CUSTOMERS}) + \underset{(2.37)^{*}}{0.04} \, (\text{MAN})$$

Multiple $R = 0.64$ Adjusted $R^2 = 0.39$
Standard error of the estimate = 0.81 $n = 163$

Note: For the equations the figures in parentheses are 't' values.
* Significant at the 0.05 level of significance.
** Significant at the 0.01 level of significance.
*** Significant at the 0.001 level of significance.

Equation 3. Level of sales by surrogate variables (all 13 significant variables at $p = 0.05$)

$$Y_2 = \underset{(0.67)}{0.02} + \underset{(2.14)^{*}}{0.12} \, (\text{SUPPLIERS}) + \underset{(3.07)^{**}}{0.39} \, (\text{MANTRAIN}) + \underset{(2.96)^{**}}{0.12} \, (\text{CUSTOMERS}) + \underset{(2.88)^{**}}{0.05} \, (\text{PLANMAN}) + \underset{(2.46)^{*}}{0.00} \, (\text{AGE}) + \underset{(2.01)^{*}}{0.06} \, (\text{SIZECOMP})$$

Multiple $R = 0.70$ Adjusted $R^2 = 0.46$
Standard error of the estimate = 0.60 $n = 111$

Note: For the equations the figures in parentheses are 't' values.
* Significant at the 0.05 level of significance.
** Significant at the 0.01 level of significance.

Equation 4. Level of sales by surrogate variables (7 variables at $p = 0.000$)

$$Y_2 = \underset{(0.31)}{0.08} + \underset{(3.51)^{***}}{0.12} \, (\text{SUPPLIERS}) + \underset{(2.73)^{**}}{0.31} \, (\text{MANTRAIN}) + \underset{(4.03)^{***}}{0.01} \, (\text{AGE}) + \underset{(3.19)^{**}}{0.08} \, (\text{SIZECOMP}) + \underset{(2.38)^{*}}{0.03} \, (\text{PLANMAN}) + \underset{(2.04)^{*}}{0.22} \, (\text{LOCATION})$$

Multiple $R = 0.63$ Adjusted $R^2 = 0.37$
Standard error of the estimate = 0.65 $n = 160$

Note: For the equations the figures in parentheses are 't' values.
* Significant at the 0.05 level of significance.
** Significant at the 0.01 level of significance.
*** Significant at the 0.001 level of significance.

Equation 5. Level of profitability by surrogate variables (all 13 significant variables)

$$Y_3 = 1.19 + 0.01\,(\text{AGE}) + 1.30\,(\text{MANTRAIN}) - 0.17\,(\text{PLANBUS})$$
$$(1.22)\ (2.23)^{*} \qquad (2.47)^{*} \qquad (-2.32)^{*}$$

Multiple $R = 0.39$ Adjusted $R^2 = 0.13$
Standard error of the estimate = 2.56 $n = 110$

Note: For the equations the figures in parentheses are '*t*' values.
* Significant at the 0.05 level of significance.

Table 3. Correlation coefficients between the level of trading profit/loss for the last financial year (Y_3) in the small firms and small firm characteristics

Independent variables	Hypothesized direction of relationship	Pearson correlation coefficient (r)	Coefficient of determination (r^2)	Level of significance of 'r'	Number of observations (n)
SHAREHOLDERS	+	0.13	0.02	*0.026*	221
OWNERS	–	0.21	0.04	*0.001*	204
EXECUTIVES	–	0.19	0.04	*0.005*	178
FOUNDERS	+	−0.02	0.00	0.385	159
AGE	+	0.35	0.12	*0.000*	230
MAN	+	0.08	0.01	0.110	230
SOLE	+	0.02	0.00	0.404	229
MANINDEX	+	−0.06	0.00	0.187	228
PLANMAN	+	0.02	0.00	0.402	234
PLANPROF	+	−0.12	0.01	*0.029*	234
PLANBUS	+	−0.17	0.03	*0.006*	234
MANTRAIN	+	−0.18	0.03	*0.003*	234
FINANCE	+	0.17	0.03	*0.005*	216
PRODUCTION	+	0.06	0.00	0.277	91
AGEPROD	–	0.40	0.16	*0.000*	94
CSADMIN	+	−0.05	0.00	0.205	232
INDUSTRY	±	0.03	0.00	0.313	233
LOCATION	+	0.16	0.03	*0.007*	229
TRAINING	–	−0.03	0.00	0.321	227
GRANTS	–	0.05	0.00	0.217	232
PRODUCT	+	−0.05	0.00	0.238	215
NEWPRODUCT	+	0.04	0.00	0.314	193
REVENUE	–	0.08	0.01	0.130	213
CUSTOMERS	+	0.21	0.05	*0.001*	232
NEWCUSTOMERS	+	0.14	0.02	*0.021*	225
SUPPLIERS	+	0.13	0.02	*0.030*	227
NEWSUPPLIERS	+	0.06	0.00	0.212	214
DISTCUSTOMERS	+	0.06	0.00	0.194	232
DISTSUPPLIERS	+	−0.04	0.00	0.253	227
COMPETITION	–	−0.06	0.00	0.180	218
SIZECOMP	±	0.14	0.02	*0.032*	183

Note: '*r*' value has a level of significance of 0.05 or less.

Level of profitability

Equation 5 is based on the 13 surrogate variables found to be statistically associated with the level of profitability for the last financial year (Y_3) at the 0.05 level of significance. This equation is statistically significant, has an adjusted R^2 value of +0.13 and a standard error value of 2.56. It can be inferred from Equation 5 that mature firms whose management has undertaken management training, and who hold irregular meetings with business contacts, will record the highest level of profitability.

A more refined model was calculated based on the eight surrogate variables found to be statistically associated with the dependent variable (Y_3) at the 0.01 level of significance. Equation 6 is based on 153 observations, and has a standard error of 2.57. The equation is statistically significant, has a slightly higher adjusted R^2 value of +0.14. In contrast to Equation 5, only two surrogate variables were found to be associated with the dependent variable; one positively (AGE) and the other negatively (FINANCE). It can be inferred from Equation 5 that mature firms which have not obtained financial investment (not including bank overdrafts) will record the highest levels of profitability.

Equation 6. Level of profitability by surrogate variables (8 variables at $p = 0.01$)

$$Y_3 = 1.93 + 0.03\,(\text{AGE}) - 0.54\,(\text{FINANCE})$$
$$(5.87)\quad (4.51)^{***}\quad (-2.45)^{*}$$

Multiple R = 0.39 Adjusted R^2 = 0.14
Standard error of the estimate = 2.57 n = 153

Note: For the equations the figures in parentheses are 't' values.
* Significant at the 0.05 level of significance.
*** Significant at the 0.001 level of significance.

DATA REDUCTION USING PRINCIPAL COMPONENTS ANALYSIS

Whilst the multiple regression analysis provides useful insights into the combination of factors which contribute to size and performance, there remains an inherent assumption of linearity—that all firms conform to the described patterns sequentially. Therefore, an R-mode principal-components analysis (PCA) was used in order to produce new combinations of the original data which could then be used as independent and orthogonal reference axes (or variables) in a classification of firm 'types' using cluster analysis.

The unrotated direct extraction of orthogonal reference axes by PCA did not adequately illuminate the interrelationships between the collection of variables. As a consequence, the reference axes were rotated in order to isolate more meaningful dimensions. After varimax rotation the first 11 components (out of a total of 31 components) accounted for 65.7 percent of the total variance (Table 4). The final model was found to be an appropriate factor-analytic model as indicated by Bartlett's test of sphericity, the Kaiser–Meyer–Olkin measure of sampling adequacy, the anti-image correlation matrix, the test for sampling adequacy and the test for communality.

On the basis of the component loadings, the 11 components were given the following descriptive labels:

Component 1 Manufacturing firms with old manual product lines but sophisticated administration bases. Firms are in competition with a small number of direct competitors whose customers are in nationwide locations.

Component 2 Firms with large and increasingly diverse customer and supplier bases.

Component 3 Relatively mature firms with current majority owners and senior executives with 'no relationship' to the original founders and executives.

Component 4 Small firms with frequent management meetings and frequent meetings with professional advisers and business contracts with diverse supplier bases. The management team has received some form of management training and has introduced a diverse computerized administration base.

Component 5 Firms with a large proportion of managerial functions the sole responsibility of one person and a high level of delegation.

Table 4. Standardization of small firm characteristics using a Varimax rotated principal components analysis

Variables	Varimax rotated components											Commu-nality (h^2)
	1	2	3	4	5	6	7	8	9	10	11	
SHAREHOLDERS	0.01	0.17	−0.13	0.07	−0.01	0.07	−0.04	0.14	0.12	*−0.78*	−0.08	0.71
OWNERS	−0.04	0.03	*0.90*	−0.00	0.01	0.02	−0.07	−0.01	0.05	0.07	−0.04	0.83
EXECUTIVES	−0.02	−0.01	*0.86*	0.13	−0.04	0.15	0.06	0.05	0.07	0.07	0.04	0.80
FOUNDERS	0.03	−0.14	−0.12	−0.05	0.05	*−0.77*	0.06	0.05	0.03	−0.01	−0.03	0.64
AGE	0.24	*0.30*	*0.35*	0.02	−0.19	*0.58*	−0.09	−0.04	0.02	−0.08	−0.02	0.66
MAN	0.24	0.21	0.02	0.09	0.04	−0.08	0.13	0.05	−0.03	0.06	*0.78*	0.75
SOLE	0.13	0.04	−0.01	0.03	*0.91*	−0.08	0.07	0.06	0.01	0.03	0.26	0.93
MANINDEX	0.03	−0.05	−0.04	0.04	*0.92*	0.01	−0.01	0.05	−0.03	−0.00	−0.25	0.92
PLANMAN	−0.04	0.03	0.11	*0.70*	0.03	−0.01	−0.00	0.10	0.09	−0.04	−0.11	0.54
PLANPROF	−0.15	−0.18	−0.11	*0.57*	0.01	−0.13	−0.04	−0.14	−0.19	−0.05	−0.13	0.49
PLANBUS	0.06	−0.12	−0.27	*0.36*	0.23	0.22	0.07	−0.05	−0.26	0.25	0.04	0.46
MANTRAIN	0.05	0.14	0.12	*0.54*	0.00	0.10	0.12	0.02	−0.04	0.01	0.14	0.37
FINANCE	0.05	0.20	0.09	0.04	−0.11	*−0.48*	−0.09	−0.09	−0.27	0.07	0.14	0.41
PRODUCTION	*0.86*	−0.06	−0.06	−0.02	0.08	−0.07	−0.00	−0.02	−0.11	0.01	0.08	0.78
AGEPROD	*0.74*	0.10	0.18	−0.02	0.04	*0.35*	−0.02	0.07	−0.02	0.02	0.03	0.72
CSADMIN	*0.45*	−0.13	−0.10	*0.48*	0.01	−0.01	−0.15	0.03	0.03	0.07	*0.35*	0.61
INDUSTRY	*−0.80*	0.20	0.07	−0.01	−0.07	0.09	−0.02	−0.02	0.10	−0.05	−0.05	0.71
LOCATION	−0.12	0.13	0.15	−0.00	0.04	0.06	−0.14	−0.08	*0.74*	−0.07	0.08	0.64
TRAINING	−0.06	−0.14	−0.06	−0.21	−0.15	−0.08	0.12	*0.36*	*0.39*	0.12	−0.19	0.45
GRANTS	−0.25	0.01	−0.15	−0.16	−0.00	*0.31*	−0.09	0.10	*0.45*	*0.38*	−0.16	0.60
PRODUCT	−0.08	0.01	−0.02	0.05	−0.03	0.14	*0.81*	−0.05	0.01	0.07	0.06	0.70
NEWPRODUCT	0.04	0.09	−0.01	−0.02	0.08	−0.21	*0.79*	−0.00	−0.08	−0.07	−0.13	0.71
REVENUE	−0.12	−0.12	−0.03	−0.20	−0.06	0.01	*−0.36*	0.00	0.01	−0.04	*0.57*	0.53
CUSTOMERS	−0.09	*0.85*	0.07	−0.03	0.02	0.15	0.07	−0.03	0.02	−0.06	0.02	0.77
NEWCUSTOMERS	−0.18	*0.81*	−0.07	−0.04	−0.03	0.01	0.05	−0.02	−0.02	−0.12	0.09	0.72
SUPPLIERS	*0.30*	*0.50*	0.07	*0.37*	0.04	0.00	0.05	0.14	0.13	*0.44*	−0.06	0.72
NEWSUPPLIERS	0.15	*0.46*	0.18	*0.35*	−0.05	*−0.34*	−0.05	0.13	0.07	*0.43*	−0.09	0.72
DISTCUSTOMERS	*0.39*	−0.03	−0.04	0.11	0.08	−0.12	−0.08	*0.64*	−0.19	−0.08	−0.03	0.65
DISTSUPPLIERS	0.16	0.14	−0.11	−0.10	0.11	−0.05	−0.17	*0.43*	*−0.54*	*0.32*	0.03	0.69
COMPETITION	*−0.42*	−0.08	0.10	0.09	0.09	0.15	−0.03	*0.38*	0.24	0.19	0.16	0.50
SIZECOMP	−0.12	0.04	0.06	0.01	0.04	0.05	−0.00	*0.76*	0.00	−0.09	0.05	0.61
Eigenvalue	2.92	2.29	2.00	1.91	1.86	1.76	1.60	1.58	1.55	1.43	1.42	20.32
Percentage of variance	9.4	7.4	6.5	6.2	6.0	5.7	5.2	5.1	5.0	4.6	4.6	
Cumulative percentage of variance	9.4	16.8	23.3	29.5	35.5	41.2	46.4	51.5	56.5	61.1	65.7	

Component 6 Very mature small firms with old manufacturing product lines which have few remaining original founders who are still partners or shareholders. Firms have not received financial investment from external sources.

Component 7 Firms with an increasingly diverse range of new as well as existing major product lines or major service groups, and which have a small proportion of sales revenue accounted for by the major product or service line.

Component 8 Firms with a large number of competitors but the major competitor is large in size. Customers are in nationwide locations and suppliers are 'non-local'.

Component 9 Small firms in the 'south' with local suppliers who have not applied for grants and training schemes.

Component 10 Concentrated ownership structure in firms with increasingly diverse supplier bases which have not applied for grants.

Component 11 Firms currently operating a diverse range of managerial functions with non-manual administration bases who are heavily dependent on the sales revenue accounted for by the major product line or service group.

It is clear from this evidence that the linked trends isolated in the component structure do have meaningful expression in terms of firm characteristics which stresses the need for a classification of firm 'types'.

CLASSIFICATION INTO 'TYPES' OF FIRMS

The simple description of component loadings is useful in that it describes the pattern of each single basic factor, but nothing other than intuitive classification can be attempted. Therefore, in order to obtain a classification of small firm 'types' based on 'internal' as well as 'external' environmental factors, Ward's error sum of squares method of cluster analysis was used to group similar firms (Ward, 1963). In this study Ward's method produces a grouping of relatively homogeneous firm 'types' which have maximum between-group variance and minimum within-group variance. A dendrogram was drawn to display each stage in the grouping process. At step 215 the grouping procedure was stopped with the 222 firms being reduced to only eight firm 'types', and with a 83.63 percent loss of original detail in return for an increased level of 'generality'.

In order to give a descriptive label to each of the eight clusters (or firm 'types'), the cluster mean for each variable was compared to the respective global mean for that variable (Table 5).

Cluster 1 This is the largest cluster of 63 generally non-manufacturing firms with diluted ownership structures which have a very diverse range of major product lines or major service groups. Firms are middle-aged and have frequent management meetings but have received no finance from external sources. Customers as well as suppliers are 'non-local', and the firms have a large number of direct competitors.

Cluster 2 Firms in which managerial functions are highly delegated and management meetings are held at quarterly intervals. These generally 'northern' firms have a small number of shareholders and for the manufacturing firms in the cluster the control technology in production lines is a manual one. This cluster contains 31 firms.

Cluster 3 A cluster of 29 service firms in which a very small number of founders are still partners or shareholders. Management meetings and meetings with professionals are infrequent, a small number of managerial functions are currently operated, and the firms have sophisticated administration bases. Firms are in competition with a small number of direct competitors and the major competitor is large in size.

Cluster 4 Small firms with highly diluted ownership structures and 'local' customers located in the 'south'. Management meetings are generally annual in frequency. This cluster contains 36 firms.

Cluster 5 Twelve very mature firms with family succession current majority owners and senior executives who have undergone some form of management training. In the firms a large number of managerial functions are operated but only a small proportion are the responsibility of one person; consequently these firms are associated with a low level of delegation. For the manufacturing firms in this cluster they operate very old manual production lines but are associated with sophisticated administration bases. Firms have diverse supplier bases with customers as well as suppliers located in nationwide locations. The firms have large major competitors.

Cluster 6 This is the second-largest cluster containing 48 very young manufacturing firms located in the 'north' associated with young production lines. The firms have modest customer bases and have contacted only a small number of new customers over the past twelve months. Grants from central or local government have been applied for.

Cluster 7 A single mature service firm located in the 'north' with the one original founder being the current majority owner and senior executive. The firm has one major service group and it obtains all of its sales revenue from it. Moreover, the business has less than 11 'local' customers and has not acquired a new customer in the past 12 months. In contrast, the firm has over 50 suppliers located in 'regional' locations. The firm faces competition from less than 11 direct competitors. Local or central government training schemes and grants have not been applied for. The firm currently operates a wide range of managerial functions but only a small proportion are the responsibility of one person. Management meetings and meetings with professionals and business advisers are held frequently, and the firm has introduced computer technology in the administration base. The owner-manager has undergone some form of management training but has not received financial investment from external sources.

Cluster 8 Two very young service firms located in the 'north' with the original owner-manager founders being the current first-generation majority owners and senior executives. The businesses are associated with a very small number of major service groups with the firms stating that the major service group accounted for all of their sales revenue. Firms in this cluster have less than 11 'nationwide' customers, the businesses are supplied by over 11 'non-local' suppliers. The two firms have not applied for training schemes or grants provided by local or central government. Both the firms operate a small number of managerial functions which generally are the responsibility of one person. Management meetings and meetings with professionals and business contracts are infrequent in nature. One of the owner-managers has received management training while the other has not. Neither of the firms has received financial investment from external sources.

TYPES OF FIRMS AND PERFORMANCE DIFFERENCES

The final stage of the analysis compared business size and performance between the identified 'types' of small firms. The aim was to test whether the cross-sectional analysis presented any evidence to support the 'stages of development' theories. Did the clusters fall into a logical sequence when measured by size or performance? For example, was cluster 6 characterized by very small firms, cluster 1 medium-sized firms, and cluster 5 large firms? Further, were the three firms which remained isolated from the rest of the sample the atypical 'high-flyers'?

The data were first subjected to exploratory chi-squared analyses. Clusters 7 and 8 were excluded from analysis in order to satisfy the assumptions of the technique. The use of the chi-squared technique also allowed the inclusion of a further performance measure which it had not been possible to use in previous analysis, since it was based upon only three categorical scores—respondents were asked to indicate whether they rated their business profit performance relative to competition as 'good', 'about average', or 'poor'. Whilst these ratings are, clearly, subjective, their inclusion adds to the overall pattern of results.

Table 6 indicates that a larger proportion of firms in clusters 1, 3, and 5 (22.6, 25.0, and 25.0 percent respectively) had 50 or more total employees. In contrast, firms in cluster 4 had a greater tendency to be less than 10 employees in size (33.3 percent), whilst firms in cluster 2 had a greater propensity to be between 10 and 25 employees in size (41.9 percent). With regard to the level of sales for the last financial year it can be inferred from Table 7 that a markedly larger proportion of firms in clusters 1, 3, and 5 (40.0,

Table 5. Cluster characteristics of small firm types

Variables	Clusters 1	2	3	4	5	6	7	8	Global mean	Standard deviation
SHAREHOLDERS	4.34	3.45	4.89	7.01	5.98	5.51	3.00	4.00	4.34	5.64
OWNERS	1.67	1.61	1.67	1.81	2.00*	1.34	1.00**	1.00**	1.63	0.83
EXECUTIVES	1.80	2.04	1.73	2.07	2.18*	1.50	1.00**	1.00**	1.82	0.94
FOUNDERS	2.65	2.60	1.83*	2.05	2.13	2.67	1.00**	2.00	2.44	1.76
AGE	28.70	19.26	32.61	34.31	45.42**	14.43*	30.00	4.50**	26.40	35.06
MAN	9.46	9.81	8.44*	9.58	10.67*	10.02	14.00***	4.50**	9.56	3.96
SOLE	4.01	5.00*	3.27	3.89	2.92*	3.66	6.00**	3.50	3.91	3.73
MANINDEX	0.46	0.50	0.46	0.44	0.30*	0.39	0.43	0.78**	0.44	0.36
PLANMAN	4.66	4.97*	3.79*	3.93*	4.46	4.83	5.00*	3.00**	4.48	1.93
PLANPROF	3.20	3.35	2.97*	3.30	3.19	3.41	4.00**	4.00**	3.26	1.12
PLANBUS	3.99	4.39	3.60	4.10	3.29	4.24	5.00*	3.00*	4.02	1.94
MANTRAIN	1.50	1.62	1.60	1.44	1.75*	1.61	1.00***	1.50	1.56	0.50
FINANCE	0.78	0.87	0.82	0.83	1.00	0.85	0.00**	0.00**	0.82	0.93
PRODUCTION	2.74	3.00*	2.80	2.83	3.00*	2.78	0.00**	0.00**	2.81	0.59
AGEPROD	157.72	121.00	167.70	179.19	247.20**	86.50*	0.00**	0.00**	142.52	149.14
CSADMIN	9.62	9.35	8.86*	9.33	10.18*	10.02	11.00**	7.50	9.53	2.21
INDUSTRY	1.86	2.00	2.21*	1.91	1.67	1.63*	3.00***	3.00***	1.89	0.94
LOCATION	1.51	1.41	1.46	1.57*	1.42	1.24*	1.00**	1.00**	1.43	0.50
TRAINING	1.89	1.87	1.81	1.89	1.92	1.87	2.00*	2.00*	1.87	0.33
GRANTS	1.84	1.74	1.86	1.75	1.83	1.63*	2.00**	2.00**	1.77	0.42
PRODUCT	204.61	41.07	6.93	14.66	16.60	7.28	1.00	5.50	68.99	708.00
NEWPRODUCT	4.15	5.46	1.27	1.46	4.90	1.45	0.00*	0.00*	2.96	11.29
REVENUE	68.82	69.85	70.76	66.25	74.38	67.80	100.00***	100.00**	69.26	28.51
CUSTOMERS	3.94	3.74	3.96	3.75	3.55	3.17*	1.00***	1.00***	3.66	1.60
NEWCUSTOMERS	2.44	2.13	2.57	2.41	2.09	1.87*	0.00***	0.00***	2.26	1.42
SUPPLIERS	2.59	2.37	2.36	2.51	3.09*	2.37	3.00*	2.50	2.50	1.11
NEWSUPPLIERS	1.31	1.24	1.21	1.18	1.60**	1.22	1.00*	1.00*	1.26	0.56
DISTCUSTOMERS	3.54	3.29	3.55	3.08*	4.09*	3.83	1.00***	5.50***	3.53	1.57
DISTSUPPLIERS	3.56	3.17	3.55	3.76	3.91*	3.46	3.00*	3.50	3.53	1.49
COMPETITION	3.93	3.74	3.35*	3.97	3.92	3.56	3.00*	3.50	3.74	1.52
SIZECOMP	3.58	3.08	4.20*	3.20	4.00*	3.31	3.00	2.50*	3.46	2.03
Number of firms in the cluster	63	31	29	36	12	48	1	2		

Notes: * Cluster mean which deviates by more than a quarter of a standard deviation from the respective global mean.
** Cluster mean which deviates by more than half a standard deviation from the respective global mean.
*** Cluster mean which deviates by more than a standard deviation from the respective global mean.

Table 6. Total employment size of the small firms

Cluster	Total employment size								Total	
	1–9		10–25		26–49		≥50			
	No.	%	No.	%	No.	%	No.	%	No.	%
1	13	21.0	20	32.3	15	24.2	14	22.6	62	100.1
2	5	16.1	13	41.9	11	35.5	2	6.5	31	100.0
3	8	28.6	9	32.1	4	14.3	7	25.0	28	100.0
4	12	33.3	7	19.4	10	27.8	7	19.4	36	99.9
5	3	25.0	4	33.3	2	16.7	3	25.0	12	100.0
6	12	25.5	14	29.8	11	23.4	10	21.3	47	100.0
Total	53	24.5	67	31.0	53	24.5	43	19.9	216	99.9

$\chi^2 = 12.20$; d.f. = 15; significance = 0.6641.

Table 7. Level of sales for the last financial year

Cluster	Level of sales for the last financial year						Total	
	≤£249,999		£250,000–£999,999		£1m or more			
	No.	%	No.	%	No.	%	No.	%
1	14	23.3	22	36.7	24	40.0	60	100.0
2	10	34.5	13	44.8	6	20.7	29	100.0
3	10	37.0	5	18.5	12	44.4	27	99.9
4	14	38.9	8	22.2	14	38.9	36	100.0
5	2	20.0	1	10.0	7	70.0	10	100.0
6	13	27.1	21	43.8	14	29.2	48	100.1
Total	63	30.0	70	33.3	77	36.7	210	100.0

$\chi^2 = 17.06$; d.f. = 10; significance = 0.0730.

44.4, and 70.0 percent, respectively) had sales of £1 million or more compared to firms in cluster 4 which had a tendency to have sales of less than £250,000 (38.9 percent). Firms in clusters 2 (44.8 percent) and 6 (43.8 percent) generally had sales between £250,000 and £999,999. In terms of the third performance measure it is apparent that the vast majority of firms in each of the clusters had made a profit in the last financial year (Table 8). However, Table 8 shows that a markedly larger proportion of firms in clusters 2, 3, and 4 had made a profit (86.2, 82.1, and 88.9 percent), whilst firms in clusters 1, 5, and 6 had a greater propensity to have made a loss (20.0, 27.3, and 18.8 percent, respectively). Finally, Table 9 indicates that the majority of firms (with the notable exception of firms in cluster 4) rated their business's profit performance as being above average relative to competition with firms in clusters 3, 5, and 6 in fact stating it was 'good' (60.0, 80.0, and 63.6 percent, respectively). Conversely, a markedly larger proportion of firms in cluster 4 (20.6 percent) stated their profit performance was 'poor' relative to competition.

Table 8. Number of businesses operating at the following levels of profitability for the last financial year

Cluster	Level of profitability for the last financial year						Total	
	Profit		Loss		Break-even			
	No.	%	No.	%	No.	%	No.	%
1	44	73.3	12	20.0	4	6.7	60	100.0
2	25	86.2	1	3.4	3	10.3	29	99.9
3	23	82.1	3	10.7	2	7.1	28	99.9
4	32	88.9	3	8.3	1	2.8	36	100.0
5	8	72.7	3	27.3	0	0.0	11	100.0
6	37	77.1	9	18.8	2	4.2	48	100.1
Total	169	79.7	31	14.6	12	5.7	212	100.0

Table 9. Rating the business's profit performance relative to competition

Cluster	Rating the business's profit performance relative to competition						Total	
	Good		About average		Poor			
	No.	%	No.	%	No.	%	No.	%
1	34	58.6	16	27.6	8	13.8	58	100.0
2	15	55.6	7	25.9	5	18.5	27	100.0
3	15	60.0	6	24.0	4	16.0	25	100.0
4	16	47.1	11	32.4	7	20.6	34	100.1
5	8	80.0	2	20.0	0	0.0	10	100.0
6	28	63.6	13	29.5	3	6.8	44	99.9
Total	116	58.6	55	27.8	27	13.6	198	100.0

The results detailed above have indicated that no statistically significant differences were observed in any of the chi-squared analyses conducted. There was no statistical relationship between cluster membership and either size or performance. However, scrutiny of the individual results does indicate the following patterns (unless stated, no particular bias is evident).

Cluster 1 Fewer firms than expected with sales of less than £250,000.

Cluster 2 Essentially small firms employing between 10 and 50 people and with sales between £250,000 and £1m.

Cluster 3 Firms in this group are polarized in size—either employing less than 10 people and with sales of less than £250,000, or employing more than 50 people and with sales of greater than £1m.

Cluster 4 Predominantly very small firms employing less than 10 people, with sales of less than £250,000, in profit, but rating their relative profit performance as 'average' or 'poor'.

Cluster 5 A large percentage of firms with sales of more than £1m, rating their relative profit performance as 'good'.

Cluster 6 A large percentage of firms with sales between £250,000 and £1m.
Cluster 7 A profitable firm which rates its profit performance as 'good' with less than 26 employees and sales less than £250, 000.
Cluster 8 Two profitable firms rating their profit performance as 'average', both firms have between 10 and 25 employees and sales between £250,000 and £999, 999.

The above analyses present *no evidence* to support the theories that small firms pass sequentially through pre-defined stages of growth. However, the chi-squared test is not particularly powerful, and so the two size measures were subjected to the more powerful analysis of variance test for differences between the mean values in each cluster. No significant differences were identified between the clusters for sales revenue (*/F/* = 0.824, d.f. = 5, significance level = 0.790) or for total employees (*/F/* = 0.824, d.f. = 5, significance level = 0.534). Therefore, it was not possible to rank the clusters in order of their size.

SUMMARY AND CONCLUSIONS

The aim of this paper has been to study the interrelationships between all the factors in the strategic profile of a sample of small firms and, by using cross-sectional analysis, to attempt to identify any evidence to support the 'stages of growth' theories. Three surrogates for comparative growth were used in the analysis—number of employees, sales turnover, and profitability. The analysis follows five sequential stages—bivariate correlation analysis, multivariate correlation and regression analysis, cluster analysis, chi-squared analysis, and, finally, analysis of variance.

The results from the bivariate correlation analyses are remarkably consistent (see Table 10). Thus, the sizes of the small firms in the sample measured in terms of both number of employees and sales revenue are characterized by ownership structure, age, and market positioning as reflected in customer, supplier, and competitor bases. There is also some indication that growing firms may develop more complex management, as reflected in the number of managerial functions and the frequency of management meetings. However, there is no evidence that this extends to the use of outside advisors (PLANPROF, PLANBUS), or to the development of a management structure through delegation (SOLE, MANINDEX).

Table 10. Bivariate correlations at the 0.05 level of significance

Small firm characteristics variables	Performance measures		
	Employees	Sales	Profit
SHAREHOLDERS	*Yes*	No	Yes
OWNERS	*Yes*	*Yes*	*Yes*
EXECUTIVES	*Yes*	*Yes*	*Yes*
FOUNDERS	No	No	No
AGE	*Yes*	*Yes*	*Yes*
MAN	*Yes*	*Yes*	No
SOLE	No	No	No
MANINDEX	No	No	No
PLANMAN	*Yes*	*Yes*	No
PLANPROF	No	No	*Yes*
PLANBUS	No	No	*Yes*
MANTRAIN	*Yes*	*Yes*	*Yes*
FINANCE	No	No	*Yes*
PRODUCTION	No	No	No
AGEPROD	*Yes*	*Yes*	*Yes*
CSADMIN	*Yes*	No	No
INDUSTRY	No	No	No
LOCATION	No	*Yes*	*Yes*
TRAINING	*Yes*	No	No
GRANTS	No	No	No
PRODUCT	No	No	No
NEWPRODUCT	No	No	No
REVENUE	No	No	No
CUSTOMERS	*Yes*	*Yes*	*Yes*
NEWCUSTOMERS	*Yes*	*Yes*	*Yes*
SUPPLIERS	*Yes*	*Yes*	*Yes*
NEWSUPPLIERS	*Yes*	*Yes*	No
DISTCUSTOMERS	*Yes*	*Yes*	No
DISTSUPPLIERS	No	No	No
COMPETITION	No	No	No
SIZECOMP	*Yes*	*Yes*	*Yes*

The results for profit are particularly interesting since many are counter-intuitive. Whilst market profile continues to be important, the more that ownership and management is divorced from the original owners, the higher the profitability; and involvement with outside advisers or trainers, and the use of outside finance, is negatively related to profitability!

Subjecting the data to the more stringent

technique of multivariate regression analysis reduces the number of variables, but reinforces the overall conclusion. In particular, there is a marked absence of any relationship between the organizational structural variables and size, although it is comforting to these authors that management training does appear to make some contribution to size and profitability!

The multiple regression analyses support the theory of a combination of factors contributing to the growth and development of the firm, but they provide little illumination as to the profile of the firms in the sample, or the extent to which firms with a particular combination of characteristics are *likely* to grow or to be profitable. Moreover, the inherent assumption of linearity implies that all small firms follow the same pattern; that, since age is one of the predictive variables, all firms must grow; and that firms adjust their rate of growth by adjusting, for example, their customer base.

This assumption, found in much of the literature, that all firms follow the same prescribed path, and that the small firm sector is essentially homogeneous has been subjected to very little empirical examination. The cluster analysis conducted in this study identified eight different types of small firms characterized by 'internal' variables of ownership, management, and product structure; and by 'external' variables of product/market positioning. Unlike the preliminary regression analyses this use of cluster analysis took account of the small firm which experienced only limited growth. For example, the manufacturing firms in cluster 2 have highly delegated management structures and hold regular management meetings, suggesting relatively large firms which have evolved through a number of 'growth stages'. However, we find that they are almost certainly 'family' (with a small number of shareholders) firms, and are primarily small, employing less than 50 people and with sales revenue of less than £1m. It would have been extremely neat to find that, having identified eight clusters of firms, three of which had potential as the 'high-flyers' of the sample, and our cross-sectional analysis had captured firms at various stages of growth. However, the chi-squared analyses and the analysis of variance tests identified no significant differences between the clusters with regard to size. Consequently, any ranking would be invalid.

These results are based upon a comprehensive analysis of the strategic profile of a random sample of small firms using 31 'internal' and 'external' variables. In the cross-sectional analysis there is no support for the theory that (all) firms pass sequentially through a series of growth stages. From our observation of the firms during the data collection period this is a conclusion that we find intuitively appealing. Clearly firms do change, but not necessarily in any prescribed sequence. Indeed, the evidence presented in this paper suggests that we should be developing theories which better describe the heterogeneity of the sector. Moreover, we should be seeking to analyze the development within clusters of firms, rather than seeking generalized over-arching theories for all firms.

REFERENCES

Bamberger, I. 'Value systems, strategies and performance of small and medium sized firms', *International Small Business Journal*, **1**, 1983, pp. 25–39.

Begley, T. M. and D. P. Boyd. 'Executive and corporate correlates of financial performance in smaller firms', *Journal of Small Business Management*, April 1986, pp. 8–15.

Birley, S. and P. Westhead. *The Cranfield Small Firms Database, 1988. Report 1: Small Firm Characteristics*. Cranfield School of Management, Cranfield, 1988.

Brockhaus, R. H. Snr. 'The psychology of the entrepreneur'. In C. A. Kent, D. L. Sexton and K. H. Vesper (eds), *Encyclopedia of Entrepreneurship*, Prentice-Hall International, London, 1982, pp. 39–71.

Calori, R. and H. Bonamy. 'Growth companies in Europe: Salomon, a case study'. In S. Birley (ed.), *European Entrepreneurship: Emerging Growth Companies*, EFER, Cranfield, 1989, pp. 27–48.

Chaganti, R. 'Industry life-stage and profitable small business strategies', *Eastern Academy of Management Proceedings*, 1986, pp. 95–99.

Churchill, N. C. and V. L. Lewis. 'The five stages of small business growth', *Harvard Business Review*, **61**, 1983, pp. 30–50.

Cooper, A. C. 'The role of incubator organizations in the founding of growth-orientated firms', *Journal of Business Venturing*, **1**, 1985, pp. 75–86.

Covin, J. G. and D. P. Slevin. 'New venture competitive strategy: An industry life cycle analysis' In B. A. Kirchhoff, W. A. Long, W. E. McMullan, K. H. Vesper and W. E. Wetzel (eds), *Frontiers of Entrepreneurship Research*. Babson College, Wellesley, MA, 1988, pp. 446–460.

Deeks, J. *The Small Firm Owner Manager: Entrepreneurial Behavior and Management Practice*. Praeger,

New York, 1976.

Del Monte, A. and A. Giannola. 'Relevance and nature of small and medium sized firms in Southern Italy'. In D. Keeble and E. Wever (eds), *New Firms and Regional Development in Europe*, Croom Helm, Beckenham, 1986, pp. 275–298.

Devine, P. J. *An Introduction to Industrial Economics*, Allen and Unwin, Hemel Hempstead, 1979.

England, G. W. *The Manager and His Values: An International Perspective from the United States, Japan, Korea, India and Australia*, Ballinger, Cambridge, MA, 1975.

Filley, A. C. and R. A. Aldag 'Venture age and growth within organization types'. Paper Presented at the Eighth Annual Babson College Entrepreneurship Research Conference, The University of Calgary, Canada, 1988.

Fombrun, C. J. and S. Wally. 'Structuring small firms for rapid growth', *Journal of Business Venturing*, **4**(2), 1989, pp. 106–122.

Gibb, A. and M. Scott. 'Strategic awareness, personal commitment and the process of planning in the small business', *Journal of Management Studies*, **22**, 1985, pp. 597–631.

Hair, J. F. , R. E. Anderson, R. L. Tatham and B. J. Grablowsky. *Multivariate Data Analysis*, PPC Books, Tulsa, OK, 1979.

Hitchins, D. W. N. and P. N. O'Farrell. 'The comparative performance of small manufacturing firms in Northern Ireland and South East England'. *Regional Studies*, **21**, 1987, pp. 543–553.

Hitchins, D. W. N. and P. N. O'Farrell. 'Comparative performance of small manufacturing companies in South Wales and Northern Ireland'. *Omega*, **16**, 1988, pp. 429–438.

Hjern, R., C. Hull, D. Finlayson, A. Gillespie and J. Goddard. *Helping Small Firms Grow*. International Institute of Management, Discussion Paper Series, Berlin, 1980.

Hornaday, R. W. and J. Aboud. 'Characteristics of successful entrepreneurs', *Personnel Psychology*, **24**, 1971, pp. 141–153.

Hornaday, R. W. and W. J. Wheatley. 'Managerial characteristics and the financial performance of small business', *Journal of Small Business Management*, April 1986, pp. 1–7.

Karger, D. W. and F. A. Malik. 'Long range planning and organizational performance—a cross validation study', *Long Range Planning*, **8**, 1975, pp. 60–64.

Kets de Vries, M. F. R. 'The entrepreneurial personality: A person at the crossroads', *Journal of Management Studies*, **14**, 1977, pp. 34–57.

Khan, A. M. 'Entrepreneur characteristics and the prediction of new venture success', *Omega*, **14**, 1986, pp. 365–372.

Kimberley, J. R., R. H. Miles and Associates. *The Organizational Life Cycle*, Jossey Bass, San Francisco, CA, 1980.

Kudla, R. J. 'The effects of strategic planning on common stock returns', *Academy of Management Journal*, **23**, 1980, pp. 5–20.

Lafuente, A. and V. Salas. 'Types of entrepreneurs and firms: The case of new Spanish firms'. *Strategic Management Journal*, **10**, 1989, pp. 17–30.

Lorenzoni, G. and O. A. Ornati. 'Constellations of firms and new ventures', *Journal of Business Venturing*, **3**, 1988, pp. 41–57.

Mason, C. M. 'Venture capital in the United Kingdom: A geographical perspective', *National Westminster Bank Quarterly Review*, May, 1987, pp. 47–59.

Mason, C. M. and R. T. Harrison. 'The geography of small firms in the UK: Towards a research agenda', *Progress in Human Geography*, **9**, 1985, pp. 1–37.

Milne, T. and M. Thompson. 'The infant business development process'. University of Glasgow, Management Studies Working Paper No. 2, 1982.

Oakey, R. P. , P. A. Nash and A. T. Thwaites. 'The regional distribution of innovative manufacturing establishments in Britain', *Regional Studies*, **14**, 1980, pp. 235–253.

O'Farrell, P. N. and D. W. N. Hitchins. 'Alternative theories of small-firm growth: A critical review', *Environment and Planning*, **20**, 1988a, pp. 1365–1382.

O'Farrell, P. N. and D. W. N. Hitchins. 'The relative competitiveness and performance of small manufacturing firms in Scotland and the Mid-West of Ireland: An analysis of matched pairs', *Regional Studies*, **22**, 1988b, pp. 399–416.

O'Neill, H. M., C. B. Saunders and A. N. Hoffman. 'Beyond the entrepreneur: Planning as the organization grows', *Business Forum*, **12**, 1987, pp. 38–40.

Perry, C., G. G. Meredith and H. J. Cunnington. 'Relationship between small business growth and personal characteristics of owner/managers in Australia', *Journal of Small Business Management*, April 1988, pp. 76–79.

Porter, M. E. *Competitive Strategy: Techniques for Analyzing Industries and Competitors*. Free Press, New York, 1980.

Porter, M. E. *Competitive Advantage: Creating and Sustaining Superior Performance*. Free Press, New York, 1985.

Roure, J. B. and R. H. Keeley. 'Comparison of predicting factors of successful high growth technological ventures in Europe and the USA'. In S. Birley (ed.), *European Entrepreneurship: Emerging Growth Companies*, EFER, Cranfield, 1989, pp. 189–222.

Steinmetz, L. L. 'Critical stages of small business growth', *Business Horizons*, **12**, 1969, pp. 29–34.

Storey, D. J., K. Keasey, R. Watson and P. Wynarczyk. *The Performance of Small Firms*. Croom Helm, London, 1987.

Storey, D. J., R. Watson and P. Wynarczyk. 'Fast growth small business: Case studies of 40 small firms in North East England'. Department of Employment Research Paper No. 67, London, 1989.

Stuart, R. and P. A. Abetti. 'Start-up ventures: Towards the prediction of initial success', *Journal of Business Venturing*, **2**, 1987, pp. 215–230.

Sweeney, G. P. *Innovation, Entrepreneurs and Regional Development*. Frances Pinter, London,

1987.

Taylor, M. J. and N. J. Thrift. 'Models of corporate development and the multinational corporation'. In M. J. Taylor and N. J. Thrift (eds), *The Geography of Multinationals*, Croom Helm, Beckenham, 1982, pp. 14–32.

Ward, J. H. Jr. 'Hierarchical grouping to optimize an objective function', *Journal of the American Statistical Association*, **58**, 1963, pp. 236–244.

Westhead, P. 'A typology of new manufacturing firm founders in Wales'. Cranfield School of Management Working Paper No. 46, 1988.

Wilson, P. and P. Gorb. 'How large and small firms can grow together', *Long Range Planning*, **16**, 1983, pp. 19–27.

APPENDIX: SMALL FIRM CHARACTERISTICS VARIABLES

SHAREHOLDERS	Number of shareholders or partners
OWNERS	Family relationship of current majority owners to founders
EXECUTIVES	Family relationship of current senior executives to founders
FOUNDERS	Number of original founders who are still partners or shareholders
AGE	Age of the small business (years)
MAN	Total number of managerial functions which currently operate within the firm
SOLE	Total number of managerial functions the sole responsibility of one person
MANINDEX	Managerial score function index (total number of managerial functions the sole responsibility of one person/total number of managerial functions which currently operate within the firm)
PLANMAN	Frequency of board and management meetings
PLANPROF	Frequency of meetings with professional advisers such as the bank, an accountant, and a solicitor
PLANBUS	Frequency of meetings with business contacts such as major customers and major suppliers
MANTRAIN	Has the small business management team received any management training?
FINANCE	Number of sources of received financial investment
PRODUCTION	Control technology for the major manufactured product lines
AGEPROD	The age of the oldest piece of production equipment (months)
CSADMIN	Control technology used in the administration base
INDUSTRY	Industrial activity of the small firm
LOCATION	Location of the small business
TRAINING	Has the small business applied for any local or central government training schemes in the last 3 months?
GRANTS	Has the small business applied for any local or central government grants in the last 3 months?
PRODUCT	Number of major product lines or major service groups
NEWPRODUCT	Number of new major product lines or major service groups added in the last 12 months
REVENUE	Percentage of sales revenue accounted for by the major product line or service group
CUSTOMERS	Total number of customers
NEWCUSTOMERS	Number of new customers in the past 12 months
SUPPLIERS	Total number of suppliers
NEWSUPPLIERS	Number of new suppliers in the past 12 months
DISTCUSTOMERS	Distribution of the majority of customers from operational premises
DISTSUPPLIERS	Distribution of the majority of suppliers from operational premises
COMPETITION	Number of direct competitors
SIZECOMP	Employment size of major competitor

[25]

CONTINUED ENTREPRENEURSHIP: ABILITY, NEED, AND OPPORTUNITY AS DETERMINANTS OF SMALL FIRM GROWTH[1]

PER DAVIDSSON
Umeå University Business School, Sweden

EXECUTIVE SUMMARY

The purpose of this research was to enhance our understanding of the growth or non-growth of individual small businesses, growth here being regarded as an indication of continued entrepreneurship.

Taken together, earlier studies have suggested a very large number of determinants of entrepreneurship and growth. Yet no very strong explanatory factors emerge. It is argued here that all of the specific low-level explanatory variables that have previously been used can be regarded as aspects of either of three major determinants: Ability, Need, and Opportunity.

A model based on these three major factors is developed, and the results of previous studies are reviewed in the light of this more abstract model. In the model, objective factors are separated from their subjective counterparts, and it is suggested that subjective factors—or reality-as-perceived—influence Growth Motivation and direct behavior. Although objective factors only partly determine subjective perceptions, they can have important direct effects on outcomes, i.e., Actual Growth.

Using survey data from more than 400 Swedish small firms and applying Partial Least Squares analysis, which is a technique for analyzing structural relations among indirectly measured concepts, the parameters of the model are empirically estimated. The results largely lend support for the usefulness of the model.

More specifically, the analyses suggest that: (1) objective measures of Ability, Need, and Opportunity can explain a substantial share of the variation in Actual (historical) Growth rates; (2) objective and subjective measures of these three factors can explain a substantial share of the variation in Growth Motivation; (3) in both cases, Need-related issues appear more important than Ability and

Address correspondence to Per Davidsson, Department of Business Administration, Umeå University Business School, S-901 Umeå, Sweden.

[1]This work was made possible through financial support from Jan Wallander's Foundation and Ruben Rausing's Foundation for Research on Innovation and New Business Venturing, whom I hereby thank. I am also indebted to Professors Clas Wahlbin and Karl-Erik Wärneryd for their valuable comments on earlier versions of this manuscript.

Journal of Business Venturing 6, 405–429 0883-9026/91/$3.50

Opportunity (which would mean that satiation is the major reason why small firms stop growing); (4) subjective factors contain growth-relevant information that is not captured by objective measures; (5) direct effects of objective variables on Actual Growth can be traced; (6) some relations are consistent whereas others seem to vary considerably across industries; and (7) while the model largely gains support, the analyses also suggest some additional relations that are theoretically reasonable and may deserve consideration in future studies.

Finally, it is argued that for the advancement of entrepreneurship research, conceptual models at a higher level of abstraction like the one developed in this article are needed. Such models can add meaning to empirical facts and have the virtue of reducing complexity without assuming away too many potential contingencies. It is also suggested that entrepreneurship is a matter of degree and can show itself in different ways, such as start-up, growth, innovation, etc. In practice, the sole measure of entrepreneurship has often been a person's current status as being or not being the founder or owner-manager of a small firm. In future studies the use of a composite measure of the degree of entrepreneurship may prove more fruitful than the comparison-of-characteristics approach has been.

INTRODUCTION

In empirical studies, the fact that an individual owns and runs his/her own firm is often used as the sole measure of entrepreneurship. A frequent approach is to compare the characteristics of small firm owner-managers to those of some other group along an unstructured array of low-level explanatory variables that appear to have been selected on a common sense basis. An almost endless list of correlates of entrepreneurship can be compiled from the results of such studies. Yet no very strong predictors emerge, and our knowledge about the mechanisms behind entrepreneurial behavior is still limited.

This author's opinion is that in order to advance further, entrepreneurship research should focus more on *continued entrepreneurship* and on *degrees of entrepreneurship*. In doing this, working with more abstracted concepts, as well as using and developing more of theory than has generally been the case, should be pursued.

The present study is an attempt in that direction. An economic-psychological model of determinants of small firm growth will be proposed and its parameters empirically estimated. A large number of low-level explanatory variables will be used, but these will be treated as aspects of more general concepts rather than as separate variables.

THEORY AND PREVIOUS RESEARCH

The Model

Figure 1 depicts the theoretical model to be evaluated. The model can be regarded as a more detailed version of Katona's notion of willingness and ability as determinants of economic behavior (Katona 1975).

In short, the model suggests that an important determinant of Actual Growth is (the manager's or management team's) Growth Motivation. Motivation is explicitly assumed to vary, to direct behavior, and thus affect outcomes.

Growth Motivation, in its turn, is determined by the perceived growth-relevant Ability, Need, and Opportunity. Motivation is enhanced, and expansion therefore pursued, if the manager believes that growth would serve personal goals. S/he also has to feel that there are external conditions that can be gainfully exploited, and that s/he is able to exploit them.

So far, the model is highly subjective. Although expected to vary also when objective conditions are the same, the perceptions are at least to some degree influenced by the objective

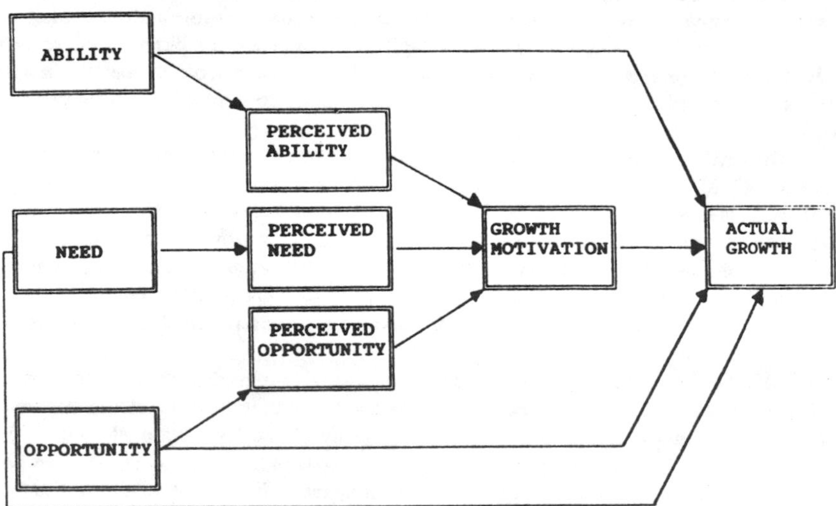

FIGURE 1 A model of determinants of small firm growth.

conditions. It is important, however, to realize that Growth Motivation is entirely the result of reality *as perceived*.

This is not necessarily true for Actual Growth. Circumstances that are not considered and thus do not affect decisions can nevertheless influence the outcomes. If, for example, an owner-manager misjudges some specific opportunities, s/he may well become growth-motivated but still not able to bring about the desired growth. Therefore, direct effects of objective Ability, Need, and Opportunity on Actual Growth are included in the model.

Now, is growth an indication of continued entrepreneurship? To the extent that the manager is free to choose, i.e. if economic behavior is discretionary (cf. Katona 1975), the answer is yes. Just as founding a firm is considered more entrepreneurial than not doing so, pursuing continued development of the firm is the more entrepreneurial choice when refraining from doing so is another feasible alternative.

Rationale for the Model

Previous research on entrepreneurship and small firm performance has used a very wide range of explanatory variables. Some of these concern external factors such as industry structure and dynamics, and various characteristics of the geographic and economic environment, including access to key resources (see Bruno and Tyebjee 1982; Cooper 1982; Doutriaux 1987; Dunkelberg et al. 1987; Keeble et al. 1990; Plaschka 1987; Reynolds 1986; Reynolds and Maki 1990; Sandburg and Hofer 1987; Stuart and Abetti 1986). While such variables often yield significant relations in the expected direction, their contribution to the explanation of micro-level variations is much smaller than one would expect on the basis of economic theory.

What all these specific aspects of external conditions have in common is that they concern (objective) *Opportunity*. Characteristics such as industry fragmentation, market size and growth, entry barriers, and access to capital and labor are all likely to be relevant indicators of Opportunity for growth. Inasmuch as the list of such specifics may be endless, it appears to be fruitful to incorporate instead the broader concept of Opportunity in the model.

The firm's age and its size have been shown to be negatively correlated with growth (Evans 1987; Kumar 1984; Boswell 1972; Doutriaux 1984; Simyar et al. 1988). A plausible explanation is that the objective *Need* for further expansion declines with increasing age and size. The older the firm, the more it has proven viable doing what it currently does. The larger it is, the more likely are profits to be high enough to ensure a satisfactory standard of living for its owner-manager(s). Numerous studies showing positive relations between survival on the one hand, and either age or size on the other (cf. March and Sevón 1988) support such an interpretation.

Also the owner-manager's age tends to be negatively related to growth (cf. Boswell 1972; Wärneryd 1988). This can be regarded as another indication that Need is important. An older individual is likely to have a lower objective Need for additional income. For example, support burden, mortgage and interest on housing, etc., generally decline with age given that demands on standard of living do not increase. In cross-sectional studies there may also be a more subjective explanation. An older individual, still being the owner-manager of a *small* firm, is more likely to have reached his/her initial aspirations at (or adjusted them to) the current state of affairs. This may also cause a negative relation between length of tenure as CEO and growth.

Ideally, objective Need should be assessed in a more direct way than by the suggested indicators. As this would require thorough insight into the financial position of the owner-manager as well as that of the firm, a more direct approach is likely to cause severe problems in empirical work.

Other explanatory variables used in previous studies clearly concern *Ability*. Examples are education, various types of experience, breadth of education and experience, and management team building (Begley and Boyd 1987; Boswell 1972; Brandstätter 1988; Dunkelberg et al. 1987; Gasse 1982; Hoad and Rosko 1964; Kayser 1987; Lamont 1972; Lorrain and Dussault 1988; Mayer and Goldstein 1964; Pickle 1964; Plaschka 1987; Smith 1967).

That Ability is needed to make desired outcomes materialize could hardly be opposed. Besides the importance of a well-balanced management team in the high-tech context (Cooper and Bruno 1977; Roberts 1972; Roure and Maidique 1986; Stuart and Abetti 1986; Utterback and Reitberger 1982), the empirical evidence is in fact very mixed. Apparently what constitutes relevant Ability depends very much on the context. By using the broader concept Ability in the model and using alternative measures of it, the questions "How important is Ability?" and "What abilities matter in this context?" can both be answered by the same empirical analysis.

Three concepts thus cover most of the objective explanatory variables suggested by previous research: Ability, Need, and Opportunity. But this is not the whole story. When a firm operates above mere subsistence level in a less than perfect market, the manager is to a considerable extent free to choose whether to pursue expansion or not. If so, differences in *Growth Motivation* are of interest.

Motivation can be conceived of as based on cognition. Examples of cognitive approaches are, e.g., Expectancy X Value models (Vroom 1964) and Cognitive Structure attitude models (e.g., Fishbein and Ajzen 1975). These theories focus on the behavioral effects of expectations concerning the consequences of performing an act in relation to personal goals. In the case of small firm growth, previous research suggests a range of expected outcomes that should be considered, the monetary outcome not being of outstanding importance (cf. Brockhaus 1982; Collins et al. 1964; Davidsson 1987, 1989b; Donckels et al. 1987; Gasse 1982; Kets de Vries 1977, 1985; Scheinberg and MacMillan 1988; Smith 1967).

Motivation may also be based on affect, i.e., a general favorable or unfavorable attitude, the cognitive bases for which may have been forgotten, towards an act or object (cf. Pieters 1988, 1989). Further, Motivation may be expressed in various ways, e.g., as aspirations or behavioral intentions. Hence, multiple indicators of Motivation are likely to be needed to get a valid overall measure.

Differences in objective Ability, Need, and Opportunity might have direct effects on the outcomes of behavior, but these variables cannot affect Motivation unless they are perceived. It is well known that human information processing is characterized by selective perception, limited processing capacity, and various kinds of processing biases. Thus, individual differences in perceptions are to be expected also when the objective conditions are equal, and yet another triplet of concepts appears to be needed. *Perceived Ability, Perceived Need,* and *Perceived Opportunity*.

Internal Locus-of-Control (Rotter 1966), self-confidence, and optimism may be regarded as indicators of Perceived Ability. Several studies have included such presumed traits of entrepreneurs (see, e.g., Begley and Boyd 1987; Brockhaus 1982; Cooper et al. 1986; Egge 1987; Hornaday 1982; Kets de Vries 1977; Wärneryd 1988). The results are mixed, but taken together they lend some support to the idea that those traits influence entrepreneurial behavior.

Some studies deal with the financial aspect of Perceived Need, viz. the satisfaction with profitability and personal economic outcome (e.g., Donckels et al. 1987). A more thoroughly researched area is the Need for Achievement (Murray 1938). This concept has been one of the most popular and at the same time most debated in entrepreneurship research (see, e.g., Begley and Boyd 1987; Borland 1974; Deeks 1976; Gasse 1982; Finison 1976; Hornaday and Aboud 1971; Khan 1986; Hull et al. 1980; McClelland 1961, 1965, 1966; McClelland and Winter 1969; Miron and McClelland 1979; Panday and Tewary 1979; Plaschka 1987; Wärneryd 1988).

There are no doubt methodological shortcomings, conflicting results, and questionable validity for some of the relationships proposed by *n* Achievement (*n*Ach) theory. McClelland's (1961) basic idea remains, however, a very plausible one: that individuals (and cultures) differ with respect to the value attributed to (economic) achievements and that these differences affect entrepreneurial efforts. Much of the doubt arises from studies where owner-managers are contrasted with hired managers. When comparisons are made between more and less entrepreneurial cultures (Bellu 1987), or between "super-entrepreneurs" and owner-managers in general (Perry et al. 1986), substantial differences are established.

Superior perception of opportunity is central in some economic theorists' conceptions of the entrepreneur (Kirzner 1979, 1982, 1983; Shackle 1979). The inclusion of aspects of Perceived Opportunity seems to have been less common in empirical studies. While judgements about the future development of the industry, the financial strength of the firm, and accessibility of needed resources occasionally appear, there are no established concepts such as Locus-of-Control or *n*Ach that recur in study after study.

METHOD

Model Development

The model in Figure 1 was not fully developed before data collection. Earlier versions of the model guided questionnaire design. The specific set of concepts and relations suggested in Figure 1 evolved over time, mainly in an attempt to summarize and make a synthesis of results from a large number of earlier studies (cf., above and Davidsson 1989a, ch. 2), but also with some knowledge of the low-level empirical relations in this particular set of data.

This means that while the model is not an outcome of analyses of this study's data, the results presented here cannot be interpreted as an "acid test" of the model. The fact that the model was not fully developed before data collection also means that the selection of indicators to measure the concepts in the model is less than ideal in some cases.

Data Collection

Telephone interviews and a mail follow-up questionnaire were used for data collection. The original sample comprised 540 firms. Thirty of these were found not to be members of the target population. Of the remaining 510 firms, the managers of 423 (83%) were interviewed and 322 (63%) also completed the mail questionnaire.

The sampling frame used was Statistics' Sweden's register of all Swedish enterprises. The sample was restricted to independent firms within four industries: (1) Manufacturing of metal products and machinery; (2) Manufacturing of (certain) electronic, electric, and optical equipment; (3) Repair Services; and (4) Retailing with clothing and home equipment. Three size strata were specified: 2–4, 5–9, and 10–19 employees, respectively. Each industry/size class stratum was given equal representation in the sample.

The questionnaires included several variables relating to each "box" in the model. As only such questions were asked that the manager would be willing and able to answer without consulting other people or written documentation, details on data on profits, assets, and such are lacking.

Data on characteristics of the industries and of different geographic areas were collected from external, secondary sources.

Data Analysis

The research problem concerns a system with direct and indirect relations between theoretical constructs that cannot be adequately captured by a single measure. A suitable method for analyzing such systems is partial least squares (PLS) analysis. This method, which was developed by Wold (1982, 1986), will be used here.

PLS is an iterative least squares technique. It embodies earlier least squares methods such as Regression, Principal Component, and Canonical Correlation analysis as special cases. The technique is prediction-oriented, optimizing the explanation of specified variances. PLS is further a "distribution-free" and "independence-free" method. Unlike Maximum Likelihood-based methods for covariance structure analysis, it can be applied to large models and small samples.

PLS permits two different kinds of latent variables (LVs). As in covariance structure analysis, an LV can be specified as a *reflective* factor. The underlying idea is that the LV causes the variation in its manifest (i.e., directly measured) indicators (MVs). Thus the latter should be highly intercorrelated, each one being an imperfect reflection of "the same thing" (cf., ordinary "exploratory" factor analysis and Cronbach's Alpha-test of index variables).

LVs in PLS can also be specified as *formative* factors. In that case the theoretical variable (LV) is constructed by a number of indicators (MVs) that are not necessarily highly correlated; yet they sum up to a meaningful construct. A Cognitive Structure attitude model (cf., Fishbein and Ajzen 1975) is an example of an index of this kind. The beliefs and evaluations for different attributes of an object contribute to, but are not caused by, the overall attitude.

With the kind of constructs and measures used in this study, the formative factor option is essential. For example, education and experience need not be correlated but can both contribute to growth-relevant Ability.

The analyst specifies the MV-LV relations, i.e., which MVs are indicators of which LV and the direction of these relationships, as well as the LV-LV relations, i.e., the causal structure. The choice of direction for MV-LV relations involves a trade-off between structural fit and explanatory power on the one hand (formative) and "good measurement" and unambiguous interpretation of the LVs on the other (reflective).

PLS models can be evaluated in several ways. The magnitudes of R^2 values, path coefficients, and total (direct + indirect) effects give the strengths of the empirical relations proposed by the model. The path coefficients and residual correlations[2] also reveal whether some relations could be excluded and/or others need to be added. Statistical tests can be computed only if the analysis is based on raw data, something that requires that no missing values exist in the data matrix.

The MV-LV relations are described by regression weights and factor loadings. The loadings are model parameters for reflective factors, but can be used for interpretation also of formative factors, whose model parameters are the weights.

The applications of PLS in this study are based on correlation data, which means that statistical tests are not provided. The variables are standardized and path coefficients can therefore be interpreted in the same manner as standardized regression coefficients. For more elaborate descriptions of PLS see Fornell (1987), Fornell and Bookstein (1982), Lohmöller (1984), and Wold (1982, 1986).

Method Problems

Figure 1 is of course a simplification. Many other contingencies than those proposed by this model are conceivable, feedback loops and interaction effects not excluded. A problem of operationalization is that while the theoretical constructs are fairly easy to separate conceptually, the dividing lines may be less clear at the manifest level. When translating the model to the empirical world, some simplifying assumptions must be made. However, simplicity should be sacred as long as it does not lead too far astray, and empirical estimation has the power of revealing at least some types of misspecifications.

A problem with this particular study is that with cross-sectional data the model as a whole cannot be tested directly. While some objective Ability, Need, and Opportunity data that may explain previous growth are available, *ex ante* data on motivation and perception variables are lacking. Growth data concern the 1984–1986 period, whereas growth motivation and perception data were collected at one point in time, viz., November–December 1986.

Therefore, partial analyses are presented. First an attempt is made to explain Actual (historical) Growth by differences in objective Ability, Need, and Opportunity in the relevant

[2]Residual correlation in this context refers to correlation among the variables that is not accounted for by the estimated structural coefficients in the causal system as specified.

time period. The subjective part of the model is thus left out. In the following two analyses are estimated the effects of Ability, Need, Opportunity, and perceptions of these, on Growth Motivation.

Although the relation between Growth Motivation and subsequent real growth cannot be tested directly, the results of the partial analyses have implications for that relation.

RESULTS

Determinants of Actual Growth

The basic assumption in this section is that more Ability, more Need, and more Opportunity lead to a higher rate of Actual Growth. Growth rates were computed from statements about current size in turnover and in number of employees, and the corresponding figures three years previously. The logarithms of the ratios of these two size measures are used as indicators of Actual Growth in the analyses.

The explanatory variables are also composite measures. In technical terms they are second-order factors, constructed as linear combinations of first-order factors that in their turn have manifest variables as indicators. As the dependent variable concerns previous growth, only such indicators were used that could reasonably be considered as not being after-the-fact. The reader is referred to Table 1 for a description of the measures.

As to the important components of growth-relevant Ability, Need, and Opportunity, the following has been assumed:

1. Industry experience, management experience,entrepreneurial experience, and education (general and business) enhance growth-relevant Ability.
2. Profitability, higher firm age, age of the manager, and firm size (1983 figures) reduce the Need for growth.
3. Opportunity for growth should be better in an industry that is less (naturally) fragmented, has a higher market growth rate, and a higher rate of (product) innovation. Growth Opportunity is also enhanced by a favorable geographic location (i.e., large local market, growth area, proximity to university).

The model arrived at is displayed in Figure 2. All variables but Age/Maturity and Firm Size are scored so that positive coefficients are expected. Coefficients for the relationships between manifest indicators and first-order factors are given in Table 1.

It turns out that the three factors, Ability, Need, and Opportunity, do explain a substantial share (25%) of the variation in Actual Growth. The path coefficients further show that Ability, Need, and Opportunity each have a unique impact on Actual Growth that is large enough to deserve consideration. Need stands out as the most important factor, but the coefficients for the other factors are not negligible.

Then what are the underlying dimensions of growth-relevant Ability, Need, and Opportunity? For Ability and Need the pattern is fairly clear-cut. In both cases, each first-order factor gets a substantial weight and loading. Entrepreneurial Experience appears to be slightly more important than formal Education, and Age/Maturity slightly more important than Firm Size. Indicators of industry and management experience, and a (weak) proxy for profitability, did not contribute to growth-relevant Ability and Need, respectively, and were excluded from the displayed analysis.

The high intercorrelations among the first-order Opportunity factors result in some negative regression weights although all loadings are positive. The weights must be regarded as unreliable indicators of relative importance. Judging from correlations and factor loadings,

TABLE 1 Explanatory Variables in Analysis of Actual (Previous) Growth

SECOND-ORDER FACTORS/ *First-Order Factors*		Manifest Indicators	Higher Value Means . . .	Weights/Loadings[a] for Indicators	Weights/Loadings[a] for *F-O Factors*
ABILITY			MORE ABILITY		
Education	1	General education	*Higher education*	.91/.99	*.64/.61*
	2	Business education		.18/.58	
Entrepreneurial Experience	3	Prior own bus. experience	*More experience*	.16/.37	*.79/.77*
	4	Business founder		.95/.99	
NEED			MORE NEED		
Age/maturity	5	Firm age (log)	*Older (= less need)*	.89/.95	*−.68/−.85*
	6	Managers' age (log)		.33/.49	
Firm size	7	Firm size 1983, empl.	*Larger (= less need)*	*/.92	*−.55/−.76*
	8	Firm size in 1983, T-O		*/.86	
OPPORTUNITY			MORE OPPORTUNITY		
Rate of innovation within industry	9	Mean judgement by resp. in category	*Higher rate*	.46/.91	*.73/.92*
	10	High-tech firm[b]		.61/.95	
Industry structure	11	Mean number of empl. for all firms in ISIC-cat.	*More concentr.*	*/.97	*−.11/.57*
	12	No. of firms with 1–4 rel. to 10–19 empl. in ISIC-cat.		*/.94	
Market growth	13	Tot. empl. in ISIC-cat. in 1986 rel. to 1980	*High growth*	*/.94	*.24/.47*
	14	Tot. empl. in ISIC-cat. in 1986 rel. to 1984		*/.84	
Character of geographical area; county	15	Total population	*More favorable*	*/.93	*.14/.28*
	16	Pop. change 1984–86		*/.92	
	17	Pop. density		*/.94	
	18	Major university[b]		*/.90	
Character of geographical area; community	19	Total population	*More favorable*	*/.95	*−.01/.25*
	20	Pop. change 1984–86		*/.91	
	21	Pop. density		*/.66	
	22	Major university[b]		*/.82	
	23	Minor university[b]		*/.07	
Geographic market dispersion; ISIC category mean	24	Percent of T-O within home county (reversed)	*More dispersed*	*/.97	*−.22/.51*
	25	Exports[b]		*/.97	
Customer structure; ISIC-category mean	26	Type of customers	*More concentr*	*/.91	*.45/.79*
	27	Importance of 3 largest cust.		*/.91	
ACTUAL GROWTH					
Actual growth	28	Annual growth rate 1983–86; no. of employees (log)	HIGHER RATE	*/.92	**/1.00*
	29	Annual growth rate 1983–86; turnover (log)		*/.93	

[a]Loadings only for reflective factors.
*denotes a left-out weight in such cases.
[b]Dummy variable. 1 = Yes; 0 = No.

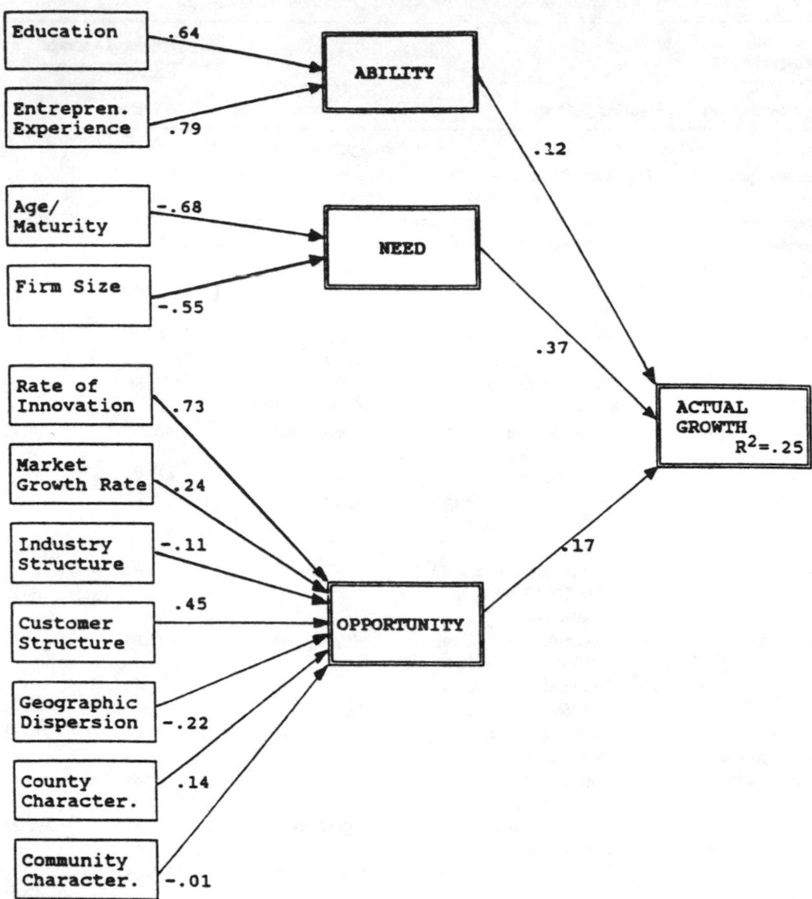

FIGURE 2 Determinants of Actual (historical) Growth.

Rate of Innovation, Customer Concentration, Industry Concentration, Geographical Market Dispersion, and Market Growth (in the order given) are the most important indicators of growth-relevant Opportunity. In terms of sampling categories, the two manufacturing subsamples have considerably higher growth rates than have retailers and repair service firms.

Geographic Characteristics of the kind captured by the measure do not seem to be important general determinants of company growth.

In all, the results confirm the importance of some of the objective factors that have been suggested by theory and previous studies, but they certainly leave room for motivation as an additional factor for explaining differences in the growth of small firms.

Determinants of Growth Motivation

Also in the analysis of Growth Motivation a two-step procedure has been followed. The central constructs thus are second-order factors.

Three first-order factors are used as indicators of Growth Motivation. The first is Cognitive Attitude towards growth. The indicators for this factor are expectations of what (positive or negative) consequences growth would have with respect to eight specific dimensions: workload, work tasks, employee well-being, private finances, control, independence, crisis survival ability, and product/service quality. For a detailed analysis of the relations between these expectations and growth aspirations, see Davidsson (1989b).

The second factor is labeled Affective Attitude. This is an "overall attitude" kind of measure, reflecting reactions towards a hypothetical increase of the firm's size by 25 and 100%, respectively.

The third Growth Motivation factor is Growth Aspirations. This factor was measured with two indicators: (1) the difference between present size and an "ideal size" five years ahead in terms of number of employees; and (2) the same for turnover. The measures used in the analyses are logarithms of size ratios.

The indicators for objective factors essentially correspond to those used in the analyses of Actual Growth. They have been regrouped somewhat to reduce the total number of first-order factors. The size measures used here are 1986 figures. Ownership Dispersion has been added as another indicator of objective Need (since there are "more mouths to feed"). In addition, some group-level proxy indicators of Opportunity have been replaced by individual-level questionnaire data, and additional indicators of Entrepreneurial Experience and Age/Maturity have been incorporated.

Perceived Ability is measured with but three manifest indicators, all being attitude items aimed at capturing Locus-of-Control and self-confidence. Two subfactors of Perceived Need are included, viz. Economic Satisfaction (two indicators) and *n*Ach (four indicators). Finally, three subaspects of Perceived Opportunity are specified: Perceived External Obstacles (4), Perceived Entry Barriers (2), and Perceived Room for growth (five indicators).

Details on the measures are given in the Table 2 and in Davidsson (1989a).

TABLE 2 Explanatory Variables in Analysis of Growth Motivation

SECOND-ORDER FACTORS/ *First-Orders Factors*		Manifest Indicators	Higher Value Means . . . (SECOND-ORDER/ *First-Order*)	Weights/Loadings[a] for Indicators	Weights/Loadings[a] for *F-O Factors*
ABILITY			MORE ABILITY		
Education	1	General education	*Higher education*	.84/.97	*.95/.96*
	2	Business education		.27/.67	*[.93/.94]*
Entrepreneurial	3	Prior own bus. experience	*More experience*	.68/.81	*.28/.31*
Experience	4	Runs multiple firms		.32/.45	*[.34/.37]*
	5	Business founder		.47/.64	
Need			MORE NEED		
Ownership dispersion	6	Resp. (+family) share (rev.)	*More dispersed (=more need)*	.02/.72	*.40/.55* *[.43/.58]*
	7	Partnership[b]		.71/.75	

TABLE 2 Explanatory Variables in Analysis of Growth Motivation

SECOND-ORDER FACTORS/ *First-Orders Factors*		Manifest Indicators	Higher Value Means . . . (SECOND-ORDER/ *First-Order*)	Weights/Loadings[a] for Indicators	Weights/Loadings[a] for *F-O Factors*
	8	VenCap[b]		.65/.69	
Age/maturity	9	Manager's age (log)	*Older (= less need)*	.26/.60	*− .70/ − .84*
	10	Firm age (log)		.56/.82	*/[− .72/ − .86]*
	11	Tenure as CEO (log)		.46/.85	
Firm size	12	Firm size 1986, empl.	*Larger (= less need)*	*/.82	*− .46/ − .42*
	13	Firm size in 1986, T-O		*/.88	*/[− .39/ − .35]*
Opportunity			MORE OPPORTUNITY		
Industry characteristics	14	Mean number of empl. for all firms in ISIC-cat.	*More favorable*	*/.88	*.23/.40 /[.28/.47]*
	15	No. of firms with 1–4 rel. to 10–19 empl. in ISIC-cat.		*/.76	
	16	Tot. empl. in ISIC-cat. in 1986 rel. to 1980		*/.49	
	17	Tot. empl. in ISIC-cat. in 1986 rel. to 1984		*/.46	
	18	Type of customers		*/.67	
	19	Importance of 3 largest cust.		*/.65	
	20	Service firm[b]		*/ − .35	
	21	Hitech firm[b]		*/.65	
Geographic market dispersion	22	Percent of T-O within home county (reversed)	*More dispersed*	.95/.97	*.64/.76 /[.67/.81]*
	23	Scand. exports[b]		− .18/.44	
	24	Global exports[b]		.28/.53	
Geographic location	25	Total population; county	*More favorable*	*/.89	*− .66/ − .64*
	26	Pop. change 1984–86		*/.87	*/[− .59/ − .56]*
	27	Pop. density		*/.91	
	28	Major university		*/85	
	29	Total population; comm.		*/.81	
	30	Pop. change 1984–86		*/.91	
	31	Pop. density		*/.70	
	32	Major university		*/.74	
PERCEIVED ABILITY			MORE ABILITY		
Perceived ability	33	Attitude item	*More ability*	.93/.94	*/1.00*
	34	Attitude item		− .21/ − .06	*/[*/1.00]*
	35	Attitude item		.29/.37	
PERCEIVED NEED			MORE NEED		
Economic satisfaction	36	With profitability	*More satisfied*	.01/.55	**/ − .61*
	37	With pesonal income	*(= lower need)*	1.00/1.00	*/[*/ − .53]*
Need for achievement	38	Attitude item	*Higher need*	.04/.17	**/.86*
	39	Attitude item		.40/.69	*/[*/.91]*
	40	Attitude item		− .09/.12	
	41	Attitude item		.78/.93	
PERCEIVED OPPORTUNITY			MORE OPPORTUNITY		
Perceived external obstacles	42	Recruiting	*More obstacles (= less opport.)*	− .50/ − .47	**/ − .54*
	43	Getting loans		.65/.71	*/[*/ − .30]*
	44	Labor market legislation		.54/.57	

TABLE 2 Explanatory Variables in Analysis of Growth Motivation

SECOND-ORDER FACTORS/ *First-Orders Factors*	Manifest Indicators	Higher Value Means . . . (SECOND-ORDER/ *First-Order*)	Weights/Loadings[a] for Indicators	*F-O Factors*
	45 Taxes		−.13/.00	
Perceived barriers to entry	46 Spin-off risk	*Higher barriers*	*/.49	*/.52
	47 Capital needed for start-up	*(=more opport.)*	*/.96	/[*/.43]
Perceived (market room for expansion)	48 Future profitabl. in industry	*More room*	.13/.27	*/.76 /[*/.91]
	49 Perc. exp. poss. with existing products		.33/.44	
	50 . . . with existing physical facilities		.13/.51	
	51 . . . with existing work force		.53/.69	
	52 Necessity of new prod. development		.60/.64	
GROWTH MOTIVATION			MORE MOTIVATION	
Cognitive attitude (expected effect of growth on . . .)	53 Manager's workload	*More positive*	*/.53	*/.83
	54 Manager's work tasks		*/.60	/[*/.82]
	55 Employee satisfaction		*/.70	
	56 Private finances		*/50	
	57 Ability to keep control		*/.59	
	58 Feeling of independence		*/.62	
	59 Crisis survival ability		*/.49	
	60 Product/service quality		*/.61	
Affective attitude	61 Moderate growth (25%)	*More positive*	*/.94	*/.77
	62 Substantial growth (100%)		*/.94	/[*/.77]
Growth aspirations (present size compared to "ideal" 5 years ahead)	63 As regards employees (log)	*Higher*	*/.91	*/.83 /[*/.83]
	64 As regards turnover (log)		*/.95	

Note: Weights and loadings for manifest variables are "frozen" after the first step and thus do not change when the model is revised. Weights/loadings for first-order factors in the revised model (Figure 4) are given within brackets below the corresponding figures for the original (Figure 3) model. While loadings are model parameters only for reflective factors, they can be used for interpretation also of formative factors.

[a]Loadings only for reflective factors.

*Denotes a left-out weight in such cases.

[b]Dummy variable. 1 = Yes; 0 = No.

Two analyses will be presented. In the first, the modeling criteria employed were the following:

1. Specify the model as in Figure 1 but with the exclusion of the "Actual Growth" variable (and causal relations to that variable).

2. Introduce direct effects of objective variables on Growth Motivation if doing so eliminates a residual correlation that is greater than ±0.10 and yields a path coefficient that is greater than ±0.10.[3]

These criteria were followed also in the second analysis. In addition, causal relations among the explanatory variables (but not suggested by Figure 1) were introduced if:

3. the relation is theoretically plausible and
4. the introduction of such a relation eliminates a residual correlation that is greater than ±0.10 and yields a path coefficient that is greater than ±0.10.

The variables are scored so that positive coefficients are expected except for the effects of Age/Maturity, Firm Size, Economic Satisfaction, and Perceived External Obstacles.

Figure 3 depicts the results of the first analysis. Some additional information from this and the following analysis can be found in Tables 2 and 3.

It can be concluded first that the model gains support insofar as a substantial part of the variation in Growth Motivation is explained (33%). Why more of the variation could not be explained is a question that will be looked at later.

The results are also largely in line with the assumption that the effects of objective variables are mediated by the perception variables. The latter are not superfluous, and only for Need did a direct effect have to be introduced to improve model fit. It should be noted that the objective variables, as measured here, explain a very modest part of the variations in perceptions.

As with Actual Growth, Need appears to be the central issue. Although the Opportunity factors also have a substantial effect on Growth Motivation, the total effect of the Need factors is much greater.

A weak part of the model is that Perceived Ability has but a very small positive effect on Growth Motivation. In part this can be explained by the small number of indicators, and presumably by their quality. In fact, the resulting factor is almost identical to one of its manifest indicators, viz. the degree of (dis)agreement with the statement "How a firm develops is actually determined mainly by factors which the manager cannot control." It should be noted, though, that the presumed weakness of the Perceived Ability measure does not necessitate the inclusion of a direct effect of Ability on Growth Motivation.

As to first-order factors, Entrepreneurial Experience appears to be relatively less important for Growth Motivation than for Actual Growth. This suggests that the lion's share of the effect of such experience on Actual Growth is direct rather than mediated by Growth Motivation. As the total effect of Education on Growth Motivation is also very small, this may hold true for the effect of Ability in general.

All three first-order Need factors appear to be relevant. As was the case with Actual Growth, Age/Maturity has the strongest influence.

For objective Opportunity, Geographic Dispersion appears most important. High values on Geographic Dispersion are much more common for firms in the manufacturing subsamples. According to the results, what was believed to be a favorable Geographic Location has a *negative* influence on Perceived Opportunity and hence on Growth Motivation. While this is not impossible, this particular result should be interpreted with caution. The various indicators of Opportunity are intercorrelated in a complex manner, and firms from different

[3]It is logically impossible for objective variables to influence motivation unless they are perceived. Because measures of perceptions are unlikely to cover all perceived aspects of the objective variables, direct effects can turn up in empirical estimation.

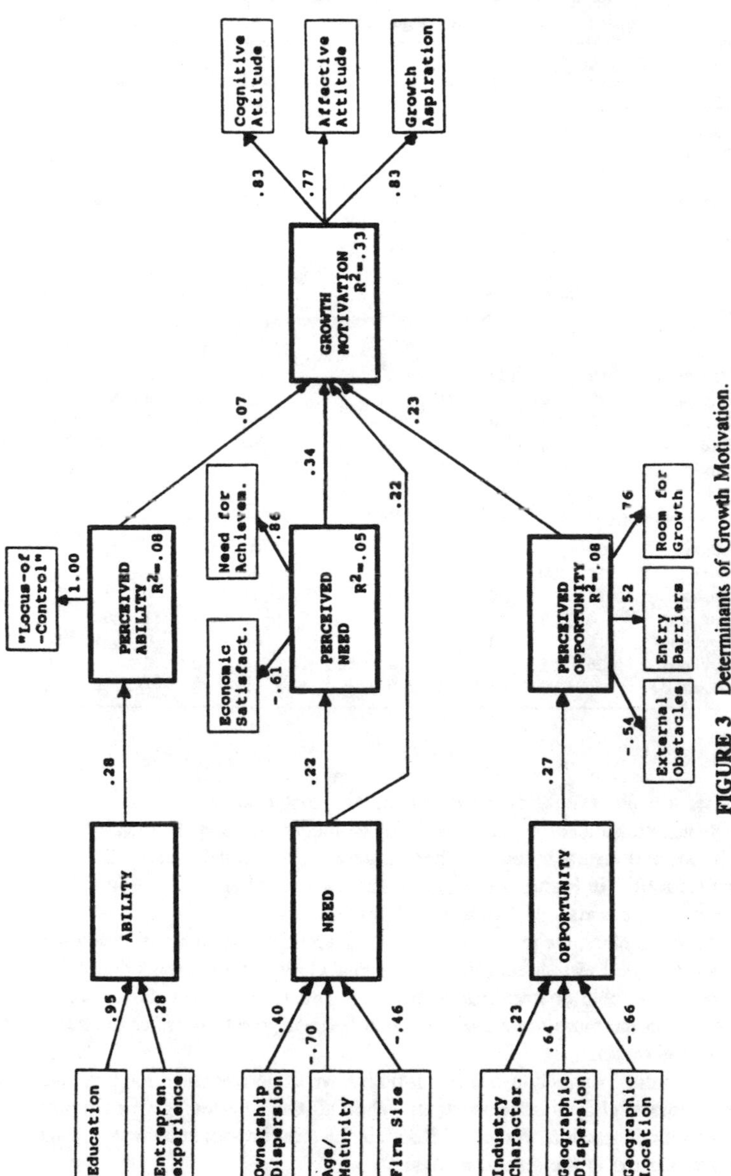

FIGURE 3 Determinants of Growth Motivation.

TABLE 3 Additional Information from the Analyses of Growth Motivation

	Correlation of Factors (× 100)													
	Original Model (Figure 3)							Revised Model (Figure 4)						
	1	2	3	4	5	6	7	1	2	3	4	5	6	7
1. Ability	100							100						
2. Need	17	100						20	100					
3. Opportunity	13	9	100					17	12	100				
4. Perc. abil.	28	5	15	100				29	6	17	100			
5. Perc. need	22	22	25	9	100			23	24	27	10	100		
6. Perc. opp.	29	10	27	16	28	100		35	13	33	23	28	100	
7. Growth mot.	21	33	17	15	46	36	100	21	33	19	15	46	36	100
Total (direct + indirect) effects (× 100)														
1. Ability	100							100						
2. Need	0	100						0	100					
3. Opportunity	0	0	100					0	0	100				
4. Perc. abil.	28	0	0	100				29	0	0	100			
5. Perc. need	0	22	0	0	100			16	18	22	0	100		
6. Perc. opp.	0	0	27	0	0	100		30	4	28	0	20	100	
7. Growth mot.	2	30	6	7	34	23	100	13	29	13	5	38	21	100
Residual correlations (× 100)														
1. Ability	100							100						
2. Need	17	100						20	100					
3. Opportunity	13	9	100					17	12	100				
4. Perc. abil.	0	1	11	92				0	1	12	92			
5. Perc. need	18	0	23	2	95			0	0	0	1	86		
6. Perc. opp.	26	8	0	5	19	92		0	0	0	9	0	76	
7. Growth mot.	1	0	−1	0	0	0	67	0	0	−1	0	0	0	69

industries are not evenly distributed over geographic areas. This adds to uncertainty of estimation, and the coefficient is likely to be highly unstable. Compared to manifest-level correlations and results based on other (more detailed) model specifications (see Davidsson 1989a) the results in Figure 3 exaggerate the negative influence of Geographic Location and understate the importance of Industry Characteristics.

Taken together, the results in Figures 2 and 3 imply that industry structure and dynamics have direct as well as indirect effects on Actual Growth. This means that firms in industries with more favorable characteristics in this regard tend to grow faster partly because the managers become more motivated, but also because growth is easier to attain regardless of level of motivation.

Economic Satisfaction and *n*Ach both have some relevance for Perceived Need. The latter appears slightly more important. While all three Perceived Opportunity factors load in the expected direction, Perceived Room is the most important indicator. This will be even more accentuated in the second analysis.

Finally, the three sub-aspects of Growth Motivation all have fairly high and essentially equal loadings.

Figure 4 displays the second analysis. Four more causal relations have been added:

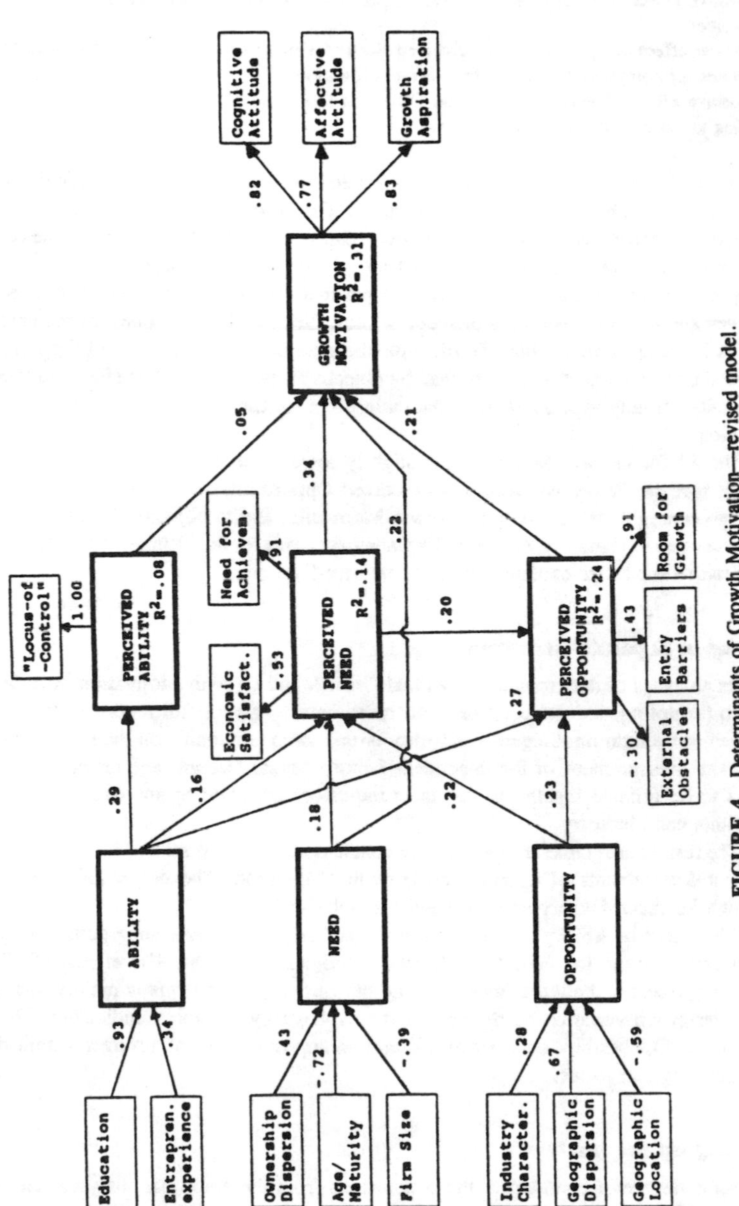

FIGURE 4 Determinants of Growth Motivation—revised model.

1. A positive effect of Ability on Perceived Need. This can be explained by people with more education and experience having higher aspirations than others (other things being equal).
2. A positive effect of Ability on Perceived Opportunity. Ability should facilitate detection of opportunities.
3. A positive effect of Opportunity on Perceived Need. An environment with more opportunity affects the bases for comparison and can thus elevate aspirations.
4. A positive effect of Perceived Need on Perceived Opportunity. Perceived Need evokes search, leading to the detection of opportunities.

Substantial coefficients for these relations emerge while the relations included already in the previous analysis are not much affected. The results suggest a pattern of relations that is more intricate than proposed by Figure 1. Substantial correlations among the objective variables also emerge, but these have not been given causal interpretations.

Some features of the revised model are particularly interesting. First, Perceived Need to an even greater extent becomes the central issue. Second, the R^2 values for the perception variables become more sizable. Third, with the measures used, Perceived Opportunity is influenced more by objective Ability than by objective Opportunity. The effect via Perceived Opportunity actually appears as to be the main route for the influence of Ability on Growth Motivation.

The R^2 for Growth Motivation is slightly lower with this model specification. The reason is that the Perceived Need and Perceived Opportunity factors are now estimated to act as "good neighbors" not only to Growth Motivation and to objective Need/Opportunity, but also to other explanatory variables. Explanatory power for the ultimate dependent variable is thus traded for better explanation of the intermediate ones.

Analyses of Separate Industries

Separate analyses of determinants of Actual Growth and Growth Motivation have been run for each (sampling) industry. There is no room here to give a full report on these, but as they shed some light on the generalizability issue, some comments on the results should be made. The measurement of the dependent factors Actual Growth and Growth Motivation appears to be reliable insofar as that their indicators correlate in approximately the same way within each industry.

The results are stable as concerns the conclusion that Need-related factors are the most important determinants of Growth and Growth Motivation. The degree of consistency is very high for Age/Maturity and for Need for Achievement.

The effect of Ability on Actual Growth is fairly stable over subgroups whereas less consistency is found for the Ability-Growth Motivation relation. The effects of objective Opportunity factors show the lowest degree of consistency, but this is mainly due to very small inter-group variation on the part of the explanatory variables' indicators. The effect of Perceived Opportunity on Growth Motivation appears to be far stronger within the two manufacturing categories.

Summing up the Analyses

With some degree of confidence, the conclusions from the empirical analyses can be summarized as follows:

- Objective measures of Ability, Need, and Opportunity can explain a substantial share of the variation in Actual (historical) Growth. Need appears to be relatively more important than the other two.

- Objective and perception-based measures of Ability, Need, and Opportunity can explain a substantial share of the variation in Growth Motivation. Again, Need-related factors appear more important than Ability and Opportunity.
- Besides the motivation-mediated effects, direct effects of objective variables on Actual Growth can be traced.
- Subjective perceptions contain growth-relevant information that is not captured by objective measures. That is, subjective factors have their own objective effects.
- Different parts of the results show varying degrees of consistency over subsamples. Especially for Need and Perceived Need the degree of consistency is impressive.
- While the proposed model (Figure 1) gains support, the analyses also suggest some additional relations that are theoretically reasonable. Whether or not these relations should be included as generally valid is a question that requires further investigation to be answered.

DISCUSSION

An Overall Interpretation of the Results

In all, the analyses in this article support the assumptions that: (1) perceptions of ability, need, and opportunity influence growth motivation; (2) objective ability, need, and opportunity can only in part explain differences in the perception of these three factors; and (3) truly direct effects of these three objective factors on growth may exist alongside the motivation mediated effects.

In particular, the results support the idea that the individual matters. The results for age of the firm and of the individual, number of years as CEO, need for Achievement, and degree of economic satisfaction, i.e., the Need factors included in the study, suggest that the core of the matter is the subjectively perceived situation and its relation to personal goals.

To many, retaining the status quo is satisfactory. Growth (and possibly other aspects of continued entrepreneurship) is then perceived as no longer serving, or even as threatening, important personal goals. This group—probably the majority of all small firm owner-managers—thus is relatively conservative in their business attitudes and behavior. It must be emphasized that their being satisfied with maintaining the status quo does not mean that easy living is characteristic for them. What it means is that neither external nor internal pressures necessitate anything more than working hard on what they are currently doing.

For others the expected (monetary and nonmonetary) gains of continued entrepreneurship exceed the expected costs, and the choices they make therefore favor growth. This may be the result of higher initial aspirations or a tendency to shift them upwards over time, which increases the subjective (and possibly objective, because of search) value of the gain side.

Some do not feel that they can choose freely. This is more common when the firm is young and small and thus does not ensure a satisfactory standard of living. Competitive pressure may also force towards continued development because it makes the status quo a non-feasible alternative.

These results have implications, e.g., for the design of policy measures directed at the small firm sector. General measures such as adjustments of taxes and other legislation probably have a small effect on most firms, while the effect on those who have the right motivation can be assumed to be quite strong. It is imperative that general measures are so designed that only those who react in the intended way are rewarded. If also those who are relatively satisfied with the status quo get the benefits, reactions that run counter to the intentions of the policy are not unlikely.

The heterogeneity within the small firm sector further suggests that selective measures often are preferable. The growth potential for individual firms varies greatly among industries. This is a question of structure and largely not contingent on whether or not the industry as a whole is growing. For industries with a high degree of natural fragmentation it might be wiser to support the start-up of new firms rather than growth of existing firms, whereas the opposite is true for other industries. Besides industry, the age of the firm can serve as an objective criterion for selection.

A large part of the heterogeneity within the small firm sector is due to subjective differences. To distribute support selectively to groups defined by subjective criteria is difficult, at least when it is not done at a very local level. Resources such as consulting, education, and financial support can, however, be supplied for those who select themselves as "growth-aspirants." It is then important that such services are designed and informed in a way that appeals to entrepreneurial people.

Finally, it is of course possible to try to affect attitudes directly. Information as such can be effective to the extent that negative expectations concerning the consequences of growth are in fact unjustified. Persuasive attempts that require that more growth-oriented ideals are established could be effective if directed at younger firms and younger managers. These have a stronger objective need for expansion, and their values, attitudes, and "company cultures" are less likely to be firmly held. Trying to influence individuals who have since long defined and lived up to a role as the manager of one particular, stable firm is much less likely to have any behavioral effects.

It should be remembered that the results and interpretations presented here are based on a Swedish sample. Judging from the literature at large there may exist a cultural difference between Scandinavian (or European) and North American business founders. The impression is that—on the average—the latter have more formal education and higher aspirations for growth and continued development from start-up on. However, the American results are frequently based on mail surveys with response rates around 30 percent. While the cultural difference may well be a real one, it is not unlikely that it is exaggerated by respondents' self-selection.

Why Was Not More of the Variation Explained?

Considering their number (on the manifest level), one could have expected the explanatory variables to account for more of the variation in Growth Motivation and Actual Growth. Now, why did the larger share of the variation remain unexplained?

As concerns Actual Growth, the model itself provides an obvious explanation: no measure of Growth Motivation was included. While this explanation is a plausible one, the fact that R^2 for Growth Motivation was not that much higher calls for other answers.

One of these is the fact that the coefficients represent average effects. The true effect for each individual or firm deviates from this effect, leaving variation unexplained. Other reasons are that linear relations have been assumed and that interaction effects were not examined.

Measurement error is likely to be a major cause of deflation of the empirically estimated relations. On the latent variable level, measurement error means that the indicators used do not adequately capture the theoretical variable we are after. All the manifest indicators used in this study are of the crude-but-useful kind.

At the manifest level, measurement error arises as a result of response style differences and because the questions do not have exactly the same meaning to each respondent. This problem would not be solved entirely by including more, or more relevant, indicators.

The problems mentioned above apply also to the dependent measures. In addition, the reason why a firm has not grown, although growth would have been predicted from measures of explanatory variables, may be that the manager has successfully started an additional firm or increased profitability and probability of survival by means of product and process innovations.

It is thus conceivable that growth is a too narrowly defined dependent variable. Continued entrepreneurship is perhaps best thought of as an array of alternative behaviors that have common underlying explanations. In future studies, therefore, the use of a composite dependent variable that captures several aspects of entrepreneurship, e.g., start-up of additional ventures, innovativeness, and growth, would be recommendable. In terms of the model in Figure 1, this means replacing "Growth Motivation" by "Entrepreneurial Motivation" and "Actual Growth" by "Observed Entrepreneurship," and selecting indicators accordingly. In fact, using such a model for study design makes it possible to capture all major aspects of what practitioners and scholars, according to Gartner's (1990) results, conceive of as "entrepreneurship."

The Contribution of this Study

The contribution of this study lies not primarily in the specific results obtained. That growth might depend on opportunity, need, and ability, and that individual differences matter are, after all, not very provocative ideas. So it is not very surprising that this turned out to be the case, although previous studies are of little help in judging the relative strength of the relationships.

The contribution lies rather in the way the problem was dealt with. In this study, more general concepts were singled out from the multitude of variables used in or suggested by previous studies. These more general concepts were then related in a theoretical model. Data were gathered directly from a representative sample of small firm owner-managers as well as from secondary sources. This, and the application of a suitable analysis method, made it possible to estimate empirically rather than judge subjectively the model parameters. This is a major advantage compared with purely theoretical and so called "qualitative" approaches.

The alternative of performing a vast number of separate analyses at the manifest level in an atheoretical way inevitably leads to our getting lost in details and losing track of the important overriding structure. Moreover, it is well established that relations at the manifest level are heavily influenced by minor alterations, e.g., in the specific wording of survey questions. Such problems are at least partly overcome when each measured variable is interpreted but as an indicator of a more general concept.

Therefore, the most important advantage compared with more conventional quantitative approaches is that, without having to make too many negligibility assumptions at the outset, it was possible to arrive at fairly simple, yet meaningful, results. While the model suggested here is by no means *the* model for entrepreneurship studies, it is this author's opinion that it is imperative to the development of entrepreneurship research that models and concepts *such as* these be used. When studying a complex real-world phenomenon such as entrepreneurship, including a large number of variables may be necessary, but the findings are likely to be more meaningful if the analyses are made at a higher level of abstraction.

REFERENCES

Begley, T. P., and Boyd, D. P. 1987. Psychological characteristics associated with performance in entrepreneurial firms and smaller businesses. *Journal of Business Venturing* 2:79–93.

Bellu, R. R. 1987. A behavioral explanation of the differential economic development of the center-north and mezzogiorno of Italy. Working Paper, Kingsborough College of the City University of New York.

Borland, C. 1974. Locus of control, need for achievement, and entrepreneurship, unpublished doctoral dissertation, University of Texas.

Boswell, J. 1972. *The Rise and Decline of Small Firms*. London: Allen and Unwin.

Brandstätter, H. 1988. Becoming an entrepreneur: a question of personality structure? In P. Vanden Abeele, ed., *Psychology in Micro and Macro Economics*. Leuven: IAREP.

Brockhaus, R.H. Sr. 1982. The psychology of the entrepreneur. In C.A. Kent, D.L. Sexton, and K.H. Vesper, eds., *Encyclopedia of Entrepreneurship*. Englewood Cliffs, NJ: Prentice-Hall, pp. 39–57.

Bruno A.V., and Tyebjee, T.T. 1982. The environment for entrepreneurship. In C.A. Kent, D.L. Sexton, and K.H. Vesper, eds., *Encyclopedia of Entrepreneurship*, Englewood Cliffs, NJ: Prentice-Hall, pp. 288–316.

Collins, O., Moore, D. and Unwalla, D.B. 1964. *The Enterprising Man*. East Lansing: Michigan State University.

Cooper, A.C. 1982. The entrepreneurship small business interface. In C.A. Kent, D.L. Sexton, and K.H. Vesper, eds., *Encyclopedia of Entrepreneurship*. Englewood Cliffs, NJ: Prentice-Hall, pp. 39–57.

Cooper, A.C., and Bruno, A.V. 1977. Success among high-technology firms, *Business Horizons*, 20:16–22.

Cooper, A.C., Dunkelberg, W.C., and Woo, C.Y. 1986. Optimists and pessimists: 2994 entrepreneurs and their perceived chances for success. In *Frontiers of Entrepreneurship Research 1986*. Wellesley, MA: Babson College.

Davidsson, P. 1987. Small business managers' willingness to pursue growth: the role of beliefs about outcomes of growth for attitudes towards growth and growth aspirations. In P. Davidsson, ed., *Growth Willingness in Small Firms: Entrepreneurship and After?* Stockholm: EFI/Stockholm School of Economics (Research Report).

Davidsson, P. 1989a. *Continued Entrepreneurship and Small Firm Growth*. Doctoral dissertation, Stockholm: EFI/Stockholm School of Economics.

Davidsson, P. 1989b. Entrepreneurship and after? A study of growth willingness in small firms. *Journal of Business Venturing* 4:211–226.

Deeks, J. 1976. *The Small Firm Owner-Manager: Entrepreneurial Behavior and Management Practice*. New York: Praeger.

Donckels, R., Bragard, L., Dupont, B., Michel, P. and Demarche, M.P. 1987. New entrepreneurship in Belgium. Paper presented at the Workshop on Recent Research on Entrepreneurship in Europe. Brussels: EIASM, May 14–15,1987.

Doutriaux, J. 1984. Evolution of the characteristics of (high-tech) entrepreneurial firms. In *Frontiers of Entrepreneurship Research 1984*. Wellesley, MA: Babson College.

Doutriaux, J. 1987. Growth pattern of academic entrepreneurial firms. *Journal of Business Venturing* 2:285–297.

Dunkelberg, W.C., Cooper, A.C., Woo, C.Y., and Dennis, Jr., W.J. 1987. New firm growth and performance. In *Frontiers of Entrepreneurship Research 1987*. Wellesley, MA: Babson College.

Egge, K.A. 1987. Expectations vs. reality among founders of recent start-ups. In *Frontiers of Entrepreneurship Research 1987*. Wellesley, MA: Babson College.

Evans, D.S. 1987. Test of alternative theories of firm growth. *Journal of Political Economy* 95:657–674.

Finison, L.J. 1976. The application of McClelland's national development to recent data. *Journal of Social Psychology* 98:55–59.

Fishbein, M., and Ajzen, I. 1975. *Belief, Attitude, Intention, and Behavior: an Introduction to Theory and Research*. New York: Addison-Wesley.

Fornell, C. 1987. A second generation of multivariate analysis: classification of methods and implications for marketing research. In M. Houston, ed., *The Review of Marketing 1987*, American Marketing Association.

Fornell, C., and Bookstein, F.L. 1982. Two structural equation models: LISREL and PLS applied to consumer exit-voice theory. *Journal of Marketing Research* 19:440–452.

Gartner, W.B. 1990. What are we talking about when we talk about entrepreneurship? *Journal of Business Venturing* 5:15–28.

Gasse, Y. 1982. Elaborations on the psychology of the entrepreneur. In C.A. Kent, D.L. Sexton, and K.H. Vespers, eds., *Encyclopedia of Entrepreneurship*. Englewood Cliffs, NJ: Prentice-Hall, pp. 57–61.

Hoad, W.M., and Rosko, P. 1964, *Management Factors Contributing to the Success or Failure of New Small Manufacturers*. Ann Arbor, MI: University of Michigan.

Hornaday, J.A. 1982. Research about living entrepreneurs. In C.A. Kent, D.L. Sexton, and K.H. Vesper, eds., *Encyclopedia of Entrepreneurship*. Englewood Cliffs, NJ: Prentice-Hall, pp. 57–61.

Hornaday, J.A., and Aboud, J. 1971. Characteristics of successful entrepreneurs. *Personnel Psychology* 24:141–153.

Hull, D.L., Bosley, J.J., and Udell, G.G. 1980. Renewing the hunt for the Heffalump: identifying potential entrepreneurs by personality characteristics. *Journal of Small Business Management* 18:11–18.

Katona, G. 1975. *Psychological Economics*. New York: Elsevier.

Kayser, G. 1987. Growth problems of young firms. Paper presented at the Workshop on Recent Research on Entrepreneurship in Europe, EIASM, Brussels, May 14–15, 1987.

Keeble, D., Potter, J., and Storey, D.J. 1990. Cross national comparisons of the role of SMEs in regional economic growth in the European community, Working Paper, University of Cambridge (UK) and University of Warwick.

Kets de Vries, M.F.R. 1977. The entrepreneurial personality: a person at the cross-roads. *Journal of Management Studies* 14:34–57.

Kets de Vries, M.F.R. 1985. The dark side of entrepreneurship. *Harvard Business Review* 63:160–167.

Khan, A.M. 1986. Entrepreneur characteristics and the prediction of new venture success. *Omega* 14:365–372.

Kirzner, I.M. 1979. *Perception, Opportunity, and Profit*, Chicago: University of Chicago Press.

Kirzner, I.M. 1982. The theory of entrepreneurship in economic growth. In C.A. Kent, D.L. Sexton, and K.H. Vesper, eds., *Encyclopedia of Entrepreneurship*. Englewood Cliffs, NJ: Prentice-Hall, pp. 272–276.

Kirzner, I.M. 1983. Entrepreneurs and the entrepreneurial function: a commentary. In J. Ronen, ed., *Entrepreneurship*. Lexington, MA: Lexington Books, D.C. Heath, pp. 281–290.

Kumar, M.S. 1984. *Growth, Acquisition, and Investment*. Occasional Paper 56. Department of Applied Economics, Cambridge, UK: University of Cambridge.

Lamont, L. 1972. What entrepreneurs learn from experience. *Journal of Small Business* 10:254–260.

Lohmöller, J.-B. 1984. *LVPLS 1.6 Program Manual*. Forschungsbericht 81.04, Fachbereich Pädagogik, Munich: Hochschule der Bundeswehr.

Lorrain, J., and Dussault, L. 1988. Relation between psychological characteristics, administrative behaviors and success of founder-entrepreneurs at the start-up stage. In *Frontiers of Entrepreneurship Research 1988*. Wellesley, MA: Babson College.

March, J.G., and Sevón, G. 1988. Behavioral perspectives on theories of the firm. In W.F. van Raaij, G.M. van Veldhoven, and K.-E. Wärneryd, eds., *Handbook of Economic Psychology*. Dordrecht, the Netherlands: Kluwer, pp. 368–402.

Mayer, C.S., and Goldstein, S. 1964. Manual workers as small businessmen. In A.B. Shostak and W. Gomberg, eds., *Blue Collar World*. Englewood Cliffs, NJ: Prentice-Hall.

McClelland, D.C. 1961. *The Achieving Society*. Princeton, NJ: Van Nostrand.

McClelland, D.C. 1965. In Achievement and entrepreneurship: a longitudinal study, *Journal of Personality and Social Psychology* 1:389–392.

McClelland, D.C. 1966. That urge to achieve (reprint: 1975). In C.M. Baumback and J.R. Mancuso, eds., *Entrepreneurship and Venture Management*. Englewood Cliffs, NJ: Prentice-Hall, pp. 3–10.

McClelland, D.C., and Winter, D.G. 1969. *Motivating Economic Achievement*. New York: The Free Press.

Miron, D., and McClelland, D.C. 1979. The impact of achievement motivation training on small business. *California Management Review* 21:13–28.

Murray, H.A. 1938. *Explorations in Personality*. New York: Oxford University Press.

Panday, J., and Tewary, N.B. 1979. Locus of control and achievement values of entrepreneurs. *Journal of Occupational Psychology* 52:107–111.

Perry, C., Macarthur, R., Meredith, G., and Cunnington, B. 1986. Need for Achievement and Locus of Control of Australian Small Business Owner-Managers and Super-Entrepreneurs. *International Small Business Journal* 4:55–64.

Pickle, H.B. 1964. *Personality and Success: An Evaluation of Personal Characteristics of Successful Small Business Managers*, Washington D.C: Small Business Administration.

Pieters, R.G.M. 1988. Attitude-behavior relationships. In W.F. van Raaij, G.M. van Veldhoven, and K.-E. Wärneryd, eds., *Handbook of Economic Psychology*. Dordrecht, the Netherlands: Kluwer, pp. 144–204.

Pieters, R.G.M. 1989. *Attitudes and Behavior in a Source-Separation Program: A Garbology Approach*. Doctoral dissertation, Rotterdam: Erasmus University.

Plaschka, G. 1987. Characteristics of successful and unsuccessful entrepreneurs. A theoretically guided empirical investigation of personrelated and microsocial factors. Paper presented at the Workshop on Recent Research on Entrepreneurship in Europe, EIASM, Brussels, May 14–15, 1987.

Reynolds, P.D. 1986. Organizations: predicting contributions and survival. In *Frontiers of Entrepreneurship Research 1986*. Wellesley, MA: Babson College.

Reynolds, P.D., and Maki, W.R. 1990. *Business Volatility and Economic Growth*. Research Report. Small Business Administration.

Roberts, E.B. 1972. Influences upon performance of new technical enterprises. In A.C. Cooper and J.L. Komvies, eds., *Technical Entrepreneurship: a Symposium*. Milwaukee: Center for Venture Management.

Rotter, J.B. 1966. Generalized expectancies for internal versus external control of reinforcement. *Psychological Monographs: General and Applied* 80:609.

Roure, J.B., and Maidique, M.A. 1986. Linking prefunding factors and high-technology venture success: an exploratory study. *Journal of Business Venturing* 1:295–306.

Sandburg, W.R., and Hofer, C.W. 1987. Improving new venture performance: the role of strategy, industry structure, and the entrepreneur. *Journal of Business Venturing* 2:5–28.

Scheinberg, S., and MacMillan, I.C. 1988. An 11 country study of motivations to start a business. In *Frontiers of Entrepreneurship Research 1988*. Wellesley, MA: Babson College.

Shackle, G.L.S. 1979. Imagination, formalism, and choice. In M.R. Rizzo, ed., *Time, Uncertainty, and Disequilibrium. Exploration of Austrian Themes*. Toronto: Lexington Books.

Simyar, F., Doutriaux, J., and Argheyd, K. 1988. Characteristics of founders and the growth of entrepreneurial high-tech Canadian manufacturing firms. Paper presented at the Conference of Small High-Tech Firms in Small Countries. EIASM, Brussels, June 27–29, 1988.

Smith, N.R. 1967. *The Entrepreneur and his Firm: the Relationship between Type of Man and Type of Company*. East Lansing: Michigan State University.

Stuart, R.W., and Abetti, P.A. 1986. Field study of start-up ventures part II: predicting initial success. In *Frontiers of Entrepreneurship Research 1986*. Wellesley, MA: Babson College.

Utterback, J.M., and Reitberger, G. 1982. *Technology and Industrial Innovation in Sweden: A Study of New Technology Based Firms*. Stockholm: Center for Policy Alternatives/Styrelsen för teknisk utveckling.

Vroom, V.H. 1964. *Work and Motivation*. New York: John Wiley.

Wärneryd, K.-E. 1988. The psychology of innovative entrepreneurship. In W.F. van Raaij, G.M. van Veldhoven, and K.-E. Wärneryd, eds., *Handbook of Economic Psychology*. Dordrecht, the Netherlands: Kluwer, pp. 404–447.

Wold, H. 1982. Models for knowledge. In J. Gani, ed., *The Making of Statisticians*, New York: Springer-Verlag, pp. 189–212.

Wold, H. 1986. Introduction to the second generation of multivariate analysis. Preliminary manuscript for: *Theoretical Empericism: A General Rationale for Scientific Model-Building*. Washington and New York: Paragon House Publishers.

[26]

Small Business and Job Creation: Dissecting the Myth and Reassessing the Facts

Steven J. Davis
John Haltiwanger
Scott Schuh

Abstract. This paper investigates how job creation and destruction behavior varies by employer size in the U.S. manufacturing sector during the period 1972 to 1988. The paper also evaluates the empirical basis for conventional claims about the job-creating prowess of small businesses. The chief findings and conclusions fall into five categories:

(1) Conventional wisdom about the job-creating prowess of small businesses rests on misleading interpretations of the data.
(2) Many previous studies of the job creation process rely upon data that are not suitable for drawing inferences about the relationship between employer size and job creation.
(3) Large plants and firms account for most newly-created and newly-destroyed manufacturing jobs.
(4) Survival rates for new and existing manufacturing jobs increase sharply with employer size.
(5) Smaller manufacturing firms and plants exhibit sharply higher *gross* rates of job creation but not higher *net* rates.

1. Introduction

Few ideas about the U.S. economy reap greater homage in public discourse than the belief that small businesses are the fountainhead of job creation. Claims about the job-creating prowess of small business appear with remarkable regularity in a wide range of public pronouncements, including speeches by prominent politicians, newspaper columns by leading opinon makers, statements from the U.S. Small Business Administration, and assessments by well-known analysts like David Birch. Box 1 contains a sampling of these claims.[1] As the quotations in the box illustrate, claims about small business's ability to generate jobs are frequently presented as justification for tax incentives, regulatory policies and other government programs that favor the small business sector.

But it is not only the public discourse that motivates our interest in the relationship between employer size and job creation. Previous academic research convincingly establishes strong connections between employer size and important economic outcomes like the level and inequality of wages, the incidence of fringe benefits, workforce quality, the pace of technological innovation, and the likelihood of unionization.[2] These findings prompt us to ask how job creation and destruction behavior varies by employer size. In this paper, we address that question for for the U.S. manufacturing sector.

We also evaluate the empirical basis for conventional claims about the job-creating prowess of small businesses. In this regard, we develop two sets of conclusions:

(1) *The conventional wisdom about the job-creating prowess of small businesses rests on misleading interpretations of the data.* One common error entails the use of changes in the size distribution of employment to draw inferences about the relationship between job creation and employer size. A second problem – the regression fallacy – leads to overly favorable assessements of small

Final version accepted on February 3, 1995

Steven J. Davis
University of Chicago
National Bureau of Economic Research

John Haltiwanger
University of Maryland
National Bureau of Economic Research

and

Scott Schuh
Federal Reserve Board

Small Business Economics 8: 297–315, 1996.

BOX 1
Small business and job creation: Reciting the conventional wisdom

From 1970 to 1980 small businesses accounted for most of the 20 million new jobs generated in the United States.
Leonard Silk, *New York Times*, April 9, 1986

Little companies currently employ 53% of the total U.S. work force, and during the past decade created virtually all net new jobs.
Adam Zagorin, *Time*, July 12, 1993

Small firms created virtually all new jobs between 1988 and 1991.
David Birch, Cognetics Inc. press release, 1993

As always, the key [to job creation] is to spur hiring by new companies, the small businesses of fewer than 500 workers that accounted for fully two-thirds of job creation in the 1980s.
Stephen Roach, *New York Times*, March 14, 1993

The term, "Great American Job Machine," is appropriately applied to American small business.
U.S. Small Business Administration, *State of Small Business Report*, 1988, p. 35.

Moreover, government regulation tends to be especially burdensome to small business, which created most of the jobs in the 1980s.
Henry F. Meyers, *Wall Street Journal* ("The Outlook" column), March 8, 1993

Small businesses have become the superstars of job creation, producing up to 80 percent of new jobs in recent years. . . . Considering the success of small businesses in today's service sector and their willingness to take on and retain new employees, it would be innovative and economically sound for the Clinton Administration and Congress to give business a tax credit for hiring additional people.
Muriel Siebert, *New York Times*, January 6, 1992

The large increase in the effective tax rate on many small firms is likely to retard the economy's recovery momentum because small firms account for practically all the job creation in the U.S. economy.
David Hale, *Wall Street Jounal*, July 30, 1993

Because small business has created such a high percentage of all the new jobs in our nation over the last 10 or 15 years, our plan includes the boldest targeted incentives for small business in history. We propose a permanent investment tax credit for the small firms in this country, . . .
President Bill Clinton, 1993 State of the Union Address

We agree with the President that we have to put more people to work, but remember this: 80 to 85 percent of the new jobs in this country are created by small business. So the climate for starting and expanding businesses must be enhanced with tax incentives and deregulation, rather than imposing higher taxes and more governmental mandates.
Representative Robert Michel, House Minority Leader, in the Republican Response to the 1993 State of the Union Address

What do Bill Clinton, George Bush and Bob Dole have in common? All have uttered one of the most enduring homilies in American political discourse: That small businesses create most of the nation's jobs. This old chestnut got a heavy workout recently as Washington wrangled over the $500 billion budget package. Clinton invoked it to defend an equipment-purchase tax break aimed mostly at small businesses; Republicans cited it while denouncing the packages's tax hike on upper-income earners.
Susan Dentzer, *U.S. News and World Report*, August 16, 1993

business job creation whenever measurement error or transitory employment movements are present in the data. Finally, a common confusion between net and gross job creation distorts the overall job creation picture and hides the enormous number of new jobs created by large employers.

(2) *The most widely cited studies of job creation rely upon unsuitable data*. We review previous research that documents severe data problems in the data base that underlies the most prominent studies of small business job creation. Our review leads us to question whether any useful information can be gleaned from these studies about the relationship between employer size and job creation.

Our analysis of job creation and destruction behavior in the manufacturing sector relies upon the Longitudinal Research Database (LRD) housed at the Center for Economic Studies in the U.S. Bureau of the Census. The LRD contains plant-level data at annual sampling intervals for the U.S. manufacturing sector from 1972 to 1988. Information in the LRD permits classification of employers by various characteristics, including plant and firm size. Among U.S. data sets that have been used to study job creation and destruction, the LRD contains the most detailed information on plant characteristics, the most careful treatment of the statistical sampling frame, and the best treatment of plant entry and exit. We exploit the LRD to deepen our understanding of job creation and destruction in the U.S. manufacturing sector and, by extension, the entire U.S. economy.[3]

The chief findings to emerge from our study of the U.S. manufacturing sector fall into three categories:

(1) *Large plants and firms account for most newly-created (and newly-destroyed) manufacturing jobs.* Plants that average at least 100 employees account for two-thirds of job creation over the 1972 to 1988 period. Firms with at least 500 employees account for more than one-half of job creation. These findings reflect the simple fact that large plants and firms account for the bulk of the manufacturing jobs base.

(2) *Survival rates for manufacturing jobs increase sharply with employer size.* The one-year job survival rate at the biggest firms is 92 percent, as compared to only 81 percent for the smallest firms. The one-year survival rate for newly-created jobs at the biggest firms is 76 percent, as compared to only 65 percent at the smallest firms. Similar patterns hold for large plants as compared to small plants, and for multi-unit firms as compared to single-unit firms. Hence, in terms of both new jobs and the typical existing job, larger employers offer greater job durability.

(3) *Smaller manufacturing firms and plants exhibit sharply higher* gross *job creation rates but not higher* net *creation rates.* The gross job creation rate averages 12.2 percent per year for firms with fewer than 100 employees, nearly double the rate for firms with 25,000 or more employees. In this sense, small businesses create a disproportionately large share of new jobs. In the same sense, however, smaller plants and firms destroy a disproportionately large share of existing jobs. The *net* job creation rate in the U.S. manufacturing sector exhibits no strong or systematic relationship to employer size.

The sections that follow explain how and why we arrived at these conclusions. The next two sections describe our measurement procedures. Subsequent sections present our results and central line of argument.

2. Measuring job creation and destruction

Although the concept of a job is easy to understand, measuring and interpreting job creation and destruction requires careful definitions. In this study, a job means an employment position filled by a worker. Our data do not distinguish among part-time, full-time and overtime employment positions; all count equally as a single job. We do not measure the number of vacancies (i.e., unfilled positions) at a point in time or the change in vacancies over time. Rather, we measure plant-level changes in the number of filled employment positions.

The basic observational unit underlying our job creation and destruction measures is the plant – a physical location where production takes place. In contrast to a plant, a company or firm is an economic and legal entity that encompasses one or more plants and, possibly, administrative offices specializing in nonproduction activities. While we provide tabulations broken down by plant and firm size, all job creation and destruction measures are cumulated from plant-level employment changes.

We calculate job creation and destruction from plant-level net employment changes over twelve-month intervals. If, for example, a plant expands by ten employees between March 1987 and March 1988, then according to our calculations the plant contributes ten jobs to the 1988 creation count. If another plant contracts by eight employees over the same time interval, it contributes eight jobs to the 1988 destruction count.

Since plants represent the observational units in the LRD, our calculations capture the effects of firms that shift employment between plants. By the same token, however, our calculations do not capture the effects of job shifts within plants. For example, if a plant replaces several secretaries with an equal number of computer programmers, no net change in plant-level employment occurs; hence, our calculations record no job creation or destruction associated with this event. Because of the point-in-time nature of LRD employment data, our calculations also do not record plant-level employment changes that are reversed within the sampling interval. For example, if a plant lays off some workers in July 1987 and recalls an equal number in September 1987, there is no net effect on the plant's employment change between March 1987 and March 1988; hence, no contribution to job creation and destruction would be recorded for this episode of layoff and recall. For both reasons – the failure to capture within-plant job shifts and the point-in-time nature of the employment data – our job creation and destruction measures understate the true magnitudes.

With these remarks as background, we supply the following definitions:

Definition 1: Gross job creation at time t equals employment gains summed over all plants that expand or start up between $t - 1$ and t.

Definition 2: Gross job destruction at time t equals employment losses summed over all plants that contract or shut down between $t - 1$ and t.

In line with these definitions, plants with unchanged employment contribute to neither job creation nor job destruction. We shall typically express job creation and destruction figures as rates by dividing through by a measure of the employment level.[4]

Definition 3: The net employment change at time t is the difference between employment at time t and employment at time $t - 1$.

A simple and important relationship links the concepts described by these three definitions: *The net employment growth rate equals the job creation rate minus the job destruction rate.* In other words, job creation and destruction figures decompose the net change in aggregate employment into a component associated with growing plants and a component associated with shrinking plants.

The job creation and destruction components of the net employment change provide insights into employment dynamics that are unavailable from traditional sources of information on employment trends. For example, suppose that aggregate employment grew 2 percent during the past year. That figure could be produced by a 4 percent rate of job creation and 2 percent rate of job destruction, or by a 22 percent rate of creation and a 20 percent rate of destruction. Important aspects of economic behavior and performance are likely to vary with rates of job creation and destruction. Higher rates of job creation and destruction mean larger numbers of workers compelled to shuffle between jobs and, most likely, a greater incidence of unemployment. For a given net growth rate, higher rates of job creation make it easier for displaced workers and labor market entrants to find employment, and higher rates of job destruction imply less job security for employed persons. Higher rates of job creation and destruction also imply greater heterogeneity in the behavior of employment growth across plants. Thus, job creation and destruction figures offer a window into the diversity of plant-level outcomes masked by aggregate employment statistics.

3. Measuring employer size

There are many related but distinct concepts of employer size. Our analysis considers four concepts: current plant size, average plant size, firm size, and ownership type. Current size equals the simple average of the plant's current employment and its employment twelve months earlier. In contrast, average plant size equals the weighted mean number of employees, computed over all annual observations on the plant during the 1972 to 1988 period. Firm size equals the number of manufacturing workers employed by the plant's parent firm in the preceding Census of Manufactures.[5] Finally, ownership type indicates whether the plant's parent firm operates one or multiple plants.

A few remarks help to clarify the usefulness, strengths and weaknesses of these alternative measures of employer size. Plant size is a natural metric for the scale of operations at a geographically distinct production unit. Since employment often fluctuates from year to year, because of demand variation and other factors, average plant size provides a better indication of the production unit's intended scale of operations. Hence, for most purposes, we prefer average size to current size.[6]

Firm size is superior to plant size as an indicator of the overall scale of operations carried out by the plant's parent firm. Firm size corresponds closely to the notion of business size that underlies most public discourse on job creation behavior. In addition, patterns of government regulation and business access to financial markets are tied more closely to firm size than to plant size. Smaller firms enjoy exemption from or weaker enforcement of many government regulations related to the environment, affirmative action, financial reporting, and occupational health and safety.[7] Larger firms enjoy greater access to certain forms of financial credit like equity and debt issues.[8]

Ownership type is a crude indicator of firm size. Its chief virtue lies in its widespread availability and easy use in government data on individual business establishments. Consequently, many other studies and government statistical publications report breakdowns of economic activity by ownership type.

4. Job creation and destruction rates by employer size

With these remarks as background, we now turn to the empirical evidence. Table I displays average net and gross job flow rates by employer size. The table reveals strong regularities in the relationship between employer size and gross job flow rates. Consider, first, the average rate of gross job creation. By all four measures, gross job creation rates decline monotonically with employer size. The job creation rate averages 16.5 percent of employment per year for firms with fewer than 20 employees, 9.3 percent for firms with 500–999 employees, and 6.3 percent for firms with 50,000 or more employees. Similar patterns prevail for the ownership-type indicator and both measures of plant size. Thus, small employers create new jobs at a much higher gross rate than large employers.

But gross job creation measures clearly reveal only part of the story. Table I also shows that the gross job destruction rate declines sharply with firm and plant size. It averages 18.8 percent of employment per year for firms with fewer than 20 employees, 9.8 percent for firms with 500–999 employees, and 8.0 percent for firms with 50,000 or more employees. Again, similar patterns prevail for the ownership-type indicator and plant size measures. Thus, small employers also destroy jobs at a much higher rate than large employers.

How does net job creation vary by employer size? On this score, the empirical evidence produces no strong pattern. Net job creation rates by firm size exhibit a ∩ shape: manufacturing firms with 100–499 employees show mild net contraction rates between 1972 and 1988, whereas smaller and larger firms show sharper contraction rates. Neither plant size measure evinces any strong relationship to net job creation rates, although the net contraction rate is substantially smaller for single-unit than multi-unit firms. In a nutshell, net job creation behavior in the U.S. manufacturing sector exhibits no strong or simple relationship to employer size.

How can we reconcile this empirical result with the widely held belief that small businesses account for a disproportionate fraction of new jobs? One might think that the answer lies in our focus on the manufacturing sector. Perhaps in the nonmanufacturing sectors of the economy, smaller firms exhibit higher net job creation rates than larger firms. But even if this were true, it is not the basis for the widespread belief about the job creation role of small business. Rather, that belief rests on fallacious and misleading interpretations of the data, as we explain in the next three sections.

5. The size distribution fallacy

Many claims about the job-creating prowess of small business appear to be based upon changes over time in the size distribution of employment. We review the calculation typically performed on the size distribution data and explain why the usual interpretation of this calculation leads to fallacious inferences about job creation.

The SBA typically defines small businesses as firms with fewer than 500 employees, although the

TABLE I
Rates of job creation and destruction by employer size, 1973–1988[a]

Size class	Gross job creation	Gross job destruction	Net job creation	Employment share
		I. *Average plant size*[b]		
0 to 19 employees	15.9	17.2	−1.3	4.4
20 to 49	12.6	13.8	−1.1	8.2
50 to 99	11.7	12.6	−0.9	10.1
100 to 249	10.0	11.5	−1.4	18.5
250 to 499	8.5	9.8	−1.3	16.6
500 to 999	7.5	8.5	−1.0	13.8
1000 to 2499	6.6	8.2	−1.6	12.5
2500 to 4999	6.5	8.2	−1.7	7.2
5000 or more	5.9	6.5	−0.6	8.8
		II. *Current plant size*[c]		
0 to 19 employees	18.7	23.3	−4.5	5.2
20 to 49	13.2	15.3	−2.1	8.6
50 to 99	12.2	13.5	−1.3	10.5
100 to 249	9.6	10.7	−1.1	18.5
250 to 499	7.7	8.7	−1.0	16.0
500 to 999	7.0	7.6	−0.6	13.5
1000 to 2499	6.3	7.3	−1.0	12.3
2500 to 4999	6.1	7.5	−1.3	7.0
5000 or more	5.4	5.6	−0.2	8.4
		III. *Firm size*[d]		
0 to 19 employees	16.5	18.8	−2.3	5.2
20 to 49	12.3	13.3	−1.0	7.0
50 to 99	11.5	11.9	−0.4	6.8
100 to 249	11.1	11.2	−0.1	9.1
250 to 499	9.8	9.9	−0.1	6.8
500 to 999	9.3	9.8	−0.4	6.2
1000 to 2499	8.8	9.5	−0.7	8.2
2500 to 4999	8.0	9.4	−1.4	7.1
5000 to 9999	7.8	9.1	−1.3	8.5
10000 to 24999	7.1	8.6	−1.5	13.6
25000 to 49999	6.5	8.1	−1.6	9.2
50000 or more	6.3	8.0	−1.6	12.4
Ownership type	**Gross job creation**	**Gross job destruction**	**Net job creation**	**Employment share**
		IV. *Ownerhsip type of parent firm*		
Single-unit	12.7	12.9	−0.2	22.3
Multi-unit	8.1	9.4	−1.3	77.7

[a] Job creation and destruction rates are defined in section 2 of the text. Table entries for the creation and destruction rates and the employment shares are means of annual values for the period 1973 to 1988.
[b] Equal to the weighted mean number of employees, computed over all annual observations on the plant during the period 1972 to 1988.
[c] Equal to the simple mean of the plant's current employment and its employment twelve months earlier.
[d] Equal to the number of manufacturing workers employed by the plant's parent firm in the preceding Census of Manufactures. Census years are 1972, 1977, 1982 and 1987.

precise cutoff is not important to the point at hand. Given a particular cutoff, let $TOTAL_t$ and $SMALL_t$ stand for total employment and small business employment, respectively, in year t. In terms of these symbols, one can calculate the small business "contribution" to 1990 job creation as the ratio,

$$\frac{SMALL_{1990} - SMALL_{1989}}{TOTAL_{1990} - TOTAL_{1989}}$$

In words, the small business contribution to 1990 job creation is equated to the ratio of net employment change among small firms to total net employment change.[9]

The fallacy arises because firms can migrate between size categories from one year to the next. An example illustrates this point.

The example considers three firms, one of which (firm 1) satisfies the SBA definition of a small business in year 1. The largest firm (firm 3) grows dramatically in year 2, while the two smaller ones shrink. As it shrinks, firm 2 migrates from the large to the small business category. On net, total employment increases by 100.

If one executes the typical calculation on data in the example, small business appears to contributes 90 percent of net job growth. But, as the construction of the example makes clear, this interpretation is fallacious. In the example, firm-level net job growth actually increases with firm size, an observation that can be made only by following individual employers over time, as in the calculations that underlie the net and gross job flow figures in Table I.

How important is such migration across firm size categories in reality? The large magnitude of gross job flows – and the concentration of job flows in plants that undergo big employment changes – indicates that migration across categories is frequent and important.[10] Especially during periods of slow employment growth, firm migration from large to small is likely to occur quite often. This pattern creates the appearance of a booming small firm sector.

In summary, many claims about the job-creating prowess of small businesses derive from a fallacious interpretation of data on the size distribution of employment. Size distribution data cannot tell us whether small businesses systematically grew faster than large businesses.

6. Netting out reality

Sophisticated proponents of the view that small businesses create a disproportionate fraction of new jobs recognize the fallacy described above.[11] Circumventing the fallacy requires longitudinal data on individual establshments or firms – i.e., data that track individual employers over time. The most widely cited studies of job creation behavior rely upon such data, but they often present results in a way that can mislead the statistically naive.[12]

To understand the potential for confusion, consider the example in Box 3. The example depicts a situation with moderate net job growth in the midst of much larger gross job flows. We know from Table I that this situation typifies the experience of the U.S. manufacturing sector. It also typifies the experience in other sectors of the U.S. economy and in other industrialized nations.[13]

In the example, 100 percent of the net job increase between years 1 and 2 is accounted for by firm 1, which is classified as small based on its

BOX 2
Illustration of the size distribution fallacy

	Firm 1	Firm 2	Firm 3	Small firms	Big firms	All firms
Year 1 employment	300	550	650	300	1200	1500
Year 2 employment	50	340	1210	390	1210	1600
Net Change	–250	–210	560	90	10	100
	Small firm share of net job creation = (390 – 300)/(1600 – 1500)					

This illustration uses data on the size distribution of employment to calculate job creation shares. The calculation uses only the data that appear in the three rightmost columns. Changes in the distribution of employment by firm size are fallaciously used to draw an inference about the share of job creation accounted for by small firms.

BOX 3
Illustration of a confusion between net and gross job creation

	Firm 1	Firm 2	Firm 3	Small firms	Big firms	All firms
Year 1 employment	300	600	600	300	1200	1500
Year 2 employment	350	400	800	350	1200	1550
Net change	50	−200	200	50	0	50

Small firm share of net job creation = 50/50 = 1

Small firm share of gross job creation = 50/(50 + 200) = 0.2

This illustration calculates job creation shares from longitudinal data on individual firms. The calculation makes use of longitudinal data to calculate net firm-level employment changes. The net firm-level employment changes are aggregated over firms within a size class and then expressed as a fraction of the aggregate net change. Following the common practice of prominent analysts and government agencies like the U.S. Small Business Administration, continuing firms are assigned to a size category using base-year employment. The last two lines show how the small firm share of net job creation misrepresents the actual distribution of newly-created jobs by size of firm.

employment in year 1. Thus, one might conclude that "small firms created virtually all new jobs" between years 1 and 2. Closer analysis reveals, however, that such a conclusion grossly mischaracterizes the distribution of newly-created jobs by size of firm. In fact, in this example large firms create 80 percent of the new jobs in year 2.

Public discourse about job creation rarely distinguishes between the small business share of gross job creation (20 percent in the example) and its "share" of net job creation. Consequently, claims about the job creation role of small business often conjure up the image of an economy in which large firms inexorably shrink and small firms struggle valiantly to replenish the stock of jobs. This image deviates sharply from the facts set out in Table I and in Table III below, which show that both large and small employers create large numbers of new jobs.

To appreciate fully the misleading character of statements about the small business "share" of net job creation, consider a particular historical episode. Between March 1973 and March 1974, manufacturing employment as reported in the LRD increased on net by about 16,000 jobs. Over this same period, manufacturing plants with fewer than 100 employees as of March 1973 experienced a net increase of about 160,000 jobs. Thus the net increase for small plants was ten times as large as the overall net increase. If we summarized these data in the usual phaseology of public discourse, we would say that "small employers created 1,000 percent of the new manufacturing jobs in 1974." Proponents of the small business job creation view would likely eschew the usual phraseology in this case, because it highlights the absurdity of the underlying calculation.

Continuing with the historical episode, manufacturing plants of more than 500 employees created about 1.3 million gross new jobs between 1973 and 1974. Since net job growth was only 16,000 during this period, we could easily identify a set of large manufacturing plants that accounted for 50 percent, 100 percent, 200 percent, or 1000 percent of net job growth. We could do so by choosing a set of large plants situated in states with robust employment growth or rapidly expanding industries. We could even identify several distinct sets of large plants, each of which accounted for, say, 100 percent of net job growth. Would useful economic policy prescriptions then follow from these characterizations of the data? Certainly not! Yet it is precisely this type of data characterization and argument that underlies claims that small businesses create most jobs and – therefore – ought to receive favorable tax and regulatory treatment.

In summary, longitudinal studies that focus on the "share" of net job growth accounted for by small businesses grossly misrepresent the actual distribution of newly-created jobs by size of employer. A more meaningful way to represent this distribution is to focus on the small employer share of gross job creation.[14]

7. The regression fallacy

Most longitudinal studies of the relationship between employer size and job creation suffer from another statistical pitfall known as the regression fallacy or regression-to-the-mean bias.[15] The potential for bias arises whenever employers experience transitory fluctuations in size, or whenever measurement error introduces transitory fluctuations in observed size. Both phenomena are important features of longitudinal data on employers.

The simple example in Box 4 illustrates the regression fallacy. The example calculates growth rates for individual firms and by size of firm for years 2 and 3. Following widespread practice, firms are assigned to size classes using base-year employment.[16] The base year means the initial year of the time interval over which a particular growth rate is calculated.

Bold face entries in the illustration represent average employment growth rates by size class in years 2 and 3. These entries convey the impression that small firms outperform large ones in both years. Yet, closer inspection reveals that each firm is the same size in year 3 as in year 1. Evidently, the seemingly appropriate calculations underlying the bold face entries provide a misleading characterization of the size-growth rate relationship. This misleading characterization is an example of the regression fallacy.

The fallacy arises because, each year, we reclassify firms into size classes using base-year employment. The interaction between this reclassification and transitory firm-level employment movements lies at the heart of the regression fallacy. On average, firms classified as large in the base year are more likely to have experienced a recent transitory increase in employment. Since transitory movements reverse themselves, firms that are large in the base year are relatively likely to contract. Likewise, firms classified as small in the base year are more likely to have experienced a recent transitory decrease in employment. Hence, firms that are small in the base year are relatively likely to expand. As in our illustration, this regression phenomenon (i.e., regression to the firm's own long run size) creates the illusion that small firms systematically outperform large firms.

The magnitude of the bias associated with the regression fallacy depends on several factors: the extent of measurement error in the data, the importance of transitory employment movements for individual employers, the size distribution of employment, and the precise size-class boundaries chosen by the analyst. As a consequence, we cannot precisely quantify the extent of regression-to-the-mean bias in previous studies without direct access to their longitudinal data. We can, however, replicate their procedure for measuring employer size in the LRD and determine the resulting relationship between size and net job growth. We can then compare this size-growth relationship to the ones that emerge under alternative size measures.

Table II carries out this comparison using LRD data for the period 1973 to 1988. Following the standard practice described above, the first panel classifies continuing plants and plant deaths by

BOX 4
Illustration of the regression fallacy

	Firm 1	Firm 2	Firm 3	Small firms	Big firms	All firms
Year 1 employment	450	550	600	450	1150	1600
Year 2 employment	550	450	600	450	1150	1600
Year 3 employment	450	550	600	450	1150	1600
Year 2 growth rate	0.22	–0.18	0	**0.22**	**–0.09**	0
Year 3 growth rate	–0.18	0.22	0	**0.22**	**–0.09**	0

This illustration calculates net job creation rates for individual firms and by size class of firms. Following the common practice of prominent analysts and government agencies like the U.S. Small Business Administration, continuing firms are assigned to a size category using base-year employment. Year 1 (year 2) is the base year when calculating year-2 (year-3) growth rates. Although each firm employs the same number of workers in year 1 as in year 3, the net growth rate for small firms – as calculated – exceeds the net growth rate for big firms in both years 2 and 3. This apparent puzzle reflects a bias in the estimated size-growth relationship induced by temporary changes in the level of employment at individual firms.

TABLE II

Job destruction and creation rates by three measures of plant size, 1973–1988[a]

Size class	Gross job creation	Gross job destruction	Net job creation	Employment share
		I. *Base-year measure of plant size*[b]		
0 to 19 employees	25.7	15.4	10.3	5.2
20 to 49	13.6	13.1	0.6	8.5
50 to 99	11.4	12.0	−0.7	10.4
100 to 249	9.5	11.1	−1.7	18.6
250 to 499	7.4	9.9	−2.5	16.0
500 to 999	6.3	9.0	−2.7	13.5
1000 to 2499	5.7	8.4	−2.6	12.3
2500 to 4999	5.4	7.9	−2.5	7.0
5000 to 9999	4.7	7.1	−2.4	8.5
		II. *Average plant size measure*[c]		
0 to 19 employees	15.9	17.2	−1.3	4.4
20 to 49	12.6	13.8	−1.1	8.2
50 to 99	11.7	12.6	−0.9	10.1
100 to 249	10.0	11.5	−1.4	18.5
250 to 499	8.5	9.8	−1.3	16.6
500 to 999	7.5	8.5	−1.0	13.8
1000 to 2499	6.6	8.2	−1.6	12.5
2500 to 4999	6.5	8.2	−1.7	7.2
5000 or more	5.9	6.5	−0.6	8.8
		III. *Current plant size measure*[d]		
0 to 19 employees	18.7	23.3	−4.5	5.2
20 to 49	13.2	15.3	−2.1	8.6
50 to 99	12.2	13.5	−1.3	10.5
100 to 249	9.6	10.7	−1.1	18.5
250 to 499	7.7	8.7	−1.0	16.0
500 to 999	7.0	7.6	−0.6	13.5
1000 to 2499	6.3	7.3	−1.0	12.3
2500 to 4999	6.1	7.5	−1.3	7.0
5000 or more	5.4	5.6	−0.2	8.4

[a] Job creation and destruction rates are defined in section 2 of the text. Table entries for the creation and destruction rates and the employment shares are means of annual values for the period 1973 to 1988.
[b] Equal to the number of employees in the initial year of the interval over which the growth rate is calculated.
[c] Equal to the weighted mean number of employees, computed over all annual observations on the plant during the period 1972 to 1988.
[d] Equal to the simple mean of the plant's current employment and its employment twelve months earlier.

base-year size. New plants are classified according to size in the entry year. As we have explained, the entries in this panel are subject to the regression fallacy. To avoid the regression fallacy, we measure employer size using average plant size or current plant size. Recall that current size equals the simple average of the plant's employment in the current and previous years, and average size equals a mean computed over all sample obervations on the plant.[17] Repeating portions of Table I, the bottom two panels of Table II display the figures for average and current plant size measures.

The results of the comparison are striking. In Panel A, the net job creation rate declines steeply over the first five size class intervals and then flattens out over the remaining intervals. Panel B presents a sharp contrast. It indicates that the net job creation rate shows no systematic relationship to average plant size. Panel C actually shows a positive relationship between net job creation and current plant size. The gross job creation and destruction patterns also look much more favorable for small plants under the base-year size measure (Panel A) than under either alternative measure. Evidently, the regression fallacy illustrated in Box 4 operates with powerful effect in the LRD data for the U.S. manufacturing sector.[18]

There is good reason to suspect that the regression fallacy operates with even greater effect in the longitudinal data sets used in the widely cited studies by Birch (1979, 1987) and the annual SBA reports. In particular, measurement error is almost certainly more serious in their data sets than in the LRD, a point we develop in the next section. Given their procedures for measuring firm size, the more serious measurement problems in their data suggest greater susceptibility to the regression fallacy.

In summary, the standard practice of measuring firm or establishment size according to base-year employment leads to a regression fallacy, which in turn paints an overly favorable picture of the relative job growth performance of small employers. Our replication analysis with LRD data finds a substantial bias in favor of small businesses under the standard practice for measuring business size using base-year employment.

8. An unsuitable data base

Still another weakness of many leading studies of the job creation process is their reliance on an unsuitable data base: the Dun and Bradstreet Market Identifier (DMI) files. David Birch and associates use these data for their studies, and until recently, so did the SBA.[19] While the Dun and Bradstreet data base has many impressive attributes and represents an unparalleled source of information for many commercial purposes, it is not designed or maintained to maximize its usefulness as a tool for statistical analysis. Numerous studies have highlighted severe problems with the DMI files as a tool for measuring job creation and destruction or business births and deaths.[20]

For the purpose of investigating the job creation process, the DMI files suffer from two key problems. First, there is an enormous discrepancy between U.S. total employment as tabulated from the DMI files and the corresponding employment figures produced by the Bureau of Labor Statistics (BLS) or the Bureau of the Census. In 1986, for example, total employment tabulated from the DMI files exceeds the corresponding BLS and Census figures by more than eight million persons.[21] In an economy with roughly 82 million private-sector payroll employees, a discrepancy of this magnitude raises serious doubts about the accuracy of any statistical portrait generated from the DMI files. Furthermore, previous research finds that the most serious data problems in the DMI files involve younger and smaller businesses. This finding suggests that DMI-based claims about small business job creation should be interpreted with special caution.

Second, the DMI files do not accurately track business births and deaths or other important employment events. The U.S. Government Accounting Office (GAO) has analyzed the accuracy of the DMI files in accounting for mass layoffs, with particular emphasis on layoffs due to plant closures. SBA provided GAO with a sample of mass layoffs and plant closures from the DMI files for the 1982–84 period.[22] The GAO study found that 81 percent of the mass layoff events in the DMI files were mistakenly identified. In reality, these 81 percent represented some other event, such as a change in ownership structure, not a mass layoff or plant closure.

The DMI files also inaccurately identify plant births. A study by Birley (1984) compares three alternative sources of data for identifying new firms: the DMI file, the ES-202 data generated from administrative records maintained by state unemployment insurance agencies, and the telephone directory. She finds that the DMI files failed to identify 96 percent of the new firms found in the ES-202 data. Using a similar methodology, Aldrich *et al.* (1988) find that the DMI files missed 95 percent of apparently new businesses in the ES-202 data and 97 percent of those in the telephone directory.

In short, previous research indicates that the DMI files are unsuitable for generating job creation and destruction figures. Identifying plant births and deaths and tracking businesses over time is most difficult for small employers. Thus the DMI files are especially ill-suited for investigating the role of small business job creation.

The LRD, in contrast, is explicitly designed and maintained to avoid the type of problems that plague the DMI files. It is based on business surveys specifically designed to provide a statistical portrait of U.S. manufacturing activity. In addition, the Census Bureau draws on payroll tax records and other government data sources to verify and enhance the quality of LRD employment data.[23] Drawing on the longitudinal data in the LRD, the next two sections report additional findings about the job creation process in the U.S. manufacturing sector.

9. What fraction of new manufacturing jobs did small employers create?

Table III reports the percentage of manufacturing employment and job creation and destruction by employer size for the period 1973 to 1988. As the table reveals, large employers created most new manufacturing jobs over the period. They also destroyed most of the lost manufacturing jobs. Panel I of the table reveals that plants averaging at least 100 employees accounted for roughly seven of every ten newly created and newly destroyed manufacturing jobs. Panel II shows that firms with at least 500 employees accounted for 53 percent of job creation and 56 percent of job destruction. Panel IV shows that multi-unit firms accounted for roughly seven of every ten newly created and newly destroyed manufacturing jobs.

The table also reveals why large employers play the dominant role in job creation and destruction, despite the higher creation and destruction rates among smaller employers. The reason is that large employers account for the bulk of the manufacturing jobs base. Over the 1972–88 period as a whole, firms with at least 500 employees accounted for 65 percent of manufacturing employment.

The SBA defines small businesses to include any firm with fewer than 500 employees. According to this definition, Panel III of Table III reveals that small manufacturing firms account for 46% of job creation. This figure reflects an expansive and generous definition of the small business sector. Political orations about the virtues of small business often bring to mind family-run businesses and struggling entrepreneurs with shoe-string operations, not firms with up to 500 employees. In addition, a host of government regulations that entail exemptions for small businesses specify a cutoff level far below 500 employees. For example, Brock and Evans (1986, p. 74) note that the "Office of Federal Contract Enforcement exempts businesses with fewer than fifty employees from filing affirmative action plans." As another example, the Worker Adjustment and Retraining Notification Act of 1988 requires employers to give workers and government officials sixty days advance notice before a plant closure or large layoff, but the Act exempts establishments with fewer than fifty employees. The Family and Medical Leave Act of 1993 exempts employers with fewer than 50 workers. Returning to Table III, firms with fewer than fifty employees account for only 19 percent of gross job creation in the manufacturing sector; plants with fewer than fifty employees account for only 23 percent. Thus, according to these definitions, only about one-fifth of all new manufacturing jobs are created by small employers.

Would this characterization of the small business role in job creation differ if we looked outside the manufacturing sector? Although we are currently unable to calculate gross job creation and destruction rates for nonmanufacturing industries, we know that small businesses account for a considerably larger fraction of the jobs base in most nonmanufacturing industries. This point stands out clearly in Table IV. Drawing on several data sources, the table reports employment shares for various concepts of large and small businesses. According to SBA figures, firms with fewer than 500 workers acount for 50 percent of private sector employment but only 36 percent of manufacturing employment. According to County Business Patterns data, establishments with fewer than 100 workers account for 64 percent of nonmanufacturing employment but only 28 percent of manufacturing employment. Thus, small businesses provide a much larger share of the jobs base outside the manufacturing sector. In addition, the available evidence indicates that the gross job creation rate declines with employer size in the nonmanufacturing sector, just as it does in the manufacturing sector.[24] These facts make us confident that small business accounts for a larger share of job creation and destruction in most nonmanufacturing industries than in the manufacturing sector. A more precise characterization awaits the development and analysis of high quality longitudinal data for nonmanufacturing

TABLE III
Shares of gross manufacturing job creation and destruction by employer size, 1973–1988[a]

	Job creation	Job destruction	Employment
Average Plant Size[b]			
0 to 19 employees	7.6	7.4	4.4
20 to 49	11.3	11.0	8.2
50 to 99	13.1	12.5	10.1
100 to 249	20.3	20.7	18.5
250 to 499	15.6	16.0	16.6
500 to 999	11.4	11.5	13.8
1000 to 2499	9.1	10.1	12.5
2500 to 4999	5.2	5.8	7.2
5000 or more	5.7	5.6	8.8
Current plant size[c]			
0 to 19 employees	10.7	11.8	5.2
20 to 49	12.5	13.0	8.6
50 to 99	14.0	13.8	10.5
100 to 249	19.5	19.5	18.5
250 to 499	13.6	13.6	16.0
500 to 999	10.4	10.1	13.5
1000 to 2499	8.5	8.8	12.3
2500 to 4999	4.7	5.1	7.0
5000 or more	5.0	4.6	8.4
Firm size[d]			
0 to 19 employees	9.5	9.6	5.2
20 to 49	9.4	9.1	7.0
50 to 99	8.6	7.9	6.8
100 to 249	11.1	9.9	9.1
250 to 499	7.4	6.6	6.8
500 to 999	6.4	6.0	6.2
1000 to 2499	7.9	7.6	8.2
2500 to 4999	6.2	6.5	7.1
5000 to 9999	7.2	7.6	8.5
10000 to 24999	10.5	11.4	13.6
25000 to 49999	6.6	7.3	9.2
50000 or more	8.6	9.7	12.4
Ownership type			
Single-unit	31.1	28.2	22.3
Multi-unit	69.0	71.6	77.7

[a] Table entries show the shares of gross job creation, gross job destruction and employment for U.S. manufacturing. Table entries are average annual values for the period 1973–1988.
[b] Equal to the weighted mean number of employees, computed over all annual observations on the plant during the period 1972 to 1988.
[c] Equal to the simple mean of the plant's current employment and its employment twelve months earlier.
[d] Equal to the number of manufacturing workers employed by the plant's parent firm in the preceding Census of Manufactures. Census years are 1972, 1977, 1982 and 1987.

businesses. Since the manufacturing sector accounts for a small and declining share of U.S. employment – only 19% in 1988 – we think the development of such data merits a high priority by government statistical agencies.

10. The durability of jobs by employer size

Laudatory claims about the job creation role of small businesses often fail to consider how the permanence of jobs varies with employer size. This failure is serious, because job durability

TABLE IV
The share of employment by employer size

Year	Sector	Data source	Number of employees < 50	< 100	≥ 500	≥ 1000
			I. By current size of establishment[a]			
1988	Private	CBP	0.43	0.56	0.19	0.13
1988	Nonman.	CBP	0.51	0.64	0.14	0.09
1988	Manuf.	CBP	0.17	0.28	0.37	0.24
1988	Manuf.	LRD	0.11	0.22	0.40	0.26
			II. By average size of establishment[b]			
1988	Manuf.	LRD	0.11	0.22	0.41	0.27
			III. By size of firm[c]			
1988	Private	SBA			0.50	
1988	Manuf.	SBA			0.36	
1987	Private	ES	0.28	0.36	0.51	0.29
1987	Nonman.	ES	0.36	0.45	0.59	0.21
1987	Manuf.	ES	0.12	0.18	0.32	0.48
1987	Manuf.	LRD	0.09	0.16	0.35	0.42

Year	Sector	Data source	Single unit	Multiple units
			IV. By parent firm ownership type	
1987	Private	ES	0 .45	0.55
1987	Nonman	ES	0 .54	0.46
1987	Manuf.	ES	0 .24	0.76
1988	Manuf.	LRD	0 .20	0.80

Notes:
[a] For the LRD, equal to the simple mean of the plant's current employment and its employment twelve months earlier. For the CBP, equal to the number of employees during March of the current year.
[b] Equal to the weighted mean number of employees, computed over all annual observations on the plant during the period 1972 to 1988.
[c] Equal to the number of workers employed by the plant's parent firm.
Data sources:
CBP: Authors' calculations from County Business Patterns (1988). The CBP covers the nonfarm private sector, excluding railroad and domestic household workers.
LRD: Authors' calculations from the Longitudinal Research Database. Unlike the other data sources, the LRD excludes administrative and auxilliary establishments not directly engaged in production activity.
SBA: From Table 17 in Small Business Administration (1991).
ES: Authors' calculations from Enterprise Statistics (1987). The ES data exclude finance, insurance, real estate, public utilities, communications and some service industries.

differs systematically by employer size. Table V documents this pattern for the manufacturing sector.

The table shows one-year survival rates for all jobs and newly-created jobs by size of employer. The one-year survival rates for all jobs rise systematically with all four measures of employer size. The one-year survival rate for the biggest firms is 92 percent, as compared to only 81 percent for the smallest firms. Furthermore, the one-year survival rates for new jobs rise systematically with average plant size, firm size and ownership type.[25] The one-year survival rate for new jobs at the biggest firms is 76 percent, as compared to only 65 percent at the smallest firms. Simply put, bigger employers offer greater job

TABLE V
Survival and persistence rates for all jobs, new jobs, and lost jobs in manufacturing, 1973–1988[a]

	One-year survival rate		One-year persistence rate
	All jobs	New jobs	Newly-destroyed jobs
Average plant size[b]			
0 to 19 employees	0.83	0.62	0.84
20 to 49	0.84	0.65	0.84
50 to 99	0.87	0.69	0.82
100 to 249	0.88	0.71	0.82
250 to 499	0.90	0.71	0.80
500 to 999	0.92	0.71	0.80
1000 to 2499	0.92	0.71	0.82
2500 to 4999	0.92	0.75	0.80
5000 or more	0.93	0.75	0.82
Current plant size[c]			
0 to 19 employees	0.77	0.70	0.86
20 to 49	0.85	0.70	0.84
50 to 99	0.86	0.71	0.83
100 to 249	0.89	0.70	0.81
250 to 499	0.91	0.68	0.79
500 to 999	0.92	0.68	0.80
1000 to 2499	0.93	0.68	0.81
2500 to 4999	0.92	0.73	0.79
5000 or More	0.94	0.71	0.83
Firm size[d]			
0 to 19 employees	0.81	0.65	0.86
20 to 49	0.87	0.66	0.82
50 to 99	0.88	0.67	0.81
100 to 249	0.89	0.70	0.81
250 to 499	0.90	0.70	0.82
500 to 999	0.90	0.69	0.81
1000 to 2499	0.90	0.70	0.81
2500 to 4999	0.91	0.70	0.82
5000 to 9999	0.91	0.70	0.81
10000 to 24999	0.91	0.71	0.81
25000 to 49999	0.92	0.70	0.82
50000 or more	0.92	0.76	0.82
Ownership type			
Single-unit firm	0.87	0.67	0.82
Multi-unit firm	0.91	0.71	0.82

[a] The one-year survival rate for all jobs equals one minus the job destruction rate, as reported in Table I. The one-year survival rate for new jobs equals the fraction created between year $t - 1$ and t that are still present at the same location in year $t + 1$. The one-year persistence rate of newly-destroyed jobs equals the fraction of jobs lost between year $y - 1$ and t that have not reappeared at the same location by year $t + 1$. All table entries are average annual values for the period 1973 to 1988.
[b] Equal to the weighted mean number of employees, computed over all annual observations on the plant during the period 1972 to 1988.
[c] Equal to the simple mean of the plant's current employment and its employment twelve months earlier.
[d] Equal to the number of manufacturing workers employed by the plant's parent firm in the preceding Census of Manufactures. Census years are 1972, 1977, 1982 and 1987.

durability. Regardless of employer size, however, new jobs are much less durable than the typical existing job.

Although the relationship is weaker, Table V also reveals that the persistence of newly-destroyed jobs is greater for smaller employers. In a nutshell, both existing and newly-created jobs are less secure at small busineses than at large businesses, and once lost, small business jobs are less likely to reappear. Thus, in terms of job durability, larger employers outperform smaller ones.

11. Conclusions

Drawing on U.S. Census Bureau data for manufacturing plants from 1972 to 1988, we report new evidence on the relationship between employer size and job growth. We find that large firms and plants dominate the creation and destruction of jobs in the U.S. manufacturing sector. This finding has a simple two-part explanation. First, for employers large and small, gross job creation and destruction rates are quite high – on the order of 10 percent of employment per year. Second, large firms and plants account for the bulk of the manufacturing jobs base.

While gross job creation rates are substantially higher for smaller plants and firms, so are gross destruction rates. We find no strong or systematic relationship between net job growth rates and either firm or plant size. However, we find clear evidence that larger employers offer greater job security. For both new jobs and the typical existing job, job durability increases with employer size.

These empirical findings clash sharply with conventional wisdom about the job-creating prowess of small business. One might suspect that the source of disagreement lies with differences between the manufacturing and nonmanufacturing sectors of the economy. We hold open the possibility that careful analysis of job creation activity in the nonmanufacturing sector might produce evidence more congenial to the conventional view, but that view does not rest upon a careful and balanced analysis of the data. Rather, the widely espoused claims about small business and job creation rest upon two common fallacies – the size distribution fallacy and the regression fallacy – and a confusion between net and gross job creation.

As illustrated by several quotations in Box 1, the job-creating prowess of small business is often touted as an argument in favor of preferential tax, subsidy, or regulatory treatment of small businesses. Aside from its questionable factual basis, this type of argument is, quite simply, a nonsequitur. It has two fundamental problems.

First, the argument neglects the issue of job quality; the mere creation of jobs is not an appropriate economic policy objective. Economic policy is appropriately directed towards wealth creation and the expansion of consumption opportunities. Here, we mean "consumption opportunities" in a broad sense that encompasses not just material goods, but the many factors that influence the quality of life. For economic policy to serve these objectives, it must promote job quality as well as job creation. While there are many exceptions to the basic pattern, the weight of evidence indicates that, on average, larger employers offer better jobs in terms of wages, fringe benefits, working conditions, opportunities for skill enhancement, and job security.[26] Few studies that purportedly demonstrate small business's disproportionate contribution to job creation effectively address the issue of job quality. Except for the matter of job durability, we have not addressed the issue in this article.

Second, the argument for preferential treatment of small business fails to comprehend the central theorem of economic policy prescription. This theorem directs attention towards marginal responses to proposed economic policy changes. In contrast, claims about the job-creating prowess of small business are statements about the average behavior of a class of firms. Even if accurate, these statements do not predict how the number (or quality) of jobs would respond to a proposed economic policy change. Careful, well-founded predictions about how the number and quality of jobs respond to changes in the economic environment are the appropriate yardstick for policy evaluation.

In practice, determining how policy changes affect job numbers and quality poses considerable challenge. Even greater challenges in the political arena confront efforts to implement economically sound policies that target specific sectors or types of firms. Targeted policy proposals invite political conflicts over the precise structure of subsidies, tax breaks, and preferential regulatory treatment. These conflicts are costly for two reasons. First, they inevitably turn into resource-consuming struggles over the redistribution of society's wealth. Second, the outcome usually reflects the relative political strengths of the parties to the conflict, rather than the economic criteria that shaped the original policy proposal. In our view, these practical barriers to successful design and implementation of targeted policies create a strong presumption in favor of neutral, untargeted policies.

Appendix

In Table V, the one-year survival rate for new jobs shows a clear relationship to average plant size but not to current size. How can we reconcile these apparently contradictory results? First, consider some hypothetical employment histories in a simplified setting with only two size classes. Suppose a plant is small at the beginning of the sample, becomes large for one period, and then returns permanently to the small category. This plant is classified as small under the average size measure. Under the current size measure, it is classified as small in most periods but as large in the period that coincides with its one episode of job creation.[27] Consequently, this plant's employment history pulls down the survival rate for small plants under the average size measure, but it pulls down the survival rate for large plants under the current size measure.

As a second hypothetical example, consider a plant that starts out large, becomes small for one period, and then returns permanently to large status. The plant's return to large status involves an episode of persistent job creation. This episode pushes up the new job survival rate for large plants under the average size measure, but it pushes up the rate for small plants under the current size measure.

These two hypothetical employment histories illustrate a more general point: under the current size measure, plant-level employment histories that involve occasional, temporary movements across size-class boundaries increase the new job survival rates for small plants relative to large plants. Just how prevalent are these occasional boundary-crossing episodes? We know from Davis, Haltiwanger and Schuh (1995, chapter 2) that job creation is concentrated among plants that experience large percentage employment changes, suggesting that much job creation involves boundary crossing. We know from other research (e.g., Lilien, 1980) that temporary layoffs in the manufacturing sector are quite important, especially during cyclical downturns. These observations suggest that the second hypothetical example, in particular, captures an important aspect of plant-level employment dynamics.

These remarks reconcile the apparent discrepancy between results based on the two alternative measures of plant size, but they do not indicate which size measure is more appropriate. As we suggested earlier, average plant size is probably a more accurate proxy for the plant's intended scale of operations. More importantly, the average size measure assigns each plant to a fixed category. In contrast, as our examples reveal, the current size measure can attribute job creation to the small plant category, even though the plant is large during most periods – and vice versa.[28] To our mind, this aspect of accounting for job creation by current size class is discomfiting. We believe that using average plant size is a more informative way to examine job creation data, although the current size measure may be preferable for some purposes.

In any case, this issue becomes less nettlesome when we examine the survival of new jobs by ownership type and firm size. A plant's ownership type seldom changes. Since firm size reflects the firm's employment level during the preceding Census of Manufactures, the measured size of a plant's parent firm is unaffected by the plant's subsequent employment history.

Notes

This authors are also research associates at the Center of Economic Studies, U.S. Bureau of the Census. This paper draws heavily on the authors' forthcoming book, *Job Creation and Destruction*. The authors gratefully acknowledge the generous support of the National Science Foundation and the U.S. Bureau of the Census. In preparing the data for this study, we have greatly benefited from the assistance of Bob Bechtold, Mark Doms, Tim Dunne, Cyr Lenience, Bob McGuckin, Jim Monahan, Al Nucci, Arnie Reznek, Ken Troske and other Census Bureau Employees at the Center for Economic Studies. Steve Strongin and Janice Weiss provided helpful comments on a previous draft of this paper. Laura Power provided excellent research assistance. This views expressed in the paper are those of the authors, and do not necessarily reflect official positions of the Census Bureau or the Federal Reserve System.

This article first appeared in *Labor Markets, Employment Policy & Job Creation* edited by Lewis C. Salmon and Alec R. Levenson. Copyright 1994 by the Milken Institute for Job & Capital Formation. Published by Westview Press, Boulder, CO.

1 See also the SBA's annual reports to the President, *The*

State of Small Business, and Birch (1979, 1987). The chorus of praise for the job creation performance of small business has been challenged by only a handful of critics. See Armington and Odle (1982a) and chapter 3 in Brown, Hamilton and Medoff (1990). For journalistic pieces that question conventional wisdom about the small business role in creating jobs see Wessel and Brown (1988), Marshall (1993) and Kinsley (1993).

[2] Recent studies include Acs and Audretsch (1988), Brown and Medoff (1989), Brown, Hamilton and Medoff (1990), Davis and Haltiwanger (1991,1992), and Hansen (1992).

[3] Our forthcoming book describes the LRD in much greater detail.

[4] To convert time-t job creation and destruction measures to rates, we divide by the average of employment at t and $t-1$. The resulting growth rate measure has several technical advantages over more conventional growth rate measures. See Davis, Haltiwanger and Schuh (1995) for further discussion of this point.

[5] Only in Cenus years can we measure total employment for every manufacturing firm. The Census of Manufactures was carried out in 1972, 1977, 1982 and 1987.

[6] Most other studies focus on yet a different measure of employer size that we describe in our analysis of the regression fallacy.

[7] See chapter 5 in Brock and Evans (1986) and pages 82–88 in Brown, Hamilton and Medoff (1990).

[8] On the relationship between firm size and financing patterns, see Walker (1989), Gaston (1989), Gertler and Gilchrist (1992), and Kashyap and Stein (1992).

[9] Zayas (1978) use data on changes in the size distribution of employment to calculate growth rates by size of business. This calculation is also subject to the size distribution fallacy identified below.

[10] Table I shows that gross job creation and destruction flows are large relative to net employment changes. Chapter 2 of Davis, Haltiwanger and Schuh (1995) contains additional evidence on this point and on the concentration of gross job flows at plants that undergo big employment changes.

[11] The SBA's 1983 report, *State of Small Business*, clearly explains the fallacy on page 62. See also Birch and MacCracken (1983).

[12] The most widely cited studies of the small business role in creating jobs are the SBA's annual *State of Small Business Report* and Birch (1979, 1987).

[13] See Davis, Haltiwanger and Schuh (1995) for a review of the evidence.

[14] For the record, we should note that not every statistical tabulation performed on longitudinal data by the SBA examines the small employer share of net job creation. For example, Table 13 in SBA (1988) reports gross job creation by firm size. Nonethelss, the surrounding text reverts to the misleading "net" calculation when characterizing the small business role in job creation.

[15] Friedman (1992) suggests that the regression fallacy "is the most common fallacy in the statistical analysis of economic data." Leonard (1986) explains how regression-to-the-mean bias can distort the estimated relationship between employer size and growth rates. Friedman (1992) and Quah (1993) focus on the regression fallacy in the recent literature that investigates whether per capita income levels are converging across countries.

[16] This classification practice is used, for instance, in the annual SBA reports to the president and in Birch (1979, 1987).

[17] To the extent that transitory employment fluctuations require more than one year to reverse themselves, our current size measure is subject to a milder and more subtle version of the regression fallacy. However, random errors in measuring employment levels do not produce a regression fallacy under any of our plant or firm size measures.

[18] Brown *et al.* (1990) stress a different potential problem with the standard size measure. They argue that classifying new firms according to size in the entry year creates a bias, because new firms often start small even when their intended scale of operations is large. This point clearly applies to new plants as well. However, a symmetric point is that dying plants often contract and become small on their way towards exit. A careful reading of Table II suggests that this latter effect dominates for manufacturing plants. Observe that, among the smallest plants, the difference between the gross destruction rate based on current size and the gross destruction rate based on average size exceeds the corresponding difference for the gross creation rate. Observe, also, that the creation and destruction rates align more closely when comparing the current and averge size measures than when comparing either of these measures to the Birch/SBA measure. This last observation indicates that the regression fallacy – not the birth problem stressed by Brown *et al.* – accounts for the striking contrast between Panel A and the other panels.

[19] The SBA has recently contracted with the Bureau of the Census to longitudinally link the federal government's Standard Statistical Establishment List for the purpose of studying job creation and destruction behavior. See Census contract number 61-93-41, "The Longitudinal Data Study".

[20] See Armington and Odle (1982b), Birch and MacCracken (1983), Birley (1984), Howland (1988, chapter 2), Evans (1987), Aldrich *et al.* (1988), and the SBA (1983, 1987).

[21] See page 514 in the 1989 *U.S. Statistical Abstract.*

[22] The GAO defined a mass layoff as the dismissal of at least 20 percent of a plant's permanent work force.

[23] Given the need of policy makers to understand the job creation process, government statistical agencies should set a high priority on developing longitudinal establishment-level data bases for other sectors of the U.S. economy. The Center for Economic Studies at the Bureau of the Census is currently conducting a pilot study to determine whether the federal government's Standard Statistical Establishment List can be effectively used to construct longitudinal data on firms and establishments for the entire U.S. economy.

[24] Unpublished tabulations prepared by Ken Troske for the finance, insurance and real estate sector in Wisconsin, and by Al Nucci for the U.S. nonmanucturing sector during the 1982–87 period, indicate that gross job creation rates decline sharply with employer size.

[25] The appendix explains why current plant size and average plant size exhibit different relationships to the one-year survival rate for new jobs. The explanation relates closely to our earlier discussion of the regression fallacy.

[26] Brown *et al.* (1990) review much of the evidence on how job quality varies with employer size.

[27] Recall that our measure of current plant size equals the simple average of current and previous period's employment. Remarks in the text presume that the plant crosses the size-class boundary – once during its job creation episode and a second time after it returns to its initial size.

[28] The same problem arises if we use base-year employment to measure employer size.

References

Acs, Zoltan and David Audretsch, 1988, 'Innovation in Large and Small Firms: An Empirical Analysis', *American Economic Review* **78** (September), 678–690.

Aldrich, Howard, Arne Kalleberg, Peter Marsden and James Cassell, 1988, 'In Pursuit of Evidence: Five Sampling Procedures for Locating New Businesses', *Journal of Business Venturing* **4**, 367–386.

Armington, Catherine and Marjorie Odle, 1982a, 'Small Business — How Many Jobs?', *Brookings Review* (Winter).

Armington, Catherine and Marjorie Odle, 1982b, 'Sources of Employment Growth, 1978-80', unpublished report, The Brookings Institution, Washington, D.C.

Birch, David L., 1979, *The Job Generation Process*, unpublished report, MIT Program on Neighborhood and Regional Change.

Birch, David L., 1987 *Job Creation in America: How Our Smallest Companies Put the Most People to Work*, New York: The Free Press.

Birch, David and Susan MacCracken, 1983, 'The Small Business Share of Job Creation: Lessons Learned from the Use of a Longitudinal File', unpublished report, MIT Program on Neighborhood and Regional Change.

Birley, Sue, 1984, 'Find the New Firm', *Proceedings of the Academy of Management Meetings*.

Brock William A. and David S. Evans, 1986, *The Economics of Small Business: Their Role and Regulation in the U.S. Economy*, New York: Holmes and Meier.

Brown, Charles and James Medoff, 1989, 'The Employer Size Wage Effect', *Journal of Political Economy* (October), 1027–1059.

Brown, Charles, James Hamilton and James Medoff, 1990, *Employers Large and Small*, Cambridge, Massachusetts: Harvard University Press.

Davis, Steven J. and John Haltiwanger, 1991, 'Wage Dispersion between and within U.S. Manufacturing Plants, 1963–86', *Brookings Papers on Economic Activity: Microeconomics*, 115–200.

Davis, Steven J. and John Haltiwanger, 1992, 'Employer Size and the Wage Structure in U.S. Manufacturing', mimeograph, University of Chicago.

Davis, Steve, John Haltiwanger, and Scott Schuh, 1990, 'Published Versus Sample Statistics from the ASM: Implications for the LRD', *Proceedings of the American Statistical Association, Business and Economics Statistics Section*.

Davis, Steve, John Haltiwanger, and Scott Schuh, 1995, *Job Creation and Destruction*, MIT Press (forthcoming).

Dentzer, Susan, 1993, 'Doing the Small-Business Shuffle', *U.S. News and World Report* (August 16), 49.

Evans, David, 1987, 'The Relationship between Firm Growth, Size and Age: Estimates for 100 Manufacturing Industries', *Journal of Industrial Economics* **XV**, 567–581.

Friedman, Milton, 1992, 'Do Old Fallacies Ever Die?', *Journal of Economic Literature* **30**(4), 2139–2132.

Gaston, Robert J., 1989, 'The Scale of Informal Capital Markets', *Small Business Economics* **1**(3), 223–230.

Gertler, Mark and Simon Gilchrist, 1992, 'Monetary Policy, Business Cycles and the Behavior of Small Manufacturing Firms', working paper, New York University.

Hale, David, 1993, 'Small Business, Tax Plan's Victim', *Wall Street Journal* (July 30), A.8.

Hansen, John A., 1992, 'Innovation, Firm Size, and Firm Age', *Small Business Economics* **4**(1), 37–44.

Howland, Marie, 1988, *Plant Closings and Worker Displacements: The Regional Issues*, W.E. Upjohn Institute for Employment Research: Kalamazoo, Michigan.

Kashyap, Anil and Jeremy Stein, 1992, 'Monetary Policy and Bank Lending', mimeograph, University of Chicago.

Kinsley, Michael, 1993, 'Small Isn't Beautiful', *The New Republic* (September 13), 6.

Leonard, Jonathan, 1986, 'On the Size Distribution of Employment and Establishments', NBER working paper 1951.

Lilien, David, 1980, 'The Cyclical Pattern of Temporary Layoffs in United States Manufacturing', *Review of Economics and Statistics*, **CXII**, 24–31.

Marshall, Jonahan, 1993, 'Dispelling a Small-Business Myth', *San Francisco Chronicle* (March 29), D1.

Meyers, Henry F., 1993, 'The Outlook', *Wall Street Journal* (March 8), 1.

Quah, Danny, 1993, 'Galton's Fallacy and Tests of the Convergence Hypothesis', Londond School of Economics Discussion Paper EM/93/265.

Roach, Stephen, 1993, 'The New Majority: White-Collar Jobless', *New York Times* (March 14), section 4, page 17.

Siebert, Muriel, 1992, 'Hire Workers. Get a Tax Credit', *New York Times* (January 6), A21.

Silk, Leonard, 1986, 'Quiet Shapers of History', *New York Times*, (April 9), D2.

U.S. Bureau of the Census, 1988, *County Business Patterns*, U.S. Summary Statistics, Volume I, Washington, D.C.: U.S. Governemnt Printing Office.

U.S. Bureau of the Census, 1987, *Enterprise Statistics*, Washington, D.C.: U.S. Government Printing Office.

U.S. Small Business Administration, 1983, 1987, 1988, 1991, *The State of Small Business: A Report of the President*, Washington, D.C.: U.S. Government Printing Office.

Walker, David A., 1989, 'Financing the Small Firm', *Small Business Economics* **1**(4), 285–296.

Wessel, David and Buck Brown, 1988, 'The Hyping of Small-Firm Job Growth', *Wall Street Journal* (November 8), 1.

Zagorin, Adam, 1993, 'How the Small Business Owner Gets Clobbered', *Time* (July 12), 32.

[27]

A TAXONOMY OF BUSINESS START-UP REASONS AND THEIR IMPACT ON FIRM GROWTH AND SIZE

SUE BIRLEY
Imperial College of Science, Technology and Medicine

PAUL WESTHEAD
Warwick Business School

EXECUTIVE SUMMARY

Based on a survey of 405 principal owner–managers of new independent businesses in Great Britain this paper explores two research questions—are there any differences in the reasons that owner–managers articulate for starting their businesses, and, if there are, do they appear to affect the subsequent growth and size of the businesses? The results of the study indicate an affirmative answer to the first question. From the 23 diverse reasons leading to start-up that were identified in the literature, an underlying pattern emerged via the Principal Components Analysis. Moreover, these were similar to those found in earlier studies. Thus, five of the seven components identified by the model correspond to those identified by Scheinberg and MacMillan (1988) in their eleven-country study of motivations to start a business: "Need for Approval," "Need for Independence," "Need for Personal Development," "Welfare Considerations," and "Perceived Instrumentality of Wealth." Two further components were identified by this current study. The first vindicates the decision to add a question not included in the previous study that related to "Tax Reduction and Indirect Benefits," and the second, the desire to "Follow Role Models" was identified by Dubini (1988) in her study in Italy.

In order to take account of possible multiple motivations in the start-up period, cluster analysis was used to provide a classification of founder "types." The seven generalized "types" of owner–managers were named as follows—the insecure (104 founders), the followers (49 founders), the status avoiders (169 founders), the confused (15 founders), the tax avoiders (18 founders), the community (49 founders), and the unfocused (1 founder). Further, evidence from the final discriminant analysis model suggested that the seven-cluster classification of owner–managers was appropriate and optimal. However, despite these clear differences between clusters, this was not found to be an indicator of subsequent size or growth, as measured by sales and employment levels. The answer to the second research question would be in the negative. Therefore, we conclude that, whereas new businesses are founded by individuals with significantly different reasons leading to start-up, once the

Address correspondence to Professor Sue Birley, The Management School, Imperial College of Science, Technology and Medicine, 53 Princes Gate, Exhibition Road, London SW7 2PG.

The authors would like to acknowledge the very helpful comments received from one of the reviewers of this paper.

Journal of Business Venturing 9, 7–31 0883-9026/94/$6.00

new ventures are established these reasons have a minimal influence on the growth of new ventures and upon the subsequent wealth creation and job generation potential.

This result is important for investors and policy-makers. It suggests that strategies for "picking winners" solely based upon the characteristics of owner–managers and their stated reasons for wanting to go into business are not supported. Thus, for example, targeting scarce resources to those with high opportunistic and materialistic reasons for venture initiation would miss those with a wider sense of community or those with personal needs for independence who establish similarly sized businesses with comparable levels of wealth creation.

INTRODUCTION

> "Personal characteristics of entrepreneurs, and especially their motivations and work experiences, are therefore relevant factors in the study of entrepreneurship, since they will lie behind the supply side of entrepreneurial activities and will have to be closely identified in any public policies orientated to promote such activities"
>
> *(Lafuente and Salas 1989, p. 18).*

Since 1979 the focus of monetarist-inspired free-market government policy in Great Britain has shifted towards the development of an active and vibrant "enterprise" culture. Associated with increasing interest in creating greater competitiveness, a desire to privatize public sector production, moves to switch resources away from traditional industries towards high-tech small firms, and an ideological objective of reducing reliance on the state by fostering the principles of "individualism," choice, and "self-help" (Martin 1985, p. 385), government has introduced a torrent of measures that have actively encouraged individuals to become self-employed or to start their own businesses (Beesley and Wilson 1982). All of these initiatives have been predicated on the assumption that it is possible to influence individuals to the extent that a larger percentage of the population than previously can be encouraged successfully to create their own businesses. Unfortunately, this was based primarily upon casual assumption rather than upon an empirical evidence. However, empirical evidence has shown that only a small proportion of businesses has the potential for significant wealth creation and job generation (Storey et al. 1987; Reynolds 1987; Storey and Johnson 1987a). As a result, a small firm's policy of "picking winners" has been suggested as a way of using scarce resources more efficiently (Storey and Johnson 1987b, Storey et al., 1987), a view that Hakim (1989) believes is unlikely to be a viable and practical strategy in a complex real world. Nevertheless, Gibb and Davies (1990, p. 16) argue that, "it is perhaps an unrealistic expectation that it will be possible definitively to pick winners or indeed to produce a comprehensive theory that leads to this. But arguably it is possible to make further strides towards better understanding of the factors that influence the growth process and therefore to better assist those who are appraising companies to make better decisions as well as assist those who are seeking to improve support for company development." Supporting this latter theme a number of recent studies have explored the influence of variety of founder- as well as business-related factors surrounding the survival and growth of new and small businesses (Davidsson 1988; Woo et al. 1988, 1991; Lafuente and Salas 1989; Birley and Westhead 1990; Westhead 1990).

Reasons and motivations leading to start-up have traditionally been regarded as an important element influencing not only the start-up of the new business but also its characteristics, survival, and performance (McClelland 1961; Brockhaus 1980; Atkinson and

Hilgard 1983; Hofer and Sandberg 1987; Begley and Boyd 1987; Jenssen and Kolvereid 1991). Results of empirical studies (summarized in Westhead 1988, p. 655) suggest that the overwhelming motivations for entrepreneurship have been an amalgam of a desire for independence and financial betterment, with frustration in previous employment playing a secondary role. However, a number of studies in the United Kingdom have also indicated that redundancy or firm closure has provided a particular trigger "pushing" founders to leave their previous jobs (Storey 1982; Keeble and Gould 1984, p. 10; Binks and Jennings 1986; Westhead 1988, p. 375; Turok and Richardson 1989, p. 29). In their "social development" model of venture initiation Gibb and Ritchie (1982, p. 27) claim that class structure, family origin, education, occupational choice and development, career and organizational history and experience, present lifestyles and attachments have marked impacts on why certain individuals are most likely to establish new businesses (Cooper and Dunkelberg 1986; O'Farrell and Pickles 1989). This approach, like the "trait approach" where entrepreneurs are born not made (McClelland 1961; Brockhaus 1980, 1982), the "psychodynamic" models (Kets de Vries 1977) associated with social marginality (Stanworth and Curran 1973, 1976; Scase and Goffee 1980, 1982) and the "person variable approach" (Chell 1985, pp. 48–51) that uses Mischel's (1973) "cognitive social learning variables," is not without its limitations (for a full discussion of these models and their limitations see Chell 1985). The "social development" model is preferred because it leaves open the possibility of the exploration of a variety of influences not only on the formation but also on the subsequent survival and growth of the new enterprises established.

Clearly, in the early days of a business, growth objectives are synonymous with those of the owner–manager (Simon 1964; O'Farrell and Hitchens 1988a, p. 1373). "And, because of the organic nature of the development process, the resource constraints and owner's limited horizons, assumptions of conventional rational economic behaviour in response to assistance stimuli cannot be made" (Gibb and Scott 1986, pp. 99–100). Consequently, it is assumed that the choice of a "growth" rather than purely a "survival" policy principally rests with the objectives of the owner–manager which are, in part, influenced by the initial reasons leading to venture initiation. Thus, future business goals are influenced not only by commercial considerations but also by personal lifestyle. However, Milne and Thompson (1982) claim that the growth of a small business is not solely related to the personal traits and characteristics of small firm founders but also to how quickly they can adapt and learn from the experience of dealing with the environment within which the new venture does its business (Hjern et al. 1980). The implication of this is twofold—original motivations may change and/or may not be related to the subsequent size and performance of the firm. Therefore, this research asks two basic questions:

1. Are there differences in the reasons that owner–managers articulate for starting their businesses?
2. Assuming that there *are* differences, do they appear to affect the subsequent growth and size of the businesses?

RESEARCH

The empirical evidence presented in this paper is derived from a wider international study of new venture creation and growth (refer to Shane et al. (1991) for a comparison of the reasons leading to start-up of new businesses in Great Britain, New Zealand, and Norway). Thirty-eight statements were identified from the literature as factors that entrepreneurs have described as reasons for starting their businesses, and were *piloted* in a survey of over 1,000 entrepreneurs in 11 countries. These data were analyzed and, using factor analysis, the 38 statements were reduced to 22 (Scheinberg and MacMillan 1988; Alange and Scheinberg 1988; Dubini 1988; Blais and Toulouse 1990). After discussion among the international collaborators, an additional tax-related statement was introduced for this current study. These 23 statements are reproduced verbatim in Table 1, but in a different order from that in the questionnaire.

Reflecting the increased recognition of the importance of both locational considerations in the functioning of the economy (Cooke 1986; Allen and Massey 1988) and of spatial variations in both business formation and small firm survival and growth (Blackburn et al. 1990; Mason 1991; Moyes and Westhead 1990), 12 contrasting locations were selected for the Great Britain database. The environments were subjectively selected by these researchers to include government designated assisted areas, rural as well as urban environments, areas with persistently high levels of unemployment, areas associated with specialized declining traditional heavy industries and high concentrations of external ownership, particularly in the manufacturing industry, as well as localities with high personal disposable income, high service new firm formation, centers covering diverse ethnic communities, and "munificent" areas with strong and varied enterprise promotion through the activities of enterprise agencies and development agencies.

Because there is no comprehensive list of new business start-ups in Great Britain, a pragmatic approach was taken in the building up of the survey frame. It was assumed that county, regional, and borough business directories contained the vast majority of all businesses in each area. The most recent available directories were cross-referenced with county and regional directories, Dun and Bradstreet, and Industrial Market Location Directories produced prior to 1986 in order to identify "potential" privately owned new businesses. The list of businesses was further cleaned and checked by cross referencing with pre-1986 Yellow Pages telephone directories, and reference was also made to the Companies House Register of Limited Companies in the United Kingdom. Community businesses and the subsidiaries and branches of companies were excluded.

On the basis of this data cleaning, a list of 4,914 names and addresses of "potential" independent new businesses was identified. Questionnaires were sent by post to the principal owner–managers of these businesses. In total, 744 questionnaires were returned of which 408 were from owner–managers of independent businesses receiving their first order between 1 January 1986 and 31 December 1990. This paper draws upon data from 405 new businesses in the database. Due to the statistical requirement to provide complete responses to the 23 reasons leading to start-up statements, responses from three owner–managers were removed from the database for this analysis. For a discussion of the limitations of this methodology see Birley and Westhead (1991).

Businesses contacted during the survey are drawn from a wide range of locations and industries. Their characteristics are:

Business Characteristics

- *Employment*: ranged from 1 to 290 total employees. Total number of employees = 3,732 people. Mean employment per firm = 9.22 (median = 4).
- *Sales*: ranged from less than £100,000 (50.8% of firms) to more than 5 million sales turnover (0.5% of firms).

TABLE 1 Reasons Leading to Start-Up of the Current Business

Reasons Leading to Start-Up	Percentages					Mean Score	Standard Deviation
	To no extent (1)	To little extent (2)	To some extent (3)	To a great extent (4)	To a very great extent (5)		
To have considerable freedom to adapt my own approach to my work	8.1	6.7	22.2	29.1	33.8	3.74*	1.22
To take advantage of an opportunity that appeared	8.6	6.9	21.7	34.1	28.6	3.67*	1.21
To control my own time	11.4	7.4	21.0	30.6	29.6	3.60*	1.29
It made sense at that time in my life	13.1	6.2	25.7	25.7	29.4	3.52*	1.33
To give myself, my spouse, and children security	17.3	5.9	22.7	23.2	30.9	3.44*	1.42
To have greater flexibility for my personal and family life	15.3	7.2	26.4	27.4	23.7	3.37*	1.33
Desire to have high earnings	17.8	11.4	31.9	19.3	19.8	3.12	1.34
To be challenged by the problems and opportunities of starting and growing a new business	18.0	14.8	24.2	24.2	18.8	3.11	1.36
To achieve something and to get recognition for it	20.2	15.1	30.1	20.5	14.1	2.93	1.31
To continue learning	19.5	15.6	33.1	20.2	11.6	2.89	1.26
To contribute to the welfare of my relatives	37.3	15.1	24.7	12.6	10.4	2.44*	1.37
To achieve a higher position for myself in society	38.5	17.0	28.6	10.1	5.7	2.27*	1.23
To be innovative and to be in the forefront of technological development	44.0	14.8	20.7	12.6	7.9	2.26*	1.34
To develop an idea for a product	49.6	8.9	18.5	13.8	9.1	2.24*	1.42
To have access to indirect benefits such as tax exemptions	50.4	21.0	20.5	4.0	4.2	1.91*	1.12
To increase the status and prestige of my family	54.3	19.3	15.6	7.2	3.7	1.87*	1.14
To contribute to the welfare of the community that I live in	57.3	18.8	17.3	5.2	1.5	1.75*	1.01
To be respected by friends	62.5	17.3	13.3	4.4	2.5	1.67*	1.03
To contribute to the welfare of people with the same background as me	72.6	14.1	9.4	2.0	2.0	1.47*	0.89
As a vehicle to reduce the burden of taxes I face	75.6	12.8	5.4	3.2	3.0	1.45*	0.95
To have more influence in my community	70.9	19.0	5.9	2.7	1.5	1.45*	0.84
To follow the example of the person that I admire	80.0	8.9	6.9	2.2	2.0	1.37*	0.86
To continue a family tradition	85.7	5.7	4.2	3.2	1.2	1.29*	0.79

**Statistically significant difference at the 0.01 level of significance (two-tailed tests).*

- *Profits*: During the past financial year the majority of businesses (58.6%) had operated at a profit, 23.5% had recorded losses, and the rest had broken even.
- *Industry*: Manufacturing—146 firms (36.0%). Service—238 firms (58.8%). Construction—21 firms (5.2%).
- *Location*: Urban locations 75.1% of firms. "Assisted" area locations 59.0% of firms.
- *Business Age*: Mean age = 3.35 years (median = 3). Range from less than 1 year to 5 years.

Owner–Manager Characteristics

- *Gender*: 90% of owner–managers in the sample were male.
- *Partners*: 66.4% of the new businesses had two or more partners or shareholders.
- *Founders' Age*: Mean age at the start of the current business = 37.3 years (median = 37.0). Age range from 18 to 75 years.

Only ten respondents (2.5%) had been unemployed prior to start-up, and so it is unlikely that many of these founders had established their new ventures with the prime intention of adhering to the "livelihood principle" by maintaining the entrepreneur in work (Oxenfeldt 1943; Wendervang 1965; Dahmen 1970). Interestingly, this proportion is markedly lower than those reported in new firm studies covering acute recessionary periods in the north-east of England (26%) (Storey 1982, p. 117), Wales[1] (29%) (Westhead 1988, p. 392), and West Lothian in Scotland (38%) (Turok and Richardson 1989, p. 28).

Data Analysis

Although the pilot study had reduced the list of reasons for start-up from 38 to 22, an underlying assumption in the design of the research was, clearly, that there would be significant inter-correlations. It is only by combining these dimensions to produce "gestalts" (Gartner et al. 1989) which "... capture the interdependencies among attributes ..." (Woo et al. 1991, p. 96) that a more holistic and realistic perspective of the entrepreneurial triggers can be obtained. Moreover, this approach is not new in the entrepreneurial field. The use of descriptive typologies to classify entrepreneurs into heterogeneous groupings had been used by, for example, Smith (1967), Stanworth and Curran (1976), and Dunkelberg and Cooper (1982a). However, a primary issue in such a process is the decision as to the choice of classification variables (or attributes). In an attempt to test the dichotomy of "craftsmen" and "opportunist" entrepreneurs, Woo et al. (1991, p. 101) suggest a hierarchical structure of dimensions as:

Classification A: Goals.

Classification B: Goals, background (education/experience).

Classification C: Goals, background (education/experience), management style.

Woo et al. (1991, p. 102) claim that, "These three schemes progress from a narrow set (special classification) to a broad scheme with all three classes of characteristics included (general classification)." In analyzing data from a group of entrepreneurs across each of these

[1] This study was concerned solely with manufacturing firms.

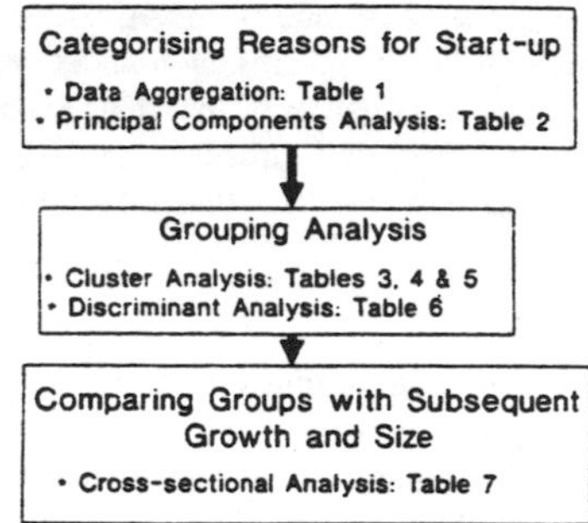

FIGURE 1 Analytical stages

dimensions, they found that the different classification criteria produced different groupings. They conclude that this particular derivation of entrepreneurial types does not appear to be robust. However, as the authors note, respondents were asked to rank individual goals but they were not able to place equal importance on more than one goal, and so the subsequent analysis was not able to detect individual "trade offs." Woo et al. (1991, p. 107) deduce from this that motivations are likely to be simultaneous rather than mutually exclusive. This is intuitively obvious to these researchers and, indeed, it is for this reason that surveyed owner–managers were asked to rate the importance of each reason leading to a start-up on a scale of 1 (to no extent) to 5 (to a very great extent).

Following from this, the most important theoretical issue is the decision as to which variables to include in the initial classification and which to use for subsequent explanatory analysis. For example, Gartner et al. (1989) followed the "Classification C" procedure and included the characteristics of the individual, the organization, the environment, and the start-up process in producing their taxonomy of new business ventures. However, on a cautionary note, Woo et al. (1991) argue in their conclusion that "Classification C" procedure is, as yet, not widely supported in the literature.

In this analysis, the focus of the "gestalt" is the combination of factors that projected the individual into starting a new business. The subsequent analysis follows the implicit research question in the papers of Gartner et al. (1989) and Woo et al. (1991)—*in what ways, if any, are the groups of entrepreneurs different in their personal background and in the particular characteristics of the businesses they created?* The analytical procedure adopted in this study is shown in Figure 1.

Not surprisingly, there was considerable inter-correlation between the 23 reasons leading to start-up variables from 405 owner–managers. Therefore, in order to develop an "objective" classification of founders based on these variables a "minimum variance" clustering procedure was used. The 23 variables were first "ortho-normalized" using Principal Components Analysis (PCA) into a smaller number of new independent orthogonal reference axes of stated reasons. This technique removed the distorting effect that strong inter-correlations among the 23 variables (or attributes) would have on the calculation of the various "distance" and "variance" measures used in the QUICK CLUSTER analysis. On the basis of the new independent and orthogonal component scores from the factor analytic model a typology of owner–managers was produced using cluster analysis. Clearly, by allocating individual founders (and businesses) to a small number of groups (in this following example, seven) there will inevitably be a loss of detail. In compensation, however, there is a considerable gain in the resultant level of generalization. Cluster analysis serves a useful purpose in helping to distinguish broad patterns of founder reasons leading to start-up "types" using multivariate sets of information (Carter and Aitchison 1986, pp. 19–20). It allows the analyst to develop an integrated classification of founder "types" while the accuracy of the typology can be assessed by discriminant analysis.

RESULTS

For the 23 statements Table 1 shows the resultant total scores ranked in order of the mean score. The first six statements show a mean score that is significantly greater than the mid-point score of 3 at a 1% level of significance. All reflect a positive economic environment combined with a personal need to change direction:

- To have considerable freedom to adapt my own approach to my work (mean score of 3.74).
- To take advantage of an opportunity that appeared (3.67).
- To control my own time (3.60).
- It made sense at that time in my life (3.52).
- To give myself, my spouse and children security (3.44).
- To have greater flexibility for my personal and family life (3.37).

The second four statements which include a "desire for high earnings" and a "need to achieve something and get recognition for it," the popular conceptions of entrepreneurial motivation, are stimuli that evenly divide the group with approximately one-third showing indifference (at a 1% significance level). The remaining 13 statements have a mean score that is significantly lower than 3 (at a 1% level of significance) and reflect reasons for start-up drawn from the literature but to which these owner–managers do not appear to subscribe strongly. So, for example, "having more influence in the community" (1.45), "following an admired person" (1.37), and "continuing a family tradition" (1.29) were hardly rated at all.

Overall, this preliminary analysis would appear to support the results found in the earlier study of new firm founders in England, Australia, Sweden, Finland, Norway, Denmark, and the United States (Scheinberg and MacMillan 1988, p. 687) that the drive to be independent was the dominant reason leading to venture initiation. However, by asking the owner–managers to rate all the 23 reasons, the researchers recognized that starting a business is a complex process which involves a variety of motivations and stimuli. Therefore, the second part of the analysis is concerned with identifying the underlying patterns in the responses.

PRINCIPAL COMPONENTS ANALYSIS

An R-Mode Principal Components Analysis (PCA) was used to transform and "ortho-normalize" the original data for the 23 selected reasons leading to business start-up. Norusis (1988, B-46) has suggested that PCA "... can be used whenever uncorrelated linear combinations of the observed variables are desired. All it does is transform a set of correlated variables to a set of uncorrelated variables (principal components)." Further, "its biggest advantage is that no assumptions are made about the size of the communality, as 1.0 is entered into all the diagonal cells of the similarity matrix. This means that each variable is given equal weight in the analysis. As such the model is best utilized either for re-writing data in a concise, parsimonious form as a prelude to some other analysis, or for simply exploring or describing the relationships in a data set" (Davies 1984, p. 131). In this study the resulting independent and orthogonal reference axes, as reflected in the component scores for each founder (or case), form the data for a general classification (Woo et al. 1991, pp. 98–99) of owner–manager reasons leading to start-up "types" using cluster analysis.

The initial extraction of orthogonal reference axes by PCA produced seven components with an eigenvalue above one but they could not be easily labeled. Here, it is appreciated that, "Rotated components do allow better group identification, which may be desirable, if, for example, the scores are to be used as independent variables . . ." (Johnston 1980, p. 172). Therefore, in order to achieve a solution in which each of the original variables was highly correlated with only one component, a varimax rotation was undertaken (see Table 2). The first seven components, all of which had sums of squares of the component loadings greater than 1, accounted for 60.6% of the total variance. Moreover, the choice of the 23 variables as representing the potential primary reasons leading to start-up of the owner–manager are justified because all load on to at least one of the components identified. This rotated component model was found to be an appropriate factor-analytic model (Norusis 1985) as indicated by Bartlett's test of sphericity, the Kaiser–Meyer–Olkin measure of sampling adequacy (0.79), the anti-image correlation matrix, the test for sampling adequacy, and the test for communality.

The following description of the components uses those variables with factor loadings greater than 0.3 (Hair et al. 1979). Description of the components here enables the data collected for new firm founders in Great Britain to be compared with the results of earlier studies using "factor analytic" methods to identify the leading or "primary" groups of reasons leading to new business start-up. Five of the components correspond to those identified by Scheinberg and MacMillan (1988) and so, for reasons of consistency, the labels that they ascribed are used in the following discussion.

Component 1: Need for Approval

All except one of the variables in this component load greater than 0.5 and so are considered to be very meaningful (Hair et al. 1979). Moreover, the component closely corresponds to Scheinberg and MacMillan's Factor 1 (1988, pp. 680–681) in the previously presented eleven-country study of reasons leading to start-up. As the earlier research suggested, this indicates a founder primarily concerned with external approval and input, a strong "Need for Approval." Linked with McClelland's theories on need for achievement (McClelland et al. 1953; McClelland 1961), the component scores highly on position and recognition and so is strongly associated with Maslow's (1943) fourth level need, "esteem" or self-actualization (Maslow 1954). Thus, venture initiation is seen as part of personal development, a means by which the founder can progress ideas and, consequently, corresponds to the traits of individualistic behavior discussed by Hofstede (1980).

Component 2: Need for Independence

This "Need for Independence" component corresponds to Scheinberg and MacMillan's (1988) Factor 5. Again, this empirical evidence provides support for Hofstede's (1980) scale of "Individualism" where personal control and freedom of choice are paramount to the new business founder.

TABLE 2 Reasons Leading to Start-Up: Varimax Rotated Component Matrix

Variables	Varimax Rotated Components							Communality
	1	2	3	4	5	6	7	(h^2)
To be challenged by the problems and opportunities of starting and growing a new business	0.292	**0.396**	0.214	0.068	**–0.358**	0.016	0.048	0.423
To continue learning	0.152	**0.353**	**0.566**	0.132	–0.092	0.071	0.181	0.532
To be innovative and be in the forefront of technological development	0.076	0.125	**0.795**	0.164	0.011	0.039	0.136	0.700
To develop an idea for a product	0.003	–0.029	**0.755**	0.123	–0.008	–0.055	0.016	0.589
To follow the example of the person that I admire	0.180	0.122	0.167	–0.091	0.039	0.087	**0.768**	0.682
To have considerable freedom to adapt my own approach to my work	0.096	**0.809**	0.099	–0.021	0.016	0.075	0.017	0.680
To control my own time	0.006	**0.779**	0.008	0.113	0.073	0.038	0.007	0.627
It made sense at that time in my life	0.067	**0.376**	0.065	–0.060	–0.077	**0.374**	0.046	0.302
To take advantage of an opportunity that appeared	0.085	–0.080	**0.382**	–0.254	**0.310**	0.223	–0.246	0.430
To give myself, my spouse, and children security	0.201	0.125	–0.034	0.021	**0.793**	–0.003	0.037	0.688
Desire to have high earnings	**0.543**	0.134	0.060	–0.253	**0.349**	0.202	–0.008	0.543
To have access to indirect benefits such as tax exemptions	0.144	0.184	0.026	0.066	0.112	**0.767**	0.062	0.664
As a vehicle to reduce the burden of taxes I face	0.029	0.005	–0.015	0.164	0.020	**0.835**	0.131	0.743
To have greater flexibility for my personal and family life	0.056	**0.792**	0.038	0.091	0.182	0.102	0.020	0.684
To achieve something and get recognition for it	**0.654**	0.283	0.264	0.031	–0.120	–0.118	–0.026	0.607
To achieve a higher position for myself in society	**0.795**	0.002	0.055	0.085	0.138	0.019	–0.058	0.665
To increase the status and prestige of my family	**0.668**	0.025	–0.022	0.166	0.278	0.131	0.181	0.602
To be respected by friends	**0.685**	0.012	–0.034	0.209	–0.075	0.156	**0.321**	0.647
To have more influence in my community	**0.443**	0.058	0.084	**0.498**	–0.074	0.203	0.299	0.591
To continue a family tradition	0.035	–0.052	0.041	0.228	0.101	0.113	0.728	0.611
To contribute to the welfare of my relatives	0.056	0.072	0.037	**0.307**	**0.696**	0.062	0.131	0.609
To contribute to the welfare of the community that I live in	0.094	0.094	0.188	**0.801**	0.106	0.042	–0.097	0.717
To contribute to the welfare of people with the same background as me	0.115	0.067	0.153	**0.696**	0.144	0.110	0.206	0.601
Sums of squares of the component loadings	2.725	2.522	1.906	1.857	1.691	1.678	1.558	13.937
Percent of variance	11.83	10.97	8.29	8.07	7.35	7.30	6.77	
Cumulative percent of variance	11.85	22.82	31.11	39.18	46.53	53.83	60.60	

Component 3: Need for Personal Development

This "Need for Personal Development" component (Factor 4: Scheinberg and MacMillan 1988) stresses reasons linked to individual personal development and to learning, traits that Scheinberg and MacMillan (1988, p. 682) indicated correspond to a "non-masculine" approach and "It is here where the personal effect of the entrepreneur is seen as directly affecting the performance of the business; while simultaneously the business is seen as the means to keep developing the entrepreneur."

Component 4: Welfare Considerations

This component is clearly strongly related to Hofstede's "Collectivism" index and Lodge's (1976) concept of "Communitarianism" (Factor 3: Scheinberg and MacMillan 1988) and may be linked to Friberg's (1976) moral and ideological "internalized incentives" group. Thus, starting a business due to "Philanthropy" is a way for the founder to contribute to the wider welfare of the group of which he is part, whether it be his community, people with the same background, or his immediate family (Dubini 1988, p. 15–16).

Component 5: Perceived Instrumentality of Wealth

This component corresponds to Factor 2 in the Scheinberg and MacMillan (1988, p. 680) study and to the "Materialism" component in Dubini's (1988, pp. 15–16) analysis of owner–managers in Italy, a component that closely relates to characteristics of ideal compensation methods reported by Peterson and Stevenson (1987).

Component 6: Tax Reduction and Indirect Benefits

This group of reasons leading to start-up were not directly identified in the earlier study. However, it must be recalled that during this current study an additional tax reduction question ("as a vehicle to reduce the burden of taxes I face") was incorporated into the revised questionnaire to take into account the importance of this reason in Scandinavian countries. The component reflects, in an indirect way, the objective of founders to increase personal wealth by retaining previously earned money, a reason that Dubini (1988, p. 17) suggests is a means of allowing for independence and freedom.

Component 7: Follow Role Models

This component more closely relates to a wider social incentive, identification with other individuals, rather than with personal initiative (Friberg 1976). Dubini (1988, p. 17) identified a similar "Role Model" component and concluded that members of this group "... confirm the importance of role models and family attitudes (Shapero and Sokol 1982) in influencing the desirability of starting a new business.

GROUPING ANALYSIS

Reassuringly, it is clear from the presented evidence that the linked trends isolated in the rotated component structure do have meaningful expression in relation to the literature. However, whereas the above analysis enables a description of the pattern for each single component, nothing other than intuitive classification can be attempted. Therefore, the responses from the 405 owner–managers were re-classified using the varimax rotated component scores—these "ortho-normalized" scores evaluate the owner–manager's ratings on the seven basic patterns of the original data identified by the Principal Components Analysis. The 405 by 7 matrix of component scores formed the basis for the QUICK CLUSTER analysis (Norusis 1988).

Determination of the appropriate number of groups or types is a key arbitrary decision in cluster analysis that must be made with strong prior theoretical assessment (Woo et al. 1991, p. 103). In this study seven clusters were specified because the PCA had identified seven themes within the database.

Scanning the data in Table 3, cluster 7 is immediately distinguishable in two ways. First, it has only one member and second, the number of variables that are significant suggests a varied and unfocused set of reasons leading to venture initiation. Therefore, this cluster was eliminated from any further analysis. For the six remaining clusters, one-way analysis of variance was conducted for each of the seven components. The results, presented in Table 4, show that six clusters are well separated based on the Euclidean distances from their centers. However, because this analysis had only accounted for 60.6% of the variance in the data, chi-square statistics were calculated between each of the six clusters with respect to the original "*raw*" data for the 23 reasons leading to start-up statements on the five-point Likert scale (Table 3). Statistically significant contrasts were recorded among the six remaining cluster groups with respect to 22 variables. Interestingly, no statistically significant difference was recorded among the clusters with regard to the reason "to take advantage of an opportunity" on which all groups scored greater than the indifference score of 3.

In order to allocate a descriptive label to each of the seven clusters, the cluster mean for each of the 23 variables from the original "raw" data was compared to the respective global mean for that variable (Table 3). The combination of variables that contributed to each of the components (discussed above and detailed in Table 2) were then scanned for each cluster. Further, the cluster mean for each of the earlier identified principal components was calculated (Table 5). Overall, the results from the two analyses are reasonably consistent. Therefore, component descriptions are used in the description of the clusters. Cases where cluster means for a variable deviate by more than a full or half a standard deviation from the respective global mean are used in the commentary below to highlight the distinguishing characteristics of each of the clusters (Openshaw 1983). Two perspectives are used—those components where the majority of the variables score significantly different from the global mean, and those components where the majority of variables score greater than the indifference score of 3. The resulting generalized description of the clusters is shown below.

Cluster 1: N = 104: The Insecure

Founders in this cluster show a significantly higher score than those in the other clusters on only one component—in their *need for approval.*

Cluster 2: N = 49: The Followers

Owner–managers in this cluster show a significant difference from the rest of the group in two out of three variables that contribute to component 7, *the need to follow role models*, although the scores are below the indifference point. There is also some indication that this group was concerned with a *need for personal development* and a *need for independence.*

TABLE 3 Cluster Characteristics of Owner–Managers Reasons Leading to Start-Up

Variables	Variables Related to Principal Components	Clusters							Global Mean	Standard Deviation
		1	2	3	4	5	6	7		
To be challenged by the problems and opportunities of starting and growing a new business (áá)	5, 2	3.48	3.41	2.69	3.53	3.00	3.43	1.00**	3.11	1.36
To continue learning (áá)	3, 2	2.86	3.63	2.51	3.60	2.67	3.34	5.00**	2.89	1.26
To be innovative and be in the forefront of technological development (áá)	3	1.81	3.20*	1.95	2.87	2.22	3.10*	5.00**	2.26	1.34
To develop an idea for a product (áá)	3	1.69	2.90	2.18	3.07*	1.61	2.94	1.00*	2.24	1.42
To follow the example of the person that I admire (áá)	7	1.29	2.57**	1.04	2.47**	1.39	1.08	5.00**	1.37	0.86
To have considerable freedom to adapt my own approach to my work (áá)	2	3.90	4.35	3.27	3.53	4.17	4.35	1.00**	3.74	1.22
To control my own time (áá)	2	3.60	4.00	3.24	4.00	4.00	4.20	1.00**	3.60	1.29
It made sense at that time in my life (á)	6, 2	3.52	3.73	3.30	4.13	4.17	3.63	5.00**	3.52	1.32
To take advantage of an opportunity that appeared (n.s.)	5, 3	3.61	3.86	3.51	3.60	4.39*	4.00	1.00**	3.67	1.21
To give myself, my spouse, and children security (áá)	5	3.55	3.96	2.92	3.93	3.56	4.39*	1.00**	3.44	1.42
Desire to have high earnings (áá)	5, 1	3.76	3.47	2.44*	3.60	3.50	3.51	1.00**	3.12	1.34
To have access to indirect benefits such as tax exemptions (áá)	6	1.85	2.04	1.54	3.27**	3.72**	2.00	5.00**	1.91	1.11
As a vehicle to reduce the burden of taxes I face (áá)	6	1.22	1.24	1.24	3.13**	4.17**	1.31	5.00**	1.45	0.95
To have greater flexibility for my personal and family life (áá)	2	3.38	3.90	2.93	3.60	3.94	4.12*	1.00**	3.37	1.33
To achieve something and get recognition for it (áá)	1	3.75*	3.12	2.21	3.60*	2.33	3.53	1.00**	2.93	1.31
To achieve a higher position for myself in society (áá)	1	3.20*	1.92	1.53*	3.47*	2.17	2.92*	1.00**	2.27	1.23
To increase the status and prestige of my family (áá)	1	2.53*	1.86	1.22*	3.40**	1.50	2.29	5.00**	1.87	1.14
To be respected by friends (áá)	7, 1	2.29*	1.68	1.14*	3.53**	1.50	1.61	5.00**	1.67	1.03
To have more influence in my community (áá)	4, 1	1.59	1.29	1.17	3.40**	1.39	1.65	5.00**	1.45	0.84
To continue a family tradition (áá)	7	1.11	1.90	1.08	3.27**	1.28	1.08	5.00**	1.29	0.79
To contribute to the welfare of my relatives (áá)	5, 4	2.22	2.78	1.98	3.47*	2.56	3.73*	5.00**	2.44	1.37
To contribute to the welfare of the community that I live in (áá)	4	1.45	1.43	1.60	2.73*	1.28	3.00**	5.00**	1.75	1.01
To contribute to the welfare of people with the same background as me (áá)	4	1.19	1.45	1.24	2.93**	1.17	2.45**	5.00**	1.47	0.89
Number of founders in the cluster		104	49	169	15	18	49	1		

Notes:
** Cluster mean which deviates by more than a standard deviation from the respective global mean.
* Cluster mean which deviates by more than half a standard deviation from the respective global mean.
(áá) Chi-square coefficient statistically different at the 0.001 level of significance for the six clusters (excluding the one founder in cluster 7).
(á) Chi-square coefficient statistically different at the 0.05 level of significance for the six clusters.
(n.s.) No statistically significant difference between the six cluster "types."

TABLE 4 Between- and Within-Cluster Mean Square Variability for the Six Cluster Solution (Excluding the Sole Founder in Cluster 7)

Variable	Between-Cluster Mean Square (Cluster MS)	d.f.	Within-Cluster Mean Square (Error MS)	d.f.	F	Probability
Component 1	42.76	5	0.48	398	89.18	0.000
Component 2	9.07	5	0.88	398	10.30	0.000
Component 3	13.29	5	0.85	398	15.68	0.000
Component 4	27.01	5	0.62	398	43.30	0.000
Component 5	11.50	5	0.86	398	13.30	0.000
Component 6	35.11	5	0.55	398	64.38	0.000
Component 7	36.78	5	0.47	398	78.56	0.000

Cluster 3: $N = 169$: The Status Avoiders

All the four variables that score significantly lower than the global means load inversely onto the component *need for approval*; the remaining three variables show the same pattern, also being below. The only other component that scores consistently above 3, although not significantly greater than the global mean, is component 2—*need for independence.*

Cluster 4: $N = 15$: The Confused

This small group shows a significant difference from the rest for the majority of variables in four of the seven components—*need for approval, welfare considerations, for reasons of tax reduction and other indirect benefits* and to *follow role models*. Overall, this group scored highly on almost all the variables measured.

Cluster 5: $N = 18$: The Tax Avoiders

This group was driven significantly more than the rest by a need for *tax reduction and other indirect benefits*. They also consistently scored highly on a *need for independence.*

Cluster 6: $N = 49$: The Community

The results for this group are less consistent with the original principal component analysis than the previous five in that four of the variables that score significantly greater than the global mean load on different components. However, the remaining three show that this group

TABLE 5 Final Cluster Centers Based on the Average Values of the Component Scores

Component	Clusters 1	2	3	4	5	6	7
1. Need for approval	1.04	−0.27	−0.66	1.01	−0.49	0.24	−0.44
2. Need for independence	0.09	0.51	−0.32	−0.36	0.18	0.50	−2.93
3. Need for personal development	−0.42	0.76	−0.11	0.14	−0.22	0.57	−0.19
4. Welfare considerations	−0.34	−0.69	−0.02	1.49	−0.53	1.12	4.53
5. Perceived instrumentality of wealth	−0.18	0.41	−0.27	0.08	0.08	0.83	−1.01
6. Tax reduction and indirect benefits	−0.22	−0.24	−0.15	1.39	2.70	−0.26	3.51
7. Follow role models	−0.20	1.34	−0.23	1.94	−0.24	−0.72	5.76

is significantly different from the rest in their concern for *welfare considerations*. For the rest *need for independence, need for personal development*, and the *perceived instrumentality of wealth* also score consistently above the indifference point.

DISCRIMINANT ANALYSIS: EVALUATION OF THE ACCURACY OF THE CLASSIFICATION

The appropriateness of the seven-cluster classification of owner–managers' reasons leading to start-up was tested using discriminant analysis (Johnston 1980, p. 239; Norusis 1985, p. 73) based on the original "raw" reasons leading to start-up data for the 405 founders (or cases). The final discriminant analysis model that minimized the Wilks' lambda included 20 out of the original 23 variables (the three reasons not included in the final model were "to control my own time," "it made sense at that time in my life," and "to have greater flexibility for my personal and family life"). Classification results from the final discriminant model presented in Table 6 show that the seven-cluster solution of reasons leading to start-up founder "types" is optimal. The vast majority of owner–managers were allocated by the model to the group specified by the cluster analysis at a level that is significantly higher than that which could be achieved by chance alone. Approximately 90% of owner–managers were correctly classified with only 41 individuals allocated to a group other than that defined by the cluster analysis.

CROSS-SECTIONAL ANALYSIS: CHARACTERISTICS OF OWNER–MANAGERS AND NEW BUSINESSES

The aim of this final section was to test whether or not the clusters fall into a logical sequence when the characteristics of the owner–managers and those of their firms are taken into account. Therefore, analysis of variance and chi-square analyses were conducted on a total of 48 variables listed in Table 7. Surprisingly, significant differences between clusters were observed in only 12.5% of the analyzed dimensions. Thus

- A significantly larger proportion of *the followers* and *the status avoiders* founders in clusters 2 and 3 were engaged in manufacturing activities, whereas over 65% of founders in the remaining clusters had established construction or service ventures.
- The mean age of owner–managers when their businesses received their first order was 37.3 years. However, the *status avoiding* founders of businesses located in cluster 3 were significantly older than their counterparts (mean = 40.1 years), particularly those in the *confused* cluster 4 (mean = 28.1 years). Although this is an unsought result, it does suggest a possible relationship between age and clarity of direction when starting a new firm.
- A significantly larger proportion of the *followers*, running primarily manufacturing firms, had parents who had been business owners (45.8%), whereas those in clusters 1, 5, and 6—the *insecure*, the *tax avoiders*, and the *community groups*—were more likely to have parents from professional or managerial backgrounds (Criteria 13). Gibb and Ritchie (1981, p. 36) suggest that a high level of formal educational attainment is not inconsistent with entrepreneurial intention (for a dissenting view see Pickles and O'Farrell 1987) and small business growth (Dunkelberg and Cooper 1982b). In terms of this study the majority of owner–managers in each of the cluster "types" had

TABLE 6 Classification Results from a Discriminant Analysis Model Evaluating the Accuracy of the Typology Produced by Cluster Analysis

Actual Cluster/Group	Number of Cases	Predicted Group Membership							Percent of "Grouped" Cases Correctly Classified
		1	2	3	4	5	6	7	
Cluster 1	104	96 92.3%	2 1.9%	5 4.8%	1 1.0%	0 0.0%	0 0.0%	0 0.0%	96 92.3%
Cluster 2	49	1 2.0%	42 85.7%	2 4.1%	1 2.0%	0 0.0%	3 6.1%	0 0.0%	42 85.7%
Cluster 3	169	3 1.8%	1 0.6%	148 87.6%	1 0.6%	4 2.4%	12 7.1%	0 0.0%	148 87.6%
Cluster 4	15	0 0.0%	0 0.0%	0 0.0%	15 100.0%	0 0.0%	0 0.0%	0 0.0%	15 100.0%
Cluster 5	18	0 0.0%	0 0.0%	0 0.0%	0 0.0%	18 100.0%	0 0.0%	0 0.0%	18 100.0%
Cluster 6	49	1 2.0%	0 0.0%	3 6.1%	0 0.0%	1 2.0%	44 89.8%	0 0.0%	44 89.8%
Cluster 7	1	0 0.0%	0 0.0%	0 0.0%	0 0.0%	0 0.0%	0 0.0%	1 100.0%	1 100.0%
Total "grouped" cases correctly classified		96 92.3%	42 85.7%	148 87.6%	15 100.0%	18 100.0%	44 89.8%	1 100.0%	364 89.9%

TABLE 7 Statistically Significant Differences Between New Firms by Owner–Manager Reasons Leading to Start-Up Cluster "Types"

Criteria	Chi-square Statistic (X^2)	Degrees of Freedom (d.f.)	Significance Level	"F" Statistic	Degrees of Freedom V^1	Degrees of Freedom V^2	Significance Level
(a) Business Data							
1. Age of the business				1.21	5	398	0.303
2. Number of shareholders or partners				1.50	5	396	0.190
3. Industrial activity of the new business	11.33	5	**0.045**				
4. Primary operational premises located in a rural area	4.51	5	0.479				
5. Primary operational premises located in an "assisted" area main operational premises	3.75	5	0.580				
6. Absolute present employment size				0.36	5	398	0.877
7. Standardized present employment size				0.40	5	398	0.847
8. Change in absolute number of employees since received first order				0.26	5	398	0.934
9. Change in standardized number of employees since received first order				0.29	5	398	0.919
(b) Personal Background of the Founder							
10. Age of founder when business received first order				7.12	5	396	**0.000**
11. Gender of founder	(a)						
12. Parents immigrants	(a)						
13. Occupational status of parents	34.49	10	**0.000**				
14. Founders' highest education level	15.18	10	0.126				
(c) Work Experience of the Founder							
15. Job title of last employer	2.47	5	0.781				
16. Business started in the same industry as last employer	4.55	5	0.474				
17. "Type" of last employer	11.04	5	0.051				
18. Employment size of last employer	2.93	5	0.710				
19. Current business relationship with last employer	4.84	5	0.436				
20. Number of organizations worked for by the founder				1.29	5	386	0.267
21. Number of businesses established prior to this current one				0.51	5	389	0.772
22. Business started on a part-time basis	6.16	5	0.291				

(continued)

TABLE 7 Statistically Significant Differences Between New Firms by Owner–Manager Reasons Leading to Start-Up Cluster "Types" *(continued)*

Criteria	Chi-square Statistic (X^2)	Degrees of Freedom (d.f.)	Significance Level	"F" Statistic	Degrees of Freedom V^1	Degrees of Freedom V^2	Significance Level
(d) Financial Base							
23. Number of sources of start-up capital				0.53	5	398	0.751
24. Number of current sources of capital				1.14	5	398	0.338
25. Level of sales for the last financial year (£'s)	8.42	5	0.135				
26. Percentage change in sales in the past year	7.78	5	0.169				
27. Percentage of sales revenue accounted for by major product line or service group				2.92	5	309	**0.014**
28. Level of profitability	6.97	5	0.223				
29. Change in the level of profitability in the last year	5.02	5	0.413				
30. Current profit performance relative to competition	1.62	5	0.899				
(e) Customer and Supplier Base							
31. Number of customers	19.49	10	**0.035**				
32. Location of majority of customers	18.90	10	**0.042**				
33. Four customers or fewer accounting for 75% of sales revenue	9.75	5	0.083				
34. Number of suppliers	8.22	10	0.608				
35. Location of majority of suppliers	15.06	10	0.130				
36. Four suppliers or fewer accounting for 75% of purchases	10.29	5	0.068				
37. Percentage of sales exported				0.52	5	395	0.763

(continued)

TABLE 7 Statistically Significant Differences Between New Firms by Owner–Manager Reasons Leading to Start-Up Cluster "Types" *(continued)*

Criteria	Chi-square Statistic (X^2)	Degrees of Freedom (d.f.)	Significance Level	"F" Statistic	Degrees of Freedom		Significance Level
					V^1	V^2	
(f) Competitive Structure							
38. Number of competitors	1.18	5	0.947				
39. Employment size of major competitor	3.94	5	0.755				
40. Price of major product or service relative to direct competitors	2.64	5	0.558				
41. Quality and finish of major product or service relative to direct competitors	5.81	10	0.831				
42. Design quality of major product or service relative to direct competitors	8.78	10	0.553				
43. Quality of labor force	3.99	5	0.551				
44. Quality of local material input supplies	7.83	5	0.166				
(g) Future of the Business							
45. Standard of living today	9.58	10	0.479				
46. Future of the business	4.01	5	0.547				
47. Desire for growth	(a)						
48. Intend to increase number of employees in the next two years	9.26	5	0.099				

Note: (a) Due to the assumptions of the chi-square test it was not possible to calculate a coefficient.

progressed beyond compulsory school education. Whereas over 50% of founders in each of the clusters had obtained technical or professional qualifications, the larger proportion of owner–managers (although not statistically significant) in clusters 2 and 3, the *followers* and the *status avoiders*, who were more likely to have established manufacturing ventures, had also obtained some form of university degree.

- More than 60% of businesses in clusters 1, 4, and 6—the *insecure*, the *confused*, and the *community* clusters—had more than 50 customers, whereas 41.2% of businesses in the *tax avoiders* cluster 5 had between 11 and 50 customers (Criteria 31). In marked contrast, those businesses located in clusters 2 and 3 with a significantly greater propensity to be engaged in manufacturing activities (Criteria 3) also had a markedly greater tendency to have fewer than 11 customers. However, in terms of the location of the majority of customers (i.e., more than 50%) founders in clusters 2 and 3 were also more likely to serve customers located outside in the county region of the businesses' primary operational premises whereas the generally more non-manufacturing positioned businesses in clusters 4, 5, and 6 had the majority of their customers within the same county.
- Only a small minority of the surveyed businesses appear to have diversified their product/market base. With the exception of the *confused* cluster 4, more than 40% of businesses in each cluster had more than 75% of their sales revenue dependent on the performance of the single major product line or service group. However, significantly more founders in this clusters were less dependent on the fortunes of their major product line or service group than their counterparts, particularly in the *tax avoiders* cluster 5.

GROWTH AND SIZE

The above analysis has indicated clear differences in the reasons that owner–managers articulate for starting their business and has shown some differences in the characteristics of their firms. However, the primary aim of the study was to determine whether or not there were any observable differences in the company size, performance, and the owner–managers' expressed desire for growth. For example, did the owner–managers in cluster 5, *the tax avoiders*, who were primarily concerned with the need to control their personal finances, grow larger, more profitable businesses than either the *confused* cluster, apparently unsure of their original goals, or the *community* cluster?

Size:

Surprisingly, there were no statistically significant differences in size, as measured by sales revenue or employment levels, among businesses located in the six clusters. However, there is some indication that owner–managers of businesses in clusters 2, 3, and 5 (*the followers, the status avoiders and the tax avoiders)* had established larger employment-sized businesses (mean values of 10.6, 10.0, and 10.0 people, respectively) than their counterparts, particularly those located in clusters 4 and 6, the *confused* and *community* groups (4.7 and 7.8 people, respectively). Similarly, *the followers, status avoiders, and tax avoiders* recorded larger mean absolute increases in total employment since start-up than did their colleagues. The lowest level of job generation was recorded by the *confused* cluster 4. Overall, these results were sustained when part-time and casual employees were taken into account by scoring full-time, part-time, and casual employees 1, 0.5, and 0.25, respectively (Cooper et al. 1989, pp. 323–324).

Growth:

As with measures of size, no significant differences emerged with regard to growth. Indeed, over 58% of all founders indicated that their sales had increased during the past year, although more founders in the *follower* cluster 2 stated their sales had declined or were about the same. Moreover, during this recessionary time period over 46% of founders in each of the cluster groups stated their businesses had made a profit during the previous financial year, with the largest proportions being recorded in the *tax avoiders* and *followers* clusters (77.8% and 65.3%, respectively). No significant differences were recorded among clusters with regard to current profit performance relative to competition.

Future of the Business

Past performances may not necessarily be an indication of future intentions. Therefore, the owner–managers were also asked to indicate their expectations for the future. No significant differences emerged. The majority of *all* founders indicated that their standard of living had been sustained since they had started the business, and over 39% indicated they were "better off." Also, the majority of founders believed that their businesses would be growing/ expanding during the next two years, with over 88% stating that they *wished* to grow their business in the future. Within this, a slightly larger proportion of founders in cluster 5, the *tax avoiders* group, indicated they had no desire for further growth! Similarly, the majority of founders (over 55%) in all except cluster 4, the *confused* cluster, stated they intended to increase the employment size of their business in the next two years.

SUMMARY AND CONCLUSIONS

The first aim of this study was to explore the ways in which owner–managers in Great Britain articulated their reasons for starting their business and to determine if these differed from those expressed by their colleagues in other countries. As expected, these surveyed "surviving" founders of new businesses are not a homogeneous group and so it would be unwise to treat them as such (Birley and Westhead 1990). However, within the diverse mix of reasons leading to start-up listed in Table 1 an underlying pattern emerged from the Principal Components Analysis. Moreover and reassuringly, linked trends isolated in the rotated component structure had meaningful expression in relation to the literature. Indeed, five of the seven components identified by the factor analytic model correspond to those identified by Scheinberg and MacMillan (1988) in their eleven-country study of motivations to start a business: "*Need for Approval,*" "*Need for Independence,*" "*Need for Personal Development,*" "*Welfare Considerations,*" and "*Perceived Instrumentality of Wealth.*" Two further components were identified by this current study. The first clearly vindicates the addition of the questions related to "*Tax Reduction and Indirect Benefits*"; the second, a desire to "*Follow Role Models,*" was identified by Dubini (1988) in her study of owner–managers in Italy. Therefore, the first important conclusion from this study is that these owner–managers would appear to be driven by similar types of start-up triggers to those of their colleagues in other countries. However, this result does not imply mutual exclusivity, that, for example, an owner–manager driven by a need for personal development may not also be concerned to reduce his tax burden. Therefore, the second stage of the analysis was concerned to determine if there was any overriding pattern in the *combination* of start-up reasons articulated by the owner–managers. This was found to be the case. The cluster analysis identified several generalized "types" of owner–managers that were named as follows—*the insecure, the followers, the status avoiders, the confused, the tax avoiders, the community, and the unfocused.* Moreover, results from the final discriminant analysis model suggested that this seven-cluster classification of owner–managers was appropriate and optimal.

The above result is important because it reinforces the view of the recent researchers that it is dangerous to dichotomize potential entrepreneurs into simple bivariate categories. However, the more important question for policy-makers and investors is whether or not these identifiable start-up triggers are predictors of the nature of the subsequent business. In other words, are they likely to be helpful in the process of directing policy and "picking winners"? The results from the final stages of analysis would suggest not. No significant differences were recorded between the defined clusters with regard to business size or business growth or, indeed, desire for further increases in growth and size. For example, the *insecure* founders, who might be expected to have a strong drive to succeed, did not consistently outperform their *community* counterparts who went into business "to give myself, my spouse, and children security" as well as wider "welfare considerations" not only to their family and relatives but to their community. Whereas the *insecure* owner–managers had a greater tendency to have established profitable business that were slightly larger in terms of present employment size, the *community* founders initiated ventures that had a greater propensity to have sales more than 100,000 and to be engaged in exporting sales abroad. This evidence supports the view of Milne and Thompson (1982) and Hjern et al. (1980) that, although new businesses are founded by individuals with significantly different reasons leading to start-up, once the new ventures are established these reasons have a minimal influence on the growth of new ventures and upon the subsequent wealth creation and job generation potential. Indeed, they would appear more likely to be influenced by market factors of industry, the diversity of the major product line or the service group, and the ability to sell to a large number of customers, many of which are outside the "local" area of the business.

This is an exploratory study and, relatively speaking, the sample size is small. Nevertheless, the findings are consistent with those of researchers elsewhere. Moreover, the most important finding is not the particular labeling of the typologies of owner–managers because these may well vary over time, but that there is no apparent relationship between the clusters and the subsequent growth of the business. This has clear implications for government and for policy-makers. There is no evidence to support strategies and policies to assist new small business start-ups based solely on the characteristics of owner–managers and their stated initial reasons for wanting to go into business. Targeting scarce resources to potential "winners" with high opportunistic and materialistic reasons for venture initiation would miss those individuals either with a wider sense of community or even personal need for independence who establish similar sized businesses with comparable levels of wealth creation.

REFERENCES

Alange, S., and Scheinberg, S. 1988. Swedish entrepreneurship in a cross-cultural perspective. In B.A. Kirchhoff, W.A. Long, W.E. McMullan, K.H. Vesper, and W.E. Wetzel, Jr., eds., *Frontiers of Entrepreneurship Research*. Wellesley, MA: Babson College, pp. 1–15.

Allen, J., and Massey, D., eds., 1988. *Restructuring Britain, The Economy in Question*. London: Sage.

Atkinson, R.L., and Hilgard, E.R. 1983. *Introduction to Psychology*. New York: Harcourt Brace Jovanovich Inc.

Beesley, M.E., and Wilson. P. 1982. Government aid to the smaller firm since Bolton. In J. Stanworth, A. Westrip, D. Watkins, and J. Lewis, eds., *Perspectives on a Decade of Small Business Research*. Aldershot: Gower, pp. 181–199.

Begley, T.M., and Boyd, D.P. 1987. Psychological characteristics associated with performance in entrepreneurial firms and smaller businesses. *Journal of Business Venturing* 2:79–93.

Binks, M., and Jennings, A. 1986. New firms as a source of industrial regeneration. In M. Scott, A. Gibb, J. Lewis, and T. Faulkner, eds., *Small Firms' Growth and Development*. Aldershot: Gower, pp. 3–11.

Birley, S., and Westhead, P. 1990. Growth and performance contrasts between "types" of small firms. *Strategic Management Journal* 11:535–557.

Birley, S., and Westhead, P. 1991. The effect of "assisted" area status on the profile of new firms. *Proceedings of Recent Research on Entrepreneurship, Rent V.* Vaxjo, Sweden: University of Vaxjo.

Blackburn, R.A., Curran, J., Woods, A., Bandey, S., Kitching, J., Lucas, P., and Roberts, L. 1990. Exploring enterprise cultures: Small service sector enterprise owners and their views. *Proceedings of the Thirteenth United Kingdom Small Firms Policy and Research Conference Towards the 21st Century*. Harrogate, England: Leeds Business School.

Blais, R.A., and Toulouse, J.-M. 1990. National, regional or world patterns of entrepreneurial motivation? An empirical study of 2,278 entrepreneurs and 1,733 non-entrepreneurs in fourteen countries on four continents. *Journal of Small Business and Entrepreneurship* 7:3–20.

Brockhaus, R. 1980. Risk-taking propensity of entrepreneurs. *Academy of Management Journal* 23:509–520.

Brockhaus, R. 1982. The psychology of the entrepreneur. In C.A. Kent, D.L. Sexton, and K.H. Vesper, eds. *Encyclopedia of Entrepreneurship*. Englewood Cliffs, NJ: Prentice Hall, pp. 39–57.

Carter. H., and Aitchison, J. 1986. Language areas and language change in Wales: 1961–1981. In I. Hume and W.T.R. Pryce, eds., *The Welsh and their Country: Selected Readings in the Social Sciences*. Llandysul, Dyfed: Gomer, pp. 1–25.

Chell, E. 1985. The entrepreneurial personality: A few ghosts laid to rest? *International Small Business Journal* 3:43–54.

Cooke, P. 1986. The changing urban and regional system in the United Kingdom. *Regional Studies* 20:243–251.

Cooper, A.C., and Dunkelberg, W.C. 1986. Entrepreneurship and paths to business ownership. *Strategic Management Journal* 7:53–68.

Cooper, A.C., Woo, C.Y., and Dunkelberg, W.C. 1989. Entrepreneurship and the initial size of firms. *Journal of Business Venturing* 4:317–332.

Dahmen, E. 1970. *Entrepreneurial Activity and the Development of Swedish Industry*. Homewood, IL: Irwin.

Davidsson, P. 1988. Type of man and type of company revisited: A confirmatory cluster analysis approach. In B.A. Kirchhoff, W.A. Long, W.E. McMullan, K.H. Vesper, and W.E. Wetzel, Jr., eds., *Frontiers of Entrepreneurship Research*. Wellesley, MA: Babson College, pp. 88–105.

Davies, W.K.D. 1984. *Factorial Ecology*. Aldershot: Gower.

Dubini, P. 1988. The influence of motivations and environment on business start-ups: Some hints for public policies. *Journal of Business Venturing* 4:11–26.

Dunkelberg, E., and Cooper, A.C. 1982a. Entrepreneurial typologies: An empirical study. In K.H. Vesper, ed., *Frontiers of Entrepreneurship Research*. Wellesley, MA: Babson College, pp. 1–14.

Dunkelberg, E., and Cooper, A.C. 1982b. Patterns of small business growth. *Academy of Management Proceedings 1982*:409–413.

Friberg, M. 1975–1976. Ar Lonen det enda som sporrar oss att arbeta? (Is the Salary the Only Incentive for Work?). *Sociologisk Forskning* 1:24–42 and 4:52–65 (in English).

Gartner, W.B., Mitchell, T.R., and Vesper, K.H. 1989. A taxonomy of new business ventures. *Journal of Business Venturing* 4:169–186.

30 S. BIRLEY AND P. WESTHEAD

Gibb, A., and Davies, L. 1990. In pursuit of frameworks for the development of growth models of the small business. *International Small Business Journal* 9:15–31.

Gibb, A., and Ritchie, J. 1981. *The "Shell" Entrepreneurs: A Study of the Efforts of a Sample of Would-Be Entrepreneurs to Get into Business*. Durham: Durham University Business School.

Gibb, A., and Ritchie, J. 1982. Understanding the Process of Starting Small Businesses. *European Small Business Journal* 1:26–45.

Gibb, A., and Scott, M. 1986. Understanding small firms growth. In M.G. Scott, A.A. Gibb, T. Faulkner, and J. Lewis, eds., *Small Firms Growth and Development*. Aldershott: Gower, pp. 81–104.

Hakim, C. 1989. Identifying fast growth small firms. *Employment Gazette* 97:29–41.

Hair, J.F., Anderson, R.E., Tatham, R.L., and Grablowsky, B.J. 1979. *Multivariate Data Analysis*. Tulsa: Oklahoma: PPC Books.

Hjern, R., Hull, C., Finlayson, D., Gillespie, A., and Goddard, J. 1980. *Helping Small Firms Grow*. Berlin: International Institute of Management Discussion Paper Series.

Hofer, C.W., and Sandberg, W.R. 1987. Improving New Venture Performance: Some Guidelines for Success. *American Journal of Small Business*. Summer: 11–25.

Hofstede, G. 1980. *Culture's Consequences: International Differences in Work Related Values*. Beverly Hills, CA: Sage Publications.

Jenssen, S., and Kolvereid, L. 1991. Reasons leading to start-up as determinants of survival among Norwegian entrepreneurs. *Proceedings of the Inaugural Global Conference on Entrepreneurship Research*. London, England: The Management School, Imperial College.

Johnston, R.J. 1980. (second edition). *Multivariate Statistical Analysis in Geography: A Premier on the General Linear Model*. London: Longman.

Keeble, D.E. and Gould A. 1984. *New Manufacturing Firms and Entrepreneurship in East Anglia: Final Report to the Económic and Social Research Council*. University of Cambridge: Department of Geography.

Kets de Vries, M.F.R. 1977. The entrepreneurial personality: A person at the crossroads. *Journal of Management Studies* 14:34–57.

Lafuente, A., and Salas, V. 1989. Types of entrepreneurs and firms: The case of new Spanish firms. *Strategic Management Journal* 10:17–30.

Lodge, G.C. 1976. *The New American Ideology*. New York: Alfred A. Knopf.

Martin, R. 1985. Monetarism Masquerading as Regional Policy? The Government's New System of Regional Aid. *Regional Studies* 19:379–388.

Maslow, A. 1943. A Theory of Human Motivation. *Psychology Review* July:370–396.

Maslow, A. 1954. *Motivation and Personality*. New York: Harper and Row.

Mason, C.M. 1991. Spatial variations in enterprise: The geography of new firm formation. In R. Burrows, ed., *Deciphering the Enterprise Culture*. London: Routledge, pp. 74–106.

McClelland, D.C., Atkinson, J.W., Clark, R.A., and Lowell, E.L. 1953. *The Achievement Motive*. New York: Appleton Century Crofts.

McClelland, D.C. 1961. *The Achieving Society*. Princeton, NJ: Van Nostrand.

Milne, T., and Thompson, M. 1982. *The Infant Business Development Process*. University of Glasgow: Management Studies Working Paper No. 2.

Mischel, W. 1973. Towards a cognitive social learning reconceptualisation of personality. *Psychological Review* 80:252–283.

Moyes, A., and Westhead, P. 1990. Environments for New Firm Formation in Great Britain. *Regional Studies* 24:123–136.

Norusis, M.J. 1985. *Advanced Statistics Guide SPSSX*. Chicago: McGraw-Hill.

Norusis, M.J. 1988. *SPSS/PC+ Advanced Statistics V2.0*. Chicago: SPSS Inc.

O'Farrell, P.N., and Hitchens, D.M.W.N. 1988a. Alternative theories of small-firm growth: A critical review. *Environment and Planning A* 20:1365–1382.

O'Farrell, P.N., and Pickles, A.R. 1989. Entrepreneurial behaviour within male work histories: A sector specific analysis. *Environment and Planning A* 21:311–331.

Openshaw, S. 1983. Multivariate analysis of census data: The classification of areas. In D. Rhind, ed., *Census User's Handbook*. London: Methuen, pp. 243–263.

Oxenfeldt, A.R. 1943. *New Firms and Free Enterprise*. Washington: American Council on Public Affairs.

Peterson, R., and Stevenson, H.H. 1987. *An Empirical Search for Entrepreneurship*. National Center for Management Research and Development, USA: Working Paper Series.

Pickles, A.R., and O'Farrell, P.N. 1987. An analysis of entrepreneurial behaviour from male work histories. *Regional Studies* 21:425–444.

Reynolds, P.D. 1987. New firms: Societal contribution versus potential. *Journal of Business Venturing* 2:231–246.

Scase, R., and Goffee, R. 1980. *The Real World of the Small Business Owner*. London: Croom Helm.

Scase, R., and Goffee, R. 1982. *The Entrepreneurial Middle Class*. London: Croom Helm.

Scheinberg, S., and MacMillan, I.C. 1988. An 11 county study of motivations to start a business. In B.A. Kirchhoff, W.A. Long, W.E. McMullan, K.H. Vesper, and W.E. Wetzel, Jr., eds., *Frontiers of Entrepreneurship Research*. Wellesley, MA: Babson College, pp. 669–687.

Shane, S., Kolvereid, L., and Westhead, P. 1991. An exploratory examination of the reasons leading to new firm formation across country and gender. *Journal of Business Venturing* 6:431–446.

Shapero, A., and Sokol, L. 1982. The social dimensions of entrepreneurship. In C. Kent, D. Sexton, and K. Vesper, eds., *Encyclopedia of Entrepreneurship*. Englewood Cliffs, NJ: Prentice-Hall, pp. 72–90.

Simon, H.A. 1964. On the concept of organisational goals. *Administrative Science Quarterly* 9:1–22.

Smith, N.R. 1967. *The Entrepreneur and His Firm: The Relationship Between Type of Men and Type of Company*. East Lansing, Michigan: Bureau of Business and Economic Research, Michigan State University.

Stanworth, M.J.K., and Curran, J. 1973. *Management Motivations in the Smaller Business*. London: Gower.

Stanworth, M.J.K., and Curran, J. 1976. Growth and the smaller firm—An alternative view. *Journal of Management Studies* 13:95–110.

Storey, D.J. 1982. *Entrepreneurship and the New Firm*. London: Croom Helm.

Storey, D.J., and Johnson, S. 1987a. *Are Small Firms the Answer to Unemployment*. London: Employment Institute.

Storey, D.J., and Johnson, S. 1987b. *Job Generation and Labour Market Change*. Basingstoke: Macmillan.

Storey, D.J., Keasey, K., Watson, R., and Wynarczyk, P. 1987. *The Performance of Small Firms*. London: Croom Helm.

Turok, I., and Richardson, P. 1989. *Supporting the Start-Up and Growth of Small Firms: A Study in West Lothian*. Glasgow: University of Strathclyde, Strathclyde Paper on Planning No. 14.

Wendervang, F. 1965. *Development of a Population of Industrial Firms*. Oslo: Scandinavian Press.

Westhead, P. 1988. *New Manufacturing Firm Formation in the Context of the Economy of Wales*. University of Wales: Unpublished Ph.D. Dissertation.

Westhead, P. 1990. A typology of new manufacturing firm founders in Wales: Performance measures and public policy implications. *Journal of Business Venturing* 5:103–122.

Woo, C.Y., Cooper, A.C., and Dunkelberg, W.C. 1988. Entrepreneurial Typologies: Definitions and Implications. In B.A. Kirchhoff, W.A. Long, W.E. McMullan, K.H. Vesper, and W.E. Wetzel, Jr., eds., *Frontiers of Entrepreneurship Research*. Wellesley, MA: Babson College, pp. 165–176.

Woo, C.Y., Cooper, A.C., and Dunkelberg, W.C. 1991. The Development and Interpretation of Entrepreneurial Typologies. *Journal of Business Venturing* 6:93–114.

Business Similarity as a Moderator of the Relationship Between Pre-Ownership Experience and Venture Performance

Gaylen N. Chandler

This research focuses on the degree of similiarity between pre-ownership experience and the work requirements of the present venture as a moderator of the relationship between pre-ownership experience and venture performance. Multiple itme scales are developed to assess two dimensions of business similarity: (1) talk environment similarity, and (2) skills/abilities similarity. The results indicate a positive main effect for task enviroment similarity and a curvilinear moderation effect for skill/abilities similarity. Qualitative interviews are used to help better explain the results.

There is little dispute among venture capitalists and practitioners that the expertise and behaviors of the founder influence the performance fo the firm. However, much of the extant entrepreneurship research dealing with the relationship between founders and their ventures has focused on years of experience aws a proxy for the knowledge and competencies developed by the founder. There is evidence tha the years of pre-ownership experience in similar businesses is positively related to the performance of the venture (Chandler & Jansen, 1992; Cooper & Gimeno-Gascon, 1992; Cooper, Gimeno-Gascon, & Woo, 1994; Dunkelberg & Cooper, 1982; Dunkelbery, Cooper, Woo, & Dennis, 1987; MacMillan, Siegel, & SubbaNarasimha, 1985; Stuart & Abetti, 1990). Other researchers (e.g. Van de Ven, Hudson, & Schroeder, 1984) have found no relationships. Thus, the evidence has been relatively weak and not entirely consistent.

The inconsistency of these finding suggests that perhaps pre-ownership exposure to business activities does not automatically translate into knowledge, skills, and abilities that can successfully be applied to the situation found in the start-up venture (Reuber & Fischer, 1994). The present research seeks to explore some of the issues involved in transferring the knowledge, skill, and abilities gained through pre-ownership activities to the application of starting a new business. In so doing, it seeks to make three contributions to our knowledge. First, it identifies two dimensions of experience: (1) task environment similarity, and (2) skills/abilities similarity. It then discusses how these dimensions relate to the performance of the venture. Second, it provides evidence supportive of the empirical validity of scales that can be used to operationalize task environment similarity and skills/abilities similarity. Third, it develops and provides tests for the theoretically based hypotheses.

KNOWLEDGE, SKILLS, ABILITIES AND PERFORMANCE

Pre-ownership experience in a highly related field is thought to be an important correlate of emerging business performance (Dunkelberg et al., 1987; Stuart & Abetti, 1990; Tyebjee & Bruno, 1984). However, if experience is to be beneficial to a start-up company, the knowledge, skills, and abilities learned through experience must be transferred from a pre-ownership situation to the setting of the emerging business. In addition, the impact of the transferred learning must be strong enough to translate into organizational-level results.

Two Dimensions of Business Similarity

To help develop hypotheses, I have relied on the literature along with insights gained through in-depth interviews with 10 business founders. The review of the literature and discussions with business founders revealed two major dimensions of knowledge, skills, and abilities: (1) task environment knowledge, and (2) specific skills and abilities.

Task environment similarity. Pre-ownership experience in a highly similar business allows founders to better understand the context within which their emerging firm will operate (Cooper et al. 1994). Drucker (1994) states that managers must make assumptions about markets, customers, and technologies when they make business decisions. Porter (1980) discusses the importance of knowing and assessing the environment. Indeed, numerous entrepreneurship researchers have emphasized the importance of recognizing opportunities and accurately evaluating the environment (e.g. Hofer & Sandberg, 1987; Kunkel, 1991; Timmons, 1990). Such research highlights the importance of understanding the context within which a firm operates.

Pre-ownership experience in the task environment can help the business founder better understand the benefits and limitations of any given technology. This knowledge is important as emerging businesses interact with three major constituencies: customers, suppliers, and competitors.

Pre-ownership experience in a highly similar business helps founders to better understand the customers. This exposure not only helps founders recognize what customers want, but also helps them meet customers and develop a working relationship with them. In our interviews with business founders we found that often pre-ownership experiences had allowed them to become acquainted with a customer base locally, nationally, and internationally.

In order to maintain good customer service it is important to identify reliable suppliers. Pre-ownership experience in similar businesses exposes founders to suppliers. Porter (1980) discusses the importance of suppliers and supplier power. As illustrated by the following anecdotes, this may be particularly important for start-up firms. In my interviews I encountered two founders who were able to start businesses because they developed contacts with suppliers and were supported financially by the supplier when the business started. In one case, the supplier provided goods on consignment until the business was established, and in the second case, the supplier provided a low-interest loan with generous repayment terms.

Understanding competitors also becomes important. Researchers have discussed the importance of hostile versus benign environments (Covin & Slevin, 1989). Understanding how competitors do business and what they focus on can help a founder to comprehend and develop a more appropriate niche (Timmons, 1990). In my interviews there were eight founders who developed products to fit niches where there were no direct competitors. In another case, however, a founder decided not to open a retail establishment because a major competitor was percieved to have enough power to create extreme competitive pressure as well as an ability to orchestrate political pressure through the zoning commission. This insight allowed the founder to avoid significant future hostilities.

The cited literature and case examples are consistent with previous arguments (Cooper et al. 1994) that business similarity implies knowledge of the task-level environment. This knowledge does not equate with any specific skill or ability, but rather provides more accurate information to increase the efficacy of decision making.

Skill/ability similarity. In addition to gaining knowledge of the task environment, individuals are thought to develop specific managerial and technical skills that can be of use in an emerging business. Numerous studies have evaluated founder experience, but two recent studies have developed models of entrepreneurial expertise. Both Chandler and Jansen (1992) and Reuber and Fischer (1994) developed models that included multidimensional measures of managerial expertise. Both models included items to measure the founder's managerial competence in organizing, coordinating, planning, and motivating people. Finally, both models included measures of technical competence such as research and development and production.

These studies suggest that pre-ownership experience can facilitate the learning of specific managerial and technical skills that will be useful to the founder in the start-up business. Specific skills and abilities are conceptually different from the broader task environment knowledge. Task environment knowledge implies that the potential founder has gained knowledge about the product, customers, suppliers, and competitors that can aid in strategy formulation. The acquisition of specific skills and abilities implies that the founder has developed managerial and technical expertise that will aid in strategy implementation.

Business Similarity and Experience

Previous researchers have stated that experience in similar businesses seems to be more valuable than experience in less similar settings. Cooper et al. (1994) operationalized the construct of business simlarity as a three-item scale measuring similarity in services, customers, and suppliers. This operationalization is consistent with my conceptualization of task environment similarity. Stuart and Abetti (1990) operationalized business similarity as the compatibility of skills learned through experience, which is more congruous with my conceptualization of skills/abilities similarity.

In each of these cases, the variables were tested as direct independent variables in the analysis. Although the direct effects are of interest, testing only the direct effects assumes that business similarity leads to performance. It can be strongly argued that it is not business similarity or years of experience that is directly related to performance, but rather the acquisition and application of knowledge, skills, and abilities (Chandler & Jansen, 1992; Reuber & Fischer, 1994). From this perspective, I expect not only verifiable relationships between the two dimensions of business similarity and performance, but also moderating effects that extend beyond the relationships exhibited by the original variables. Thus, I expect task environment similarity and skills/abilities similarity to moderate the relationship between years of pre-ownership experience and the performance of the emerging venture. This suggests the model displayed in Figure 1.

Figure 1

A Model of the Moderating Effects of Task Environment and Skills/Abilities Similarity on the Relationship Between Pre-ownership Experience and Venture Performance

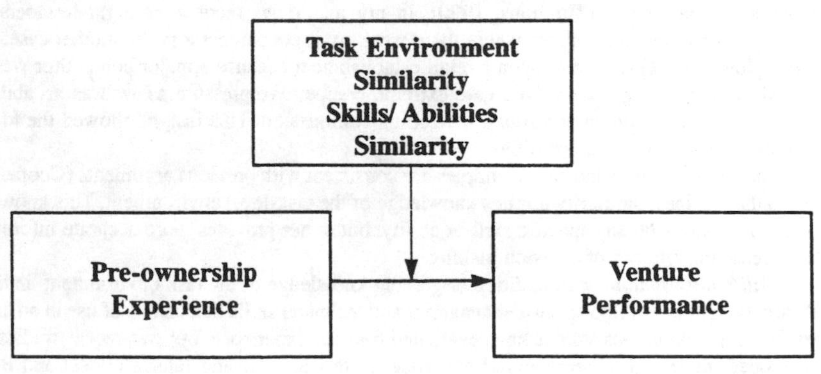

The preceding discussion leads to the statement of the following hypotheses:

H1: There are two conceptually distinct dimensions of knowledge, skills, and abilities gained through experience. The first is knowledge of the task environment, the second is specific managerial and technical skills.
H2: Task environment similarity is positively related to venture sales/earnings and growth.
H3: Skills/abilities similarity is positively related to venture sales/earnings and growth.
H4: Task environment similarity positively moderates the relationship between experience and new venture performance.
H5: Skills/abilities similarity positively moderates the relationship between experience and new venture performance.

Issues Obscuring Relationships

With respect to skills/abilities similarity there may be founders who believed they learned appropriate skills and abilities from the prior firm, and yet in the prior firm they did many things wrong! Thus, the skills/abilities similarity measure may be clouded by inappropriate learning in the prior firm.

Even if positive transfer of experience occurs, research focusing on founder competencies and venture performance must overcome the liabilities associated with cross-level research (Rousseau, 1985). Frequently such relationships are difficult to verify because firm performance is a function of environmental, firm, and individual-level constructs (Chandler & Hanks, 1994). Thus, existing relationships might be obscured by extraneous factors. This is less likely to occur, however, in the setting of emerging businesses. Start-up firms are characterized by simple structure and a culture defined by the founder's vision; hence, more internal consistency in culture and climate and fewer diverging internal forces. Therefore, in the setting of start-up firms, more evidence of cross-level responsiveness between individual and firm-level constructs and stronger evidence of coupling between the founder's learning transfer and the performance of the emerging venture are expected than if larger, more complex firms were analyzed.

In addition to the difficulties associated with cross-level research, the research model proposed in this paper is not intended to be a comprehensive model of venture performance. Researchers have proposed and tested variables at environmental, organizational, and individual levels of analysis (e.g. Chandler & Hanks, 1994; Hofer & Sandberg, 1987; Covin & Slevin, 1989). Even comprehensive models rarely explain large proportions of the total variance in venture performance. This may occur because the models are not adequately specified, there is error in measurement, there is inherent randomness, or a combination of the above.

For these reasons, the models tested in this paper are not expected to explain large amounts of variance; rather they seek to provide greater insights into the phenomenon of how knowledge gained through experience is related to venture performance. This is done by evaluating relationships between these constructs and new venture performance. Only modest magnitude of effects is expected; however, given the complexities inherent in this type of research, significant findings provide relatively strong evidence of the importance of the identified constructs.

Control Variables

Because the research seeks to evaluate differences between individual- and organizational-level constructs, a number of control variables are appropriate. The dependent variables are business growth and business volume. Research shows that as firms age, growth tends to slow (Hanks, Watson, Jansen, & Chandler, 1993). In addition, we expect eight-year-old firms on average to have higher sales levels than two-year-old firms. Thus, in the context of emerging businesses, business age is an appropriate control variable.

There is some evidence that the industry in which a firm competes may have some impact on the performance of the firm. Firms for the study were selected from manufacturing, retail, wholesale and business services industries. To provide controls for potential differences in these areas, business type is a control variable.

Pre-ownership experience is not the focal point of this study, but rather the interaction between experience and task environment and skills/abilities similarity. Thus it is necessary to include experience as a control variable in order to capture interaction effects beyond the main effects explained by experience.

METHODS

The research is cross-sectional and cross-level in nature. It is designed to provide evidence for the validity of measurement of the task environment similarity and skills/abilities similarity constructs. It also seeks to assess the relationship between these constructs and new venture performance.

Sample

The sample was selected from State of Utah records of business incorporations. Questionnaires were mailed to the founders of all firms (n = 431) in four types of businesses — manufacturing, retail, wholesale, and business services—that met the following criteria: (1) they incorporated between January 1985 and June 1988; (2) they were in good standing with the state as of February, 1990; and (3) they were not subsidiaries of parent corporations. The data collection procedure followed that was proposed by Dillman (1978). Of the 431 questionnaires mailed, 35 were returned by the post office marked "not deliverable." There were 134 completed questionnaires returned that included performance information, for an effective response rate of 35 percent. Questionnaires requesting supporting performance data were mailed independently to individuals listed as vice-presidents in each of the firms. Complete matching firm performance data were returned for 38 of the firms.

Respondents. The respondents were 92 percent male and 96 percent caucasian. Eighty-five percent were married. Education levels were above average for Utah, with 88 percent having at least some college and 47 percent holding at least a bachelor's degree. Ages ranged from 25 to 65 with a mean of 43 years. Founders reported working a mean of 53 hours per week and had been intensively involved in a median of one previous business start-up.

Firms. Completed questionnaires were returned for 134 manufacturing and service firms. The manufacturing firms (45 percent of the sample) represented both low-technology and high-technology industries, with a variety of products ranging from ceramic pottery, upholstered furniture, and animal kennels, to medical devices, electronic instruments, and ion lasers. The service firms included retailers (20 percent), wholesalers, (14 percent) and business services, (21 percent). The firms reported median sales of $100,000 to $500,000 and median sales growth of 15 percent to 19 percent. Median earnings, including the salary of the founder, ranged from $50,000 to $100,000. The median number of employees was six. Although the data came from businesses incorporating between 1985 and 1988, 32 of the 134 companies reported that they were in business before 1985. Nineteen companies had been in business between six and 10 years; the remaining 13 companies had been in business from 11 to 25 years.

Measures

In past research business similarity has been operationalized as the degree of similarity between the product or service offered by the pre-ownership business and the product or service offered by the emerging business (Dunkelberg et al., 1987). Cooper et al. (1994) operationalized business similarity as the similarity of services, customers, and suppliers. These approaches are consistent with my conceptualization of task environment similarity. The present research has extended the construct of business similarity and operationalized measures of skills/abilities similarity, consistent with the concept of competencies as suggested by Chandler and Jansen

TABLE 1
Task Environment And Skills/Abilities Similarity Items

Rate the following items for similarity. A "1" means that the two compared items are very dissimilar. A "5" means the two items are very similar. Please circle the most appropriate response.

very dissimilar	somewhat dissimilar	neutral	somewhat similar	very similar
1	2	3	4	5

PREVIOUS JOB OR BUSINESS						CURRENT VENTURE
customers	1	2	3	4	5	customers
suppliers	1	2	3	4	5	suppliers
competitors	1	2	3	4	5	competitors
product/service	1	2	3	4	5	product/service
technology	1	2	3	4	5	technology
tasks performed	1	2	3	4	5	tasks performed
skills/abilities used	1	2	3	4	5	skills/abilities used
managerial duties	1	2	3	4	5	managerial duties
technical/functional duties	1	2	3	4	5	technical/functional duties

Principal Components Analysis
Varimax Rotated Factor Matrix:
Task Environment and Skills/Abilities Similarity

ITEM	Task Environment	Skills/Abilities
Product/Service	**.89**	.15
Competitors	**.85**	.17
Suppliers	**.84**	.17
Customers	**.81**	.26
Technology*	**.64**	.50
Managerial Duties	-.01	**.85**
Skills/Abilities	.20	**.82**
Technical Duties	.38	**.76**
Tasks Performed	.40	**.71**
Alpha	**.90**	**.86**
Eigenvalue	4.58	1.53
% Variance Explained	58.90	17.00

**Omitted from the scale because of a strong loading on both factors*

(1992), and matching abilities as suggested by Stuart and Abetti (1990).

Task environment and skills/abilities similarity. The measures of task environment and skills/abilities similarity are founders' self-reported perceptions of the degree of similarity between their pre-ownership experience and the current venture. Founders were asked to rate the similarity of several items on 5-point scales (1 very dissimilar, 5 very similar). Based on the discussion earlier in this paper, two *a priori* dimensions were hypothesized.

(1) The first group of measures operationalized context issues. It is referred to as **task environment similarity**, and incorporates the similarity of customers, suppliers, competitors, product/service, and technology.
(2) The second construct is referred to as **skills/abilities similarity** and incorporates content issues including tasks performed, knowledge, skills, and abilities required, managerial duties, and technical-functional duties.

Items as they appeared in the questionnaire and principal components analysis results using a varimax rotation are displayed in Table 1. The results show that the business and task similarity dimensions factor as hypothesized. The first factor includes the work context items that I refer to as **task environment similarity**. The similarity of technology loaded heavily on both scales, and was thus omitted from the measure. Coefficient alpha for the remaining four-item scale is .89 and does not improve if additional items are excluded from the analysis. The second group of items comprises the job content items that we refer to as **skills/abilities similarity.** Coefficient alpha for this four-item scale is .86 and does not improve if items are deleted from the scale. The principal components and alpha analysis results provide evidence for the validity and reliability of these constructs (Nunnally, 1978).

Control variables. Pre-ownership experience was measured by requesting the number of years spent prior to founding the business as a general manager, managing their own business, and in technical/specialist positions. Each of these was coded from zero to three: 0 = no prior experience; 1 = some, but less than one year prior experience; 2 = one to three years prior experience; 3 = more than three years experience in this area. The areas were then summed to form one variable that reflects both the depth and breadth of experience.

Business age was calculated by subtracting the year the business was founded from 1990, the year the data were collected. Business types were coded using dummy variables: manufacturing, retail, and business services are entered into the regression equation to capture the variance accounted for by business type.

Firm level performance indicators. This research focuses on two performance dimensions that have been identified as being particularly releant to start-ups (Chandler & Hanks, 1993): sales/earnings, and growth. Because most emerging businesses are privately held and have no legally mandated requirement to disclose performance information, only self-report data were available. Two items each are used to measure earnings and growth.

Principal components analysis with varimax rotation was used to investigate the structure of measures of venture performance. Items used, descriptive statistics, and factor loadings of the four items measuring firm performance are displayed in Table 2. Individual items measuring each construct were combined to create two variables: sales/earnings, and growth. Coefficient alpha for the sales/earnings variable is .76; coefficient alpha for the growth variable is .65. Both approach or exceed the .70 recommended by Nunnally (1978).

All founders provided performance data; the subsample of 38 companies with two respondents was used to provide evidence of inter-rater reliability for performance measures. Interrater reliability for the sales/earnings and growth variables are .83 and .73 (Pearson correlation coefficients) respectively (n = 38); there was substantial rater agreement on the performance measures. Firm performance data were requested for the most recent three years for sales, earnings, and sales growth. In the study, only the most recent year's figures were used. The correlation between the most recent year and the year preceding were .86 for sales, .81 for earnings, and .79 for growth. However, inter-rater reliabilities (Pearson correlation coefficients) for the previous year were only .58 for sales/earnings and .45 for growth. The reliabilities for the second preceding year were .42 for sales/earnings and .23 for growth. This suggests that self report measures of performance are only reliable for the most recent year. Because of these results, the lack of reliability appears to be a greater concern than the concern for volatility, thus only the most recent years figures were used. The content of the items and the statistical results provide evidence supporting the reliability and validity of the performance measures for the most recent year.

TABLE 2
Frequencies for Firm Performance Indicators

Item	Value label	Frequency	Valid percent
Market share	Decreasing moderately	5	3.9
	Holding its own	30	23.3
	Increasing moderately	73	56.6
	Increasing rapidly	21	16.3
Sales growth	Under 5%	18	14.4
	5% to 9%	24	19.2
	10% to 19%	22	17.6
	20% to 49%	37	29.6
	50% to 99%	11	8.8
	More than 100%	13	10.4
Earnings	Less than 10K	18	15.0
	10K to 25K	19	15.8
	25K to 50K	18	15.0
	50K to 100K	26	21.7
	100K to 500K	35	29.2
	More than 500K	4	3.3
Sales	Less than 25K	7	5.4
	25K to 100K	20	15.5
	100K to 500K	42	32.6
	500K to 2.5 million	47	36.4
	2.5 million to 10 million	12	9.3
	More than 10 million	1	.8

Principal Components Results (varimax rotation)

Item	Sales/Earnings	Growth
Earnings	.94	-.01
Sales	.83	.24
Sales Growth	-.05	.90
Market Share Growth	.26	.85
Alpha	.76	.65
Eigenvalue	2.10	1.23
% Variance Explained	52.60	30.90

ANALYSIS AND RESULTS

Descriptive statistics and simple correlations are displayed in Table 3. The correlations between independent variables are relatively small, indicating there should be no serious problems due to multi-collinearity.

The univariate tests of significance displayed in the correlation matrix in Table 3 indicate that experience is positively related to sales/earnings. Task environment similarity is positively related to venture growth. However, skills/abilities similarity is negatively related to sales/earnings.

Hypothesis 1

As previously discussed in the measurement section, the principal components results support the hypothesis that there are two separate dimensions of the knowledge, skills, and abilities gained through experience. The items dealing with task environment issues load heavily on the first factor, while items dealing with specific skills and abilities load heavily on the second factor. The pattern of factor analysis results supports the operationalization of two dimensions as used in this study.

Hypotheses 2 and 3

To test the second and third hypotheses, hierarchical multiple regression analysis was used. The second hypothesis stated that significant relationships between task environment similarity and venture performance was expected. As can be seen in the upper half of Table 4, the hypothesis was supported when growth is the dependent variable ($p < .05$). There was no significant relationship between task environment similarity and sales/earnings.

The third hypothesis stated the expectation of positive relationships between skills/abilities similarity and venture performance. In the case of growth there is no significant relationship; however, in the case of earnings the relationship is negative. This is contrary to the hypothesis. The implications of these findings will be discussed later.

Hypotheses 4 and 5

The final hypotheses stated that it was expected that task environment similarity and skills/abilities similarity would moderate the relationship between experience and performance. To test moderation effects it is appropriate to use complementary moderated regression analysis

Table 3
Descriptive Statistics and Correlations

Variable	Mean	SD	1	2	3	4	5	6	7	8
1. Business Age	6.07	5.59								
2. Retailer*	.20		-.07							
3. Wholesaler*	.11		.10	-.18b						
4. Manufacturer*	.45		-.14	-.44a	-.32a					
5. Experience	6.40	1.59	.05	.03	.15	.07				
6. Task Environment Similarity	2.99	1.27	-.17	-.05	.00	.27a	.06			
7. Skills/Abilities Similarity	2.62	1.20	-.09	.05	-.04	.15	-.09	.53a		
8. Sales/Earnings	6.78	2.33	.33a	-.03	.00	.03	.22b	-.11	-.20b	
9. Growth	7.18	2.03	-.18b	-.18b	.04	.33a	-.02	.22a	.07	.20b

[a] *p less than or equal to .01*
[b] *p less than or equal to .05*
**Standard Deviations are not meaningful for dummy coded variables. In addition, the business services category has not been included as a control variable in the analysis, although 24% of the firms in the sample are business services. Since entering three of four variables into the equation accounts for all variance due to business type (the fourth is a linear combination of the first three, and will not enter a regression equation), only manufacturing, wholesale, and retail were entered into subsequent analysis.*

Table 4
Moderated Regression Analysis Results

Variable	Sales/Earnings Beta Coefficient		Growth Beta Coefficient	
	Equation I	Equation II	Equation III	Equation IV
Analysis Part 1: Test of Initial Hypotheses				
Business Age	.36[a]	.42[a]	-.11	-.06
Retailer	.01	-.01	.05	.03
Wholesaler	-.01	-.01	.15	.09
Manufacturer	.07	.07	.40	.35[a]
Experience	.19[b]	.26[a]	.01	-.01
Task Environment Similarity		.04		.23[b]
Skills/Abilities Similarity	-.18[c]		-.01	
Interaction 1 Task Environment x Experience		-.05		-.12
Interaction 2 Skills/Abilities x Experience	-.24[a]		-.01	
Analysis Part 2: Tests for Curvilinear Relationships				
Curvilinear Interaction 1 x Interaction 1		-.12		.09
Curvilinear Interaction 2 x Interaction 2	-.19[b]		-.26[a]	
Partial Equation F (Curvilinear part of the equation)	5.90[a]	1.77	2.54[c]	1.68
Adjusted R-square	.23	.16	.14	.13
F	5.09[a]	3.46[a]	3.00[a]	2.89[a]

a Significant p le to .01
b Significant p le to .05
c Significant p le to .10

(Venkatraman, 1989). To model moderation the two original variables are entered into a regression equation (in this case experience and skills/abilities similarity) to predict an outcome variable (in this case sales/earnings and growth). The same variables are then multiplied together and entered into the equation after the original variables are entered. If there is a significant interaction between the two original variables such that jointly they explain more variance than they do separately, the multiplicative term will be statistically significant. This perspective can be represented in the following two equations:

$$Y = a0 + a_1X + a_2Z + e \quad (1)$$

$$Y = a0 + a_1X + a_2Z + a_3XZ + e \quad (2)$$

This multiplicative effect sometimes results in high levels of multicollinearity. However, Southwood (1978) demonstrated that a simple scale of origin transformation reduces multicollinearity and the transformed multiplicative interaction remains a valid analytical tool for testing moderation. After the transformation, the t-score associated with a3 is a valid estimator of the significance of the interacti... term (Venkatraman, 1989). In all cases business age and business type are entered into the equations to partially control for differences in performance based on the age and stage of development of the firm and industry differences. The top half of Table 4 summarizes the results of the multiple regression analysis.

The fourth hypothesis was that task environment similarity would be a positive moderator of the relationship between experience and venture performance. Growth and sales/earnings are the two dependent measures of venture performance. Business age and three categorical business-type variables are entered into the equations first. These are followed by experience and task environment similarity. Finally, the multiplicative interaction term is entered into the equation. Although task environment similarity is significant as a direct independent variable with respect to growth, there are no significant interaction effects. Equation II and Equation IV show the results for Sales/Earnings and Growth respectively.

The final hypothesis was that skills/abilities similarity would be a positive moderator of venture performance. This was tested in a similar manner as was the fourth hypothesis. The control variables were entered first, experience was allowed to enter the equation, followed by skills/abilities similarity. The interaction of skills/abilities similarity is negative, and significantly so in the case of sales/earnings ($p < .05$). Equation I and Equation III include the results for sales/earnings and growth respectively. These results are contrary to our hypothesis.

DISCUSSION

Although not the direct object of this study, some ancillary results in this study confirm previous research findings. The breadth and depth of experience gained by years spent in technical and managerial positions appear to be positively related to sales/earnings (Dunkelberg & Cooper, 1982; Dunkelberg et al., 1987; Stuart & Abetti, 1987, 1990).

Task Environment Similarity.

In general, task environment similarity appears to be positively related to firm performance; the strongest effects are evidenced in terms of venture growth. This is congruent with previous research findings (e.g., Cooper et al, 1994; Dunkelberg et al; 1987). It is intuitively and theoretically reasonable that this should be the case. The overall results suggest that familiarity with the task environment is an important correlate of new venture performance.

These results are supportive of the statement by Cooper et al. (1994) that the similarity of the task environment implies knowledge of the task environment. The relative weakness of the interaction term suggests that the major benefits of task environment exposure are captured by the task environment similarity measure; there is no significant interaction between experience and task similarity that explains more than the original variables.

An underlying implication of this finding is that it may not be necessary to have experience in a highly similar business to gain familiarity with the task environment. In the 10 interviews, I found six high-tech start-ups in which the pre-ownership experience was scientific research. These founders perceived a need for a product that could be used in their research that was not readily available on the market, or whose quality was previously inadequate. They were well acquainted with the research community and knew other potential customers. They knew about potential competitors because they had been suppliers of materials used in the research. Another founder of a highly successful plastic injection molding business was a tool and die maker, supplying injection dies to molding companies. He learned about the industry through contact with his customers. He learned about potential margins, met suppliers, and came into contact with customers for plastic injection molded parts as he designed dies to meet their needs.

Both the quantitative and anecdotal evidence associated with this study suggest that experience in and familiarity with the task environment is important. Among the 10 in depth interviewees only two came from a business with a highly similar product and started a business based on that product. The remaining eight were familiar with the task environment, but gained that familiarity either by being potential customers of the product they developed or suppliers to companies producing products similar to those produced by the new venture after start-up.

Skill/Ability Similarity

According to the research model, skills/abilities similarity should be a positive moderator of the relationship between experience and performance. However, in the case of skill/ability similarity and sales/earnings the interaction term is significantly negative. This finding is contrary to expectations. Theoretically, both task environment similarity and skills/abilities similarity should be positively related to venture performance. A possible explanation of this phenomenon is that many of the perceived skills and abilities learned through prior experience were learned incorrectly. In spite of this possibility, I attempted to better understand these findings by pursuing *post hoc* analyses. First, I plotted the regression residuals against the predicted values for the interaction term. In the case of skills/abilities similarity and both sales/earnings and growth, the patterns indicated that the residuals were not uniformly distributed. The observed

Figure 2

Curvilinear Interaction Terms

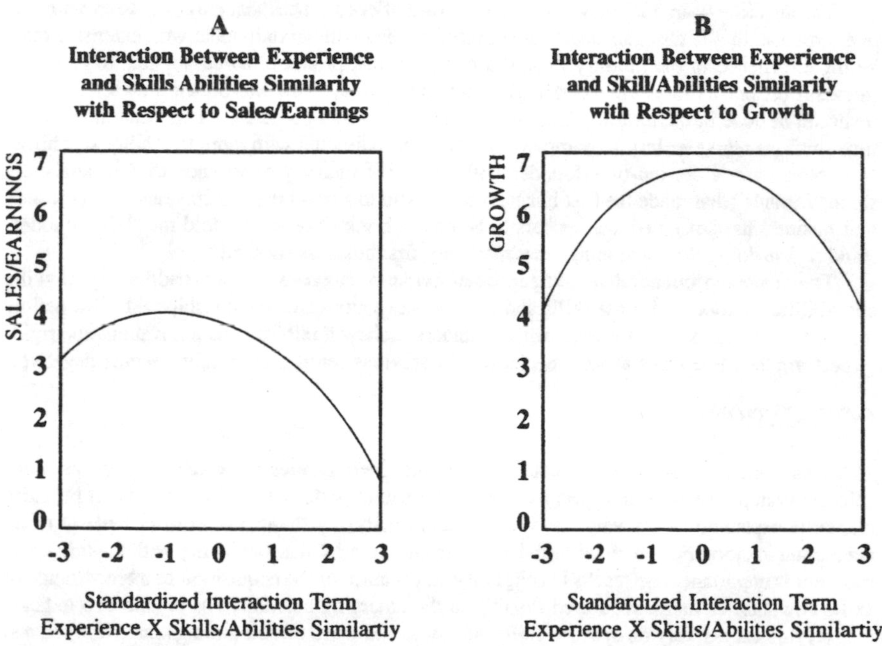

The units on the Y axes are combined sales/earnings and combined sales growth/market share growth. The scores are simply the summation of the two measures as displayed in Table 2. The X axis in each plot is the standardized score of Experience X Skills/Abilities Similarity. The Curve is the plot of the equations represented in the bottom half of Table four, Equations 1 and 3.

patterns were consistent with expected results when there is a curvilinear relationship. In accordance with this insight I followed the procedure described by Billingsley, Croft, Huntsberger, and Watson (1986) to fit a quadratic regression model to the data according to the following equation:

$$Y = a_0 + a_1X + a^2X^2 + e \qquad (3)$$

The results are displayed in the bottom half of Table 4 and Figure 2. The significance of the curvilinear relationship is evaluated with an F-test of the partial regression equation . This test *is* significant for the *curvilinear skills/abilities interaction* term with *both* sales/earnings and growth .

Taken in concert, the results suggest that the acquisition of a broad variety of managerial and technical skills is beneficial to both the sales/earnings and growth of a new venture. Founders need a broad mix of skills and abilities that will enable flexibility and creativity. This is important because in the context of an emerging business, the specific role demands of the founder may be different from the role expectations in previous experience. The curvilinear nature of the relationship suggests that a moderate level of skills and similarity is optimal. A low experience and similarity interaction suggests inadequate acquisition and transfer of skills and abilities. On the other hand, a high experience and similarity interaction indicates that the founder may be inappropriately performing the same tasks in the new venture as were performed in previous businesses and suggests that entrenchment in specific job behaviors affects firm performance negatively.

Through follow-up interviews, I became aware of occurrences that may help to explain this phenomenon. In one case, an electrical engineer teamed with an individual with extensive marketing experience in the industry to start a company that produced a data logging device. The marketer became a blocker of technological advances because that was not the way he perceived it should be done in the industry. Growth and earnings were inhibited for a substantial period of time until the marketer left the company and another individual with more flexibility was hired. In another case, a second-time founder with extensive industry experience tried to apply the same "formula" that made the first business successful to a new business 20 years later. The second business has struggled and appears to be on the brink of death. He told me "I don't understand it, I'm doing the same things that made my first business succeed."

The combined quantitative and anecdotal evidence suggests that a broad variety of skills and abilities is good and those skills and abilities have a positive relationship with firm performance to a certain point. However, when founders eschew flexibility and innovation, and rigidly perform the same tasks as were performed in previous settings the results become negative.

IMPLICATIONS

This research provides significant insights into the dynamics associated with the relationship between pre-ownership experience and new venture performance. I believe that it provides plausible explanations for why previous research analyzing these relationships have at times been contradictory. For potential founders the results suggest that familiarity with the task environment is important. The results highlight the importance of the acquisition of a broad range of skills and abilities that can be used flexibly in the emerging business. The results also indicate that relying excessively on specific skills, abilities, and ways of doing things that were learned previously can be associated with negative performance results.

The research has some inherent limitations. The cross-sectional design captures associations between perceived task environment and skills/abilities similarity and firm performance, even after the effects of business age, business type, and years of experience variables are accounted for; however, the evidence is correlational rather than causal. In addition to the limitations imposed by cross-sectional data, there may be some self-selection bias among those who chose to return the questionnaire. Also, the sample frame comprised a limited geographic area (Utah). The research also may be affected by restriction of range, which means that the relationships might be stronger if the sample included founders whose businesses failed. Finally, only a small part of the total variance in venture performance appears to be explained by biographical measures of founder experience. Therefore, more research emphasis should be placed on the development of a comprehensive multilevel model of venture performance that incorporates, but does not rely exclusively on, individual-level variables.

In spite of the limitations, the findings have some interesting implications. First, the findings imply that the distinction between task environment and skills/abilities similarity is important. Working in the task environment provides founders with important exposure to information. Although the acquisition of broad skills and abilities is important, the research suggests that founders should be especially careful to guard against entrenchment in specific skills and abilities. Thus, the distinction between the two dimensions, task environment similarity and skills/abilities similarity, should be preserved.

Most of the studies related to experience and performance have relied on biographical measures, such as years of experience, as indicators of learning. Although objectively measured, this is at best a crude indicator of knowledge, skills, and abilities. In the area of personnel selection a number of different tools have been developed to help assess the skills and abilities of potential employees. Paper-and-pencil skills tests have been developed that are relatively successful. In addition such methods as assessment centers have been developed that require candidates to participate in a number of different managerial tasks on which they are evaluated by a panel of experts. Likewise, in-depth behavioral interviewing can give information not only about the time spent in particular pursuits, but also the skills and abilities learned and the accomplishments made. Particular insights could be gained if a panel of potential founders were evaluated and then reevaluated at several subsequent times to track the acquisition and transfer of knowledge, skills, and abilities. In addition, future studies might develop and operationalize measures of role flexibility or adaptability (or alternatively inflexibility and entrenchment). In conclusion, the present study highlights some of the complexities associated with the acquisition and transfer of learning that can enhance venture performance. There is substantial room in the field for additional studies that will move beyond years of experience as a performance indicator and focus on the process of acquiring and successfully using individual and organizational competencies.

REFERENCES

Billingsley, P., Croft, D. J., Huntsberger, D.V., & Watson, C. J. (1986). *Statistical inference for management and economics*. Boston: Allyn and Bacon.

Chandler, G. N., & Hanks, S. J. (1993). Measuring the performance of emerging businesses: a validation study. *Journal of Business Venturing, 8*(5), 391-408.

Chandler, G. N., & Hanks, S. J. (1994). Market attractiveness, resource-based capabilities, venture strategies, and venture performance. *Journal of Business Venturing, 9*(4), 331-349.

Chandler, G. N., & Jansen, E. J. (1992). The founder's self-assessed competence and venture performance. *Journal of Business Venturing, 7*(3), 223-236.

Cooper, A. C., & Gimeno-Gascon, F. J. (1992). Entrepreneurs, processes of founding, and new firm performance. In D. Sexton & J. Kasarda (Eds.), *The state of the art in entrepreneurship*, pp. 301-340 &. Boston, MA: PWS Kent Publishing Co.

Cooper, A. C., Gimeno-Gascon, F. J., & Woo, C. (1994). Initial human and financial capital as predictors of new venture performance. *Journal of Business Venturing, 9*(5), 371-396.

Covin, J. G., & Slevin, D. P. (1989). Strategic management of small firms in hostile and benign environments. *Strategic Management Journal, 10*(1), 75-87.

Dillman, D. A. (1978). *Mail and telephone surveys: The total design method.* New York: John Wiley & Sons.

Drucker, P. F. (1994). The theory of the business. *Harvard Business Review, 72*(5), 95-104.

Dunkelberg, W. C., & Cooper A. C. (1982). Patterns of small business growth. In K. H. Chung (Ed.), *Proceedings of the Academy of Management, 1982*, pp. 409-413. New York: Academy of Management.

Dunkelberg, W. C., Cooper, A. C., Woo, C., & Dennis, W. (1987). New firm growth and performance. In N. C. Churchill, J. A. Hornaday, B. A. Kirchhoff, O. J. Krasner, & K. H. Vesper (Eds.), *Frontiers of entrepreneurship research*, pp. 307-321. Wellesley, MA: Babson College.

Hanks, S. H., Watson, C. J., Jansen, E., & Chandler G. N. (1993). Tightening the life cycle construct: A taxonomic study of growth stage configurations. *Entrepreneurship Theory and Practice, 2*(18), 5-30.

Hofer, C. W., & Sandberg, W. R. (1987). Improving new venture performance: Some guidelines for success. *Entrepreneurship Theory and Practice, 12*(3), 11-21.

Kunkel, S. W. (1991). *The impact of strategy and industry structure on new venture performance.* Ph.D. dissertation, University of Georgia.

MacMillan, I. C., Siegel, R., & SubbaNarisimha, P. N. (1985). Criteria used by venture capitalists to evaluate new venture proposals. *Journal of Business Venturing, 1*(1), 119-128.

Nunnally, J. C. (1978). *Psychometric theory.* New York: McGraw-Hill.

Porter, M. E. (1980). *Competitive strategies: Techniques for analyzing industries and competitors.* New York: Free Press.

Reuber, A. R., & Fischer, E. M. (1994). Entrepreneurs experience, expertise, and the performance of technology-based firms. *IEEE Transactions on Engineering Management, 4*(41), 365-374

Rousseau, D. M. (1985). Issues of level in organizational research: Multilevel and cross level perspectives. In B. M. Stan & L. L. Cummings (Eds.), *Research in Organizational Behavior, 7*, 1-37. Greenwich, Conn: JAI Press.

Southwood, K. E. (1978). Substantive theory and statistical interaction: Five models. *American Journal of Sociology, 83*, 1154-1203.

Stuart, R. W., & Abetti P. A. (1987). Start-up ventures: Towards the prediction of early success. *Journal of Business Venturing, 2*, 215-230.

Stuart, R. W., & Abetti P. A. (1990). Impact of entrepreneurial and management experience on early performance. *Journal of Business Venturing, 5*, 151-162.

Timmons, J. A. (1990). *New venture creation: Entrepreneurship in the 1990s.* Homewood, IL: Irwin.

Tyebjee, T. T., & Bruno, A. V. (1984). A model of venture capitalist investment activity. *Management Science, 30*(9), 1051-1066.

Van de Ven, A. H., Hudson, R., & Schroeder, D. M. (1984). Designing new business start-ups: Entrepreneurial, organizational, and ecological considerations. *Journal of Management, 10*(1), 87-107.

Venkatraman, N. (1989). The concept of fit in strategy research: Toward verbal and statistical correspondence. *Academy of Management Review, 14*(3), 423-444.

Gaylen N. Chandler is an Associate Professor of Management at Utah State University.

I wish to recognize the contributions of David Baucus and Steven Hanks who encouraged me to use anecdotes from a broader project involving in-depth interviews to illustrate major points. I also wish to recognize the inputs of Kelly Shaver and several anonymous reviewers who have provided valuable insights in the development of this paper.

[29]

Long Range Planning, Vol. 20, No. 3, pp. 45 to 52, 1987
Printed in Great Britain

Five Stages of Growth in Small Business

Mel Scott and Richard Bruce

As a small business develops it moves through five growth stages, each with its own distinctive characteristics. Because the transition from one stage to the next requires change, it will be accompanied by some crisis or another. Crises tend to be disruptive and the problems of change can be minimized if managers are proactive rather than reactive. Prior knowledge of what generates crises and what to expect in each stage will smooth the process of change. This article proposes a model of small business growth to enable managers of small businesses to plan for future growth. The model has been successfully tested and used by the authors in analysing and solving the problem of growing small businesses. The model isolates the five growth stages, the sort of things that will precipitate crises and the major strategies that should be considered at each stage. Its main purpose is as a diagnostic tool in analysing the firm's present position and in planning what will be required as it progresses to the next stage of its development.

Introduction

All businesses pass through distinctive stages (each with its own characteristics) as they develop. This development process can be likened to the product lifecycle. Like products, businesses do not move through the cycle at the same speed but unlike most products businesses can stay in the same stage for a considerable period of time.

Whilst it is clear that each business is different our research has shown that there are sufficient similarities in the problems that they face to make a general growth model useful to the management of a small business. It is prior knowledge of what can be expected in the next stage of development that makes the growth model useful in planning the future of the business.

Because of the different characteristics of each stage the transition from one to the next is often accompanied by a crisis[1] which may be either external or internal to the firm. It follows that the small businessman has two major concerns in moving from one stage of development to the next. Firstly he will be concerned with handling the crisis itself. If he succeeds in this he is faced with the second problem of managing the 'new company'. This will clearly involve managing change and because the successful management of change is both difficult and often time consuming,[2] planning is crucial. This means that events likely to precipitate a crisis should be constantly monitored so that the manager can be proactive rather than reactive in moving from one stage of development to the next.

The use of the model lies in anticipating when a crisis is likely to arise and what will be necessary to successfully negotiate the next stage of growth.

Objective

Not all businesses that survive grow to be large businesses. This is due either to the nature of their industry or simply the personal desires or ambitions of the owner/manager. The objective of this article is to develop a model of small business growth to isolate the main factors which will be important in each stage of growth and the type of crises to be faced in moving from one to the next so that managers can more successfully plan the future of their businesses, i.e. to assist in formulating feasible strategies.

What is a Small Business?

Defining a small business is necessary to avoid misunderstanding of the term. Several attempts have been made at a definition.[3-6] For the purposes of this article that of the American Committee for Economic Development[7] has been adapted.

This is:

(i) Management is independent. Usually the managers are also owners.

Mel Scott is a Senior Lecturer in Business Policy at the University of Cape Town Graduate School of Business, currently on sabbatical leave in Britain. Richard Bruce is also at the University of Cape Town Graduate School of Business.

(ii) Capital is supplied and ownership is held by an individual or small group.

(iii) Area of operations is mainly local. Workers and owners are in one home community, *but markets need not be local.*

Selected Research

Several growth models were analysed and drawn on in the development of the model. These models can be broken down into the following categories:

☆ Industry Growth Models.
Wright,[8] Little[9] and Porter[10] used the product lifecycle concept to illustrate how industries develop and how businesses react to these pressures.

☆ Large Business Growth Models.
Channon[11] and Salter[12] showed the characteristic changes in businesses as they grow into large multidimensional units which become geographically decentralized.

☆ Small Business Growth Models.
Maher and Coddington,[13] Bruce,[14] Steinmetz,[4] Churchill and Lewis[15] and Barnes and Hershon[16] developed models for small businesses per the above definition.

☆ General Growth Models.
Scott,[17] Greiner[5] and Lippitt and Schmidt[18] developed models that can be applied to businesses of all sizes.

The methodology followed in developing the model is one of drawing on the work of previous researchers as well as that of the authors. The proposed model has drawn extensively on the work of Churchill and Lewis.[15] Their model, however, concentrates mainly on organization structure whereas the proposed model is much broader.

Because the authors believe that each stage of a business is preceded by a crisis the model developed by Greiner[5] (Figure 1) is important. As this model deals exclusively with small businesses the nature of the crises are somewhat different from those described by Greiner. Changes in both external and purely internal factors can precipitate these crises. As the external factors are usually beyond the manager's control, monitoring the key issues is

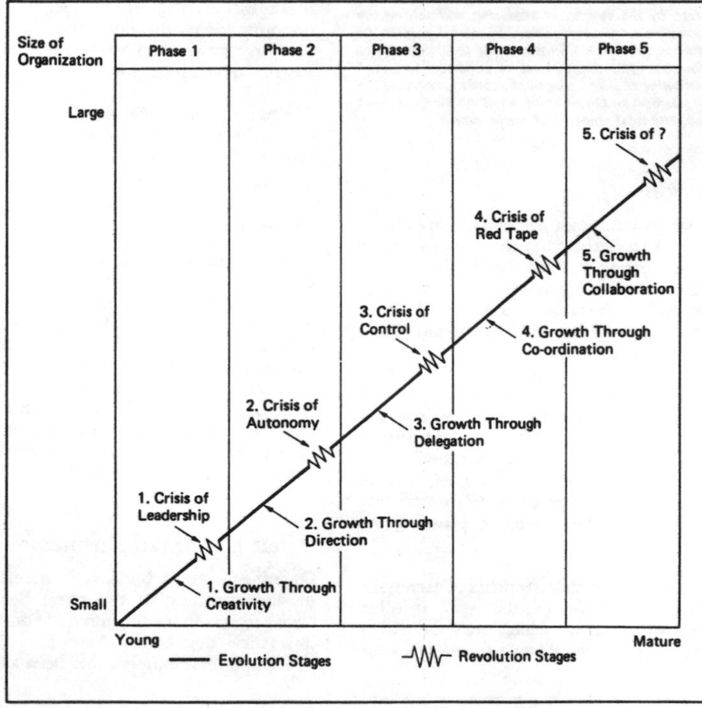

Figure 1. The Greiner Model of the five stages of growth (Greiner, 1978)

important so that he is prepared for possible change. It is being proactive rather than reactive that can spell success or failure in moving from one stage to the next. The transition will often involve relatively major change and the importance of being prepared cannot be overemphasized.

The Proposed Model

The model is developed in two stages. The first is in the form of the classic product lifecycle and is set out in Figure 2. It is important to remember that the shape of the curve and the speed at which the firm moves through each stage will vary from business to business. This part of the model does not attempt to act as a predictor as to when it will move from one stage to the next but rather to show the relationship between time, size of the firm and the stages of growth.

It must be emphasized, as is shown in the model, that although the business may fail at any time it is most likely to happen at one of the crisis points. These crises are extremely important to the entrepreneur in terms of both his business and personal life.

Table 1 sets out details of the proposed model. Expansion of and comments on the model follow.

The Question of Size

We use size to describe one of the axes in Figure 2 with some trepidation. It begs a definition in terms of something like sales, total assets or number of employees. It also hints that there is some finite level of, say, sales which launches a firm from one stage to the next. It is not any single measure that precipitates change but rather a combination of all of them accompanied by some external factor or another that forces a business into the next stage if it is to survive. The actual combination will vary from one business to the next depending on both internal factors (such as condition of the plant or the aspirations of management) and external factors (such as the entry of a new competitor into the market or a change in technology). Size is not dealt with in absolute terms but rather as something which is unique to each business. It is the concept that is important here.

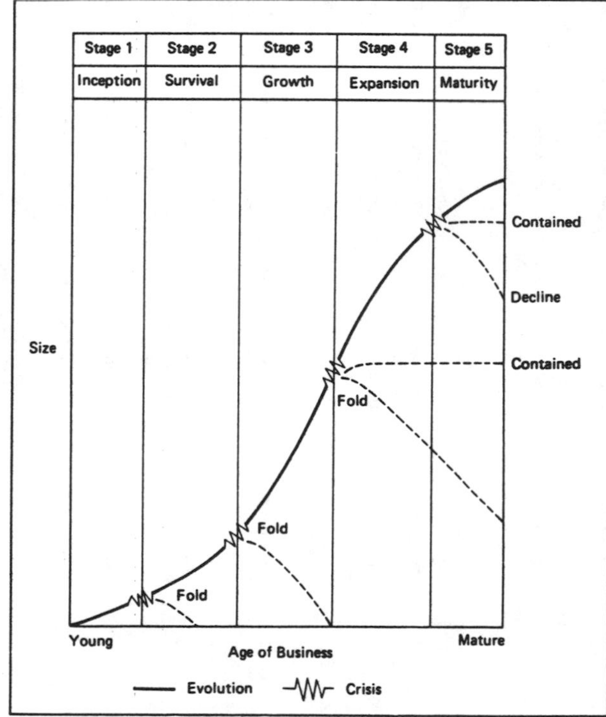

Figure 2

Table 1. A model for small business growth

	Stage 1. Inception	Stage 2. Survival	Stage 3. Growth	Stage 4. Expansion	Stage 5. Maturity
Stage of industry	Emerging, fragmented	Emerging, fragmented	Growth, some larger competitors, new entries	Growth, shakeout	Growth/shakeout or mature/declining
Key issues	Obtaining customers, economic production	Revenues and expenses	Managed growth, ensuring resources	Financing growth, maintaining control	Expense control, productivity niche marketing if industry declining
Top management role	Direct supervision	Supervised supervision	Delegation, co-ordination	Decentralization	Decentralization
Management style	Entrepreneurial, individualistic	Entrepreneurial, administrative	Entrepreneurial, co-ordinate	Professional, administrative	Watchdog
Organization structure	Unstructured	Simple	Functional, centralized	Functional, decentralized	Decentralized functional/product
Product and market research	None	Little	Some new product development	New product innovation, market research	Production innovation
Systems and controls	Simple bookkeeping, eyeball control	Simple bookkeeping, personal control	Accounting systems, simple control reports	Budgeting systems, monthly sales and production reports, delegated control	Formal control systems, management by objectives
Major source of finance	Owners, friends and relatives, suppliers leasing	Owners, suppliers, banks	Banks, new partners, retained earnings	Retained earnings, new partners, secured long-term debt	Retained earnings, long-term debt
Cash generation	Negative	Negative/breakeven	Positive but reinvested	Positive with small dividend	Cash generator, higher dividend
Major investments	Plant and equipment	Working capital	Working capital, extended plant	New operating units	Maintenance of plant and market position
Product-market	Single line and limited channels and market	Single line and market but increasing scale and channels	Broadened but limited line, single market, multiple channels	Extended range, increased markets and channels	Contained lines, multiple markets and channels

Stage 1—Inception

The Basic Features

The reasons for starting the business will be varied but in all cases the main values driving the firm will be those of the founder(s). The basic skills of the founder also determine the functional emphasis (for example if he is an engineer we can expect the main concentration of effort to be on production rather than on sales), and management will be by direct supervision. The main efforts will hinge around developing a commercially acceptable product and establishing a place for it in the market-place. The difficulty of doing this will depend in part on the stage of the industry lifecycle.[10]

The result will normally be one operating unit operating in a single market with limited channels of distribution. Sources of funds will be haphazard and will place heavy demands on the founder, his partners (if any), and his 'friends and relatives'. With the high level of uncertainty the level of forward planning is low.

The Most Likely Crises

If owners can accept the demands that the business places on their finances, energy and time, they become stage 2 enterprises. If not the firm will fold because it can only spend a limited time in this stage.

(1) *The emphasis on profit*. The major focus switches from establishing itself and its product to profitability (or are least curbing losses). More important perhaps is the necessity for generating a positive cash flow in order to survive. This requires a different management attitude and concentration of effort on new and different aspects of the business. The firm will disappear if the manager is unaware of the new demands or chooses to ignore them.

(2) *Administrative demands*. With the push for profits and the increased business activity will come the need for some formalization of systems and record keeping. This is likely to create demands on the manager that he may not have the skills to handle or quite simply does not want to handle. The crisis arises when it is ignored in the forlorn hope that it will go away. It will not.

(3) *Increased activity and its demands on time*. It is likely that because of increased activity demands on the manager's time will become excessive. This along with the increased administrative load will call for a change in management style. He will have to delegate supervisory tasks. This may escape his attention causing backlogs, bottlenecks and confusion. The result is a crisis of management style and an organization structure requiring change (or at least adaptation) if the firm is to survive.

Stage 2—Survival

The Basic Features

If a company has reached this stage it is potentially a workable business entity. As the business expands the financing emphasis will swing to working capital and the need to finance increased inventories and receivables. The owner and his personal sources of financing continue to bear the brunt although more use may be made of creditor financing if the firm has established credibility with its suppliers. Bank overdrafts or short-term loans are common at this stage.

The level of competition is still uncertain but it is likely that if the business is doing well the industry will be attracting new entrants. If barriers to entry are low (which they often are at this stage) the entry of new businesses will be simplified, increasing competition and making success based purely on differentiation more difficult.

The product line is normally still single or at least limited with growth coming from market expansion. Expanded channels of distribution may well be needed to reach the expanded market.

The Most Likely Crises

Many firms remain in the survival stage for some time earning marginal returns but once they decide to grow of their own accord or because competition intensifies they must to move to the next stage.

(1) *Overtrading*. From this point onwards overtrading is an ever present threat. It is possibly wrong to include it here as a crisis as its occurrence will not necessarily push the firm into the next stage. On the other hand if it is not properly handled it will certainly lead to the demise of the business. Because uncontrolled growth is what overtrading is all about there are two possible remedies. The first is to curb that growth which will mean that the firm stays in the survival stage. Here it will not be a catalyst for change. The second is to continue to grow but to bring this growth under control. This will certainly need a move to stage 3 as more control systems are required. Some of the specific issues that will arise are dealt with below.

(2) *The increased complexity of expanded distribution channels*. As the drive for sales growth increases so the existing customer base will need to be expanded. If this requires operating in new geographic areas or selling to a different type of customer some major changes in the way business is done is likely. Operating in new geographic locations broadens spans of control so that 'supervised supervision' management style at present in place will be sorely tried. The result is a need to restructure the firm and with it the adaptation of management style to one with even more emphasis on delegation and co-ordination from a distance. Selling to a new type of customer will probably mean that the rules of the game are different. Norms vary from industry to industry and from market to market, forcing the firm to adapt its practices if it is to succeed. The existing resources will be sorely tried and the new

skills necessary will put pressure on 'the way things are done around here'. To succeed, management style will need to adapt accordingly. Again greater delegation is indicated.

(3) *Change in the basis of competition.* If new competitors enter the market and the firm wishes to maintain market shares and relative competitive strength, changes will be necessary. The increase in competition is likely to place greater emphasis on price at the expense of differentiation. If the firm chooses the price path economies of scale become necessary and with it plant modernization and expansion. Apart from further stretching spans of control, and the need for new skills, financing will be required. To maintain a sound equity base further capital will need to be issued. If, as is usually the case, the founder(s) is unable to raise the cash himself he will have to consider admitting new partners. All of this is likely to lead to new demands on the business and hence on management.

(4) *Pressures for information.* All of the above crises will put huge demands on the firm's information systems. Price competition will demand cost control which in turn requires formalized control systems. If they include a budgetary control system it is almost inevitable that financial expertize will have to be bought with, at the very least, a full-time book-keeper. This will bring a change in management style and threaten the existing power base.

Stage 3—Growth

The Basic Features

By the time the firm reaches this stage it should be profitable but is unlikely to generate cash for the owner. It will be ploughed back into the business to help finance the increased working capital demands. More time will have to be spent on co-ordinating the efforts of the functional managers. This will mean a more formal organization structure based on functional lines. Normal accounting systems will now be in place. Depending on the nature of the product the firm may have to embark on formal research and development to expand the product range. It is likely to be on a small scale, however, due to the lack of resources available to the firm. If management can adapt to the changing environment the firm can continue in this stage for quite some time. In some cases the owner may be able to sell the business prior to stage 4 at a substantial capital gain. If the growth gets out of hand and the firm falls into the trap of overtrading it could find its resouces overstretched. Liquidity can be a major problem and despite the acceptance of its products in the market-place the firm can fold. If sufficient opportunities are seen for new products and/or operating in different markets the enterprise will enter stage 4.

The Most Likely Crises

(1) *Entry of larger competitors.* As the industry moves through its lifecycle[10] and starts to consolidate or at least attract larger competitors the basis of competition will once again change. These larger firms often use economies of scale as a major competitive weapon. The result—pressure on price. Response can take one of two forms. The first is to respond in kind. The implications of this are dealt with in (2) below. The second is to forfeit market share and to compete on a differentiation basis exchanging volume for margin. To succeed this will require considerable investment of time and resources in product or service development. This strategy effectively means staying in stage 3.

(2) *The demands of expansion into new markets or products.* Hand-in-hand with the first response above is the strategy of expanding into new markets and/or new products. Both of these will stretch both managerial and financial resources. Key issues facing management will be financing the growth and maintaining control of operations. To cope with this the organization structure will need to change again and for the first time a professional rather than entrepreneurial approach may be necessary. Heavy emphasis will fall onto administrative issues to control and co-ordinate the expanded and more diverse operation. A degree of decentralization is probably necessary. This sort of change is probably the most demanding on management style and as such represents a major crossroads for the entrepreneur. He may well have to relinquish some of his power base if the firm is to grow further. This is easier said than done.

Stage 4—Expansion

The Basic Features

Budgetary control, regular management reports and decentralized authority accompanied by formalized accounting systems are the order of the day. The need to systemize most administrative functions will be a fundamental to survival through this stage.

As in the growth stage long-term funds will be necessary and if further equity partners were not introduced in that stage they will almost certainly have to be sought now. Retained earnings are still a major form of finance but dividends, especially to sweeten new investors, are by now virtually inevitable. The company's track record of successful operation will now allow it to seek long-term debt but it will have to provide security in the form of its assets.

It is during this stage that company politics are likely to become a major issue for the first time. To cope with the enlarged scope of the business and the formalized systems that have been introduced 'professional' managers will have been introduced. They will not have the commitment to the business that those who were with the business from the early stages had and are unlikely to be prepared to make the same sacrifices 'for the sake of the business'. This situation is potentially dangerous and can cause a crisis not indicated in Figure 2. This is essentially a crisis of culture.

The company may continue to operate successfully on this scale depending upon the competitive environment. If the industry is growing then there may well be opportunities to sell out and take what could be a substantial capital gain. If the firm is not well managed it may drop back to the growth stage or even disappear completely if growth has got out of control. Once again if there is the desire and opportunity for growth then the company may proceed to the next stage.

The Most Likely Crises

(1) *The distance of top management from the 'action'.* If growth is maintained decentralization will continue apace and the entrepreneur/founder will find himself getting further and further from the coal face and thrust more into the role of watchdog and planner. This is often completely against his nature—the nature that allowed him to set up the new business in the first place. The professional managers gather more power and hold greater sway in decision making further diluting the entrepreneur's traditional power base.

(2) *The need for external focus.* Up to this point many firms have been internally focused with the product dominant. As the industry matures and consolidates so competition for sales grows and product differentiation, although possible, becomes more and more difficult. To maintain a competitive advantage through a differentiated product requires greater focus on customer needs and adapting the product offering (including promotion) to meet those needs. The intensified competition often causes a more turbulent operating environment which in turn increases the need to be proactive and anticipatory. This again calls for greater external emphasis and an adaptation of management style.

Stage 5—Maturity

The Basic Features

It is important to realize that unlike the conventional lifecycle concept the company is still growing in the maturity phase. Most companies in this stage are on the verge of moving out of being small businesses in terms of the earlier definition.

The key issues facing management are expense control, productivity and finding growth opportunities. The lines of authority may continue along functional lines or be reorganized along product lines. Because of price competition productivity is fundamental to success and a major innovative thrust should be towards improving this.

Major investments are now into the marketing effort and plant upgrading and maintenance. Earnings are normally sufficient to handle this but sometimes further long-term debt (or at least bridging finance) may prove necessary. The firm may stay in this stage, shrink its operations or go on, normally after a flotation or acquisition, to becoming a large corporation.

Whatever happens the manager will come under pressure from 'shareholders' to ensure the future of the company. This hinges around succession. Whilst this is undoubtedly correct and sound business practice it is a move that will not come naturally to the entrepreneur. He founded and built up the business with a great deal of effort and often sacrifice. Now he is asked to give it away. As an unknown entrepreneur said, 'My banker has suggested that I bring along a potential successor. In effect he is asking me to supply the plank and then walk it.'[19]

Conclusion

The model developed isolated five stages through which a small business grows. It also identified four crisis points that precede the advance into the next stage of development. It is the anticipation of these crises and the successful management of the change that they cause that ensures the survival of the growing small business. Small businesses may not follow all of the paths suggested and may in fact appear to be a hybrid of two or more stages. This may be perfectly rational if that firm is in a stage of transition or if it has an operating environment peculiar to itself which indicates that such courses may be correct.

The model is not intended as a panacea for strategy formulation. It is rather a diagnostic tool to assist in analyzing a firm's present situation. It is also meant to be an indicator of what strategies appear suitable at various stages in an organization's growth. It is, however, only a tool and cannot make the decisions for management. They must rely on their judgement for that. Hopefully the model will add to their information and thus enable them to make better judgements.

References

(1) Larry E. Greiner, Evolution and revolution as organizations grow, *Harvard Business Review*, July/August (1972).

(2) James Brian Quinn, *Strategies for Change: Logical Incrementalism*, Richard D. Irwin, Homewood, Illinois (1980).

(3) W. J. Baumol, *Business Behavior, Value and Growth*, Harcourt Brace & World, New York (1967).

(4) L. L. Steinmetz, Critical stages of small business growth, *Business Horizons*, February (1969).

(5) Larry E. Greiner, Evolution and revolution as organizations grow, *Harvard Business Review*, July/August (1972).

(6) C. M. Boardman, J. W. Bartley and R. L. Ratliff, Small business growth and characteristics, *American Journal of Business*, 3, January–March (1981).

(7) P. C. Kelly, K. Lawyer and C. M. Baumback, *How to organize and Operate a Small Business*, Prentice-Hall, Englewood Cliffs (1968).

(8) R. V. L. Wright, Strategy centres: a contemporary managing system, unpublished paper, A. D. Little Inc. (undated).

(9) A. D. Little, A system for managing diversity, unpublished paper, A. D. Little Inc. (undated).

(10) Michael, E. Porter, *Competitive Strategies: Techniques for Analyzing Industries and Competitors*, The Free Press, New York (1980).

(11) J. I. Channon, *Business Strategy and Policy*, Harcourt Brace Javonovich, New York (1968).

(12) M. S. Salter, Stages of corporate development, *Journal of Business Policy*, 1 (1) (1970).

(13) J. R. Mahar and D. C. Coddington, in H. N. Broom and J. G. Langenecker (Eds), *Small Business Management*, South Western, Cincinnati (1966).

(14) R. Bruce, *The Entrepreneurs: Strategies, Motivations, Successes and Failures*, Bedford Libertarian Books (1978).

(15) N. C. Churchill and V. L. Lewis, The five stages of small business growth, *Harvard Business Review*, May/June (1983).

(16) L. B. Barnes and S. A. Hershon, Transferring power in the family business, *Harvard Business Review*, July/August (1976).

(17) B. R. Scott, Stages of corporate development. Part 1, unpublished paper, Harvard Business School (1971).

(18) G. L. Lippitt and W. H. Schmidt, Crisis in developing organizations, *Harvard Business Review*, November/December (1967).

(19) C. Roland Christensen, Management succession in small and growing enterprises, unpublished paper, Graduate School of Business Administration, Harvard University (1954).

[30]

Management Training and Small Firm Performance: Why is the Link So Weak?

by Paul Westhead and David Storey

TO IMPROVE THE INTERNAL EFFICIENCY and business performance of small- and medium-sized enterprises (SMEs) a number of training initiatives have been introduced in the United Kingdom over the last decade (Watkins, 1983; Curran and Stanworth, 1989). The provision of training to SMEs has been based upon the premise that,

> ". . . training can, and should, be a powerful agent of change, facilitating and enabling a company to grow, expand and develop its capabilities thus enhancing profitability" (Jennings and Banfield, 1993, p3).

Documents prepared by the Confederation of British Industry (1986, 1993), Midland Bank (1993) and the Small Business Bureau (1993) suggest such relationships exist. All four documents make virtually identical statements. '*Finance for Growth*' produced by the Confederation of British Industry (1993) may be regarded as typical:

> "In the SFC 1988 report it was recommended that lending should be made on more favourable terms to businesses whose managers had undertaken prescribed training. This carrot and stick approach is justified by figures from the DTI which showed that failure rates could fall from one-in-three in the first three years, to one-in-ten where training was undertaken."

Our efforts to locate the ultimate source of this information proved unsuccessful. The closest results seem to be those referred to by the National Audit Office (1988) who say:

> "A detailed follow-up by the Training Commission of the first 200 trainees on the New Enterprise Programme found

that 82 per cent had started business and of these only 2 per cent failed after three years."

Whilst these figures do not precisely correspond to those being quoted in 1993, their orders of magnitude are broadly similar. Hence it is disconcerting that 'received wisdom' has to rely upon the New Enterprise Programme which dealt with people starting their businesses at the end of the 1970s as a justification for training policies in the 1990s.

This paper seeks to review research which has examined the relationship between small firm performance — profits, growth or survival — and participation in management training. Although the prime focus of the current paper is upon the United Kingdom context, an earlier paper (Storey and Westhead, 1994) examined research literature from elsewhere in Europe, Canada, the United States and Australia. Its conclusion was that the relationship between participation in management training and small business performance is currently *not* well established. The current paper briefly reviews these issues but is primarily concerned to establish reasons for the weak relationship between management training and small business performance in well-conducted research.

The Provision of Management Training in SMEs

Management training is defined as:

"... the process by which managers acquire the knowledge and skills related to their work requirements by formal, structured or guided means" (Deloitte Haskins and Sells, 1989, p3).

The acquisition of knowledge and skills can include informal-on-the-job training, formal-in-house training and external training. A second distinction is between management training for the *owner* and that for the non-*owner* managers.

Our earlier review of the literature (Storey and Westhead, 1994) clearly demonstrated participation in some form of external training for either owners or managers was positively related to firm size. For example, the Cambridge Small Business Research Centre (1992) national study found only 25 per cent of larger SMEs in the United Kingdom which provided formal workforce training relied exclusively upon insiders, compared with 51 per cent of micro firms. In addition, Blackburn (1990) in his study of small electronic and engineering firms in Dorset, England, noted, although only 3 per cent of the total workforce of firms in his sample were engaged in formal training, these places were provided by one-third of the firms in the sample. These participating firms were, on average, three times as large as the non-participants. Similarly, Mangham and Silver (1986) in their national level study in the United Kingdom also noted the tendency to utilise informal in-house training occurred with increasing business size.

The Impact of Management Training on SMEs

This section briefly reviews those studies which have attempted to relate the performance of SMEs to whether or not these businesses had participated in formal management training. It distinguishes between enterprise training for owner managers and management training for non-owner managers in SMEs.

Enterprise Training for Owner Managers

After 1979, several schemes were

introduced in the United Kingdom to encourage people to enter self-employment or start their own business. One such scheme was the Enterprise Allowance Scheme (EAS) and its successor the Business Start-up Scheme (BSUS). Their objective was to provide financial assistance to help unemployed people create viable new businesses which would not otherwise exist. From 1987 onwards participants in EAS and BSUS were generally provided with a single day's training on, for example, how to develop a business plan. EAS and BSUS entrants have been tracked and the performance of the new businesses have been monitored over relatively short time periods. The most recent eighteen-month study of BSUS is by Tremlett (1993) and the most recent three-year study of EAS is by Maung and Erens (1991). From a review of these evaluations there appears little evidence that businesses where the founder received training performed better than those which had not. Indeed, the Tremlett (1993) study suggests businesses founded by individuals who had participated in training had a (non-significantly) *higher* probability of closure than those who had not.

In 1987, it was claimed by Business in the Community (BIC) that the local network of advice and assistance provided by Enterprise Agencies (EAs) in England and Wales contributed to a higher survival rate among businesses they had helped to start. In fact, BIC (1987) claimed,

> "the failure rate of EA assisted firms in the first three years after start-up is one of the order of 1 in 6 (16 per cent) compared with 1 in 3 (33 per cent) for all new firms, based on data drawn from the VAT register."

However, considerable doubt can be cast upon this statement. First, it is not valid to simply compare EA clients with VAT registered businesses in general, since deregistration of the latter includes reasons such as take-over and change of legal status, in addition to closure. Second, Smallbone (1989) studied the survival of new firms who had received free business counselling from an EA in an outer London borough. During the 1980s, Smallbone found 42 per cent of new firms had ceased trading within three years of start-up and he concluded:

> "the presence of the EA cannot be said on this evidence to increase the chances of survival for clients who approach it" (p145).

In addition, Stanworth *et al* (1992) examined the development needs of 120 manufacturing and service SMEs in three regions in England. They monitored the impact, in terms of performance, of attending Business Development workshops but found no evidence that performance over the 1989–91 period, when the workshops were taking place, was superior to that in the three prior years. The problem here, however, as the authors acknowledge, is that macro-economic conditions were very different since the workshops were held in the depth of a recession in the United Kingdom. Nevertheless, the absence of a direct effect upon 'performance' has to be highlighted.

Further, based on data from a non-random postal survey of twenty-five firms in the Mezzogiorno region of Southern Italy, Gray (1989) monitored the effectiveness of enterprise training. The study focused on measurable objective changes to business performance one year after the completion of an enterprise training course. Gray concluded the training course had been beneficial.

Nearly three-quarters of firms reported an increase in sales turnover and 60 per cent reported they had increased the size of their workforce. This favourable conclusion, however, on a number of counts, needs to be treated with some caution. First, the sample size of the study was very small. Second, responses were not gathered from a random sample of firms attending the enterprise courses. Third, the performance of firms were not analysed in a multivariate framework. Fourth, the performance of firms attending the training course were not compared against a similar group of firms that had not attended a training course.

Overall, our much more extensive review of the evidence presented in Storey and Westhead (1994) was unable to provide clear support for the assertion made by CBI (1986, 1993), Midland Bank (1993) or the Small Business Bureau (1993) that training for the entrepreneur prior to starting the business is a factor likely to lower business failure rates. It is also ambiguous about the impact of training for SME owner managers once the business is in operation.

Management Training for Non-owner Managers

A number of schemes to improve the quality of non-owner managers in SMEs have been introduced in the United Kingdom. For example, the Business Growth Training, (BGT), Option 3, scheme was introduced in 1989 by the Training Agency. It was designed to overcome the perception that smaller firms were less likely to train managers primarily because of scepticism on the part of owner-managers surrounding the value of this training. To overcome this, BGT Option 3 provided smaller firms with up to half of the costs, to a maximum of £15,000, of employing a consultant to train and develop their management staff. One objective was to persuade small firms of the benefit of such training so that, once the subsidy had been paid, firms would choose to continue to purchase training at full market rates. Another objective was to observe improvements in firm performance associated with the provision of training.

A careful assessment of BGT was conducted by Marshall *et al* (1993, 1995). These researchers noted the provision of the subsidy led to a significant one-off rise in the quantity of training undertaken by small firms. Marshall *et al*, also found the scheme encouraged firms, once the subsidy had been exhausted, to continue with a higher level of management training than had been the case prior to the provision of the subsidy. Yet, on the key area of whether training influenced firm performance, the researchers were much more equivocal. They noted:

> "We were less successful in demonstrating that human resource development thereby improves business performance . . . and the lack of a clearly demonstrable link between training and firm performance is one of the reasons why many firms are reluctant to invest in human resources" (Marshall *et al*, 1993, p346).

Additional case study evidence revealed that if the conditions are not right management development projects had a modest impact. Marshall *et al* (1995, p88), concluded:

> "Management training projects are less effective in the very smallest firms; they work best in firms that have the management capacity to make the necessary commitment and absorb

both management and business development. The research also shows that firms carrying out narrowly defined management training projects, or those that have carried out significant amounts of management training before, and already had a staff and business plan, may not benefit as much as other SMEs from training and development projects in the future. In contrast, where managers in firms have limited experience of management training, and the firm has attendant problems such as a weak management structure, the research suggests it will not normally be possible, given the pressures of running a small business, to make real gains in much less than one year."

A study by Wynarczyk *et al* (1993) of fast-growth SMEs in the United Kingdom was also unable to find a link, once a variety of variables were held constant, between firm performance and the provision of training. They were, in addition, unable to find a link between salaries paid to managers in SMEs and whether those managers had received some form of training. Further, the Cambridge Small Business Centre (1992) survey in the United Kingdom was unable to demonstrate a clear link between firm growth and whether or not training had been undertaken.

Finally, based on responses from a large postal and telephone survey of 1,480 growing SMEs (defined as those businesses that had grown in employment, sales and assets between 1984 and 1988) in five regions and ten industries in Canada, Baldwin *et al* (1994) found business success was not associated with training alone. In fact, they concluded, labour issues played a minor role in discriminating between more-successful (with regard to growth in profitability) and less-successful groups of firms. Their univariate empirical analysis revealed that both the proportion of employees and the expenditure per employees on training were negatively correlated with business profitability. They also observed that the most-successful businesses tended to train fewer workers than a less-successful group of firms. In addition, the more-successful firms were more likely to provide formal training and less likely to undertake informal training. With regard to Government programmes to encourage training in SMEs the results for procurement were found to be interesting. Baldwin *et al* (1994, p78), concluded:

> "The more-successful group of firms are not characterised by greater training intensity and, therefore, this group does not place a higher value on government training programs.
>
> The results for training might disappoint the advocates of the importance of training. This should not be so. The results do not mean that training is counter-productive. They only indicate that the more-successful do no more training than the less-successful firms."

Towards an Understanding of Why Management Training may be Less Relevant in SMEs than in Large Firms

Evidence that management training either for owner managers or non-owner managers enhances SME performance is rather sparse (Birley and Westhead, 1990; Bell *et al*, 1992; Hewitt, 1993; Kinsella *et al*, 1994). To explain this dearth of supporting evidence Storey and Westhead (1994) in their recent review focused their explanation primarily upon the limitations of the studies conducted in this area to date. We emphasised that comparatively few studies have tracked groups of firms over time; we emphasised the limitations of 'quantitative' performance related indicators; we emphasised the inadequacy of examining the impact of management training solely within a univariate framework; and the difficulties of attempting to assess what would have happened to these firms had they not participated in any form of management training. It also seemed to be the case that the most technically sophisticated studies to date have been the least likely to observe a clear link between the receipt of management training and enhanced SME performance. This suggests that, if such a positive link exists, it either requires considerably more analytical sophistication than has been applied to date, or that such a link does not exist for SMEs.

This section of the paper seeks to examine, virtually from first principles, the factors influencing the demand for management training by SMEs. This is an illustration of the need to build theory based on SME experience. Fundamental to this is the recognition that the small firm is not a 'scaled-down' version of a large firm. In short, theories relating to SMEs must consider the motivations, constraints and uncertainties facing smaller firms and recognise these differ from those facing larger firms.

Leading theorists have clearly recognised that the central characteristic which distinguishes small from large firms, other than size *per se*, is that of uncertainty (Casson, 1982). It is, however, necessary to distinguish between 'internal' and 'external' uncertainty. This paper argues it is 'external' uncertainty which is particularly characteristic of small firms whereas 'internal' uncertainty is more characteristic of larger firms.

For larger firms the key issue is to ensure that decisions being made at the top of the organisation are delivered 'on the ground'. A key uncertainty facing Chief Executives in large organisations is that many of their decisions are actually implemented by others. An objective of the Chief Executive must be to ensure that decisions made at the top are appropriately implemented throughout the organisation. Internal monitoring, however, in small firms is very much easier since the owner-manager has a greater awareness of what is going on. The opportunity for internal inefficiency is less and the small firm owner-manager can feel more certain that decisions made by him/her will be carried out. Therefore, 'internal' uncertainty is much lower in small than in large firms.

On the other hand, the small firm experiences considerably greater 'external' uncertainty than a large firm, primarily because of its lack of power in the marketplace. It is clearly at the mercy of single large purchasers of output, since many small firms are sub-contractors heavily dependent on a dominant customer. Smaller firms are also more likely to have a single or restricted range of products/services so they are more 'exposed' by changes in the marketplace. On the other hand, large firms are more likely to have a range of customers and products/services and to have greater financial resources to overcome temporary problems.

Given this 'external' uncertainty the small firm responds by generally having a shorter time horizon than a large firm so that the small firm favours projects with short-term rather than long-term returns.

The Balance Sheets of small firms emphasise heavier contributions from Current, rather than Fixed Assets, on the grounds that the former provide greater 'flexibility' (Hughes and Cosh, 1994). In this sense, 'flexibility' is the small firms response to 'external' uncertainty. The main benefits of training are, however, apparent to owners in the long, rather than the short run. As a result, smaller firms will invest less in all forms of training than larger firms. It is important to note this conclusion is independent of any assumptions made about the 'quality' of the training.

We now turn to understanding why *non-owner managers* in SMEs are less likely to be in receipt of management training than similar individuals in larger firms. In part, this reflects the reluctance of the owner to invest in long-term projects, which was noted above, but it also emphasises the particular characteristics of the non-owner managerial labour market. Wynarczyk *et al* (1993) argue that internal labour markets (ILMs) exist in large firms but do not exist in small firms. The key element of an ILM is that individuals expect to obtain their next job within the organisation for which they currently work. This means it is in the interests of that organisation to provide training to improve the performance of the non-owner manager, not only in their current job, but also in anticipation of their next job. The role of the ILM is to ensure non-owner managers stay with the enterprise and do not move. Hence, the training provided by the enterprise is argued to be 'narrowing' in the sense that it focuses upon business procedures and, in so doing, makes the individual less attractive to other businesses (Creedy and Whitfield, 1988).

However, ILMs are unlikely to exist in most small firms. Non-owner managers in small firms recognise their next job will *not* be in that firm, since often the only more senior manager is the owner. The non-owner manager, therefore, recognises their next job move may be outside the firm. Since this is also recognised by the owner, management training is not seen to be in the interests of either party (Curran *et al*, 1993) — the owner does not wish to make the investment on the grounds that the manager is likely to leave, and the non-owner manager does not wish to participate in management training on the grounds that this may be 'narrowing'.

In principle, of course, the purpose of training is to 'widen' rather than to 'narrow' the non-owner manager and this is the case for qualification-based training. The problem is that it is precisely this type of training which the small firm owner is less likely to provide for the non-owner manager since the returns are long-term and, by its provision, the non-owner manager becomes more attractive in the labour market. Thus, the small firm non-owner manager him/herself may pay for and undertake such training, but it is unlikely to be provided by small firm owners.

These issues can be presented in tabular form. Table 1 examines four groups of reasons why small firms purchase less management training than large firms. They broadly relate to the elementary economics textbook factors influencing demand for a product.

The first is price. Although the market price of management training may be identical between small and large firms, the 'real' price paid by small firms exceeds that of large firms. This is because the price paid includes not only the market price, but also the cost of

Table 1
Why Do Small Firms Buy Less Management Training Than Large Firms?

Reasons	
1. Price:	The 'real' price of training is higher in small firms.
2. Income:	Small firms are more financially 'constrained'.
3. Tastes:	— Greater uncertainty means a short-term view.
	— Absence of an internal labour market (ILM).
	— Training perceived not to be appropriate.
4. Information:	Scale economies for trainers in dealing with large firms.

management supervision and the opportunity cost of his/her absence from the workplace during the training period (Vickerstaff, 1992). The opportunity cost of management time may differ between small and large firms, with the cost being higher in smaller rather than larger firms, although the market price for the training may be identical the real price paid will differ[1]. If the price is higher for small firms than for large, then less management training would be purchased by SMEs. A second dimension is that the cost of providing training to small firms is higher because a more 'differentiated' product has to be provided. For larger firms management training development costs can be spread over more personnel — so lowering unit costs.

A second reason shown in Table 1, which has been found to influence the purchase of a commodity, is income. Those on lower incomes, other things being equal, would be expected to purchase less of a commodity than those on higher incomes. Small firms are likely to be more 'financially constrained' than large firms, with their smaller size and often their lack of 'track record' and collateral restricting their access to loan capital, compared with medium- and large-sized firms. For this reason, small firms are less likely to purchase commodities on credit, than large firms.

The third set of reasons identified in Table 1 relate to 'tastes'. Three separate elements are identified: the first is that the nature of uncertainty facing large firms differs fundamentally from those facing small firms and the second is the absence of an ILM in small firms. Both these points were discussed earlier. The third element relates to the perception that the management training on offer is not appropriate. Here it is assumed the small firm owner does not purchase the management training on offer for a number of non-price reasons. The first is that the training may be 'too general' and not of specific relevance to his/her business. The second may be that it is not provided by people with sufficient 'understanding' or 'business nous'. The familiar cry is that 'training' is provided by teachers rather than by practitioners. A third aspect may be that training is not conveniently provided — either in terms of location, form of training or media. The key point here is that these different reasons have been frequently presented to 'explain' why small firms are less likely to participate in management training (Kirby, 1990, Cambridge Small Business

Research Centre, 1992; Johnson and Gubbins, 1992; Vickerstaff, 1992). Our argument is that they are only one of a number of factors pointing in this direction.

The final reason in Table 1 relates to information. Here, it is argued, small firm owners may be less well-informed about the availability of management training (Fuller *et al*, 1991) than their large firm counterparts. This is because there is less incentive on the part of training providers to contact small firms than large firms. In short, there may well be scale economies in the provision of information surrounding management training since it is easier to identify and contact large firms than small firms.

Overall, virtually all of the reasons in Table 1 point to the expectation that larger firms are more likely to provide management training than smaller firms. This is partly because the 'price' which they pay is lower, and partly because they are more able to 'internalise' any benefits obtained.

Conclusions

Over the last decade there has been a huge growth in the 'training industry', much of it supported from the public purse. Small firms which have participated in management training schemes generally suggest their business have derived some benefit from this participation. Most notably, staff in receipt of training are generally more confident. Careful empirical research has, however, failed to link the provision of management training in small firm with enhanced performance in the recipient firm. This paper has attempted to provide a greater insight into this funding by examining the demand for management training by SMEs.

Our view is that the supply of management training for SMEs is not homogeneous. Some training may focus upon developing particular functional skills, others may focus upon SMEs at particular business development stages — start-up, growth businesses, etc. Some training is provided by public organisations such as universities and colleges whereas for others it is provided by private sector training consultants. Some courses are for one-day or less, whereas others are in a distance learning format or taken over a long period of time.

Our highly subjective impression is that some types of management training may be effective in enhancing firm performance whilst others are not. However, our review is unable to consistently document methodologically well conducted research evidence which show the provision of management training for SMEs clearly leads to improved performance on the part of a recipient firm. This may either be because of a lack of impact or because of the difficulties of attributing cause and effect.

The reasons for an absence of impact may be the poor quality of the training provided, the fact that it is often over too short a period to exert an influence upon the firm, that perhaps some forms of training are more effective than others or that the poorer providers dominate the rest. In its defence, the 'training industry' can claim that the scale, variety and quality of management training in small firms has yet to be adequately monitored and evaluated. Most notably, the majority of evaluations have tracked firms which have received management training over relatively short time periods. 'Snap shot' studies clearly fail to fully capture the long-term benefits of management training schemes. Further, most studies have concentrated on highly 'quantitative' outcomes. Only a small number of studies have related management training to 'qualitative' improvements in SME performance. Based upon this review, we believe there is an urgent need for additional carefully conducted research, from a variety of perspectives, surrounding the relationship between management training and small firm performance.

Acknowledgements

This paper draws upon a much broader study of management development in SMEs (Storey and Westhead, 1994) which was sponsored by the Confederation of British Industry. The views expressed here do not necessarily reflect those of the CBI, but have benefited considerably from the comments received from two anonymous ISBJ referees.

Notes

1 In a world of perfect markets there should be no difference with wages related to marginal productivity. In practice, numerous surveys of small firms have identified constraints upon managerial time being particularly characteristic of smaller firms (Cambridge Small Business Research Centre, 1992). Furthermore, if larger firms are more likely to have 'market power' then they are also more likely to exhibit managerial X-inefficiency (Liebenstein, 1966) so the absence of such individuals from work has less impact upon business performance than in smaller firms.

References

Baldwin, J., Chandler, W., Le, C., and Papailiadis, T. (1994), *Strategies for Success: A Profile of Growing Small- and Medium-sized Enterprises (GSMEs) in Canada*. Ottawa: Statistics Canada.

Bell, J., Murray, M., and Maddon, K. (1992), Developing Expertise: An Irish Perspective. *International Small Business Journal*, 10, pp37–53.

Birley, S., and Westhead, P. (1990), Growth and Performance Contrasts Between 'Types' of Small Firms. *Strategic Management Journal*, 11, pp535–557.

Blackburn, R. (1990), Job Quality in Small Businesses: Electrical and Electronic Engineering Firms in Dorset. *Environment and Planning*, A, 22, pp875–892.

Business in the Community (1987), *Small Firms: Survival and Job Creation — The Contribution of Enterprise Agencies*. London: Business in the Community.

Cambridge Small Business Research Centre (1992), *The State of British Enterprise: Growth, Innovation and Competitive Advantage in Small- and Medium-sized Firms*. Cambridge: University of Cambridge.

Casson, M. (1982), *The Entrepreneur: An Economic Theory*. Oxford: Martin Robertson.

Confederation of British Industry (1986), *Management Training for Small Businesses*. London: Confederation of British Industry.

Confederation of British Industry (1993), *Finance for Growth: Meeting the Financing Needs of Small and Medium Enterprises*. London: Confederation of British Industry.

Creedy, J., and Whitfield, K. (1988), The Economic Analysis of Internal Labour Markets, *Bulletin of Economic Research*, 4, pp247–267.

Curran, J., and Stanworth, J. (1989), Education and Training for Enterprise: Some Problems of Classification, Evaluation, Policy and Research, *International Small Business Journal*, 7, pp11–22.

Curran, J., Kitching, J., Abbott, B., and Mills, V. (1993), *Employment and Employment Relations in the Small Service Sector Enterprise — A Report*. Kingston University: ESRC Centre for Research on Small Service Sector Enterprises.

Deloitte Haskins and Sells (1989), *Management Challenge for the 1990s: The Current Education, Training and Development Debate*. Sheffield: Department of Employment.

Fuller, M. F., Murphy, M. P., and Vickerstaff, S. A. (1991), Training in the Kent Economy: Present and Prospects, *Regional Studies*, 25, pp563–569.

Gray, C. (1989), Enterprise Training as a Development Strategy: Evidence from Southern Italy, *Piccola Impresa/Small Business*, 1, pp89–108.

Hewitt, N. (1993), Elephants and Wallflowers at the Global Dance: A Comparative Analysis of the Quality of Training Within Small Manufacturing Firms in Northern Ireland and Massachesetts. *Proceedings of the 16th National Small Firms Policy and Research Conference*. Nottingham: The Nottingham Trent University.

Hughes, A., and Cosh, A. (1994), Size, Financial Structure and Profitability: UK Companies in the 1980s, in Hughes, A., and Storey, D. J. (eds.), *Finance and the Small Firm*, London: Routledge, pp18–63.

Jennings, P. L., and Banfield, P. (1993), Improving Competence in Small Firms. *Proceedings of the 16th National Small Firms Policy and Research Conference*. Nottingham: The Nottingham Trent University.

Johnson, S., and Gubbins, A. (1992), Training in Small- and Medium-sized Enterprises: Lessons from North Yorkshire. In Caley, K., Chell, E., Chittenden, F., and Mason, C. (eds.) *Small Enterprise Development: Policy and Practice in Action*. London: Paul Chapman Publishing Ltd., pp28–42.

Kinsella, R., Clarke, W., Storey, D. J., Mulvenna, D., and Coyne, D. (1994), *Fast-Growth Small Firms: An Irish Perspective*. Dublin: Irish Management Institute.

Kirby, D. A. (1990), Management Education and Small Business Development: An Exploratory Study of Small Firms in the UK, *Journal of Small Business Management*, 28, pp78–87.

Liebenstein, H. (1966), Allocative Efficiency vs. 'X-efficiency', *American Economic Review*, 56, pp392–415.

Mangham, I., and Silver, M. (1986), *Management Training: Context and Practice*. London: ESRC/DTI.

Marshall, J. N., Alderman, N., Wong, C., and Thwaites, A. (1993), The Impact of Government-Assisted Management Training and Development on Small- and Medium-sized Enterprises in Britain, *Environment and Planning C.*, 11, pp331–348.

Marshall, J. N., Alderman, N., Wong, C., and Thwaites, A. (1995), The Impact of Management Training and Development on Small- and Medium-sized Enterprises, *International Small Business Bournal*, 13, pp73–90.

Maung, N. A., and Erens, R. (1991), *Enterprise Allowance Scheme: A Survey of Participants Two Years After Leaving*. London: Social and Community Planning Research.

Midland Bank (1993), *The Changing Financial Requirements of Smaller Companies.* London: Midland Bank.
National Audit Office (1988), *Department of Employment/Training Commission: Assistance to Small Firms.* London: Report to the Comptroller and Auditor General, HMSO.
Smallbone, D. (1989). Enterprise Agencies and the Survival of New Business Start-ups, *Local Economy*, 4, pp143–147.
Small Business Bureau (1993), *Enhanced Loan Guarantee Scheme Report.* London: Small Business Bureau.
Stanworth, J., Purdy, D., and Kirby, D. (1992), *The Management of Success in 'Growth Corridor' Small Firms.* London: SBRT Monograph.
Storey, D. J., and Westhead, P. (1994), *Management Development in Small- and Medium-Sized Enterprises with Growth Potential.* London: Confederation of British Industry.
Tremlett, N. (1993), *The Business Start-up Scheme: 18 Months Follow-up Survey.* London: Social and Community Planning Research.
Vickerstaff, S. (1992), The Training Needs of Small Firms, *Human Resource Management Journal*, 2, pp1–15.
Watkins, D. (1983), Developing Training and Education for the Small Firm: A European Perspective, *European Small Business Journal*, 1, pp29–44.
Wynarczyk, P., Watson, R., Storey, D., Short, H., and Keasey, K. (1993), *Managerial Labour Markets in Small- and Medium-Sized Enterprises.* London: Routledge.

Name Index

UNIVERSITY OF GLAMORGAN
PRIFYSGOL MORGANNWG